Edinburgh

timeout.com/edinburgh

Time Out Guides Ltd
Universal House
251 Tottenham Court Road
London W1T 7AB
United Kingdom
Tel: +44 (0)20 7813 3000
Fax: +44 (0)20 7813 6001
Email: guides@timeout.com
www.timeout.com

Published by Time Out Guides Ltd, a wholly owned subsidiary of Time Out Group Ltd.
Time Out and the Time Out logo are trademarks of Time Out Group Ltd.

© **Time Out Group Ltd 2010**
Previous editions 1998, 2000, 2002, 2004, 2006.

10 9 8 7 6 5 4 3 2 1

This edition first published in Great Britain in 2009 by Ebury Publishing.
A Random House Group Company
20 Vauxhall Bridge Road, London SW1V 2SA

Random House Australia Pty Ltd 20 Alfred Street, Milsons Point, Sydney, New South Wales 2061, Australia

Random House New Zealand Ltd 18 Poland Road, Glenfield, Auckland 10, New Zealand

Random House South Africa (Pty) Ltd Isle of Houghton, Corner Boundary Road & Carse O'Gowrie, Houghton 2198, South Africa

Random House UK Limited Reg. No. 954009

For further distribution details, see www.timeout.com.

ISBN: 978-1-84670-066-8

A CIP catalogue record for this book is available from the British Library.

Printed and bound by Firmengruppe APPL, aprinta druck, Wemding, Germany.

The Random House Group Limited supports The Forest Stewardship Council (FSC), the leading international forest certification organisation. All our titles that are printed on Greenpeace approved FSC certified paper carry the FSC logo. Our paper procurement policy can be found at http://www.rbooks.co.uk/environment.

Time Out carbon-offsets its flights with Trees for Cities (www.treesforcities.org).

Contents

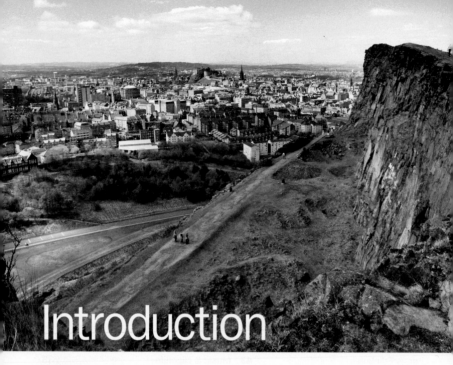

Introduction

The marketing machine would have you believe that for one month of the year, when all the festivals hit in August, Edinburgh is the most important city in the world. In cultural terms, the marketing machine is correct. Nowhere else brings together the programme that the International Festival, the Fringe, the Tattoo, the Book Festival and others collectively offer, and nowhere else draws international audiences on such a massive scale. The sense of event is palpable, the excitement infectious, the celebration an antidote to the concerns of day-to-day life in the 21st century.

This upside implies a downside, of course, that for the other months of the year, the city simply isn't quite as thrilling. Yes, it has its castles and its galleries, its acclaimed restaurants and its museums, its medieval fabric and its Georgian neo-classicism, but it can't claim to be on a par with the likes of London, New York or Paris. Its population and location lead to suggestions that the city's more obvious peers are, perhaps, Copenhagen or Dublin, Helsinki or Oslo. Yet Edinburgh has a more resonant reputation than comparable northern capitals; internationally, it's held in regard for more than just August.

Perhaps Sir Walter Scott pulled off this trick nearly 200 years ago, spinning the very idea of Scotland from a matrix of noble clansmen, stark mountains and enduring romance. Even though Edinburgh is resolutely urban, visitors can still see 12th-century ruins or rugged topology in the city centre, a fix of Caledonian mythos without travelling to the Highlands. The legacy of the Scottish Enlightenment also underpins its status, and not just statues of men such as David Hume or Adam Smith. For a period in the 18th century, Edinburgh was the world's intellectual proving ground, helping form a framework for the very nature of academic and intellectual enquiry that has followed ever since. The New Town is a living monument to the ambition and self-conscious rationality of that age.

It's narratives such as these, historical fact or literary fiction, that are the city's real strength. Tales twisting round its cobbled streets and sandstone façades elevate and engage, capturing the attention of visitors. Away from the incandescence of August, the city's stories are well told whatever the month. And the pages keep turning. *Keith Davidson, Editor*

Edinburgh in Brief

IN CONTEXT

For many visitors, Edinburgh's history is one of its main attractions. The opening section of this book illuminates this rich and tangled past, before bringing the story up to date with discussion of the city today. There are also extensive features on the city's architecture, its literary heritage and the Enlightenment, an 18th-century flourishing of cultural, economic and scientific achievement.

▶ For more, see pp15-50.

SIGHTS

Neatly linking Edinburgh Castle with the Palace of Holyroodhouse, the Royal Mile is the first port of call for most first-time sightseers. But there's plenty of interest beyond its confines: to the north and north-west, the elegant New Town and genteel Stockbridge; to the east, the dominant hulk of Arthur's Seat; and the coastal town of Leith, undergoing rapid change in the 21st century.

▶ For more, see pp51-112.

CONSUME

Edinburgh's eating options have long been impressive and they're still improving today, with Michelin-starred high-end venues at one extreme and a bright array of budget cafés at the other. The pubs and bars, too, are many and varied, historic pubs supplemented by sleek style bars. Also in the section, there's coverage of Edinburgh's shopping choices, and a guide to the best hotels in the city.

▶ For more, see pp113-204.

ARTS & ENTERTAINMENT

Most of the highlights of Edinburgh's cultural scene are crammed into a single month: August, when an array of arts festivals draws thousands to the city from far and wide. But outside the chaos of summer, there's plenty here that appeals, from the improving local art scene to the cluster of bring-an-instrument folk sessions held in tiny Old Town pubs.

▶ For more, see pp205-254.

ESCAPES & EXCURSIONS

It's less than an hour from Edinburgh by train, but Glasgow is a very different city to its near-neighbour: bigger, brasher and arguably a little livelier. There's extensive coverage of the town in this section here, from its mainstream sights via its much-praised restaurants to its vital nightlife. And there's also information here on other, more rural highlights within easy reach of Edinburgh.

▶ For more, see pp255-300.

Edinburgh in 48 Hrs

Day 1 The Old Town Redux

8AM Before exploring the historic Old Town, go back in time even further by taking a brisk hike up **Arthur's Seat** (*see p96*), formed some 350 million years ago. It's an invigorating start to the day.

9.30AM Back at the bottom of the **Royal Mile**, the **Palace of Holyroodhouse** (*see p70*) gives an excellent grounding in Edinburgh's royal history going back 500 years. Art-lovers should divert to the **Queen's Gallery**, which shows paintings from the Royal Collection. If monarchy bores you, tour the modern **Scottish Parliament** (*see p70*).

11.30AM Low-key attractions dot the Canongate, among them the **Museum of Edinburgh** (*see p69*) and the **Scottish Storytelling Centre** (*see p66*). Dip into them as you wander the Royal Mile before stopping for lunch: French at **La Garrigue** (*see p137*), tapas at **Barioja** (*see p135*) or Scottish at the St Mary's Street branch of **Stac Polly** (*see p146*).

2PM After lunch, continue east to the **High Kirk of St Giles** (*see p64*), its Thistle Chapel an ornate must-see, before exploring into the atmospheric labyrinth of closes and wynds that run off the Royal Mile (*see p60*).

3PM **Edinburgh Castle** (*see p56*) dominates the city from the top of Castlehill. From the simplicity of St Margaret's Chapel to the haunting Scottish National War Memorial, it's an extraordinary place.

6PM After the castle, head for the **Bow Bar** on Victoria Street (*see p167*), to sample some excellent single malt Scotch while you consider your options for the evening. If you're taking in a show before eating, the post-theatre supper at the **Witchery** on Castlehill (*see p139*) is an ideal way to close your day on the Royal Mile. Stepping out of the restaurant late at night, on to the cobbles, takes you back to an Edinburgh of centuries ago.

NAVIGATING THE CITY

The best way to negotiate your way around central Edinburgh is to pay almost no attention to the street names. Instead, navigate according to the compass points in relation to the three major landmarks: Arthur's Seat, Edinburgh Castle and Calton Hill. Major streets change names constantly: the Royal Mile labours under four identities (Castlehill, Lawnmarket, High Street and Canongate) in 1,600 cobbled metres; crossing it, North Bridge becomes South Bridge becomes Nicolson Street becomes Clerk Street, and so on. It can be a little confusing.

Many venues in Edinburgh are reachable on foot, assuming you're staying in a central hotel. However, there's also a comprehensive bus network that covers most corners of the city, and the next few years – 2011, it's hoped – will see the opening of Edinburgh's much-anticipated and by no means controversy-free tram network.

Day 2 North of the Castle

10AM At the foot of the Mound, the **National Gallery of Scotland** (*see p79*) is a gentle way to start a day's exploration. There's more art at the comparatively low-key **Fruitmarket Gallery** (*see p230*) along Market Street; alternatively, head north into Princes Street Gardens and climb the **Scott Monument** for excellent city-centre views.

NOON From here, head north into the **New Town** (*see pp77-85*) and explore its handsome Georgian roads. **Dundas Street** has private art galleries and a view to Fife; **Heriot Row** maintains a patrician air; and **Northumberland Street** is as understated as **Great King Street** or **Moray Place** are grand. When you've seen enough, head west into the genteel neighbourhood of **Stockbridge**.

1PM Looking for lunch in Stockbridge, you'll be spoiled for choice on St Stephen Street; two worthwhile options include the café-bar simplicity of the **Saint** and the pub grub at the **Baillie** (for both, *see p173*). The area is also full of independent shops worth a browse, as is the **Raeburn Estate** up Leslie Place, another impressive neo-classical neighbourhood.

2.30PM Nearby, Dean Terrace nearby runs along the lovely **Water of Leith**, which winds its way all the way north to Leith. After a little stroll along it, cut north into Inverleith Park and the **Royal Botanic Garden** (*see p89*), which pleases both plant-lovers and casual strollers. As well as the greenery and the various glasshouses, you'll find fine art exhibitions in **Inverleith House** (*see p89*). Check the opening hours before setting out: the Botanics' closing time varies by season.

6.30PM After this gentle, cultured day, it's time to experience the less prim side of north Edinburgh. Stop for a pre-dinner cocktail at **Bramble** (*see p169*) on Queen Street, then try **Centotre** on George Street (*see p143*) for dinner. And after that? Check the **Pubs & Bars** and **Music & Nightlife** sections (*see pp167-182 and pp235-244*) and pick your poison…

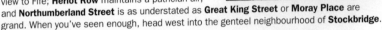

For more on getting to, from and around the city, *see pp302-304*.

PACKAGE DEALS

If you're planning to visit a number of venues run by Historic Scotland, it may be worth getting an **Explorer Pass**. There are two versions of the pass: one covering three days of sightseeing (valid for any three days over a five-day period; £21, £10.50-£15.50 discounts, £42 family) and one covering seven days (valid over a 14-day period; £30, £15.50-£22.50 discounts, £60 family). You can buy the pass at any Historic Scotland attraction or online from www.historic-scotland.gov.uk, which is also the place to go for further information on the pass. Edinburgh attractions covered by the pass include Edinburgh Castle (where cardholders get fast-track access) and Craigmillar Castle; many of the sites featured in the Around Edinburgh chapter of this guide (*see pp292-300*) also qualify.

Edinburgh in Profile

THE OLD TOWN

Nearly 900 years ago, Edinburgh started to take on a recognisable shape in the Old Town, and the area still has many of the city's major tourist sites. But don't mistake it for some medieval wonderland preserved in aspic. Its backbone, the **Royal Mile**, has a range of 21st-century additions, from designer hotels to Scotland's parliament, plus vibrant street performance during the Fringe every August.

▶ For more, see pp52-76.

THE NEW TOWN

Perhaps the apogee of Scottish Enlightenment thinking in practice, the squares and streets of the New Town, created in the late 18th and early 19th centuries, have an unparalleled Georgian elegance. This is an area for walking and gawking. At its southern extent, **Princes Street** is the main thoroughfare for the entire city; **George Street** has the more aspirational shops, plus any number of restaurants and bars.

▶ For more, see pp77-85.

STOCKBRIDGE

A Bohemian little enclave to the north-west of the New Town, the old village of Stockbridge is best approached for its fine selections of restaurants, cafés and bars, its quirky little shops and delicatessens, and – perhaps the key to its appeal – the faintly exclusive sense it offers of being a remove or two from the big city. It's also the home of Scottish cricket, and is handy for the **Royal Botanic Garden**.

▶ For more, see pp86-90.

CALTON HILL & BROUGHTON

The appeal of this quarter of the city is stretched between two extremes: the heights of **Calton Hill**, with its array of unusual monuments and its 360-degree views of Edinburgh; and buzzing **Broughton Street**, with its complement of pubs and café-bars edging into the heart of the city's gay scene. Pay your respects at the grave of philosopher David Hume or go clubbing until 3am. Or, of course, do both.

▶ For more, see pp91-95.

ARTHUR'S SEAT & DUDDINGSTON

Holyrood Park is an oasis of wilderness in the middle of the Scottish capital. Its centrepiece is **Arthur's Seat**, a hill formed by ancient volcanic action that now stands an impressive 251 metres above the city. On a clear day, you can see 40 miles from the top, assuming you're not just concentrating on the fauna and flora around you. To the south-east, the village of **Duddingston** completes the bucolic picture.

▶ For more, see pp96-99.

sit The
Scotch Whisky
Experience

Sensational Journey

- Amber Restaurant
- Whisky Bar
- Whisky and Gift Shop
- Whisky Tour

**NEXT TO
EDINBURGH CASTLE**

WWW.SCOTCHWHISKYEXPERIENCE.CO.UK

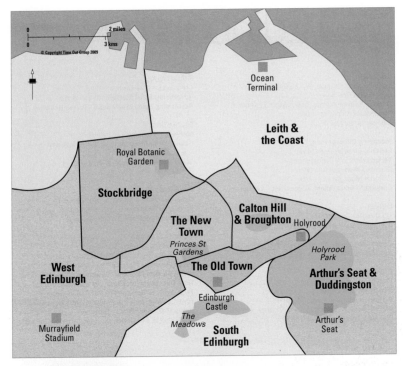

South Edinburgh
West Edinburgh
Stockbridge
The New Town
Princes St Gardens
Calton Hill & Broughton
Holyrood
Holyrood Park
Royal Botanic Garden
Leith & the Coast
Ocean Terminal
The Old Town
Edinburgh Castle
The Meadows
South Edinburgh
Arthur's Seat & Duddingston
Arthur's Seat
Murrayfield Stadium

2 miles
3 kms
© Copyright Time Out Group 2009

SOUTH EDINBURGH

With the **Meadows** and **Bruntsfield Links**, then **Blackford Hill** and the **Braid Hills** ebbing towards the **Pentlands**, South Edinburgh doesn't lack for green spaces. It's also home to some attractive neighbourhoods – **Bruntsfield**, **Marchmont**, **Morningside** – and some of the city's more exclusive streets.

▶ For more, see pp100-102.

WEST EDINBURGH

Not an obvious port of call for visitors, this is where you visit a specific place for a specific purpose: **Edinburgh Zoo** for the animals, **Murrayfield** for rugby, **Tynecastle** for football or the **Union Canal** towpath for a walk. The village of **Cramond** in Edinburgh's far north-west has a river walk and a fine coastline.

▶ For more, see pp103-106.

LEITH & THE COAST

A working deepwater port, **Leith** was once a town in its own right and still feels separate from Edinburgh. It's been transformed since the 1980s and is now a centre for fine dining and café-bars. Like its coastal neighbours **Granton** and **Newhaven**, it's undergoing massive residential development; further east, **Portobello** is the city's beach suburb.

▶ For more, see pp107-112.

Time Out Edinburgh

Editorial
Editors Keith Davidson, Will Fulford-Jones
Copy Editor Ros Sales
Listings Editors William Crow, Gemma Pritchard
Proofreader Mandy Martinez
Indexer Ismay Atkins

Managing Director Peter Fiennes
Editorial Director Ruth Jarvis
Series Editor Will Fulford-Jones
Business Manager Dan Allen
Editorial Manager Holly Pick
Assistant Management Accountant Ija Krasnikova

Design
Art Director Scott Moore
Art Editor Pinelope Kourmouzoglou
Senior Designer Henry Elphick
Graphic Designers Kei Ishimaru, Nicola Wilson
Advertising Designer Jodi Sher

Picture Desk
Picture Editor Jael Marschner
Deputy Picture Editor Lynn Chambers
Picture Researcher Gemma Walters
Picture Desk Assistant Marzena Zoladz
Picture Librarian Christina Theisen

Advertising
Commercial Director Mark Phillips
Advertising Sales Manager Alison Wallen
Advertising Sales (Edinburgh) Christie Dessy

Marketing
Marketing Manager Yvonne Poon
Sales & Marketing Director, North America & Latin America Lisa Levinson
Senior Publishing Brand Manager Luthfa Begum
Art Director Anthony Huggins

Production
Group Production Director Mark Lamond
Production Manager Brendan McKeown
Production Controller Damian Bennett

Time Out Group
Chairman Tony Elliott
Chief Executive Officer David King
Group Financial Director Paul Rakkar
Group General Manager/Director Nichola Coulthard
Time Out Communications Ltd MD David Pepper
Time Out International Ltd MD Cathy Runciman
Time Out Magazine Ltd Publisher/MD Mark Elliott
Group IT Director Simon Chappell
Marketing & Circulation Director Catherine Demajo

Contributors
Introduction Keith Davidson. **History** Will Fulford-Jones (*Murders Most Horrid* Kaye McAlpine; *Just for Laughs, Banking on the Capital* Mark Fisher). **Edinburgh Today** Mark Fisher. **Architecture** Keith Davidson. **Literary Edinburgh** Isla Leaver-Yap (*All Plays, No Work* Mark Fisher). **The Brains Trust** Mark Fisher. **Sights** Keith Davidson (*Enter the Labyrinth* Isla Leaver-Yap; *Go Figure* Kaye Davidson; *Walk: The Newest in New Town, In Praise of Old Women, Park Life, On the Waterfront* Mark Fisher). **Hotels** Keith Davidson. **Restaurants & Cafés** Keith Davidson (*Tea for Two* Ian Sclater). **Pubs & Bars** Keith Davidson (*Fancy a Pint?* Ian Sclater). **Shops & Services** Kaye McAlpine (*The Gift of Scotland* Ian Sclater). **Festival Edinburgh** Mark Fisher. **Calendar** Keith Davidson. **Children** Kaye McAlpine. **Comedy** Mark Fisher. **Film** Mark Fisher. **Galleries** Mark Fisher. **Gay & Lesbian** Robin Lee. **Music & Nightlife** Neil Cooper. **Sport & Fitness** Keith Davidson (*Riding the Rails* Ian Sclater). **Theatre & Dance** Mark Fisher. **Glasgow** Keith Davidson. **Around Edinburgh** Keith Davidson (*Fishing for Culture* Ian Sclater). **Directory** Will Fulford-Jones.

Maps john@jsgraphics.co.uk.

Photography Olivia Rutherford, except: page 24 Camera Press/Mander & Mitchenson; page 26 Rex Features; page 43 Jane Barlow/Camera Press; page 46 Douglas McBride; page 50 Getty Images; page 67, 251 Nadin Dunigan; page 206 Peter Sandground; page 208 (top, left & bottom) Paul Lopez; page 208 (right) Callum Bennetts; page 211 (left & top right) Helena Smith/EIFF; page 211 (bottom right) Peter Ross; page 213 Rob McDougall; page 216 courtesy of www.ceilidhculture.co.uk; page 225 Britta Jachinski; page 227 Allstar; page 236 Tom Finnie; page 241 Guillam Lopez/Camera Press; page 252 (top) Rebecca Marr; page 252 (bottom) Ellis Parrinder. The following images were provided by the featured establishments/artists: page 45, 208, 212, 260, 253 (right), 288, 292, 294, 297.

The Editor would like to thank all contributors to previous editions of *Time Out Edinburgh*, whose work forms the basis for parts of this book.

About the Guide

GETTING AROUND

The back of the book contains street maps of Edinburgh, as well as overview maps of the city and its surroundings. The maps start on page 321; on them are marked the locations of hotels (❶), restaurants and cafés (❶), and pubs and bars (❶). The majority of businesses listed in this guide are located in the areas we've mapped; the grid-square references in the listings refer to these maps.

THE ESSENTIALS

For practical information, including visas, disabled access, emergency numbers, lost property, useful websites and local transport, please see the Directory. It begins on page 301.

THE LISTINGS

Addresses, phone numbers, websites, transport information, hours and prices are all included in our listings, as are selected other facilities. All were checked and correct at press time. However, business owners can alter their arrangements at any time, and fluctuating economic conditions can cause prices to change rapidly.

The very best venues in the city, the must-sees and must-dos in every category, have been marked with a red star (★). In the Sights chapters, we've also marked venues with free admission with a FREE symbol.

PHONE NUMBERS

The area code for Edinburgh is 0131. You don't need to use the code when calling from within Edinburgh: simply dial the seven-digit numbers as listed in this guide.

From outside the UK, dial your country's international access code (011 from the US) or a plus symbol, followed by the UK country code (44), 131 for Edinburgh (dropping the initial '0') and the seven-digit number as listed in this guide. So, to reach Edinburgh Castle, dial +44 131 225 9846. For more on phones, including information on calling abroad from the UK and details of local mobile-phone access, *see p310.*

FEEDBACK

We welcome feedback on this guide, both on the venues we've included and on any other locations that you'd like to see featured in future editions. Please email us at guides@timeout.com.

Time Out Guides

Founded in 1968, Time Out has grown from humble beginnings into the leading resource for anyone wanting to know what's happening in the world's greatest cities. Alongside our influential weeklies in London, New York and Chicago, we publish more than 20 magazines in cities as varied as Beijing and Beirut; a range of travel books, with the City Guides now joined by the newer Shortlist series; and an information-packed website. The company remains proudly independent, still owned by Tony Elliott four decades after he launched *Time Out London*.

Written by local experts and illustrated with original photography, our books also retain their independence. No business has been featured because it has advertised, and all restaurants and bars are visited and reviewed anonymously.

ABOUT THE EDITORS

Based in Edinburgh, **Keith Davidson** has worked on every edition of this guide since it was launched in 1998, and has also contributed to a number of other Time Out titles. **Will Fulford-Jones** is the Series Editor of Time Out City Guides.

A full list of the book's contributors can be found opposite. However, we've also included details of our writers in selected chapters through the guide.

Time Out
Travel Guides

British Isles

Written by local experts

In Context

Palace of Holyroodhouse. *See p36*.

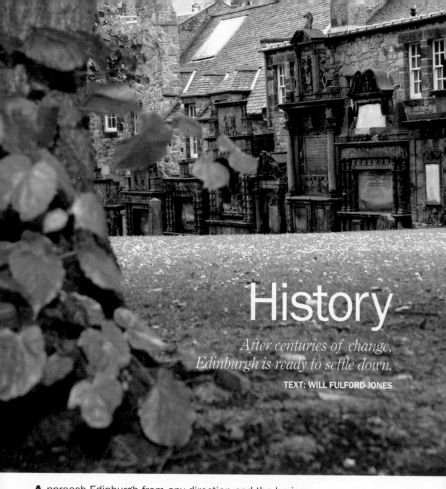

History

After centuries of change,
Edinburgh is ready to settle down.

TEXT: WILL FULFORD-JONES

Approach Edinburgh from any direction and the horizon will be dominated by Edinburgh Castle, welded to its basalt outcrop. Catching the rays of the westering sun, visible from halfway to Glasgow and from the opposite shores of Fife, here is a natural fortress whose occupants, secure on their dizzying heights, could survey the flowing waters of the Firth of Forth and watch for raiders approaching in the distance.

The city of Edinburgh grew from this natural vantage point. The fortress on the rock was followed by the city itself, flowing down the castle's ridge into the major roads and tiny passages of what would become the Old Town. Then, when it could no longer be contained, Edinburgh spilled northwards across the intervening valley to create the elegant New Town, neatly ordered and regimented with its Georgian grids. Into the 21st century, the city continues to grow.

IN THE BEGINNING

Edinburgh's dramatic setting is the result of a landscape shaped by fire and ice. More than 300 million years ago, volcanoes spewed molten lava across desolate landscapes to form the hills of the city. Creeping northwards as the continents played their slow game of marriage and divorce, Scotland vanished under vast rivers of grinding, groaning ice, which carved out a mountainous landscape across it. With the disappearance of the final Ice Age glaciers 15,000 years ago, the stage was set for the emergence of this most visually striking of cities.

Traces of human occupation here go back more than ten millennia. Rewind 5,000 years and you'd have seen hunter-gatherers foraging along the Water of Leith; go back three millennia and you would have witnessed the introduction of farming (evidence of which can still be detected in the terraces on the flanks of Arthur's Seat). The hills of Edinburgh bear the signs of early fortification and hut settlements: when dredged in the 18th century, the waters of Duddingston Loch revealed caches of Bronze Age weapons.

It's not known whether the Romans occupied the Castle Rock, although from their fort at Inveresk, five miles away, they would have had a fine view of its imposing bulk. However, the Rock is known to have been a stronghold for Celtic tribes. King Mynyddog ruled from the Rock at the start of the seventh century; it was he and his people who named it Dun Eidyn, meaning 'hill fort'.

In AD 638, southern Scotland was conquered by the Northumbrians, who built on the Rock and Anglicised its name to Edinburgh. But in the middle of the tenth century, the MacAlpin kings repelled the Northumbrians southwards. When, in 1018, Malcolm II defeated them at Carham, the Rock and the area surrounding it became Scottish.

THE FIRST CASTLE

The first known castle on the hill was established by Malcolm's grandson Malcolm III, on the throne from 1058 to 1093. Also known as 'Canmore' ('big head' or 'great leader'), Malcolm is best remembered for his appearance in Shakespeare's *Macbeth* and for his marriage to Margaret, the Saxon princess who, fleeing the arrival of the Normans to England, arrived on the shores of the Forth in 1070 and wed the king. Margaret proved a pious but energetic queen: in between producing nine children, she played a central role in the introduction of Roman Catholicism to Scotland, founded a priory at Dunfermline in Fife and established a ferry service for pilgrims across the Forth. The oldest extant building on the Rock, the 12th-century St Margaret's Chapel, is dedicated to her.

After a brief period when Malcolm's brother Donald sat on the throne in a joint rule with his nephew Edmund, three of Malcolm and Margaret's six sons went on to rule Scotland. Of these, it was David, the youngest, who had the greatest impact. During his three decades on the throne, he established a royal mint in Edinburgh, introduced feudalism to Scotland and established the first royal burghs (towns granted charters to hold markets and fairs).

Edinburgh folklore has it that David was hunting one day when he was knocked from his horse and attacked by a stag, only to be saved when a cross (or 'rood') appeared in his hand. His gratitude to God found a lasting monument in the shape of Holyrood Abbey, which he founded in 1128 with the help of some construction-savvy Augustinian friars. The Gothic ruins of the Abbey can still be seen in the grounds of Holyroodhouse.

With the Abbey in place, Edinburgh began to creep down the spine of the volcanic ridge from the Castle Rock. The houses of the city's burgesses faced on to the High Street; behind them, long gardens rolled downwards, their lower walls used as part of the city defences. Parallel to the Canongate, the deep valley of the Cowgate developed into an entrance through which cattle were herded to market; the newly arrived Black Friars (Dominicans) established a friary at its eastern end in 1230. With a succession of religious orders arriving in the town, Edinburgh became an ecclesiastical centre of some importance.

IN CONTEXT

BRUCIE BONUS

While riding his horse along the coast one stormy night in 1286, Scotland's King Alexander III fell to his death over a cliff at Kinghorn. Alexander left no living children to inherit his title; his young granddaughter, the so-called 'Maid of Norway', died before she could be brought to the throne. With his demise began a long and sombre chapter in Scotland's history of warfare with England.

Repeatedly ravaged by English armies, Scotland nevertheless secured its independence after Robert the Bruce's victory at Bannockburn in 1314. The Treaty of Edinburgh was signed in 1328, ending hostilities between the two kingdoms. The following year, Bruce granted Edinburgh the status of royal burgh, giving its burgesses important fiscal privileges. However, Bruce died mere months later. David II, his son and successor, was only five years old when he ascended to the throne, a position of weakness that left the kingdom vulnerable to renewed strikes by the English. Edward III attacked first in 1333; and then, nine years after David's death in 1371, Richard II followed suit, besieging the castle and burning both the Canongate and St Giles.

David II had died without producing an heir and was succeeded by Robert II, the son of Walter the Steward and Robert the Bruce's daughter, Marjorie. Through this dynastic marriage, Robert II was able to start a dynasty of his own: the House of Stewart. It was during this period that Edinburgh emerged as Scotland's most populous burgh, a position it was to hold for the next 400 years.

A DRAMATIC DYNASTY

The Stewarts proved to be dynastically tenacious, and went on to rule Scotland for three centuries. As individuals, however, they were somewhat short-lived. Being king was a dangerous occupation: this was a period of lawlessness that saw successive monarchs murdered or killed in battle, the throne then passing to children who were too young to rule in their own right. This succession of Stewart child-kings in turn left Scotland vulnerable to the machinations of rival court factions. The family also, as we shall see, proved somewhat unimaginative in their choice of baby names.

James I (1406-37) tried to curb the power of the nobles, but himself became a victim of their power struggles and was murdered at Blackfriars in Perth in 1437. His six-year-old son was hastily crowned James II by his mother at Holyrood Abbey, but his reign, during which the Old Town took shape and the city's first defensive wall was constructed, ended with standard abruptness in 1460 when he was killed by an exploding cannon while besieging the English occupiers of Roxburgh Castle.

ANOTHER JAMES

Like his father and his grandfather, James III (1460-88) inherited the throne as a child, at a time when his kingdom was riven by warring factions and power struggles. Despite the turbulence, the Cowgate emerged as a fashionable quarter during James's reign, the French writer Froissart remarking on its fine aristocratic mansions, gardens and orchards. From around 1485, dwellings were also built in the Canongate. But the lack of a defensive wall left the area open to attack, and the Abbey itself was regularly sacked and looted.

Commerce was also flourishing. As the only major town with a port between the Tweed and the Forth, Edinburgh was ideally placed to capitalise on foreign trade opportunities. But when, in 1469, the town ceased to be ruled by the merchant burgesses, it became a self-electing corporation. Cloth sellers, beggars and fishwives plied their trade from booths around St Giles on the High Street; their stalls eventually became permanent fixtures. In 1477, James III chartered markets to be held in the Grassmarket, partly to alleviate the congestion caused by traders on the High Street. He granted the citizens of Edinburgh the Blue Blanket just five years later, a symbol of the independence of the municipality and the exclusive rights of the town's craftsmen.

Holyrood Abbey. *See p17.*

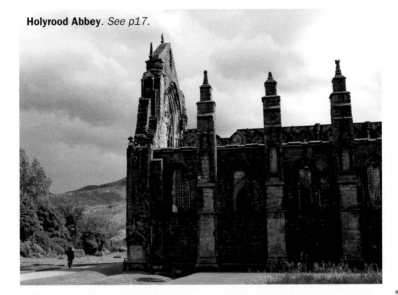

SCOTLAND 2, ENGLAND 2

Holyrood witnessed an occasion of some grandeur on 8 August 1503, when the educated, cultured King James IV married Henry VII's 12-year-old daughter, Margaret Tudor. The events that followed were less splendid. As part of the marriage settlement, James had signed the Treaty of Perpetual Peace with England, but it failed to live up to its name. Only a decade after the accord, the French persuaded James to attack England, and the two countries went to war once more.

In 1513, James IV led his army into Northumberland. Despite their numerical superiority, the Battle of Flodden was a disaster for the Scots: 10,000 were killed, among them the king himself. In Edinburgh, disbelief at the defeat turned to panic when it was realised the English might press north and attack the city. Work on the Flodden Wall began, though the attack never materialised. Still visible in parts today, it had six entry points; when it was eventually completed in 1560, it formed the town's boundary for a further two centuries.

The life and death of James's son James V, who ascended to the throne in 1513 at the age of one, continued the dynastic turmoil but added to it a religious element. When James died in 1542, it was thought that stability could be ensured by marrying off his six-day-old daughter, the future Mary, Queen of Scots. But to whom? The Scots were split between those who wanted a French alliance (Cardinal Beaton and Mary's mother, Mary of Guise, among them) and those who preferred an English match.

Henry VIII of England sent the Earl of Hertford's army to Scotland to 'persuade' the Scots that a marriage to his son, Edward, was preferable. After landing at Leith in the early summer in 1544, Hertford went on to loot both the Abbey and the Palace of Holyroodhouse in an episode that has come to be known as the 'rough wooing'. Hertford's 10,000-strong forces then stormed the Netherbow, but were repulsed.

Three years later, though, in September 1547, the English returned. The Battle of Pinkie Cleuch was fought at Musselburgh, just outside the town, between the insurgent English and the defensive Scots. The Scots lost and were chased back to the gates, but the castle was held; after French and Dutch reinforcements arrived in Leith the following year, the English were finally repelled and the port was reinforced

Murders Most Horrid

Edinburgh's past is awash with grisly tales.

Edinburgh's history is defined by nasty death, its landscape dotted with grim reminders of those who died in less than fortunate circumstances. Few boast grimmer histories than the **Grassmarket**, one of Edinburgh's chief execution sites. A Covenanter memorial on the raised ground next to the zebra crossing marks the spot where the gallows once stood. However, it wasn't just Covenanters who died here: dozens of people had the life choked out of them here. In this light, the name of the Last Drop pub takes on a new meaning; next to it is Maggie Dickson's, named for a woman ('Half-Hangit Maggie') who survived her execution. It's hardly surprising that the area is said to be haunted by a man with rope burns around his neck.

Captain John Porteous was one of many who died here, but not at the gallows. On 14 April 1736, Porteous, Captain of the City Guard, broke up a riot that followed the hanging of smuggler Andrew Wilson by ordering his troops to fire at will, wounding or killing more than 30 people. Found guilty of murder, Porteous was sentenced to death. But when news came through that he was to be reprieved, a furious mob liberated him from prison, dragged him to the Grassmarket and strung him up from a dyer's pole.

The **High Street** also had its share of dramatic executions, including that of William Burke on 28 January 1829 (*see p27*) at the **Lawnmarket**. By all accounts, the day was like a public holiday: although many wanted him 'burked' or strangled by hand, the crowd's roar when he was hanged could be heard in the New Town.

Petty treason – acts of violence or murder against your father, master or husband – could also reap a dreadful punishment, and few were more terrible than that suffered by Robert Weir.

Apprehended in 1604 for the murder four years earlier of the Laird of Warriston, for whom he had worked as a servant, Weir was one of only a few people in Scotland ever to be broken on the wheel, his bones smashed one by one with the cutting edge of a plough. Weir was left to die a slow and agonising death; records show that after 24 hours at the Mercat Cross, Weir (plus wheel) was transported to the scene of his crime near Warriston.

Weir was not the only person implicated in the murder: Jean Livingstone, the Laird's wife, and several other servants were also executed for the crime. Livingstone's serving women were strangled and then burned on Castlehill, close to the spot where today stands the **Witches' Memorial**. The lady herself was beheaded at the Maiden, Edinburgh's guillotine (now on display at the Museum of Scotland), at the Girth Cross of Holyrood.

Witches Memorial.

'John Knox hated Mary, and the period of her reign saw much friction between the Catholic monarchy and the Protestant church.'

to prevent further invasion. At the age of five, Mary was sent to live in France; by the time she returned, Scottish politics was dominated by religious unrest.

MARRIAGE AND MURDER

The Reformation Parliament declared Protestantism to be Scotland's official religion in 1560, and John Knox became the leader of the Reformed Church. The faction that had previously been pro-French and pro-Mary now also became pro-Catholic, while the Protestant forces rallied against them. Knox hated Mary, and the period between her arrival at Leith from France in August 1561 and her abdication in 1567 saw much friction between the Catholic monarchy and the Protestant church.

Mary married Henry Darnley, a cousin, in 1565. Darnley was a grandchild of Margaret Tudor, which made Elizabeth I even more suspicious of their claims on the English throne. Darnley was also a shameless manipulator: it has been suggested that the brutal assassination at Holyrood in 1566 of David Rizzio, Mary's favoured Italian secretary, was engineered by him in an attempt to cause Mary to miscarry, and perhaps even kill her, leaving the throne vacant for his assumption.

The couple's relationship became increasingly fractious until, in 1567, Darnley's house was blown up with him inside. While no proof of Mary's involvement emerged, suspicions fell on Lord Bothwell, one of her most loyal supporters. When the pair subsequently married, public opinion turned violently against the Queen. Forced to abdicate in favour of her infant son, the future James VI, Mary escaped from imprisonment at Loch Leven Castle, only to have her army defeated near Glasgow. She took refuge in England, spending 19 years as the prisoner of Elizabeth I before her execution in 1587.

THE WISEST FOOL IN CHRISTENDOM

Born in a tiny room in Edinburgh castle, James VI (1567-1625) was brought up by Protestant tutors, alienated from his mother, and subject to several kidnapping attempts as a child. By the time he assumed the reins of government, he had grown into a suspicious and wary man. His reign was a permanent headache, thanks to tussles with the economy, the nobles and, above all, the Church.

James VI's long-term ambition was to inherit the English crown from Elizabeth I. Elizabeth, meanwhile, was reluctant to formally recognise 'that false Scotch urchin' as her heir. However, on her death in 1603, Sir Robert Carey galloped up from London to Holyrood in an incredible 36 hours to announce that James VI of Scotland was now James I of England. James, once described as 'the wisest fool in Christendom', left for London to be crowned king, an event known as 'the Union of the Crowns'. He promised to return to Scotland every three years, but it was 16 years before Scotland saw its monarch again.

The years following James's departure were characterised by social unrest, religious turmoil and a loss of national identity, as Scotland came to terms with absentee rule. Even so, the first years of the 17th century were not unprofitable for Edinburgh. Local merchants thrived, with goldsmiths, watchmakers and bookbinders all flourishing in Parliament Square, and the University of Edinburgh, founded in 1582 as the Tounis College, continued to grow. The east wing of the Castle was rebuilt by Sir James Mason; Parliament House was begun in 1632 (the Scottish Parliament was, by then, resident in the city); and, a year later, Holyroodhouse was extended.

IN CONTEXT

MERRY MONARCHS

James died in 1625 and was succeeded by his son, Charles I, who was crowned King of Scots in 1633. Charles made it his mission to impose uniformity throughout the kingdom, but his attempt to force a new liturgy on the Presbyterian Church met with strong resistance (not least from a market-trader named Jenny Geddes, who famously hurled her wooden stool at the pulpit in disgust during a service at the High Kirk of St Giles in 1639). As a result of this perceived assault on their freedoms, a document called the National Covenant was drawn up in order to assert the Scots' rights to both spiritual and civil liberty. On the last day of February 1638, it was read from the pulpit of Greyfriars Kirk; over the next two days, a host of lairds and burgesses came to sign it. Thus began the Covenanting Wars, which continued into the reign of Charles II. The city suffered: trade dropped off and, in 1644, plague killed a fifth of the population.

Charles had been distracted from events in Edinburgh by the outbreak of civil war in England. Although Edinburgh Castle was held by forces loyal to the King, the rule of the Covenant held sway elsewhere in the town. By 1649, Oliver Cromwell had assumed power in England; on 30 January, Charles I was executed. The Scots were outraged that their Parliament hadn't been consulted; but six days later, they proclaimed Charles II to be the King of Scotland, on the condition he accepted the Covenanters' demands.

Charles refused, and instead asked the Marquis of Montrose, who had been loyal to his father, to conquer Scotland for him. However, Montrose was defeated and captured by the Covenanters, brought to Edinburgh and, on 21 May 1650, executed. Cromwell's response was to invade, defeating the Scots under General Leslie at the Battle of Dunbar on 3 September 1650.

RESTORATION, RESTORATION

Although Cromwell's government and the Scots' Presbyterian Church shared the same values, Cromwell's Scottish occupation proved increasingly unpopular. Charles II's return to the throne after Cromwell's death in 1658, an event that became known as the Restoration, was therefore greeted with relief.

It didn't last. When Charles reneged on acts made in favour of Covenanters, discontent simmered once again. After the Covenanters won a crucial victory at the Battle of Drumclog in 1679, Charles sent the Duke of Monmouth to crush them, which he did at the Battle of Bothwell Brig later that year. In a period since nicknamed 'the Killing Time', the survivors were marched to Greyfriars Kirkyard in Edinburgh and imprisoned for five months with little food, shelter or water. Many died or were executed; several hundred others were sent as slaves to Barbados.

James VII of Scotland (simultaneously James II of England) ascended the thrones of both countries on the death of his brother Charles in 1685, but his Catholicism made him unpopular. The Dukes of Argyll and Monmouth tried and failed to unseat him. But when James finally fathered a male heir, a group of English noblemen sought to replace him with William of Orange, a Protestant, and his wife Mary (James's daughter). James fled to France and the protection of Louis XIV.

AN END TO AN OLD SONG

Many in Edinburgh and the Scottish Parliament were delighted by William's ascension to the throne. However, supporters of James VII, named 'Jacobites' after the Latin for James (*Jacobus*), mounted resistance. The misery of civil war was exacerbated by wretched living conditions. And when, in 1698, the so-called Darien Scheme, designed to establish a trading colony in Central America, virtually bankrupted the nation, the citizens cracked, storming the Tolbooth and setting fire to the Cowgate.

The collapse of the Darien Scheme strengthened the hand of those who promoted a union of the Scottish and Westminster parliaments. After much discussion, argument and lavish bribery, the Act of Union became law in January 1707. It would be nearly 300 years before the Scottish Parliament sat again.

THE AGE OF IMPROVEMENT

The 18th century is known in Edinburgh as the 'Age of Improvement'. The phrase refers to the massive building programme that was implemented in the 1760s, but also to the influence of the Enlightenment – the spirit of intellectual inquiry that flourished in the 18th century – among the lawyers, academics and churchmen of the city. Social and cultural improvements arrived apace. For more, see pp48-50.

However, at the start of the 18th century, the city's geography was still profoundly medieval in its nature; a cramped, towering whole clinging grimly on to the hillside. By and large, the old city walls still formed the town boundaries, so as the population grew to well over 50,000 during the 18th century, the only way to build was up. This resulted in the 'lands'; six-, seven-, and even eight-storey buildings that were prone to collapse. Something needed to be done, but what?

REBELLION AND ENLIGHTENMENT

Gradually, southern Scottish cities such as Edinburgh and Glasgow came to realise that their union with Great Britain offered beneficial opportunities for commerce and trade. Edinburgh was initially seduced by the glamour of Charles Edward Stuart, better known as Bonnie Prince Charlie: he 'took' the city in 1745 with the assistance of a number of Highland clans, before heading southwards in an attempt to claim the British throne. However, the sympathies of the townspeople ultimately remained Hanoverian.

Shortly after Charlie's last stand at Culloden, the city embarked on an ambitious building programme: the expansion of Edinburgh across the valley north of the castle. The scheme was influenced by the appalling living conditions in the plague- and epidemic-prone Old Town, but it also had a political motivation: to demonstrate that Edinburgh was a civilised, cultured city. The competition to design the New Town was won in 1766 by a 22-year-old architect named James Craig, with a simple, elegant and harmonious plan (see p38). The two million cartloads of earth dug from the foundations of the New Town formed the basis for the Mound, begun in 1781 but not finished until 1830.

Around the same time, Edinburgh also pushed southwards: George Square was laid out in 1766, and a new college for the university was built in 1789 at the old Kirk O'Fields. But it was the New Town that proved most popular. As the wealthier classes moved north, a social apartheid of sorts formed. The contrast between the gentility of the New Town and the low-life of the Old Town, with its cock-fighting dens and brothels, became a recurring theme that even 21st-century Edinburgh has found hard to shift.

The Geddes Stool.

Just for Laughs

Edinburgh's comedy tradition extends far beyond the Fringe.

Glasgow's place as Scotland's first city of comedy is assured. Generations of comedians, from Stanley Baxter to Billy Connolly and from Armando Iannucci to Frankie Boyle, have seen to that. However, although Edinburgh isn't in the same comedic league, it has generated a fair few comedians of its own.

It helps that the world's biggest collection of stand-ups come together every year on the Fringe, but the city has a record for variety entertainment that stretches back much longer. In the case of **Harry Lauder**, it stretches all the way back to the 19th century. Born in Portobello in 1870 (he later moved to Fife and Lanarkshire), Lauder developed his music-hall act as a singer and comic, dressed in tartan with a trademark twisted walking stick. He was a huge hit in Edinburgh but also found success abroad, especially in Australia and the US.

Maidie Murray emerged from a similar background, developing her accordion act at the Capitol Theatre in Leith as a child performer in the 1930s. She came to prominence in a double-act with her husband, the Greenock-born **Chic Murray**. 'I was bright and peppy while he was sombre,' she recalled, 'so I think we just fitted each other fine.'

In the modern era, Edinburgh's biggest comedy export has been **Ronnie Corbett**. The Edinburgh-born son of a local baker, Corbett grew up in Marchmont and got involved in amateur dramatics before moving to London. After appearing in cabaret and on BBC television's *The Frost Report*, Corbett hooked up with Ronnie Barker for a 16-year run of sketch shows under the umbrella of *The Two Ronnies*.

During the late 1970s, at the fee-paying Clifton Hall School just outside

Harry Lauder.

Edinburgh, Morningside-born **Rory Bremner** honed his gift for mimicry. After studying in London, he turned his talents into a career with *Now, Something Else*, his debut TV series in 1986. By the '90s, his act had become more satirical and political on the long-running Channel 4 show *Bremner, Bird and Fortune*.

In recent years, the city has spawned comics such as **Danny Bhoy** and **Alan Francis**, both of whom have found success at home and elsewhere. For more on the city's contemporary comedy scene, *see pp223-224*.

GREAT SCOTT

The rise of the New Town virtually parallels the increased influence of Edinburgh-born Sir Walter Scott (1771-1832), a titan of the late 18th and early 19th centuries. Scott's character and interests were largely influenced by time spent as a child in the Borders, where he had been sent to recuperate from the polio that would leave him with a permanent limp. The romance of Borders legends and ballads enthralled the imaginative child, and the collection of similar stories from all parts of Scotland became a life-long passion.

After an education at the Royal High School and the Law Faculty of the University, Scott embarked on a starry legal career, while simultaneously finding great acclaim as a writer. But while his literary and legal works are rightly famed, his wider influence should not be underestimated: his tireless efforts almost single-handedly awakened the world to the romantic potential of Scotland, and paved the way for its rehabilitation after the Jacobite debacle. It was thanks to Scott's enthusiasm and perseverance that the long-lost 'Honours of Scotland' – the crown, sceptre and sword of state – were uncovered from their hiding place in Edinburgh Castle and put on public display. He was also responsible for the first visit to Scotland of a British monarch since the reign of Charles II, when, in 1822, he persuaded George IV to visit the capital of 'North Britain'.

VICTORIAN EDINBURGH

Edinburgh added a number of notable features to its townscape in the first three decades of the 19th century, among them Waterloo Bridge in the east and Melville Street in the west. However, not every construction project ended in success; or, for that matter, ended at all. Begun in 1822, William Playfair's National Monument to honour the dead of the Napoleonic Wars was never completed but never destroyed: the Parthenon-like structure, long ago dubbed 'Scotland's Disgrace', stands on Calton Hill to this day. Power was held by London and the intellectual activity of the Enlightenment was declining. Edinburgh's glory days were behind it.

Nevertheless, the city underwent a third period of expansion during the Victorian era, when suburbs such as Marchmont, Morningside and Bruntsfield were erected. The city that had become two-part when the New Town was built found itself with still more

IN CONTEXT

The Darien Chest, used to store assets of the **Darien Scheme**.
See p22.

'Riots in 1812 and 1818 were blamed on poor economic conditions; by the 1830s, cholera and typhoid had decimated the Old Town.'

faces, each with its own character. The solid Victorian suburbs were peopled by the growing middle classes; the grand New Town remained the area of choice for lawyers and judges; and the teeming Old Town became a slum.

Through it all, the population of greater Edinburgh spiralled, growing from 100,000 at the start of the 19th century to 320,000 by 1881. One of the reasons for the dramatic increase was the influx of people from Ireland and the Scottish highlands; displaced by the Clearances, they moved to the city in search of work. Among them were William Burke and William Hare, a pair of Irish labourers who came to work on the Union Canal to the west of the city, but eventually abandoned digging ditches in favour of a more lucrative trade supplying corpses to the University's Anatomy School. Burke and Hare infamously spurned the established – if somewhat unsavoury – practice of digging up recently buried bodies in favour of providing fresh ones, unfortunate by-products of a killing spree the pair carried out from their lodgings in the West Port off the Grassmarket. Convicted of 16 murders in 1829, Burke was hanged on the evidence of his turncoat partner. A pocketbook made from his skin is still on display in the medical museum at Surgeon's Hall on South Bridge.

With the increase in population came unemployment. Riots in 1812 and 1818 were both blamed on poor economic conditions; by the 1830s, outbreaks of cholera and typhoid had decimated the Old Town. The misery was compounded in 1824 when a fire destroyed much of the High Street, leading to the formation of the world's first municipal fire service.

A study conducted by Dr George Bell in the 1850s found that 159 of the Old Town's closes lacked drainage and fresh water; Bell also bemoaned the alcoholism. A decade or so earlier, a separate study undertaken by a young doctor named William Tait had found that the area contained an impressive 200 brothels. Attempts were made to restore the neighbourhood, particularly by William Chambers (Lord Provost from 1865-69), but it was on a downward spiral that was to continue into the 20th century.

When the neglected Paisley Close on the High Street collapsed in 1861, killing 35 people, public outrage caused the Town Council to agree to the adoption of proper health and safety regulations. Dr Henry Littlejohn was appointed as the first Medical Officer of Health in Scotland. Littlejohn's report on sanitary conditions in Edinburgh coincided with the election of the philanthropic publisher William Chambers as Lord Provost, resulting in the improvement scheme of 1866 that cleared some of the slums of the Old Town and created new streets such as St Mary's and Blackfriars.

FASTER THAN WITCHES

The Victorian era was also defined by technological advances, particularly in the fields of transport and medicine. In the early 1600s, London was 13 days away by coach; towards the end of the century, the journey could be done in a 'mere' four days. But with the advent of the age of steam, travel became far easier, to the benefit of all concerned.

Between 1845 and 1846, rail tunnels were built between Haymarket and Waverley Stations, through the south flank of Calton Hill and under the Mound. Trains travelling through them brought tourists and travellers straight into the heart of the city, where they would emerge to face the Castle, the Gothic bulk of the Scott Monument (begun in 1840), the galleries at the foot of the Mound and the splendour of the Princes Street

IN CONTEXT

Work

※RBS
The Royal Bank of Scotland Group

Making **Fred Goodwin**.

Banking on the Capital

The rise and fall of the Royal Bank of Scotland.

If you're in the middle of Edinburgh and have a few minutes to spare, seek out the St Andrew Square branch of the Royal Bank of Scotland, housed in a converted 18th-century mansion set back from the road. When you're inside the circular banking hall, look upwards and marvel at the domed ceiling, all gold-lined, star-shaped panels. Reach for your wallet and take out a Royal Bank of Scotland (RBS) banknote, and you'll see the same design etched in the centre. It's a poignant reminder of the key role played by the RBS in making Edinburgh the fifth largest financial centre in Europe.

The RBS was founded in 1727 as a rival to the then 30-year-old Bank of Scotland, which the British government suspected of harbouring Jacobite sympathies. After a period of intense rivalry, the two banks began to expand, opening new branches and acquiring smaller institutions throughout the 19th and 20th centuries. The Bank of Scotland was the first in Europe to print its own bank notes, while the RBS pioneered the concept of the overdraft.

However, when the RBS Group beat the Bank of Scotland in a battle to take over NatWest in the late 1990s, it became the second largest bank in the UK. The takeover helped to secure Edinburgh's place as the UK's biggest financial centre outside London, a position further bolstered by RBS's aggressive expansion in the following half-decade.

All of which meant that when the banking crisis hit in the autumn of 2008, the RBS had a long way to fall. By February 2009, it had announced the biggest annual loss in British corporate history: a scarcely credible £24 billion. After talk of 20,000 job losses and a virtual nationalisation of RBS, not to mention the injection of more than £30 billion of public money, chief executive Sir Fred Goodwin came in for fierce vilification, especially when it was discovered that he'd walked away with a pension worth £16 million. Some protestors even went so far as to break the windows of Goodwin's home in the Grange while the banker was abroad.

The bank remains in business, but only just. It's now propped up by the UK Treasury, which owns more than 70 per cent of the business. St Andrew Square is still a grand old building. However, the bank's glory days are surely all behind it.

Gardens. In 1890, the completion of the Forth Bridge, hailed as the eighth wonder of the world, linked the city with towns beyond the Forth, while a network of suburban lines facilitated expansion into outlying villages.

And yet for all Edinburgh's optimistic expansion, Glasgow had begun to assume increasing importance in Scotland by the end of the Victorian era. The two international festivals held in Glasgow in 1888 and 1901 far outshone the one staged at the Meadows in Edinburgh in 1886; at the same time, Glaswegians such as designer Charles Rennie Mackintosh were creating an artistic and architectural legacy that is still revered today. As the historian and journalist Allan Massie has pointed out, Edinburgh at the end of the 19th century was just the biggest small town in Scotland.

THE 20TH CENTURY

The history of the first half of the 20th century was dominated by the two world wars. Scots made up ten per cent of British recruitment in the Great War, with 25 per cent of the Scottish male population marching off to war. Long lists of the many who did not return can be seen on Lorimer's Scottish National War Memorial at the Castle.

Although a Zeppelin raid in 1916 caused damage in Leith (and also, with ironic accuracy, scored a direct hit on the German Church at Bellevue), Edinburgh itself suffered very few direct attacks in the first war. The city's lack of heavy industry meant it also escaped the worst ravages of the Depression in the 1930s. Although it was a peripheral victim of the first air raid of World War II in October 1939, when the Luftwaffe attacked Royal Navy cruisers off Inchgarvie in the Forth, it was spared the worst of the aerial attacks during the conflict. Still, Edinburgh already had plenty on its plate.

The suburbs went on creeping outwards, but buildings were in general more likely to be pulled down than put up. At last, the city fathers (and private contractors) got to grips with the decaying Old Town, upgrading the city's infrastructure while also moving the population to outlying areas such as Niddrie and Craigmillar. Even today, visitors to Edinburgh are often left unaware that the city's centre is ringed by poorly resourced housing schemes.

END OF THE MILLENNIUM

Many of Edinburgh's traditional industries, among them publishing, declined during the 20th century. However, the addition of two new universities helped to boost the city's already strong academic reputation, and the city has also become one of Europe's top financial centres, specialising in banking, fund management and insurance. As in the rest of Scotland, the tourist industry continues to be vital to the local economy.

The city's most notable cultural phenomenon of the 20th century was the establishment of the Edinburgh International Festival in 1947. The opening event featured music from the Vienna Philharmonic Orchestra, ballet from Sadler's Wells and theatre from the Old Vic. Just as crucial, though, were the eight theatre companies that, excluded from the official programme, staged shows in smaller venues. Others followed suit in subsequent years, and the ebullient, ever-expanding Fringe began to make a reputation all of its own.

A decade or two before the festival was launched, Edinburgh saw a brief cultural flowering known as the Scottish Renaissance, centred around writers and artists such as Hugh MacDiarmid, James Bridie, Edwin Muir, Lewis Grassic Gibbon and Neil M Gunn. Something of that feel returned during the 1990s, thanks to the presence of a few vibrant publishing houses, such as Canongate, and the international success of Irvine Welsh's *Trainspotting*. The novel brought some realism to the city's image by throwing the spotlight on its ills, chiefly the heroin epidemic that swept through it in the 1980s.

But the event that history may come to regard as the century's most significant came right at its close, with the partial devolution of Scotland and the establishment of a Scottish Parliament in the capital. Edinburgh today is looking to its capital city status, rather than its striking physical landscape, to define itself anew.

Key Events

Edinburgh in brief.

c1-c300AD The rock is the fortress of Votadini, tribal allies of Romans.
c300-c700 The rock becomes the stronghold of the Gododdin, a British tribe.
638 Northumbrians take over southern Scotland.
c950 The Northumbrians are defeated by Kenneth MacAlpin.
1070 Malcolm Canmore marries Margaret. The first castle is built on Castle Rock.
1084-1153 David I reigns, during which he founds the Augustinian Priory at Holyrood.
1243 The High Kirk of St Giles is consecrated.
1286 Alexander III is killed. Scotland is invaded by Edward I of England.
1314 Thomas Randolph retakes the castle from English occupation.
1329 Robert the Bruce gives the Royal Charter to Edinburgh.
1333 Berwick falls to the English.
1349 The Black Death arrives, with further epidemics in 1362 and 1379. One third of the Scots population dies.
1488-1513 James IV's reign; the Great Hall is built at the castle.
1513 The Scots are defeated at Flodden, and James IV is killed.
1542 Mary, Queen of Scots inherits the throne from James V. Holyroodhouse and the Abbey are attacked in the 'Rough Wooing'.
1560 John Knox declares Protestantism the official religion of Scotland.
1561 Mary returns from France to rule.
1582 Edinburgh University is founded.
1603 James VI accedes to the English throne as James I; the Court moves to London.
1638 The National Covenant is signed in Greyfriars Kirkyard.
1639 Parliament House is completed.
1681 James Dalrymple publishes *Institutions of the Law of Scotland.*
1695 The Bank of Scotland is set up.

1699 The Darien Scheme collapses.
1707 The Act of Union; Parliament moves to Westminster.
1726 The city's last witch-burning.
1727 The Royal Bank of Scotland is founded.
1736 The Porteous Riots take place.
1767 Work on the New Town begins.
1784 The last execution in the Grassmarket.
1824 The Great Fire destroys much of the High Street and results in the formation of world's first municipal fire brigade. The Botanic Garden is established at Inverleith.
1836 Work on begins on the building of Waverley Station.
1843 The church is split by the Disruption.
1865 The city's last public hanging.
1871 The first international rugby match is played at Raeburn Park.
1874 Heart of Midlothian FC is founded; Hibernian follows in 1875.
1890 The Forth Rail Bridge opens.
1903 Edinburgh Zoo opens.
1925 Murrayfield Stadium opens.
1947 The first Edinburgh International Festival is staged.
1964 Heriot-Watt University is founded.
1996 The Stone of Destiny returns to Edinburgh Castle.
1997 Scotland votes in favour of establishing a Scottish Parliament.
1998 The Royal Yacht *Britannia* is berthed permanently at Leith.
1999 The Scottish Parliament starts to meet once more.
2002 Fire destroys a block of the Old Town on the Cowgate.
2004 The new Scottish Parliament building is opened by the Queen.
2005 An estimated 225,000 join the Make Poverty History march.
2006 Smoking is banned in all enclosed public spaces.
2009 The collapse and bailout of the Royal Bank of Scotland.

IN CONTEXT

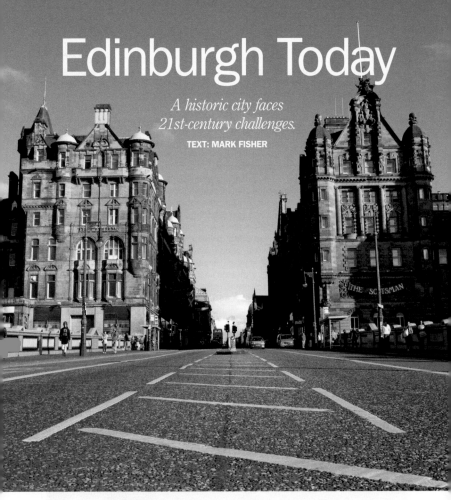

Edinburgh Today

A historic city faces 21st-century challenges.

TEXT: MARK FISHER

A former editor of The List, **Mark Fisher** *is now the Scottish theatre critic for* Variety *and the* Guardian, *and the editor of the Theatre Scotland website (www.theatre scotland.com).*

Read the newspapers, and you'd be forgiven for thinking that Edinburgh's days are numbered. The city's financial institutions are in trouble, the recession has caused deeper unemployment, the local property market has ground to a standstill, and the once-mighty Scotsman newspaper is feeling the severe strain of reduced advertising revenues.

So much for the headlines. Without wishing to belittle the severity of the global slowdown, the impression you get wandering round Edinburgh today is quite different. Far from being a city on the verge of collapse, it appears to be a place of transition, a capital poised on the edge of a new lease of life. Having acclimatised to the arrival of the Scottish Parliament, the city is focusing on itself once more and undergoing a steady process of renewal.

IN CONTEXT

BUILDING ON HISTORY

Although the developers of some large-scale projects in the city centre may beg to differ (*see p40* **Arrested Development**), Edinburgh has long been adept at shedding its skin. Just as the city built the New Town without losing the Old Town (no doubt people grumbled about the inconvenience back then, too), it's repeatedly managed to reinvent itself while retaining the qualities that made it so distinctive in the first place. By the time the first tram hums its way through the streets, all manner of refits and new buildings will have been completed, helping to create a cityscape considerably different from the one criss-crossed by the city's previous tram network just over 50 years ago.

At the Royal Botanic Garden, the gift shop at the west entrance has been demolished to make way for the John Hope Gateway, a new visitors' centre. Over in Chambers Street, the Royal Museum has been undergoing a three-year refit, a £46m scheme designed with the aim of improving the special exhibitions space, introducing a learning centre and adding 16 new galleries to increase the number of exhibits on show.

At the heart of the Lothian Road arts quarter, the Usher Hall – sandwiched between the Royal Lyceum and Traverse theatres and over the road from the Filmhouse – has undergone a £25m refurbishment and expansion, introducing a glass-covered wing to allow more space for audiences, performers and educational work, and better accessibility. The management believes that, construction delays notwithstanding, the changes will return the hall to its status as one of Europe's finest. Efforts are also being made to raise funds for the refurbishment of the century-old King's Theatre, which suffers from dry rot and poor air circulation. Some £6 million has been promised by the council, topped up by £500,000 from Historic Scotland, but more is needed.

On the edge of Calton Hill, meanwhile, the former Royal High School will not be turned into a museum of photography as planned. Instead, the council has launched a competition to encourage developers to suggest imaginative uses for the landmark building which was once in the running to house the Scottish parliament. Sadly, a hotel is a more likely option than a cultural centre.

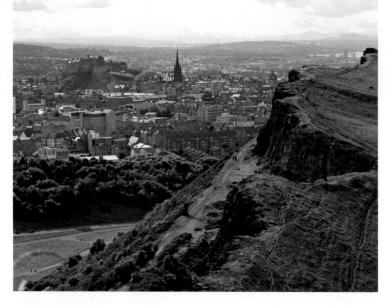

Under Construction

Will Edinburgh's tram network ever get completed?

In spring 2009, a series of posters appeared on lampposts proclaiming 'I ❤ Leith'. One featured a picture of the Royal Yacht *Britannia*; another contained a close-up of a delicacy from Valvona & Crolla. So far, so uncontroversial, but it's a wonder that a third image didn't provoke a riot. The poster pictured a tram. And if there's one thing the people of Leith absolutely did not love in 2009, it was trams.

Once upon a time, Edinburgh had a tram network. It closed in 1956, though, and the decision to build a replacement caused controversy from the start. For one thing, setting up a new tram system from a standing start requires mountains of money: the first phase of the Edinburgh network has a budget of £512 million. And for another, it causes huge disruption. Transport Initiatives Edinburgh (TIE), the council-owned company charged with building the network, couldn't consider laying the rails until it had first repositioned the service pipes beneath the roads. The result was month upon month of traffic delays, precarious pedestrian crossings and a severe drop in trade for shops on the route.

As the scheme moved forward, it grew even less popular. In late 2008, TIE chief executive Willie Gallagher, who had come under pressure from councillors after road closures caused gridlock, left the firm, citing family reasons. Then, at the start of 2009, construction was halted on Princes Street after a financial dispute between TIE and contractor Bilfinger Berger (at that year's Fringe, a team of comics nodded at the delays by calling their show *The Silence of the Trams*). Work on Leith Walk fell eight months behind schedule, and the proposed spur line from Roseburn to Granton was shelved. At present, the only part of the network under construction is the section from Edinburgh Airport out to Newhaven via Princes Street and Leith Walk.

Public opinion on the network may change once the trams are running, hopefully in July 2011. But even then, there will be questions about why there are fewer stops than planned, and whether the same money could have been better spent elsewhere on the transport infrastructure.

▶ *For updates on the tram network, see www.edinburghtrams.com.*

IN CONTEXT

BUY, BUY, BUY

In the field of commerce, the city is forever fretting about holding its own as a shopping destination, faced by tough competition from out-of-town malls and the fashionable boutiques of Glasgow. So it will be interesting to see precisely what becomes of the plans to demolish the architecturally ghastly St James Centre on the east end of Princes Street and build something more attractive in its place. Locals are used to the area being a bit of a building site: the construction of the Omni Centre and two nondescript office blocks next door, blocking the previously clear view of Calton Hill from Leith Street, has gone on for the best part of a decade. The structural changes required by the trams will also result in a new layout in front of St Mary's Catholic Cathedral where currently a set of Paolozzi sculptures sit.

And if this is a city in recession, nobody told Missoni. The Milan-based fashion house opened Hotel Missoni, the first of a planned chain, on George IV Bridge in spring 2009. It's the kind of swanky joint where, on a June afternoon, you're likely to overhear Film Festival directors discussing their newspaper reviews while eager-to-please bar staff work the espresso machine beneath a dozen designer chrome lightshades. The £180 rack rate suggests the economy has a way to go before it hits rock bottom.

Not that Edinburgh has ever been big on flashing the cash. Even in the boom periods – the first years of the 21st century, most recently, when property prices tripled and the city's economy grew faster than those of London, Paris and Dublin – residents kept their consumption inconspicuous. Put it down to the Presbyterian work ethic or to living in a compact city in which rich and poor have always lived at close quarters. But whatever the reason, the moneyed crowd get no more ostentatious than splashing out in the upmarket bars on George Street. Not exactly *Trainspotting* territory, but still pretty discreet.

KEEPING THE CITY MOVING

How long the good times will continue to roll for Edinburgh's good-time crowd and the rest of the population remains to be seen. Certainly, and despite some appearances to the contrary, the city was hit by the global financial slowdown, most dramatically in the case of the Royal Bank of Scotland Group. The bank was on the verge of collapse before being bailed out by the government to the tune of countless billions, to the point where 70 per cent of the banking group is owned by British taxpayers. The demise of the bank would have left a massive hole in the city's economy, not least because after the NHS and the local council, RBS is the city's biggest employer. The collapse of the bank would have introduced shocking levels of joblessness to a city that traditionally hasn't suffered as badly with unemployment as other major UK cities.

Financial problems were also behind the month-long impasse that delayed construction work on the city's controversial tram network in 2009; and when things did get under way again, major disruption ensued. From Leith Walk to Haymarket, the city centre became a warren of metal cages as the workmen dug holes, relaid pipes and set tracks in place, closing roads and diverting traffic as they went. Perhaps it will seem worth it once passengers can make a smooth journey all the way from Newhaven to the airport. But until then, there's nothing about which the locals enjoy complaining more than the nascent tram system.

Summer 2009 saw one piece of good news for the city. After the ticketing shambles of 2008, when the Fringe's box-office computer system collapsed and caused chaos for promoters, venue managers and festivalgoers, sales for the summer festivals remained defiantly healthy in 2009. There's a residual worry, though, that the arts are next in line for financial cutbacks, which can't be good for a local economy so dependent on cultural tourism.

But the city will surely survive. From the volcanic rock of Castle Hill to the ancient closes of the Royal Mile, Edinburgh retains has a sense of permanence, resilience and confidence that, if nothing else, puts its current financial woes into perspective.

Architecture

The past mixes easily with the present in the Scottish capital.

TEXT: KEITH DAVIDSON

Topographically, Edinburgh has been dealt a spectacular hand. The Pentland Hills lie to the south and a coastal plain stretches north and east to the Firth of Forth; Arthur's Seat and Castle Rock, along with Calton Hill and the Salisbury Crags, lend geographical drama.

This magnificent setting has helped shape a city of two distinct characters: the architectural chaos of the Old Town looks across to the regularity of the New Town, a triumph of classical formality played out in a gridiron of well-disciplined streets. In 1995, UNESCO designated the Old Town and the New Town a World Heritage Site, an honour that underlines the city's knack for seducing its visitors. For the visitor interested in architecture, Edinburgh's 800-year building history should prove endlessly rewarding.

Moray House.

IN CONTEXT

EARLY DAYS

Under the ambitious rule of the Malcolm III, Edinburgh's Castle Rock emerged as a fortified stronghold: today's **Edinburgh Castle** (*see p56*). Named for Malcolm's wife, **St Margaret's Chapel** is the earliest architectural survivor from those times. Built around 1120, the small stone building has a chevron-decorated chancel arch. The expanding settlement was declared a royal burgh in 1125 AD; three years later, **Holyrood Abbey** (*see p69*) was founded. Linear development gradually linked Holyrood to the Castle Rock, defining today's **Royal Mile**.

Architecturally, little remains from Edinburgh's infant years. Instability and limited funds meant few structures were built of stone; most houses were instead crudely constructed from wattle and post, covered in clay for insulation, thatched with straw, rushes or heather, and built to last decades at best. Of the handful of medieval stone structures still standing in Edinburgh, St Giles (today's **High Kirk of St Giles** on the Royal Mile; *see p64*) dates from the 12th century, but only fragments of the original building remain; the church was extensively remodelled in the late 14th century.

As its national stature grew during the reign of James III (1460-88), Edinburgh witnessed a surge in confidence. Holyrood Abbey became a royal residence and was expanded, leading to the 1498 addition of the **Palace of Holyroodhouse** (*see p70*). The castle was augmented by Crown Square and its baronial Great Hall, topped with a hammerbeam roof. Money was also pumped into houses of worship, Trinity College Church perhaps most notable among them. The building has long since been demolished, but its magnificent altarpiece, by Hugo van der Goes, was preserved, and is now on display in the **National Gallery of Scotland** (*see p79*). Similar grand gestures resulted in a distinctive crown steeple being added to the central tower of St Giles around 1500. The resulting structure became a template for the numerous crown steeples built in subsequent years on churches across Scotland.

'After the 1707 Act of Union with England, Edinburgh soon came to see architecture as an essential way of asserting its character.'

LIVING ARRANGEMENTS

Narrow lanes, known locally as wynds and closes, developed like ribs from the spine of the Royal Mile during medieval times. Simultaneously, many existing houses had extra storeys tacked on to them, often haphazardly. **John Knox's House** (c1490) is one of the few remaining examples (*see p66*), but it's a relatively restrained one; some timber-framed structures protruded as far as seven feet into the street.

Eventually, building regulations began to rein in the speculators. But even as far back as the 15th century, local architects were experimenting with new ideas in a bid to solve a housing crisis brought on by a rising population. The rocky and uneven terrain of the Old Town, combined with the ancient 'feu' system of land tenure that granted leases in perpetuity, made horizontal development problematic. Expansion was thus forced upwards, leading to the birth of the tenement. Standing cheek by jowl along the Royal Mile, the sandstone or harled (a mix of small stones and lime plaster) tenements had more in common with northern Europe than England. The five-storey **Gladstone's Land** (c1620-30; *see p62*) retains the once commonplace street arcade and an oak-panelled interior.

With the upper Royal Mile awash with merchants, its lower reaches soon became the location of choice for the nobility. **Moray House** (c1628, with its pyramid-topped gate piers, and the vast **Queensberry House** (c1634; *see p69*), now part of the new Scottish Parliament complex, are the grandest of the buildings that survive. Around this time, buildings regulators began introducing measures intended to reduce the risk of fire: a law in the 1620s stipulated that all buildings must have tile or slate roofs, and a 1674 edict forced developers to give their properties stone façades. The Palace of Holyroodhouse was rebuilt in the 1670s with a triumphant blend of Scottish and European influences, creating a thickset façade with turreted towers fronting an inner courtyard lined with classical arcades.

New wealth brought along in its well-heeled wake a new **Parliament House**; built next to St Giles in 1637, its presence added weight to Edinburgh's role as Scotland's capital. The building was given a classical overhaul in the early 19th century. Elsewhere, the city flaunted its internationalism, exemplified by its easy (if rather tardy) handling of the Renaissance 'palace' style in the grandly ornamented **George Heriot's School** (1628), south of the Royal Mile. Churches were regularly built along the Royal Mile, among them John Mylne's handsome **Tron Kirk** (1663; *see p65*) and the aristocratic, Dutch-looking **Canongate Kirk** (1688; *see p68*), with its delicate, curving gables.

TIME FOR A MAKEOVER

The 1707 Act of Union with England provoked an identity crisis for Edinburgh, and some dubbed the city 'a widowed metropolis'. But the capital, not given to extended periods of mourning, soon came to see architecture as an essential way of asserting its character.

The collapse in 1751 of a Royal Mile tenement highlighted the run-down state of the Old Town and the need for 'modern' living quarters. George Drummond, the city's Lord Provost, drew up proposals the following year to expand Edinburgh, creating the grandiose **Exchange** (now the **City Chambers**; *see p64*) on the Royal Mile and, in 1765, the **North Bridge** (*see p65*). The bridge, the first to cross Nor' Loch, offered

IN CONTEXT

'The city liked the idea of being an intellectual "Athenian" metropolis, compared with the imperial "Roman" English capital of London.'

easy access towards the port of Leith and, importantly, to a swathe of redundant land north of the Old Town. This was to become the site of the 'new towns', collectively known as today's New Town.

Conceived as Edinburgh's 'civilised' face, the first **New Town**, designed in 1766 by James Craig, was built to a regimented layout with proportion and grandeur as its hallmarks. One leading practitioner of this new style was Robert Adam, who designed the residential enclave of **Charlotte Square** (from 1792; *see p83*) as a grand full-stop to the west end of George Street. **General Register House** (1789; *see p80*), on the axis of North Bridge, is another example of Adam's well-mannered classicism, its cupolas and pedimented portico a gracious retort to the haphazard gables of the Old Town.

CLASSICAL REINVENTION

By the early 1800s, architecture had taken on an increasingly crucial role in expressing the city's newly cultivated identity. Edinburgh had been dubbed the 'Athens of the North' as early as 1762; though the nickname still raises eyebrows, the city's topography made the analogy plausible. What's more, Edinburgh liked the idea of being an intellectual 'Athenian' metropolis, especially compared with the imperial 'Roman' English capital of London. As the Scottish Enlightenment held sway, architect William Playfair provided a stone and mortar representation of Calton Hill's status as Edinburgh's Acropolis with his **City Observatory** (1818; *see p93*), a cruciform mini-temple capped by a dome.

The Observatory stands next to another Playfair construction. Begun in 1826 to commemorate the Napoleonic Wars, the Parthenon-inspired **National Monument** (*see p93*) is built around 12 huge columns, set on a vast stepped plinth in an attempt at classical allusions. However, a funding crisis meant the structure was never completed; ever since, it's laboured under the nickname 'Edinburgh's Disgrace'. The monument later formed a visual link to Thomas Hamilton's **Royal High School** (1825) on the lower slopes of Calton Hill. Described as the 'noblest monument of the Scottish Greek revival', the structure was neo-classicism at its most authoritative.

Playfair's work can be seen elsewhere in the city. Even after the funding debacle that put paid to his plans for the National Monument he remained a busy man, producing further classical expression in the forms of the **Royal Scottish Academy** (1823; *see p79*) and the **National Gallery of Scotland** (1850; *see p79*), a monumental, temple-inspired duo on the Mound, parading an army of columns and classical trimmings.

SCOTTISH BARONIAL: TRIUMPH OF THE FICTIONAL

George IV visited Edinburgh in 1822 at the behest of Sir Walter Scott, campaigner for the 'tartanisation' of Scotland. Scott's campaign bore fruit in brick and stone when the 1827 Improvement Act advised that new buildings and those in need of a facelift should adopt the 'Old Scot' style. Turrets, crenellations and crows' feet elbowed their way back into the city's architecture; **Cockburn Street** (*see p65*) is a determined example of the style.

Elsewhere, several new public buildings masqueraded as rural piles airlifted from the Scottish Highlands. The old **Royal Infirmary** (1870; *see p73*), to the south of the Royal Mile, sports a central clock-tower and an array of turrets. **Fettes College** (1865-70), north of the New Town, is an exuberant intermarriage of Highland baronial seat and French chateau. Its construction inspired JK Rowling when she was dreaming up Hogwarts School of Witchcraft & Wizardry.

This growing adventurousness soon gave way to architectural promiscuity. The city's well-off institutions showed confident but sometimes florid excess, with a pick-and-mix approach to building style. The **Bank of Scotland** office building, grandly posed on the precipice of the Mound, was given a neo-baroque makeover. The **British Linen Bank** on St Andrew Square, now owned by the Bank of Scotland, instead opted for the Renaissance palazzo look, its Corinthian columns topped by six colossal statues.

The Gothic revival also made its mark. Augustus Pugin, the master of the decorated pinnacle and soaring spire, designed the **Highland Tolbooth** (1844) below Castle Esplanade; today, it's the Hub (*see p59*), headquarters of the Edinburgh International Festival. But the finest line in romantic Gothic came in the shape of George Meikle Kemp's **Scott Monument** (1844; *see p80*) on Princes Street, a fitting memorial to the man who reinvented Scotland's medieval past.

PRETTY VACANT

Little disturbed by industrialisation, late 19th-century Edinburgh saw no huge bursts of construction; in the 20th century, the impetus to build was further anaesthetised by two world wars. Clean-cut 1930s modernism made scant impression, save for **St Andrew's House** (1937-39; *see p92*) on the lower reaches of Calton Hill. Designed by Thomas Tait, with an imposing, symmetrical façade, it's a true heavyweight.

With upwardly mobile residents siphoned off to the New Town, a large part of the Old Town had, by the Victorian era, developed into an overcrowded slum. As early as

Scottish Parliament. *See p41.*

Leith.

Arrested Development

The city centre struggles to change.

The World Heritage status of both the Old Town and the New Town and the complexity of the planning process combine to mean that constructing new buildings in Edinburgh is rarely simple. It can be years before even the best-laid plans make it off the drawing board, and the torporous nature of the process occasionally leaves huge holes in the city's streetscape for extended periods. Locals still remember the 'hole in the ground', an ugly gap site between Lothian Road and Castle Terrace that's now home to a cluster of modern buildings but that had previously lain derelict for an astonishing 25 years.

The **Caltongate** project, around the Canongate, is a prime example. The original £300 million proposal called for the demolition of an unremarkable old bus depot, with a view to replacing it with a hotel, a conference centre, apartments and more. The plan was controversial, partly because it required the destruction of two blocks of occupied tenements on the Canongate. All the same, the depot was levelled in 2006 and Caltongate got the green light two years later... just in time for the credit crunch, which led the developer into administration. Then, in 2009, while other developers vied to take over, UNESCO called for changes. By then, Caltongate had already been a 'hole in the ground' for three years.

That's nothing when compared with an equally ill-starred project nearby. At the end of 2002, a city block located where South Bridge crosses the Cowgate burned to the ground (*see p71*). It took four years for a developer to put forward the **SoCo** proposal, a £40 million multi-use venture (hotel, restaurant, nightclub and so on), and a further three years for the complex to receive planning permission despite local objections. If everything continues on schedule, SoCo (the name comes from 'South Bridge' and 'Cowgate') should be finished by 2011, nine years after the original building vanished.

Some say this dissent is legitimate given the general blandness of modern architecture and its disregard for local communities; others say it's simply conservatism dressed up as high-minded concern. Certainly, the problem in getting anything built in the middle of town contrasts starkly with the massive rebuilding in and around **Leith**, accomplished without anything like the same level of difficulty. Back in town, on the east end of Princes Street, the massive plan to replace the **St James Centre** and **New St Andrew House** shouldn't face any opposition, given the disdain Edinburghers have for the existing buildings. But given the city centre's struggles with major change, it's impossible to know for sure.

1892, influential urban planner Sir Patrick Geddes, who inspired the revamp of Ramsey Gardens just below Castle Esplanade, had proposed seeding the area with members of the university as a means of adding to its intellectual weight, but his plan was not adopted. Instead, in the years before and after World War II, Edinburgh's residents were encouraged to decamp to a series of council-built satellite townships on the periphery of the city. This social engineering was a crude mirror of the earlier and socially exclusive New Town. Through it all, the fate of the crumbling Old Town remained in the balance.

In 1949, as part of a scheme drawn up by town planner Patrick Abercrombie, slum tenements and the grander George Square were demolished to create space for a new university campus. The sacrifice of George Square sent a rallying call to the preservation troops, and much of the Old Town was saved as a result. But other parts of the city suffered through explosions of 1960s brutalism: the ugly, block-like **St James Centre** is the most conspicuous example. The subsequent backlash sent city planners retreating into an ultra-cautious approach. Accusations of architectural timidity reached their height in 1989, when a prime redundant site on the Royal Mile was given over to the Scandic Crown Hotel (now the **Radisson SAS Hotel**; see p118), constructed in a Disneyfied, imitation-Old Town style.

A few modern buildings did sneak past the planning department, most notably around the **Exchange**, the city's new financial quarter to the west side of Lothian Road. Terry Farrell's **Edinburgh International Conference Centre** (1995; see p103) on Morrison Street forms the nucleus of the area, with big-name companies inhabiting the surrounding office blocks. The central parabolic sweep of the **Scottish Widows Building** (1998; see p103) on Morrison Street, while hardly the stuff of no-holds-barred invention, offers the only bold design gesture in the whole precinct.

VOICE OF THE PEOPLE

Although Edinburghers are notoriously unforthcoming, for some years it wasn't hard to coax them into sharing their views on one key building: the **Scottish Parliament** at Holyrood (see p70), the construction of which was a textbook example of poor project management.

The building was first discussed in 1997, although its original budget of £40 million seemed to have been plucked from thin air by an apparatchik. Two years later, there was a site, a plan, an architect – celebrated Catalan Enric Miralles – and an apparently more realistic budget of £103 million. Partly inspired by the hull shapes of some small upturned boats he saw in Northumberland, Miralles' initial vision was far from conservative, but we'll never know how it would have developed under his watch: he died in 2000, aged just 44. The political driving force behind the project, Scottish First Minister Donald Dewar, himself passed away little more than three months later.

As the early years of the 21st century ticked by, the building became a national joke, and its potential architectural merit was eclipsed by more pressing concerns: when would it open, and how much would it cost? The answers were autumn 2004 and a staggering £414.4 million, more than ten times the original think-of-a-number budget.

Up close, the building's exterior can seem fussy and overly detailed, but it's impressive at a distance; take a walk up the Radical Road, under Salisbury Crags in Holyrood Park, and you'll get a much better sense of what Miralles was perhaps trying to achieve. Inside, themes of transparency and accountability are carried through in the design, while the main chamber combines the feel of a television studio with an achingly modern church and even echoes of boat rigging. Since the building opened, outrage about its cost has subsided as more people have seen and been impressed by its interior, and – whisper it – some Scots are now quite proud of the boldness and the philosophy behind the building. Then again, since 2008, Edinburghers have had the trams to moan about instead (see p33 **Under Construction**).

IN CONTEXT

Familiarity failing to breed contempt, as per the parliament, also holds for Michael Hopkins' vast, tent-like **Our Dynamic Earth** adjacent (*see p69*), a huge marquee structure completed in 1999. The only other building of interest up Holyrood Road is the **Tun** (2002), Allan Murray Architects' reinvention of a former brewery building. That said, the tragic **Dumbiedykes** housing estate to the south side of the road did get a facelift between 2003 and 2008, so as not to embarrass its more chi-chi neighbours.

ONWARDS AND OUTWARDS

Despite city-centre headline-grabbers such as **Caltongate** and **SoCo** (*see p42* **Arrested Development**), Edinburgh's main architectural focus of late has been its coastline. When Forth Ports was privatised in 1992, it started to consider new commercial uses for its derelict land; the result was a number of residential developments, the enormous **Scottish Government** building at Victoria Quay in Leith (1996) and the nearby **Ocean Terminal** shopping mall nearby (2001; *see p185*). However, these projects are mere dots on the horizon when compared with the grand plan for Edinburgh Waterfront, which calls for thousands of homes and all kinds of commercial and retail properties between Granton in the west and Leith in the east. It's a long-term venture that may take decades to come to fruition.

The waterfront redevelopment has not been without its hiccups – most recently during the credit crunch of 2008-09, when several property developers went bust and work on some apartment complexes was put on hold. These events are dramatised neatly on the reclaimed land to the seaward side of the Western Harbour between Leith and Newhaven. Home to a row of three plush, contemporary complexes (**Platinum Point**, **Western Harbour** and the **Element**), this stretch should eventually form the centre of a whole new suburb rising from the sea, but for the time being it looks more like a trio of space arks that have crash landed on a grim mudbank. Regardless, the local householders seem confident that it will all turn out well in the end.

Back in the city centre, the big residential news of recent years has been **Quartermile**, a complex of more than 900 apartments at the site of the old Royal Infirmary between Lauriston Place and the Meadows. Down the side of the development, at Simpson's Loan on Middle Meadow Walk, you can find **Peter's Yard**, an airy Swedish bakery and café that opened in 2007. The Union Canal at **Lochrin Basin** in West Edinburgh (*see p104*) has also been a popular site for new-build apartments, albeit on a smaller scale.

Although new buildings with panache can be found around the Old and New Towns, they tend to be discreet, as if the city fathers retain strong memories of the planning decisions that blighted the city in the '60s and are fearful of making similar mistakes. The **Scottish Poetry Library** off the Canongate (*see p73*) and Richard Murphy Architects' apartments on Old Fishmarket Close are two recent, subtle success stories; neat architectural conversions include the **Architecture+Design Scotland** building on Bakehouse Close (*see p68*) and the **Scottish Storytelling Centre** on the Royal Mile (*see p66*). Meanwhile, thousands of people walk past Robert Adam's **General Register House** each day without even noticing the recent changes, the most prominent of which are at the back with the development of **Scotland's Family Centre** (*see p80*).

This is typical of Edinburgh. Modern office blocks that are inoffensive at best are visible all over the city, while more interesting buildings are hidden from passers-by. Unless you walk up Calton Hill, you'd never know the **Glasshouse** hotel (*see p126*) had an attractive roof terrace; unless you walk along Regent Road, it would come as a surprise that the City of Edinburgh Council's new administrative offices over in East Market Street also had grass on the roof. You have to go the furthest for the funkiest new building in town: the sci-fi organics of the Egg lecture theatre (2004), over at **Napier University**'s Craiglockhart campus. Fortunately, neither distant nor hidden, the **National Museum of Scotland** (1998; *see p76*) remains quite the gem: all of Scotland's history in an Old Town building with unexpected visual drama and style.

Literary Edinburgh

Tales of the city.

TEXT: ISLA LEAVER-YAP

The fiction spawned by the Scottish capital has traversed both the grandeur and the gutter with equal relish. Some of Edinburgh's scribes have hurled themselves into the city's netherworlds with rare and committed abandon; take the truculent patter of Irvine Welsh's *Trainspotting*, for instance. Others, though, have sought to cover up the malaise of poverty and marginalisation with the kind of quiet civility for which the city has long been renowned.

Alongside the idealised myth of the Scottish literary tradition has run a simultaneous eagerness to avoid discussing some of the city's harsher realities. For more than 150 years, Scott and the poet Robert Burns have remained the stalwart figureheads of the romantic and tourist-friendly tropes of Scottishness, shot through with lilac hues of heather and heroic scenery. The highbrow status of literature in Edinburgh rests upon the recollections of a decidedly selective memory.

'Rebus continues to tread his fearless path through the perils of Edinburgh's iniquitous side-streets and housing schemes, some purely fictitious but others very much based on reality.'

EARLY PIONEERS

During the late 18th and 19th centuries, Edinburgh's bookselling and publishing industries rivalled those of London, as the city busily preened itself in the wake of the success of its biggest national export: the Scottish Enlightenment. Yet the city responsible for publishing the first *Encyclopaedia Britannica* was by no means one big culture club. The smart drawing rooms of the New Town, favoured by those connected to Edinburgh's publishing industries, stood in stark contrast to the dank closes and squalid alleys of the working-class and still-shambolic Old Town.

The most influential literary figure of this period was **Sir Walter Scott**, who combined a soaraway legal career with a prolific sideline as a writer. Scott's blockbuster poems and novels introduced readers to the hitherto neglected landscape and heritage of the Scottish Borders and Highlands: epic poems such as *The Lay of the Last Minstrel* and *The Lady of the Lake*, and novels such as *The Heart of Midlothian* and *Rob Roy*, communicated the writer's deep knowledge of and love for his Scottish heritage to the literary world of the early 19th century.

One writer who adapted well to the two-faced nature of Edinburgh in the late 18th century was poet **Robert Burns**, a regular visitor. On the one hand, he enjoyed charming polite society in opulent Georgian villas following the success of his Kilmarnock poems in 1786; on the other, he wasn't averse to indulging in the licentiousness of the public inns. But it was left to **Robert Louis Stevenson** to pass comment on the city's curious duplicity in *The Strange Case of Doctor Jekyll and Mr Hyde*. Although the book is purportedly set in London, the topography it depicts is undeniably that of Edinburgh, with its veneer of bourgeois propriety casually bordering on impoverished slums.

Jekyll and Hyde scavenges its plot from the tale of Deacon Brodie, a wealthy Edinburgh cabinet-maker by day but a thief by night, who ended up hanged on gallows he himself had designed. However, the tale also recalls the infamous Edinburgh murderers William Burke and William Hare, who suffocated the incapacitated and elderly before selling their bodies as specimens for use on the university's dissecting tables (*see p25*). Against such a coarse backdrop of real-life violence, *Jekyll and Hyde*'s Manichean tension between enlightened science and inexplicable savagery smacks of wry local satire, with a fitting taste for the gothic that remains alive in the city's literature even today.

ARRIVALS AND DEPARTURES

Like many Edinburghers during the 19th century, Stevenson had a love-hate relationship with the city, finally abandoning its keen winds for the sunnier climes of Western Samoa in the 1890s. National treasure **Muriel Spark** also left the capital, although not before taking inspiration from James Gillespie's High School, her alma mater, while devising the setting for her 1961 novel *The Prime of Miss Jean Brodie*. Spark's old school still sits near the leafy surrounds of Morningside, but the book's shrewd take on Edinburgh's tempestuous religious history and schism between Calvinism and Catholicism takes its backdrop from the Tolbooth, St Giles Cathedral, and, of course, John Knox's house on the High Street. The book's title character even mentions her own lineage back to her cabinet-making namesake.

Edinburgh's uncommon literary talents and its even rarer topography have also pricked the interest of visiting writers. **George Eliot**, **Daniel Defoe**, and **William Makepeace Thackeray** all spent time here, while **Mary Shelley** gave the city a rather unflattering cameo in *Frankenstein*. Although **William Wordsworth** dropped in on Sir Walter Scott, the *Edinburgh Review* of the time had little praise for the emerging poet. Wordsworth and his sister Dorothy spent a couple of nights at the Grassmarket's White Hart Inn; **Thomas de Quincey**, author of the celebrated *Confessions of an English Opium Eater*, went one better and moved here from London in 1826. Residing in a variety of addresses across town, partly in an effort to evade his creditors, the novelist died in the city in 1859.

NATIONAL PRIDE

The city's shape-shifting literary style is due in part to the problematic negotiations of its many identities, since it is a tradition unevenly built upon three languages: English, Scots and Gaelic. From the Union of the Crowns in 1603 and the subsequent shift in the dynamics of power between Scotland and London, through to the failure to secure a Scottish referendum in 1979, and even the comedown that followed the formation of the Scottish Parliament in 1999, the literature of the city has moved with the often volatile rise and ebb of nationalism.

Scottish literature also has enduring links with the legal world, with a preponderance of lawyers and judges among its leading lights. **James Boswell**, Sir Walter Scott, Robert Louis Stevenson, **Henry Cockburn** and **Francis Jeffrey**, the first editor of the *Edinburgh Review*, were all scholars of law before they were writers. Even the *Review*'s motto carried judicial weight: '*judex damnatur ubi nocens absolvitur*', or 'the judge is condemned when the guilty is acquitted'. The *Review* was one of the most influential magazines of the 1800s before closing in 1929; four decades after its demise, its name was recycled to launch a new publication, which continues to print the work of authors local, national and international.

The University of Edinburgh has educated many notable writers. Among them are **JM Barrie**, best known for his ever-young creation Peter Pan, and Edinburgh-born

PENGUIN CLASSICS

SIR WALTER SCOTT

Waverley

The Prime of Miss Jean Brodie

Muriel Spark

IN CONTEXT

Sunshine on Leith.

All Plays, No Work

Edinburgh as seen on the stage.

IN CONTEXT

The way Edinburgh has been represented on stage down the years has had as much to do with novelists as playwrights. Ever since the speedy stage adaptations of the novels of Sir Walter Scott in the early 19th century, it's the fiction writers who have given the city its starring roles through works such as Robert Louis Stevenson's *The Strange Case of Doctor Jekyll and Mr Hyde*, Muriel Spark's *The Prime of Miss Jean Brodie* and Christopher Brookmyre's *Boiling a Frog*. Even *Trainspotting* was adapted for the stage before the famous film was made; several more of Irvine Welsh's novels later made the same journey.

For all that, though, some playwrights have brought the city directly to the stage, often using real-life events as inspiration. **James Bridie**'s 1930 play *The Anatomist* concerns Edinburgh's notorious Dr Robert Knox and the gruesome price of his success. Other writers have taken a historical perspective without necessarily leaning on facts. In 2003, playwright **Peter Arnott** put the city in the psychiatrist's chair in *The Breathing House*, a Victorian-style melodrama about people leading a well-to-do life in a city seething with cholera and syphilis. A different kind of social hypocrisy is lampooned by **Robert McLellan** in his 1948 comedy *The Flouers o'Edinburgh*, which describes an 18th-century capital city acclimatising itself to the union of the crowns and learning to act like the English.

The prolific **David Greig** used the city as a player in two feelgood comedies, *Caledonia Dreaming* and *Midsummer*, while **David Harrower**'s second play, *Kill the Old, Torture Their Young*, was about a city that had changed so much it could even support an events guide such as *The List*. But few plays can match **Stephen Greenhorn**'s *Sunshine on Leith* for the sheer volume of Edinburgh references. Built around the songs of the Proclaimers, the musical went so far as to make jokes about individual shops such as Borlands on Leith Walk, which boasts the unlikely twin specialities of darts and televisions. The jokes didn't all travel; the proud locals, though, didn't mind one bit.

Sir Arthur Conan Doyle, who took inspiration from his professor, Dr Joseph Bell, as he went about devising the character of Sherlock Holmes. More recently, **Alexander McCall Smith**, author of the *No.1 Ladies' Detective Agency* series, studied at the university and went on to become a professor in medical law at the institution. Even after shifting thousands of books on both sides of the Atlantic, he continued teaching until 2005 and has retained his status as a local academic.

THE MODERN WORLD

Despite McCall Smith's success, the city's two most notable contemporary novelists are probably **JK Rowling** and **Ian Rankin**, a pair of writers who embrace the city's taste for the gothic in very different ways. Rowling's Harry Potter books have done much to colour the imaginations of youngsters attending Fettes College, on which Hogwarts may or may not have been partly modelled, but has also provided a not unwelcome fillip to the city's café culture. Rowling, famously, began sketching out her books in local coffeehouses; unsurprisingly, a host of Old Town establishments have since laid claim to being the birthplace of her first novel, *Harry Potter and the Philosopher's Stone.*

Rankin's series of bestsellers exposes the tartan noir of the town and its less touristy vistas, as his characters pass through Edinburgh's brothels, bars and banks with a world-weary demeanour. Rankin, born in Fife but resident in Edinburgh since his days at the university, has built a veritable industry from unassuming beginnings: his crime novels have been adapted for TV and translated into more than 27 different languages, and form the basis for online quizzes, fan gatherings and tours of the city.

While Rankin's life is now a comfortable one, and Rebus has been officially retired since 2007's *Exit Music*, Malcolm Fox, who was introduced by Rankin in *The Complaints* (2009), now treads a fearless path through the perils of Edinburgh's iniquitous side-streets and housing schemes, some purely fictitious but others very much based on reality. But one delight shared by both Rebus and his maker is the Oxford Bar on Young Street in the New Town. A literary landmark since the days of Sydney Goodsir Smith, who was a regular during the 1950s, the bar has long been a favourite both with Rankin and his most famous invention.

Iain Banks lives just outside Edinburgh, but the city and its environs regularly crop up in his work or even inspire it: *Complicity, Whit* and *The Bridge* all carry with them shades of the city. Banks may not enjoy the blockbuster sales of Rowling (or even, for that matter, Rankin), but his novels and epic space operas (*The Algebraist, Excession*) have carved him an important place in the local literary pantheon.

But the novelist who most radically changed the outside world's view of contemporary Scots literature has been Leith-born **Irvine Welsh**, another in a long line of writers keen to expose an urban underbelly that the city fathers would rather conceal. In novels such as *The Acid House* and *Trainspotting*, Welsh writes of a town guilty of self-gentrification and of pushing its predominantly working-class inhabitants into an outer ring of 'problem' housing schemes. A far cry from Muriel Spark's decorous aspersions, lovingly voiced in a clipped Morningside accent, Welsh's Edinburghers are afflicted by privation, AIDS and drug addiction, and bawl their complaints in the legendarily impenetrable Scottish vernacular.

The prose of Scott, Spark, Rowling, Rankin and even Welsh earned Edinburgh the title of UNESCO's first City of Literature in 2004, while the presence of two major annual book festivals on the city's cultural calendar (*see pp206-215*) has been of further benefit to the boom of literary tourism in the capital. With an abundance of endearingly haphazard second-hand bookshops, numerous bars bearing the names of famous local novels and authors, literary pub crawls around the Old Town and even a museum devoted to local scribes, the city has leapt at the chance to articulate and exploit its literary flair. It's to be hoped that the writers the city celebrates continue to expose the corners it doesn't want you to see.

IN CONTEXT

The Brains Trust

How Edinburgh benefited from the Enlightenment.

TEXT: MARK FISHER

Start with the statues. On the Royal Mile by the High Court sits David Hume (*pictured above*), cast as a Roman senator. Opposite the City Chambers, is Adam Smith, upright in his university gown. Down the hill, outside the Canongate Kirk, stands a youthful Robert Fergusson.

There are others. The corner of the National Portrait Gallery yields three more: artist Henry Raeburn, with paint palate; surgeon John Hunter, with skull; and geologist James Hutton, with lump of rock. On a high plinth in West Princes Street Gardens, Allan Ramsay wears a silk nightcap. And then there's a seated Walter Scott (with dog) in the Scott Monument, the world's biggest memorial to a writer.

What connects these men is the Scottish Enlightenment. During the 18th century, Edinburgh set the cultural pace across Europe for cutting-edge scientific, artistic and philosophical thought. According to academic Arthur Herman, writing in *The Scottish Enlightenment* (2001), their intellectual adventurousness created the modern world. We still view our environment and ourselves through their framework.

SO WHY EDINBURGH?

The reasons for this flowering are hard to establish. Perhaps it was the less-than-equal union between Scotland and England in 1707 that led Edinburgh intellectuals to look to Europe, where Enlightenment ideas were taking hold. Perhaps it was the circulation of people passing through on their way to the Americas, bringing with them new ways of thinking. Perhaps it was the unusually high levels of literacy born from the free Scottish education system. Or perhaps it was a mere historical fluke that so many gifted people arrived here in quick succession.

Whatever the explanation, Edinburgh epitomises the dramatic shift from an era of religious doctrine, superstition and subservience to an age of reason, individual will and rational thought. This approach laid the ground rules for a secular society and governs the western mindset to this day. The significance of the men now enshrined in the city's statues is not only in the brilliance of their theories, discoveries, poetry, novels and paintings, but also in their embracing of a radical vision of human society.

Edinburgh cannot take all the credit. It was the German philosopher Immanuel Kant who coined the term 'Enlightenment', and the movement would have been nothing without the contributions of French intellectuals such as Denis Diderot, François Voltaire and Jean-Jacques Rousseau. It was Voltaire, however, who acknowledged Edinburgh's influence; 'We look to Scotland,' he said, 'for all our ideas of civilisation.'

Thanks to advances in science and the cool-headed logic of the scientific method, this was the era when people realised the world was best explained not by blind faith but empirical observation. Such a view encouraged a spirit of questioning that threatened the old orthodoxies, not least that of the church. In place of faith came rational thought; in place of belief in the afterlife came the pursuit of happiness in this world. No wonder accusations of heresy abounded.

In this way, the movement affected all aspects of civilisation, from medicine to religion, from philosophy to literature, each development emboldening the other. As a result, by the following century, it had become possible for Charles Darwin to put forward an idea as iconoclastic as the theory of evolution without being burned at the stake. It was, incidentally, the geological work of James Hutton laid out in *A Theory of the Earth* (1785) and presented to the Royal Society of Edinburgh that helped set Darwin on his pioneering path. Hutton and the other figures who came to prominence in 18th-century Edinburgh represented the whole spectrum of human endeavour, their achievements embracing everything from economics to poetry.

IN CONTEXT

THE LEADING FIGURES

Born in the city in 1711, **David Hume** was the pre-eminent figure in the Scottish Enlightenment, versed in philosophy, history, economics and diplomacy. His first published work, *A Treatise on Human Nature* (1739), had the subtitle 'an attempt to introduce the experimental method of reasoning into moral subjects', which gives a clear indication of how the different academic disciplines were influencing each other. His atheism stood in the way of a university career, and it was only posthumously that his *Dialogues Concerning Natural Religion* was published. However, his ideas were debated vigorously in France at the time, and his influence was still felt among empiricist philosophers in the 20th century.

It was Hume's *Essays Moral and Political* that set the agenda for the science of economics, of which his friend the Kirkcaldy-born **Adam Smith** was a master. Linked to the key Enlightenment thinkers of the day, Smith taught logic and moral philosophy at Glasgow University. In his book *An Inquiry into the Nature and Causes of the Wealth of Nations*, published in 1776, he set out the idea that economic growth was fuelled by the division of labour and made observations about the free-market economy.

In his monument on the Royal Mile, not far from Smith's grave in the Canongate Kirkyard, sculptor Alexander Stoddart kept one of Smith's hands hidden in reference to the economist's description of the 'invisible hand' that seemed to guide the economy in a way that made everyone better off. Although Smith was championed by free marketers in the 1980s, he was also a moralist, one who was writing decades before the word 'capitalism' was even coined, and would have been shocked by the levels of rampant greed encouraged by the laissez-faire economists who claim his name.

His thoughts on ethics did not go unnoticed. According to the academic Robert Crawford, **Robert Burns** produced a 'straight versification of something in Adam Smith' when he wrote: 'O wad some Pow'r the giftie gie us/To see oursels as others see us.' Contrary to his image of an unschooled poet, Burns was a keen reader of Smith's *The Theory of Moral Sentiments* (1759, the year of Burns' birth). Although more closely associated with Alloway and Dumfries, Burns spent time in Edinburgh in the 1780s, and was toasted by the literary establishment as a major Enlightenment figure.

Robert Fergusson was another influence on Burns. The poet died tragically young, succumbing in 1784 at the age of 24, but not before making significant inroads in the writing of vernacular Scots. In turn, Fergusson had been influenced by **Allan Ramsay**, author of *The Gentle Shepherd* (1725) and a leading exponent of Scots language. Emerging from the literary scene created by these writers, **Sir Walter Scott**, born in 1771, went on to popularise the historical novel, which he effectively invented, and established an international career unparalleled in his day.

To these names can be added those of architect **Robert Adam**, whose works include General Register House; **James Boswell**, a noted diarist and the biographer of Samuel Johnson; philosophers **Francis Hutcheson** and **Thomas Reid**; scientists **John Playfair**, **William Cullen** and **Joseph Black**; **James Hutton**, who essentially invented modern geology; historian **Adam Ferguson**, the father of modern sociology; and economist **James Anderson**. Many were painted by the celebrated portraitist **Henry Raeburn**, himself an Enlightenment figure. And to underline the point, Edinburgh was where the first editions of the *Encyclopaedia Britannica* were published, between 1768 and 1771.

Perhaps the most fitting memorial to the Enlightenment, which ended two centuries ago, is not the collection of statues commemorating its leading figures, but the chaotic cultural bonanza of the summer festivals. In some wayward fashion, August in Edinburgh is a perfect tribute to the intellectual curiosity that defined the most vivacious intellectual shindig in history.

James Boswell.

Sights

The Old Town

Edinburgh's historic centre continues to draw the crowds.

SIGHTS

Historians sometimes talk of the 'herringbone' pattern that defines the structure of old Scottish towns and villages, and Edinburgh's Old Town is essentially no different. With the castle in place up on its rock and Holyrood Abbey located a mile to the east, a medieval backbone was created that endures today: the Royal Mile. The streets, wynds and closes falling away north and south complete a picture that now takes in more historic attractions and key sites than anywhere else in Scotland. Against a background of political and religious drama, the Old Town attests to a story of life and death that has spanned nearly a thousand years and left much behind in terms of notable architecture.

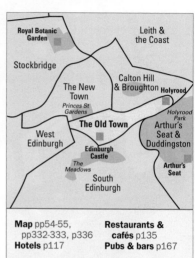

Map pp54-55, pp332-333, p336	**Restaurants & cafés** p135
Hotels p117	**Pubs & bars** p167

INTRODUCING THE OLD TOWN

Edinburgh loosened her stays and expanded in the late 18th century, when the New Town was built (*see pp77-85*). Since then, further urban development has seen it transformed into a sprawling city of 470,000 people. As a result of this expansion, the boundaries of the Old Town can seem compromised or mysterious, but the area still retains its own identity beneath these hidden borders.

In 1513, the Scots suffered a catastrophic defeat to an English army at Flodden in Northumberland. Edinburgh's citizens feared a subsequent invasion, and threw up the Flodden Wall to protect themselves. The course of the wall, or what remains of it, gives a good idea of the city boundaries at the time. Nearly 500 years later, the most apparent parts of the wall still standing are beside **George Heriot's School** and at the east end of the **Cowgate** (for both, *see p73*).

To the north, where Waverley Station and Princes Street Gardens now sit, the town was traditionally protected by the Nor' Loch. However, the wall provided extra insurance, running from the eastern bounds of the loch, up and over the Royal Mile, south up the Pleasance

and west along what's now Drummond Street, then on to Teviot Place and north past George Heriot's and the West Port to the Castle Rock. The enclosed area, plus the environs of Holyrood Abbey, essentially was Edinburgh from the medieval period onwards.

When finding your way around the streets and narrow thoroughfares of the Old Town, bear in mind that a close is a narrow alleyway that usually opens up into a courtyard of some sort (check out Trunk Close or Lady Stair's Close, and read the Scottish poetry extracts carved into the flagstones); a wynd is a narrow winding lane leading off the main thoroughfare; a pend is a narrow, covered entryway to the backcourt of a block of houses; and a vennel is simply a narrow alley. Indeed, narrow is the key word in the Old Town. The buildings were traditionally crammed together, and the streets off the Royal Mile are outlandishly skinny.

In the 15th and 16th centuries, the Old Town was home to two main types of resident: those with money and those without. For residents in the former category, life could be comfortable, if not ostentatious. Even the better houses were sparsely furnished, but they were at least prettified by painted rafters and wall tapestries. The poor, though, suffered, especially as the population grew and sanitation worsened. The Nor' Loch and the Burgh Loch (now the **Meadows**; *see p101*) were dumping grounds for all kinds of waste; householders got rid of slops by heaving them out of the window on to the street below with a warning cry, 'Gardy loo!'

Typhus was rife in the Old Town and, inevitably, plague struck. By the end of the 16th century, it had wiped out a third of the population. One visitor likened Edinburgh to a comb: filthy at the teeth, but with some clean parts in between. Planning for the expansion of the city began in 1752, and construction in the New Town started just a few decades later, but it wasn't until the middle of the 19th century that the cramped environs of the Old Town really became too much for its population, and the Great Flitting' north to the New Town began.

Nearly two centuries later, the residential population of the Old Town is comparatively small, but tourists now make up the numbers. Parts of the area are like a huge open-air museum; the Royal Mile, the area's central street, is neatly bookended by buildings that were completed 900 years apart. At the western end, in the castle, you'll find St Margaret's Chapel, which dates to the early 12th century. And at the street's eastern extremity, at the foot of the Canongate, sits the Scottish Parliament, completed only a few years ago. It's little wonder that UNESCO declared the Old Town a World Heritage Site in 1995.

THE ROYAL MILE

Running between the Castle Esplanade and the Palace of Holyroodhouse, the Royal Mile is a catch-all term for a thoroughfare that comprises four distinct streets: **Castlehill**, the **Lawnmarket**, the **High Street** and the **Canongate**. Key events in Scotland's history have been played out here: kings and queens have sallied from the castle to the palace and back, men have been hanged for criminality and treason, and women have been burned for witchcraft. It's more sedate these days, at least for 11 months of the year.

The Royal Mile is busy with tourist foot-traffic most of the time; unsurprisingly so, since many of Edinburgh's main attractions sit on or near it. It's flanked on both sides by around 60 closes and wynds, which are home to tightly packed clusters of residential tenements, pubs, restaurants and cafés. These skinny streets also provide an eerie setting for many of Edinburgh's popular ghost tours (*see p304*).

Between George IV Bridge and the Tron, the Royal Mile becomes the focal point of August's **Edinburgh Festival Fringe** (*see pp206-215*), as hundreds of street performers and souvenir-hawkers descend upon it to sell their wares. Members of the public not paying total attention may find themselves enlisted as the unwitting star or victim of an amateur juggling act, or the reluctant paperweight for thousands

SIGHTS

Royal Mile.

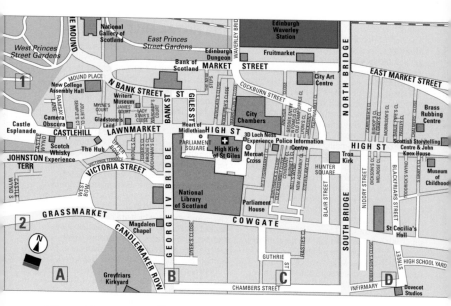

of fliers and free newspapers. The street is also popular year-round with buskers, especially pipers playing reels, airs and the inevitable renditions of *Flower of Scotland*.

This section of the book maps out the Royal Mile from west to east, starting at the castle.

Castlehill

The Royal Mile begins at Castlehill, home – naturally – of **Edinburgh Castle** (*see p56*). The fortress stands on the towering basalt hunk of Castle Rock; one of Edinburgh's extinct volcanoes, it stands 435 feet (130 metres) tall, and has long provided Edinburghers with a vantage point over the city. The rock has been inhabited by humans since at least the ninth century BC; over the ages, a succession of wooden and stone fortifications were built on site, although most of the buildings visible today date from the 18th and 19th centuries.

The castle was a royal residence until the Lang Siege of 1571-73, when supporters of Mary, Queen of Scots were bombarded by troops led by James Douglas. At the time, Douglas was the Regent Morton and governed on behalf of Mary's son, the infant King James VI of Scotland. (He later became the King of England; as England had never before had a king named James, he was styled James I & VI.) The royal home was then moved to the Palace of Holyroodhouse at the other end of the Mile, and the castle was refurbished and heavily fortified. It last heard shots fired in anger in

1745, when its cannons were used to repel the invading forces of the Young Pretender, Charles Edward Stewart (aka Bonnie Prince Charlie, the son of deposed monarch King James II & VII).

The approach to the castle runs through the **Esplanade**, where the almost invariably sold-out **Edinburgh Military Tattoo** (*see p207 and p215*) has been held every August since 1950. When the Tattoo's temporary seating isn't in place, the castle's imposing Half Moon Battery dominates the Esplanade. Built after the Lang Siege to defend the eastern side of the stronghold (the other sides are sheer), it provided the basis for the castle's massive artillery strength. Behind it on the left are the palace apartments, now one of the castle's museums. A small gate at the eastern end of the north side of the Esplanade leads down winding paths to **Princes Street Gardens** (*see p78*).

The view from the Esplanade's southern parapet looks out over the suburbs of Edinburgh as far as the Pentland Hills, while

INSIDE TRACK
STONE ON SCREEN

The supposed mystery surrounding the **Stone of Destiny**, housed at Edinburgh Castle (*see p56*), was dramatised in a 2008 movie starring Billy Boyd and Robert Carlyle, predictably titled *The Stone of Destiny*.

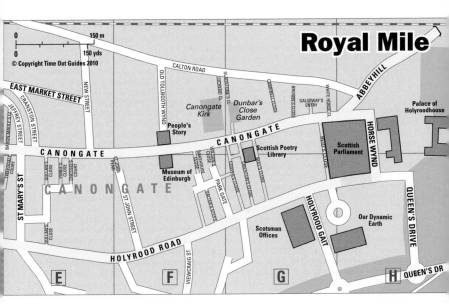

the northern aspect leads the eye over the New Town and across the Firth of Forth to Fife. Various military memorials on the Esplanade serve as sombre remembrance to the many Scottish soldiers killed in action overseas. Also here is the tomb of Ensign Charles Ewart, who single-handedly captured the standard of the famous French Invincibles at the Battle of Waterloo. His memory is celebrated in the name of a nearby pub (521 Lawnmarket, 225 7440).

Look out, too, for the **Witches' Memorial**, a lasting epitaph to a dreadful historical trend Edinburgh shares with much of Europe. Although it's often said to date to the Middle Ages, witch-burning was actually a popular sport of Renaissance and Enlightenment man, and was a paranoid passion of James VI. A bronze, wall-mounted well marks the spot where more than 300 women were burned as witches between 1479 and 1722. It's little comfort to learn that in Scotland, the victims were usually strangled before the fire was lit.

On the extreme left, as you face away from the castle, stands **Ramsay Gardens**, an irregular complex of romantic baronial buildings bristling with spiral staircases and overhangs. Constructed around the poet Allan Ramsay's octagonal 'goose-pie' house, the buildings were erected (for the most part) in the late 19th century in a bid to lure the upper classes back to the Old Town. Today, all of them in private hands, they're some of the city's most desirable and expensive real estate. The low, flat building next to them is less attractive,

but originally performed an important function: as the Castlehill reservoir, built in 1851, it supplied water to Princes Street. It now houses the **Edinburgh Old Town Weaving Co** (*see p59*), an all-round-tourist emporium.

The **Camera Obscura** (*see p56*), the city's oldest official tourist attraction, stands next door in a striking black and white tower. Best visited on clear days, it's akin to an 18th-century CCTV system. Nearby **Cannonball House** is named for the two cannonballs lodged about halfway up the west gable end wall. They're said to have marked the level to which water piped from Comiston Springs in the Pentland Hills would rise, proving that it could be used to feed the Castlehill reservoir. Just opposite is the **Scotch Whisky Experience** (*see p59*), which occupies a former school building. Regular tours offer insight into the history of whisky-making; there's also a well-stocked shop (samples are available) and an educational amusement ride.

A few metres away, where Castlehill meets the top of Johnston Terrace, stands a grand building by James Graham and Augustus Pugin, the latter famed for designing London's Houses of Parliament. Completed in 1844 as the Victoria Hall, it later become the **Highland Tolbooth St John's Kirk**, complete with a towering 240-foot (75-metre) Gothic spire. The church was reopened by the Edinburgh International Festival in 1999 as its base; it's now known as the **Hub** (*see p59*), and has a serviceable café-restaurant (*see p135*).

Camera Obscura & the World of Illusion

*Castlehill (226 3709, www.camera-obscura.co.uk).
Bus 23, 27, 41, 42, 45.* **Open** *July 9.30am-
7.30pm daily. Aug 9.30am-7.30pm Mon-Sat;
9.30am-8pm Sun. Sep, Oct 9.30am-6pm daily.
Nov-Mar 10am-5pm daily. Apr-Jun 9.30am-7pm
daily.* **Admission** £8.50; £4.25-£6.75 discounts.
Credit MC, V. **Map** p54 A1, p332 G7 & p336 D4.
Created by optician Maria Short in the 1850s, the
Camera Obscura is a system of mirrors that projects
a periscope image of the city on to a white disc in
the centre of a small darkened room. Major landmarks are pointed out by the guides as they pan the
lens across Edinburgh. While the camera is no
longer as thrilling as it must have been in Victorian
times, its innate cleverness is still engaging. (Note
that the last camera presentation usually begins an
hour before scheduled closing, sometimes earlier in
winter depending on the levels of daylight.) More
impressive to the modern tourist, perhaps, is the set
of powerful telescopes on the roof, which offer
superb views across the city. Once you've spied on
Edinburghers going about their business from up
here, you'll really begin to notice the CCTV cameras
on the city's street corners.

Before you reach the camera, you'll pass through
three floors of exhibits, including holographs, pin-
hole cameras, morphing machines and other visual
and interactive technology. Kids, though, seem just
as happy playing outside with the distorting mirrors set into the exterior of the building.

★ Edinburgh Castle

*Castlehill (225 9846, www.edinburghcastle.gov.
uk). Bus 23, 27, 41, 42, 45.* **Open** *Apr-Sept
9.30am-6pm daily. Oct-Mar 9.30am-5pm daily.
Last entry 45mins before closing.* **Admission**
£13; £6.50-£10.50 discounts; free under-5s.
Credit MC, V. **Map** p332 F7 & p336 C3.
Military barracks, prison, royal residence, murder
scene, birthplace of kings and queens… Edinburgh
Castle has served a variety of purposes during the
centuries that it's stood high above the city. While
its lofty position was employed to military advantage in years gone by, it's now extremely useful as
a navigational guide if you get lost in the surrounding warren of streets and closes. For most visitors,
however, it's the city's main tourist attraction.

Built on centuries of older structures, the castle
now comprises of a collection of buildings housed
within the protective enclave of the battery walls
(the other sides are protected by the sheer drop of
the basalt cliffs). Many of the buildings were constructed and altered over several centuries, which
can prove confusing for visitors. Although the Great
Hall was originally built in 1511 under the instruc-
tion of James IV, for instance, almost everything
there today dates from an extensive restoration that
began in 1886. The main exception is the incredibly
ornate hammerbeam roof, one of the foremost architectural treasures within the castle.

The oldest extant building is **St Margaret's
Chapel**. Dating from the 12th-century reign of
David I, it fell out of use in the 16th century and was

Bang!

Why are cannons still fired each day at Edinburgh Castle?

The gunfire that emanates from Edinburgh
Castle each lunchtime isn't a tribute to its
military history. The tradition arose in the
19th century as an aid to sailors out in
Leith Harbour, and an echo of the time
ball atop Nelson's Monument on Calton

Hill. Starting in 1861, the ball was raised
and then dropped at precisely 1pm to
allow seamen to check their chronometers
were set correctly. Unfortunately, the ball
was often shrouded in fog, and it was
decided that a cannon should be fired
simultaneously. That way, if sailors couldn't
see the signal, they could at least hear it.

Technology has moved on a little since
then, but the tradition continues. At 1pm
daily (except Sundays), a burst of shellfire
booms from a field gun on the castle walls,
terrifying unprepared tourists while amusing
the locals. Since the death in 2005 of local
hero Tom McKay (aka 'Tam the Gun'), who
performed the task for 27 years, the task
has been shared by various bombardiers.
McKay's long service was commemorated
by the 2006 arrival of a memorial bench
close to the gun; if you think your eardrums
can take the noise, it affords a good view
of the action.

Edinburgh Castle.

employed as a gunpowder store for years. Its intended use was rediscovered in 1845, and it was restored to a serene simplicity. **David's Tower** – or, rather, the ruins of it – is another remnant of early royal constructions, although most of what can be seen in the dank vaults dates from rebuilding after the Lang Siege. The **Royal Palace** in Crown Square (originally the Palace Yard) requires far less imagination to visualise its regal history. The redoubtable Mary of Guise, mother to Mary, Queen of Scots, died here in 1560, while Mary herself gave birth to James VI in the birthing chamber, a small, panelled room. The last sovereign to sleep within this royal residence was Charles I in 1633.

The **Honours of Scotland Exhibition** is housed in the Royal Palace, in the first floor's Crown Room. Alongside the Crown, commissioned in 1540 by James V from local goldsmith John Mossman, the Sceptre, presented to James IV by Pope Alexander VI around 1494, and the Sword of State, presented to James IV by Pope Julius II in 1507, you can see the Stone of Destiny (aka the Stone of Scone), on which Scottish kings were crowned for centuries. Or, at least, you can see what staff believe to be the Stone of Destiny. In 1950, four Scots students swiped it from Westminster Abbey, which had been its home since Edward I removed it from Scone Abbey in 1296. Three months later, a similar stone turned up outside Arbroath Abbey, and was taken back to London. It was eventually returned to Scotland in 1996, but opinion is split as to its legitimacy.

The castle is steeped in military history, but it's also still a British Army barracks: it's currently the home headquarters of the Royal Regiment of Scotland and serves as a locus for some of the work of 52 Infantry Brigade. The castle also hosts the **National War Museum of Scotland**, which charts four centuries of Scottish involvement in wars in a humbling and largely objective way.

A more sombre military note is sounded by the imposing **Scottish National War Memorial** on Crown Square. Designed in 1924 by Sir Robert Lorimer and opened in 1927 by the Prince of Wales

(later Edward VIII), it's a shrine to Scotland's war dead. (If you're at the castle solely to visit the memorial, you don't need to pay the entrance fee.) Below Crown Square are the castle vaults, where you'll find an effective reconstruction of the conditions endured by prisoners of war from successive skirmishes with France in the 18th and 19th centuries, and even the American War of Independence.

The buildings are the main attractions at the castle, but it's worth keeping your eyes peeled for more ephemeral bits and pieces: the **Dog Cemetery** on the Upper Ward; the graffiti scrawled by Napoleonic and American POWs (and their banknote forgery equipment); the 'Laird's Lug' spying device in the Great Hall; and Mons Meg, the huge six-ton cannon next to St Margaret's Chapel. Representing the height of technological advancement in her time, she was presented to James II in 1457 and last fired in 1681, when her barrel burst. While you're enjoying the views or scaring yourself with a peep over the drops, spare a thought for Sir Thomas Randolph and his men, who scaled the northern precipice in 1314 in order to wrest the castle from the English.

The most illuminating way of exploring the castle is with one of the audio guides (available in six languages; £3.50, £1.50-£2.50 discounts). The gift shop's offerings cover all bases, from tartan tat and pocket-money treats to toys, shirts and full-size replica weaponry. Disabled visitors should note that a wheelchair-accessible courtesy vehicle runs from the Esplanade to the upper reaches of the castle.

INSIDE TRACK
CASTLE FOR SALE OR RENT

Tourism is vital for Edinburgh's economy, but corporate hospitality forms a useful sideline. Among the venues for hire are parts of **Edinburgh Castle** (*see left*), the **Hub** (*see p59*) and the huge ground floor expanse of **Our Dynamic Earth** (*see p69*).

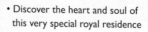

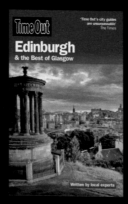

FREE **Edinburgh Old Town Weaving Co**
555 Castlehill (226 1555, www.geoffreykilts.co.uk).
Bus 23, 27, 41, 42, 45. **Open** *Apr-Oct* 9am-6.30pm
Mon-Sat; 10am-6.30pm Sun. *Nov-Mar* 9am-5.30pm
Mon-Sat; 10am-5.30pm Sun. **Admission** free.
Map p54 A1, p332 G7 & p336 D3.
Occupying the building that held the old Castlehill
reservoir, this establishment is like an extensive
complex of concessions where you can do everything from grab an ice-cream to snack in a conservatory café, have your picture taken in full
Highland dress or simply buy a kilt. The weaving
mill itself is run by Geoffrey (Tailor), a respected
Highland outfitters. As well as being a working
mill, this is a Victorian building bang in the heart
of tourist country, and it can get pretty hot and
busy in summer.
▶ *For a more sedate tartan window-shopping*
experience, Geoffrey (Tailor) has another store
further down the Royal Mile; see p193.

FREE **Hub**
348 Castlehill (473 2015 enquiries, 473 2000
tickets, 473 2067 café, www.thehub-edinburgh.
com). Bus 23, 27, 41, 42, 45. **Open** *Café*
9.30am-10pm Mon-Sat; 9.30am-6pm Sun. *Tickets*
& festival office hours vary by season; call for
details. **Admission** free. **Credit** AmEx, MC, V,
Map p54 A1, p332 G7 & p336 D4.
The Grade A-listed Highland Tolbooth St John's
Kirk started life as the Victoria Hall for the
Established Church General Assembly in 1844, following the religious 'Disruption' of the previous
year. After it was bought by the Edinburgh
International Festival in the late 1990s, it was
renamed and extensively refurbished; a fantastic
mix of Victorian Gothic and contemporary style,
it's a prime example of how the architectural
approaches of different eras can be sympathetically
blended. The bold colour scheme of the Assembly
Hall upstairs, said to adhere to Augustus Pugin's
original palette, is particularly noteworthy. The
rich red stairwell is decorated with 200 plaster statues by Jill Watson, representing people who have
performed in the EIF in years gone by. It's now an
information point, a ticket office and a restaurant-
café (*see p135*); if the weather's good, action spills
on to a terrace.

Scotch Whisky Experience
354 Castlehill (220 0441, www.whisky-heritage.
co.uk). Bus 23, 27, 41, 42, 45. **Open** *June-Aug*
9.30am-6.30pm daily. *Sept-May* 10am-6pm daily.
Last tour 1hr before closing. **Admission** £11;
£5.95-£8.50 discounts; free under-5s; £25 family.
Credit AmEx, MC, V. **Map** p54 A1, p332 G7
& p336 D4.
The shop alone makes this tourist-orientated whisky
centre worth a visit. The selection of blended whisky
and single malts, some popular and some obscure,
often includes some nifty limited editions at pre-

> **INSIDE TRACK**
> **LEARN TO DRINK**
>
> Interested in whisky? The **Scotch Whisky**
> **Experience** (*see left*) runs a one-day
> course that covers the drink's history,
> production, blending and marketing. It's
> a serious undertaking – there's even an
> exam at the end.

mium prices: a 40-year-old Dalmore from an oloroso
sherry cask, for instance, at £1,425 per bottle.
However, the hour-long tour remains the main
attraction. Visitors are guided through a series of
displays, exhibitions and finally a theme-park style
ride, which together chart the history of whisky production since the 15th century. Scotland's national
drink is shown in all its constituent parts, with the
tastes, smells and noises of its production cleverly
intertwined in an educational (if light-hearted) sen-
sory journey. If you're over 18, the charge includes
a dram, designed in part to entice drinkers down to
the well-stocked bar below the exhibition.
▶ *There's more whisky nearby at Royal Mile*
Whiskies on the High Street and Cadenhead's
on the Canongate; for both, see p197.

The Lawnmarket &
George IV Bridge

Stretching between the Hub and George IV
Bridge, the Lawnmarket draws its name not
from a grassy history, but from the fine linen
cloth called 'lawn' that was once sold here. The

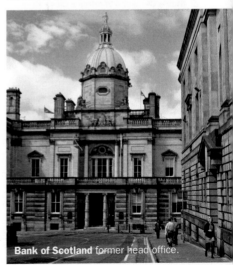

Bank of Scotland former head office.

SIGHTS

SIGHTS

Enter the Labryrinth

The secrets of Edinburgh's closes.

Its one-way streets, labyrinthine topography and devious parking restrictions mean that Edinburgh is best traversed on foot. And nowhere is better suited to pedestrian exploration than the Old Town, thanks to the array of narrow lanes, wynds, stairs, courts and closes that cut across the various levels of the High Street and feed off into the depths of the city.

These cramped, narrow streets originally slipped between Edinburgh's tenements, accommodating taverns, shops and thousands of the city's residents. Their floors were once dirt tracks, with the emphasis on the word 'dirt': all Edinburghers were legally permitted to throw their daily waste out on to the closes. The closes heaved with people; in 1774, it was recorded that they housed more people per square metre than anywhere else in Europe. Living conditions remained dire right up until the early 20th century, and many of the original closes remain condemned these days. However, plenty remain open, and the ability to negotiate them successfully tends to be what separates the seasoned local from the visitor.

Starting from the top of the Lawnmarket at castle level, the **Castle Wynd Steps** will take you right to the bottom of the Grassmarket, while **James's Court**, **Lady Stair's Close** and **Wardrop's Close** all lead in the opposite direction, between the Lawnmarket and the top of the Mound. These latter three closes are a particularly rewarding find, with the Writers' Museum (*see p63*) on one side and the Jolly Judge pub on the other. Directly opposite Lady

Stair's Close is the less inviting **Fisher's Close**, which heads down on to Victoria Terrace and then, a few steps later, on to Victoria Street.

On the south side of Lawnmarket, opposite Gladstone's Land (*see p62*), run two other closes with interesting histories. Leading into two courtyards, **Riddle's Close** was where philosopher David Hume wrote his *Political Discourses*, while nearby **Brodie's Close** was home to the rather less savoury Deacon Brodie, a respectable

street is now dotted with pubs and souvenir shops, but isn't without its appeal, especially once you get off the main drag and explore some of the surrounding closes.

The Lawnmarket's most handsome building is **Gladstone's Land** (*see p62*), a plush and well-maintained 17th-century townhouse. There's another fine building from the same era down nearby Lady Stair's Close: Lady Stair's House, where Robert Burns stayed on his first visit to Edinburgh. Appropriately, it now holds the **Writers' Museum** (*see p63*), which celebrates the work of Burns, Sir Walter Scott and Robert Louis Stevenson. Indeed, thanks in part to the onetime presence of Burns and James Boswell, who used to live on nearby James

Court, this area is now known as Makars' Court from 'makar', the Scots word for poet. Quotations in Scots, Gaelic and English from 17 Scottish writers of note are engraved on paving stones approaching the museum.

Bank Street, which winds around to the left before becoming the Mound, is home to the grand former **Bank of Scotland** head office. Designed in the 1860s along classical lines but embellished with baroque flourishes, the building has a gold statue-topped roof, a highlight of Edinburgh's central skyline. The Bank of Scotland itself merged with Halifax in 2001 to become HBOS, which was then folded into Lloyds during the 2008 banking crisis. Regardless, the **Museum on the Mound**

member of Edinburgh society who led a double life as a burglar. He was put to death outside St Giles on gallows he had designed himself, an irony remembered in the plaque on the wall of Deacon Brodie's Tavern (435 Lawnmarket, 225 6531).

With the exception of a few dead-ends, all the closes along the High Street either feed on to the parallel artery that runs at a lower level – the Cowgate and the Grassmarket – or run towards Princes Street. In the centre of the High Street are **Advocate's**, **Roxburgh's** and **Warriston's Closes**, which bring you to the foot of Cockburn Street. In the 15th century, these tributaries would have taken you down to the Nor' Loch, created as part of the city's defences but eventually a breeding ground for the plague. The water was drained in 1817 to make way for the New Town; the closes are now a handy route to the more pleasant Princes Street Gardens.

Perhaps the most infamous of all the Old Town alleys was lost for two centuries. As part of efforts to gentrify the Old Town in 1753, the grand Royal Exchange (now the City Chambers) was built over part of **Mary King's Close**, the lower floors of which acted as the new building's foundations. The construction was a conscious effort literally to bury the memories of disease, starvation and desperation that lurked in the close, which was quarantined during the plague that struck in 1645. It's said that the whole street was blocked up and its inhabitants left to die; it's now reputed to be one of the most haunted places in Scotland. Forgotten for years, the

underground lane was re-opened to the public in 2003 and is now open for tours (*see p304*).

If you're in a hurry to catch a train, **Fleshmarket Close** cuts through from the High Street right down to Market Street, where a side entrance to Waverley Station sits at the bottom of the close steps. Further down the High Street towards Holyrood, you'll find **Carruber's Close**, once home to the theatre of literary great Allan Ramsay. However, magistrates gave it the final curtain only one year after its opening in 1736. Before this short-lived thespian invasion, the close was a refuge for Jacobites in the late 1600s.

Walk past the Tolbooth and turn left after Canongate Kirk, and you'll find a rather inconspicuous lane that leads to **Dunbar's Close**, perhaps the most rewarding of all the city's closes. At the end is a tranquil garden, with ornamental flower beds and manicured hedges; it's laid out in a 17th-century style, but was created less than 30 years ago by the Mushroom Trust, a local charity.

Nearby, **Lochend**, **Little Lochend** and **Campbell's Closes** all lead on to Calton Road, while picturesque **White Horse Close**, named in honour of Queen Mary's palfrey horse, formed part of the Royal Mews in the 1700s. Nowadays, the old inn building on the close is let as self-catered accommodation. Further up, on the other side is **Crichton's Close**; although not as lavish as its regal counterpart, it leads on to Holyrood Road and is home to the unassuming Scottish Poetry Library (*see p73*).

inside (*see p62*) still offers its engaging history of banking. From here, the Mound continues down to **Princes Street** (*see p77*).

Opened in 1834 to complement the parallel South Bridge, **George IV Bridge** heads south from the Lawnmarket and crosses the Cowgate. The latest addition to the area, at the corner with the Lawnmarket, is the **Hotel Missoni** (*see p117*). Walking across the bridge, a trio of libraries dominate: the **National Library of Scotland** (*see p63*), the **Central Library** (incorporating the Children's Library; *see below*) and the **Music Library**. Numerous bars and cafés dot the length of the bridge; continuing south will eventually lead you to the famous **Greyfriars Kirk** (*see p75*).

FREE **Central Library**

George IV Bridge (242 8020, www.edinburgh. gov.uk/libraries). Bus 23, 27, 41, 42, 45. **Open** 10am-8pm Mon-Thur; 10am-5pm Fri; 9am-1pm Sat. **Admission** free. **Map** p54 B2, p332 H7 & p336 D4.

Built in 1870, the headquarters of the city's library service today houses the Edinburgh Room, the Scottish Department, and reference, fiction and lending libraries. The Edinburgh Room contains over 100,000 items pertaining to the city, from newspaper cuttings to historical prints. It's a reference library only, but some of its items are available on loan from the Scottish Department beneath it.

An adjacent building is home to the Central Children's Library and the Music Library, the latter with an extensive selection of sheet music, biographies and recordings. You have to be a local resident to borrow items, but all are welcome to browse.

Gladstone's Land

477b Lawnmarket (226 5856, www.nts.org.uk).
Bus 23, 27, 41, 42, 45. **Open** *Apr-June, Sept,*
Oct 10am-5pm daily. *July, Aug* 10am-5pm daily.
Closed Nov-Mar. **Admission** £5.50; £4.50
discounts; £10-£15 family. **Credit** MC, V.
Map p54 B1, p332 G7 & p336 D3.

Built in 1550 and extensively rebuilt 70 years later by Merchant Burgess Thomas Gledstanes, an ancestor of prime minister William Gladstone, Gladstone's Land is a typical example of the lands (tenements) that once lined the Royal Mile, right down to the high-level entry to the dwelling up a flight of narrow stairs. The National Trust for Scotland (NTS) maintains the property in the 17th-century style of its former owner; room reconstructions include a bedchamber, complete with painted wooden ceilings and an ornately carved bed, while the inevitable gift shop is found in the restored 'luckenbooth' premises below.

▶ *If you like it, perhaps you'd like to stay in Gladstone's Flat? The NTS rents it out as holiday accommodation; see p133.*

FREE Museum on the Mound

The Mound (243 5464, www.museumonthe
mound.com). Bus 23, 27, 41, 42, 45. **Open**
Aug 10am-5pm Mon-Sat; 1-5pm Sun. *Sept-July*
10am-5pm Tue-Fri; 1-5pm Sat, Sun. **Admission**
free. **Map** p54 B1, p332 H7 & p336 E3.

Opened in September 2006, the Museum on the Mound is housed within the former Bank of Scotland head office (it's now the Scottish headquarters for the Lloyds Banking Group) and is one of only three

---

Go, Figure

Five of the city's most interesting statues.

David Hume.

a talented and prolific poet who died in the city's Bedlam at the age of just 24. Robert Burns had no doubt that Fergusson's fame should have been as great as his own. However, Edinburgh didn't honour him with this statue until 2004, some 230 years after his death.

THE BEST CONCEALED
Visit the Dean Gallery (*see p90*) to be faced with Sir Eduardo Paolozzi's towering **Vulcan**. The creation is a human-mechanoid hybrid that connects past and present: while the subject matter harks back to ancient times (Vulcan was the Roman god of fire), the sculpture's physicality stands as testament to the Modern Age.

THE MOST VENERABLE
There are plenty statues of royalty, but the most interesting royal statue is probably that of **Charles II**, outside St Giles Cathedral in Parliament Square (*see right*). Edinburgh's oldest statue, erected in 1685, it's made of lead with an oak and steel infrastructure, which means it's pretty delicate. Previous restorations have ensured that it's still standing, but currently, like many old men, Charles II is in need of a replacement hip.

THE MOST BELATED
Outside Canongate Kirk (*see p68*), you'll find a statue of a small chap hurrying down the road. This is **Robert Fergusson**,

THE MOST INCONGRUOUS
Officially called **Dreaming Spires**, Helen Dennerly's two giraffe sculptures stand outside the Omni Centre (*see p94*). Made out of scrap metal culled from motorcycles and cars, they're endearing figures. But they also couldn't look much more out of place in their surroundings.

THE OLDEST... OR IS IT?
The statue of **David Hume** on the High Street (*see right*), the work of Edinburgh-born sculptor Alexander Stoddard, is a perfect example of neo-classical composition. But although it looks like it's been there for centuries, it was unveiled as recently as 1996.

SIGHTS

banking museums in the UK. Showcasing a unique collection of artefacts and memorabilia, it has a mix of static and interactive displays to keep visitors entertained. There's a section on forgers and forging, plus a gallery dedicated to the history of Bank of Scotland at the Mound that's set in context alongside the development of the city. The bank itself was founded by the Parliament of Scotland back in 1695; to this day it issues its own banknotes.

FREE National Library of Scotland

George IV Bridge (623 3700, www.nls.uk). Bus 23, 27, 41, 42, 45. **Open** *General & North Reading Rooms* 9.30am-8.30pm Mon, Tue, Thur, Fri; 10am-8.30pm Wed; 9.30am-1pm Sat. *Exhibitions & shop* 9.30am-8pm Mon-Fri; 9.30am-5pm Sat; 2-5pm Sun. **Admission** free. **Map** p54 B2, p332 H7 & p336 E4.

The NLS is one of the UK's deposit libraries, entitled to request a copy of every printed item published in the UK and Ireland. It contains around 14 million printed items, 25,000 newspaper and magazine titles, more than 100,000 manuscripts, and rare books dating to the 16th century (including the first ever printed Scottish history book, *Scotorum historiae a prima gentis origine*). Items can be viewed on here for research purposes, or in the Causewayside building in South Edinburgh, for those 'requiring material not readily available elsewhere'. Admission is by ticket, for which ID is required. Sporadic exhibitions cover various Scottish themes.

FREE Writers' Museum

Lady Stair's House, Makars' Court, Lawnmarket (529 4901, www.cac.org.uk). Bus 23, 27, 41, 42, 45. **Open** *Aug* 10am-5pm Mon-Sat; noon-5pm Sun. *Sept-July* 10am-5pm Mon-Sat. **Admission** free. **Map** p54 B1, p332 G7 & p336 D3.

The only original dwelling of Lady Stair's Close still standing, Lady Stair's House is remarkable for its sharp turnpike staircases and maze-like layout. Built by William Gray in 1622, it was given to the City of Edinburgh in 1907, and now contains curiosities and memorabilia relating to three of Scotland's most celebrated writers: Sir Walter Scott, Robert Burns and Robert Louis Stevenson. Early editions are supplemented by personal effects, including a chessboard and a large ornate pipe once belonging to Scott and one of Burns' snuffboxes. A small corner of the museum contains a selection of the authors' works and comfy chairs in which to curl up and read them. There's also a 'trip step' staircase – a 17th-century burglar alarm – in situ. The museum's permanent displays are supplemented by a programme of temporary exhibitions on Scottish writers past and present.

▶ *The museum is run by Edinburgh Council, which also oversees the Museum of Childhood (see p66), the People's Story (see p70), the Museum of Edinburgh (see p69) and the Brass Rubbing Centre (see p66). All are free.*

High Street, west of the Bridges

Just below the crossroads between George IV Bridge, the Mound and the Royal Mile, the High Street broadens for a short while, with a sense of ordered elegance brought about by Georgian and Victorian planning. A 1997 statue of Edinburgh-born philosopher and historian David Hume, a key figure in the Scottish Enlightenment, watches over proceedings (*see pp48-50 and left* **Go, Figure**). Although it's modern, the bronze is fashioned on classical lines, lending its subject a pedagogic gravitas. Three innocuous brass bricks laid into the opposite pavement mark the site of the city's last public hanging: on 21 June 1864, murderer George Bruce was put to death in front of 20,000 people. The public hangman was busy with other duties at the time, so another prisoner obliged.

This section of the Royal Mile, east of George IV Bridge but west of the North and South Bridges, is an impressive part of town. It's dominated by the suitably imposing **High Kirk of St Giles** (*see p64*), where Scottish Reformer John Knox once preached and where, in 1639, stallholder Jenny Geddes is said to have hurled her three-legged creepie stool at the Dean of Edinburgh as he read from the Anglican Book of Common Prayer, an act viewed by many post-Reformation Scots as being a deal too close to Catholicism. 'Deil colic the wame o' ye, fause thief,' she cried, adding, 'Daur ye say Mass in my lug?'

In the 15th century, the area outside St Giles were crammed with shops and luckenbooths (lockable stalls). Now **Parliament Square**, it's empty save for the occasional ambling tourist. **Parliament House** runs along the back of the square; its plush Parliament Hall is worth a visit. Home to the Scottish Parliament in the 17th century, it's now used by lawyers discussing cases from the adjoining District Court, Court of Session and High Court. It's not unusual to find solicitors marching up and down Parliament Hall, usually in pairs, engaged in earnest discussion about cases on which they're working. The area was once St Giles's churchyard, which explains why John Knox's grave can be found in the middle of a car park.

In front of St Giles, in Parliament Square, is the **Heart of Midlothian**, a heart shape set into the cobblestones of the street that marks the spot where Edinburgh's Tolbooth prison stood (not to be confused with the Canongate Tolbooth, which still survives; *see p68*). Built as a town hall, the Tolbooth became a multifunctional civic building and was used by the Scottish Parliament in the 16th and 17th centuries, until Charles I demanded that a new parliamentary building be built. It continued to house the HQ of the city guard, who often

SIGHTS

High Kirk of St Giles

displayed the severed heads of executed criminals outside the prison. After the building was demolished in 1817, its stones went to build the sewerage system of Fettes Row in the New Town. However, the long-held habit of spitting on the Heart of Midlothian, begun by the criminal fraternity when the land was still held the Tolbooth, is upheld by locals today.

To the east of the kirk stands the **Mercat Cross** ('market cross'), identifiable by the white unicorn holding a Saltire flag at the top of its turret. Reconstructed in the 19th century, the cross once stood at the top of Old Fishmarket Close; the site is marked on the pavement with a pattern of bricks. Among the many unfortunates executed here was James Graham, the dashing Marquis of Montrose. Nearby in Parliament Square sits the **3D Loch Ness Experience** (*see p65*); along the High Street is the **Police Information Centre** (*see p65*) and the **Edinburgh Festival Fringe** office (*see p214*), which sells tickets and souvenirs.

Across the High Street from St Giles are the **City Chambers**, where the city council sits. Completed in 1761 and one of the first truly Georgian buildings in Edinburgh, the premises were originally part of the Royal Exchange. However, when it failed to thrive (traders still preferred to do their business in the open air at the Mercat Cross), the city council moved into the building in 1811. The chambers were built on top of three closes; the most famous, **Mary King's Close**, is today a spooky museum accessible only as part of a tour (*see p304*).

★ FREE High Kirk of St Giles

High Street (225 9442, www.stgilescathedral.org. uk). Bus 23, 27, 35, 41, 42, 45 or Nicolson Street–North Bridge buses. **Open** *May-Sept* 9am-7pm Mon-Fri; 9am-5pm Sat; 1-5pm Sun. *Oct-Apr* 9am-5pm Mon-Sat; 1-5pm Sun. Call for service times. **Admission** free; donations welcome. **Map** p54 B1, p332 H7, & p336 E4.

There's been a church on this site since AD 854. Nothing remains of the earliest structures, but the four pillars that surround the Holy Table in the centre have stood firm since around 1120, surviving the desecration of armies during the Reformation. The kirk was considerably refurbished in the 19th century; much of what can be seen today dates from this period. Pedants should note that the fabric of the building is referred to as St Giles, while the church itself is known as the High Kirk of Edinburgh. Either way, it's the mother church of Presbyterianism.

John Knox became minister here in 1560, 12 years before his death. This was a tumultuous time for religion in Scotland, with Edinburgh – and Knox – very much at the heart of the Scottish Reformation. The kirk has changed status many times through the years, and today is often referred to as a cathedral even though it's only had two bishops in its history. As a Presbyterian place of worship, it cannot technically be considered a cathedral at all.

Inside, a great vaulted ceiling shelters a medieval interior dominated by the banners and plaques of Scottish regiments. The main entrance takes visitors past the West Porch screen, originally designed as a royal pew for Queen Victoria. Newer features include the 1911 Thistle Chapel, an intricately decorated chamber built in honour of a chivalric order named the Knights of the Thistle. The intimate panelled room was designed by Robert Lorimer, who

---

INSIDE TRACK DEAR JOHN

John Knox (*see p21*) may have been the dominant figure in the Scottish Reformation, but he spent most of the period 1547-1559 outside Scotland. He had little choice over his initial departure: while chaplain to a garrison at St Andrew's Castle in Fife, he was captured by the French and spent the next 19 months on slave galleys.

also designed the Scottish National War Memorial at Edinburgh Castle (see p57). Installed in 1992, the organ is an even more recent addition, and features a glass back that reveals its workings.

Memorials and statues pay tribute to the likes of Knox, Robert Louis Stevenson and even Jenny Geddes, but the most notable feature may be the magnificent stained-glass windows. Constructed in the workshops of William Morris, the richly-hued Edward Burne Jones window was designed to be enhanced by the western light it catches. The dazzling West Window, dedicated to Robert Burns by Icelandic artist Leifur Breidfjord in 1984, is also noteworthy, while Douglas Strachan's North Window is a blaze of rich, cold colours and swirling designs.

3D Loch Ness Experience

1 Parliament Square, Royal Mile (225 2290, www.3dlochness.com). Bus 23, 27, 35, 41, 42, 45 or Nicolson Street–North Bridge buses. **Open** *July, Aug* 9.30am-7.30pm daily. *Sept-June* 10am-5.30pm daily. **Admission** £5.95; £3.95-£4.50 discounts; free under-5s; £16.50 family. **Credit** MC, V. **Map** p54 C1, p332 H7 & p336 E4.

No, Loch Ness hasn't been piped down to the city: this is simply a multilingual exploration of the facts and myths that surround this most infamous body of water. You can decide for yourself whether Nessie exists, but most people enjoy the 3D displays.

FREE Police Information Centre

188 High Street (226 6966, www.lbp.police.uk). Bus 23, 27, 35, 41, 42, 45 or Nicolson Street–North Bridge buses. **Open** *May-Aug* 10am-9.30pm daily. *Mar, Apr, Sept, Oct* 10am-7.30pm daily. *Nov-Feb* 10am-5.30pm daily. **Admission** free. **Map** p54 C1, p332 H7 & p336 E4.

Staffed by friendly coppers (indeed, it's a working police office), this small room has information on almost every aspect of policing in Edinburgh both past and present. Historic exhibits include a macabre business-card holder made from the cured skin of grave-robber William Burke (see p27), vicious weapons and some rather splendid truncheons.
▶ *During the Festival, the Lothian & Borders Police Pipe Band plays near the Scott Monument down on Princes Street at noon each weekday.*

Cockburn Street, Market Street & the Bridges

Cockburn Street has long been the city centre's home of alternative culture, ornamented by skiving youths loitering outside record shops. Two galleries (**Collective** and the **Stills Gallery**; *see p229 and p231*) add variety; there's more art to be found if you walk to the bottom of Cockburn Street, turn right on to Market Street and continue past the **Edinburgh Dungeon** (*see right*) to the fine **Fruitmarket Gallery** (*see p230*) and the **City Art Centre** (*see p228*).

INSIDE TRACK
CARRY THE WEIGHT

The **Tron Kirk** (*see below*) derives its name from 'salt tron' (abbreviated to 'tron'), a pillar mounted on steps with a beam and scales, standing on the High Street. This was the public weighing scales for commodities sold in the city in the 17th century; the kirk itself was built close by.

Back up on the High Street, the **Tron Kirk** sits almost opposite the junction with Cockburn Street. Built in the 17th century, it survived as a church into the 1950s and then lay derelict for a time. Excavations in 1974 uncovered a 16th-century thoroughfare named Marlins Wynd beneath the church floor; it was eventually opened as a kind of unofficial tourist information centre and shop. However, the Tron Kirk is now empty once more, after proposals for a café-restaurant ran into financial problems. Just behind it is Hunter Square, a favoured haunt of Edinburgh's homeless fraternity. Some of them can be a little aggressive, so use caution.

At the traffic lights, the High Street is cut in two by North Bridge and South Bridge. Collectively known as the Bridges, they were built to provide access to the south of the city, and hastened expansion into the New Town in the late 18th century. Although the South Bridge looks like a continuous street, it's actually supported by 19 massive arches, only one of them visible.

Looking up North Bridge towards the New Town, the last building on the left of North Bridge formerly housed the offices of the *Scotsman* newspaper. Built for the company in 1905, the rugged, iconic edifice was vacated by the company 94 years later, since when it has been transformed into an impressive luxury hotel (*see p117*). At the front of the building, an enclosed spiral staircase provides a short cut down to Market Street and Waverley Station. This dank stairway has been the setting for foul murder in several Edinburgh-set detective thrillers, and is an entirely credible one at that. Unless you enjoy the stench of stale urine, you may want to take the long way around.

Edinburgh Dungeon

31 Market Street (240 1001, www.thedungeons. com). Princes Street buses. **Open** *Mid Mar-June, Sept, Oct* 10am-5pm daily. *July, Aug* 10am-7pm daily. *Nov, Dec* 11am-4pm Mon-Fri; 10am-5pm Sat, Sun. *Jan-mid Mar* 11am-4pm Mon-Fri; 10.30am-4.30pm Sat, Sun. **Admission** £15; £11-£14 discounts; free under-5s. **Credit** AmEx, MC, V. **Map** p54 C1, p332 H7 & p336 E3.

SIGHTS

If you like your history packed with facts, this might not be for you. However, if disease, murder, exaggerated pantomime mayhem and the pornography of violence are more your bag, then a trip to the Edinburgh Dungeon – run by the folks behind similar operations in London and York – is an entertaining way to find out about Scotland's murky past. Exhibits focus on local horrors, from the plague-ridden streets and brutal judicial executions to the murderous trade of Burke and Hare. There are all sorts of diabolical torture instruments on show, and a reconstruction of the cave that was home to notorious (and, quite possibly, wholly mythical) 14th-century cannibal Sawney Bean. Costumed guides do their utmost to scare you through the place. Tickets are often cheaper if you book in advance online.

High Street, east of the Bridges

Beyond the traffic lights, just behind the Bank Hotel, Niddry Street dips steeply down towards the Cowgate. Behind its shabby walls, which have been done up to represent 19th-century Edinburgh in at least one BBC drama, is a warren of cellars built into the arches of South Bridge, atmospheric places that are brought to life through a number of guided tours (*see p304*). **Nicol Edwards** (556 8642), touted as the city's most haunted pub, is found here.

A little way down the High Street, past the self-consciously historical exterior of the modern **Radisson SAS Hotel** (*see p118*) and hostel-heavy Blackfriars Street, sits the glass façade of the **Museum of Childhood** (*see below*), the first museum of its type in the world. Children who favour a more hands-on experience may prefer the **Brass Rubbing Centre** (*see below*), located just opposite on Chalmers Close. Down from here is the **Scottish Storytelling Centre** (*see below*), which incorporates John Knox House.

If you've time, nip down Trunk Close, just behind the Storytelling Centre. If you're in luck, the gate will be open and you can access a small landscaped garden, one of the many little treasures that lurk behind the gloomy entrances of the city's closes. Another of them, nearby Tweeddale Court, holds one of only a few surviving stretches of the old city wall. The Netherbow, the eastern city gate, used to stand at roughly this point on the High Street.

INSIDE TRACK
THE BELLS! THE BELLS!

The understated modern bell tower at the Scottish Storytelling Centre (*see right*) contains the original **Netherbow Bell**, the official city bell that dates back to 1621.

FREE **Brass Rubbing Centre**
Trinity Apse, Chalmers Close, High Street (556 4364, www.cac.org.uk). Bus 35, 36 or Nicolson Street–North Bridge buses. **Open** *Apr-Oct* 10am-5pm Mon-Sat. Closed Oct-Mar. **Admission** free. **Map** p52 D1 & p333 J7.
The Brass Rubbing Centre is housed in an atmospheric location: the apse that is the only surviving remnant of the Gothic Trinity College Church, founded in 1460. The centre demonstrates that although brass-rubbing might be a good kids' activity, it also can have an artistic side, particularly when Celtic knots are involved. Cheery, friendly staff and good schematic guides show you how it's done.

FREE **Museum of Childhood**
42 High Street (529 4142, www.cac.org.uk). Bus 35, 36 or Nicolson Street–North Bridge buses. **Open** 10am-5pm Mon-Sat; noon-5pm Sun. **Admission** free. **Map** p52 D1 & p333 J7.
This popular attraction was founded in 1955 by local councillor Patrick Murray, who made sure that visitors understood the difference between a museum of childhood and a museum for children. While grins of recognition are usually spread wide across the faces of kids-at-heart of all ages, older generations may enjoy their trip down memory lane more than pre-teens. While there are hundreds of bygone toys on display, many displaying a level of craftsmanship absent on today's shelves, there's a lack of the kind of interactivity that 21st-century kids are growing up to expect from museums. That said, a few early automaton boxes – the Haunted House, Sweeney Todd et al – do provide entertainment. There's a small shop at the entrance; check online for details of guest exhibitions.

Scottish Storytelling Centre & John Knox House
43 High Street (556 9579, www.scottishstory tellingcentre.co.uk). Bus 35, 36 or Nicolson Street–North Bridge buses. **Open** *July, Aug* 10am-6pm Mon-Sat; noon-6pm Sun. *Sept-June* 10am-6pm Mon-Sat. **Admission** *Scotland's Stories* free. *John Knox House: Inside History* £3.50; £1-£3 discounts. **Map** p54 D2 & p333 J7.
The Scottish Storytelling Centre opened in 2006 in a space that was formerly home to the Netherbow Theatre. Now visitors are ushered through the unassuming doorway and past the bright café into a light, airy space holding a free permanent exhibition entitled Scotland's Stories. Aimed at all ages, it contains an interactive wall that serves as an introduction to all kinds of Scottish tradition and literature (Finn MacCuill to Katie Morag); it's full of mini tableaux behind doors, and touchy-feely boxes for the littl'uns. There's also a recess with a sound and vision display on Robert Louis Stevenson. The fully refurbished theatre has been acoustically designed to meet the needs of the unamplified human voice,

Scottish Storytelling Centre & John Knox House.

but the wall can be swung out into the exhibition space to provide a more intimate storytelling room.

The venue also offers access to John Knox House. The building was saved from demolition in 1830 out of reverence for the belief that it was the last home of Knox, the founder of Scottish Presbyterianism. However, there's little conclusive evidence that he ever lived here, and the house is now believed to have been the home of goldsmith James Mossman; certainly, it's Mossman's initials, along with those of wife Mariota Arres, that can be seen on the lintel above the entrance. The museum covers its tracks by offering biographical insights on both Mossman and Knox with a string of treasures and curios. Take time to admire the exterior of the building, with its first-floor entry door, lintel stone, and the exhortation 'Luf God abufe al and yi nychtbur as yi self'.

The Canongate

The Canongate takes its name from the route used by Augustinian canons, who arrived at Holyrood Abbey in 1141, to reach the gates of Edinburgh. Situated outside the old city walls, the Canongate was separate from Edinburgh as recently as 1856; the Netherbow Port marks the spot where one burgh ended and the other began. Now mostly residential, it's dotted with museums and shops offering everything from bagpipes to occult paraphernalia.

Despite the area's history, not everything here is old – the Canongate is no stranger to modern-day architectural controversies (*see p40* **Arrested Development**). Nearby, along East Market Street, a block north, sit Edinburgh Council's modern administrative offices. At the door is *Everyman* by the German sculptor Stephan Balkenhol, which resembles a small oil derrick with a full-colour bronze man on top. The locals were not amused by its reported £100,000 price tag.

By contrast, the Canongate Tolbooth was built back in 1592 and is instantly recognisable by its clock, bell tower and external stairway. The building has served at various points as a council chamber, a police station and a prison; it now houses the **People's Story** (*see p70*), a social history museum.

Opposite sits the **Museum of Edinburgh** (*see right*), which offers fascinating insights into the other end of the social spectrum. The museum is contained within the former Huntly House, three adjoining timber-framed buildings dating to the 16th century that were later extended; they're surmounted by three overhanging white-painted gables of a kind that were once common in the Old Town. Under Huntly House, **Bakehouse Close** leads to the offices of the Architecture+Design Scotland (formerly the Royal Fine Art Commission for Scotland), a national body responsible for

Palace of Holyroodhouse. *See p70.*

promoting high standards of planning and architectural design. An old building made new, it's worth a peek.

The bell-shaped Dutch design of **Canongate Kirk** stands out from the tenement buildings on the Royal Mile. Its construction was ordered in 1688 to house the displaced congregation of Holyrood Abbey, after James II & VII turned the Abbey into a royal chapel for the use of the Knights of the Thistle. It remains Edinburgh's official military church; the royal family often worship here when they're staying in the Palace of Holyroodhouse. Outside on the pavement is a statue to local poet Robert Fergusson, cited by Burns as an inspiration. Fergusson's mental health was fragile and he died in the city asylum in 1774 at the age of just 24.

Canongate Kirkyard has excellent views over Calton Hill, and is the resting place for some well-known figures. Among them are Burns' muse Clarinda, further commemorated in the name of a nearby tearoom (*see p136*). Just the right side of twee, it's a sedate place to relax over a nice cup of tea. Works by Burns and many other poets through the ages, including Fergusson, can be found at the **Scottish**

Poetry Library down Crichton's Close (*see p73*). Nearby is **Dunbar's Close Garden**, at the end of an unassuming close on the north side of the Canongate; it's a lovely place to linger for a few moments.

Further east along Canongate sit some hugely attractive houses, most obviously the two well-kept, gleaming white edifices of **Canongate Manse** and **Whitefoord House**. The latter is now a residence for Scottish war veterans. **White Horse Close** is also very pretty; the gabled building at the end was once a coaching inn, and the departure point for the stage coach to London. It was called into service in 1745 as the officers' quarters of Prince Charles Edward Stuart's army.

At the bottom of the Royal Mile is the **Palace of Holyroodhouse** (*see p70*), one of the Queen's official residences. From a distance, the building appears perfectly symmetrical, but on closer inspection, it becomes clear that the left tower is much older than the right. The palace was damaged by Cromwell's forces, who accidentally burned down the south wing. However, it was restored in the reign of Charles II and lovingly decorated by Queen Victoria, whose influence can still be seen today during the guided audio tours that run when the royals aren't in residence. The purpose of the strange, squat building straddling the fence along Abbeyhill is unknown: it might have been a bathhouse, or perhaps a doocot (where 'doos', or pigeons, nest).

The grounds of the palace contain the ruins of **Holyrood Abbey**, founded by David I in 1128 and irrevocably linked with the Scottish monarchy. James II, born in the abbey lodgings, was married there, as were James III, James IV and Mary, Queen of Scots. James V and Charles I were crowned there; David II, James II, James V and Lord Darnley were all buried within its walls. The abbey suffered extensive attacks throughout the centuries, motivated by politics and religion: it was sacked by Edward II in 1322, damaged in 1544 and again in 1570 (with the loss of the choir and transepts) and violated yet further by a mob of Presbyterian vandals in 1688. It was finally abandoned in 1768.

Close by Holyrood sits Enric Miralles' **Scottish Parliament** complex, controversial from the outset but now settling into its neighbourhood. The complex features an array of distinctive buildings made from glass, concrete and wood, but also takes in the restored and refurbished original buildings, among them the 17th-century, Grade A-listed **Queensberry House**. The second Duke of Queensberry returned home here in 1707 after attempting to placate crowds opposed to the dissolution of the original Scottish parliament. After a hard day at the office, he was probably none too pleased to find that his lunatic son had escaped his guards and spit-roasted the kitchen boy. The oven he used still exists, though the building is now used as parliamentary offices.

The Scottish Parliament is just one of several new constructions around Holyrood Road. Close by are the offices of the *Scotsman*, the modern glass façade of the **Tun** (home to BBC Scotland, the Commission for Racial Equality and the British Council, among others) and the **Macdonald Holyrood Hotel** (*see p118*). And just next to the Parliament buildings sits **Our Dynamic Earth** (*see below*).

FREE Museum of Edinburgh

Huntly House, 142-146 Canongate (529 4143, www.cac.org.uk). Bus 35, 36. **Open** *Aug* 10am-5pm Mon-Sat; noon-5pm Sun. *Sept-July* 10am-5pm Mon-Sat. **Admission** free. **Map** p55 F2, p333 K7.
While the People's Story across the road is a tribute to hardship and to Edinburgh's redoubtable working class folk, the Museum of Edinburgh smacks more of the burgesses and the patrician classes. Housed in three interconnected old townhouses, the displays are fabulously eclectic: glass, silver, pottery, the collar and bowl of Greyfriars Bobby, James Craig's original plans for the New Town and most important in historical terms, the National Covenant of 1638 with some of its signatures written in blood. The creaky wooden floors and view out to the rear courtyard give some sense of what the Old Town was like in the 16th century.

Our Dynamic Earth

Holyrood Road (550 7800, www.dynamicearth. co.uk). Bus 35, 36. **Open** 10am-6pm daily (last admission 4.50pm). **Admission** £9.50; £5.95-£7.50 discounts; free under-5s. **Credit** MC, V. **Map** p55 H2 & p333 L7.
Our Dynamic Earth is near the former home of Edinburgh-born James Hutton, the father of geology. It's anyone's guess what he'd make of its modern, tent-like exterior, but he'd surely approve of its educational aims: to take visitors back to the creation of the universe 14 billion years ago, then bring them forward to the present day. Aimed primarily at school-age children, it's a science museum that takes a gee-whizz approach to the Big Bang, the

---

INSIDE TRACK
GONE FOR A PINT

Holyrood Road is now home to Our Dynamic Earth (*see above*) and the Scottish Parliament (*see p70*), but it used to serve a very different purpose. The land around here used to belong to brewers **Scottish & Newcastle**, until its Holyrood Brewery complex closed in 1986.

SIGHTS

formation of the planet, tectonics and vulcanism, weather, evolution, ecology, climate and more.

There's only one way through the galleries, stuffed with interactive displays, so it's worth taking your time. Staff enter into the spirit of things; while kids squeal during an earthquake simulation, they can touch a real mini-iceberg, and gaze quizzically at bubbling primordial 'soup'. The accompanying scientific explanations are simplistic without being patronising. A major addition in 2009 was the We Are Astronomers movie in the FutureDome planetarium space; narrated by David Tennant, it explains why astronomy is a good thing with the aid of cute graphics and impressive 360° film projection.

★ Palace of Holyroodhouse & the Queen's Gallery

Holyrood Road (524 1120, www.royalcollection. org.uk). Bus 35, 36. **Open** *Apr-Oct* 9.30am-6pm daily (last entry 5pm). *Nov-Mar* 9.30am-4.30pm daily (last entry 3.30pm). Occasionally closed for royal visits and other special events; call or check online. **Admission** *Palace only* £10; £6-£9 discounts; free under-5s; £26.50 family. *Palace & Gallery* £14; £8-£12.50 discounts; free under-5s; £38.50 family. **Credit** AmEx, MC, V. **Map** p55 H1, p329 & p333 L6.

The Palace of Holyroodhouse has its origins in the Abbey of Holyrood (now picturesque ruins), established in 1128 by David I. When Edinburgh was confirmed as the nation's capital, royal quarters were built adjacent to the abbey and have been gradually upgraded and renovated over the years. The building is still used by the Queen as an official residence. When she's elsewhere, parts of it are open to the public, with an audio tour detailing the history of a series of plush bedrooms, galleries and dining rooms.

The tour takes you back to 1566 when, six months pregnant, Mary, Queen of Scots watched as four Scottish noblemen murdered her secretary David Rizzio here, with the consent of Mary's husband, Lord Darnley. Some say Darnley wanted to kill the baby she was carrying (the future James I & VI), believing it not to be his. Darnley died soon after in deeply suspicious circumstances (*see p21*).

After Queen Victoria acquired the Balmoral estate, she began to use Holyroodhouse as a stop-off point on the long journey north. It was Victoria who extensively redecorated the building's then-drab

INSIDE TRACK
THE PRICE OF DEMOCRACY

In 1999, the first realistic cost estimate for the **Scottish Parliament** (*see right*) was £109 million. Within a year that had almost doubled. In 2007, two and a half years after the official opening, the final cost was reported as £414.4 million.

walls with the paintings and tapestries that remain on view today, just a small part of the extensive Royal Collection housed here.

The intricate and ornate entrance to the Queen's Gallery adjacent to the palace leads most visitors to expect a grand, ornate and old-fashioned room; in fact, the interior is surprisingly contemporary. Made up of a series of flexible spaces, the gallery hosts exhibitions from the Royal Collection, with a focus on works from the Royal Library at Windsor Castle. There's also computer access to an e-Gallery, with interactive online exhibition catalogues and details of other works from the collection. *Photo p68.*

FREE People's Story

Canongate Tolbooth, 163 Canongate (529 4057, www.cac.org.uk). Bus 35, 36. **Open** *Aug* 10am-5pm Mon-Sat; noon-5pm Sun. *Sept-July* 10am-5pm Mon-Sat. **Admission** free. **Map** p55 F1, p329 & p333 K6.

With Edinburgh's Tolbooth long since consigned to history, the Canongate Tolbooth is one of the most emotionally resonant buildings in the Old Town. It's where justice was dispensed and prisoners awaited their fate, whether hanging, beheading, branding, burning or transportation. These days, it houses the People's Story museum, but visitors are reminded of its history by the ground-floor tableau of three of the city's less illustrious citizens.

The museum itself is dedicated to the lives of Edinburgh's working classes over the last four centuries or so. The exploits of the feared Edinburgh mob are recorded, but most displays are concerned with more sedate day-to-day life, concentrating on the role of Edinburgh's guilds, unions and friendly societies. Various trades are represented: printers, ship-builders, fishwives and even the redoubtable tram clippies. The exhibits continue to the 1980s or so, including a section on Thatcher's Scotland (complete with an amusing mannequin punk) and testimonies from fans of the city's football teams. The museum also affords a glimpse into the grinding poverty that some of Edinburgh's citizens endured long into the 20th century, and continue to endure to this day in run-down estates. Read their testimonials and a very different side to the city is revealed.

★ FREE Scottish Parliament

Canongate (348 5200, www.scottish.parliament. uk). Bus 35, 36. **Open** *Business weekdays (usually Tue-Thur when parliament is in session)* 9am-6.30pm. *Non-business days (usually Mon, Fri and during parliamentary recess)* 10am-5.30pm weekdays; 11am-5.30pm Sat. **Admission** free. *Tours* £5.85; £3.50 discounts; free under-5s; £17.60 family. **Map** p55 H2, p329 & p333 L6.

The people of Edinburgh had a long wait to see the building that houses their new parliament. When the scaffolding and coverings were finally removed, a confident, dynamic and innovative complex was revealed, different from any other parliamentary

Burning Down the House

Old Town disasters, then and now.

SIGHTS

Before the modern era, the Old Town was characterised by tightly-packed tenements, open fires, lamps, candles and an absence of effective building regulations. Given such a state of affairs, it's hardly surprising that the area has long been plagued by collapses and conflagrations.

Although fire was far from unknown prior to the 19th century, the most terrible blaze on record took place over two days in November 1824. It spread from a printer's shop on the High Street, before apparently been brought under control by the local fire brigade (formed the same year). But then, just when the alarm was over, someone noticed the steeple of the Tron Kirk was burning. Sparks and embers were carried across town on the wind, and yet another fire broke out at Parliament Square a few hours later. When the blaze finally ended the following day, ten people had been killed, hundreds had been left homeless and the Tron Kirk's steeple had collapsed.

The death toll was even higher in November 1861 with the collapse, without warning, of ancient tenements at 99 and 103 High Street. As rescuers scoured the debris, a boy's voice was heard calling, 'Heave awa lads, I'm no deid yet!' An Anglicised version of his cry is carved at the site, above the entry to Paisley's Close. In all, 35 people died in the incident.

Given today's culture of safety and risk-aversion, you might think that comparable disasters would be rare as hen's teeth, but no. In 1989, tenements on Guthrie Street, between Chambers Street and the Cowgate, collapsed because of a gas explosion; one person died. Then immediately before Christmas 2002, a huge fire broke out in the confusing warren of buildings bordering the Cowgate and South Bridge. There were no deaths, but several famous names on the city's arts and leisure scene – La Belle Angele nightclub, the Gilded Balloon fringe venue – were destroyed. The site then lay derelict for years, although redevelopment plans have now been approved (*see p40* **Arrested Development**).

Then, in December 2008, it was the turn of Victoria Street. A fire started in an early Victorian building used as an Indian restaurant, sparking further flames in the roof space. The premises were gutted and the roof was destroyed, putting an end to that incarnation of the restaurant (Khushi's, now relocated) as well as two neighbours: Finnegan's Wake, a pub, and the Liquid Room, a nightclub and music venue. No one died in the fire. But still, when it comes to emergencies and disasters, today's Old Town residents have more in common with their less regulated predecessors than they might think.

Profile Dovecot Studios

Arts and crafts in a swimming pool? The Old Town gets a new resident.

Opened in 1887, the Infirmary Street Baths were the product of Victorian public health improvements. The bathhouse gave people from the neighbourhood somewhere to swim and, more importantly, to wash, making a stand against cholera and other infectious diseases; modern-style bathrooms were not a common feature in the city's working class households at the time. The baths remained in use for more than a century, eventually closing in 1995. They lay derelict for more than a decade, but have now found an unlikely new lease of life.

The roots of **Dovecot Studios** (*listings p73*) go back to 1912, when the fourth Marquess of Bute created a tapestry studio in Corstorphine with the help of two craftsmen who had previously worked with William Morris. The venture worked regularly with artists of a high calibre, among them Stanley Spencer, Henry Moore and Graham Sutherland. Around the turn of the millennium, the seventh Marquess of Bute no longer felt able to lend support to the

studios, which were threatened with closure. But with assistance from Alastair and Elizabeth Salvesen from the family behind transport and logistics company Christian Salvesen, the studios were reborn in 2001. And in August 2008, Dovecot moved into its new home – the old Infirmary Street Baths, transformed with £8 million of the Salvesens' money by Malcolm Fraser Architects.

At the entrance level, there's a reception and exhibition space, in which the studio stages a rotating programme of temporary exhibitions dedicated to art, crafts and design (not solely tapestry). Further inside, the old swimming pool has been converted into an impressive weaving studio, complete with its own mezzanine viewing gallery (open one morning a month). All told, it's a fresh, attractive space, certainly one of the more engaging Edinburgh galleries to have opened in recent years.

MORE FROM MALCOLM
Malcolm Fraser Architects designed several other buildings here, among them **Dance Base** (*see p254*), the **Scottish Poetry Library** (*see right*) and the **Scottish Storytelling Centre** (*see p66*).

building in the UK. If you've time, take the 45-minute tour (check online for times), which explores areas not normally accessible to the casual visitor. If you just want to drop in, however, there's an exhibition about the building, plus a café, a shop and crèche facilities. On business days, tickets are available for the public gallery in the debating chamber for those who book ahead. Seating is limited.

Even if you don't have the time or inclination to venture inside, the building's exterior, along with the garden areas and water features, provides plenty of points of interest. The parliament's dedicated arts strategy is reflected by design components and art installations. Among them is the Canongate Wall, which is covered with quotations from centuries of Scottish writers engraved into blocks of different types of Scottish stone. At the end of the wall is a line drawing of the Old Town based on a sketch made by the building's architect Enric Miralles, who died before the project's completion.

FREE Scottish Poetry Library

5 Crichton's Close, Canongate (557 2876, www.spl.org.uk). Bus 35, 36. **Open** 11am-6pm Mon-Fri; 1-5pm Sat. **Admission** free; donations welcome. **Map** p55 G1, p329 & p333 L6.
Founded in 1984, the Scottish Poetry Library has been housed in this award-winning building since 1999, one of the unlikely architectural surprises concealed down Edinburgh's closes. Robert Burns is well represented on the shelves, but so are scores of other poets, writing in Scots, English, Gaelic or perhaps a language of their own invention. The library also has a small selection of books for sale, including works by local poets. Staff are happy to help with recommendations and will even try to help you track down a poem, even if you can only remember a line or two.

THE COWGATE & SOUTH

At the junction of the Cowgate and Holyrood Road, turn off and head south along the Pleasance. Halfway up is the 16th-century boundary of the Old Town, marked by a remaining corner of the Flodden Wall. Turning from here on to Drummond Street provides a neat shortcut to the **National Museum of Scotland** on Chambers Street (*see p76*). Alternatively, turn north where the Cowgate and Holyrood Road meet, up shop-packed St Mary's Street towards the Netherbow. This crossroads was at one time an entrance to the Old Town, known as the Cowgate Port.

The Cowgate

The Cowgate was originally used by cows and herdsmen passing to and from the fields. However, little of its history is tangible today. Later developments have obscured its distant

INSIDE TRACK IRISH QUARTER

Until the middle of the 20th century, the Cowgate was known as the Irish Quarter, due to the thousands of Irish immigrants who arrived here following the Great Famine in 1846. Many chose to settle in the area because of the presence of **St Patrick's Church** on South Gray's Close, a Catholic church built in 1771.

past; the Old Town fire of 2002 (*see p71* **Burning Down the House**) didn't help.

By the middle of the 19th century, the Cowgate had become one of the most densely populated areas of the city, crammed with impoverished inhabitants. Today, it's a popular centre for alcohol-fuelled hedonism. Come the weekend, the huge **Three Sisters** pub (no.139, 622 6801) takes the lion's share of the street's punters, with the nearby **Subway** nightclub (no.69) providing cheap and cheerful competition to similar spots on Lothian Road. In an attempt to reduce the number of drink-related accidents, the Cowgate is now closed to traffic at night.

On the corner of Blackfriars Street sits **St Cecilia's Hall**, which houses the Russell Collection of Early Keyboard Instruments. Owned by the University of Edinburgh, the hall also hosts musical performances and recitals (*see p235*). Infirmary Street, opposite, leads up to the **Old High School** (1777), the **Old Surgeon's Hall** (1697) and the Victorian premises that once housed the Royal Infirmary, where Joseph Lister discovered the benefits of antiseptic surgery. It's also home to the **Dovecot Studios** (*see left* **Profile**). Near the end of Infirmary Street, on Nicolson Street, is **New Surgeon's Hall**, built in 1832.

Beyond the towering backs of the Sheriff's Court buildings, the Cowgate passes under George IV Bridge. Immediately on the left is the **Magdalen Chapel** (*see p74*), dwarfed by surrounding tenements. In the bloody days of the late 17th century, the chapel served as a mortuary for the executed Covenanters, whose bodies were to be buried around the corner in **Greyfriars Kirkyard** (*see p75*).

FREE Dovecot Studios

10 Infirmary Street (315 3054, www.dovecot studios.com). Bus 2, 23, 27, 41, 42, 45. **Open** *Exhibitions* 11am-5pm Tue-Fri. *Weaving Balcony* 10.30am-12.30pm first Tue of mth. **Admission** *Exhibitions* free. *Weaving Balcony* £3; £2 discounts; free under-16s. **Map** p54 B2, p333 H8, p336 D4.
See left **Profile**.

SIGHTS

INSIDE TRACK
THE OLD CURIOSITY SHOPS

The south-east corner of the Grassmarket where it meets Cowgatehead has the quirkiest row of shops in the city: **Fabhatrix** (hats; *see p195*), **Transreal Fiction** (sci-fi books), **Mr Wood's Fossils** (fossils; *see p199*) and **Armstrongs** (vintage clothes; *see p195*).

FREE Magdalen Chapel

41 Cowgate (220 1450, www.magdalenchapel. org). Bus 2, 23, 27, 41, 42, 45. **Open** 9.30am-4pm Mon-Fri. **Admission** free. **Map** p54 B2, p333 H8, p336 D4.

Built between 1541 and 1547 (the steeple was added in 1626), Magdalen Chapel is the headquarters of the Scottish Reformation Society. The chapel held the first congregation of the Church of Scotland in December 1560, which included John Knox. Its walls are lined with 'brods' (receipts for gifts of money or goods donated to the Chapel) from the 16th to the 19th centuries, which wrap round the walls like a frieze. The chapel also contains the only surviving pre-Reformation stained-glass window in Scotland – modest but significant.

The Grassmarket

There's been a market of some sort at the Grassmarket since at least 1477, when the area received its charter from James III; look out for a plaque laid on the 500th anniversary. Later, the Grassmarket developed a darker history as a venue for executions (*see p20*); these days, though, it's a little more approachable. Indeed, thanks to a £6 million makeover completed in 2008, the **Grassmarket** now looks rather smart. The new plaza feel allows ample space for drinkers and diners to do so alfresco (weather permitting, of course) at pubs such as the **White Hart Inn** (no.34), where Robert Burns is said to have written 'Ae Fond Kiss' here (and where the protagonist in Iain Banks' novel *Complicity* gets some hints about the whereabouts of a dismembered body). There are more events at the Grassmarket than ever, not to mention the occasional market.

At the west end of the row are **Granny's Green Steps**, which lead up to Johnston Terrace and, for the intrepid stroller, a possible walk around the base of Castle Rock. If you don't fancy it, head up the West Bow, which quickly turns into steep, bending and quirky Victoria Street. There's an eclectic range of shops here, selling everything from antique lace and hand-stitched leather bags to henna tattoos. Sadly, a fire just before Christmas 2008 badly

damaged the building containing a restaurant, a pub and a nightclub (*see p71* **Burning Down the House**).

Greyfriars & Chambers Street

Candlemaker Row, off the Cowgate, leads up to where Greyfriars Kirk overlooks George IV Bridge. At the top of Candlemaker Row stands one of Edinburgh's more curious attractions, a small statue of a dog named **Greyfriars Bobby**. When a man named John Gray was buried in the kirk's graveyard, so the story goes, his loyal Skye terrier Bobby kept constant watch over his grave for 14 years until his own death in 1872. It's not uncommon to see passers-by kiss the doggy statue.

However, Bobby's long vigil is far from the strangest occurrence reputed to have happened at **Greyfriars Kirk** (*see right*), said to be one of the most haunted burial grounds in Britain. Sightings of ghosts and ghouls have been recorded at regular intervals; some night-time visitors have even reported receiving scratches and bruises. The 'violence' is often attributed to the ghost of the 17th-century judge and Lord Advocate Sir George Mackenzie. Commonly known as Bluidy Mackenzie, he was the scourge of the Covenanters, many of whom were buried here after being executed. Perhaps it's the undulating ground or the result of centuries of burials, but even hardened sceptics admit to finding the place spooky.

Greyfriars Kirk and its kirkyard have played a pivotal role in the history of Scotland. The National Covenant was signed before the pulpit in 1638; later, the survivors of the Battle of Bothwell Brig (1679) were kept in the south-west corner of the yard in the Covenanters' Prison for five months under desperate living conditions. Not all of them survived their incarceration; the **Martyrs' Monument**, with its chilling inscription ('Halt passenger, take heed of what you do see, This tomb doth shew for what some men did die'), is their memorial, and stands in the north-eastern part of the yard.

Opposite the entrance to Greyfriars, the bold, impressive lines of the **National Museum of Scotland** (*see p76*) mask a warren of winding corridors that opens up on to spectacular drops

---

INSIDE TRACK BOMBS AWAY

The **Grassmarket** was an early victim of modern warfare in April 1916 when it was hit by a bomb dropped by a German Zeppelin. An inscription on the pavement marks the spot. The Castle Rock was hit on the same notorious raid.

and huge spaces. The museum's roof and its **Tower** restaurant (*see p139*) boast fantastic views of Arthur's Seat and the castle. The adjacent **Royal Museum** was designed by Captain Francis Fowke along conventional, Victorian lines and completed in 1888. A major refurbishment project is scheduled to last until 2011, during which time the museum will remain closed to visitors.

Bordered on its northern edge by Chambers Street, **Old College** is the oldest of the city's university buildings. Architect Robert Adam began work on the building in 1789, only to be interrupted by the Napoleonic Wars. William Playfair then finished it, and Rowand Anderson added the landmark dome in 1883. Entrance to the main courtyard is either through the small entrance of the **Talbot Rice Gallery**, up West College Street (*see p76*), or through the monumental arch on South Bridge.

Some areas of Old College are open to the public. Most notable are the **Playfair Library**, with its superb classical interior and the old Upper Museum, now part of the Talbot Rice Gallery. The museum features a table from Napoleon's lodgings on St Helena, complete with a cigar burn that was allegedly made by the little Corsican. The University of Edinburgh has put a couple of self-guided tours online; see http://websiterepository.ed.ac.uk/explore/places.

Two of the university's student unions are nearby, on either side of Bristo Square. **Teviot Row House** is the grander of the two (and is the world's oldest purpose-built student union); Potterrow is easily identifiable by its domed roof. Next to Teviot Row House is the **Reid Concert Hall** (*see p236*), which hosts classical concerts and houses the Edinburgh University Collection of Historic Musical Instruments.

George Heriot's School, off Lauriston Place, was used in its early days as a military hospital for Cromwell's troops. School prefects sometimes give historical tours of this fine 17th-century building, named for the goldsmith and jeweller to James I & VI.

FREE Greyfriars Kirk

2 Greyfriars Place, Candlemaker Row (225 1900, www.greyfriarskirk.com). Bus 2, 23, 27, 41, 42, 45. **Open** *Apr-Oct* 10.30am-4.30pm Mon-Fri. *Nov-Mar* by appointment. **Admission** free. **Map** p333 H8.

On the site of a Franciscan friary, Greyfriars dates back to 1620. The west end of the church was reduced to ruins in 1718 after the local council's gunpowder store exploded; 127 years later, much of the kirk was then gutted by a fire. After recent renovations, both the exterior and the interior are impressive once more, with some sympathetic, traditional harling on the outer walls and elegantly sparse spaces within.

Worshippers from the Highland Tolbooth St John's (now the Hub; *see p59*) joined the Greyfriars congregation in 1979. Known as the Highland Kirk, St John's held services in Gaelic; alongside its regular services in English, Greyfriars now does the same each Sunday. The small visitors' exhibition on

SIGHTS

Greyfriars Kirkyard.

INSIDE TRACK
LITERARY MARTYRS

The **Martyrs' Monument** in Greyfriars Kirkyard (*see p75*) crops up in local author Ken MacLeod's 2008 novel *The Night Sessions*, which blends near-future science fiction with Scotland's Presbyterian heritage.

---

the church's 400-year history contains a display about the National Covenant, but most people go to see the portrait of Greyfriars Bobby, painted by John MacLeod in 1887. Check online for details of the regular musical recitals held here.

★ FREE National Museum of Scotland & Royal Museum

Chambers Street (247 4422, www.nms.ac.uk). Bus 2, 23, 27, 41, 42, 45. **Open** *National Museum of Scotland* 10am-5pm daily. *Royal Museum closed until 2011.* **Admission** free. **Credit** *Shop* MC, V. **Map** p333 H8.

Designed by Benson & Forsyth, the NMS was judged to be the Scottish Building of the Year after opening in 1998. The huge, airy complex is full of stairways and windows that lead to or look out on other levels, reminiscent of the city's architecture of centuries gone by. Ever since it opened, the NMS has been physically linked to the Victorian-era Royal Museum next door; you can usually walk through from one to the other. As such, it's a stretch to consider the pair as two museums: they're more like two complementary parts of one large complex.

The NMS displays cover everything from Scotland's geological origins to Neolithic artefacts, Roman silver, Dark Age stone carvings, medieval reliquaries and the like, through the industrial period and right up to the modern day. Thousands of items are on display, from everyday objects to a whisky still. Grim relics of the darker side of Edinburgh's past are also on show, among them the Maiden of Edinburgh guillotine and an iron gaud used to restrain prisoners on the old Tolbooth. It's really all you need to know about Scotland under one roof.

The Royal Museum, meanwhile, is known for its special exhibitions, and displays on natural history and engineering. Or, at least, it was until it closed in 2008 for a £46 million refurbishment. It will be closed to the public until some time in 2011; the National Museum of Scotland, though, remains open as usual.

FREE Talbot Rice Gallery

Old College, South Bridge (650 2210, www.trg. ed.ac.uk). Nicolson Street–North Bridge buses. **Open** *Aug* 10am-5pm Mon-Sat; noon-5pm Sun. *Sept-July* 10am-5pm Tue-Sat. **Admission** free. **Map** p333 J8.

Situated off William Playfair's stately, grand Old Quad in Old College, the Talbot Rice Gallery is named after the Watson Gordon Professor of Fine Art, David Talbot Rice, famed for his writings on Islamic art. There are three main exhibition spaces: the White Gallery, which stages five temporary exhibitions per year on mid-career artists and emergent talents; the Georgian Gallery, a neo-classical room designed by Playfair that houses a permanent exhibition of works from the Torrie Collection of Dutch & Italian Old Masters; and the Round Room, home to small-scale exhibitions and experimental artwork.

National Museum of Scotland.

The New Town

Edinburgh's handsome heart has mostly retained its Georgian beauty.

Edinburgh's New Town arrived by means of a succession of construction projects that started in 1767. Their combined legacy is some of the finest neo-classical architecture in the world. From the West End to the edge of Broughton, Princes Street to the fringes of Stockbridge, the entire area merits its status as a UNESCO World Heritage Site.

Despite the presence of commerce at its southern reaches, Edinburgh's modern-day city centre, the New Town is still chiefly residential, home to some of Edinburgh's wealthiest residents. The richest pitch in for townhouses, which often come with keys to fabulous but exclusive communal gardens; those with lesser budgets inhabit the still-expensive tenement blocks that dot the area.

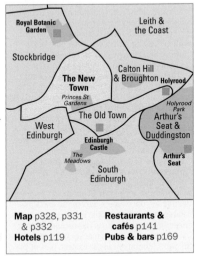

Map p328, p331 & p332
Hotels p119

Restaurants & cafés p141
Pubs & bars p169

INTRODUCING THE NEW TOWN

As the Old Town became more and more congested in the 18th century, the city fathers realised that they needed to provide alternative housing for the city's residents. However, this wasn't social housing as we understand the term today. The scheme was motivated not by concern for the general populace's health and welfare, but to allow the city's monied classes a means of escape from the tumbling tenements and questionable hygiene in what then constituted the town centre.

More salubrious districts had already been erected to the south of the Old Town's confines, most notably Brown Square in 1763 and George Square three years later, but more were needed. A competition was announced in April 1766, inviting architects to submit plans for an area north of the castle that was more accessible thanks to the draining of the Nor Loch and the construction of the original North Bridge. The contest was won by a then-unknown 22-year-old architect named James Craig, whose genteel, regimented vision remains in place today.

While the warren-like Old Town was Scottish through and through, from the architecture to the street names, the New Town's identity centred

around wider British influences. Although his designs were altered prior to construction, Craig's plans echoed the lines of the Union Flag; even the street names honoured the House of Hanover (Hanover Street), George III and his family (George Street, Charlotte Square, Frederick Street, Princes Street) and the Act of Union of 1707 (Rose and Thistle Streets).

The new quarter was initially shunned by Edinburghers, who considered it too exposed to winds blowing in from the Firth of Forth. But they soon saw the error of their ways, abandoning the chaotic jumble of the Old Town for the new refined streets and mansions. It remains the home of many of Scotland's most important players; those who believe the country is run by a small, conspiratorial elite look towards these streets for their evidence.

PRINCES STREET

Although **Princes Street** was part of the first phase of New Town construction, it's suffered more than any other thoroughfare since it was built. Today, it's an unsympathetic jumble of Edwardian aesthetic delights, functional 1970s blocks and modern glass-fronted edifices, all of which presumably seemed a good idea at the

SIGHTS

time. All the same, its mix of high-street chain stores, homeware retailers and cheap souvenir shops continues to attract sizeable crowds.

In recent years, there have been discussions on how to improve the street. The latest proposal is to overhaul it, block by block, to a framework known as the 'string of pearls'. The local authority hopes to add new walkways to Rose Street and public courtyards behind some of the buildings, all helping to create an environment where each block has a distinct character. This is all in the long term; even if the plan holds together, work won't start for several years and could take a couple of decades to complete.

The verdant **Princes Street Gardens**, protected by an Act of Parliament since 1816, act as a buffer between the New Town and Old Town. Indeed, the first thing that strikes most visitors about Princes Street is how lopsided it appears, with solid rows of buildings fronting on to this green expanse. Various statues are dotted around the gardens, and the far western end is home to two churches: **St John's Episcopal Church** (*see right*) and, at the foot of Edinburgh Castle, the Presbyterian **St Cuthbert's Parish Church** (*see below*). In summer, the western part of the gardens is often awash with people listening to music emanating from the Ross Bandstand. During the winter, a Christmas market is set up behind the Scott Monument in the eastern part of the gardens, and an ice rink is installed (*see p250*).

Princes Street has long had extensive traffic controls, including one-way systems and areas where access is restricted to bikes, buses, taxis and emergency vehicles. The latest fuss concerned its closure because of the trams project (*see p33* **Under Construction**); it should be running smoothly again by 2011, if it all goes to schedule, but there's still regular talk of closing the street permanently to cars.

FREE **St Cuthbert's Parish Church**
5 Lothian Road (229 1142, www.st-cuthberts. net). Princes Street buses. **Open** *Apr-Sept* 10am-4pm Mon-Sat. *Oct-Mar* 10am-4pm Mon-Thur; 10am-2pm Fri. **Admission** free. **Map** p332 E7 & p336 A2.
St Cuthbert's has claim to being one of the oldest places of worship in or around the city. However,

INSIDE TRACK
DON'T ADJUST YOUR WATCHES

The prominent clock outside the **Balmoral Hotel** on Princes Street famously runs three minutes fast in order to hurry passengers to the adjacent Waverley Station.

although its steeple dates to 1789, the church's current incarnation was built as recently as 1894. Its kirkyard is the resting place of some notable names: writer Thomas de Quincey, mathematician John Napier and the Reverend David Williamson, the church's covenanting minister celebrated in song as 'Dainty Davie'. When Williamson was buried here in 1706, no stone was erected by his widow, presumably because she would have had to list on it the names of her six predecessors. Indoors, there's a frieze behind the apse modelled on Leonardo's *Last Supper*.

FREE **St John's Episcopal Church**
3 Lothian Road (229 7565, www.stjohns-edinburgh.org.uk). Princes Street buses. **Open** 8am-4.45pm Mon-Fri; 8am-noon Sat. **Admission** free. **Map** p332 E7 & p336 A2.
Designed in the perpendicular Gothic style by William Burn, who also built the Melville Monument in St Andrew Square, St John's began life in 1816, just before the Act of Parliament that outlawed any further building on Princes Street Gardens; as such, the church's view of Edinburgh Castle is legally protected. The collection of stained glass is said to be the finest in Scotland, although the church's relentless 19th-century worthiness and sheer Victorian vulgarity can be overwhelming. At the north-eastern end of the church, the external mural area often features thought-provoking, politicised images.
▶ *Among the enterprises on the basement terrace is a branch of Henderson's, Edinburgh's original vegetarian food café; see p145.*

The Mound

On the west side of the intersection of the Mound and Princes Street stands a handsome 1903 statue of wigmaker-turned-poet Allan Ramsay. However, the area is dominated by the twin Doric temples of the **Royal Scottish Academy** and the **National Gallery of Scotland** (for both, *see right*), two 19th-century buildings designed by prolific architect William Playfair. The plainer and more refined National Gallery was built 20 years after the more florid Academy, topped by sphinxes and an incongruous statue of the young Queen Victoria. Completed by John Steell in 1844, the statue was originally displayed at street level, but it's said that Victoria, displeased by her chubby appearance, demanded that it was elevated to a rooftop location in order that she should avoid close scrutiny by her subjects.

Extensive work has taken place in and around these galleries in recent years. Both appear traditional from the outside, but refurbishments mean that the gallery spaces within are state of the art, with temperature and humidity controls, air conditioning and specialised lighting. While the two buildings seem to stand in splendid isolation of each

other, they're connected by the Weston Link, which runs under both and can be accessed from Princes Street Gardens. It contains an IT gallery, an education centre (comprising a 200-seat lecture theatre and cinema), a restaurant, a café and a shop. The existence of the link means that the two buildings are sometimes jointly referred to as the National Gallery Complex.

★ FREE National Gallery of Scotland

The Mound (624 6200, www.nationalgalleries. org). Princes Street buses. **Open** 10am-5pm Mon-Wed, Fri-Sun; 10am-7pm Thur. **Admission** free; charges for special exhibitions vary. **Credit** *Shop* MC, V. **Map** p332 G7 & p336 D3.

Edinburgh has a wealth of institutions serving the visual arts, but perhaps none is as grand as the National Gallery. Built by William Playfair in 1848, it opened 11 years later as the home to both the Royal Scottish Academy and the National Gallery, before becoming sole home to the latter in 1910.

The gallery contains excellent collections of sculpture and paintings, some of the latter fairly crowded together on the walls of the larger ground-floor rooms. However, the wealth of great works is undeniable, from Byzantine-like Madonnas through the Northern Renaissance and High Renaissance (highlights include Raphael's *Bridgewater Madonna* and a handful of pieces by Titian) and on to the early 20th century. Impressionist and post-Impressionist work includes Monet's *Haystack*, Gauguin's *Vision After the Sermon* and Cézanne's *Montagne Sainte-Victoire*.

The permanent collection of Scottish art encompasses works by artists such as Ramsay, Wilkie and McTaggart. Among the favourites is Raeburn's *The Reverend Walker Skating on Duddingston Loch* (aka the 'Skating Minister'), although the landscape looks unlike any view possible at Duddingston. The management of the gallery's shop are unconcerned by such trifling details, and sell the work in print, jigsaw, mug and even fridge-magnet form. Check online for details of temporary exhibitions.

FREE Royal Scottish Academy

The Mound (225 6671, www.royalscottish academy.org). Princes Street buses. **Open** 10am-5pm Mon-Sat; noon-5pm Sun. **Admission** free. **Credit** MC, V. **Map** p328 & p332 G6, p336 D2.

This grand structure was completed in 1826 to the designs of William Playfair, but its exterior dates from eight years later, after Playfair was asked to remodel his work. The building's 16 columns give it a Grecian air that finds echoes in other Playfair buildings around the city. It was originally built for the Royal Institution for the Encouragement of Fine Arts in Scotland, and dramatically renovated in the 1910s to accommodate the Royal Scottish Academy. The 21st century saw another overhaul of the building, including the addition of cruciform-shaped lower-level galleries.

The building is effectively a large-scale space for temporary exhibitions, supplementing big-ticket blockbusters with shows devoted to less well-known artists. A number of annual events focus on Scottish art, chief among them the RSA Annual Exhibition (usually May/June). Each January, the gallery also displays the Turner watercolours, bequeathed in 1900 by Henry Vaughan on the condition that they were only shown when daylight was at its weakest. Given the environmental controls now in place, they could be displayed more often but breaking out the Turners once a year has become quite a tradition.

The eastern end of Princes Street

Edinburgh offers medieval authenticity, Georgian loveliness and much more besides, but its architectural history does contain a few aesthetic disasters. Together at the eastern end of Princes Street, the **St James Shopping Centre** and the derelict **New St Andrew's House** behind it are perhaps the ugliest examples of 1960s design in the city. Happily, they may not be here for much longer. Both were bought by an investment firm several years ago before, in early 2009, outline planning permission was granted for an £850 million redevelopment that would raze them to the ground and replace them with a galleria-style retail centre, hotels, leisure facilities, office space and housing. If all goes to plan, the bulldozers will arrive in 2011, with the entire scheme completed five years later.

This end of Princes Street does have its good points. Among them is the **Scotland's People Centre** (*see right*), which encompasses both the 18th-century General Register House and the adjacent, 19th-century New Register House. Designed by Robert Adam and planned while North Bridge was being built, General Register House first opened in 1789, despite being only half complete. Under Robert Reid's supervision, it was finished in the 1820s; the Corinthian pillars, beautifully balanced front elevation and restrained frieze work are magnificent. Completed in 1863, the adjacent New Register House sits on West Register Street, which leads through to St Andrew Square past Victorian-era pubs the **Guildford** and the **Café Royal** (for both, *see p170*) en route. The interior of the latter is particularly spectacular, its central bar offset by a succession of ceramic murals depicting inventors such as Faraday and Watt.

Back on Princes Street, outside General Register House, is Sir John Steell's dramatic statue of the **Duke of Wellington** on his horse Copenhagen. Most equestrian statues have four feet on the ground, but Wellington's horse here rears up on its hind legs as his master points symbolically towards Waterloo Place.

The best feature of the nearby **Princes Mall** shopping centre is the view of the Old Town from its grassy roof terrace. Nearby along Princes Street is **Jenners** (*see p183*), the city's grande dame of retail therapy. Founded in 1838 by two Leith drapers, the shop was rebuilt in 1893 after a fire. An estimated 25,000 people gathered for the unveiling of its elaborately carved, statue-encrusted frontage, inspired by the façade of Oxford's Bodleian Library.

If this stretch of Princes Street exemplifies the city's 19th-century extravagance, no one structure exemplifies it better than George Meikle Kemp's colossal **Scott Monument**, which points 200 feet (61 metres) towards the clouds. It was originally meant to have been sited in Charlotte Square, but instead dominates the skyline on the corner of **Waverley Bridge** (named for Scott's *Waverley* novels) and rather overshadows the statue of Lanarkshire-born explorer **David Livingstone**. Close by are statues of **Adam Black**, twice Lord Provost of Edinburgh and founder of the *Edinburgh Review*, and **John Wilson**, a professor of moral philosophy at the University of Edinburgh.

★ Scotland's People Centre
2 Princes Street (314 4300, www.scotlands peoplehub.gov.uk). Princes Street buses. **Open** 9am-4.30pm Mon-Fri. **Admission** free-£10. **Map** p328 & p332 H6, p336 F2.

Opened by the Queen in summer 2008, Scotland's People Centre is the country's leading facility for family research, describing itself as the 'official government source of genealogical data for Scotland'. It brings together the resources of the General Register Office for Scotland, the National Archive of Scotland and the Court of the Lord Lyon; they hold material on everything from births, deaths and marriages to parish registers, census results, wills and coats of arms. Anyone can visit the shop or the café, or attend taster sessions on family history, for free. Access to the centre for research costs from £10 a day, but some of the research rooms are stunning (particularly the Matheson Dome and Adam Dome).

★ Scott Monument
East Princes Street Gardens (529 4068, www.cac.org.uk). Princes Street buses. **Open** *Apr-Sept* 9am-7pm daily. *Oct-Mar* 9am-3pm daily. **Admission** £3. **No credit cards**. **Map** p328 & p332 G6, p336 E2.

Travellers emerging from Waverley Station expecting to see austere classical architecture may gawp in disbelief at the Victorian Gothic ostentation of the Scott Monument. Designed by the self-taught architect George Meikle Kemp, the monument houses a vast white marble statue of Sir Walter Scott (by John Steell) as well as 64 statuettes, mostly of Scott's characters but with a few notable figures from Scottish history thrown in for good measure. It was completed in 1846, 14 years after Scott's death, using funds raised from public donations, which shows how dearly Edinburghers felt about the famous author. The views from the top are superb, but the final flight of steps up to the pinnacle is a squeeze.

ST ANDREW SQUARE

Named after Scotland's patron saint, **St Andrew Square** sits at the eastern end of George Street, a grassy haven adding punctuation to one of the city's more upmarket thoroughfares. In the centre stands the **Melville Monument**, a 135-foot (41-metre)

SIGHTS

Tower of Power

So who was Harry the Ninth?

Although St Andrew Square Garden formed part of the original 18th-century plan for the New Town, its gates had remained locked to the hoi polloi for more than two centuries. In 2008, things changed. The local authority and the local enterprise agency forked out £2.6 million between them to renovate and open up the garden, which became an instant hit with local office workers and passing shoppers.

The garden is dominated by a massive monument to a curious figure from the city's past. Born in 1742 to an aristocratic family in Dalkeith and educated in Edinburgh, **Henry Dundas** rose to become a senior politician and lawyer, holding a string of important offices in Edinburgh and London. While Great Britain was getting to grips with an independent United States, the French Revolution and the Napoleonic Wars, Dundas served variously as Treasurer of the Navy, Home Secretary, Secretary of State for War and First Lord of the Admiralty. Dundas was rewarded with the title Viscount Melville in 1802, nine years before he died. Modelled on Trajan's Column in Rome and designed by William Burn, the St Andrew Square monument to him was completed in 1823.

The interesting part of all this is that no one up here liked him much at the time. For much of his career, Dundas ran things north of the border by manipulating elections through influence and patronage; he was popularly known as Harry the Ninth, the Uncrowned King of Scotland. When the French Revolution inspired dissent in Scotland, effigies of Dundas were burned. He later watered down Wilberforce's effort to abolish the slave trade. But the final nail in the coffin of his reputation was his impeachment in 1806 for the misappropriation of public funds. He was acquitted, but it was the end of his career.

Historian Michael Fry tried to reinterpret matters in his 1992 book *The Dundas Despotism*, describing him as a man whose ideals of good government stemmed in some regard from the Scottish Enlightenment but whose thinking was firmly rooted in its time. Not corrupt, in other words, but simply misunderstood by posterity. Whether or not you buy his explanation, you can sit in St Andrew Square Garden and look up at someone who was once more important than all contemporary Scottish politicians put together.

SIGHTS

Doric column topped by a statue of Henry Dundas. For more on recent redevelopment of the square and on Dundas, *see p81* **Tower of Power**.

For years, St Andrew Square was the heart of Edinburgh's financial industries, until regeneration programmes encouraged key institutions to move west into glass and brick new-builds. Among them was the **Royal Bank of Scotland**, now based in Gogarburn on Edinburgh's western edge, but the bank's registered office remains a former mansion on the square. Set behind a lawn, this Palladian-style edifice was built in 1772 for Sir Laurence Dundas on a site that, in Craig's plan for the New Town, had been reserved for St Andrew's Church; it's a mark of Sir Laurence's political muscle that he was able to overrule the council. The building is still a working branch of the bank; the sumptuously decorated iron

dome of the Telling Room, added by J Dick Peddie in 1857, is open during banking hours. Next door sit more more outlandish bank premises: a branch of the **Bank of Scotland**, in an 1851 pseudo-*palazzo* complete with rooftop statues.

The north-eastern corner of the square has been the subject of a multi-million-pound redevelopment programme in the last decade. First to be completed was **Harvey Nichols** (*see p183*), which provided a shot in the arm for the town's shopping scene when it opened in 2002. The town's new bus station opened next, albeit without attracting the same levels of media coverage as its neighbour. Between them sits **Multrees Walk**, a tidy pedestrianised road lined with smart designer boutiques (*see p190*); it's Edinburgh's own little Bond Street.

The **Scottish National Portrait Gallery** (*see below*) sits just north of the square, at the

eastern end of Queen Street. Designed by Sir Robert Rowand Anderson and completed in the late 19th century, it's a confident building, its neo-Gothic style representing a departure from the Georgian neo-classical constraint of much of the New Town. Its red sandstone façade is best seen in the late evening summer sun.

Scottish National Portrait Gallery

1 Queen Street (624 6200, www.nationalgalleries. org). Princes Street buses. **Open** closed until late 2011. **Map** p328 G5.

The Scottish National Portrait Gallery's collection takes in everything from historic figures (the mural in the foyer depicts key moments in the country's past) to cultural figures (Sirs Alex Ferguson and Sean Connery among them). The museum closed in 2009 for a major programe of refurbishments and won't reopen until late 2011 at the earliest. Call or check online before setting out.

GEORGE STREET

Named in honour of King George III, **George Street** was conceived as the New Town's main thoroughfare. It quickly became Edinburgh's financial district, but many of the banking institutions once resident here have been transformed to meet more modern needs. The street is now a major shopping drag with more than its fair share of bars, but the ambience is different from that of nearby Princes Street: the pace is more leisurely and the price tags are higher. One constant throughout the street's history has been the excellent views afforded from here of the steep descent down to north Edinburgh and, on clear days, the hills of Fife, particularly down Dundas Street.

Through all the changes, the street has retained its dignity. National fashion chains – and the ubiquitous Starbucks – have crept in behind the street's toned-down façades, but many of the city's traditional names remain; among them are **James Gray & Son** (No.89, 225 7381), which has offered household wares from this location for around a century, and the jewellers **Hamilton & Inches** (*see p196*). Other buildings lend a suitably stylish austerity to an array of new restaurants, bars and hotels.

The **Assembly Rooms**, built by public subscription, have been a feature of the street since 1787. The rooms became a favoured haunt of Edinburgh's Regency partying set: it was here, in 1827, that local resident Sir Walter Scott revealed that he was the author of the *Waverley* novels. Though it briefly served as a labour exchange and recruiting centre during World War I, it's remained a popular venue for concerts, plays and performances of all kinds, and is busy throughout August.

INSIDE TRACK
MAXWELL REMEMBERED

The influential and gifted scientist **James Clerk Maxwell** was born in Edinburgh in 1831. His importance is such that a crater on the Moon and a mountain range on Venus have been named in his honour, but it took until 2008 for his home city to unveil to the man. It's at the eastern end of George Street.

This stretch was once a popular quarter for Edinburgh's literary types. The poet Shelley and his first wife Harriet Westbrook honeymooned at **84 George Street**, and Sir Walter Scott lived around the corner at **39 North Castle Street**. **45 George Street** was once the headquarters of the influential literary journal, *Blackwood's Magazine*, which counted Henry James and Oscar Wilde among its contributors.

St Andrew's & St George's Church, built in 1787, was originally intended for a plot of land on St Andrew Square. However, the site was appropriated by the entrepreneur and politician Sir Lawrence Dundas, and the New Town's first church was instead built on George Street. It was later the site of what became known as 'the Disruption' of the Church of Scotland: in 1843, 472 ministers marched from here to the Tanfield Hall at Canonmills and established the Free Church of Scotland.

CHARLOTTE SQUARE

Designed by Kirkcaldy-born architect Robert Adam in 1791, a year before he died, **Charlotte Square** is one of the most pleasant spaces in the city centre. Initially named St George's Square, it was planned by New Town architect James Craig to mirror St Andrew Square to the east. But when George III's daughter Charlotte was born, the square was renamed in her honour. Adam designed the palatial frontages, discreetly ornamented with sphinxes and pediments, but each house was then built separately by the owners of the individual plots, creating an effect of harmony in diversity. Many illustrious types have lived here down the years; among them was Alexander Graham Bell, the inventor of the telephone, who was born at 16 South Charlotte Street in 1847.

The best preserved façades are on the north side of the square, an excellent example of Adam's famous 'palace-front' design. At no.7 is the **Georgian House** (*see p84*), now run

SIGHTS

INSIDE TRACK
THE MAN WHO WOULD BE KING

Frederick Street is named for Frederick, Prince of Wales, the father of George III. Only his early death, at the age of 44 in 1751, prevented him becoming king; as a result, the crown skipped a generation. Frederick's own father was George II who reigned until 1760.

by the National Trust for Scotland. (The NTS itself was based at no.28 for years, but financial difficulties saw the organisation put its building up for sale in 2009.) Next door to the Georgian House, the **Bute House** is the official residence of Scotland's First Minister.

The imposing, domed building on the west side of the square is **West Register House** (535 1314), a stuffy edifice that contains the National Archives of Scotland's collection of maps as well as government and court records. In the grassy centre of the square, which hosts August's **Edinburgh International Book Festival** (*see p210 and p215*), there's a monument to Prince Albert.

Reached via the north-eastern corner of Charlotte Square and tucked away from the grander streets, **Young Street** was once home to the New Town's less financially blessed residents. In recent years, though, it's become a favoured haunt of one Inspector John Rebus, who drinks at the **Oxford Bar** (*see p170*) in Ian Rankin's best-selling detective novels. To the north of Young Street, parallel to George Street, lie **Queen Street** and the **Queen Street Gardens**. Like many of the green spaces that punctuate the New Town, they were created as retreats for the residents of the grand squares and terraces to enjoy, and are still open only to residents. Further along Queen Street, at no.8, is a townhouse built by Robert Adam; at no.9 stands Thomas Hamilton's neo-classical **Royal College of Physicians**.

Georgian House

7 Charlotte Square (226 3318, www.nts.org.uk). Princes Street buses. **Open** *Mar* 11am-3pm daily. *Apr-Jun, Sept, Oct* 10am-5pm daily. *July, Aug* 10am-6pm daily. *Nov* 10am-4pm. *Dec-Feb* closed. **Admission** £5.50; £4.50 discounts; £10-£15 family. **Credit** *Shop* MC, V. **Map** p331 D6 & p336 A1.

When John Lamont, the 18th Chief of Clan Lamont, bought this house in 1796, it cost him the princely sum of £1,600. It's now run by the National Trust for Scotland (NTS), with excellent reconstructions that open a window on to how the upper classes lived during the late 18th and early 19th centuries.

The rooms are packed with period furnishings and details, right down to sugar cones, locked tea caddies and newspapers. The basement contains an informative video presentation; well-informed guides are happy to answer questions.
▶ *Other NTS attractions include Gladstone's Land in the Old Town; see p62.*

DUNDAS STREET

Dundas Street is the backbone of what was known as 'the Second New Town', a further stage of development in the early 19th century built as landowners cashed in on the city's need for upmarket dwellings. Scottish property laws allowed them to stipulate the architectural style, so the New Town's cohesive classical formality is played out with little interruption.

Resolutely residential and exclusive, these new areas were designed to deter outsiders or Old Town riff-raff. Churches aside, there were originally no public buildings, squares or markets. Shops and restaurants have opened along the main roads in recent decades, and Dundas Street itself contains a number of art galleries (*see p228*), but this remains the New Town's residential heart. The best way to explore is simply follow your feet; it's almost impossible to get lost.

The immediate area has a literary heritage. At **17 Heriot Row**, look for the stone-carved inscription commemorating the fact that author Robert Louis Stevenson lived here as a child. It's said the gardens here influenced his novel *Treasure Island*, and the gas light that once stood outside the house inspired his poem *The Lamplighter*. Nearby, JM Barrie, author of *Peter Pan,* lodged at **3 Great King Street** when he was a student. Just beyond lies **Drummond Place**, a crescent-shaped street once called home by *Whisky Galore* author Compton Mackenzie (at no.31). And just over the intersection is **Scotland Street**, the setting for bestselling Edinburgh writer Alexander McCall Smith's novel *44 Scotland Street*.

Further west is the **Moray Estate**. Designed by James Gillespie Graham in 1822 at the behest of the Earl of Moray, it's one of the grandest of the New Town's residential quarters.

THE WEST END

The western end of the New Town, also known as the **West End**, is a quiet and pleasant place for a wander. But away from the bustle of Shandwick Place and Queensferry Street, it's almost entirely bereft of activity. With most of the buildings now either high-rent offices or apartment complexes, the architecture pales in comparison to the New Town's core. One notable exception is the **Caledonian Hilton**

Hotel (*see p121*), a colossal red sandstone and brick edifice built in 1903. It was originally the subject of complaints, with many locals suggesting that such a vulgarian effort was better suited to Glasgow, but more than a century of respectability has helped it blend in.

The only thoroughfare of any distinction is **Melville Street**, which ends with the episcopal **Cathedral of St Mary's** (enter from Palmerston Place). The foundation stone was laid in 1874, complete with what would

now be called a time capsule. The main building was completed and consecrated five years later, but the triple spires, which form an integral part of Edinburgh's skyline, were not finished until World War I. With its 270-foot (82-metre) central spire, the rose window of the south transept and the fossils in the granite steps of the High Altar, the cathedral is filled with artistic and ecclesiastical points of interest; Edinburgh has many beautiful churches, but perhaps none more beautiful than this.

Walk The Newest in New Town

On this tour of recent additions, the New Town lives up to its name.

Start on **Circus Lane**, a pretty 19th-century mews that features two designs by Richard Murphy Architects. No.10a, with its slatted wood frontage, known as the Japanese house (spot the Japanese no-parking sign), won an award from the Royal

Institute of British Architects (RIBA) in 2007; further along, behind the clean stone, chic drainpipe and lead panels, no.17 consists of two upmarket holiday lets (Jimmy Carr and Sir Ian Botham have both signed the guest book).

Turn left at the end of the lane and cross diagonally to the elegant classical curve of **St Vincent Place**, a mock-Georgian street completed in 2007. From here, work your way to **NE Cumberland Street Lane**, one of a number of New Town backstreets on which former stables have been converted into well-to-do homes. Those at numbers 19, 21 and 22 are typically handsome.

South-east of here on **Northumberland Place** (not clearly signposted, but look out for the Star Bar and the pretty cottages of Nelson Place), take in the courtyard conversions of **Dublin Meuse** by Michael Laird Architects. Across the road on Dublin Street Lane North, where the road slopes down, you'll discover a small colony of modern houses, painted white like a secret Mexican village. Also the work of Richard Murphy Architects, they won a RIBA award in 2000.

Further east, clock the new children's playground on **Barony Place**, then cross the main road to Broughton Place and then turn right on to Hart Street. The airy, stainless-steel house down here was designed by Zone Architects in 2002.

SIGHTS

Stockbridge

A village within a city? The locals like to think so.

SIGHTS

Once a small village to the north of Edinburgh by the banks of the Water of Leith, Stockbridge was incorporated into the city through the 19th century expansion of the New Town. For a time in the 1970s, it had the air of a Bohemian enclave, although the legacy of that period involves galleries, delicatessens and bric-a-brac emporia rather than cultural revolution.

The architecture around here is as varied as the shopping; several centuries' worth of building styles can be seen during the course of a stroll. The sense of gentility associated with the area is best reflected in the elegant curves of **Royal Circus**, a William Playfair creation, and the similarly neo-classical **Raeburn Estate**, parts of which survive at the top of Leslie Place. Conversely, the path alongside the Water of Leith heading towards **Dean Village** is an unexpectedly sylvan escape from the city.

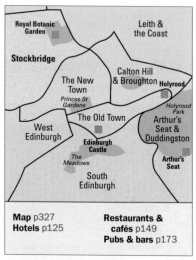

Map p327
Hotels p125

Restaurants & cafés p149
Pubs & bars p173

HOWE STREET TO THE BOTANICS

You can take the well-trod path to Stockbridge via Howe Street and Circus Place in the New Town, but there is a short and worthwhile detour. If you continue north along Howe Street where it turns into St Vincent Street (just after

INSIDE TRACK
RAEBURN'S PLACE

Born in Stockbridge, **Sir Henry Raeburn** (1756-1823) painted some iconic Scottish images. The shape of *The Reverend Robert Walker Skating on Duddingston Loch* (aka *The Skating Minister*) was a key theme in the design of the Scottish Parliament at Holyrood; you can see the work at the National Gallery of Scotland (*see p79*). Raeburn was honoured in Stockbridge in the name of Raeburn Place.

Great King Street), you'll get a close-up look at Thomas Playfair's impressive **St Stephen's Church** (1828), which dominates the view all the way downhill from the city centre. The huge arched entrance was Playfair's answer to the awkward shape and sloping ground of the site.

Bear left by the church and you'll be at the less interesting end of **St Stephen Street**. Continue along it, though, and things soon get more engaging. Along St Stephen Street, round the corner into **North West Circus Place**, down **Deanhaugh Street** and into **Raeburn Place** (Stockbridge's main drag), there's a huge concentration of independent shops selling everything from wedding dresses to carpets (**Anta**; *see p203*), crystal chandeliers to original works of art. Food specialists include eminent delicatessen **Herbie of Edinburgh** (*see p198*) and cheesemonger **IJ Mellis** (*see p199*); among the charity shops are specialist book and music stores run by **Oxfam** (nos.25 and 64 Raeburn Place, 332 9632 and 332 7593). Health remedies are provided by the **Edinburgh Floatarium** and a branch of long-established herbalist

Royal Botanical Garden. *See p89*.

In Praise of Older Women

Two mature ladies once helped to lend Stockbridge a very different character.

Think 'Mrs Doubtfire' and you think Robin Williams in a blonde wig, a flowery dress, a pastel blue cardigan and something approximating to a lilting Scottish accent. In the 1993 movie, the American star plays a down-on-his-luck divorcé who disguises himself as an elderly female housekeeper in order to see more of his children.

Before *Mrs Doubtfire* was a film, it was a novel for older children by Anne Fine called *Madame Doubtfire* (the movie producers presumably thought 'madame' was too exotic a word for the mass market). But before it was a book, it was a sign in big gold letters above an old Stockbridge shop.

Fine lived in Edinburgh as a young mother in the mid 1970s. As she trundled past with a pushchair, Madame Doubtfire's basement junk shop by the corner of South East Circus Place and Howe Street always caught her eye. Sometimes Fine would venture inside, only to find that anything she bought there 'smelled of cat pee'. She never got to know the elderly proprietor, who died in 1979 and whose real name was reputed to be Annabella Coutts. But she always remembered the name on the shop front and put it to use as the title of her novel.

The connection between fact and fiction ends there, but the story gives an insight into a very different Stockbridge to the well-to-do, vaguely bohemian quarter that stands today. Famed for smoking a clay pipe, Coutts had run the rag-and-bone shop since the 1920s. It's said that she was good friends with one Dora Noyce, a polite and smartly dressed woman who ran the city's most notorious brothel at 17 Danube Street.

For years, Noyce ran a 'house of leisure and pleasure' in this heartland of gentility, serving liquid refreshments out of silver teapots as her clients selected and then retreated upstairs with one of 15 live-in girls. A local legend, Noyce was charged 47 times for living on immoral earnings and was even sent to jail in 1972, at the age of 71, but carried on working when she emerged four months later.

Although Noyce's house of ill repute operated under the veneer of respectability, it contributed to an image of Stockbridge as the kind of place your mother would warn you against. Gentrification, which began in the 1960s, when the middle-classes began to buy run-down properties, makes such an idea laughable today. All the same, the friendly neighbourhood retains something of the flavour of the close-knit community of old, even if it has lost some of its old rag-and-bone charm.

Napiers (*see p201*). There are also a lot of bars and cafés, among them the venerable **Bell's Diner** (*see p149*), the modern **Saint** café-bar (*see p173*) and the reliable **Baillie** (*see p173*).

Still, there's more to Stockbridge than eating and shopping, as you'll see if you wander up to the corner of India Place and Gloucester Street (opposite the west end of St Stephen's Street). Built in the 1790s using stones recovered from buildings in the Lawnmarket that had been demolished during construction of the Mound, **Duncan's Land** was the birthplace of artist David Roberts (1796-1864), who specialised in visions of souks, monuments of Egypt and the vistas of the Holy Land, and who was known for dressing in exotic clothing. Look out for the higgledy-piggledy doors and windows, and the lovely lintel that reads 'Fear God Onlye' (now above the front door of a Thai restaurant).

Another memento of the area's past can be found in the form of the gateway that once led to Stockbridge's meat and vegetable market. It now stands in attractive isolation off St Stephen Street, at St Stephen Place, but still announces the availability of 'Butcher Meat, Fruits, Fish and Poultry'. Built in 1826 after a public campaign, the market was a poke in the eye for city officials who hoped that Stockbridge would leave such undignified practices behind and remain market-free, much like the neighbouring New Town.

Nearby, there's more evidence of such working-class history. Where Deanhaugh Street crosses the Water of Leith, down the stairs next to Pizza Express, you can join the waterside path that comes out at Bridge Place and takes you along to the **Stockbridge Colonies** (off Glenogle Road). Following the curve of the river, this group of 'one-ended' streets were conceived by the Edinburgh Co-operative Building Company and named after its members and supporters. The design of the buildings is two-storey but double-sided: the entrance to the upper dwelling is accessed from stairs on one street, with access to the ground floor from the street on the opposite side. Once humble workers' homes, their cuteness now makes them highly desirable.

At the bottom of one of the colony streets, Bell Street, you can pick up the Water of Leith Walkway again, heading towards **Canonmills**. On the other side of the river from the colonies, Arboretum Avenue takes you towards Arboretum Place and the West Gate of the **Royal Botanic Garden** (*see below*), with **Inverleith House** (*see below*) at its heart.

FREE Inverleith House

Royal Botanic Garden, Inverleith Row (552 7171, www.rbge.org.uk). Bus 8, 17, 23, 27. **Open** *Aug* 10am-5.30pm daily. *Mar-July, Sept, Oct* 10am-5.30pm Tue-Sun. *Nov-Feb* 10am-3.30pm Tue-Sun. **Admission** free. **Map** p327 D2.

Bang in the middle of the Botanics, this imposing, austere, late Georgian building was designed in 1774 by David Henderson for James Rocheid, whose family owned the Inverleith estate. The house eventually became the home of the garden's Regius Keeper and then, from 1960 until 1984, the Scottish National Gallery of Modern Art, but it's now owned and run by the Royal Botanic Garden. Exhibitions are largely contemporary, with the likes of Louise Bourgeois and John McCracken having featured in recent years, although at least one botanical exhibition is usually staged each year for good measure.

★ FREE Royal Botanic Garden

Inverleith Row (552 7171, www.rbge.org.uk). Bus 8, 17, 23, 27. **Open** *Apr-Sept* 10am-7pm daily. *Mar, Oct* 10am-6pm daily. *Nov-Feb* 10am-4pm daily. **Admission** *Garden* free. *Glasshouses* £3.50; £1-£3 discounts; £8 family. **Credit** *Shop* V. **Map** p327 D2.

The Royal Botanic Garden has delighted both plant-lovers and casual strollers for almost two centuries. Edinburgh's most peaceful tourist attraction, it's also a noted centre for botanical and horticultural research, and houses the oldest botanical library in Britain. Access to its grand Victorian palm house is free, although it costs to delve deeper into the themed zones of the '60s-era glasshouses. Still, it's worth the modest fee for the privilege of viewing all kinds of orchids, ferns, tropical plant life, rainforest species and other bits and pieces. The Plants & People glasshouse, for example, shows off rice, sugar and cocoa as vegetation; the pond in the middle is covered with freakishly large water lily leaves every summer.

INSIDE TRACK
THE VIEW FROM THE BOUNDARY

Stockbridge is the home of Scottish cricket with matches played at the **Grange** on Raeburn Place (*see p86*). In the last decade, Scotland have taken on Pakistan, England and Australia here in one-day internationals.

In autumn 2009, the Botanics welcomed a major new arrival with the opening of the John Hope Gateway at the West Gate, a carbon-neutral biodiversity and information centre with shop, restaurant, plant nursery and education rooms. With a wood-and-slate exterior and a rooftop wind turbine, the Gateway is the Botanics' leap into the 21st century.

Another highlight is the Chinese Hillside, which focuses on intrepid Scottish plant-hunters such as George Forrest and Robert Fortune. Specimens grow in drifts beside winding paths and carved bridges; there's also a t'ing, a traditional poolside pavilion.

The Botanics is a controlled space (no ball games, no bikes, no dogs, no jogging). However, during the Edinburgh International Festival and the Fringe, outdoor art installations are often set up around the site. Year-round, there's plenty here that appeals to children. The pond, with its ducks and swans, and the waterfall in the rock garden area, where a heron sometimes fishes, are particularly popular.

The Terrace Café, by Inverleith House, is good for a quick coffee, but the food is hardly bargain basement. Sitting outside may find you pestered by pigeons, the odd squirrel or one of the city's assertive seagull population. But even the mighty gulls are intimidated by Edinburgh's middle-class mothers, many of whom stroll here all year round. *Photos p87*.

▶ *There's more of this sort of thing at the smaller but quite lovely Inveresk Lodge Garden near Musselburgh; see p292.*

THE RAEBURN ESTATE

Back in Stockbridge again, at the top of Leslie Place (off Deanhaugh Street) sits **St Bernard's Crescent**. It's all that remains of the **Raeburn Estate**, a grandiose property development financed by artist and Stockbridge native Sir Henry Raeburn. Although St Bernard's House, the central focus of the development, is long gone, the Georgian crescent remains a fine example of neo-classical elegance. The central section, with Doric columns, is unexpectedly impressive, hidden off the main streets. It's a regular star of period dramas.

Nearby **Ann Street**, thought to have been designed by James Milne and named after Raeburn's wife, may be the prettiest street in the city, and is unusual in Edinburgh for the fact that each of its Georgian houses has its own front garden. Thomas de Quincey, the author of *Confessions of an English Opium Eater*, lived here for a time.

DEAN VILLAGE & THE GALLERIES

To reach Dean Village from Stockbridge, simply follow the **Water of Leith** upstream by taking the path at the south-west end of Saunders Street, off Deanhaugh Street. Within minutes,

SIGHTS

SIGHTS

you'll find yourself in a very different kind of environment, with the shops and the bustle replaced by trees. You won't get to enjoy the rural idyll for long, as it's less than half a mile to Dean Village, but you will pass **St Bernard's Well** en route. Around 30 years after a mineral spring was discovered here in 1760, the landowner commissioned a pump house modelled on the Temple of Sybil at Tivoli, complete with a statue of Hygeia, the goddess of hygiene and good health. Now run by the City of Edinburgh Council, the decorative pump house is open to the public on some Sunday afternoons in August (see www.edinburgh.gov.uk).

Dean Village itself was named for the dean, or deep valley, in which it sits. It's best seen from the surprisingly tall **Dean Bridge**, designed by Thomas Telford, which crosses the Water of Leith between Stockbridge and the West End. From at least the time of David I, who ruled in the 12th century, flour was milled for Edinburgh and the surrounding area here. The old buildings were largely replaced in the 19th century by breweries and distilleries; they now form part of a conservation area that's resolutely residential. The cobbled streets, varied architecture and steep braes form an attraction all by themselves, although mementos of the milling trade remain.

At the top of Bell's Brae stands the quirky **Kirkbrae House**. Eagle-eyed visitors will spot a panel taken from the ruins of a granary named Jericho, which was built for the Incorporation of Baxters (bakers) in 1619 and once stood in the dean immediately below the house. The ornate panel depicts the sun and cherubic heads with an inscription reading 'In the sweat of thy face shalt thou eat bread, Gen.3 verse 19'. Down the hill by **Bell's Brae Bridge** is another old panel, carved with two crossed bakers' peels (used for taking hot loaves out of ovens). The nearby window lintels with inscriptions are now getting too weathered to be read easily.

From Dean Village, you can follow the Water of Leith further upstream to the **Scottish National Gallery of Modern Art** (*see below*) and the **Dean Gallery** (*see below*); cross Bell's Brae Bridge into Damside and the Water of Leith Walkway continues, on the north side of the

river. In less than half a mile, there are some steps leading up to Belford Road; the galleries are around the corner to the right. Alternatively, continue along the walkway under the **Belford Bridge**; you'll soon reach a gate and some steps behind the Scottish National Gallery of Modern Art. Don't tarry, though: the gate is locked at 6pm from April to September, and at dusk during the rest of the year.

FREE Dean Gallery
Belford Road (624 6200, www.nationalgalleries. org). Bus 13 (or free shuttle from the Mound). **Open** 10am-5pm daily. **Admission** free; charges vary for special exhibitions. **Credit** MC, V. **Map** p331 A7.
Housed in an impressive 1831 building that was originally an orphanage, the Dean Gallery offers an impressive range of modern art. The permanent collection features one of Britain's largest bodies of surrealist and Dadaist art, with pieces by the likes of Dalí, Miró and Picasso. Leith-born sculptor Sir Eduardo Paolozzi is allocated a room all to himself, with a mock-up of his studio and his soaring sculpture of Vulcan (*see p62*). Temporary shows range from the populist (Mario Testino) to the more cerebral (contemporary artists' interpretation of the Enlightenment). It's directly across the road from the Scottish National Gallery of Modern Art (*see below*); you can comfortably visit both in a day.

★ FREE Scottish National Gallery of Modern Art
Belford Road (624 6200, www.nationalgalleries. org). Bus 13 (or free shuttle from the Mound). **Open** 10am-5pm daily. **Admission** free; charges vary for special exhibitions. **Credit** MC, V. **Map** p331 A7.
Since 1984, Scotland's national collection of modern art has been housed in this neo-classical structure, designed by William Burn in the 1820s as an institution for fatherless children. High-profile temporary exhibitions in recent years have covered Brit-art names such as Tracey Emin and Steve McQueen. However, there's also a strong permanent collection with pieces from Freud, Mondrian, Hepworth and the Scottish Colourists, plus a few Damien Hirsts thrown in; the most beautiful work may be Picasso's blue, beautiful *Mère et Enfant* (1902). As you walk downstairs to the café, which has a pleasant terrace, look across to the supporting wall on the stairwell. It's been given over to the artist Douglas Gordon, who has neatly printed on it the name of every person he has ever met and whose name he can remember.

The fun continues outside. At the front, the lawn has been remodelled by American landscape architect Charles Jencks into a sculpture entitled *Landform* And at the back, you'll find a Richard Long environmental sculpture (*Cornish Slate Cross*, 2007) insinuating itself into the grass, or vice versa .

▶ *For more contemporary art, see pp228-231.*

Calton Hill & Broughton

Broad views, historic monuments and fashionable modern Edinburgh.

Robert Louis Stevenson was not popularly known as a laugh-a-minute writer, but his description of **Calton Hill** as the city's best vantage point does have a certain witty merit. In *Edinburgh: Picturesque Notes*, published in 1878, Stevenson wryly points out that you can't see the castle from the castle, and you can't see Arthur's Seat from Arthur's Seat, but you can see both from Calton Hill. The views are supplemented by an array of historic monuments, some of which have fallen into sad decay.

Back at the bottom of the hill, just north of the Omni Centre, stands the adjacent district of **Broughton**. One of Edinburgh's more fashionable neighbourhoods, it's home to the city's small but cultured gay scene.

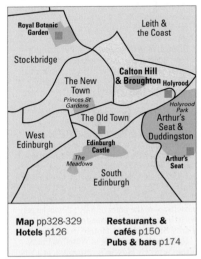

Royal Botanic Garden

Leith & the Coast

Stockbridge

The New Town

Calton Hill & Broughton Holyrood

Princes St Gardens

Holyrood Park

The Old Town

Arthur's Seat & Duddingston

West Edinburgh

Edinburgh Castle

The Meadows

Arthur's Seat

South Edinburgh

Map pp328-329
Hotels p126

Restaurants & cafés p150
Pubs & bars p174

SIGHTS

INTO THE NEIGHBOURHOOD

Calton Hill was formed in the same geological upheaval that created the Castle Rock and Arthur's Seat. The area may have been occupied during the Bronze Age, up to 4,000 years ago, but there's far more documentary evidence covering the last 550 years. In the middle of the 15th century, for instance, James II gave an amphitheatre to the city on Greenside, modern-day Greenside Place. It remains a focus for entertainment today, thanks chiefly to the Playhouse Theatre and the adjacent Omni Centre.

This confection of history and fun, ancient and modern, is typical of the area. On Waterloo Place, the Old Calton Cemetery dates to 1718 but sits opposite a hotel that opened as recently as 2009; not far away, on Royal Terrace, one of Edinburgh's most creative and contemporary restaurants, **21212** (*see p126 and p150*), offers 21st-century dining in a 19th-century townhouse. And in Broughton, brand new bars

and cafés appear regularly in a district that was first documented – as Bruchtoun – all the way back in the early 12th century.

In practical terms, the area known as Calton Hill is marked out by Calton Road in the south (Waterloo Place and Regent Road running more obviously above), and London Road and its environs in the north. Leith Street and the neighbourhood of Broughton are to the north-west, the latter eventually linking to the genteel suburb of Canonmills.

WATERLOO PLACE

Waterloo Place effectively forms an eastern entrance to the modern city centre, an impression aided by the austere façades on either side of the street and the twin ceremonial archways of Regent Bridge that carries the thoroughfare over Calton Road below. Both the bridge and the original Waterloo Hotel building on the north side (now the **Apex Waterloo Place**; *see p126*) opened in 1819, just four years after the celebrated battle at which the Anglo-Irish Duke of Wellington and Prussian Marshal Blucher saw off Napoleon once and for all.

As the Old Calton Cemetery had already been in situ on this side of Calton Hill for a century or so, the creation of Waterloo Place in the years immediately after the Battle of Waterloo effectively sliced the graveyard in two. The greater part is still accessible on the south side up some obvious steps, and serves as the final home for a number of figures from the Scottish Enlightenment; David Hume is the most celebrated, with a monument by Robert Adam that befits his status. For more on Hume, *see pp48-49*.

Elsewhere in the cemetery stand a couple of other memorials that resonate with more modern sensibilities. One of them, a towering obelisk that dates to 1844, is a tribute to a group of late 18th century political reformers led by Thomas Muir, who were transported for sedition after having had the audacity to demand parliamentary reform. The other, a 1893 monument that features Abraham Lincoln and a freed slave, was designed to commemorate the Scots who died during the American Civil War. Elsewhere, up against the graveyard's east wall, sits the **Governor's House** (1817), from the now-demolished Calton Gaol. Described by Robert Louis Stevenson as 'castellated to the point of folly', it was largely swept away during the construction of the nearby **St Andrew's House** (*see below*).

Back on the north side of Waterloo Place, at the corner by **Howie's** restaurant, is a lane called Calton Hill. Down here, you'll find the **Parliament House**, a hotel (*see p127*), and the old Rock House to the end of the residential tenements opposite. The building was home to a succession of photographers from the 1830s, among them David Octavius Hill. Working in collaboration with Robert Adamson, Hill helped to give photography credibility as a modern art form; 5,000 of the pair's calotypes and negatives now form a major part of the Scottish National Photography Collection, held by the National Galleries of Scotland and normally on display at the Scottish National Portrait Gallery (closed for renovations until 2011; *see p83*).

Waterloo Place also offers one of the most obvious routes up Calton Hill. Take the steps to your left as the street morphs into Regent Road.

REGENT ROAD

One of the two truly imposing buildings along Regent Road, **St Andrew's House** on the south side was created as a home for Scottish civil servants and is now part of the Scottish Government apparatus. It may be historically

**INSIDE TRACK
OLD SCHOOL TIES**

The origins of the **Royal High School** run back as far as the 12th century. The school has been based at various city locations in its long history. Before it moved to the Regent Road building in 1829, it spent 52 years on Infirmary Street in the Old Town. And when it left Regent Road in 1968, it rolled to the northwestern suburb of Barnton, where it remains today.

and aesthetically important, but it does smack of authoritarianism, all the more unsettling since construction was completed in 1939.

By contrast, the old **Royal High School** building a little further along on the north side is perhaps the finest example of neo-classical architecture in the city. Completed in 1829, it was designed by Glasgow-born architect Thomas Hamilton, a renowned Greek revivalist, and modelled on the Temple of Theseus in Athens (since reassigned to the god of fire and called the Hephaisteion). Because of the old pile's monumental size, it's difficult to get a proper perspective on it, even from the other side of the road. It's best to focus on the detail, then contemplate its grandeur from one of the closes at the lower end of the Royal Mile.

The school was the site of a round-the-clock, 1,980-day vigil in the 1990s by protestors campaigning for Scottish devolution. The vigil was triggered by the 1992 General Election, which once again returned a unionist-minded Conservative government to Westminster, at odds with public opinion in Scotland. The Royal High building seemed an auspicious location for a protest, as it had been made ready to house a parliamentary chamber before a referendum for a Scottish Assembly back in 1979. At that time, the vote didn't carry. But at a second referendum in 1997, the Scottish people finally said 'yes' in sufficient numbers; two years later, a parliament was convened. A cairn up on nearby Calton Hill commemorates the vigil.

The Royal High had previously been vacated in 1968, when the teachers and pupils moved to new premises. Vigil aside, the last 40 years have been quiet here, although the City of Edinburgh Council now sees Hamilton's masterpiece as part of its long-term 'string of pearls' development plan. There's long been talk that the school could house a photography museum, a nod to the area's associations with pioneering photographers Hill and Adamson (*see left*), but no one's holding their breath.

Just across the road from the old school is another Hamilton effort: the **Robert Burns**

Memorial, a small Greek temple that seems completely out of sync with its purpose. It's worth straying this far in order to take in the fantastic view up to the castle and down to the environs of Holyrood. Alternatively, head along Regent Terrace (closed to through traffic since shortly after 9/11 to protect the US Consulate) for a stroll by the elegant townhouses around that side of the hill, before heading around to Royal Terrace and back to the top of Leith Walk.

CALTON HILL

Calton Hill yields a multitude of handsome views. Looking west, you'll see the clock tower of the Balmoral Hotel, with the castle behind. To the south, you can take in the diagonal slash of Salisbury Crags. On the eastern horizon, look out for the volcanic pimple of North Berwick Law. But for the most immanent sense of space, look north-east, up to where the land falls away to Leith and the Firth of Forth beyond it opens up towards the North Sea. Catch it at the right time, when a chilly sea mist blankets the Forth, encroaching on the city, and it appears quite magical. Locals call this mist a 'haar'.

Although the views from it are terrific, **Calton Hill** is most famous for its array of bizarre architecture, and no single structure is more bizarre that the 12 Doric columns that form the **National Monument** to the dead of the Napoleonic Wars. Designed by William Playfair, the architect responsible for some of Edinburgh's finest neo-classical architecture, the monument was designed to be a replica of the Parthenon in Athens. Sadly, the funds ran

out in 1829 before the building was completed. The still-unfinished structure came to be known as 'Scotland's Disgrace', although that title might now be better applied to the old **City Observatory** complex nearby.

The enclosed precinct on Calton Hill singularly referred to as 'the Observatory' contains a number of buildings. The oldest is the rather gothic 1776 creation at the western side, designed by New Town architect James Craig but never properly completed nor used for stargazing; instead, it served as lodgings for the man who ran the first observatory here.

In the middle of the precinct sits Playfair's elegant Royal Observatory, based on the Temple of the Winds at Athens. Construction on the building began in 1818; four years later, it was given a regal imprimatur, although it wasn't fully functional until 1831. As an institution, the Royal Observatory moved away to Blackford Hill in 1896 (*see p102*); the buildings became known simply as the City Observatory, and another dome was added at the north-east of the complex. Also on the site, at the south-eastern corner, is a neo-classical monument that stands as a memorial to Playfair, who died in 1823.

The Astronomical Society of Edinburgh began using the observatory buildings in 1938, but persistent vandalism and theft from what is an insecure site caused them to think again. In early spring 2009, the society held what they described as a 'quiet closing event', and then vacated the buildings forever. Although the site may be in a line for some maintenance work before 2012, thanks to local authority cash, it was a sad ending to 233 years of astronomy on Calton Hill.

SIGHTS

National Monument.

City Observatory. *See p93.*

Other buildings on the hill include the towering **Nelson Monument** (*see below*) and, nearby, the Playfair-designed **Monument to Dugald Stewart** (1753-1828), professor of moral philosophy at the University of Edinburgh. Taken together, the monuments provide a dramatic backdrop to the annual **Beltane** celebration (*see p217*), a modern interpretation of the ancient rites of spring that draws thousands of people on the night of 30 April every year. However, the festivals predate the monuments: fairs such as Beltane have been held on Calton Hill since at least the 18th century, and probably much earlier.

Nelson Monument

Calton Hill (556 2716, www.cac.org.uk). Playhouse buses. **Open** *Apr-Sept* 1-6pm Mon; 10am-6pm Tue-Sat. *Oct-Mar* 10am-3pm Mon-Sat. **Admission** £3. **No credit cards. Map** p329 K5.

If the views from Calton Hill aren't grand enough for your liking, you can get an even better all-round vantage point from the top of the Nelson Monument. Designed to mimic the shape of Nelson's telescope, it was built to commemorate his victory at Trafalgar and completed in 1816. Some 36 years later, a time-ball mechanism was added at the very top; weighing

a mighty 762kg (1,680lbs), the ball and the One O'Clock Gun at the castle (*see p56* **Bang!**) were synchronised, helping shipping captains in Leith Harbour to reset their chronometers. By 2009, many years of ball-dropping and the tower's exposed position had taken their toll, but a few months of tender loving care saw the monument back in good nick.

BROUGHTON TO CANONMILLS

Broughton has long been a cultured and unconventional part of the city. Once a notorious centre for witchcraft, it's been home to Edinburgh's gay community for many years, and the area around Broughton Street, Picardy Place and the top of Leith Walk has been nicknamed 'the pink triangle' (*see pp232-234*). However, there's more to the neighbourhood, which has steadily become one of the most fashionable corners of the city.

The approach down **Leith Street** from the east end of Princes Street has been hugely altered in recent years with a row of modern offices and, to the south side, the huge **Omni Centre**, filled with chain eateries, a health centre, a comedy club (**Jongleurs**; *see p223*), a cineplex (*see p226*) and even a hotel (the **Glasshouse**; *see p126*). The northern side of Leith Street may also soon alter beyond all recognition if the St James Quarter development goes ahead (*see p40*). One of the few constants is the **Edinburgh Playhouse** (*see p253*), here since 1929 and not going anywhere.

Flanking the huge roundabout at the top of Leith Walk, **Picardy Place** was named in honour of a colony of Protestant French silk weavers who fled to Edinburgh from Picardy in 1685. Today, assuming you're not staying at the **Holiday Inn Express** (*see p118*) or popping into one of the local bars (*see pp174-175*), the

Park Life

Two hidden green spaces offer Calton Hill a little verdant competition.

Calton Hill is one of the most famous green spaces in the city, and with good reason: the monuments are fascinating and the views are sensational. But it's not the only historic green space in this part of town. North-east and north-west of the hill sit two parks with long and interesting histories of their own, both of them still popular with locals.

Hopetoun Crescent need not detain you for long; it's probably best used as a pleasant shortcut from Annandale Street to McDonald Road. Still, this modest patch of land has a significant history: it was here, in 1763, that John Hope, the king's botanist in Scotland, established what would become the precursor of today's Royal Botanic Garden. The site we know today at Inverleith was established in 1822, but it still has trees that began their life here. Today, the local community does a splendid job of landscaping and maintaining the gardens.

At the bottom of Scotland Street, meanwhile, **George V Memorial Park** – known locally as Scotland Yard – has an even more colourful history. The recently reopened tunnel connecting the park to the Broughton Road Tesco and the cycle paths along the Water of Leith is a reminder of the train network that once

passed this way; looking in the direction of the town centre, you can still see the tunnel entrance that would take you underground all the way to Waverley Station aided by cables that pulled the trains up a 1:27 gradient. The hairy return journey depended on two men operating brakes by hand.

The attractively wooded park was once the site of the Canonmills Loch, where the local curling club would skate in cold winters during the 1700s. After the water was drained in the middle of the 19th century, philanthropist John Cox opened the Royal Patent Gymnasium Grounds, which featured a massive see-saw for 200 people, a bicycle roundabout and a 60-foot 'boat' that would rotate on a circular pond. The gymnasium's pitch became home to St Bernard's football club, Scottish champions in 1895 and a popular draw until World War II.

The present-day park was established to commemorate George V after his death in 1936. It was upgraded in 1988, and is now a very handsome place. The park's steep path winds down to two playgrounds and a centre for children with special needs, making it a favourite of local parents.

main reason to visit is for a peek at the statue of **Sherlock Holmes**; his creator, Sir Arthur Conan Doyle, was born at a now-demolished property at no.11.

Nearby, in front of **St Mary's Roman Catholic Cathedral**, are a set of outsize sculptures by the late Sir Eduardo Paolozzi, born in Leith and a favourite son of the city; there's more of his work in the **Dean Gallery** (*see p90*). Outside the Omni Centre, opposite the Paolozzi works, stand a more populist pair of scrap metal giraffes, created in 2005 by Helen Denerley; *see p62* **Go, Figure**.

Heading downhill (north-west) from Picardy Place, **Broughton Street** is the heart of the neighbourhood. It's lined with a number of decent shops, cafés and restaurants, many listed in the relevant parts of this guide. You can stroll down here with no intention to stop or buy anything and then, hours later, retreat back to your hotel well fed, well watered and armed with several carrier bags containing anything from decent bottles of wine to hypoallergenic sex toys.

At the bottom of the street, across the roundabout, is **Mansfield Church**, the

walls of which are covered in murals by leading Arts and Crafts artist Phoebe Traquair. The church was bought by the Mansfield Traquair Trust in the 1990s and now houses voluntary organisation offices, but the murals were restored in 2005 for public display. Continuing down the hill, a look down Bellevue Crescent on the left reveals more elegant New Town façades. Eventually, via Rodney Street, you come to the suburb of **Canonmills**.

Over time, old Canonmills has been obscured by various waves of civic improvement, losing its loch, its mills, and even the historic Tanfield Hall. In 1843, a number of ministers broke away from the Church of Scotland to form the Free Kirk; when they did so, they marched from a meeting in George Street to Tanfield Hall in an event known as the Disruption, which had a profound effect on Victorian Scotland. Modern-day Canonmills offers nothing quite so dramatic: just a couple of pleasant cafés along Brandon Terrace, access to the **Water of Leith Walkway** and easy access to the **Royal Botanic Garden** (*see p89*).

SIGHTS

Arthur's Seat & Duddingston

Breathtaking views and beautiful nature… but who's Arthur?

Those who make it to the top of **Arthur's Seat**, which dominates the city's skyline, will be rewarded with fantastic views. The glorious 360-degree panorama encompasses the Bass Rock and the hills of North Berwick Law and Traprain Law to the east, the Lammermuir and Moorfoot hills to the south-east, the Pentland Hills to the south and the Firth of Forth and Fife to the north. On clear days, you can see up to 40 miles, to the fringe of the southern Highlands.

The hill's deep geological history of vulcanism adds to its lustre, as does the variety of wildlife scattered across its wild expanses. Edinburghers walk to the top of the hill, run and cycle round its flanks or linger by its lochs; some end

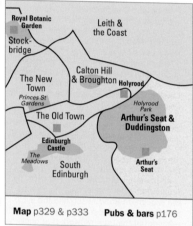

Map p329 & p333   Pubs & bars p176

their visit by wandering to the quiet and charming village of **Duddingston**, tucked away to the south-east of the grand old hill.

ARTHUR'S SEAT

Although Arthur's Seat is commonly referred to as Edinburgh's volcano, it hasn't erupted for a while. Its last explosion was roughly 350 million years ago, when it was on a different part of the Earth's crust and standing in a shallow sea. What remains today is not the volcano itself, but a basalt lava plug that choked its neck. The intervening hundreds of millions of years have seen it subject to all kinds of geological stresses (tilting it around 25 degrees off its original plane, for example); more recent erosion and glaciation created the shape that now stands. You can learn about how the landmark was formed at **Our Dynamic Earth** (*see p69*).

The earliest evidence of human industry on Arthur's Seat is the series of linear bumps in the grass just above Dunsapie Loch, the remains of cultivation terraces that may date to the Bronze Age. Further below, Duddingston Loch has

more solid evidence of Bronze Age occupation (*see p99*). And above Dunsapie Loch on **Dunsapie Hill**, there are traces of a later Iron Age hill fort.

No one really knows why the main hill is called Arthur's Seat. Some maintain that it's a corruption of the Gaelic Ard-na-Saighead, 'the height of arrows', or even of Archer's Seat. This explanation gains currency from both those old Iron Age fortifications and the fact that during the 12th century, the parkland was used as a royal hunting ground.

Climbing Arthur's Seat

Several paths lead to the top of Arthur's Seat. Some are simple and others tougher, but all are within the ability of any moderately fit adult or child, and can be taken at an easy pace with plenty of pauses to take in the view. Some cross-country runners ascend the hill every day; drink-fortified teens have been known

SIGHTS

Where the Wild Things Are

Glamour birds and sticky catchfly in Holyrood Park.

Managed by Historic Scotland and designated as a Site of Special Scientific Interest, Holyrood Park has rocky cliffs, marsh, lochs, unimproved grassland and deep undergrowth. The environment is great for visitors who want to get away from the city streets, but it's even better for the assorted species of animals and plants who live in it.

The story behind the 12th-century creation of Holyrood Abbey at the park's northern edge involves a deer (*see p17*), but you won't find mammals quite so large grazing here these days. Look out, instead, for plenty of brown hares and grey squirrels. At quieter times, you might catch a hedgehog scuttling about (or squashed on the road), a fox or even a weasel. And at Duddingston Loch, which is also an important site for a wide variety of birds (swans, geese, ducks, coots, grebes and, in the surrounding trees, Edinburgh's colony of herons), keep your eyes peeled for water voles and otters. Common in central Scotland in the middle of the last century, otters were almost wiped out by agricultural pesticides. However, they have gradually been moving back into suitable habitats in recent years; you may also see one or two on the Water of Leith.

Elsewhere in the park, St Mary's Loch and Dunsapie Loch are both frequented by plenty of waterfowl, and there's more bird life in the shape of tits, finches, skylarks and summer visitors such as sedge warblers. The unsettling squawk of carrion crows is common – you might have one perching near you as you catch your breath up Arthur's Seat – but the glamour birds are the raptors. You can often see kestrels hovering above, as well as sparrowhawks, short-eared owls and the occasional buzzard.

Toads, frogs and smooth newts also call the park home, as do all kinds of bats, damselflies, butterflies and moths. And it's estimated that there are around 350 plant species in the park, with as many as one-sixth of them quite rare in Scotland. While many people come here for the fresh air, fewer are willing to get down on their knees and check whether that dark pink flower is really a sticky catchfly. But for the enthusiast, the various micro-environments can provide all kinds of surprises and delights.

▶ For more on the park's nature, check the Holyrood Park Information Centre; see p98.

to climb the peak after a night out. A word of warning, though: while it's basically safe, the park has cliffs, precipices and sudden drops. Wear strong shoes or boots that won't slip on the grass or slopes, and take an extra layer of clothing: even on mild days, there's no shelter from the wind.

The easiest route to the top of Arthur's Seat is from **Dunsapie Loch** on the eastern part of Queen's Drive. From here, it's a straight and easy pull from the loch up a grass slope to the summit. No matter which approach you take to the top, this is also the best way down; it's an easy walk from here to the Sheep Heid Inn (*see right*) for some deserved refreshment.

If you're after a more challenging hike to the top, enter the park through the **Holyrood Park Road** entrance. Once inside, go right at the second, upper roundabout and walk uphill a short way on Queen's Drive. An obvious track soon cuts in to your left, between the south end of Salisbury Crags and the massif of Arthur's Seat itself. The track leads down into a small valley known as Hunter's Bog. At the lip of the valley, immediately up to the right, you'll see a zig-zagging and rough-cut stone pathway leading directly up the gully between Arthur's Seat and Nether Hill. It's arduous for much of the way, and you'll certainly need a head for heights but it's a great way to access the peak.

An alternative route, from the same Holyrood Park Road entrance, is to bypass the track into Hunter's Bog and continue around Queen's Drive for another 50 metres or so, where there are steps leading directly off the road. Again, it's a very steep ascent and the steps only go so far; when they end, you'll have a little scramble to reach the upper slopes. This track joins up on Nether Hill with the one from the entrance to Hunter's Bog, effectively offering two routes around and through the crags that buttress Nether Hill to its south-west. If such scrambles don't appeal, the secluded Hunter's Bog itself is a placid space, enclosed by Arthur's Seat on one side and the slopes behind Salisbury Crags on the other.

Perhaps the least punishing route to the top is via the northern approach. Enter the park via the **Holyrood Park Information Centre** (*see p99*), then head along Queen's Drive in the direction of the man-made St Margaret's Loch to the north-east. The loch itself, created in 1856 as part of a series of works drawn up by Prince Albert, is a picturesque spot and good for those who can't manage a more strenuous hike. Walking in its direction takes you past a grille set into the wall on the right; this is **St Margaret's Well**, which, during plague years, was relied upon as a source of clean and safe drinking water. Before reaching the loch, walk in behind the ruins of the 15th-century **St Anthony's Chapel**, obvious on its crag.

Here, an easy rising glen, the Dry Dam, leads uphill. The path to the rocky outcrops at the top of Arthur's Seat is plain to see.

Elsewhere in the park

Even if you don't fancy the climb to the top, there's some fine walking around. Skirting the foot of Salisbury Crags, the **Radical Road** was built in 1820 as a means of providing work for downtrodden locals, at the suggestion of the novelist Sir Walter Scott; it's named for the apparently outré political views held by the group of unemployed weavers who built it.

Part of the rock face alongside the road is known as **Hutton's Section**. In the late 18th century, it was used by James Hutton, the so-called 'father of modern geology', to show that the ochre sill of Salisbury Crags was formed by molten lava forcing its way into older layers of sedimentary rock. In later years, it was said to be a favourite spot of George VI, father of the current Queen, who took regular early-morning strolls along here when he was staying at the Palace of Holyroodhouse. Today, it's the best place from which to make sense of the architectural complexity of the **Scottish Parliament** (*see p70*), while also affording fine views over the rest of the Holyrood area.

The park offers more than just exercise. Every May Day, faithful souls take a pre-dawn jaunt to follow the pagan tradition of washing their faces in the dew at sunrise, said to bring clear skin and great beauty. The precise origins of the ritual are unknown; as, for that matter, is the identity of

Duddingston Kirk.

the person or persons who left 17 miniature coffins, each containing a tiny wooden doll, in a hillside cave at some point in the 18th or 19th centuries. The coffins were found in 1836 by boys out looking for rabbits; the surviving coffins can be seen in the **National Museum of Scotland** (*see p76*).

FREE Holyrood Park Information Centre
Horse Wynd, by the Scottish Parliament at Holyrood, Old Town (no phone, www.historic-scotland.gov.uk). **Open** 9.30am-3pm daily.
Map p329 & p333 L6.
Housed in an old stone lodge, this unstaffed information centre has displays on the park's history, geology and archaeological features, along with useful leaflets and up to date information about wildlife. It shouldn't be confused with the similarly named Holyrood Park Education Centre, a modern building just east of the Palace of Holyroodhouse perimeter wall; this latter facility serves as a base for the park rangers and police, and is not generally open to the public. However, park rangers do run guided walks and other activities; contact them on 652 8150 or at hs.rangers@scotland.gsi.gov.uk.

DUDDINGSTON

People have lived in Duddingston for thousands of years. The shores of Duddingston Loch were settled during the Bronze Age, perhaps as far back as 800 BC; a cache of broken Bronze Age weapons and tools was dredged up here in 1778, though it's unknown if they were thrown in as some sort of offering or because they were scrap. The first documentary evidence of the area concerns David I, who gifted lands here to Kelso Abbey in the early 12th century.

For years, the villagers made a living weaving a coarse linen cloth known as 'Duddingston hardings'. Parishioners also made use of the benign environment: farming was a common occupation, as the land surrounding Arthur's Seat is very fertile, and there was also a small salt industry. No longer, though. Designated an Outstanding Conservation Area in 1975, the village today is smart, residential and tranquil. It effectively comprises two parallel streets: **Old Church Lane** has the church (*see below*), while the **Causeway** has the pub (*see below*).

If you're walking around Queen's Drive, the road that rings Holyrood Park, you can descend into the village from the steps to the south of the man-made Dunsapie Loch. Otherwise, the easiest stroll is from the park's Holyrood Park Road entrance, taking a right at the first roundabout and following the 'low road' that skirts under the cliffs of the Lion's Haunch and then along past Duddingston Loch (*see p97* **Where the Wild Things Are**). It's an easy walk, but it does miss the view of the loch itself

**INSIDE TRACK
WHAT'S IN A NAME?**

Duddingston's old Brythonic name was Treverlen, which persisted into the medieval period. From 1124, the land was feued, or rented, from its church owners by a Norman knight, Dodin de Berwic; his name resulted in the village's name changing to Dodin's Toun and, eventually, Duddingston.

and the adjacent nature reserve afforded by the 'high road' above, which also overlooks Prestonfield Golf Club.

The aforementioned church is **Duddingston Kirk** (661 4240, www.duddingstonkirk.co.uk), built in 1124 and one of the oldest churches in Scotland still used for regular worship. There are services on Sundays at 10am and 11.30am; otherwise, though, the church is usually only open for limited hours during August (call or check online before setting out). Next to the church's gates is a two-storey tower, once used as a graveyard lookout point and now called the Session House. Such features were common in Edinburgh kirkyards in the 19th century, with grave-robbers such as Burke and Hare on the prowl for fresh cadavers to sell to the medical schools. Look out, too, for the 'loupin'-on-stane' (jumping-on stone), used for mounting horses, and a punishment collar known as 'the jougs'.

The small, octagonal building at the foot of the Duddingston Kirk manse, and the edge of the loch, is **Thomson's Tower**. The structure was named after the Reverend John Thomson (1778-1840), one of the parish's best-known ministers and also a landscape painter. It was Thomson who coined the Scots phrase, 'We're a' Jock Tamson's bairns' (All men are equal in the eyes of God). Thomson's visitors included the artist JMW Turner and the writer Sir Walter Scott, who wrote part of *The Heart of Midlothian* in the tower. In the mid 1790s, the loch also provided the setting for Scotland's most famous painting: Sir Henry Raeburn's *Reverend Robert Walker Skating on Duddingston Loch*, better known as 'The Skating Minister'. You can see the original in the National Gallery of Scotland (*see p79*).

Back in the village, most visitors end up in the **Sheep Heid Inn** (*see p176*) on the Causeway, a country pub that feels far removed from urban life. There's been an inn on this spot since 1360; one of its incarnations was a favourite of James VI (later James I & VI of England and Scotland), who presented the innkeeper with a snuffbox decorated with a ram's head, which later inspired the pub's name. With its dark wood circular bar, leaded glass partitions and knick-knack-festooned walls, the pub still oozes atmosphere.

SIGHTS

South Edinburgh

Where the city heads for the hills…

From the fringes of the Old Town to the Pentlands, South Edinburgh encompasses the urban, the suburban and the positively bucolic. Close to the heart of the city, **Lothian Road** boasts what is almost an arts village, while the grassy expanse of the **Meadows** offers accessible green space. Discrete attractions such as the Surgeons Hall Museums and the Edinburgh College of Art are also held tight to Edinburgh's bosom, but single items of interest become rarer in the great residential sweep from **Merchiston** in the west to **Newington** in the east. The commanding views of **Blackford Hill** deconstruct the geography. And then, just where you least expect it, you'll find Edinburgh's other castle.

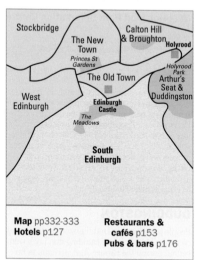

Map pp332-333	**Restaurants &**
Hotels p127	**cafés** p153
	Pubs & bars p176

Map pp332-333 **Hotels** p127 **Restaurants & cafés** p153 **Pubs & bars** p176

LOTHIAN ROAD & TOLLCROSS

Running south from the western end of Princes Street is **Lothian Road**. The thoroughfare has long had a reputation for carousing: when Robert Louis Stevenson was a student, more than 135 years ago, he came here with his friends in search of beer and bawdiness. Later, in **St Cuthbert's Kirk** (5 Lothian Road), Stevenson was said to have found a gravestone bearing the name 'Jekyll', which he went on to use in his most famous book.

Over the years, a degree of respectability has crept in to the area. The construction of the **Royal Lyceum Theatre** (*see p253*) in 1883

and the elegant **Usher Hall** (*see p236*) three decades on helped; much later, the arrival of the **Filmhouse** (*see p226*) and the **Traverse Theatre** (*see p254*) created an artistic cluster. However, seediness remains. As darkness falls, the area's pubs and clubs become magnets for young drinkers. Within the space of a block or two, you could watch traditional ballet or exotic dancing, get into a discussion about Lars von Trier or get into a fight. Jekyll and Hyde indeed.

At the south end of Lothian Road sits Tollcross, a major junction now dominated by the **Princes Exchange**. Built in 2001 to house financial-sector offices, it may be big but it's hardly beautiful. For something with a little more soul, keep walking up Home Street and Leven Street until the **Barclay Church** looms out of nowhere. With one of the tallest spires in Edinburgh, this Franco-Venetian, Gothic extravaganza was created by FT Pilkington in 1864. So much for progress.

FREE Edinburgh College of Art
Lauriston Place (221 6000, www.eca.ac.uk). Bus 23, 27, 35, 45. **Open** 9am-5pm Mon-Fri; 10am-2pm Sat, Sun. **Admission** free. **Map** p332 F9.
The ECA operates a year-round programme of exhibitions by artists from all over the world, but there

---

INSIDE TRACK GIRLS, BEHAVE!

Cartoonist Ronald Searle based his fictional St Trinian's School on a real establishment: St Trinnean's in South Edinburgh. The school opened in 1922 at 10 Palmerston Road, and later moved to St Leonard's House (now part of the University of Edinburgh's Pollock Halls complex), before closing in 1946.

---

are three key local events in amongst them: the May fashion show, the June degree show, and the August Festival exhibition. For many, the highlight is the degree show, when the public can flood in and possibly buy something from an up-and-coming name. The website has full details of upcoming exhibitions.

▶ *For the ECA's Wee Red Bar, see p244.*

GEORGE SQUARE & AROUND

Located between Bristo Square and the Meadows, **George Square** should cause the city fathers of yore to hang their heads in shame. Built around handsome central gardens, the square was once lined by elegant houses dating to the 18th century; no.25 was home to a young Walter Scott. Some survive along the west side of the square, but many were levelled in the 1960s for the University of Edinburgh. The central gardens are open during the week (until 7pm in summer, 4pm in winter).

Around the gardens, the squat **University Library** (1967) by Sir Basil Spence on the south-west corner was constructed to replace the more elegant library in Old College (*see p75*); the south-east corner commemorates the city's most famous philosopher son in the shape of the **David Hume Tower** (1963). The **Appleton Tower** (1966), set back from the east side of the square on Crichton Street, is widely regarded as one of the city's more objectionable buildings. Refurbishment work in the last decade hasn't improved its aesthetics to any great degree, although the university's latest round of construction at Crichton Street, known as the **Informatics Forum** (2008), serves to obscure it from some angles.

To the north, **Bristo Square** is also home to some modern-era university buildings, but also squeezes in a riot of architectural Victoriana. Highlights include **Teviot Row House** (1889), Britain's oldest, purpose-built student union; the **Reid Concert Hall** (1859; *see p236*); the **McEwan Hall** (1897), designed by Sir Robert Rowand Anderson and funded by brewing magnate Sir William McEwan; and, next door on Teviot Place, the **Medical School** (1888).

A little further west on Lauriston Place is the extensive **Quartermile** development, a whole new neighbourhood on the site of the old Royal Infirmary. Its mix of residential and commercial space blends Victorian and contemporary, with some of the original hospital buildings standing alongside blocks constructed since 2006.

Head in the opposite direction from Bristo Square, and you'll find another building by the celebrated architect Sir William Playfair. Completed in 1832, **Surgeons Hall** was where Burke and Hare brought their freshly deceased victims. It remains home to the Royal College

INSIDE TRACK THE MEADOWS

The **Meadows** is famous as the host of Fringe Sunday (cancelled in 2009, though it's hoped that it'll return in future years). However, back in 1886, it welcomed a very different event: the International Exhibition of Industry, housed in a temporary structure at its western end. The event left the city with several souvenirs; among them are the whale jawbones at Jawbone Walk, a gift of improbable provenance that came from the Zetland & Fair Isle knitting stand, and the memorial pillars, where Melville Drive joins Brougham Place.

of Surgeons of Edinburgh, a body that can trace its roots to 1505, and to the celebrated **Surgeons Hall Museums** (*see below*).

★ Surgeons Hall Museums

18 Nicolson Street (527 1649, www.rcsed.ac.uk). Nicolson Street–North Bridge buses. **Open** *Aug* 10am-4pm Mon-Fri; noon-4pm Sat, Sun. *Sept-July* noon-4pm Mon-Fri. **Admission** £5; £3 discounts. **Credit** MC, V. **Map** p333 J8.

The collections at the Surgeons Hall Museums allow visitors to trace the history of medicine in the city from 1505, when the Barber Surgeons of Edinburgh were incorporated, to the development of modern surgical techniques. One of the real curios is a pocketbook covered with the tanned skin of William Burke who, with William Hare, killed at least 16 Edinburgh citizens in 1827-28 and sold their bodies for dissection. Also of note are the John Menzies Campbell dentistry section and exhibits devoted to 'the real Sherlock Holmes': Joseph Bell, a former president of the college. (Arthur Conan Doyle attended lectures by Bell when studying medicine in the city.)

However, the main attraction is the celebrated pathology collection, the largest in the UK. The museum helpfully suggests that some people find the pickled remains 'unsettling', and under-15s must be accompanied by an adult. Still, seeing the workings and failing of the human body is never less than fascinating.

▶ *There's also a hotel in the building, Ten Hill Place; see p129.*

THE SOUTHERN SUBURBS

The immediate centrepiece of South Edinburgh is the **Meadows**, stretching east to west from Newington to Tollcross and north to south from Quartermile to Marchmont. Formerly the site of the Burgh Loch, it was drained in the late 17th century, leaving the distinctive flat, grassy area known today. Tree-lined paths, complete with cycle lanes, cut across in every direction; it's a

SIGHTS

popular spot for joggers and amateur sports. A lack of lighting means caution should be taken at night, but it's generally a safe place.

South of the Meadows, **Marchmont** is composed almost entirely of grand tenement buildings, built between 1876 and 1914. The cobbled sweep of Warrender Park Road gives a flavour of the district, which has long had the atmosphere of a student ghetto thanks to its proximity to various colleges. The nearby **Warrender Swim Centre** at 55 Thirlestane Road (*see p250*), housed in a beautiful Victorian building (1887), is an impressive place for a dip.

To the south-west, the Meadows opens out into **Bruntsfield Links**, all that's left of the old Burgh Muir ('town heath') gifted to the city by David I in 1128. It's long been associated with golf: there are records mentioning golf at Bruntsfield in the 17th century and there was an official Bruntsfield Links Golfing Society from 1761, although it eventually moved elsewhere in the city. A short-hole course was set up in 1895; it still exists, effectively a 36-hole pitch-and-putt (see www.golf.tollcross.org). The claim that Bruntsfield Links is the oldest golf course in the world may have some merit.

Bruntsfield itself is a thriving locale, mostly residential away from its main thoroughfare and the commercial-minded Bruntsfield Place. Further south sits **Morningside**, once notoriously snooty but now merely exclusive.

Beyond these suburbs is **Blackford Hill**. At its top stands the twin-teacake structure of the **Royal Observatory**, moved here in 1896 after the facilities on Calton Hill (*see p93*) were deemed to be no longer fit for purpose. The Blackford Hill observatory has a visitor's centre, but it's only open for pre-booked group visits and special events (see www.roe.ac.uk). Further south still lie the **Braid Hills**; like Blackford Hill, these offer amazing views back over the city. And east of the summit of Blackford Hill sits **Craigmillar Castle** (*see below*).

Craigmillar Castle

Craigmillar Castle Road (668 8600, www. historic-scotland.gov.uk). Bus 33, 48, X48, 49. **Open** *Apr-Sep* 9.30am-5.30pm daily. *Oct* 9.30am-4.30pm daily. *Nov-Mar* 9.30am-4.30pm Mon-Wed, Sat, Sun. **Admission** £4.20; £2.10-£3.20 discounts. **Credit** AmEx, MC, V.
See below **Edinburgh's Other Castle**.

Edinburgh's Other Castle

Craigmillar delivers all of the history and none of the crowds.

A fabulous and largely complete ruin with parts dating back more than 600 years, **Craigmillar Castle** is a little out of the way; two and a half miles south of the city centre, give or take. However, there's an advantage to its relative isolation: visitors can get a taste of the city's history with none of the Old Town queues. Some 200 visitors during a peak summer day constitutes 'busy'. Sometimes, you could be here on your own.

The L-shaped tower house at the castle's core dates to around 1400, and was built by a notable local family called the Prestons. They later added a mighty curtain wall and, in the early 16th century, yet more layers of defence and protection. After it was captured by the English in 1544, the castle got another makeover, and it was in this condition that it greeted its most famous guest: Mary, Queen of Scots, who stayed here in 1563 and 1566. Mary had been born in Scotland, but spent the majority of her childhood in France. When she came to Craigmillar Castle, she brought a large French retinue; it's this that explains why a nearby hamlet came to be known as Little France, a name that persists to this day.

The castle later passed out of the hands of the Prestons. In the 18th century, it was abandoned and left to decay, a sad state of affairs that persisted until the state stepped in just after World War II. Today, it's the responsibility of Historic Scotland. The castle is a shell, with none of the museum ambience that defines Edinburgh Castle. However, the atmosphere and the views make the detour worthwhile.
▶ For listings, *see above*.

West Edinburgh

An unusual mix of urban renewal and rural wonders.

Away from a few big attractions (the zoo, Murrayfield Stadium), West Edinburgh doesn't generally detain or divert visitors. But it's here that layers of Edinburgh's economic history fit together like a topological puzzle, just as a few old buildings hidden away in residential warrens hint at a less urban past. Many modern-day business-world big hitters are clustered around the western side of Lothian Road and Morrison Street in an area known as the **Exchange**, not far from the echoes of Victorian brewing found at **Fountainbridge**. Meanwhile, picturesque **Cramond** and the **Craiglockhart Hills** offer a break from the urbanity; as, too, does the surprising **Union Canal**, its terminus tucked discreetly away off Lothian Road.

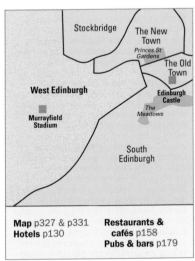

Map p327 & p331	Restaurants &
Hotels p130	cafés p158
	Pubs & bars p179

THE EXCHANGE

The first recognised name to put down roots in what is now the Exchange business district wasn't a bank or a life insurance company but the **Sheraton Grand** hotel on Festival Square (*see p130*), which was built in 1985. It wasn't until three years later that the local authority decided to promote the locale as a dedicated financial district. So began a construction boom, the most important in the city for many years (although it's now been surpassed by the goings-on at Leith and the coast).

At first, development centred around the **Edinburgh International Conference Centre**, which arrived on Morrison Street in 1995. Designed by Sir Terry Farrell, this circular, flat-topped structure beats its own drum. New buildings followed: in 1997, the **Standard Life** head office at the corner of Lothian Road and the West Approach Road; four years later, the sweeping crescent roof of **Scottish Widows** on Morrison Street. Also in 2001, the Sheraton Grand redeemed itself for its brutalist façade with the addition, at the rear, of the colourful, Farrell-designed One Spa. And then, in 2009, a giant outdoor television screen appeared on Festival Square, paid for by the

committee for the 2012 Olympics in London, as part of a move to spread the joie de vivre of the games around the UK.

Today, every scrap of land around the Exchange seems to be taken up with functional, identikit offices. The paucity of imagination is only too evident when they're compared with the tenements at the corner of Fountainbridge and Grove Street nearby. Built in the mid 1860s by maverick Victorian architect FT Pilkington, they offer a hint of fantasy that's a welcome relief from the area's orthogonal orthodoxy.

FOUNTAINBRIDGE

South-west of the Exchange and sliced in two by the West Approach Road, Fountainbridge doesn't win many beauty contests. The arrival of the **FountainPark Centre** in 1999 – bowling, bingo and a cineplex – added amenities, but it didn't improve the look of the place. Still, this is the only neighbourhood within a mile or two of the castle to betray any hint of the industries that once drove the local economy; *see p170* **Inside Track**. Economic obsolescence is just another facet of modern capitalism, but one that holds special resonance for West Edinburgh; this kind of shift has been

SIGHTS

Down on the Farm

The Royal Highland Show brings the country to the city.

The Royal Highland & Agricultural Society of Scotland was founded in 1784 to promote the regeneration of rural areas. Nearly four decades later, it chose to do so by staging a little event in Edinburgh. The first ever **Royal Highland Show** was held in 1822 at Holyrood, the site of the modern Scottish Parliament. Nearly two centuries later, it's one of the biggest events on the local calendar, and its appeal isn't limited only to farmers.

The Royal Highland Show moved around through the years before, in 1960, settling on Ingliston (next to Edinburgh Airport) as its permanent home. The site is now officially known as the Royal Highland Centre; for four days towards the end of June, it's the centre of the universe for all things agricultural. Farmers show their animals in competitions; trade exhibitors sell everything from tractors to slurry-handling equipment; and there are displays on equestrianism, falconry, drystane dyke building and other rural crafts.

If the show was just a bunch of farmers talking about milk yields, the public would not have taken it to heart. In reality, it's both a serious agricultural event and, for the outsider, a lot of fun. Getting close enough to touch thoroughbred beasts – Aberdeen Angus, Highland and other cattle breeds you can't even name – is

surprisingly enjoyable. The rare breeds of sheep and goats are even more novel and beguiling to uneducated urban eyes. And there's plenty for kids, too, which is one reason why the show is more popular than ever. In 2009, it drew the biggest single-day crowd (51,307 visited on the Saturday) and the largest four-day aggregate attendance (176,522) in its history.

Airport expansion had threatened to push the show from its Ingliston site, but those plans were shelved in 2008. Instead, the existing site is soon to get a £75 million upgrade, starting immediately after the 2010 show and due for completion in 2014.

► *For listings, see p216.*

played out in the area before, with a superhighway that predates the Victorian era.

THE UNION CANAL

Completed by Irish navvies and French stonemasons in 1822, the Union Canal once ran all the way from Lothian Road (where the Odeon cinema now stands) to Camelon, near Falkirk, linking with the Forth & Clyde Canal that ran on to Glasgow. Coal, building materials and passengers came in to Edinburgh; merchants' goods, horse manure and more passengers went out. However, the waterway's heyday proved short-lived, and the canal was bought out by a competitor railway company in 1848. Traffic died out after the 1860s; the Lothian Road terminus was built over in 1922, and the waterway was mothballed in the 1960s.

It took a while for the idea of reopening the canal as a civic amenity and a potentially green transport network to gain support, but it eventually achieved critical mass. The Forth & Clyde Canal was reopened in 2001 with the Union Canal following a year later; the new city-centre terminus was established at Lochrin Basin, off Fountainbridge. A new housing development, offices, restaurants and cafés arrived, lending it the air of a prosperous little yacht marina. Formally known as Edinburgh Quay, it won an award for the best regeneration project in Scotland in 2005.

Popular with walkers, joggers and cyclists, the towpath runs from Lochrin Basin right through the city. If you leave the towpath as it goes through the suburb of Craiglockhart, just over a mile from Lochrin Basin, you'll be within a stroll of the Craiglockhart Hills; among them is the **Easter Craiglockhart Hill**, a local nature reserve with great views and a welcome diversion from the necessarily flat canal. Also around here, you'll find **Napier University Business School** (off Colinton Road) and the **War Poets Collection** (*see right*).

Back on the canal, you can keep going as far as your stamina will take you; even, perhaps, as far as Glasgow. If you make it to the village of Ratho, around eight miles from the city centre, reward yourself with a pint at the **Bridge Inn**, which has outdoor seating overlooking the canal (27 Baird Road, 333 1320, www.bridgeinn.com).

FREE War Poets Collection

Edinburgh Napier University Business School, Craiglockhart Campus, 219 Colinton Road (455 6021, www2.napier.ac.uk/warpoets). Bus 10, 18, 45. **Open** *Jun-Aug* 8.45am-8pm Mon-Thur; 8.45am-5pm Fri; 10am-4pm Sat. *Sept-May* 8.45am-9pm Mon-Thur; 8.45am-8pm Fri; 10am-4pm Sat, Sun. **Admission** free.

This Victorian building at Craiglockhart was used as a sanatorium for shell-shocked soldiers during World War I. Among them were Wilfrid Owen and Siegfried Sassoon, who met here in 1917 and wrote some of their best work while recovering from their front line experiences. The place gives a hint of the world of nearly a century ago, when Craiglockhart offered the men brief respite before they were sent back into battle. Sassoon survived, but Owen was killed a mere week before the war ended.

▶ *For a fictional account of Sassoon and Owen's meeting at Craiglockhart, check out Pat Barker's acclaimed 1991 novel* Regeneration.

GORGIE & DALRY

West of the castle, Edinburgh was once a bucolic stretch of farms and small hamlets. Given the riot of tenements and modern developments crammed into the area, such rural tranquility hardly seems credible today. But seek out some of the older buildings, and a different picture emerges. Down Distillery Lane, for instance, off Dalry Road at Haymarket Station, sits a simple 18th-century mansion called **Easter Dalry House**. It's now occupied by offices.

Further along Dalry Road at Orwell Terrace is **Dalry House** (1661), originally the country seat of the Chiesley family. Hemmed in by tenements, it was restored as an old folks' home in the 1960s, then transformed into apartments in 2006. Back in 1689, though, John Chiesley, the son of the original owner, was found guilty of murder, had his hand hacked off before being hanged, and was then apparently buried in the back garden. The building is said to be haunted by 'Johnny One-Arm', Chiesley's ghost.

Keep going and you'll reach Gorgie, where **Heart of Midlothian** (or, simply, Hearts) play their football at Tynecastle Stadium (*see p246*). Nearby is the child-pleasing **Gorgie City Farm** (*see p221*). And at the junction of Gorgie Road and Balgreen Road, look out for **Saughton Park**. Complete with beautifully kept winter gardens, a sunken Italian garden

Lauriston Castle.

SIGHTS

INSIDE TRACK
GAMES WITHOUT FRONTIERS

Local science fiction author Charles Stross made use of the Corstorphine Hill nuclear bunker (*see p106*) in his 2008 book, *Halting State*. In the novel, it was the headquarters of a computer games company.

and a celebrated rose garden, it's a good point to access the Water of Leith Walkway.

Just off the western end of Gorgie Road sits **Saughton Prison**, Edinburgh's lock-up since 1919. Four men have been executed here, the most recent in 1954. By contrast, the Families' Reception Centre is a peaceful space that allows prison visitors, usually women and children, to prepare for and wind down from their visits. Built in 2000, it's an architectural award-winner.

Close to Saughton, and even more anomalous than its fellow old country houses in West Edinburgh, is **Stenhouse Mansion**, a solid old pile built in 1623 on a meander of the Water of Leith. It's used by Historic Scotland as a conservation centre and isn't open to visitors. The motto above the door reads 'Blisit be God for all his giftis', which, nearly 400 years ago, would have included an uninterrupted view of the castle over open land.

THE REST OF THE WEST

Directly west of Haymarket Station and Fountainbridge, **Murrayfield Stadium** (*see p247*) is the 67,130-capacity home of Scottish rugby union. An extraordinary place during any Six Nations match, it's one of the UK's largest sporting arenas, but also hosts major gigs: Live8 took place here in 2005, and Oasis sold out the place in 2009.

Further west still is **Edinburgh Zoo** (*see p221*), open since 1913. While it's principally a family-orientated attraction, its penguin parade is one of the most bizarre and hilarious sights in the city, whatever your age. Legend has it that the parade began in the 1950s, when a keeper accidentally left the door to the penguin enclosure open and they all followed him out.

Behind the zoo, **Corstorphine Hill** is a favourite with cyclists, joggers and walkers. Trees hide many of the best panoramas, but there is one fabulous lookout point, east of the higher reaches of the zoo. Known as 'Rest-and-be-thankful', it's where travellers journeying in from the west once got their first real glance at

INSIDE TRACK
CHARLIE ARRIVES

On 16 September 1745, Bonnie Prince Charlie and his army reached **Slateford** in West Edinburgh and set up camp. The very next day, the city was theirs without a fight and the prince headed to Holyrood. He held court there for some weeks before continuing on his way south where his attempt to reach London, and the British throne, ultimately failed.

Edinburgh. However, the hill's quirkiest claim to fame is down to the Cold War nuclear bunker that sits here. Built in 1952, it remained secret for a decade until protestors made its existence public in 1963. The local authority eventually inherited the complex and sold it to a developer, who struggled to do anything worthwhile or lucrative with it. In 1992, a fire caused major damage; the bunker has lain derelict ever since.

Near the city limits by the airport, **Ingliston** is the long-time home to the annual Royal Highland Show (*see p104* **Down on the Farm**). If you swing back towards the Firth of Forth instead, though, the road to Cramond in the north-west of the city passes **Lauriston Castle** (*see below*). The magnificent lawns at the front are home to the **Edinburgh Croquet Club** (www.edinburghcroquetclub.com).

Cramond

Cramond is the earliest known settlement in the Lothians. Waste has been found from the camps of Mesolithic people who inhabited the area in 8,500 BC. The Romans arrived in about AD 140 and made themselves at home, even building a bath house; just by **Cramond Kirk**, you can see the floor-plan remains of their old fortification. Finds have included a remarkable sandstone statue of a lioness that was discovered in the River Almond; it's now held by the National Museum of Scotland (*see p76*).

During the 18th century, the water power available from the Almond proved irresistible to industrialists, who built iron mills along its banks; the village became an exporter of nails around the world. On the quayside, the small **Cramond Heritage Trust** exhibition (www.cramondheritagetrust.org.uk, open Apr-Sept 2-5pm Sat, Sun) offers an intriguing slant on local history. These days, Cramond is a handsome and desirable commuter satellite town.

Lauriston Castle

Cramond Road South, Davidsons Mains, Cramond (336 2060, www.edinburgh.gov.uk). Bus 1, 41, 42. **Open** *House tours* Apr-Oct 2pm Mon-Thur, Sat, Sun. Nov-Mar 2pm Sat, Sun. *Grounds* dawn-dusk daily. **Admission** *House* £5; £3 discounts. *Grounds* free. **No credit cards**.
Set in large, reasonably well-kept grounds and now in the care of the local authority, this neo-Jacobean fortified property was built in the 1590s (as a tower house for Sir Archibald Napier), extended during the 1820s and last used as a private home in 1926, when then-owner William Reid left it to the nation. Reid and his wife were enthusiastic antiques collectors who furnished the house with their finds; the property's Edwardian interiors have been carefully preserved. Access is by tour only (around 50 minutes); special group tours can be arranged if you call ahead.

Leith & the Coast

It's all change along the Edinburgh shoreline.

Despite its proximity to the centre of Edinburgh (it's only around two miles north-east of the Old Town), Leith is very much a separate place, with a history and a modern-day atmosphere all of its own. At various points, it's been a medieval fishing settlement, a port, a shipbuilding centre and a crime-riddled suburb. More recently, though, a paradigm of revitalisation has taken hold, which has seen the formerly depressed docks area and its surrounding streets transformed by apartments, restaurants, bars and shops. Ambitious development plans are in place that are designed to create a entirely new 'city by the sea' in the coming years. For now, though, Leith remains in flux.

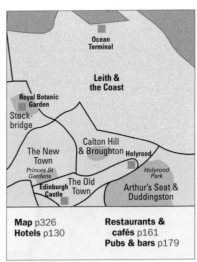

Map p326	Restaurants &
Hotels p130	cafés p161
	Pubs & bars p179

LEITH

When David I founded Holyrood Abbey in 1128, he endowed it with various patches of land. Among them was a small area around the Water of Leith, which included a sparse fishing settlement. David himself built another fishing village nearby, roughly around the site of what's now the Shore. It grew neatly enough and became a conduit for international trade. But in 1329, Robert the Bruce, in one of his last acts as King of Scotland, granted Leith Harbour to the burgesses of Edinburgh, a move that was to have dramatic repercussions.

Edinburgh tried to keep Leith under its thumb for the next 500 years – despite the fact that for much of that time, it was Scotland's

INSIDE TRACK STEADY EDDIE

Celebrated sculptor Sir Eduardo Paolozzi (1924-2005) was born to first-generation Italian immigrants in Leith. His work can be found outside **St Mary's Cathedral** at the top of Leith Walk (*see p95*) and at the **Dean Gallery** (*see p90*).

premier port. When cargoes were landed at Leith, for instance, someone had to walk or ride all the way to the Edinburgh Tolbooth, up on the High Street, to pay duty before the cargo could be unloaded. This absurd situation sums up the relationship between the two: Leith the doorway to the wider world, the commanding capital skimming a share of its trade. Mutual mistrust simmered down the years, with Leith always maintaining a sense of distance.

Leith was often caught in the middle of the conflicts between Scotland and England. But locals viewed such distractions as a minor impediment. By the second half of the 18th century, strong trade links had been forged with the Baltic, the Low Countries, Scandinavia and further afield, and the harbour had capacity for hundreds of ships. Brandy, wine and citrus fruits arrived from France, Spain and Portugal, with rum, rice and timber coming from America and the West Indies. Business boomed.

The tensions between Leith and Edinburgh never went away, and the pair divorced in 1833 over mismanagement of the docks, corruption and other financial issues. But then, in 1920, the expansion of Edinburgh saw Leith swallowed up again, before it was left to crumble in the post-war doldrums. The port's struggles were

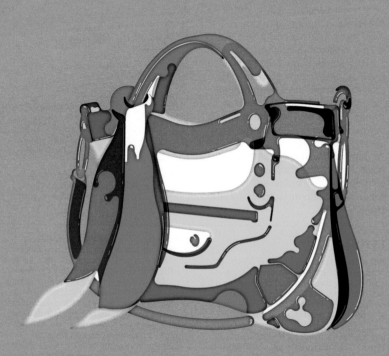

NYC

Ask New York City about New York City fabulous

nycgo.com

compounded into the 1970s by ill-advised public
housing, unemployment, prostitution and drugs.

In the 1980s, encouraged by cheap rents,
a few intrepid entrepreneurs set up in Leith,
leavening the social mix while also encouraging
others to follow. Things began to improve, but
Leith really took off when, in 1992, the docks
were privatised, and the newly created Forth
Ports PLC looked at alternative uses for its
land. Flagship projects followed: the first
Malmaison opened here in 1994, the Scottish
Government building arrived at Victoria Quay
in 1996, the Royal Yacht *Britannia* shipped up
in 1998 and the Ocean Terminal mall was
completed in 2001, all joined in recent years
by new residential construction (*see p111*). But
despite all the changes, Leith retains an element
of its disreputable past. It's still a working port,
after all, and the new gentility occasionally sits
cheek-by-jowl with pre-1980s style deprivation.

One other novelty in recent years has been
the number of Polish voices. Following the 2004
EU expansion, thousands of young Poles
headed for Scotland to find work, and many
gravitated to Leith. The relationship between
Poles and Leithers seems to be an economic
symbiosis, the modern equivalent of the Baltic
trade from centuries past. While the Leith of
today is a different proposition to the Leith of
25 years ago, some things simply don't change.

Leith Walk & the Kirkgate

The most direct route to Leith from Edinburgh
city centre, **Leith Walk** only came into its
own after the construction of North Bridge in
1769. The road was built on the line of an old
earthwork running from Calton Hill to Leith,
which had been thrown up as a defence against
Cromwell's invading army in 1650. These days
it's flanked by tenements, with shops, pubs and
cafés running all the way from the **Edinburgh
Playhouse** at the city end (*see p253*) down to
Leith's **New Kirkgate Shopping Centre**.

The pedestrianised **Kirkgate**, which used to
link the foot of Leith Walk to the Shore, was
once Leith's main street. Its tenements were
demolished and its memory obliterated by
1960s public housing, but two structures give
any clue as to what the road was once like. The
first is **Trinity House** (*see below*), approaching
its 200th birthday; the other is the somewhat
gothic **South Leith Parish Kirk**, a Victorian
structure erected on the site of a 15th-century
church that was damaged when the English
besieged Leith in 1560. Both are still handsome
buildings, but they're overwhelmed by the crass
modern architecture that surrounds them.

Trinity House

*99 Kirkgate (554 3289, www.historic-scotland.
gov.uk). Bus 1, 7, 10, 11, 12, 14, 16, 22, 25,
34, 35, 36.* **Open** 10am-3.30pm Mon-Fri.
Admission £4.20; £2.10-£3.20 discounts.
No credit cards. Map p326 Y4.

The original Trinity House was built in 1555 as the
Hospital for the Fraternity of Masters & Mariners
of Leith. Completely rebuilt in classical Georgian
style in 1816 by Thomas Brown, it has a fabulous
interior, and still serves as a museum to Leith's sea-
faring history. Your tour starts with a short film,
shown in the original cellars to the rear of the building; highlights of the main house include portraits
by Raeburn and the impressive Convening Room
upstairs. Trinity House is little visited and does
smack of a bygone era, but it remains one of the most
affecting museums in the city. Book your spot in
advance, as hours can be erratic. *Photo p110.*
▶ *As part of its charitable work, Trinity House
was a major contributor to the construction of
both North Leith Parish Kirk on Madeira Street
(1816) and the South Leith Parish Kirk.*

Leith Docks.

Trinity House. *See p109.*

Leith Links

Before the development of Leith's docks and the addition of the various waves of urban housing in the 19th and 20th centuries, **Leith Links** was a flat, grassy stretch of land by the Firth of Forth that stretched off to the east. This was the site of Edinburgh's first racecourse; there are records of silver cups being presented as prizes as far back as 1655, although the course was eventually moved east to Musselburgh in 1816. The racecourse isn't Leith Links' sole claim to sporting fame. The Honourable Company of Edinburgh Golfers, the oldest golf club in the world, teed off here in 1744, and drew up the rules that were adopted by the Royal & Ancient Club at St Andrews ten years later.

What's left of the old links, now stretching for half a mile from the foot of Easter Road, is surrounded by houses and tenements, and is popular with amateur footballers, cricketers and others simply out to enjoy the sunshine. At night, though, it can be a different story. For a time, Leith Links was a haunt for street prostitution. A 2007 crackdown introduced kerb-crawling laws and fines for male customers, but the new edicts only served to push street girls into areas where they're more vulnerable to attack. Single women should be particularly wary of the area after dark.

The Shore

Leith's Shore is where it all began, the site of the 12th-century fishing settlement that grew

into a major international port. The Shore itself is actually the name of the street running down the south bank of the Water of Leith, home to an assortment of bars and restaurants that face across to modern apartments on the north bank. A stroll along it reveals just how dramatic the area's recent regeneration has been. However, it's by no means the whole story.

Just behind the Shore is a maze of narrow old streets that gives some indication of what the area was like before redevelopment. The oldest building is **Andrew Lamb's House** on Burgess Street, a warehouse with merchants' quarters that's now owned by the National Trust for Scotland. Its existence was first recorded in the 1500s, when it was visited by Mary, Queen of Scots; however, experts reckon the architecture is more 17th century, and the current building may be on the site of an earlier version.

After a spell in which Andrew Lamb's House served as a day care centre for the elderly, the last few years have seen it pretty much left to decay. Critics point at the millions being spent on new developments in the area while such living history gets shabbier and shabbier. A short walk away, at the corner of Giles Street and in much better condition, is the **Vaults**, a 1682 wine warehouse topped with an upper storey added in 1785. The ground floor is home to the **Vintners Rooms** (*see p166*); above is the **Scotch Malt Whisky Society** (*see p182*).

Signs of Leith's 19th-century prosperity are visible just a few minutes' walk from the Shore. Look out for grand, confident edifices such as the old, domed **Leith Bank** in Bernard Street (1804); the **Custom House** at the east end of Commercial Street (1812); the **Exchange Buildings** and the **Assembly Rooms** in Constitution Street (1809); the **Municipal Buildings**, also on Constitution Street (1827) and now a police station; and the **Corn Exchange** (1862) at the corner of Baltic Street, now the **Corn Exchange Gallery** (*see p229*). Back on the quayside, opposite 30 The Shore, a plaque commemorates the arrival here in 1822 of George IV, the first British monarch to set foot in Scotland for nearly two centuries. 'Geo IV Rex O Felicem Diem,' it reads, or 'George IV rules on this happy day'.

North Leith

Described by Robert Louis Stevenson as 'that dirty Water of Leith', Edinburgh's urban river meets the sea at Leith Docks and is not the most bucolic of waterways. However, it's been cleaned up in recent years, if not completely, and can be a good site for a daytime stroll. Start at the northern end of the Sandport Place Bridge and follow it upstream; it's a great way to see behind the façade of the city.

The Water of Leith also serves to divide Leith, north and south. It flows under Junction Bridge at the corner of Ferry Road and North Junction Street, overlooked by a gable-end mural depicting the history of Leith as a jigsaw. The final piece of the puzzle is a picture of a Sikh man reaching to take the outstretched hand of the community. Many of Edinburgh's Sikhs live in Leith; a Sikh temple now occupies a converted church, back over the bridge and down Mill Lane towards the Shore. To the left of the mural are two imposing but unfussy buildings, **Leith Library** and the **Leith Theatre** (28-30 Ferry Road). Both opened in 1932 and are curious examples of between-the-wars design.

Along the otherwise unremarkable North Junction Street, the **Leith School of Art**

(no.25) inhabits the oldest Norwegian seamen's church outside Norway, a small Lutheran kirk dating from 1868. Walk on a little way to the corner of Prince Regent Street and at its far end you'll discover the Doric portico and classical steeple of **North Leith Parish Kirk**, dating from 1813. New Leith, in the shape of the Sir Terence Conran-designed **Ocean Terminal** shopping mall (*see p185*) and the **Royal Yacht Britannia** (*see p112*), is just a few minutes further along.

East of Conran's retail shed is **Commercial Quay**, a row of bonded warehouses that have been renovated and converted into apartments, upmarket shops, restaurants and offices. Facing them across the quayside is an implacable chunk of modern architecture

On the Waterfront

The Leith coast gets a 30-year upgrade – if the money doesn't run out first.

Although you can see the Firth of Forth from vantage points on the Royal Mile, Princes Street and Calton Hill, it's easy to forget Edinburgh is close to the coast. The focus of the city is inland; even in Leith, it's taken gentrification to make the waterside seem an attractive proposition and not just inhospitable dockland. The 2001 opening of the Ocean Terminal shopping mall helped kick off a major regeneration programme, latterly coalesced around the name **Edinburgh Waterfront** (www.theedinburghwaterfront.com), that now extends from Leith west around the coast to Newhaven and Granton.

Preferring to think of global warming in terms of balmy Mediterranean temperatures and not the threat of rising sea levels, the city has set about transforming an unloved area of industrial coastland into a substantial residential zone. Numerous new apartment blocks have sprung up in every nook and cranny, some affordable and some decidedly plush. The original plan was to build 30,000 houses over 30 years; the scheme was running several years late even before the recession made such an ambition seem unlikely. But even a more modest increase in population on a site as big as Holyrood Park will bring with it shops, offices and schools, as well as hotels, leisure centres, a museum and the prospect of a rejuvenated beach between Granton and Newhaven.

There was only enough money in the pot for the first phase of the new tram system to be extended as far as Ocean Terminal,

which seems an oversight given the council's ambition to create 'one of the world's great waterfronts for living, working, learning and leisure'. At present, the area is a mixture of quaint remnants of Granton's village past and a rather bleak stretch of main road, but you can already see apartment blocks and office buildings setting the ball rolling. Whether it ever challenges Dubai for the tourist dollars, as was once claimed, is another matter.

SIGHTS

housing the **Scottish Government** (*see p42*). The design may not be to everyone's taste, but its brashness epitomises modern-day Leith to a tee. And the Edinburgh Waterfront plan (*see p111*) suggests that there's much more of this to come.

★ Royal Yacht Britannia

Ocean Terminal, Ocean Drive (555 5566, www.royalyachtbritannia.co.uk). Bus 1, 11, 22, 34, 35. **Open** *Apr-June, Oct* 10am-4pm daily (last admission). *July-Sept* 9.30am-4.30pm daily (last admission). *Nov-Mar* 10am-3.30pm daily (last admission). **Admission** £10.50; £6.75-£9 discounts; free under-5s; £31 family. **Credit** AmEx, DC, MC, V. **Map** p326 X1.

Launched in 1953, the year of Queen Elizabeth II's coronation, the Royal Yacht *Britannia* was used by the royal family for state visits, holidays and diplomatic functions for more than four decades. After it was decommissioned at the end of 1997, it was left in permanent residence in Leith, where it's consistently drawn big crowds. Since the 2009 addition of the Royal Deck Tea Room, you can even linger a while with tea and cake.

Although the ship's exterior has an art deco beauty, stepping on board – enter from the second floor of Ocean Terminal, through the Britannia Experience – is like regressing into a 1950s nightmare of suburban taste. You'll get to see the large state dining room, which has entertained everyone from Gandhi to Reagan, and the engine room, favoured more by grease monkeys. The many photographs of the royals, dating back more than 50 years, give a top-down flavour of British social history in the second half of the 20th century.

NEWHAVEN & GRANTON

Following the shore west along Lindsay Road, past the gleaming white silos of Chancelot Mill and the new housing developments to that side of the Western Harbour, will lead you to the old fishing village of **Newhaven**. Until the 20th century, this was an insular community whose residents are thought to have descended from the intermarriage of locals and the shipbuilding craftsmen brought over from France, Spain, Portugal and Scandinavia by James II. It became famous for its colourfully dressed fishwives, who used to carry creels full of fresh fish up to Edinburgh to sell every morning. Much of the original village has been pulled down, but there are still some fishermen's cottages in the streets near the shore. The harbour is the departure point for **Seafari**'s boat tours (*see below*).

The former St Andrew's Kirk in Newhaven is now an indoor climbing centre by the name of **Alien Rock** (*see p249*). However, the major recreational centre in Newhaven is the huge

Next Generation Club (Newhaven Place, 554 5000, www.nextgenerationclubs.co.uk). When the club first opened back in the 1990s, it was an anomaly on what was then a sparse stretch of waterfront. However, with the Newhaven side of the Western Harbour area now part of the mammoth Edinburgh Waterfront development, it looks rather less lonely.

Further west still, **Granton Harbour** was built by the fifth Duke of Buccleuch as part of his estate and opened in 1838. Engineering expertise for the project came courtesy of one of the lighthouse-building Stevenson family, relatives of Robert Louis. Like Newhaven, Granton was once the base for a fishing fleet, but only small leisure craft are found there today. It also once boasted the world's first ferry train, offering the most direct route to Fife before the construction of the Forth Rail Bridge in 1890. And yes, there are new waterfront apartments here, too.

Seafari Adventures Forth

Sailings from Newhaven Harbour (331 4857, www.seafari.co.uk). Bus 7, 10, 11. **Times** check online for a schedule. **Rates** *Seafari Adventure* £20; £18 discounts. **Credit** MC, V.

Seafari runs popular one-hour jaunts around the Forth from Newhaven on an 11-metre rigid inflatable boat (RIB); waterproofs are provided for passengers. Other Seafari services run from Newhaven Harbour to Inchcolm, home to the 12th century Inchcolm Abbey; the company also launches from North Berwick.

PORTOBELLO

The current focus of attention on Edinburgh's coastline is very much on Leith and points west. However, to the east, **Portobello** is worth a peek. The town was founded in 1739 by George Hamilton, a retired sailor. Having fought in Panama against the Spanish, Hamilton was part of the successful capture of Puerto Bello; when he retired to the shore of Edinburgh, he named his house 'Portobello' in its honour. For a time, the town consisted more or less solely of Hamilton's home, but it soon became a staging post for passengers travelling on the stagecoach to Musselburgh and on towards London.

Once a proper Victorian holiday resort, Portobello has followed other British seaside towns in fading down the years. Still, on sunny days, its seafront and long stretch of sand can get packed. There's a mood of determined enjoyment whatever the weather that is peculiarly British; but if things get too inclement, the **Portobello Swim Centre** (*see p250*) is worth a look. Afterwards, catch a drink or some pub grub at either the **Dalriada** or the **Esplanade** (for both, *see p180*).

Consume

Concrete Wardrobe. *See p191.*

Hotels

Big choices, big fun, big August prices…

With a wide array of new hotels supplemented by a string of high-profile renovations, the range of accommodation in Edinburgh is wider now than at any time in the city's history. Choices range from venerable, old-school behemoths, such as the **Balmoral** and the **Caledonian Hilton**, to a wave of modish establishments that appeared in the mid noughties, chief among them the **Glasshouse**, **Le Monde** and **Tigerlily**. And no sooner had these latter upstarts got their feet under the table that the refurbished **Rutland**, **Hotel du Vin**, **Apex Waterloo Place** and **Hotel Missoni** brought even more upmarket competition to the city.

Set against all this activity at the higher end of the market, budget chains have also been expanding: **Premier Inn** and **Travelodge** now have as many as 15 properties between them. But whatever your budget and wherever your preferred location, it's still vital to book ahead, especially during the chaos of August and the run-up to Hogmanay.

STAYING IN THE CITY

In Edinburgh, you can bunk with backpackers on the Royal Mile, share a modern apartment with friends, bed down in lush rooms attached to a couple of the city's finest restaurants, and even camp outside in a tent. But it's the hotels in Scotland's capital that really add a sense of occasion. At the **Prestonfield** (*see p127*), for example, you can rest easy amid the splendour of a late Jacobean mansion that's been refurbished with contemporary fabrics and gadgets. The **Howard** (*see p121*) jumps forward by more than a century, allowing guests to share in the class of a Georgian townhouse. And in the here and now, any number of design-led hotels have opened here since 1994, the year when the country's first **Malmaison** (*see p132*) created a stir in Leith.

If you're working with a healthy budget and like the idea of staying in a home from home (but with more antiques), the **Edinburgh Residence** (*see p121*) has suites rather than

> ❶ Red numbers given in this chapter correspond to the location of each hotel on the street maps. *See pp326-333.*

rooms. The landmark **Balmoral** (*see p119*), another five-star venue, is a more traditional hotel, and has hosted everyone from J Lo to JK Rowling. Away from the top end, the **Hotel Ceilidh-Donia** (*see p129*) has quietly built a reputation for value and friendliness in the south of the city. And the **Mercure Point** (*see p127*), the most futuristic hotel in Edinburgh when it opened in 1995, often offers fine deals.

Prices & booking

Bad news first. Edinburgh is the most expensive place to stay in Scotland. What's more, it's often busy. Average occupancy rates hover near the 75 per cent mark thanks to near-constant business travel, the city's capital status and year-round tourism.

In truth, though, this average disguises an annual trough and peak. The habitual August festival rush sees nearly 90 per cent of rooms taken by travellers, often at extraordinarily high tariffs that reflect the clamour for beds. Other major events – Hogmanay, big rugby matches – have the same effect. Conversely, during the dog days of winter before Christmas and after New Year, trade slackens off, with more than a third of rooms empty. At times like these, there are definitely bargains to be had.

If you're able to book ahead, preferably by several months, you should benefit from your foresight. Discounts can run to 50 per cent or more on standard advertised rates, especially out of peak season and even in some of the city's more desirable and fashionable properties. Last-minute travellers may also get lucky with cheap rates out of season, but deep discounts are far from guaranteed.

When booking, always check the hotel's individual website first; some deals are only available online. It's also worth checking consolidators such as Hotels.com and Lastminute.com, which often offer good rates, but be sure to check the small print (especially with regard to cancellation charges).

If you do arrrive without pre-booking, the Edinburgh branch of the national tourist agency **VisitScotland** (www.edinburgh.org) runs an accommodation service and can usually find you somewhere to stay for a small fee. It has a desk at Edinburgh Airport and an office above Princes Mall at the east end of Princes Street (*see pp310-311*). It's a better bet than simply walking into a hotel and asking for a room, a method that may result in paying more than necessary.

About the chapter

Hotels in this chapter have been arranged by area and placed into four price bands: **Deluxe**, **Expensive**, **Moderate** and **Budget**. For each

INSIDE TRACK PARKING

City-centre hotels don't always have car parking, and those that do can charge high rates (and may not have many spaces). Central Edinburgh is fairly compact and well served by buses and taxis: unless you really need private transport, it's best to just leave the car at home.

property, we've listed a range of room rates for a double room or equivalent, but these are only for guidance: the variation within these rates, top to bottom and over the course of the year, can be staggering. Make a booking months ahead with a budget chain and you could get a double room, out of season, for the price of little more than two hostel bunks. On the other hand, a standard room for two in a Deluxe hotel in August, booked even a few weeks in advance, can easily top £300 or even £400 a night.

At the end of each review, we've listed a selection of hotel services: restaurants and bars, internet access, spas and the like. If you're bringing a car to the city (and we don't recommend doing so; *see above and p303*), always check with the hotel before you arrive; at some hotels, parking is limited and may need to be reserved in advance, while others don't offer any parking facilities whatsoever.

CONSUME

Hotel Missoni. *See p117.*

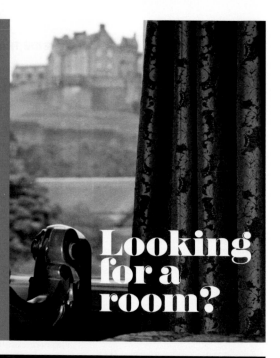

Hotels

THE OLD TOWN

Deluxe

★ Hotel Missoni
1 George IV Bridge, EH1 1AD (220 6666, www.hotelmissoni.com). Bus 23, 27, 42, 45. **Rates** £280-£310 double. **Rooms** 136. **Credit** AmEx, DC, MC, V. **Map** p332 H7 & p336 D4 ❶

Aficionados will know Missoni as an Italian fashion house, celebrated for its bold colours and designs. However, it's branched out of late, most recently hatching a deal with the Rezidor Hotel Group to get into hospitality. Edinburgh was chosen as the host for the first Missoni-branded hotel, which opened in summer 2009 with a characteristic aesthetic splash. Guests have been wowed by the service, the comfort, the Cucina restaurant (*see p137*) and the suave Bar Missoni. In summary: style with knobs on, and lots of stripes. *Photo p115.*

Bar. Business centre. Concierge. Disabled-adapted rooms. Gym. Internet (wireless, free). Parking (limited, £35). Restaurant. Room service.

Scotsman
20 North Bridge, EH1 1YT (556 5565, www.thescotsmanhotel.co.uk). Nicolson Street–North Bridge buses. **Rates** £200-£350 double. **Rooms** 69. **Credit** AmEx, DC, MC, V. **Map** p332 H7 & p336 F3 ❷

Filling the historic premises vacated by the *Scotsman* newspaper, this hotel leapt straight into the city's upper echelon of places to stay when it opened in 2001. It subsequently struggled financially, but new ownership has brought fresh investment. The buzzing and ornate North Bridge Brasserie (*see p139*) was relaunched in 2008 and the Spa & Healthclub followed in 2009, retaining its funky stainless-steel pool. The rooms have contemporary elements but remain in keeping with the building's Edwardian-baronial origins. Its sister hotel in the city is the Glasshouse (*see p126*).

Bar. Business centre. Concierge. Disabled-adapted rooms. Gym. High-speed internet (wireless, £15; also shared terminal). Pool. Restaurant. Room service. Spa.

★ Witchery by the Castle
352 Castlehill, Old Town, EH1 2NF (225 5613, www.thewitchery.com). Bus 35 or Nicolson Street–North Bridge buses. **Rates** £295 suite. **Rooms** 7. **Credit** AmEx, MC, V. **Map** p332 G7 & p336 D4 ❸

Seven suites, some with kitchens, are hidden away in two buildings at the top of the Royal Mile; two are in the 16th-century building in Boswell's Court, with the other five in a 17th-century house off Sempill's Court. Each of them is dark, theatrically gothic and

lavishly furnished with antiques, leather and velvet, Victorian baths and grand beds, complementing the magical atmosphere at the Witchery dining rooms (*see p141*). Impure indulgence. *Photo p118.*
Restaurant.

Expensive

Apex International
31-35 Grassmarket, EH1 2HS (300 3456, www.apexhotels.co.uk). Bus 2, 23, 27, 41, 42. **Rates** £135-£235 double. **Rooms** 171. **Credit** AmEx, DC, MC, V. **Map** p332 G8 & p336 C4 ❹

This 1996 debut venture from Apex was refurbished and extended just a couple of years later; more than a decade on, it remains a slick, contemporary venue in a brilliant location (the deluxe rooms look directly across to the castle). The pedestrian-friendly Grassmarket is on the doorstep, with a range of busy bars, although the hotel has its own bar-brasserie as well as a restaurant (also with castle view) and a dinky little spa.

There are also branches of the Apex chain at 61 Grassmarket, Old Town, EH11 2JF (242 3456) and 90 Haymarket Terrace, New Town, EH12 5LQ (474 3456). For Apex Waterloo Place, *see p126*.
Bar. Business centre. Concierge. Disabled-adapted rooms. Gym. Internet (wireless, free; also shared terminal). Parking (limited, £8). Pool. Restaurants (2). Room service.

Hotel du Vin
11 Bristo Place, EH1 1EZ (247 4900, www.hotelduvin.com). Bus 2, 41, 42. **Rates** £125-£300 double. **Rooms** 47. **Credit** AmEx, DC, MC, V. **Map** p332 H8 ❺

Edinburgh joined the select posse of UK towns and cities with a Hotel du Vin in late 2008, and its sheer, well-executed reliability has made it a discreet hit ever since. Jammed ergonomically into what seems like an impossible urban space, it has a busy, traditional bistro, a bar, a whisky lounge, a courtyard with 'cigar shack', a wine-tasting room and characteristically lush, modern decor in all the bedrooms.
Bar. Concierge. Disabled-adapted rooms. Internet (wireless, £10). Parking (£12). Restaurant. Room service.

CONSUME

Witchery by the Castle. *See p117.*

Moderate

Barceló Edinburgh Carlton
19 North Bridge, EH1 1SD (472 3000, www.
barcelo-hotels.co.uk). Nicolson Street–North
Bridge buses. **Rates** £100-£240 double. **Rooms**
177. **Credit** AmEx, DC, MC, V. **Map** p333 J7 &
p336 F3 **⑥**
This big old city centre hotel has gone through three
different identities in the last decade or so, becoming the Barceló Edinburgh Carlton in early 2008. Not
quite in the same class as the Scotsman opposite or
the Balmoral nearby, it's large and functional. The
interior decor is grand in a 1980s kind of way, the
rooms have great views – although those facing on
to North Bridge can be a little noisy – and there's a
small pool with a sauna and a steam room.
Bar. Business centre. Concierge. Disabled-adapted
rooms. Gym. Internet (wireless, £15). Pool.
Restaurant. Room service. Spa.

Holiday Inn Express Royal Mile
300 Cowgate, EH1 1NA (524 8400, www.
hiexpressedinburgh.co.uk). Bus 35 or Nicolson
Street–North Bridge buses. **Rates** £79-£199
double. **Rooms** 78. **Credit** AmEx, DC, MC, V.
Map p333 J7 **⑦**
Sitting along the Cowgate, this establishment is very
close to the Royal Mile, although not actually on it.
The bedrooms lack character, as you might expect of
a big chain. But on the plus side, the hotel is a dependable outpost of a generally reliably chain, blessed with
a very central location and professional staff.
   Holiday Inn has another centrally located Express
at Picardy Place (EH1 3JT, 558 2300), plus two more

traditionally branded hotels (107 Queensferry Road,
EH4 3HL, 0871 942 9025; Corstorphine Road, EH12
6UA, 0871 942 9026). For the Holiday Inn Express
at Leith, *see p130*.
Bar. Business centre. Disabled-adapted rooms.
Internet (wireless, free). Parking (limited, £16).

Macdonald Holyrood
81 Holyrood Road, EH8 8AU (0870 194 2106,
www.macdonaldhotels.co.uk/holyrood). Bus 35,
36. **Rates** £75-250 double. **Rooms** 156. **Credit**
AmEx, DC, MC, V. **Map** p333 L7 **⑧**
Opened in 1999 to capitalise on the other developments around Holyrood, chief among them the
Scottish Parliament, the Macdonald has always had
a business feel. There's a gym, a small swimming
pool and beauty treatment rooms, but it's the exclusive Club Floor, with its upgraded rooms and views
of Holyrood Park, that's the stand-out feature. The
decor is a little bit dated these days, but the location
makes up for it.
Bar. Business centre. Concierge. Disabled-adapted
rooms. Gym. Internet (wireless, £10; also shared
terminal). Parking (£20). Pool. Restaurant. Room
service. Spa.

Radisson SAS
80 High Street, Royal Mile, EH1 1TH (557
9797, www.radissonsas.com). Bus 35 or Nicolson
Street–North Bridge buses. **Rates** £100-£300
double. **Rooms** 238. **Credit** AmEx, DC, MC, V.
Map p333 J7 & p336 F4 **⑨**
Sympathetic in situ or just historical pastiche?
Originally the Scandic Crown, this hotel divided
opinion when it opened just over 20 years ago. Either

way, it got a multi-million-pound internal revamp in 2005, thanks to new owners Radisson SAS and Glasgow design experts Graven Images. The result is a clean-cut, sleek and monochromatic look with subtle Scottish motifs. Service standards are high, and you'll walk out of reception on to the Royal Mile. *Bar. Concierge. Disabled-adapted rooms. Gym. Internet (wireless, free; also shared terminal). Parking (£8.50). Pool. Restaurant. Room service. Spa.*

Budget

Ibis Edinburgh Centre
6 Hunter Square, EH1 1QW (240 7000, www.ibis hotel.com). Nicolson Street–North Bridge buses. **Rates** *£57-£135 double.* **Rooms** 99. **Credit** AmEx, DC, MC, V. **Map** p333 J7 & p336 F4 ⑩
Efficient, reasonable value, mere seconds from the Royal Mile and with few defining characteristics, this branch of the midmarket Ibis tends to inspire little in the way of enthusiastic praise but also very few criticisms from the travellers who stay. The location is very handy for both Waverley Station and the Airlink shuttle bus to the airport that leaves from Waverley Bridge, a short walk down Cockburn Street. *Bar. Disabled-adapted rooms. Internet (web TV). Parking (£12.80).*

Jurys Inn
43 Jeffrey Street, EH1 1DH (200 3300, http:// edinburghhotels.jurysdoyle.com). Nicolson Street –North Bridge buses. **Rates** *£59-£250 double.* **Rooms** 186. **Credit** AmEx, DC, MC, V. **Map** p333 J6 ⑪
If it looks like an old office block, that's because it is an old office block. The Edinburgh branch of this hotel chain is nothing out of the ordinary, but the location is every tourist's dream, two minutes from Waverley Station and only a very short hop to the Royal Mile. Although it's clean, tidy and safe, you probably won't want to spend much time here, but it's decent value if you book in advance. *Bar. Business centre. Disabled-adapted rooms. High-speed internet (shared terminal, wireless; £10). Restaurant.*

Hostels

Brodies Backpackers *93 High Street, EH1 1SG (556 6770, www.brodieshostels.co.uk). Bus 35 or Nicolson Street–North Bridge buses.* **Open** *Reception 7am-midnight daily. No curfew.* **Rates** *£11-£25 dorm bed; £42-£64 double.* **Credit** MC, V. **Map** p333 J6 & p336 F4 ⑫
Budget Backpackers *37-39 Cowgate, EH1 1JR (226 6351, www.budgetbackpackers.com). Nicolson Street–North Bridge buses.* **Open** *Reception 24hrs. No curfew.* **Rates** *£18-£35 dorm bed; £18-£43 double.* **Credit** MC, V. **Map** p332 H8 & p336 D4 ⑬

Castle Rock Hostel *15 Johnston Terrace, EH1 2PW (225 9666, www.castlerockedinburgh.com). Bus 2, 23, 27, 41, 42.* **Open** *Reception 24hrs. No curfew.* **Rates** *£12-£15 dorm bed; call for double prices.* **Credit** AmEx, DC, MC, V. **Map** p332 F8 & p336 B4 ⑭
Edinburgh Backpackers Hostel *65 Cockburn Street, EH1 1BU (220 1717 reception, 220 2200 reservations, www.hoppo.com/edinburgh). Bus 35 or Nicolson Street–North Bridge buses.* **Open** *Reception 24hrs. No curfew.* **Rates** from *£12.50 dorm bed.* **Credit** MC, V. **Map** p332 H7 & p336 F3 ⑮
Edinburgh Metro SYHA Hostel *11 Robertson's Close, Cowgate, EH1 1LY (556 8718 hostel, 0870 004 1115 reservations, www.syha.org.uk). Nicolson Street–North Bridge buses.* **Open** *Reception 24 hrs. No curfew.* **Rates** *£21.50-£42.50 single, plus membership.* **Credit** MC, V. **Map** p333 J7 ⑯
High Street Hostel *8 Blackfriars Street, EH1 1NE (557 3984, www.highstreethostel.com). Bus 35 or Nicolson Street–North Bridge buses.* **Open** *Reception 24hrs. No curfew.* **Rates** *£13.50-£18 dorm bed.* **Credit** AmEx, DC, MC, V. **Map** p333 J7 & p336 F4 ⑰
Royal Mile Backpackers *105 High Street, EH1 1SG (557 6120, www.royalmilebackpackers. com). Bus 35 or Nicolson Street–North Bridge buses.* **Open** *Reception 7am-3am daily. No curfew.* **Rates** *£13-£15 dorm bed.* **Credit** AmEx, MC, V. **Map** p333 J7 ⑱

THE NEW TOWN
Deluxe

★ Balmoral
1 Princes Street, EH2 2EQ (556 2414, www.thebalmoralhotel.com). Nicolson Street –North Bridge buses or Princes Street buses. **Rates** *£120-£290 double.* **Rooms** 188. **Credit** AmEx, DC, MC, V. **Map** p328 & p332 H6, p336 F2 ⑲
With a Michelin-starred restaurant (Number One; *see p146*), an acclaimed spa, the elevated service standards you would expect from a Rocco Forte hotel and a clock tower that has been a defining feature of the Edinburgh skyline for more than a century, the Balmoral pretty much has the lot. The rooms and suites, some of which have iconic castle views, factor modern lines and design elements into an Edwardian fabric for an overall package that easily merits five-star status. Other amenities include the Palm Court, great for tea in the afternoon and champagne in the evening, an amenable brasserie, and a recently refurbished bar. *Bars (2). Business centre. Concierge. Disabled-adapted rooms. Gym. Internet (wireless, £15; also shared terminal). Parking (£25). Pool. Restaurants (2). Room service. Spa.*

CONSUME

Caledonian Hilton

4 Princes Street, EH1 2AB (222 8888, www. hilton.com/caledonian). Princes Street buses. **Rates** £140-£400 double. **Rooms** 254. **Credit** AmEx, DC, MC, V. **Map** p332 E7 & p336 A2 ⑳

Originally an Edwardian railway hotel, the Caledonian Hilton is often cited as Sir Sean Connery's Edinburgh favourite. Hilton manages the property but sold it in 2007 to new owners, who initially announced a rolling, multi-millionpound refurbishment programme; 89 bedrooms were revamped by 2008. There are still whispers about a covered courtyard and a much-needed upgrade for the leisure facilities. Until that happens, the rooms are generally modern but in sympathy with the hotel's origins.

Bars (2). Business centre. Concierge. Disabled-adapted rooms. Gym. Internet (wireless, £15; also shared terminal). Parking (limited, £9.50). Pool. Restaurants (2). Room service. Spa. **Other locations** Grosvenor Street, New Town, EH12 5EF (222 6001).

Chester Residence

9 Rothesay Place, EH3 7SL (226 2075, www. chester-residence.com). Bus 13. **Rates** £165-£399 suite. **Rooms** 19. **Credit** AmEx, DC, MC, V. **Map** p331 C7 ㉑

The Chester Residence isn't exactly a hotel, but it's certainly close enough to merit inclusion here. It's a collection of 19 fully serviced, luxury suites, all within a West End Georgian townhouse. It's like staying in your own apartment but with house-keeping and a 24-hour concierge to take care of you. The suites range in size and price, but all are designer-plush and rather beautiful, and all are located just a placid ten-minute stroll from the west end of Princes Street.

Concierge. Internet (wireless, free). Parking (£15). Room service.

★ Howard

34 Great King Street, EH3 6QH (557 3500 information, 274 7402 reservations, www. thehoward.com). Bus 13, 23, 27. **Rates** £105-£290 double. **Rooms** 18. **Credit** AmEx, DC, MC, V. **Map** p328 F4 ㉒

A New Town Georgian fantasy of a hotel, the Howard occupies three adjacent buildings that date to the 1820s. You can almost imagine King George IV fiddling with the television remote while Mrs Fitzherbert dallies in a voluminous, free-standing bath. There are butlers to look after you, modern comforts alongside period fixtures, and one of the city's most discreet dining rooms: the Atholl. It's as romantic as anything; no wonder it's so popular with honeymooners. Even if you're not staying here, try to pop in for afternoon tea.

Concierge. Disabled-adapted rooms. Internet (wireless, free; also shared terminal). Parking (limited, free). Restaurant. Room service.

Le Monde

16 George Street, EH2 2PF (270 3900, www.le mondehotel.co.uk). Bus 13, 23, 27, 42 or Princes Street buses. **Rates** £125-£295 double. **Rooms** 18. **Credit** AmEx, DC, MC, V. **Map** p328 & p332 G6, p336 D1 ㉓

Le Monde is more than just a hotel: there's a base-ment nightclub here as well as a restaurant and bar. Design is guided by a more-is-more mantra. Bedrooms each have a theme: the St Petersburg takes its inspiration from Catherine the Great's palace, for example, while the New York junior suite is apparently inspired by loft apartment liv-ing. Some people find it gimmicky; most, though, think it's a hoot. Just don't expect a bucolic coun-try house.

Bars (3). Disabled-adapted rooms. Internet (wireless, free). Restaurants (2). Room service.

Expensive

Bonham

35 Drumsheugh Gardens, EH3 7RN (226 6050 information, 623 9300 reservations, www.the bonham.com). Bus 13, 19, 37, 41, 47. **Rates** £125-£280 double. **Rooms** 48. **Credit** AmEx, DC, MC, V. **Map** p331 C7 ㉔

Originally three Victorian townhouses, the Bonham has at various points been used for private housing, a medical practice and a hall of residence for female medical students. It opened as a hotel in 1998, with contemporary art (all of it by young Scottish artists), stylish furniture, attractive bedrooms and a plain, spacious restaurant. More than a decade on, it's lasted very well indeed. Sister hotels in the Town House Collection include the Howard and the Edinburgh Residence, both just as impressive.

Concierge. Disabled-adapted rooms. Internet (wireless, free). Parking (limited, free). Restaurant. Room service.

★ Edinburgh Residence

7 Rothesay Terrace, EH3 7RY (623 9304, www.theedinburghresidence.com). Bus 13. **Rates** £135-£500 suite. **Rooms** 29. **Credit** AmEx, DC, MC, V. **Map** p331 C7 ㉕

One of the city's most popular hotels, the Edinburgh Residence is part of the Town House Collection, which also includes the Bonham, Channings and the Howard; all of them are listed on these pages because they're all pretty good. More a collection of large suites stuffed with antique furniture and hotel services attached, the Edinburgh Residence is far from a typical hotel; the drawing room contains an honesty bar, breakfast is served in your room and more formal in-room dining is positively encouraged (a decent menu is available 2.30-9.15pm daily). Aficionados wouldn't stay anywhere else.

Concierge. Disabled-adapted rooms. High-speed internet (wireless, free; also shared terminal). Parking (limited, free). Room service.

CONSUME

CONSUME

George

*19-21 George Street, EH2 2PB (225 1251,
www.principal-hayley.com). Bus 13, 23, 27, 42
or Princes Street buses.* **Rates** £99-£309 double.
Rooms 249. **Credit** AmEx, DC, MC, V. **Map**
p328 & p332 G6, p336 D1 ㉖

The core of the George, one of Edinburgh's old
stagers, dates back to the late 18th century, although
the building has only been a hotel since 1881. The
business was taken over in 2005 by Principal Hotels
(now Principal Hayley), and subjected to a £20 million refurbishment that was finally completed in
summer 2009. The rooms are all quietly contemporary; some have fantastic views north to the Forth
and Fife. The EH2 Tempus bar-restaurant is modern and slick, but this remains an Edinburgh hotel
of some tradition.

*Bar. Business centre. Concierge. Disabled-adapted
rooms. Internet (wireless, £9.95). Parking (£17).
Restaurant. Room service.*

Roxburghe

*38 Charlotte Square, EH2 4HQ (240 5500,
www.macdonaldhotels.co.uk/roxburghe). Princes
Street buses.* **Rates** £99-£245 double. **Rooms**
198. **Credit** AmEx, MC, V. **Map** p332 E7 &
p336 A1 ㉗

The Roxburghe is a deceptively large venue with
an elegant address, no distance at all from the west
end of Princes Street. Lurking away behind the
classical New Town façade (the building is the
work of Robert Adam) is a small pool, a gym and
198 bedrooms done up in a style not uncommon in
the city: the 19th century meets the 21st. The location is good all year round, but the Roxburghe is
particularly handy during the Edinburgh
International Book Festival, which is staged right
on its doorstep.

*Bars (2). Business centre. Concierge. Disabled-
adapted rooms. Gym. Internet (wireless, £10;
also shared terminal). Parking (£19). Pool.
Restaurant. Room service. Spa.*

Royal Scots Club

*29-30 Abercromby Place, EH3 6QE (556 4270,
www.royalscotsclub.com). Bus 13, 23, 27.* **Rates**
£200-£260 double. **Rooms** 20. **Credit** AmEx,
DC, MC, V. **Map** p328 G5 ㉘

The Royal Scots Club was founded in 1919 as a
tribute to those who died in World War I. Nearly a
century later, it still exudes a sense of history and
tranquility; the atmosphere may be more akin to
an old-fashioned private gentlemen's club than a
hotel, but the Club is actually open to all. The
rooms have been furnished in traditional style,
some with four-poster beds, but aren't averse to
modern comforts; a few rooms offer views north to
the Firth of Forth. There's an open fire in the lounge
during the winter.

*Bar. Disabled-adapted rooms. Internet (wireless,
free). Restaurant. Room service.*

Rutland

*1-3 Rutland Street, EH1 2AE, (229 3402,
www.therutlandhotel.com). Princes Street buses.*
Rates £105-200 double. **Rooms** 12. **Credit**
AmEx, MC, V. **Map** p332 E7 & p336 A2 ㉙

Long regarded by locals as 'that bar at the West
End', the Rutland underwent a transformation in
2008 and from the chrysalis of scaffolding emerged
something with a Le Monde (*see p121*) or Tigerlily
(*see below*) atmosphere in mind: basement nightclub, achingly contemporary bar and restaurant,
boutique bedrooms upstairs (including a couple
with excellent castle views). Much in the manner
of its peers, the Rutland offers lavish decor and a
modish experience that may once have seemed too
ostentatious for Presbyterian old Edinburgh, but
now feels quite at home.

*Bar (2). Concierge. Disabled-adapted rooms.
Internet (wireless, free). Restaurant. Room
service.*

★ Tigerlily

*125 George Street, EH2 4JN, (225 5005, www.
tigerlilyedinburgh.co.uk). Bus 13, 23, 27, 42 or
Princes Street buses.* **Rates** £110-£235 double.
Rooms 33. **Credit** AmEx, MC, V. **Map** p328
& p332 E6, p336 B1 ㉚

Tigerlily really did break the mould when it arrived
on the scene in 2006, representing the apogee of
demotic chic near the height of an economic boom
when anyone with a credit card could have the kind
of experience usually reserved for the Victoria
Beckhams of this world. The bedrooms are
designed to the hilt, but somehow the effect isn't
overwhelming; this remains one of the best-loved
hotels in the city, to say nothing of its visually opulent bar, restaurant or nightclub. The place is best
appreciated by a certain demographic of course;
your gran probably wouldn't like it, nor that
curmudgeonly uncle.

*Bars (2). Business centre. Concierge. Disabled-
adapted rooms. Internet (wireless, free; also
shared terminal). Restaurant. Room service.*

Moderate

Christopher North House & Number 10

*6 & 10 Gloucester Place, EH3 6EF (225 2720,
www.hoteledinburgh.co.uk, www.hotelnumberten.
com). Bus 24, 29, 36, 42.* **Rates** £98-£168
double. **Rooms** 15. **Credit** AmEx, DC, MC,
V. **Map** p328 E5 ㉛

Perhaps one of the most confusing hotels in
Edinburgh, Number 10 is tucked away at 10
Gloucester Place on the fringes of the New Town
and Stockbridge. Two doors along, meanwhile, sits
Christopher North House. Although they don't
adjoin each other and have two websites (and, for
that matter, two names), they are in fact the same
hotel. At any rate, there's a lovely Georgian feel to
the establishment, traditional touches to the decor,

Against the Grain

Economic gloom? Countrywide misery? Why not open some luxury hotels…

At first glance, the timing could not have been more inauspicious. While banks were being taken into public ownership and people muttered darkly about the worst recession since the 1930s, three ambitious hotels opened in central Edinburgh. Shoehorned into the block between Bristo Place and Forrest Road, Edinburgh's first **Hotel du Vin** (*see p117*) opened in December 2008. It was followed in 2009 by the **Apex Waterloo Place** (*see p126*), the company's grandest property to date, and **Hotel Missoni** (*see p117*), the first luxury hotel from the Italian designer brand of the same name. But why now?

The short answer is that hotel developments aren't thrown together in five minutes. Missoni decided to move into the hotel business back in 2005, the same year that MWB Group Holdings, which owns the Hotel du Vin and Malmaison chains, announced an expansion plan for both brands. Meanwhile, Apex Hotels spent 13 years building its portfolio from one property to six. All three companies had committed to their new hotels way before anyone had coined the phrase 'credit crunch'.

Beyond that, however, more far-reaching considerations come into play. A 2007 report commissioned by the local enterprise body, the tourist authority and four local councils called for 5,000 more hotel rooms across the region by 2015, four-fifths of them in the city. The extra rooms were needed to keep up with growing demand, the report said. Since tourism is so important to the local economy, the stage was set for new hotels to pop up everywhere.

Hotel du Vin, Apex Waterloo Place and Hotel Missoni muster a modest 370 rooms between them, small potatoes in terms of strategic planning. It's hardly surprising, then, that hotel-building in Edinburgh continues to be smiled on from on high. Major development schemes such as Caltongate and SoCo (*see p40* **Arrested Development**) include large hotels as a part of the package, and well-known hotel chains continue to see the city as a prime site for expansion. Edinburgh's third **Holiday Inn Express** (*see p118*) was unveiled in early 2008; there are also now seven **Premier Inns** (*see p129, p132*) and no fewer than eight **Travelodges** (*see p130*). Whatever the overall economic climate, this frenzy of hotel development in Scotland's capital seems set to continue.

Hotel du Vin.

CONSUME

artmag
EAST OF SCOTLAND GALLERY GUIDE

Gallery guide
Complete directories & maps for Edinburgh, East Lothian, Fife & the Borders
Free in galleries, museums & art spaces

art**news**
art**world**

Previews
50+ exhibitions
in every issue

www.artmag.co.uk

Chinese antiques, some Philippe Starck bathrooms and a Kaffe Haus. When booking by phone, though, just be clear which one you favour.
Bar. Internet (wireless, free; also shared terminal). Restaurant. Room service.

Old Waverley

43 Princes Street, EH2 2BY (556 4648, www. oldwaverley.co.uk). Princes Street buses. **Rates** £169-£219 double. **Rooms** 85. **Credit** AmEx, MC, V. **Map** p328 & p332 H6, p336 E2 ❸❷
Dating back to 1848, the Old Waverley is one of the capital's oldest hotels. Although it's been undergone refurbishment in recent years, it still retains a genteel, traditional look; tartanphobes may want to avert their eyes. Some rooms face south, giving rather splendid castle views; if yours doesn't, you could always try for a window seat in the bar as recompense. Either way, you'll step out of the front door straight on to Princes Street, so the location couldn't be more central.
Bar. Concierge. Internet (wireless, free). Restaurant. Room service.

Rick's

55a Frederick Street, EH2 1HL (622 7800, www.ricksedinburgh.co.uk). Bus 13, 23, 27, 42 or Princes Street buses. **Rates** £130-£175 double. **Rooms** 10. **Credit** AmEx, MC, V. **Map** p328 & p332 F6, p336 C1 ❸❸
If 'boutique' means in some way 'small and individual', then Rick's deserved the epithet when it opened in 2000: a city centre bar-restaurant with ten modish rooms above. The location, the atmosphere and the sense of style were all praised, although a decade of wear and tear didn't do it any favours. Happily, though, the rooms and the bar-restaurant were freshened up in 2009. The accommodation still has a quiet, understated chic; as long as the staff aren't run off their feet, breakfast is pretty good, as are the cocktails in the bar (*see p173*).
Bar. Business centre. Disabled-adapted rooms. Internet (wireless, free; also shared terminal). Restaurant. Room service.

Budget

Frederick House

42 Frederick Street, EH2 1EX (226 1999, www.townhousehotels.co.uk). Bus 13, 23, 27, 42 or Princes Street buses. **Rates** £50-£190 double. **Rooms** 45. **Credit** AmEx, MC, V. **Map** p328 & p332 H6, p336 E2 ❸❹
Frederick House is a former office space in an old listed building in the southern, consumer-oriented part of the New Town, which has loads of shops, pubs, cafés and restaurants – and it's close to Princes Street too. Its conversion to a hotel saw traditional decor throughout; it may be a little chintzy for some, but there's little quibbling with the value. The prices, already very decent, get even cheaper out of season;

---

check the website for special offers. There's no dining room or bar, but there are lots of options nearby.
Internet (wireless, free).

Hostels

Belford Backpackers *6-8 Douglas Gardens, EH4 3DA (220 2200, www.hoppo.com/belford). Princes Street buses.* **Open** *Reception* 24hrs daily. No curfew. **Rates** £10-£18 dorm bed. **Credit** AmEx, MC, V. **Map** p331 B7 ❸❺
Caledonian Backpackers *3 Queensferry Street, EH2 4PA (226 2939, www.caledonian backpackers.net). Princes Street buses.* **Open** *Reception* 24hrs daily. No curfew. **Rates** £11-£30 dorm bed. **Credit** MC, V. **Map** p331 D7 ❸❻
Princes Street East Backpackers *5 West Register Street, EH2 2AA (556 6894, www. edinburghbackpackers.com). Nicolson Street–North Bridge buses or Princes Street buses.* **Open** *Reception* 24hrs daily. No curfew. **Rates** £11-£15 dorm bed; £30-£40 double. **Credit** MC, V. **Map** p328 & p332 H6, p336 A2 ❸❼

STOCKBRIDGE

Expensive

Channings

12-16 South Learmonth Gardens, EH4 1EZ (315 2226 information, 623 9302 reservations, www.channings.co.uk). Bus 19, 37, 41, 47. **Rates** £110-£185 double. **Rooms** 41. **Credit** AmEx, MC, V. **Map** p327 B4 ❸❽
Noted polar explorer Sir Ernest Shackleton once lived in these premises, which is why, in recent years, the owners of Channings created three suites and two rooms on a Shackleton theme. Guests can now lie in an enormous bathtub and soak up the narrative from a huge print of his ship, the *Endurance*, on the wall adjacent. The hotel's other rooms are equally crisp and handsome, with the north-facing accommodation giving views to the Firth of Forth and Fife. It's a discreet hotel that feels far away from central Edinburgh but isn't, and with a decent basement bistro to boot.
Bar. Business centre. Concierge. Internet (wireless, free). Restaurant. Room service.

Budget

Inverleith Hotel

5 Inverleith Terrace, EH3 5NS (556 2745, www.inverleithhotel.co.uk). Bus 8, 23, 27. **Rates** £59-£119 double. **Rooms** 10. **Credit** MC, V. **Map** p362 E2 ③⑨

Sitting cheek by jowl with the beautiful Royal Botanic Garden (*see p89*), the Inverleith Hotel is a small and traditionally furnished townhouse dating to the early Victorian period. There's no restaurant and the bar is residents only, but guests tend to be unremittingly positive about the service, friendliness and comfort of the rooms (especially the suite with the four-poster bed). Staying here can be quite a bargain in the off-season; the owners also have a self-catering New Town apartment for let; check the website for details.

Bar. Internet (wireless, free). Room service.

CALTON HILL & BROUGHTON

Deluxe

★ Glasshouse

2 Greenside Place, EH1 3AA (525 8200, www.theetoncollection.com). Playhouse buses. **Rates** £150-£295 double. **Rooms** 65. **Credit** AmEx, MC, V. **Map** p329 J5 ④⓪

Behind the façade of the former Lady's Glenorchy Church, between the Playhouse Theatre and the Omni, the Glasshouse has been delighting guests with its contemporary design, roof terrace (with views up to Calton Hill), comfortable beds and amenable service since 2003. The clean, modern lines of the hotel's design make for a cultured and classy atmosphere; the name is echoed in the floor-to-ceiling windows that offer impressive views over the city. It's just a stone's throw (no, don't!) from the commotion of the capital, but a world apart.

Bar. Business centre. Concierge. Disabled-adapted rooms. Internet (wireless, free). Parking (£17). Room service.

★ 21212

3 Royal Terrace, EH7 5AB (0845 22 21212, www.21212restaurant.co.uk). Bus 1, 4, 5, 15, 15A, 19, 26, 34, 44, 45. **Rates** £250-£325 double. **Rooms** 4. **Credit** AmEx, MC, V. **Map** p329 K5 ④①

The four guestrooms above Paul Kitching's restaurant, which opened here in spring 2009 (*see p151*), have the same visual panache as his celebrated cooking. Each room has a slightly different decorative theme, but all of them are spacious, super-plush and clearly cut from the same cloth. Two of them have great views north over the city to the Forth; the other pair overlook the gardens behind

Bar. Internet (wireless, free). Restaurant.

Expensive

Apex Waterloo Place

23-27 Waterloo Place, EH1 3BH (523 1819, www.apexhotels.co.uk). Nicolson Street–North Bridge buses. **Rates** £119-£260 double. **Rooms** 187. **Credit** AmEx, DC, MC, V. **Map** p329 & p333 J6 ④②

Glasshouse.

Established as a hotel in 1819, this building has been used for a variety of different purposes uses during its 180-year life, most recently as local authority offices. However, after a refurbishment, it reopened in 2009 and became the Edinburgh flagship for the Apex chain. Modern, comfortable and handsome in a 21st century sort of way, the rooms at the front of the building overlook the historic Old Calton Cemetery across the road. Some premium rooms in a 1970s-era extension at the back have expansive views but others don't; ask when booking. *Photos p131.*
Bar. Business centre. Concierge. Disabled-adapted rooms. Gym. Internet (wireless, free; also shared terminal). Parking (£15). Pool. Restaurant. Room service. Spa.

Parliament House
15 Calton Hill, EH1 3BJ (478 4000, www. parliamenthouse-hotel.co.uk). Playhouse buses. **Rates** *£80-£210 double.* **Rooms** 53. **Credit** AmEx, DC, MC, V. **Map** p329 & p333 J6
Parliament House opened back in the days when people thought the new Scottish Parliament would be at the former Royal High School building on Regent Road nearby, which explains the slightly off-kilter name. Still, the location is pretty decent, tucked away down a lane at Calton Hill. Jacobean and Georgian buildings were connected to create the hotel premises, and rooms vary in outlook and size as a result. With a clean, crisp design, some of them are cavernous while others are cosy; a number are blessed with views of Arthur's Seat or the Old Town.
Bar. Disabled-adapted rooms. Internet (wireless, £12). Restaurant. Room service.

Moderate

Ballantrae Albany
39-47 Albany Street, EH1 3QY (556 0397, www.ballantraealbanyhotel.com). Playhouse buses. **Rates** *£90-£160 double.* **Rooms** 22. **Credit** AmEx, MC, V. **Map** p328 H5
A Georgian townhouse just along Albany Street from the bars and restaurants of Broughton Street, the Ballantrae Albany is a fairly small property, but a fairly characterful one. You'll either love the rooms here or loathe them; fans will consider them dark, romantic and boutiquey, while others may find them gothic and oppressive. The property lacks its own restaurant but does have a pretty good one in the basement (Haldane's; *see p151*).
Bar. Concierge. Internet (wireless, £10). Parking (£15). Restaurant. Room service. Spa.

Hostels

Edinburgh Central SYHA Hostel
9 Haddington Place, EH7 4AL (524 2090, www.syha.org.uk). Bus 7, 10, 12, 14, 16, 22, 25, 49. **Open** call for details. No curfew. **Rates** *£16-£27, plus membership.* **Credit** MC, V. **Map** p329 J4

SOUTH EDINBURGH

Expensive

★ Prestonfield
Priestfield Road, Prestonfield, EH16 5UT (225 7800, www.prestonfield.com). Bus 2, 14, 30. **Rates** *£160-£275 double; £275-£350 suite.* **Rooms** 24. **Credit** AmEx, DC, MC, V.
Set in parkland just south of Arthur's Seat, the main building here dates to 1687. Much of its original, last-gasp-Jacobean character remains, from the approach along a tree-lined drive to the ornate fixtures and fittings inside. Opulent antique furniture and lush upholstery complement the look of the hotel and its well-known restaurant, Rhubarb (*see p158*); the guestrooms, both in the old house or the modern extension out back, are similarly sumptuous, although contemporary comforts abound (plasma-screen TVs, free Wi-Fi). Peacocks and Highland cattle amble around outside in the grounds. Genuinely impressive.
Bar. Business centre. Concierge. Disabled-adapted rooms. Internet (wireless, free) Parking (free). Restaurant. Room service.

Moderate

Mercure Point
34 Bread Street, EH3 9AF (221 5555, www. mercure.com). Bus 1, 2, 10, 11, 15, 15A, 16, 23, 24, 27, 34, 35, 45. **Rates** *£75-£165 double.* **Rooms** 139. **Credit** AmEx, MC, V. **Map** p332 E8 & p336 A4

CONSUME

The designer hotel concept came to Edinburgh way back in 1995, when the Point opened on Bread Street. Award-winning in its day, it's since been refurbished and is now more user-friendly than it used to be, although still very contemporary. Originally a grand department store showroom, the hotel is now an extensive venue with conference facilities, a restaurant, a bar and some 139 rooms, many of which have great views across to Edinburgh Castle. There was a change of ownership in 2008, which ushered in the worldwide Mercure chain to manage the property.
Bar. Disabled-adapted rooms. Internet (wireless, £15). Parking (£13). Restaurant. Room service.
▶ *For a bargain, upmarket lunch try Abstract nearby on Castle Terrace (see p153).*

Novotel Edinburgh Centre
80 Lauriston Place, EH3 9DE (656 3500, www.accor-hotels.com). Bus 1, 2, 10, 11, 15, 15A, 16, 23, 24, 27, 34, 35, 45. **Rates** £69-£209 double. **Rooms** 180. **Credit** AmEx, DC, MC, V. **Map** p332 F9 ❼
Novotel's central-Edinburgh property is pretty typical of the chain: clean, straightforward and moderately modern rooms; a small pool, with a sauna and a jacuzzi accommodation; efficient staff; and a bar and a restaurant that are both functional at best. The city's other Novotel, at Edinburgh Park on the western outskirts, tends to be cheaper. Fancy a beer? Cloisters (see p176), one of the city's best cask ale pubs, is just a short walk away.
Bar. Business centre. Disabled-adapted rooms. Gym. Internet (wireless, £10; also shared terminal). Parking (limited, £10). Pool. Restaurant. Room service. Spa.

★ Salisbury
43-45 Salisbury Road, EH16 5AA (667 1264, www.the-salisbury.co.uk). Nicolson Street–North Bridge buses. **Rates** £70-£140 double. **Rooms** 18. **Credit** MC, V. **Map** p333 L11 ❾
Discreetly tucked away on a side road in Newington, the Salisbury merits praise for the standard of accommodation ('now' meets 'then' decor with all mod cons), the friendly approach from its staff, the breakfasts, the food in its Gabbro bistro and even the mellow space of its walled garden. You could splash out on a four-poster if you wanted, but all the rooms are handsome and very good value. It's about a mile from the Royal Mile.
Bar. Concierge. Internet (wireless, free). Parking (free). Restaurant. Room service.

Ten Hill Place
10 Hill Place, EH8 9DS (662 2080, www.tenhillplace.com). Nicolson Street buses. **Rates** £65-£210 double. **Rooms** 78. **Credit** MC, V. **Map** p333 J8 ❾
Home to the Royal College of Surgeons for years, Surgeons' Hall is a grand classical building. Behind

the frontage, however, it's an extensive complex, with a modern extension to the original Georgian premises that includes a conference venue and this hotel (access is around the corner on Hill Place). The rooms at Ten Hill Place are slick and modern, and the central location is a selling point – the premium fourth-floor Skyline rooms have brilliant views across the city. There's a basic café-bar on site, but you're better off looking elsewhere for food and drink. For those with a strong constitution, the pathology exhibition at Surgeons' Hall is a must-see (see p101).
Bar. Disabled-adapted rooms. Internet (wireless, free). Parking (limited, free). Restaurant. Room service.

Budget

★ Hotel Ceilidh-Donia
14-16 Marchhall Crescent, EH16 5HL (667 2743, www.hotelceilidh-donia.co.uk). Bus 2, 14, 30, 33. **Rates** £65-£120 double. **Rooms** 17. **Credit** MC, V.
The Hotel Ceilidh-Donia is in the suburbs, around a mile and a half south of Princes Street (ten minutes on the bus on a good day). But that's the only downside with this fine property, a much-loved, family-run bargain in an attractive Victorian terrace. The rooms are comfortable, the rates are appealing and the bistro is decent, and the entire property has a fair amount of character. The dog-averse or dog-allergic should note that the owners have two golden retrievers.
Bar. Disabled-adapted room. Internet (wireless, free). Restaurant.

Premier Inn
82 Lauriston Place, EH3 9DG (0870 990 6610, www.premierinn.com). Bus 1, 2, 10, 11, 15, 15A, 16, 23, 24, 27, 34, 35, 45. **Rates** £65-£139 double. **Rooms** 112. **Credit** AmEx, DC, MC, V. **Map** p332 F9 ❺⓿
Like all members of this chain, Edinburgh's Premier Inn is a budget bed box where form is usurped by function, but this one delivers thanks to its fairly

---

THE BEST CONVERSIONS

Malmaison
Originally a waterside seaman's mission.
See p132.

Mercure Point
A pre-war department store showroom.
See p127.

Tigerlily
Once offices for a life insurance company.
See p122.

CONSUME

central location and helpful staff. There are six other Premier Inns around the city, all offering the same combination of cheap rooms and anticharismatic decor; check the website for details.
Bar. Disabled-adapted rooms. Internet (wireless, £10). Parking (£12). Restaurant.

Salisbury Green
Pollock Halls, 18 Holyrood Park Road, EH16 5AY (651 2001, www.salisburygreen.co.uk). Bus 2. 14. 30. 33. **Rates** *£89-£134 double.* **Rooms** 36. **Credit** MC, V. **Map** p333 M11 ⑤
Not to be confused with the Salisbury relatively nearby (*see p129*), Salisbury Green opened for business in 2006. It's an impressive mid 18th-century residence, which has been converted into a hotel but retained many of its original fixtures and fittings in public areas. Technically part of the University of Edinburgh, it sits within the grounds of Pollock Halls (*see p134*), so there are lots of students around in term time. Rooms are in that IKEA-modern style, but most people love the location (by Holyrood Park) and the value.
Concierge. Disabled-adapted rooms. Internet (wireless, free). Parking (limited, free). Restaurant. Room service.

WEST EDINBURGH
Expensive

Sheraton Grand
1 Festival Square, Lothian Road, EH3 9SR (229 9131, www.sheraton.com). Bus 1, 2, 10, 11, 15, 15A, 16, 23, 24, 27, 34, 35, 45. **Rates** *£105-£300 double.* **Rooms** 260. **Credit** AmEx, DC, MC, V. **Map** p331 D8 ㉒
Built in the mid 1980s and an early pioneer among the various developments to the immediate west side of Lothian Road, the Sheraton Grand has a bland façade and an interior that could almost be any Sheraton on earth. The hotel has the chain's typical international-traveller aesthetic throughout; its main defining feature, aside from the castle views from some windows, is the world-beating One Spa, which has a fantastic thermal suite, a 19-metre swimming pool, an outdoor hydropool and various other facilities. Guests may have to pay a supplement for some of the facilities.
Bar. Business centre. Concierge. Disabled-adapted rooms. Gym. Internet (wireless, £10; also shared terminal). Parking (£9). Pool. Restaurants (2). Room service. Spa.

Moderate

Dunstane House
4 West Coates, Haymarket, EH12 5JQ (337 6169, www.dunstane-hotel-edinburgh.co.uk). Bus 12, 26, 31, 38. **Rates** *£98-£178 double.* **Rooms** 16. **Credit** AmEx, MC, V. **Map** p331 A8 ㉓

A mid 19th-century villa around a third of a mile west of Haymarket railway station, Dunstane House has been a hotel for more than 40 years. The slightly gothic frontage gives way to a handsome interior, with many period features (including, in some rooms, four-poster beds). The current owners hail from Orkney, which explains the Orcadian influence in the hotel restaurant (Skerries). Across the road and under the same ownership, Dunstane City has a more modish, boutiquey interior.
Bar. Business centre. Internet (wireless, free). Parking (free). Restaurant. Room service.

Edinburgh Marriott
111 Glasgow Road, EH12 8NF (334 9191, www.marriott.co.uk). Bus 31, 48, X48, Airlink 100. **Rates** *£87-£190 double.* **Rooms** 245. **Credit** AmEx, DC, MC, V.
Way out west, around four miles from Princes Street en route to the airport, the Marriott is one of those hotels that many visitors pass by without noticing. That's a pity. It is very consciously a business hotel and not exactly awash with character, but the location and market position of the property can mean decent special offers and weekend deals, especially out of season. The guestrooms are comfortable, modern and well-equipped, and amenities include a small pool.
Bar (2). Business centre. Concierge. Disabled-adapted rooms. Gym. Internet (high-speed, wireless; £15). Parking (free). Pool. Restaurant. Room service. Spa.

Budget

Travelodge Shandwick Place
25 Shandwick Place, EH2 4RG (08719 846398, www.travelodge.co.uk). Princes Street buses. **Rates** *£30-£90 double.* **Rooms** 146. **Credit** AmEx, DC, MC, V. **Map** p331 D7 ㉔
Rather like its fellow Travelodges and other competing budget hotels, there's not a lot to say about this venue except that it's cost-effective, functional and does the job if you're looking for somewhere in town with no frills that won't break the bank. You know what you're getting when you stay here. Having opened in summer 2009, it's the newest of the eight Travelodges in the city, and it's also one of the most central.
Internet (wireless, £10).

LEITH & THE COAST
Moderate

Holiday Inn Express
Britannia Way, Ocean Drive, EH6 6JJ (555 4422, www.hiex-edinburgh.com). Bus 1, 10, 16, 22, 35, 36. **Rates** *£79-£165 double.* **Rooms** 145. **Credit** AmEx, DC, MC, V. **Map** p326 X2 ㉕

Apex Waterloo Place. *See p126.*

CONSUME

Malmaison.

Just on the other side of a roundabout from Ocean Terminal shopping mall (not on the water, but pretty close), this Holiday Inn Express is one of only a few hotels in Leith. Just as one might expect, it's fairly large and functional, with modern, iden-tikit rooms: it provides a solid standard of service without stirring the soul. There are lots of restaurants and bars nearby at the Shore; access to the Royal Yacht Britannia (*see p112*) is via the Ocean Terminal mall.
Bar. Business centre. Disabled-adapted rooms. Internet (wireless, £10). Parking (free).

Malmaison

1 Tower Place, EH6 7DB (468 5000, www. malmaison.com). Bus 1, 10, 16, 22, 35, 36. **Rates** £135-£155 double. **Rooms** 100. **Credit** AmEx, DC, MC, V. **Map** p326 Y2 ⑤⑥
There are now 12 Malmaison hotels across the UK, but this property was the first to arrive. Launched in 1994, it's housed in a former seaman's mission in a grand building where the Water of Leith meets the docks. When it opened, it brought a sense of boutique style to the waterfront; it's now showing its age in some ways, but the suites and rooms still have a plush feel to them. There are three Michelin-starred restaurants within walking distance: Restaurant Martin Wishart (*see p166*), the Plumed Horse (*see p166*) and Kitchin (*see p165*).
Bar. Disabled-adapted rooms. Gym. Internet (wireless, £10). Parking (free). Restaurant. Room service.

Budget

A-Haven Townhouse

180 Ferry Road, EH6 4NS (554 6559, www.a-haven.co.uk). Bus 11, 14, 21. **Rates** £60-£130 double. **Rooms** 14. **Credit** AmEx, DC, MC, V. **Map** p326 V3 ⑤⑦
Despite Leith's regeneration, it still seems short on decent hotels. Thank goodness, then, for the A-Haven Townhouse, a Victorian-era venue on Ferry Road (the centre of old Leith at the Shore is around half a mile away). It's more of a guesthouse, and the decor may be a little fussy for some. But it's good value, owner-manager David Kay is an affable host, and it's just a 15-minute bus ride from the centre of Edinburgh.
Bar. Internet (wireless, free). Parking (free). Room service.

Premier Inn Edinburgh (Leith)

51-53 Newhaven Place, EH6 4NS (08701 977 093, www.premierinn.com). Bus 7, 11, 16. **Rates** £60-£90 double. **Rooms** 85. **Credit** AmEx, DC, MC, V. **Map** p326 U1 ⑤⑧
Technically not in Leith but at Newhaven, a little way west, this is simply another functional Premier Inn but with a rare waterfront position. It's tucked away by the historic little Newhaven Harbour. The location is good for those who want to escape the city centre after a day's sightseeing and smell the sea air, but don't want to pay too much for the privilege.
Disabled-adapted rooms. Internet (wireless, £10). Parking (free). Restaurant.

Other Accommodation

APARTMENTS

If you're here for more than a few nights, as many visitors are during the festival, it may pay to investigate a short-stay apartment, or a suite in an aparthotel. Some are basic and cheap, while others are much more luxurious and expensive. During the various August festivals and in the run-up to Hogmanay, the short lettings market is busy and prices inflate. As with hotels, book as early as possible for the best deals. Always bear in mind that many of these properties will offer a minimum stay, which could be anywhere from a few nights to a fortnight.

Historic properties

Although many short-stay apartments are in modern blocks, or buildings of Victorian or Georgian origin, a number have even more historical resonance. Operated by the National Trust for Scotland, **Gladstone's Flat** is housed in a 17th-century building off the Royal Mile. **Pilrig House** is another 17th-century property, refurbished recently, that's located in a park halfway between Leith and the city centre. And on the south side of the city, by the Pentland Hills, sit **Swanston Cottages**, traditional farm cottages renovated to modern standards.

Gladstone's Flat *477B Lawnmarket, Old Town, EH1 2NT (243 9331, www.nts.org.uk). Bus 2, 23, 27, 41, 42.* **Rates** £100-£150/night. **Credit** MC, V. **Map** p54 B1, p332 G7 & p336 D3 ⑤⑨
★ **Pilrig House** *30 Pilrig House Close, Leith, EH6 5RF (554 4794, www.pilrighouse.com). Bus 11, 36.* **Rates** £80-£250/night. **No credit cards**.
Swanston Cottages *Swanston Farm, 111 Swanston Road, South Edinburgh EH10 7DS (445 5744, www.swanston.co.uk). No bus.* **Rates** £382-£633/week. **Credit** AmEx, MC, V.

Apartments

Apartments and apart-hotels vary in size, quality and price. However, whether you're a couple looking for a two-week stay or whether you need to house a largeish party over a long weekend, you may find something to suit.

Calton Apartments
44 Annandale Street, Calton Hill & Broughton, EH7 4AW (556 3221, www.townhouse hotels.co.uk). Bus 7, 10, 12, 14, 16, 22, 25, 49. **Rates** £50-£300/night. **Credit** AmEx, MC, V. **Map** p329 J3 ⑥⓪
Eight apartments in one building. They may not win any interior design prizes, but they're fairly central and pretty cheap at certain times of year. The owners also operate Frederick House; *see p125*.

Canon Court Apartments
20 Canonmills, New Town, EH3 5LH (474 7000, www.canoncourt.co.uk). Bus 8, 23, 27, 36. **Rates** £89-£240/night. **Credit** AmEx, MC, V. **Map** p328 F3 ⑥①
Simple, modern self-catering accommodation not far from the Royal Botanic Garden. Amenities include free wireless internet access.

★ Fountain Court Apartments
Administrative office: 115 Lauriston Place, EH8 8PE (622 6677, www.fountaincourtapartments. com). **Rates** vary. **Credit** AmEx, MC, V.
Fountain Court rents a variety of modern serviced apartments in several locations, most just west of the city centre. The most popular are known as EQ-2 (Edinburgh Quay 2), and are found in a waterfront block at the Lochrin canal basin.

> ### INSIDE TRACK BRUNCH
>
> The room might have been fine – but if you've been disappointed by an expensive hotel breakfast, try brunch at a local café instead. For the very best, *see p163* **The Breakfast Club**, or just check out the Restaurants & Cafés chapter (*see pp135-166*).

CONSUME

★ Holyrood Aparthotel

1 Nether Bakehouse, Holyrood, Old Town EH8
8PE (524 3200, www.holyroodaparthotel.com).
Bus 35. 36. **Rates** £230-£290. **Credit** AmEx,
DC, MC, V. **Map** p55 F2 & p333 L7 ⑫
Modern serviced apartments tucked away just a few
minutes from the Royal Mile, the Scottish Parliament
and Palace of Holyroodhouse.

James Square Apartments

James Square, 51 Caledonian Crescent, West
Edinburgh EH11 2AT (225 7808, www.
edinburghathome.com). Bus 2, 3, 3A, 4, 25, 33,
44, 44A. **Rates** £60-£195. **Credit** MC, V. **Map**
p331 B10 ⑬
Located off Dalry Road, out past Haymarket Station,
these upscale, luxury apartments offer a private
swimming pool, a sauna and a roof terrace.

Kew House & Balbirnie Apartments

1 Kew Terrace, West Edinburgh, EH12 5JE (313
0700, www.kewhouse.com). Bus 12, 26, 31.
Rates £100-£200/night. **Credit** AmEx, MC, V.
Kew House is effectively a B&B but with two separate, serviced apartments to let nearby in a modern
terrace. There's not much character, but the apartments are roughly halfway between Murrayfield
and the West End and are thus handy for both.

No.5 Self-Catering Apartments

3 Abercorn Terrace, Portobello, EH15 2DD
(669 1044, www.numberfive.com). Bus 12, 15,
15A, 26, 42, 49. **Rates** £13-£75/night. **Credit**
AmEx, MC, V.
This seaside special sits just 300 yards from the
beach. The accommodation is fairly basic, but there
is a good discount for stays of more than six weeks.

★ Royal Garden Apartments

York Buildings, Queen Street, New Town EH2
1HY (625 2345, www.royal-garden.co.uk).
Princes Street buses. **Rates** £110-£295/night.
Credit AmEx, MC, V. **Map** p328 G5 ⑭
At the east end of Queen Street, this is a handy and
centrally located aparthotel within easy walking distance of Princes Street and Broughton Street.

West End Apartments

2 Learmonth Terrace, Stockbridge, EH4 1PQ
(332 0717, www.edinburghapartments.biz). Bus
24, 29, 42. **Rates** £35-£65/night. **No credit**
cards. Map p327 B4 ⑮
Housed in a Victorian terrace, these apartments have
a traditional feel, and some come with great views.
They're located just on the other side of Dean Bridge
from the West End.

Apartment agencies

The agencies and websites listed below all offer
a variety of self-catered accommodation around

the city, ranging from luxurious family houses
to more basic and affordable apartments. Some
properties are let out for as little as a week at
a time; others require minimum terms of a
month or longer. **Festival Beds** differs from
the others in that it deals not in self-catered
apartments but in B&B accommodation, and
rents properties only during August (the other
companies all operate year-round).

Apartments in Edinburgh *556 8309,*
www.apartmentsinedinburgh.com.
Clouds *550 3808, www.clouds.co.uk.*
Edinburgh Apartments
www.festivalapartments.com.
Edinburgh Holiday Flats
www.edinburghholidayflats.com.
Factotum *0845 119 6000, www.factotum.co.uk.*
Festival Beds *225 1101, www.festivalbeds.co.uk.*
Festival Flats *01620 810620,*
www.festivalflats.net.
Glen House Apartments *228 4043,*
www.edinburgh-apartments.co.uk.
Mackay's Agency *550 1180,*
www.mackays-self-catering.co.uk.

STUDENT ACCOMMODATION

The city's universities rent out rooms in their
halls of residence during academic vacations.
The University of Edinburgh alone has some
2,000 rooms available in summer under its
Edinburgh First brand; at its Pollock Halls
of Residence, many rooms face Arthur's Seat,
offering some of the best views of any university
accommodation in the UK. Some halls have a
detached campus feel and are a bus ride away
from the centre of town – particularly Queen
Margaret University, which moved out to East
Lothian in 2007 – but prices are keen.

Edinburgh Conference Centre (Heriot-Watt
University) *Heriot-Watt University, Riccarton*
Campus, Riccarton, EH14 4AS (451 3115,
www.edinburgh-conference.com/stay). Bus 25,
34, 45. **Rates** B&B £41-£59. **Credit** MC, V.
Edinburgh First (University of Edinburgh)
Pollock Halls: 18 Holyrood Park Road, South
Edinburgh, EH16 5AY (667 1971, www.
edinburghfirst.com). Bus 2, 14, 30, 33. **Rates**
B&B £42-£99. **Credit** MC, V. **Map** p333 M10 ⑯
Napier University Student Accommodation
Office *Craiglockhart Campus, 219 Colinton*
Road, South Edinburgh, EH14 1DJ (455 3738,
www.napier.ac.uk/accommodation). Bus 10, 27,
45. **Rates** call for details. **Credit** MC, V.
Queen Margaret University *Queen Margaret*
University Drive, by Musselburgh, East Lothian
EH21 6UU (474 0000, www.qmuc.ac.uk).
Bus 30 or Musselburgh rail. **Rates** £51-£79.
Credit MC, V.

CONSUME

Restaurants & Cafés

It's not just haggis, neeps and tatties.

Edinburgh's dining scene doesn't always operate according to logic. A decade into the 21st century, key local restaurateurs such as Dave Ramsden and Tony Singh faced down the recession by opening value-for-money eateries. But elsewhere, the number of Michelin stars in the city grew to four thanks to the arrival of Paul Kitching's daringly upmarket **21212**, with cooking so creative it bordered on the baroque. Against the tide of financial failure, bistros seemed to spring up every five minutes, adding to a backbone of existing venues that already covered most styles and nationalities. And, of course, the city's café scene remains lively, with countless places offering light snacks during the day and richer meals in the evening.

In other words, there's no narrative here. Chaotic? Certainly, but the Edinburgh food scene is the most fun you have can have with a fork in Scotland.

CONSUME

PRACTICALITIES

Few restaurants in Edinburgh have a dress code, and the smart-casual look for both men and women is acceptable almost everywhere. As a general rule, however, the pricier the joint, the smarter the clientele; if you're unsure, call ahead first. As for tipping, it's standard practice to pay ten per cent on top of the bill for service. Some restaurants will add a service charge automatically, even while insisting that it's 'optional'; if service wasn't up to scratch, ask for it to be deducted. Be wary of places that include a service charge on the bill but still leave a space for a gratuity on your credit card slip.

During the festival month of August, many restaurants and cafés remain open beyond their regular hours; it's worth checking if you want a late meal. Conversely, though, it becomes even more crucial than normal to book a table during August; booking ahead becomes key.

Throughout the chapter, we've listed the price of an average main course (or equivalent, such as a sandwich price in a café) to give a rough indication of price. Budget venues, most of them cafés, are denoted by the **£** symbol.

> ❶ Blue numbers given in this chapter correspond to the location of each venue on the street maps. *See pp326-333.*

THE OLD TOWN

£ Always Sunday
170 High Street (622 0667, www.alwayssunday. co.uk). Bus 35 or Nicolson Street–North Bridge buses. **Open** 8am-6pm Mon-Fri; 9am-6pm Sat, Sun. **Main courses** £7. **Credit** MC, V. **Map** p332 H7 & p336 F4 ❶ Café
Thanks to its prime site, this contemporary café can get terribly crowded in August. But it's worth trying for a table: the quality of food (soups, salads, decent bread and daily specials) means it's a great place for lunch, a snack or even a leisurely breakfast. No frills, no dawdling, but quite a gem.

Barioja
19 Jeffrey Street (557 3622, www.iggs.co.uk/ barioja). Bus 35 or Nicolson Street–North Bridge buses. **Open** 11am-10pm Mon-Sat. **Main courses** *Tapas* £5.50. **Credit** AmEx, DC, MC, V. **Map** p333 J7 ❷ Tapas
The sister venture to Igg's next door (*see p139*), Barioja is an accomplished modern take on a tapas bar. The menu lists just over 30 starter-sized portions: dishes like asparagus with romesco sauce, clams with almonds and seaweed, or eggs with carpaccio of smoked cod. Good grazing fare.
▶ *For more, see p163 The Breakfast Club.*

£ Café Hub
Castlehill (473 2067, www.thehub-edinburgh.com). Bus 2, 23, 27, 41, 42. **Open** 9.30am-6pm Mon,

Sun; 9.30am-10pm Tue-Sat. **Main courses** £6. **Credit** AmEx, MC, V. **Map** p332 G7 & p336 D4 ❸ **Café/bistro**

The catering wing of the Edinburgh International Festival home base, Café Hub sits in a building dating to 1845, which originally served as an assembly hall and offices for the Church of Scotland. The menu is flexible, ranging from salads and sandwiches to more substantial dishes such as poached salmon. Thanks to the terrace, it's also a great place to have an alfresco beer on a sunny day. Of course, it gets stupidly busy in August.

▶ *For more on the Hub, see p59.*

Caffè Lucano

37-39 George IV Bridge (225 6690, www.caffe lucano.co.uk). Bus 23, 27, 42, 45. **Open** 7am-10pm Mon-Fri; 8am-10pm Sat; 9am-8pm Sun. **Main courses** £10. **Credit** MC, V. **Map** p332 H8 ❹ **Café**

A simple Italian establishment, Caffè Lucano offers breakfast (scrambled egg and smoked salmon on toast), filled ciabattas and focaccias, cakes, coffees and even full-on plates of fettucini, steak or chicken; the house wines are reasonable. The good-natured staff and sheer lack of whimsy or pretension combine to make it a welcome find.

£ Clarinda's

69 Canongate (557 1888). Bus 35, 36. **Open** 9am-4.45pm Mon-Sat; 9.30am-4.45pm Sun. **Main courses** £5. **No credit cards**. **Map** p333 L6 ❺ **Tearoom**

Hanging baskets of flowers outside, politesse inside: nothing changes at this classic Royal Mile tearoom. Along with your pot of tea, sample a chocolate crispy, a sherry trifle or a melting moment; the menu also runs to breakfasts, sandwiches and lunches. It's all very sweet and home-made, with cakes and biscuits your Scottish grandmother might have baked.

▶ *It's named in honour of Robert Burns' muse; for more, see p68.*

Creelers

3 Hunter Square (220 4447, www.creelers.co.uk). Bus 35 or Nicolson Street–North Bridge buses. **Open** noon-2.30pm, 5.30-10.30pm Mon-Thur; noon-2.30pm, 5.30-11pm Fri; noon-3pm, 5.30-11pm Sat; 1-3pm, 6-10.30pm Sun. **Main courses** £18. **Credit** MC, V. **Map** p332 H7 & p336 F4 ❻ **Seafood**

Tim and Fran James opened this accessible seafood restaurant, a sister to the Arran original, in 1994. The formula is simple: good produce sourced from Scotland's west coast. Food may arrive unadorned (a signature seafood platter) or with more elaborate preparation (chargrilled salmon with blackbean, honey and soy). The menu includes one or two meat and vegetarian options for those not fishily inclined.

Cucina

Hotel Missoni, 1 George IV Bridge (220 6666, www.hotelmissoni.com). Bus 23, 27, 42, 45. **Open** 6.30-10.30am, 12.30-3pm, 6-10pm Mon-Thur; 6.30-10am, 12.30-3pm, 6-11pm Fri; 7-11am, 12.30-3pm, 6-11pm Sat; 7-11am, 12.30-3pm,

La Garrigue.

CONSUME

6-10pm Sun. **Main courses** £16. **Credit** AmEx, DC, MC, V. **Map** p332 H7 & p336 D4 ❼ Italian
Some people regard the styling at the Hotel Missoni's restaurant, all blacks, whites and aquamarines, as *ne plus ultra*; others have retinal seizures. The food brooks fewer arguments: it's Italian (octopus and potato salad, prawn risotto) but with a contemporary gloss thanks to the celebrated chef Giorgio Locatelli, who acted as menu consultant.
▶ *For the hotel, see p117.*

★ **David Bann**
56-58 St Mary's Street (556 5888, www.david bann.com). Bus 35 or Nicolson Street–North Bridge buses. **Open** 11am-10pm Mon-Thur, Sun; 11am-10.30pm Fri, Sat. **Main courses** £10. **Credit** AmEx, MC, V. **Map** p333 J7 ❽ Vegetarian
There are Indian vegetarian venues in Edinburgh, and Michelin-starred establishments with meat-free menus. But among modern restaurants with wholly vegetarian menus, David Bann dominates. The approach is flexible: it's fine to have a quick coffee and a light snack, but there are also full menus for lunch or dinner. Try blue cheese and tomato tart to start, then aubergine and chickpea cake with mash and gravy. There's a short, affordable wine list.

Dubh Prais
123b High Street (557 5732, www.dubhprais restaurant.com). Bus 35 or Nicolson Street– North Bridge buses. **Open** 5-10.30pm Tue-Sat. **Main courses** £18. **Credit** AmEx, DC, MC, V. **Map** p333 J7 ❾ Scottish

THE BEST VEGETARIAN EATS

Ann Purna
Gujarati cooking since 1983. *See p153.*

David Bann
Modern European and meat-free. *See left.*

Kalpna
Thaalis, dosas and specials. *See p157.*

This discreet cellar has been offering Scottish cuisine for more than 20 years and locals tend to take it for granted. Pity: chef James McWilliams has a great culinary CV, and his cooking has been praised by the likes of Raymond Blanc. His kitchen delivers well-executed food with robust flavours, as demonstrated by dishes such as seafood soup or saddle of venison. It's a tiny venue, though, so book ahead.

£ **Elephant House**
21 George IV Bridge (220 5355, www.elephant-house.co.uk). Bus 23, 27, 42, 45. **Open** 8am-11pm daily. **Main courses** £6. **Credit** MC, V. **Map** p332 H8 ❿ Café
This popular café draws everyone from skiving students to grannies out with the grandkids. The food menu runs to salads, baguettes and savouries; some of the teas and coffees are first-rate, and there's also a short and affordable wine list. The main room at the back has fantastic views out over the Old Town. Given the associations with JK Rowling (she wrote some early Harry Potter here), muggle memento photography outside the front door comes as no surprise.

£ **Fruitmarket Gallery**
45 Market Street (226 1843, www.fruitmarket. co.uk). Bus 35 or Nicolson Street–North Bridge buses. **Open** 11am-5.30pm Mon-Sat; noon-4.30pm Sun. **Main courses** £7. **Credit** MC, V. **Map** p332 H7 & p336 F3 ⓫ Café
This modern art gallery challenges the viewer to ponder what they've seen long after they've left the exhibits. Just as well, then, that this light, airy café is on the premises, providing some space to think along with some excellent salads, sandwiches and deli platters. Drinks run to a few wines and beers.
▶ *For the gallery itself, see p230.*

★ **La Garrigue**
31 Jeffrey Street (557 3032, www.lagarrigue. co.uk). Bus 35 or Nicolson Street–North Bridge buses. **Open** noon-2.30pm, 6-9.30pm Mon-Sat. **Main courses** £15. **Credit** AmEx, MC, V. **Map** p333 J7 ⓬ French
The designer-rustic decor of Edinburgh's specialist Languedoc restaurant – tables and chairs are by the late, great furniture-maker Tim Stead – are in keeping with chef Jean-Michel Gauffre's philosophy. The

CONSUME

FORTH FLOOR
RESTAURANT · BAR · BRASSERIE

THE FORTH FLOOR RESTAURANT, BAR AND BRASSERIE BOASTS STUNNING VIEWS OVER EDINBURGH CASTLE AND THE RIVER FORTH

Combined with outstanding modern European cuisine,
the Forth Floor is destination dining at its best.

To make a reservation, please call reception on 0131 524 8350
or book online at www.harveynichols.com

HARVEY NICHOLS
ST ANDREW SQUARE EDINBURGH 0131 524 8388
www.harveynichols.com

food is top-quality regional cooking (duck galantine to start, then Castelnaudary cassoulet, perhaps) and there are some predictably good wines. One of Edinburgh's best-loved venues.

Grain Store
30 Victoria Street (225 7635, www.grainstore-restaurant.co.uk). Bus 2, 23, 27, 41, 42. **Open** noon-2pm, 6-11pm Mon-Thur; noon-2pm, 6-11pm Fri; noon-3pm, 6-11pm Sat; noon-3pm, 6-10pm Sun. **Main courses** £20. **Credit** MC, V. **Map** p332 G7 & p336 D4 ⑬ **Modern European**
Looking out from the first-floor level down a curving, cobbled brae, the Grain Store has been a comforting presence for a couple of decades. The cooking is Franco-Scots: oysters with spinach and hollandaise, followed by venison, lamb or fresh fish. It's particularly good for a casual, good-value lunch (£10 for two courses, £13.50 for three) with a bottle of wine. A stone-walled, wooden-floored, candlelit local favourite.

Igg's
15 Jeffrey Street (557 8184, www.iggs.co.uk). Bus 35 or Nicolson Street–North Bridge buses. **Open** noon-2.30pm, 6-10.30pm Mon-Sat. **Main courses** £6. **Credit** AmEx, MC, V. **Map** p333 J7 ⑭ **Spanish**
Iggy Campos's upmarket Iberian restaurant has been charming diners since 1989. Even after all these years, the table linen is still white and the glassware shines. The food relies on good ingredients presented with no small degree of craft: langoustine with garlic butter and vanilla salt, for example, or rib-eye steak with red onion marmalade; drinks stretch to interesting Spanish wines and sherries.
▶ *For the informal Barioja next door, see p135.*

Maison Bleue
36-38 Victoria Street (226 1900, www.maison bleuerestaurant.com). Bus 2, 23, 27, 41, 42. **Open** 5-11pm Mon-Thur; noon-11pm Fri, Sat; noon-10pm Sun. **Main courses** £12. **Credit** MC, V. **Map** p332 G7 & p336 D4 ⑮ **French/ North African**
Maison Bleue is a French restaurant with North African influences that uses Scottish ingredients; and despite the slightly cluttered nature of that description, it works. The menu consists of *bouchées* (one as a starter, two or three as a main), *bouchées doubles* (more substantial dishes) and brochettes (chargrilled skewers), so it's flexible; you could have anything from steak and chips to seafood ceviche, peppered Camembert fondue to lamb tagine.

★ Mother India Café
3-5 Infirmary Street (524 9801, www.mother indiascafe.info). Nicolson Street–North Bridge buses. **Open** noon-10.30pm Mon-Fri; noon-11pm Sat, Sun. **Main courses** £5. **Credit** MC, V. **Map** p333 J8 ⑯ **Indian**

Mother India's empire in Glasgow expanded east in 2008 and set up here, offering an entire menu of starter-sized, tapas-style Indian dishes. The decision proved a very shrewd one: the restaurant has been a great success, and with good reason. The decor is simple and the cooking is impressive, with dishes that range from simple chickpeas and potatoes in yoghurt-based sauce to the livelier likes of king prawns and spiced haddock.

North Bridge Brasserie
Scotsman Hotel, 20 North Bridge (556 5565, www.thescotsmanhotel.com). Nicolson Street– North Bridge buses. **Open** noon-2pm, 5.30-10pm daily. **Main courses** £15. **Credit** AmEx, DC, MC, V. **Map** p332 H7 & p336 F3 ⑰ **Modern European**
As the street-front brasserie of the Scotsman Hotel, formerly the headquarters of the *Scotsman* newspaper (from 1904 to 1999), the fixtures and fittings here are Edwardian-plush with a modern makeover. The seating is split over two levels, and the cooking is aspirational and very 'now' (baby artichoke and truffle salad, then sea bream with basil minestrone for example). It all buzzes along nicely when it's busy.

£ Spoon
15 Blackfriars Street (556 6922). Bus 35 or Nicolson Street–North Bridge buses. **Open** 9am-5pm Mon-Fri; 10am-5pm Sat. **Main courses** £7. **Credit** MC, V. **Map** p333 J7 ⑱ **Café**
This fresh, modern café has a reputation for the quality of its food, cakes and smoothies. Despite its proximity to the Royal Mile, it can be a great escape from the tourist madness a few feet away. The menu features everything from ham and cheese croissant at breakfast to blue cheese, chicory, pear and walnut salad for lunch; you can tackle an antipasti plate later in the day.

Tower
National Museum of Scotland, Chambers Street (225 3003, www.tower-restaurant.com). Bus 23, 27, 42, 45. **Open** noon-4.30pm, 5-11pm daily. **Main courses** £20. **Credit** AmEx, DC, MC, V. **Map** p332 H8 ⑲ **Modern European**
The Tower offers self-conscious chic, good views and a terrace, weather permitting. The menu has an emphasis on fresh seafood and well-sourced meat – grilled sardines to start, perhaps, and Borders beef fillet to follow. The wine list is one of the best in the city, with bottles from £13.95 to £1,000.
▶ *It's atop the National Museum of Scotland; see p76.*

★ Witchery & the Secret Garden
352 Castlehill (225 5613, www.thewitchery.com). Bus 2, 23, 27, 41, 42. **Open** noon-4pm, 5.30-11.30pm daily. **Main courses** £25. **Credit** AmEx, DC, MC, V. **Map** p332 G7 & p336 D4 ⑳ **Modern European**

CONSUME

WHEREVER CRIMES AGAINST HUMANITY ARE PERPETRATED.

Across borders and above politics.
Against the most heinous abuses
and the most dangerous oppressors.
From conduct in wartime
to economic, social, and cultural rights.
Everywhere we go,
we build an unimpeachable case
for change and advocate action
at the highest levels.

HUMAN RIGHTS WATCH TYRANNY HAS A WITNESS

WWW.HRW.ORG

**HUMAN
RIGHTS
WATCH**

One historical venue, two dining rooms and tons of ambience. James Thomson opened the Witchery in 1979, its wood panelling, red leather and candlelit interior lending it a classy reputation; the even more romantic Secret Garden followed in 1989. Neither are cheap and the cooking perhaps hasn't kept up with the Kitchins or Kitchings of this world (*see p150 and p163*). However, the food – mains might include saddle of rabbit or monkfish ossobuco – is still of a good standard and the wine list is a local legend.

▶ *For the hotel side of the operation, see p117.*

Wedgwood

267 Canongate (558 8737, www.wedgwood therestaurant.co.uk). Bus 35. **Open** noon-3pm, 6-11pm Mon-Sat; 12.30-3pm, 6-11pm Sun. **Main courses** £18. **Credit** AmEx, DC, MC, V. **Map** p333 J7 ㉑ **Modern European**

This site has housed a number of restaurants over the years, with Wedgwood having occupied the site since 2007. Small and contemporary, it's somewhere to pop in for some confit duck with artichoke, then pollock on wilted spinach; a haven in tourist country. If you're undecided about what to order, try the Deciding Time pre-starter (champagne plus canapés for £9.75) as you browse the menu.

THE NEW TOWN

Atholl

Howard Hotel, 34 Great King Street (557 3500, www.townhousecompany.com). Bus 13, 23, 27. **Open** 7.30-10am, noon-2pm, 7-9pm Mon-Sat; 8-10.30am, noon-2pm, 7-9pm Sun. **Main courses** £22. **Credit** AmEx, DC, MC, V. **Map** p328 F4 ㉒ **Modern European**

INSIDE TRACK LATE DINING

Have you left it late to eat? The post-theatre supper at the **Witchery** (*see p139*) remains one of the most romantic dining experiences in Edinburgh. It's served daily from 10.30pm until 11.30pm; two courses cost £13.95.

It's always worth keeping an eye on the Town House Collection, one of Edinburgh's boutique hotel companies, to see how it adapts its dining options. Here at the Howard, the Atholl dining room was formerly residents-only, but no longer. Now anyone can work their way through smoked oysters to start, followed by venison with sweet and sour red cabbage, then summer fruit pudding with clotted cream. Tiny, Georgian and elegant, the Atholl is smart and discreet, almost secret, and has so few tables that booking ahead is essential.

▶ *For the hotel, see p121.*

★ Balmoral Hotel

Balmoral Hotel, 1 Princes Street (556 2414, www.thebalmoralhotel.com). Princes Street buses. **Open** 9am-1am daily. *Afternoon tea* 2.30-6pm. **Main courses** *Afternoon tea* £21-£37.50. **Credit** AmEx, DC, MC, V. **Map** p328 & p332 H6, p336 F2 ㉓ **Café**

Afternoon tea at the Balmoral has an honourable pedigree. In both the elegant Palm Court and the Drawing Room, you can order the Balmoral Tea (2.30-6pm, £21), which includes sandwiches, scones, shortbread, cake and tea or coffee, then kick back

CONSUME

Centotre. See p143.

CONSUME

The Dogs.

and feel like an old-school aristocrat. Add a glass of Bollinger, though, and the price can reach £37.50. Coffee and snacks are served in the morning and the early afternoon.

▶ *For the Balmoral's Number One restaurant , see p146; for the hotel itself, see p119. For more on afternoon tea, see p154 Tea for Two.*

Bonham
35 Drumsheugh Gardens (623 9319, www.the bonham.com). Bus 13, 19, 37, 41, 47. **Open** 7am-10pm Mon-Sat; 12.30-3pm, 6.30-10pm Sun. **Main courses** £20. **Credit** AmEx, DC, MC, V. **Map** p331 C7 **㉔ French**
Although it's just a few minutes' walk from the west end of Princes Street, the Bonham feels secluded. The menu in its light, spacious dining room reflects head chef Michel Bouyer's French origins – vichyssoise followed by tuna niçoise – but also offers a modern take on his native cuisine. Set lunches (£13.50 for two courses, £16 for three) are good value, as is the weekend Boozy Snoozy lunch for four (£79.95 for three courses with two bottles of wine).

▶ *For the hotel, see p121.*

Café Marlayne
76 Thistle Street (226 2230, www.cafemarlayne. com). Bus 13, 23, 27, 42 or Princes Street buses. **Open** noon-2pm, 6-10pm Tue-Sat. **Main courses** £13. **Credit** MC, V. **Map** p328 & p332 F6, p336 C1 **㉕ French**
Wicker chairs and wooden tables create a relaxed environment at this small restaurant, tucked away just off Frederick Street, where you can count on finding solid French cuisine based around such raw materials as duck, boudin noir, venison or seabass. Puddings are decent (prune and Armagnac tart for example) and the wine list won't break the bank. **Other locations** 7 Old Fishmarket Close, Old Town (225 3838).

Centotre
103 George Street (225 1550, www.centotre.com). Bus 13, 23, 27, 42 or Princes Street buses. **Open** *Italian Bar* 8am-11pm Mon-Thur; 8am-midnight Fri, Sat; 11am-6pm Sun. *Café* 9am-10pm Mon-Thur; 9am-10.30pm Fri, Sat; 11am-5pm Sun. **Main courses** £12. **Credit** MC, V. **Map** p328 & p332 F6, p336 B1 **㉖ Italian**
In 2004, Victor and Carina Contini, part of the family behind the celebrated Valvona & Crolla delicatessen and café (*see p149 and p198*), decided to set up on their own in this former bank, grandiose but done out with modern fixtures and fittings. The aim is simple: to produce high-quality Italian food, from pizza and pasta to Milanese-style veal and other more involved dishes. At the front of the premises, the Italian Bar caters to coffee fiends, wine-sippers and snackers. *Photo p141.*

▶ *The Continis also run Zanzero in Stockbridge; see p150.*

£ Chez Pierre
18 Eyre Place (556 0006, www.pierrelevicky.com). Bus 8, 23, 36. **Open** noon-10pm Mon-Sat, noon-9pm Sun. **Main courses** £9. **Credit** MC, V. **Map** p328 F3 **㉗ French**
Pierre Levicky's back. The man behind the Pierre Victoire restaurant chain, which bloomed across the UK between 1988 and 1998, returned to Edinburgh in 2008 to open this New Town venue. The decor is simple and modern, the menu informal and French (snacky starters such as ham and bread with olives, mains such as devilled chicken or salade Lyonnaise, inventive desserts). Good value, as you might expect.

Dining Room
Scotch Malt Whisky Society, 28 Queen Street (220 2044, www.smws.com). Bus 4, 8, 10, 11, 12, 15, 15A, 16, 26, 44, 45. **Open** noon-3pm Mon, Tue, Sun; noon-3pm, 5-9pm Wed-Sat. **Main courses** £15. **Credit** AmEx, DC, MC, V. **Map** p328 F5 **㉘ French**
Complementing the Leith original, the Scotch Malt Whisky Society has this second members' room in a restored Georgian townhouse with modern interior design touches. The ground floor holds the Dining Room, open to members and non-members alike; food has a pronounced French flavour (tian of crab to start, poussin to follow, pistachio mousseline to finish). Sadly, after your meal, you can't go upstairs for a whisky unless you join the society.

▶ *For the Leith branch, see p166.*

★ £ The Dogs
110 Hanover Street (220 1208, www.thedogs online.co.uk). Bus 13, 23, 27, 42 or Princes Street buses. **Open** noon-4pm, 5-10pm daily. **Main courses** £11. **Credit** AmEx, MC, V. **Map** p328 G5 **㉙ British**
Dave Ramsden ran two of the most celebrated Edinburgh restaurants of modern times (FitzHenry and Rogue, both now gone) and in 2008 he went down the value route with the Dogs. The decor is simple (huge dog picture excepted), and the food is both good and good value: three courses at dinner (sardines on toast, followed by liver casserole then rice pudding, for instance) weighs in at under £18.

▶ *Ramsden opened an Italian version, Amore Dogs, in 2009, a couple of doors down (no,104, 220 5155, www.amoredogs.co.uk).*

Dusit
49a Thistle Street (220 6846, www.dusit.co.uk). Bus 13, 23, 27, 42 or Princes Street buses. **Open** noon-3pm, 6-10.45pm Mon-Sat; noon-11pm Sun. **Main courses** £13. **Credit** AmEx, MC, V. **Map** p328 & p332 F6, p336 C1 **㉚ Thai**
Over the last decade, Edinburgh experienced a huge increase in the number of Thai restaurants, many of which fell by the wayside. Dusit, around since 2002, has survived, and is one of the best Thai venues in the city. For the most part traditional, it does make

CONSUME

a few concessions to its Scottish location (whisky-marinated chicken dishes, stir-fried venison), and also has decent vegetarian options.

£ Eteaket
41 Frederick Street (226 2982, www.eteaket. co.uk). Bus 13, 23, 27, 42 or Princes Street buses. **Open** 8am-7pm Mon-Sat; 10am-7pm Sun. **Main courses** £4. **Credit** MC, V. **Map** p328 & p339 F6, p336 C1 ③ **Tearoom**

Locals walking along Frederick Street at Christmas 2008 were confronted by a wholly new concept for Edinburgh: a tea boutique. Eteaket is the street-trading face of an online tea vending business where customers can choose from all kinds of quality varieties. These New Town premises act as a lush but polite café where you can have a cake or ciabatta to go with your Gyokuro or Big Red Rooibos.
► *For more, see p154 Tea for Two.*

Fishers in the City
58 Thistle Street (225 5109, www.fishersbistros. co.uk). Bus 13, 23, 27, 42 or Princes Street buses. **Open** noon-10.30pm. **Main courses** £15. **Credit** AmEx, MC, V. **Map** p328 & p332 F6, p336 C1 ② **Seafood**

The owners of the long-established Fishers in Leith ventured into the city centre in 2001 with this smart, modern seafood eaterie. Hardy perennials include excellent creamy fish soup, oysters and a seafood platter; alternative mains might include herring fillet with salad or whole lemon sole with Pernod and caper butter. Slick and snappy.
► *For the Leith original, see p163.*

★ Forth Floor
Harvey Nichols, 30-34 St Andrew Square (524 8350, www.harveynichols.com). Princes Street buses. **Open** *Brasserie* 10am-5.30pm Mon-Sat; 11am-4pm Sun. *Restaurant* noon-3pm Mon; noon-3pm, 6-10pm Tue-Fri; noon-3.30pm, 6-10pm Sat; noon-3.30pm Sun. **Main courses** *Brasserie* £11. *Restaurant* £24. **Credit** AmEx, DC, MC, V. **Map** p328 H5 ③ **Modern European**

Even the anti-fashion brigade admit that Harvey Nicks' fourth floor restaurant and brasserie are pretty good. The views are tremendous, the interior design lends a spacious feel, and the kitchen operates at an elevated standard. The restaurant has a slightly more elaborate menu than the adjacent brasserie, but it's all effectively one space with a discreet partition; there's also a cocktail bar on the same floor. Special events – dinner during the Festival Fireworks, for example – are always popular.
► *For more, see p154 Tea for Two.*

£ Glass & Thompson
2 Dundas Street (557 0909). Bus 13, 23, 27. **Open** 8am-6pm Mon-Sat; 10.30am-4pm Sun. **Main courses** £8. **Credit** AmEx, MC, V. **Map** p328 F5 ③ **Café**

Ever since it opened in the mid 1990s, G&T has been on every list of Edinburgh's best cafés. Given the New Town location and premium prices, it's not the most populist of places, but the food is excellent: the cakes are sublime, while the assorted tarts and platters would put some local restaurants to shame. The decor is modern, with a couple of outside tables for sunny days.

£ Henderson's
94 Hanover Street (225 2131, www.hendersons ofedinburgh.co.uk). Bus 13, 23, 27, 42 or Princes Street buses. **Open** noon-10pm daily. **Main courses** £8. **Credit** MC, V. **Map** p328 & p332 G6, p336 D1 ③ **Vegetarian**

Open since 1963, this basement vegetarian restaurant was a true pioneer back in its day and is still going strong. Food – hearty soups, stews, salads and desserts – is served canteen-style: you queue, you pay, you find a table. The Henderson's empire has expanded over time; there's now a bistro with table service round the corner (25c Thistle Street, 225 2605); a café in the basement of St John's Episcopal Church at the west end of Princes Street (*see p78*), as well as a gallery and shop (*p230*).

Iglu
2b Jamaica Street (476 5333, www.theiglu.com). Bus 24, 29, 36, 42. **Open** *Bar* noon-1am Tue-Sun. *Restaurant* noon-3pm, 6-10pm Tue, Sun. **Main courses** £13. **Credit** MC, V. **Map** p328 F5 ③ **Modern European**

The ground floor bar at Iglu is pleasingly modern; upstairs is a small organic restaurant, added in 2005 by energetic proprietor Charlie Cornelius (who also founded the Wild in Scotland tour business). Dishes might include wild boar burger, duck salad, escalopes of wild venison or chargrilled Aberdeen Angus rump steak; there are vegetarian options too. Popular and innovative.

Kweilin
19-21 Dundas Street (557 1875, www.kweilin. co.uk). Bus 13, 23, 27. **Open** noon-2pm, 5-11pm Tue-Sat; 5-11pm Sun. **Main courses** £14. **Credit** MC, V. **Map** p328 F5 ③ **Chinese**

This Cantonese establishment has been ploughing the same furrow for three decades or so. A change of management in 2008 didn't seem to make a huge amount of difference to the menu (sweet and sours, beef with black bean sauce, lemon chicken), and Kweilin remains a hit with New Town locals and visiting businessmen.

Nargile
73 Hanover Street (225 5755, www.nargile. co.uk). Bus 13, 23, 27, 42 or Princes Street buses. **Open** noon-2pm, 5.30-10pm Mon-Thur; noon-2pm, 5.30-11pm Fri, Sat. **Main courses** £12. **Credit** AmEx, MC, V. **Map** p328 & p332 G6, p336 D1 ③ **Turkish**

CONSUME

Sit-down cuisine from Turkey and the wider Middle East is still rare in Scotland, so praise is due to host Seyhan Azak for carving out this unique and enduring fixture back in 2000. Meze features prominently on the menu, but kebabs, couscous, veggie options and specials such as chargrilled swordfish are also on offer, as are Turkish wines.

★ Number One

Balmoral Hotel, 1 Princes Street (557 6727, www.restaurantnumberone.com). Princes Street buses. **Open** 6-10.30pm daily. **Main courses** £24. **Credit** AmEx, DC, MC, V. **Map** p328 & p332 H6, p336 F2 ❸ **Modern European**

An enviable address, a keen reputation and a very talented executive chef (Jeff Bland) all make this a first-class restaurant, one of only four venues in Edinburgh with a Michelin star in 2009. The spacious room is both contemporary and classic at once; the heady menu might include crab millefeuille with brown crab pannacotta and wasabi mayo, or vegetarian pithivier of squash, chickpeas and spinach with red onion marmalade.

▶ *For the afternoon teas, see p141; for the hotel, see p119.*

Oloroso

33 Castle Street (226 7614, www.oloroso.co.uk). Bus 13, 23, 27, 42 or Princes Street buses. **Open** noon-2pm, 7-10.15pm daily. **Main courses** £13. **Credit** AmEx, MC, V. **Map** p328 & p332 F6, p336 B1 ❹ **Modern European**

Since opening in 2001, this destination bar-restaurant has, under Tony Singh's ever-watchful eye, steadily built a fine reputation for the quality of its cooking. The restaurant leads on its beef, lamb and seafood grills (premium prices) and a modish à la carte menu. The bar is usually buzzing; many people head there simply to drink or snack on high-quality fishcakes, burgers or pasta from the bar menu. There's a roof terrace for the ephemeral Scottish summer.

▶ *For a cheaper Tony Singh meal, try Tony's Table; see right.*

Pompadour

Caledonian Hilton Hotel, Princes Street (222 8888, www.hilton.com). Princes Street buses. **Open** 12.30-2.30pm, 7-10pm Tue-Fri; 7-10pm Sat. **Main courses** £15. **Credit** AmEx, DC, MC, V. **Map** p332 E7 & p336 A2 ❹ **Modern European**

This dainty venue at the Caledonian Hilton has endured for nearly a century, its ice-cream rococo decor endearing it to tourists and couples on romantic breaks (especially the window table with the classic castle view). Since new owners took over, there have been whispers that the dining room may be relocated. In the meantime, though, it's still a great place for posh nosh.

▶ *For the hotel, see p121.*

Stac Polly

29-33 Dublin Street (556 2231, www.stacpolly. co.uk). Bus 10, 11, 12, 23, 27. **Open** noon-2pm, 6-10pm Mon-Fri; 6-11pm Sat, Sun. **Main courses** £19. **Credit** AmEx, DC, MC, V. **Map** p328 G5 ❷ **Scottish**

A small family of restaurants, Stac Polly makes a virtue of its Scottishness, offering the likes of haggis in filo with plum and red wine sauce to start; or calves liver with mustard mash, sherry vinegar and game reduction for a main. This branch was the 1990 original, the others arriving in 1993 and 2007. **Other locations** 8-10 Grindlay Street, South Edinburgh (229 5405); 38 St Mary's Street, Old Town (557 5754).

Tony's Table

58a North Castle Street (226 6743, www.tony stable.com). Bus 13, 23, 27, 42 or Princes Street buses. **Open** 8-10am, noon-2.30pm, 3-5pm, 6.30-10pm Tue-Fri; noon-2.30pm, 3-5pm, 6.30-10pm Sat. **Main courses** £15. **Credit** AmEx, MC, V. **Map** p328 & p332 E6, p336 B1 ❸ **British**

Formerly Cosmo, this building was taken over in 2009 by Tony Singh of Oloroso fame (*see left*). He's retained the elegance of the old interior but added a veneer of contemporary art and a tangible informality. Dishes are both big on flavour and decent value: dinner has a set price of £18 for two courses, £20 for three, and the lunchtime fish pie (£6) is a winner.

Urban Angel

121 Hanover Street (225 6215, www.urban-angel.co.uk). Bus 13, 23, 27, 42 or Princes Street buses. **Open** 9am-10pm Mon-Sat; 10am-5pm Sun. **Main courses** £11. **Credit** MC, V. **Map** p328 G5 ❹ **Modern European**

Urban Angel has a smart country-city crossover look, with wooden floors and white walls. It maintains high ethical standards, using organic, free range and Fair Trade ingredients. In the daytime, it's a café serving brunches, sandwiches and salads, but it comes into its own in the evening as a relaxed and popular restaurant. Try the fantastic tapas to start, followed by lamb meatballs and coriander mash. **Other locations** 1 Forth Street, Calton Hill & Broughton (556 6323).

▶ *For more, see p163 The Breakfast Club.*

Valvona & Crolla Vin Caffè

Multrees Walk, St Andrew Square (557 0088, www.valvonacrolla.com). Princes Street buses. **Open** 9.30am-10.30pm Mon-Sat; noon-5pm Sun. **Main courses** £11. **Credit** AmEx, MC, V. **Map** p328 H5 & p336 F1 ❺ **Italian**

The esteemed Valvona & Crolla company saw the success of its deli and attached Caffè Bar, so decided to open this Vin Caffè in 2004. A modern space with a café on the ground floor and restaurant upstairs, it's bang in the heart of Multrees Walk, Edinburgh's upscale shopping thoroughfare. Inside, the look is

Market Forces

Food from the country, once a week in the city.

You can blame the inexorable, post-war rise of supermarkets, you can blame alienation from the countryside or you can blame the weather. Whatever the precise cause, the tradition of the outdoors food market faded a long, long time ago in most parts of Scotland, including Edinburgh.

Towards the end of the 1990s, however, the local authority felt that reviving some sort of Saturday market could kill two birds with one stone: it would bring fresh, healthy food into the heart of the city on the busiest shopping day of the week, and it would give small Scottish farmers and producers another outlet for their produce. The synergy of economic development and the green notion of 'eating local' was irresistible, so in 2000 the **Edinburgh Farmers' Market** was born. It was monthly at first, but proved so successful that it soon came to be held every week.

The market now takes place every Saturday from 9am to 2pm; you can find it on Castle Terrace, just under the south-west side of the Castle Rock. Around 5,000 shoppers, foodies and random passers-by each week – more on a sunny day in August, fewer on a cold, wet morning in February – stroll past upwards of 50 stalls selling everything from mini-kegs of cask ale to organic chickens, fresh herbs to pots of home-made soup. In its time, the market has even been an award-winner, picking up accolades from *Country Life* magazine in 2006 (Britain's Favourite Farmers' Market) and from the Farmers' Retail & Markets Association in 2007 (Certified Farmers' Market of the Year).

Although there are luxury purchases that would count as a treat for most people, there are also basics: fruit and vegetables, free-range eggs, bread, cheese, meat and fish. You can pick up food to eat on the spot, such as toasties and burgers, as well as items that would make for a fantastic picnic. Anyone seeking an iconic Scottish purchase won't have to look too hard for smoked salmon or venison, but the market also springs some endearing surprises: water buffalo steak from Fife, for example. Whether you want to browse or buy, it's a nice way to pass an hour on a Saturday.

CONSUME

dark wood and leather banquettes, and the food is accomplished; dishes include tapas-style snacks, antipasti, pizza and pasta, plus a full dinner menu.
▶ *For the deli, see p198.*

£ Wok & Wine
57a Frederick Street (225 2382, www.wokand wine.co.uk). Bus 13, 23, 27, 42 or Princes Street buses. **Open** 5.30-11pm daily. **Main courses** £10. **Credit** AmEx, MC, V. **Map** p328 & p332 F6, p336 C1 ㊻ **Chinese**
Some Chinese restaurants in Edinburgh have been trading for decades without changing, but the arrival of Wok & Wine in 2003 changed the nature of the game. The restaurant's modern interior and tapas-like 'wok bites' menu (which sits alongside the main menu, along with some Japanese and Thai dishes) brings the Chinese restaurant experience up to date.

STOCKBRIDGE

£ Bell's Diner
7 St Stephen Street (225 8116). Bus 24, 29, 36, 42. **Open** 6-10.30pm Mon-Fri, Sun; noon-10.30pm Sat. **Main courses** £10. **Credit** MC, V. **Map** p328 E4 ㊼ **American**
Bell's Diner has been pursuing its simple formula on St Stephen Street since 1972, which should tell potential customers something about the effectiveness of the approach. It's a small, simple room that sells fabulous burgers (including vegetarian versions), good steaks and hearty desserts to delight your inner child. No frills, no messing; and they'll even do mini-burgers for kids.

£ Maxi's
33 Raeburn Place (343 3007). Bus 24, 29, 42. **Open** 8.30am-6pm Mon-Wed; 8.30am-10.30pm Thur-Sat; 10am-5pm Sun. **Main courses** £4. **Credit** MC, V. **Map** p327 D4 ㊽ **Café**
A popular café with a few deli bits and bobs for sale, Maxi's has now been around for more than ten years. A light and airy space with blond wood tables, it's modern but accessible, and a good stop for breakfast, coffee, cake, sandwiches or fresh soup.

★ Redwood
33a St Stephen Street (225 8342, www.redwood-restaurant.co.uk). Bus 24, 29, 36, 42. **Open** 6-10pm Wed, Thur; noon-2.30pm, 6-10pm Fri; noon-3pm, 6-10pm Sat; 11.30am-3.30pm Sun. **Main courses** £15. **Credit** AmEx, MC, V. **Map** p328 E4 ㊾ **American**
Opened in late 2008, this basement restaurant offers Californian cuisine with flair and enthusiasm. Simple modern decor complements a kitchen that produces successful dishes such as goat's cheese, blueberry and prosciutto salad, or glazed pork with coriander-chilli salsa. The dinner menu is kept to a sensible size (three choices at each course); there's also a mean Sunday brunch.

21212. *See p150.*

Artisan Roast.

Stockbridge Restaurant

54 St Stephen Street (226 6766, www.the
stockbridgerestaurant.com). Bus 24, 29, 36, 42.
Open 7-9.30pm Tue-Fri; 7-10pm Sat; 7-9.30pm
Sun. **Main courses** £22. **Credit** AmEx, MC, V.
Map p328 E4 ⑩ **Modern European**

One of Edinburgh's leading neighbourhood restaurants, this is a very smart basement venue indeed.
With award-winning chef and proprietor Jason
Gallagher (formerly of the Bonham) still at the helm,
the cooking betrays no lack of ambition: Scottish
ingredients such as venison, salmon or halibut are
treated in a Franco-European style to create complex analogues of meat and two veg. There are also
good vegetarian choices, such as goat cheese and
walnut gateau, and a rather sweet Tot's Taster
menu for children.

Zanzero

15 North West Circus Place (220 0333,
www.zanzero.com). Bus 24, 29, 36, 42.
Open 10am-11pm Mon-Sat; 10am-9pm Sun.
Main courses £14. **Credit** AmEx, MC, V.
Map p328 E5 ⑪ **Italian**

The shocking green decor might not appeal to everyone, but the food here holds wider appeal. The
kitchen takes the best Italian ingredients and transforms them into everything from afternoon cake to
three-course dinners. There are favourites such as
bruschetta, pizza and pasta but also substantial
dishes involving steak or salmon, done in Italian
style. Informal but impressive.

▶ *The owners also run Centotre on George*
Street; see p143.

CALTON HILL & BROUGHTON

★ 21212

3 Royal Terrace (0845 222 1212, www.21212
restaurant.co.uk). Bus 1, 4, 5, 15, 15A, 19, 26,
34, 44, 45. **Open** noon-1.45pm, 6.45-9.30pm Tue-
Sat. **Main courses** £13. **Credit** AmEx, MC, V.
Map p329 K5 ⑫ **Modern European**

Chef Paul Kitching and manager Katie O'Brien made
their names at Juniper in Manchester; when they
moved north in 2009, their new venue instantly
joined Edinburgh's top tier. The name comes from
the dining structure at dinner (choice of two starters,

one interim course, choice of two mains, another interim course, then a choice of two desserts). The decor is lush and the cooking extraordinary: white asparagus with caviar, dried cherries, cauliflower and shitake mushroom makes a starter, with the rest of the meal following in the same vein. *Photo p149.*
▶ *There are four upscale rooms above the restaurant; see p126.*

£ Artisan Roast
57 Broughton Street (07789 840776, www. artisanroast.co.uk). Bus 8, 13 or Playhouse buses. **Open** 8am-7.30pm Mon-Fri; 10am-7.30pm Sat; 10am-6pm Sun. **Main courses** £1. **No credit cards. Map** p328 H4 ❸ **Café**
Artisan Roast supplies quality coffee to cafés and restaurants, but in Broughton Street it has its very own premises. It's a laid-back spot, far from po-faced, dealing cakes and croissants, but the main attraction is the fresh-roast arabica. A sign wryly comments that JK Rowling did not write any Harry Potter on the premises, a claim made by all too many cafés these days.

£ Blue Moon Café
1 Byron Street (556 2788). Bus 8, 13 or Playhouse buses. **Open** 10am-11pm daily. **Main courses** £7. **Credit** MC, V. **Map** p328 H4 ❺❹ **Café**
Gay-run but straight-friendly, the Blue Moon is a popular meet-and-eat place during the week, but the atmosphere steps up a notch to accommodate the pre-club crowd at weekends. The food tends to be simple and filling (burgers, nachos, macaroni cheese), and there are some good bottled lagers and economy wines. If you want to know anything about the city's gay scene, ask the friendly staff.

Circle
1 Brandon Terrace, Canonmills (624 4666, www.thecirclecafe.com). Bus 8, 23, 27, 36. **Open** 8.30am-5pm Mon-Sat; 9am-4.30pm Sun. **Main courses** £8. **Credit** MC, V. **Map** p328 F3 ❺❺ **Café**
Walk past the counter at the entrance and you'll discover a long, thin, stone-walled café offering decent breakfasts, lunches and afternoon teas. Whether you're after eggs Benedict for breakfast, a chocolate brownie and an espresso, or a glass of merlot accompanied by brie and oatcakes, Circle can deliver.

£ Embo
29 Haddington Place, Leith Walk (652 3880, www.embo-deli.com). Bus 7, 10, 12, 14, 16, 22, 25, 49. **Open** 8am-4pm Mon-Fri; 9am-4.30pm Sat. **Main courses** £5. **No credit cards. Map** p329 K4 ❺❻ **Café**
Up a short flight of steps from the pavement on one of Leith Walk's terraces, Embo is a small but well-run establishment. If you're in the area and fancy a high-quality focaccia, salad or wrap, then head here.

You can eat in or take out; either way, the food is very good. The decor is simple but attractive, and the staff are a matey lot.

L'Escargot Bleu
56 Broughton Street (557 1600, www.lescargot bleu.co.uk). Bus 8, 13 or Playhouse buses. **Open** noon-3pm, 5.30-10pm daily. **Main courses** £15. **Credit** AmEx, DC, MC, V. **Map** p328 H4 ❺❼ **French**
With wood floors, white walls, a bistro feel and French waitresses, this 2009 arrival feels surprisingly authentic, especially when customers and staff trip over French-English comprehension. As for the food, snails with parsley risotto, pig's trotter and potato salad, rib eye steak with Roquefort sauce and a classic beef bourguignon all feature. Accompany with some *vin rouge* and you'll be a contented diner.

Haldane's
39a Albany Street (556 8407, www.haldanes restaurant.com). Playhouse buses. **Open** 5.30-9.30pm daily. **Main courses** £16. **Credit** MC, V. **Map** p328 H5 ❺❽ **Modern European**
Sitting along Albany Street, just off Broughton Street, this basement restaurant just on the eastern fringes of the New Town. Chef-owner George Kelso's food is solid and traditional in a classic Franco-Scots style: haggis bon bons to start, herb-crusted Borders lamb as a main. The friendly, informal approach and good cooking make for a happy experience.

★ £ Manna House
22-24 Easter Road (652 2349, www.manna-house-edinburgh.co.uk). Bus 1, 35. **Open** 8am-6pm Mon-Sat. **Main courses** £3. **No credit cards. Map** p329 M4 ❺❾ **Café**
Although the housing market finally cooled down in 2007 and 2008, enormous change was brought to bear in the preceding decade on solid working-class neighbourhoods such as Easter Road. Property prices boomed and a wave of new residents appeared, with new tastes and expectations. Catering to just this market, Manna House is a brilliant pâtisserie with coffee, cake, elaborate tarts and savouries. There are few seats, but you can always take something away.

> ### INSIDE TRACK
> ### COFFEE CONFIDENTIAL
>
> Looking for a decent Americano? The company behind **Artisan Roast** is a coffee supplier and roasts its own beans around three times a week. This guarantees the maximum aromatic hit from the varieties used in its specialist Broughton Street café (*see left*).

CONSUME

£ Renroc

91 Montgomery Street (556 0432, www.renroc. co.uk). Bus 1, 7, 10, 12, 14, 16, 22, 25, 35, 49. **Open** 7.30am-6pm Mon-Wed; 7am-7.30pm Thur, Fri; 9.30am-7.30pm Sat; 10.30am-6pm Sun. **Main courses** £5. **Credit** AmEx, MC, V. **Map** p329 K4 **60** Café

If Manna House (*see p151*) demonstrates the gentrification of the southern end of Easter Road, nearby Renroc goes one better, offering not only an extensive café menu but also a complementary health studio in its basement. Sample soups, sandwiches, panini and other specials; ideally at one of the tables outside, a suntrap on the right day.

▶ *The Renroc people also run the Earl of Marchmont pub in South Edinburgh; see p176.*

Rivage

126-130 Easter Road (661 6888). Bus 1, 35. **Open** noon-2pm, 5.30-11pm Mon-Sat; 12.30-2.30pm, 5.30-11pm Sun. **Main courses** £7. **Credit** AmEx, MC, V. **Map** p329 M4 **61** Indian

Done out with chunky decor and bare brickwork, the family-run Rivage has won over the Easter Road locals. It goes beyond the basics to provide some elaborate starters and inventive mains (such as whole baby aubergines in a peanut-yoghurt sauce), while substantial side dishes such as tarka daal weigh in at under £3. A great neighbourhood venue.

£ Tailend Restaurant & Fish Bar

14-15 Albert Place, Leith Walk (555 3577, www.tailendrestaurant.com). Bus 1, 7, 10, 12, 14, 16, 22, 25, 35, 49. **Open** 11.30am-10pm daily. **Main courses** £9. **Credit** AmEx, MC, V. **Map** p329 K3 **62** Fish & chips

Tailend is a simple fish-and-chipper with an adjacent sit-down space. Unlike some of the more downmarket examples of the genre, it uses good fish and offers a decent choice: langoustine, scallops and lemon sole sit alongside the expected battered haddock, chips (fantastic) and mushy peas. Some say this is now the best fish and chip shop in the city.

★ Valvona & Crolla Caffè Bar

19 Elm Row, Leith Walk (556 6066, www. valvonacrolla.com). Bus 7, 10, 12, 14, 16, 22, 25, 49. **Open** 8am-6pm Mon-Sat; 10.30am-4.30pm Sun. **Main courses** £10. **Credit** AmEx, MC, V. **Map** p329 J4 **63** Italian

Still the most celebrated delicatessen in Scotland, Valvona & Crolla also encompasses this simple and tasteful space at the rear of the shop, a converted stables. The food includes breakfast, toasted panini and more substantial dishes, drawing on the top-quality raw materials shipped direct from Italian markets. The deli also has an award-winning Italian wine section – pick any bottle to drink in the Caffè Bar with your meal and you'll pay £6 corkage.

▶ *For the deli, see p198. And for more, see p163 The Breakfast Club.*

SOUTH EDINBURGH

★ Abstract

33-35 Castle Terrace (229 1222, www.abstract restaurant.com). Bus 1, 2, 10, 11, 15, 15A, 16, 23, 24, 27, 34, 35, 45. **Open** noon-2pm, 6-10pm Tue-Sat. **Main courses** £22. **Credit** MC, V. **Map** p332 E8 & p336 A3 **64** Modern European

A key part of the Edinburgh restaurant scene, Abstract puts the fun back into fine dining with inventive dishes, ambitious decor and winning service. The two-course lunch menu, quite a bargain, might bring the likes of pickled herring with curry mayonnaise, followed by hake with cavalo nero, smoked potato and mushrooms. Modern European cooking with élan.

Ann Purna

45 St Patrick Square (662 1807). Nicolson Street–North Bridge buses. **Open** noon-2pm, 5.30-11pm Mon-Fri; 5.30-11pm Sat. **Main courses** £13. **Credit** MC, V. **Map** p333 J9 **65** Indian

The Pandyas, who opened this restaurant back in the '80s, have now retired, but their nephew remains in charge of this family-run gem, which offers vegetarian cooking on a Gujarati-style menu. It's close to assorted University of Edinburgh buildings and is popular with staff and students, as well as long-standing regulars who have been eating here since Frankie Goes to Hollywood topped the singles chart.

Apartment

7-13 Barclay Place (228 6456). Bus 11, 15, 15A, 16, 23, 45. **Open** 5.30-11pm Mon-Fri; noon-11pm Sat, Sun. **Main courses** £11. **Credit** MC, V. **Map** p332 E10 **66** Modern European

Kicking around for more than a decade now, the Apartment was a trend-setter when it opened, offering a different menu structure to the standard starter/main/dessert. The food still features those mould-breaking Chunky Healthy Lines, chargrilled chunks on skewers (monkfish and pepper, chicken and prawn) served with signature coleslaw-stuffed pitta bread. But you can also have assorted fish dishes, lamb shank or steak instead. For South Edinburghers, still a hip joint.

Other locations Outsider, 15-16 George IV Bridge, Old Town (226 3131).

★ Atrium

10 Cambridge Street (228 8882, www.atrium restaurant.co.uk). Bus 1, 2, 10, 11, 15, 15A, 16, 23, 24, 27, 34, 35, 45. **Open** noon-2pm, 6-10pm Mon-Fri; 6-10pm Sat. **Main courses** £20. **Credit** AmEx, MC, V. **Map** p332 E8 & p336 A3 **67** Modern European

Innovative, interesting and influential for nearly 20 years, Andrew Radford's flagship changed the rules of Edinburgh fine dining when it opened back in 1993. A revamp in 2007 didn't really change the overall look, and the kitchen still reaches for good

CONSUME

Tea for Two

Enjoy an Edinburgh afternoon in unusually civilised fashion.

Afternoon tea is thought to have been invented in 1841 by Anna Maria, the seventh Duchess of Bedford, as a snack to tide her over between lunch and dinner. Nearly two centuries on, several Edinburgh venues carry on the tradition of serving dainty sandwiches, home-made scones and the fabled tiered cake stand.

A number of hotels offer cut-above tea services. At the **Balmoral** (*see p119 and p141*), afternoon tea is served to the sound of a harpist in the Palm Court and comes with a choice of twenty loose leaf teas or, with a supplement, a glass of Bollinger. There's more opulence at the **Prestonfield** (*see p127*), a 1687 Jacobean manor house that's now a hotel and restaurant. In summer, afternoon tea is served in the gothic tea house, on the croquet lawns surrounded by fragrant rose bushes or overlooking the gardens; in winter, you can take it by a roaring log fire. And there's also a splendid high tea served daily at the **Howard** (*see p121*), a handsome hotel in the New Town.

Transformed from a former office, the self-styled 'tea boutique' **Eteaket** (*see p145*) offers a relaxing retreat from the bustling city centre. Like the afternoon tea it serves, the decor is traditional but brought slyly up to date. There's more modernity at South Edinburgh favourite **Loopy Lorna's** (*see p157*) in the shape of Loopy's Amazing Traditional Afternoon Tea, served amid pink, black and silver paisley-patterned decor.

Afternoon tea at **Harvey Nichols** (*see p145*) comes with fine views from the fourth-floor picture windows. The tea concept has evolved a little here to include with ham and pickle open sandwiches, lemon chicken wraps, smoked salmon and brioche or leek and cheddar quiche, as well as the traditional standbys.

Finally, Lovejoy would have loved the blend of tea and antiques at – wait for it – **Anteaques** (*see p202*), where fine loose teas are a passion. You can 'try before you buy' a Georgian silver tea set from the collection of antique accoutrements.

CONSUME

Howard.

local ingredients to turn into dishes such as West Coast scallops with home-cured bacon and tomatoes, or North Sea halibut with Shetland mussels and herb cream; there's also an acclaimed wine choice.

▶ *The Atrium shares a building with both Blue Bar-Café (see below) and the Traverse (see p254).*

Blonde
75 St Leonard's Street (668 2917, www.blonde restaurant.com). Nicolson Street–North Bridge buses. **Open** 6-10pm Mon; noon-2.30pm, 6-10pm Tue-Sun. **Main courses** £11. **Credit** MC, V. **Map** p333 K9 ❻❾ **Modern European**
This modern neighbourhood restaurant, named for its blond-wood interior, has become a real asset to the area. The menu takes an eclectic approach: dishes such as chicken terrine with chorizo and green peppercorns as a starter, grilled hake with couscous and sorrel cream as a main, perhaps. The wine list is brief and affordable, and the waitresses are as sharp as tacks.

Blue Bar-Café
10 Cambridge Street (221 1222, www.bluebar cafe.com). Bus 1, 2, 10, 11, 15, 15A, 16, 23, 24, 27, 34, 35, 45. **Open** noon-2.30pm, 5.30-11pm Mon-Sat. **Main courses** £12. **Credit** AmEx, MC, V. **Map** p332 E8 & p336 A3 ❻❾ **Modern European**
Upstairs from the Atrium and also run by Andrew Radford, Blue was a real smash when it opened in 1997. It's moved in and out of vogue over the years, but it's still hugely popular. On a good day, it can pull off some of the best café-bar food in town: pork belly with an apple and black pudding tart tatin for example. The front of the premises has a large, open dining space; there's a bar area to the rear.

▶ *For Atrium, see p153.*

Bonsai
46 West Richmond Street (668 3847, www. bonsaibarbistro.co.uk). Nicolson Street–North Bridge buses. **Open** noon-10pm Mon-Fri; noon-10.30pm Sat, Sun. **Main courses** £6. **Credit** MC, V. **Map** p333 K8 ❼❶ **Japanese**
The team in this small establishment produces a range of dishes, a good proportion designed not to spook the local palate: cheese *gyoze* (cheddar in pastry with soy-chilli dip), prawn tempura, vegetable tempura, beef teriyaki or California *gaijin-zushi* (featuring avocado and crabstick). If you want to go with the raw fish, however, Bonsai serves sashimi, maki-sushi and nigiri-sushi, making it feel more like Japan rather than Japan-catering-for-Scotland.

Calistoga Southside
91-93 St Leonard's Street (668 4207, www. calistoga.co.uk). Nicolson Street–North Bridge buses. **Open** 5-10pm Mon-Fri; noon-2.30pm, 5-10pm Sat, Sun. **Main courses** £14. **Credit** AmEx, MC, V. **Map** p333 K9 ❼❶ **American**

Critics say that Californian eclecticism sometimes equates with culinary incoherence, but fans of Calistoga just enjoy the informal bistro style and the dishes that range from avocado and grapefruit salad to rib eye steak with sweet chilli sauce. Calistoga also scores on its specialist Californian wine list, which offers bottles you'll find nowhere else in the country; the associated wine shop, Sideways, is next door.
Other locations Calistoga Central, 70 Rose Street Lane North, New Town (225 1233).

£ Engine Shed
19 St Leonard's Lane (662 0040, www.engine shed.org.uk). Nicolson Street–North Bridge buses. **Open** 10am-3.30pm Mon-Sat. **Main courses** £5. **No credit cards**. **Map** p333 L9 ❼❷ **Café**
Based in a former train maintenance depot, this vegetarian/vegan wholefood café may have limited opening hours, but it's a good pit-stop if you've been hiking around Arthur's Seat. Mains such as cashew nut pie and spinach bake are wholesome and hearty, the bread is excellent and there is a Saturday brunch menu, but what really sets this venture apart is its training role for adults with learning difficulties, who work behind the counter. Worth supporting.

£ Falko Konditorei
185 Bruntsfield Place (656 0763, www.falko. co.uk). Bus 11, 15, 15A, 16, 27, 23, 45. **Open** 8.30am-6.30pm Mon; 8.45am-6.30pm Wed-Fri; 9am-6pm Sat; 10.30am-6pm Sun. **Main courses** £5. **Credit** MC, V. **Café**
This German bakery and café is just the place to sit down with a generous lump of Black Forest gateau and a strong coffee to cut through the sweetness. The cakes are made fresh every day; if you turn up in the late afternoon, the best ones might be gone. Also on offer: great bread, creative sandwiches, good soups and decent teas and coffees.

Hotel du Vin Bistro
11 Bristo Place (247 4900, www.hotelduvin.com). Bus 2, 41, 42. **Open** 7-10am, noon-2.30pm, 3-5pm, 5.30-10.30pm Mon-Fri; 8-11am, noon-2.30pm, 3-5pm, 5.30-10.30pm Sat; 8-11am, 12.30-5pm, 5.30-10.30pm Sun. **Main courses** £16. **Credit** AmEx, DC, MC, V. **Map** p332 H8 ❼❸ **Modern European**
This is a typical Hotel du Vin-style restaurant, with a retro-French feel, but none the worse for its predictability; indeed, it's been very popular with locals since the hotel landed in Edinburgh at the end of 2008. The bistro offers a bargain one-dish lunch with wine and coffee (£10.95) or dinner choices such as chilled pea and broad bean soup with parmesan ice-cream to start, beef and snail pie to follow.

▶ *For the hotel, see p117.*

Jasmine
32 Grindlay Street (229 5757). Bus 1, 2, 10, 11, 15, 15A, 16, 23, 24, 27, 34, 35, 45. **Open** noon-2pm, 5-11.30pm Mon-Thur; 1-2pm, 5pm-

CONSUME

12.30am Fri; 1pm-12.30am Sat; 1-11.30pm Sun.
Main courses £9. **Credit** AmEx, MC, V. **Map**
p332 E8 & p336 A4 **74** **Chinese**
Jasmine has been around at this address since the
mid 1990s, although the premises have been regularly spruced up and refurbished along the way.
Local workers are lured in with a bargain lunch
menu; regulars rave about the almond chicken with
orange sauce. It's worth keeping an eye out for the
regular seafood specials.

Kalpna
2-3 St Patrick Square (667 9890, www.kalpna
restaurant.com). Nicolson Street–North Bridge
buses. **Open** noon-2.30pm, 5.30-10pm Mon-Sat.
Main courses £12. **Credit** MC, V. **Map** p333
K9 **75** **Indian**
A purveyor of Indian vegetarian food for nearly three
decades, Kalpna has stayed much the same over the
years, although the interior and menu got an overhaul in 2008. The lunchtime buffet is cheap (£7), but
you need to catch the dishes when they're fresh. At
dinner, try a thaali, a dosa or *dam aloo kashmeri*, the
restaurant's signature dish: potato 'barrels' filled
with vegetables, nuts and paneer in a complex sauce.

£ Khushi's Diner
32b West Nicolson Street (667 4871, www.
khushisdiner.com). Nicolson Street–North Bridge
buses. **Open** noon-11pm Mon-Sat; 5-10pm Sun.
Main courses £8. **Credit** AmEx, MC, V.
Map p333 J9 **76** **Indian**
Edinburgh's original Indian restaurant (1947)
moved premises on several occasions before settling
into a grand old building on Victoria Street in the
Old Town in 2006. Just before Christmas 2008, the
place burned down, but Khushi's was soon reborn
on West Nicolson Street. With a fair number of main
courses pegged at £7.95 or under, it's not a bank-
breaker. There's no drinks licence, but you can bring
your own alcohol.

£ Kwok
44 Ratcliffe Terrace (668 1818). Bus 3, 3A, 7, 8,
29, 31, 37, 49. **Open** noon-2pm, 5pm-midnight
Tue-Thur; 5pm-1am Fri, Sat; 5-11.30pm Sun.
Main courses £7. **Credit** MC, V. **Chinese**
This great little Chinese eaterie gets less recognition
than it should because of its location south of the
Meadows, in lands where visitors generally fail to
tread. Dark red decor and a backdrop of jazz and
lounge music set the scene, a brasserie-like atmosphere that's quite unlike that of any other Chinese
establishment in the city. The food is of an impressive quality and freshness.

★ £ Loopy Lorna's
370-372 Morningside Road (447 9217, www.
loopylornas.com). Bus 11, 15, 15A, 16, 27, 23,
45. **Open** 9am-6pm daily. **Main courses** £7.
Credit AmEx, MC, V. **Tearoom**

With its smart pink-and-black decor and waitresses
in pinnies, this is every inch a modern take on the
traditional tearoom. The teas and coffees are both
great quality, the cakes are sublime, and the breakfasts (scrambled eggs with hot-smoked salmon) are
joined on the menu by salads, sandwiches, soups
and main meals. Lorna's is also one of the most child-
friendly venues in the city.
▶ *For more, see p154 Tea for Two.*

£ S Luca
16 Morningside Road (446 0233, www.s-luca.
co.uk). Bus 11, 15, 15A, 16, 41. **Open** 9am-
10pm daily. **Main courses** £3. **Credit** MC, V.
Café
S Luca is famed for the ice-cream served at its legendary Musselburgh café. This branch – located
near Holy Corner, so named because it has more
churches per square foot than Vatican City – also
offers a range of sandwiches and panini melts as
well as pizza. Still, who needs them when there are
nut sundaes and Caribbean longboats to be scoffed?
Other locations 28-32 High Street,
Musselburgh (665 2237).

New Bell
233 Causewayside (668 2868, www.thenewbell.
com). Bus 42. **Open** 5.30-9pm Mon-Thur; noon-
2pm, 5.30-9pm Fri, Sat; 12.30-2pm, 5.30-9pm
Sun. **Main courses** £15. **Credit** MC, V.
Modern European
Few visitors find a reason to head into this slightly
suburban part of town, but the New Bell might be
worth the trip. Owned by Richard and Michelle
Heller, the restaurant occupies the neatly, traditionally decorated first floor of a 17th-century building,
above a pub called, yes, the Old Bell. The menu
offers bistro-style cooking with mains such as duck
breast with barley, black pudding and anise jus.

£ Peter's Yard
27 Simpson Loan, off Middle Meadow Walk
(228 5876, www.petersyard.com). Bus 42.
Open 7am-7pm Mon-Fri; 9am-7pm Sat, Sun.
Main courses £5. **Credit** MC, V. **Map** p332
H9 **77** **Café**
Part of the Quartermile development that's brought
hundreds of new luxury apartments to the site of the
former Royal Infirmary, Peter's Yard appeared at
the end of 2007. It's a bright, airy café with a
Swedish slant; its 'breakfast basket' includes crisp-
bread and rye, for instance. Sandwiches can be
excellent, but they're not cheap. A handy stop for a
coffee near the Meadows.

★ Rhubarb
Prestonfield, Priestfield Road (225 7800, www.
rhubarb-restaurant.com). Bus 2, 14, 30. **Open**
noon-2pm, 3-6pm, 6.30-10pm Mon-Fri; noon-2pm,
3-11pm Sat, Sun. **Main courses** £26. **Credit**
AmEx, DC, MC, V. **Modern European**

CONSUME

James Thomson, the brains behind the Witchery and the Tower, took over the old Prestonfield House Hotel, gave it a sumptuous makeover and reopened it as Prestonfield in 2003. Rhubarb, its restaurant, offers the likes of squat lobster minestrone to start, guinea fowl with truffled sweetcorn as a main. The set lunch doubles as a pre-theatre menu and is the economical way to experience at this opulent venue.
▶ For more, see p154 Tea for Two. For the hotel, see p127.

Sweet Melinda's

11 Roseneath Street (229 7953, www.sweet melindas.co.uk). Bus 24, 41. **Open** 6-10pm Mon; noon-2pm, 6-10pm Tue-Sat. **Set meal** £22. **Credit** MC, V. **Map** p332 H11 ⑦ Seafood
The compact Sweet Melinda's brightens the culinary desert of Marchmont. With an acclaimed fishmonger on the same street, it's no surprise that seafood is the order of the day, with dishes such as grilled trout with herb crostini to start and roast cod with squid and chorizo as a main. The kind of neighbourhood spot that diners leave with a smile on their faces.

Thai Lemongrass

40-41 Bruntsfield Place (229 2225, www.thai lemongrass.net). Bus 11, 15, 15A, 16, 23, 45. **Open** noon-2.30pm, 5-11.30pm Mon-Thur; noon-11.30pm Fri, Sat; 1-11.30pm Sun. **Main courses** £10. **Credit** AmEx, MC, V. **Map** p332 E10 ⑦ Thai
When it opened in 2002, Thai Lemongrass was acclaimed as one of the best Thai eateries in the city. It's proved enduringly popular, which explains why the winning formula hasn't changed. Staff in traditional costume serve fresh dishes that command attention with their punchy flavours. The main menu is extensive, and includes vegetarian options. Try the intense coconut ice-cream to finish.

Toast

146 Marchmont Road (446 9873, www.toast edinburgh.co.uk). Bus 5, 24, 41. **Open** 10am-2.30pm, 6.30-9.30pm Mon-Fri; 10am-3pm, 6.30-9.30pm Sat; 10am-3pm Sun. **Main courses** £12. **Credit** MC, V. Café
With art on the walls and lots of blond wood, Toast looks smart and contemporary. The menu changes as the day progresses, kicking off with some excellent breakfast choices (French toast with bacon and maple syrup), moving through to sandwiches, salads and light meals, then becoming bistro-like in the evenings. It's also an ideal place to relax and cast an eye over the Sunday papers.
▶ For more, see p163 The Breakfast Club.

£ Two Thin Laddies

103 High Riggs (229 0653). Bus 11, 15, 15A, 16, 23, 45. **Open** 8am-6pm Mon-Fri; 9am-5pm Sat, Sun. **Main courses** £6. **No credit cards.** Map p332 F9 ⑧ Café

This friendly café in the heart of Tollcross opens early for those seeking breakfast en route to work. It's bright and wholesome, with a menu featuring bakes, salads, and more, plus the enduring local legend that is the Two Thin Laddies' macaroni cheese.

£ Karen Wong's

107-109 St Leonard's Street (662 0777, www. karenwongchineserestaurant.co.uk). Nicolson Street–North Bridge buses. **Open** 4-11pm Mon, Wed-Sun. **Main courses** £9. **Credit** AmEx, MC, V. **Map** p333 K9 ⑧ Chinese
From the outside, Karen Wong's looks like just another anonymous Chinese restaurant, and the familiar pre-theatre menu choices (barbecue spare ribs followed by spicy kung po chicken, £10.45 for two courses) only serve to confirm that view. But the conviviality of the hostess helps things no end, and the cooking is altogether pretty decent.

£ Zulu Lounge

366 Morningside Road (466 8337, www. thezululounge.com). Bus 11, 15, 15A, 16, 27, 23, 45. **Open** 7.30am-6pm Mon-Fri; 8am-5pm Sat, Sun. **Main courses** £4. **No credit cards.** Café
Quietly working away at the southern end of Morningside Road, this tiny café can be a squeeze but it does have a stand-out feature: if you want a South African breakfast (*boerewors* in tomato sauce with fried eggs) or a toastie featuring biltong, mozzarella and avocado, you'll find it here.

WEST EDINBURGH

La Bruschetta

13 Clifton Terrace (467 7464, www.labruschetta. co.uk). Bus 2, 3, 3A, 4, 12, 25, 26, 31, 33, 38, 44, 44A. **Open** noon-2pm, 6-10.30pm Mon-Sat. **Main courses** £14. **Credit** MC, V. **Map** p331 C8 ⑧ Italian
There's nothing elaborate about La Bruschetta: it's just a fabulous little Italian restaurant. The interior is neat and modern, but the focus is very much on owner Giovanni Cariello's food, familiar Italian dishes such as bruschetta Romana, lasagne and *agnello al carciofini*. No surprises, then, but it is a joy to see this kind of thing done with such skill.

£ Chop Chop

248 Morrison Street (221 1155). Bus 2, 22, 30. **Open** noon-2pm, 5.30-10.30pm Tue-Fri; 5-11pm Sat, Sun. **Main courses** £7. **Credit** AmEx, MC, V. **Map** p331 C8 ⑧ Chinese
This sparse room certainly isn't a romantic venue – or, indeed, an eatery where you might linger at all – but it has secret weapons in the form of an amazing bargain lunch (£5.50) and excellent boiled or fried dumplings (*guo tie* and *jiao zi*). It's a rewarding pit-stop on a night out and perfect for larger groups who're happy to share.

CONSUME

A Learning Process

Teach yourself how to cook at one of Edinburgh's food schools.

Edinburgh School of Food & Wine.

CONSUME

Cookery shows are among the most popular programmes on television, and the general level of interest in cooking across Scotland and the rest of the UK has never been higher. A little learning, though, sometimes proves a dangerous thing. Thanks in part to such shows, people are now keener to learn even more about food than the TV shows are able to teach, which is why it's no real surprise that Edinburgh supports several cookery schools.

The daddy is the **Edinburgh School of Food & Wine** (Coach House, Newliston, West Edinburgh, 333 5001, www.esfw. com). Established in 1987 and based at an old coach house in the grounds of a handsome 18th-century mansion, it's a serious venue that offers a full-time, six-month diploma for budding professionals. However, it also does a roaring trade in sessions for hobby cooks and enthusiasts. Class sizes are usually limited to 16; one-day courses focus on fish, game, Indian, Mediterranean or Thai cuisine and more. There are also food and wine evenings, and the one-day gourmet course for men is often booked up months in advance.

In a completely different vein, **Krua Thai** (19 Liberton Brae, South Edinburgh, 664 3036, www.kruathai.co.uk) opened for business in 1997. As its name suggests, it's a specialist Thai establishment with almost bespoke tuition. You can pretty much arrange your day to suit; you might spend a morning on fruit carving and food presentation and an afternoon on Thai cookery, preparing four dishes to take away. If it's just yourself and a friend attending, that's fine with Krua Thai.

Martin Wishart had been running his Michelin-starred restaurant in Leith for eight years before he branched out with the **Cook School by Martin Wishart** (14 Bonnington Road, Leith, 555 6655, www.cookschool.co.uk), which runs day and evening classes, lessons for children, organised tours of local food suppliers and wine tastings. The Practical Modern Cookery day is fairly typical, covering ingredients and how to source them before dealing with the hands-on preparation of a three-course meal. There are only eight work stations and thus numbers are limited, which means lots of interaction with the staff.

Prices for classes vary widely across the schools, but you can expect to pay £35-£55 for an evening class or £120-£325 for a day course. For more details and to book, which is essential, see the websites.

£ First Coast
99-101 Dalry Road (313 4404, www.first-coast.co.uk). Bus 2, 3, 3A, 4, 25, 33, 44, 44A. **Open** noon-2pm, 5-10.30pm Mon-Sat. **Main courses** £10. **Credit** AmEx, MC, V. **Map** p331 B9 ❷❹ **Modern European**

The MacRae brothers, from the Isle of Skye, opened this bistro on unfashionable Dalry Road in 2003, and it's been an oasis of decent cooking ever since. The food, like the general atmosphere, is approachable and eclectic (spinach and egg dahl to start, then roast chicken with Puy lentils, say). Affordable wines add to the appeal.

Roti
73 Morrison Street (221 9998, www.roti.uk.com). Bus 2, 22, 30. **Open** noon-2.30pm, 6-10.30pm Mon-Sat; 6-10.30pm Sun. **Main courses** £13. **Credit** AmEx, MC, V. **Map** p331 D8 ❸❺ **Indian**

Launched in 2005 at Rose Street Lane North, Roti has always been far more than your run-of-the-mill Indian restaurant. Its tasting menu, for example, features dishes such as mango and chestnut salad, or roast duck marinated in coriander, black pepper and fenugreek. Success saw a move to bigger premises in Morrison Street in 2007, a year before original owner Tony Singh handed the reins to his cousin, Glaswegian restaurateur Ryan Singh. Debate continues as to whether West Coast populism has since overtaken East Coast finesse.

Santini
Sheraton Grand, 8 Conference Square, Western Approach Road (221 7788, www.sheraton edinburgh.co.uk). Bus 2, 3, 3A, 4, 25, 33, 44, 44A. **Open** noon-2.30pm, 6.30-10.30pm Mon-Fri; 6.30-10.30pm Sat. **Main courses** £8. **Credit** AmEx, DC, MC, V. **Map** p331 D8 ❸❻ **Italian**

On the ground floor of One Spa behind the Sheraton Grand Hotel, and with a look that's characterised by clean lines and modern decor, Santini is a sister venue to the original on London's Ebury Street. The menu features familiar starters, pizza and pasta, plus *secondi* based around sirloin, veal and swordfish. Set lunch and evening menus are a little more economical, but look out for the service charge.

▶ *For the hotel, see p130.*

Shapes
Bankhead Avenue, Sighthill (453 3222, www.shapesrestaurant.co.uk). Bus 3, 3A, 20, 25, 32, 34, 35. **Open** 9am-4pm Mon-Fri; 9am-2pm, 7-9.30pm Sat. **Main courses** £18. **Credit** MC, V. **Modern European**

Part of an auction house and furniture business, Shapes has the most unlikely restaurant address in the city, on an unlovely, far-flung industrial estate. It looks like a big green shed, but the interior decor is an eclectic riot of expensive fixtures and fittings, stopping just short of overkill. There's morning coffee and afternoon tea but the main features are lunch and, on Saturdays only, dinner, with the likes of potted crab followed by chargrilled Aberdeen Angus sirloin, then sticky toffee pudding. Worth the schlep.

Sushiya
19 Dalry Road (313 3222). Bus 2, 3, 3A, 4, 25, 33, 44, 44A. **Open** noon-2pm, 5-10pm Mon-Thur, Sun; noon-2pm, 5-10.30pm Fri; noon-2.30pm, 5-10.30pm Sat. **Main courses** £8. **Credit** MC, V. **Map** p331 C9 ❸❼ **Japanese.**

It's not the most relaxing room, it's small and fills up pretty quickly, and it's not on Edinburgh's loveliest street (Dalry Road leads from Haymarket Station towards the less agreeable western suburbs), but Sushiya is just a great spot for some quick, fresh sushi. Those antipathetic to raw fish may prefer the tempura or noodle dishes instead; the drinks list includes saké.

LEITH & THE COAST

Bonoful
13-17 Brighton Place, Portobello (669 8000, www.bonoful.com). Bus 12, 15, 15A, 26, 42, 49. **Open** noon-2pm, 5-11.30pm daily. **Main courses** £10. **Credit** MC, V. **Indian**

Portobello is not known for its restaurants, perhaps because the grand villas in the neighbourhood are mostly occupied by families who spend their money on the mortgage and the kids. As such, the endurance of the slick, modern Bonoful is worthy of note. The menu isn't innovative (bhuna, korma, rogan josh, some specials) but the food's decent. A good option after a beachside walk.

Britannia Spice
150 Commercial Street, Leith (555 2255, www.britanniaspice.co.uk). Bus 1, 10, 16, 22, 35, 36. **Open** noon-2pm, 5-11.45pm Mon-Sat; 5-11.45pm Sun. **Main courses** £13. **Credit** AmEx, DC, MC, V. **Map** p326 W2 ❸❽ **Indian**

This nautical-themed venue tries to cover the whole subcontinent rather than just India, with some Thai dishes thrown in for good measure. The menu has all the usual suspects but plenty more besides: you can have Himalayan trout or lamb jalfrezi, tandoori chicken or Bangladeshi-style prawns. A popular and populist feature of the new Leith.

THE BEST LOCAL CHEFS

Tom Kitchin
In the **Kitchin** since 2006. *See p163.*

Paul Kitching
Launched **21212** in 2009. *See p150.*

Martin Wishart
At his Leith venue since 1999. *See p166.*

CONSUME

CONSUME

E:S:I.

Café Fish

*60 Henderson Street, Leith (538 6131, http://cafe
fish.net). Bus 1, 10, 16, 22, 35, 36.* **Open** noon-
8pm Tue-Sat, 11am-5pm Sun. **Set meal** £20.
Credit AmEx, MC, V. **Map** p326 Y3 ❸❾ **Seafood**
A 2009 arrival in a downmarket block of Leith that
is heading upmarket (thanks to this place and the
nearby Plumed Horse, for which *see p166*), Café Fish
looks the part. Lunch or dinner might bring smoked
haddock with rarebit topping to start, followed by
roast spiced cod with olive oil mash as a main. An
accessible and informal 21st-century seafood spot.

£ Café Truva

*77 The Shore, Leith (554 5502, www.cafetruva.
com). Bus 1, 10, 16, 22, 35, 36.* **Open** 9am-
6.30pm daily. **Main courses** £6. **Credit** MC, V.
Map p326 Y3 ❸⓿ **Café**
This Turkish delight of a café, located down by the
Water of Leith, serves the kind of light meals and
sweets that may remind you of holiday excursions
to that end of the Mediterranean: not only moussaka
and meze, but also breakfasts, filo pastry savouries
and teeth-melting baklava. Try to nab one of the outside seats on a sunny day.
Other location 251-253 Canongate, Old Town
(556 9524).

£ Cairn Café at Tiso Edinburgh Outdoor Experience

*41 Commercial Street, Leith (555 2211, www.
thecairncafe.co.uk). Bus 1, 10, 16, 22, 35, 36.*
Open 9am-5pm daily. **Main courses** £5.
Credit MC, V. **Map** p326 X2 ❸❶ **Café**

This handy addition at the back of Scotland's premier outdoors activity store offers breakfast rolls,
some serious panini, quiches, soups and salads, plus
pies and baked potatoes. There's nothing compli-
cated or surprising; it's just a dependable café serving decent food in bright, breezy surroundings.
▶ *For Tiso itself, see p204.*

Daniel's

*88 Commercial Street, Leith (553 5933, www.
daniels-bistro.co.uk). Bus 1, 10, 16, 22, 35, 36.*
Open 10am-10pm daily. **Main courses** £12.
Credit AmEx, MC, V. **Map** p326 X2 ❸❷ **French**
One stretch of Leith's Commercial Street is occupied
by refurbished warehousing. It's unremarkable
enough on its south side, but the north side has
premises with conservatory extensions facing over
to the huge Scottish Government building. Many
bars and restaurants have opened here since the
1990s; the most enduring is Daniel's, an Alsace-influ-
enced modern French bistro that still packs 'em in
with dishes such as beef bourguignon or tartiflette.

E:S:I

*46 Queen Charlotte Street, Leith (555 3103,
www.esibrasserie.com). Bus 1, 10, 16, 22, 35,
36.* **Open** noon-3pm, 6-10pm Tue-Sat; 5-10pm
Sun. **Main courses** £12. **Credit** AmEX, MC, V.
Map p326 Y3 ❸❸ **Modern European**
Named for its founders, an Englishman, a Scotsman
and an Irishman, E:S:I is a modern, spacious
brasserie that arrived in Leith in 2008, serving three-
course dinners featuring the likes of chicken caesar
salad to start, pot-roast pork belly with apricot and

red cabbage as a main, and rhubarb and Buckfast crumble for dessert. Deservedly popular, it also does a mean haddock and chips.

Fishers

1 The Shore, Leith (554 5666, www.fishers bistros.co.uk). Bus 1, 10, 16, 22, 35, 36. **Open** noon-10.30pm daily. **Main courses** £15. **Credit** AmEx, MC, V. **Map** p326 Y2 ❾❹ Seafood

The nautical theme in the decor and fittings at Fishers, one of the city's leading seafood restaurants for two decades, is justified by the fact that the docks are on the doorstep; you can see working ships as you're walking down the Shore. Eat in the bar or the adjacent raised area, choosing from starters such as queenie scallops with wasabi and seaweed mayo, and mains such as whole grilled lemon sole. *Photo p165.*
▶ *There's a sister establishment in the New Town (see p145); the owners also operate the Shore, a nearby pub (see p182).*

★ Kitchin

78 Commercial Quay, Leith (555 1755, www.the kitchin.com). Bus 1, 10, 16, 22, 35, 36. **Open** 12.15-2pm; 6.30-9pm Tue-Sat. **Main courses** £30. **Credit** AmEx, MC, V. **Map** p326 Y2 ❾❺ **Modern European**

CONSUME

The Breakfast Club

Start the day in style with a sturdy feast.

A while ago, a number of forward-thinking pubs and café-bars in Edinburgh realised they could draw a whole new clientele by offering breakfast. The carbs helped kick-start sightseeing, remedied the excesses of the night before, or simply served as a weekend treat.

Breakfast and brunch are now well established features of the city's dining scene but familiarity doesn't guarantee quality. In some establishments, dishes aren't cooked as much as assembled, then microwaved. Fortunately, though, there are still a decent number of venues where you can emerge to face the rest of the day with a smile.

At **Porto & Fi** in Newhaven (*see p166*), staff serve what might be the best version of eggs Benedict in the city: a toasted muffin, smoked salmon, poached eggs and tangy hollandaise sauce. In contrast, a little further along the coast at Leith, **Roseleaf** (*see p182*) does an expansive fry-up called the Big One that features smoked bacon, pork sausage, black pudding, mushroom, potato scone, home-made 'funky beans', poached egg and organic toast. There's also a vegetarian version – or you can opt for some muesli with fruit and crème fraîche if you feel the main event would defeat you.

The bar-restaurant at **Rick's** boutique hotel in the New Town (*see p125*) does a mean fry-up, this one by the name of Rick's Grill, but also offers something for the sweeter tooth: ricotta and ginger hotcakes with honeycomb and bananas, which goes very well indeed with a sharp black coffee. The sweet theme carries through at both branches of **Urban Angel** on Forth Street

Urban Angel.

and Hanover Street (*see p146*), where staff drizzle maple syrup over French toast with Virginia smoked bacon. Alternatively, have scrambled eggs on toast, buttressed by Stornoway black pudding.

Wherever you go, fry-ups and scrambled eggs are fairly common, so a growing number of places look to provide more extensive menus. At **Toast** in South Edinburgh (*see p158*), there's porridge with raisins, cream and brown sugar, or Belgian waffles with goat cheese and tomato chutney. For a completely foreign flavour, go to **Barioja** in the Old Town (*see p135*), which does a very Spanish *huevos revueltos* (eggs with carpaccio of smoked cod). In a similar but Italian vein, the **Valvona & Crolla Caffè Bar** (*see p153*) has a selection of fine and hearty dishes, among them *frittata panatella* (omelette with Parmesan and parsley in a panatella roll) or the *verdure* breakfast (intensely flavoured roast Mediterranean vegetables with mushroom, fried egg and grilled polenta). Wash that down with a solid coffee and you'll be ready for anything.

Whatever your carbon footprint, we can reduce it

For over a decade we've been leading the way in carbon offsetting and carbon management.

In that time we've purchased carbon credits from over 200 projects spread across 6 continents. We work with over 300 major commercial clients and thousands of small and medium sized businesses, which rely upon our market-leading quality assurance programme, our experience and absolute commitment to deliver the right solution for each client.

Why not give us a call?

T: London (020) 7833 6000

Tom and Michaela Kitchin set up in Leith in summer 2006, and had a Michelin star within the year. Since then, they've operated at the apex of the city's restaurant scene. The quality of raw materials is impeccable (hand-dived scallops, Anstruther langoustine, Dornoch lamb), and Tom's cooking has a little more edge than the classic French approach in evidence elsewhere; look out for dishes such as boned and rolled pig's head with crispy ear salad.

Leith Lynx

102 Constitution Street, Leith (538 4796, www. leithlynx.co.uk). Bus 1, 10, 16, 22, 35, 36. **Open** noon-9.30pm Mon-Wed, Sun; noon-10pm Thur-Sat. **Main courses** £9. **Credit** AmEx, DC, MC, V. **Map** p326 Z3 **96** Modern European

This 2009-vintage bistro takes its name from Leith Links, just around the corner. Happily informal with chatty waiters, it's a good place to come for some lobster soup with brandy, perhaps, then slow-cooked game pie with mushrooms and port. The style of cooking may seem a little old-fashioned but it's big on flavour, which draws in the punters.

Loch Fyne

25 Pier Place, Newhaven (559 3900, www.loch fyne.com). Bus 7, 10, 11. **Open** noon-10pm daily. **Main courses** £14. **Credit** AmEx, MC, V. **Map** p326 U1 **97** Seafood

Now a countrywide chain, Loch Fyne started life in Argyll. It took until 2007 for a second Scottish out-

---

THE BEST SEAFOOD

Fishers
A pillar of the Leith scene since 1991.
See p163.

Ship on the Shore
Nautical but nice. *See p166.*

Sweet Melinda's
Fresh fish in landlocked Marchmont.
See p158.

---

let to open, here at Newhaven Harbour. Housed in a late Victorian fishmarket, the restaurant is modern and spacious with sea views; the menu features the famous oysters along with other shellfish, salmon, lemon sole, haddock and more.

Osteria di Domenico

30 Sandport Street, Leith (467 7266, www. osteriadidomenico.co.uk). Bus 1, 10, 16, 22, 35, 36. **Open** noon-3pm, 5-10.30pm Mon-Fri; noon-10.30pm Sat, Sun. **Main courses** £10. **Credit** AmEx, MC, V. **Map** p326 Y3 **98** Italian

This tiny, informal Italian sits just around the corner from Commercial Street, and isn't immediately apparent to passers-by. The food combines heartiness with *joie de vivre*, and makes up in personality

CONSUME

Fishers. *See p163.*

what it lacks in finesse. Once you've struggled through the generous antipasti (assorted charcuterie, cheeses and roast vegetables), the impending plate of *spaghetti alla vongole* might just finish you off. Book ahead and bring an appetite.

★ Plumed Horse

50-54 Henderson Street, Leith (554 5556, www. plumedhorse.co.uk). Bus 1, 10, 16, 22, 35, 36. **Open** 12.30-1.30pm, 7-9pm Tue; 12-1.30pm, 7-9pm Wed-Sat. **Set menu** 3 courses £43. **Credit** AmEx, MC, V. **Map** p326 Y3 **99** **Modern European**

Chef Tony Borthwick ran a Michelin-starred restaurant in south-west Scotland before moving to Leith and opening the Plumed Horse. The Michelin star was regained in 2009 for Borthwick's careful, considered cuisine: dishes such as twice-baked parmesan and truffle soufflé, or poached and roasted organic quail with Puy lentils. The midweek supper (Tue-Thur, three courses, £30) is the most affordable way to sample his talents.

★ £ Porto & Fi

47 Newhaven Main Street, Newhaven (551 1900, www.portofi.com). Bus 7, 10, 11. **Open** 8am-8pm Mon-Sat; 10am-6pm Sun. **Main courses** £6. **Credit** AmEx, DC, MC, V. **Map** p326 U1 **100** **Café**

Porto & Fi opened opposite Newhaven Harbour in 2008, aimed at residents of the new housing developments along the coast. A neat, modern café, it does seriously good breakfasts (eggs Benedict or French toast with Ayrshire bacon and maple syrup), light meals (smoked chicken and mango salsa salad), coffee, tea and fabulous cake (beetroot and chocolate). It does get very busy at peak times, especially for weekend brunch, so it's worth booking ahead.

▶ *For more, see p163 The Breakfast Club.*

★ Restaurant Martin Wishart

54 The Shore, Leith (553 3557, www.martin-wishart.co.uk). Bus 1, 10, 16, 22, 35, 36. **Open** noon-2pm, 6.45-9.30pm Tue-Sat. **Set menu** 3 courses £60. **Credit** AmEx, MC, V. **Map** p326 Y3 **101** **Modern European**

INSIDE TRACK LET'S DO LUNCH

The more affordable way of dining at Edinburgh's most illustrious restaurants is to sidestep dinner and aim for lunch. There's a two-course lunch for £20 per head at **21212** (*see p150*), a three-course set lunch for £24.50 at the **Kitchin** (*see p163*) and a three-course lunch for £23 at the **Plumed Horse** (*see above*), while the three-course *lunch du jour* at **Restaurant Martin Wishart** (*see above*) is £24.50.

Located in the historical heart of Leith, Wishart's establishment has retained a Michelin star since 2001. The food is sublime, and a meal might take in *tarte fine* of Cornish sardines to start, squab pigeon as a main and then raspberry soufflé to finish. Vegetarians are very well catered for, with a tasting menu all to themselves. The front of house staff are the slickest in the city, approachable and efficient.

▶ *Martin Wishart also runs a cooking school in Leith; see p159 A Learning Process.*

Ship on the Shore

24-26 The Shore, Leith (555 0409, www. theshipontheshore.co.uk). Bus 1, 10, 16, 22, 35, 36. **Open** noon-10pm daily. **Main courses** £17. **Credit** AmEx, MC, V. **Map** p326 Y2 **102** **Seafood**

The Ship has been part of the Leith scene since the 1980s, but in 2007, a change in management saw things move up a notch. The premises are split in two, with a dining room to one side and a pub to the other, both with nautical fixtures and fittings. You can snack in the bar, but the menu in the dining room offers greater variety: hot smoked salmon to start, or mains such as roast hake, and scallops with black pudding.

Skippers

1a Dock Place, Leith (554 1018, www.skippers. co.uk). Bus 1, 10, 16, 22, 35, 36. **Open** noon-2pm, 6.30-10pm Mon-Thur; noon-2pm, 6-10pm Fri; noon-2.30pm, 6-10pm Sat, Sun. **Main courses** £14. **Credit** AmEx, MC, V. **Map** p326 Y2 **103** **Seafood**

A pioneer of the Leith dining scene, Skippers opened back in 1979, when the surrounding area was very different. For more than three decades, it's served simple seafood – fishcakes, *moules marinière*, oysters with shallot vinegar, whole grilled lemon sole – in an accessible bistro style. A change of ownership in 2008 didn't alter the approach too much; the set lunch (two courses for £11.95) remains popular.

Vintners Rooms

Vaults, 87 Giles Street, Leith (554 6767, www.thevintnersrooms.com). Bus 1, 10, 16, 22, 35, 36. **Open** noon-2pm, 7-10pm Tue-Sat. **Main courses** £23. **Credit** AmEx, MC, V. **Map** p326 Y3 **104** **Modern European**

At the corner of a Leith backstreet sits a former wine warehouse with a long history. Its first floor is home to the esteemed Scotch Malt Whisky Society, while the ground floor hosts the Vintners Rooms, a classy French-style fixture since 1985. Diners have the choice of the homelier bar area or a small adjacent space with elaborate stucco – a late 18th-century auction room. Dinner features accomplished dishes such as smoked trout with horseradish cream, followed by stuffed saddle of rabbit with green bean salad.

▶ *For the Scotch Malt Whisky Society, see p182.*

CONSUME

Pubs & Bars

Drinking remains a national pastime in Scotland.

Like most towns and cities in the UK, Edinburgh has a full complement of hectic establishments that only seem to exist in order to part tottering girls and Diesel-clad boys from their wages on a Saturday night. Fortunately, though, such venues are far from the whole story. Edinburgh offers far more: Victorian drinking palaces, traditional alehouses, whisky specialists, gastropubs, cocktail bars, even the odd homely neighbourhood pub with its own knitting group. The traditional Scottish vision of a bar was of a smoke-filled room in which men can drink away the cares of the day. However, times have long since changed in the city. Old-timers may have frowned upon such progress, but they're well and truly in the minority.

DRINKING IN EDINBURGH

In the beginning, it was simple. Restaurants were for food, pubs were for beer and cafés were for either scones or egg-and-chips platters, and the idea of a venue that served alcohol, coffee and food throughout the day was anathema.

However, the Edinburgh scene started to change back in the 1980s. And today, trying to draw dividing lines between pubs, gastropubs, bars and café-bars is like pushing water uphill. Some venues that seem plainly identifiable as traditional pubs also serve food from breakfast to dinner; many cafés also offer a fine range of wine. And at a typical, contemporary café-bar, one table might be taken by a group of women sharing a bottle of sauvignon blanc, one by a student nursing a latte, and another by a couple wolfing down bowls of Creole gumbo with an accompanying pint or two.

That said, one general distinction can be made. In Edinburgh, bars and pubs tend to be places where people go for a drink, regardless of whether the venue serves. By comparison, café-bars exist somewhere at the intersection of bar, café and restaurant. The listings in this section are divided accordingly into pubs and bars on the one hand and café-bars on the other.

> ❶ Green numbers given in this chapter correspond to the location of each pub on the street maps. *See pp326-333.*

THE OLD TOWN
Pubs & bars

Black Bo's
57-61 Blackfriars Street (557 6136, www.black-bos.co.uk). Nicolson Street–North Bridge buses.
Open 4pm-1am daily. *Food served* 6-10.30pm daily. **Credit** AmEx, MC, V. **Map** p333 J7 ❶
This relaxed and bohemian little *howf* (meeting place) has been around for more than 20 years now, but with no style bar flourishes in sight. The pub itself is a winning little spot; next door is an often-adventurous vegetarian restaurant.

★ Bow Bar
80 West Bow (226 7667). Bus 2, 23, 27, 41, 42.
Open noon-11.30pm Mon-Sat; 12.30-11pm Sun. *Food served* noon-2pm Mon-Sat. **Credit** MC, V. **Map** p332 G8 & p336 D4 ❷
This small and simple one-room pub has one of the largest and most interesting ranges of single malt Scotch, not just in the city but in Scotland. The Port Ellen distillery on Islay was mothballed in 1983, for instance, but the Bow may still have several different bottlings on offer. There's also a good choice of cask ales, and on a typical night your only problem might be finding a seat. *Photos pp168-169.*

Canons' Gait
232 Canongate (556 4481). Bus 35, 36. **Open** noon-11.30pm Mon-Thur, Sun; noon-12.30am Fri, Sat. *Food served* noon-8pm Mon-Sat; noon-5pm Sun. **Credit** AmEx, MC, V. **Map** p333 K7 ❸

Roomy and comfortable, with a pub-grub menu and music on some evenings, the Canons' Gait offers a modern take on what a Royal Mile bar should be. Despite its location in the middle of tourist country, the place still attracts its share of locals. The pub is named after the route taken by the Augustinian canons from Holyrood Abbey as they entered medieval Edinburgh.

Medina

45-47 Lothian Street (225 6313). Nicolson Street–North Bridge buses. **Open** 10pm-3am daily. **Credit** MC, V. **Map** p332 H8 ④
The sister venue to Negociants (*see right*), Medina is a late-opening and often lively basement with a North African theme. Although it's a kind of club-bar crossover, with DJs, drinks promos and a young profile, you can just lie on the cushions, relax and listen to music. There's usually a cover charge, but it's no bank-breaker.

Monteith's

Monteith's Close, 57-61 High Street (557 0330, www.monteithsbar.co.uk). Bus 35 or Nicolson Street–North Bridge buses. **Open** noon-10pm Mon-Thur, Sun; noon-10.30pm Fri, Sat. *Food served same hours.* **Credit** MC, V. **Map** p333 J7 ⑤
Hidden down a close just a few yards from the main tourist street, this is one of the Old Town's better-kept secrets. The other-worldly atmosphere is strong, thanks to the fairy lights and antique fittings. It's a secluded place for a beer; the food is ambitious and resolutely Franco-Scots.

Royal Oak

1 Infirmary Street (557 2976, www.royal-oak-folk.com). Nicolson Street–North Bridge buses. **Open** 11.30am-2am Mon-Sat; 12.30pm-2am Sun. **No credit cards. Map** p333 J8 ⑥
Fall through the doors of this tiny, two-floor pub and you're virtually guaranteed to be regaled with a flurry of fiddles, squeezeboxes and guitars. There are nightly folk sessions, with the Wee Folk Club taking over the Lounge Bar on Sundays for a programme of guest artists. No frills: just beer and tunes.

★ Sandy Bell's

25 Forrest Road (225 2751). Bus 35/Nicolson Street–North Bridge buses. **Open** noon-1am Mon-Sat; 12.30-11pm Sun. **No credit cards. Map** p332 H8 ⑦
Like the Royal Oak (*see above*), this is a folkies' hangout: there's an open session every night from around 9pm. Also like the Royal Oak, there are no frills, but if you're looking for a traditional Scottish pub that draws everyone from bus drivers to philosophers (the University of Edinburgh is nearby), this is the place.

Whistlebinkies

7 Niddry Street (557 5114, www.whistle binkies.com). Nicolson Street–North Bridge buses. **Open** 5pm-3am Mon-Thur; 1pm-3am Fri-Sun. **Credit** MC, V. **Map** p333 J7 & p336 F4 ⑧
Edinburgh's primary live music pub, Whistlebinkies takes in rock and pop acts along with singer-songwriters, troubadours and indie kids. On Fridays and Saturdays, there's a cover charge later on.

Bow Bar. *See p167.*

CONSUME

Café-bars

City Café
*19 Blair Street (220 0125). Nicolson Street–
North Bridge buses.* **Open** 11am-1am daily.
Food served 11am-10pm daily. **Credit** MC, V.
Map p332 H7 & p336 F4 ⑨
The City Café was one of the first modern café-bars
on the scene in the 1980s; these days, it feels as much
a part of Edinburgh as the castle. The ground floor
features a pool table and fill-you-up meals, to be
devoured in the booths at the back or the more open
seating at the front. It's packed with pre-clubbers at
weekends; the late mornings bring a clientele in
search of a serious breakfast.
▶ *Cabaret Voltaire is just a few doors down on
the other side of the street; see p239.*

Ecco Vino
*19 Cockburn Street (225 1441, www.eccovino
edinburgh.com). Bus 35/Nicolson Street–North
Bridge buses.* **Open** noon-midnight Mon-Thur;
noon-1am Fri, Sat; 12.30pm-midnight Sun. *Food
served* noon-10pm Mon-Thur; noon-10.30pm Fri,
Sat; 12.30-10.30pm Sun. **Credit** AmEx, MC, V.
Map p332 H7 & p336 E3 ⑩
The formula at this perennial Old Town favourite
has a simplicity bordering on genius. Create a basic
Italian menu (antipasti, risotto, panini, pasta) and
throw in the odd special. Devise an Italian-slanted
wine list. Store the bottles of wine along one wall as
a design feature, run the bar along the other side of
the room, light some candles… and abracadabra.

Negociants
*45 Lothian Street (225 6313, www.negociants.
co.uk). Nicolson Street–North Bridge buses.*
Open 10am-1am Mon-Thur, Sun; 10am-3am
Fri, Sat. *Food served* 10am-midnight Mon-Thur,
Sun; 10am-2am Fri, Sat. **Credit** MC, V.
Map p332 H8 ⑪
A café-bar scene pioneer, Negociants is both student
hangout and late-night bar, somewhere people while
away afternoons with coffee and an improving book,
or a place to drop by for eats. You can get everything
from an all-day weekend breakfast to a late-night
menu. Equally laid-back sister operation Medina (*see
left*) is downstairs.

THE NEW TOWN
Pubs & bars

Abbotsford
*3 Rose Street (225 5276, www.theabbotsford.
com). Bus 13, 23, 27, 42 or Princes Street buses.*
Open 11am-11pm Mon-Sat; 12.30-11pm Sun.
Food served noon-3pm Mon-Sat; 12.30-3pm Sun.
Credit MC, V. **Map** p328 & p332 G6, p336 E1 ⑫
The Abbotsford has been a no-nonsense drinking
den since 1901: dark wood, bench tables, a fine central island bar, a decorative ceiling, some cask ales
and virtually no concessions to modernity. The bar
food here is better than you might imagine, but
there's also a restaurant upstairs (called Above).

★ Bramble
*16a Queen Street (226 6343, www.bramblebar.
co.uk). Bus 13, 23, 27, 42 or Princes Street
buses.* **Open** 4pm-1am daily. **Credit** MC, V.
Map p328 G5 ⑬
A 2006 arrival in a sub-basement space on Queen
Street, Bramble doesn't exactly announce itself
to the planet, but over the last few years it has been,
simply, the best cocktail bar in the city. With a
cultured feel, young staff who take pride in their
handiwork and a neat attention to detail (Buffalo
Trace bourbon in the mint julep, for instance), it's
unmatched in Edinburgh.

CONSUME

CONSUME

★ Café Royal Circle Bar

19 West Register Street (556 1884). Princes Street buses. **Open** 11am-11pm Mon-Wed; 11am-midnight Thur; 11am-1am Fri, Sat; 12.30-11pm Sun. *Food served* 11am-10pm Mon-Sat; 12.30-10pm Sun. **Credit** AmEx, MC, V. **Map** p328 & p332 H6, p336 F2 ⑭

An island bar dominates this attractive and elegant pub, where the walls are decorated with Royal Doulton tiles of famous inventors. You find all sorts here, from tourists to people dropping in after work, and it gets very busy after Scottish rugby internationals. The bar menu got a shot in the arm in 2008, and the food is better now than it has been for years.
▶ *For more formal eats, try the beautiful Café Royal Oyster Bar adjacent (no.17a, 556 4124).*

Clark's Bar

142 Dundas Street (556 1067). Bus 13, 23, 27. **Open** 11am-11pm Mon-Wed; 11am-11.30pm Thur-Sat; 12.30-11pm Sun. *Food served* same hours. **No credit cards.** Map p328 F4 ⑮

Sparse and traditional, this old *howf* opened in 1899 and hasn't changed in years: the decor still features red leather seats, shiny brass table tops and a dark red ceiling. You'll find a reasonable malt whisky selection, a few cask ales and basic bar food. It's an antidote to the excesses of George Street up the hill.

★ Cumberland

1-3 Cumberland Street (558 3134, www.cumber landbar.co.uk). Bus 13, 23, 27. **Open** 11am-1am Mon-Sat; 12.30pm-1am Sun. *Food served* noon-3pm daily. **Credit** MC, V. **Map** p328 G4 ⑯

The Cumberland is perhaps the most user-friendly of the city's acclaimed cask ale bars (four regular ales on tap, another four guest beers). It feels light and spacious during the day, and the leafy beer garden is a joy in the summer. There's a fair choice of wine and bar food, including – inevitably – Cumberland sausage with mash and gravy.

INSIDE TRACK
HERE FOR THE BEER

Edinburgh was once a world centre for beer production. Among its many breweries was Scottish & Newcastle, with a brewing plant at Fountainbridge. The last beer was brewed here in 2005, since when the land has been redeveloped with new apartment blocks. Its demise would have meant the end of a long brewing tradition but for the **Caledonian Brewery** (www.caledonian-brewery.co.uk), which survives a little further west at Slateford Road. Founded in 1869, it continues to produce award-winning ales such as Caledonian 80/– and Deuchars IPA.

★ Guildford

1-5 West Register Street (556 4312, www.guild fordarms.com). Princes Street buses. **Open** 11am-11pm Mon-Thur; 11am-midnight Fri, Sat; 12.30-11pm Sun. *Food served* noon-2.30pm, 6-9.30pm Mon-Fri; noon-10pm Sat; 12.30-3pm, 6-9.30pm Sun. **Credit** AmEx, MC, V. **Map** p328 & p332 H6, p336 F2 ⑰

Established in 1898 (the building dates back a further 60 years), the Guildford is one of Edinburgh's most accessible Victorian pubs, just a hop, skip and jump from Waverley Station. The rotating selection of cask ales is excellent, the whisky choice is decent and the bar food is better than average; try to eat in the small gallery overlooking the main bar.
▶ *Scotland's People, the genealogical research centre, is next door; see p80.*

Kay's

39 Jamaica Street (225 1858). Bus 24, 29, 36, 42. **Open** 11am-midnight Mon-Thur; 11am-1am Fri, Sat; 12.30-11pm Sun. *Food served* noon-2.30pm daily. **Credit** MC, V. **Map** p328 E5 ⑱

Drink has been a mainstay here for nearly two centuries: before morphing into a pub in 1976, these premises housed a wine merchant. Now, along with a reputation as a patrician New Town *howf*, this historic spot offers an excellent choice of single malt whiskies and a perfect environment in which to sample them. There's some basic bar food, too.

Living Room

113-115 George Street (0870 442 2718, www.the livingroom.co.uk). Bus 13, 23, 27, 42 or Princes Street buses. **Open** 11am-1am Mon-Sat; 11am-12.30am Sun. *Food served* noon-10pm Mon, Tue, Sun; noon-11pm Wed; noon-11.30pm Thur; noon-midnight Fri, Sat. **Credit** AmEx, MC, V. **Map** p328 & p332 E6, p336 B1 ⑲

Part of a UK-wide chain, Edinburgh's Living Room has collected a reputation as a somewhat more mature venue in a part of the city where office nights out are common; every evening, for instance, sees someone tinkling on the baby grand. While there is a big restaurant here, the clubbish bar area is the main feature.

Oxford Bar

8 Young Street (539 7119, www.oxfordbar.com). Bus 13, 23, 27, 42 or Princes Street buses. **Open** 11am-midnight daily. **No credit cards.** Map p328 & p332 E6, p336 B1 ⑳

Cramped, dowdy and clannish, the Oxford's bar area offers no space whatsoever; although there's a room adjacent, it's all still pretty basic, and it sometimes feels as if you have to be a member to drink here. So why come? Because it ploughs its own furrow, and doesn't give a monkey's about the white noise of contemporary style. It enjoys minor celebrity status as a favoured haunt of Ian Rankin's Inspector Rebus (and, for that matter, Rankin himself). *Photos p175.*

Size Matters

Some local bar owners are proving that small is beautiful.

In the last decade, a phenomenal amount of money has been ploughed into George Street in the New Town. The investment has created gee-whiz hotels such as Le Monde (*see p121*) and Tigerlily (*see p1222*), paid for a major refurbishment at the George (*see p122*), and seen the arrival of plush venues including the Living Room (*see left*). Looking at such changes, it's easy to conclude that the only way to make money from a new pub or café-bar in Edinburgh is through a big-concept approach and expensive design. But elsewhere in the city, a number of more low-key neighbourhood venues are bucking the trend and succeeding regardless.

Back in 2003, Swedish couple Anna and Mike Christopherson opened **Boda** on Leith Walk (*see p179*). The Christophersons kept the venue's original pub fittings but painted over them, adding further simple, homely touches to the space. The punters seemed to like it, so the Christophersons went on to do the same with **Sofi's** on Henderson Street, the **Victoria** on Leith Walk and **Joseph Pearce's** on Elm Row. All four are characterised by their sociability: Sofi's runs knitting evenings and film nights, while Joseph Pearce's hosts a jogging group and has a children's corner with a microwave so that parents can heat up baby food. It's all a very long way from *Trainspotting*.

Also in Leith, a small group of people have made an excellent job of **Roseleaf** (*see p182*), a 2007 makeover of an old Sandport Place pub. The group included Australian Amanda Caygill, who's since branched out by revamping yet more pub premises to launch the **Esplanade** and **Guilty Lily** (for both, *see p180*).

Then there's Billy and Jane Ross who started in the café business at **Renroc** (*see p153*) in 2006. The premises look small at street level, but open out downstairs with more café seating and a complementary health studio that occupies an old bakery. Rhe duo's belief that they could apply what they'd learned at Renroc elsewhere led to their takeover of the **Earl of Marchmont** (*see p176*), which has gained a new lease of life under their watch.

What the Christophersons, Caygill and the Rosses have in common is their willingness to trust their own judgement. In some ways, they must. Returning to glamorous George Street, it took a reputed £12 million to get Le Monde up and running in 2006. Small local entrepreneurs don't have that kind of leverage. Instead, perhaps both by choice and by necessity, they've shied away from a commodified, capital-intensive approach, and brought a more individual sensibility to bear on their venues. It seems to be working.

Joseph Pearce.

Café-bars

Dome
14 George Street (624 8624, www.thedome edinburgh.com). Bus 13, 23, 27, 42 or Princes Street buses. **Open** *Grill Room* noon-late daily. *Club Room* 10am-5pm Mon-Wed; 10am-late Thur-Sat. *Food served* same hours. **Credit** AmEx, MC, V. **Map** p328 & p332 G6, p336 E1 ㉑
In the 1840s, the Commercial Bank of Scotland built this grand old pile as its head office. There's a striking classical frontage, and the whole thing is crowned by the eponymous dome, now housing a bar and restaurant (the Grill Room); the building also has a separate and more discreet but very ornate dining space called the Club Room. Even with the recent outlandish bar and hotel additions to George Street, the Dome still has the biggest wow factor.

Indigo Yard
7 Charlotte Lane (220 5603, www.indigoyard edinburgh.co.uk). Princes Street buses. **Open** 8.30am-1am Mon-Fri; 9am-1am Sat, Sun. *Food served* 8.30am-10pm Mon-Fri; 9am-10pm Sat, Sun. **Credit** AmEx, MC, V. **Map** p331 D7 ㉒
It's perhaps not quite the market leader it used to be in the style-bar stakes, but Indigo Yard's popularity endures, with post-work drinkers during the week and a more mixed clientele during the day and at weekends. Available to tables on the ground floor or the mezzanine, the menu offers pretty good breakfasts, plus simple mains (pastas, fajitas, steaks).

Rick's
55a Frederick Street (622 7800, www.ricks edinburgh. co.uk). Bus 13, 23, 27, 42 or Princes Street buses. **Open** 7am-1am daily. *Food served* 7am-10pm Mon-Wed, Sun; 7am-11pm Thur-Sat. **Credit** MC, V. **Map** p328 & p332 F6, p336 C1 ㉓
On busier evenings, the café-bar at Rick's hotel tends to attract girls with a certain look (that blonde hair, that black top) and guys with a certain demeanour (that wristwatch), but it's still a lively spot. You can grab a very decent breakfast (*see p163*); later in the day, the menu offers the likes of oysters, dressed crab or lamb rump.
▶ *For the hotel, see p125.*

Whigham's Wine Cellars
13 Hope Street, Charlotte Square (225 8674, www.whighams.co.uk). Princes Street buses. **Open** noon-midnight Mon-Thur; noon-1am Fri, Sat. *Food served* noon-10pm Mon-Sat. **Credit** AmEx, MC, V. **Map** p332 E7 & p336 A2 ㉔
The old alcoves, candles and low ceilings give this well-established basement wine bar a cosy, intimate feel, but it's not completely subterranean: an expansion into next door's basement created a brighter, more open space. The menu tends towards good bistro fare (including a signature seafood platter); the wine list is a decent international mix.

STOCKBRIDGE

Pubs & bars

Avoca
4-6 Dean Street (315 3311). Bus 24, 29, 42. **Open** 11am-midnight Mon-Thur, Sun; 11am-1am Fri, Sat. *Food served* noon-2.30pm, 6-8.30pm Mon-Thur; noon-7.15pm Sat, Sun. **Credit** MC, V. **Map** p327 D4 ㉕
Despite bearing the name of a village in County Wicklow, this is no Oirish theme bar. Instead, it's a compact, modern pub in one of the city's most bourgeois quarters, with wooden fittings, friendly staff and decent bar food (including late breakfasts).

Bailie
2 St Stephen Street (225 4673). Bus 24, 29, 42. **Open** 11am-midnight Mon-Thur; 11am-1am Fri, Sat; 12.30-midnight Sun. *Food served* 11am-9pm Mon-Thur, Sat, Sun; 11am-5pm Fri. **Credit** MC, V. **Map** p328 E5 ㉖
This old-style pub somehow combines New Town money with Stockbridge bohemia. Food is typical pub grub with a few more ambitious dishes. The old regulars look testier than ever these days, presumably because they have to go outside to smoke.

Café-bars

Hector's
47-49 Deanhaugh Street (343 1735, www.hectors stockbridge.co.uk). Bus 24, 29, 42. **Open** noon-midnight Mon-Wed, Sun; noon-1am Thur-Sat. *Food served* noon-10pm Mon-Fri; noon-4pm, 5-10pm Sat, Sun. **Credit** AmEx, MC, V. **Map** p327 D4 ㉗
Formerly a pioneering designer restaurant, Hector's is now a less ostentatious style bar, good for cosy chats by candlelight or nestling by the fire. The menu features the usual suspects (nachos, burgers, salads). It's a handy stop if you've been wandering around the nearby Royal Botanic Garden.

Saint
44 St Stephen Street (225 9009, www.thesaint edinburgh.co.uk). Bus 24, 29, 42. **Open** noon-midnight Mon-Wed, Sun; noon-1am Thur-Sat.

THE BEST COCKTAILS

Bond No.9
Belvedere Intense and Noilly Prat make for a memorable vodka martini. *See p182.*

Bramble
A cultured New Town favourite. *See p169.*

Dragonfly
Still doing the business. *See p176.*

CONSUME

Food served noon-10pm daily. **Credit** AmEx, MC, V. **Map** p328 E4 ㉘

The Saint arrived in early 2009, a basement café-bar with wooden floor and furniture, white walls and straightforward cooking; a hot-smoked salmon starter with chicory, walnut and crunchy strips of potato scone may be easy to assemble, but it works well. Weekend brunch also features.

▶ *The Saint is owned by the people behind Bramble; see p169.*

CALTON HILL & BROUGHTON

Pubs & bars

Barony
81-85 Broughton Street (558 2874). Bus 8, 13 or Playhouse buses. **Open** 11am-midnight Mon-Thur; 11am-1am Fri, Sat; 12.30-11pm Sun.

Food served 11am-10pm Mon-Sat; 12.30-7pm Sun. **Credit** MC, V. **Map** p328 H4 ㉙

The Barony is a very traditional-looking pub, but comes with a fair amount of character. The clientele is pretty mixed, and wouldn't seem entirely out of place in one of the more contemporary café-bars nearby. There's pub grub, various cask ales and occasional live music.

★ Cask & Barrel
115 Broughton Street (556 3132). Bus 8, 13 or Playhouse buses. **Open** 11am-1am Mon-Sat; 12.30pm-12.30am Sun. *Food served* noon-2pm daily. **Credit** MC, V. **Map** p328 H4 ㉚

Beer heaven – this old-fashioned pub offers local brews, obscure artisan cask ales from around the UK, and bottled beers from Germany and the Low Countries. You'll be able to watch the football on one of the screens.

Fancy a Pint?

Scottish brewing goes beyond the big names.

Scotland's brewing industry, like those of so many countries around the world, is now dominated by multinationals. However, look beyond the likes of Tennents and you'll find a handful of microbreweries around the country, producing hand-crafted premium beers in small runs for a dedicated market of enthusiasts. Many of these brews can be found on tap in Edinburgh's pubs, or in bottles from a handful of local stores.

In Edinburgh, there's Steve Stewart, who started **Stewart Brewing** (www.stewart brewing.co.uk) in his garage in 2004. He's since won the Supreme Champion Award from the Society of Independent Brewers Scotland for his Edinburgh Gold. Far to the north, the folks at **Orkney Brewery** (www.sinclairbreweries.co.uk) say that the unrushed culture of the Orkney Islands influences the way they brew. Their strongest beer, Skull Splitter (8.5 per cent ABV), is named not for its effect but in honour of a Viking Earl of Orkney.

Innis & Gunn (www.innisandgunn.com) ages its beer in oak barrels, a technique that can infuse the brew with new depths of taste; hints of vanilla, toffee and orange, for example. The transformative power of oak on beer was discovered by accident in 2002, when the whisky producer William Grant & Sons commissioned brewer Dougal Sharp to formulate a beer that would impart a smooth character to bourbon barrels and, in turn, help to produce an ale-finished whisky. The resulting batch was so tasty

that he decided to brew some more. At Innerleithen in Peeblesshire, the **Traquair House Brewery** (www.traquair.co.uk) also ferments beer in oak vessels. The water in its signature Traquair House Ale comes from an underground spring in the hills of the estate on which the brewery is located.

Some brewers have gone beyond oak barrels in pursuit of flavour. The first and most popular product created by **Williams Bros** (www.williamsbrosbrew.com), based north-west of Edinburgh in Alloa, is Fraoch, a heather ale inspired by a traditional recipe. The brewery specialises in revivals of historic Scottish beers, made using unfamiliar ingredients such as Scots pine and seaweed. Further north-west in the village of Kinlochleven, the **Atlas Brewery** (www.atlasbrewery.com) has produced a ruby ale called Red Squirrel, a percentage of profits going towards preserving the dwindling numbers of – yes – red squirrels.

Finally, no round-up of Scottish beers is complete without a mention of the **Harviestoun Brewery** (www.harviestoun. com). Its Schiehallion lager, named after a Perthshire mountain and available in cask form or by the bottle, has won more gold awards than any other Scottish cask-conditioned ale, including three at the Great British Beer Festival and the World's Best Pils/Pilsner prize at the 2008 World Beer Awards. Harviestoun is also responsible for the peerlessly named Bitter 'n' Twisted, another award-winner.

CONSUME

Oxford Bar. *See p170.*

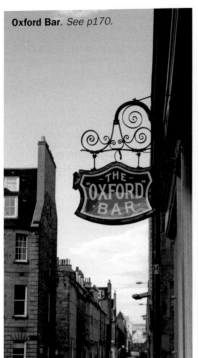

CONSUME

Pivo

2-6 Calton Road (557 2925). Leith Street buses.
Open 7pm-3am Mon-Thur, Sun; 5pm-3am Fri, Sat.
Credit AmEx, MC, V. **Map** p329 & p333 J6 ③
It's not so much a Czech bar as a Czech-themed bar,
but Pivo has the look (and the beer) all the same.
Two minutes from the east end of Princes Street, it's
a popular late-night DJ bar among cheery, up-for-it
crowds; if you want to savour a Staropramen in relative peace and quiet, go early in the evening.

Café-bars

Basement

*10a-12a Broughton Street (557 0097, www.the
basement.org.uk). Playhouse buses.* **Open** noon-
1am daily. *Food served* noon-10.30pm daily.
Credit AmEx, MC, V. **Map** p328 H5 ㉜
Broughton Street's original style bar still feels much
the same as it did back when it opened in 1994, albeit
with the odd decorative improvement. Incorporating
a dimly lit, split-level room and a separate dining
space, it can get pretty buzzy in the evenings, when
the music is even louder than the staff's trademark
Hawaiian shirts. The menu offers the likes of steak
pie or sea bass for lunch during the week, and gets
more Mexican at weekends.

Elbow

*133-135 East Claremont Street (556 5662,
www.elbowedinburgh.co.uk). Bus 8, 13, .* **Open**
9am-1am daily. *Food served* 9am-10pm daily.
Credit AmEX, MC, V. **Map** p328 H2 ㉝
Summer 2009 saw the former Claremont Bar transformed into a brighter and breezier café-bar featuring quirky art, bare brick, banquettes and a more
feminine touch. It's less eccentric than in its previous guise, but with better food and tunes; you could
pop in for a drink, or for cider-battered fish of the
day with duck-fat chips and mushy peas. It's something of an oasis on the backroads between
Broughton and Leith.

Treacle

*39-41 Broughton Street (557 0627, www.treacle
edinburgh.co.uk). Bus 8, 13 or Playhouse buses.*
Open 10am-1am daily. *Food served* 10am-10pm
daily. **Credit** AmEx, MC, V. **Map** p329 J5 ㉞
Formerly a long-running style bar called Baroque,
these premises morphed into Treacle in 2009 after a
revamp that included a massive manga mural.
Overall, with the exposed stone and fresh decor, the
place is looking a lot better. Food includes breakfast,
weekend brunch, sandwiches and main meals
(lemon chicken skewers, pan-fried duck).

CONSUME

ARTHUR'S SEAT & DUDDINGSTON

Pubs & bars

★ Sheep Heid Inn

43-45 The Causeway (661 7974, www.sheepheid. co.uk). Bus 4, 44, 44A, 45. **Open** 11am-11pm Mon-Thur; 11am-midnight Fri, Sat; 12.30-11pm Sun. *Food served* noon-8pm Mon-Sat; 12.30-8pm Sun. **Credit** AmEx, MC, V.

Legend has it that this place got its name from the motif on a snuff box presented by King James VI some years before he legged it to London to become James I of England. For many, the enticing bar menu and selection of guest beers is a reward for tramping over Arthur's Seat. This place is as close as you'll get to an historic country pub in Edinburgh: Duddingston Loch is virtually on the doorstep of the Sheep Heid, as are the wildlife delights of Holyrood Park (*see pp96-99*).

SOUTH EDINBURGH

Pubs & bars

Bennet's

8 Leven Street (229 5143). Bus 11, 15, 15A, 16, 23, 45. **Open** 11am-1am daily. *Food served* noon-2pm, 5-8.30pm Mon-Sat. **Credit** MC, V. **Map** p332 F10 ③⑤

A marvel of Victorian design. A long wooden bar occupies one side of the room, with alcoves along the top of the gantry accommodating a huge selection of single malts, while the opposite wall has fitted red leather seats and more wooden fittings. Enjoy the whisky selection and hearty pub grub.

▶ *It's an ideal place for a drink before or after a show at the King's Theatre next door; see p253.*

Blue Blazer

2 Spittal Street (229 5030). Bus 1, 2, 10, 11, 15, 15A, 16, 23, 24, 27, 34, 35, 45. **Open** 11am-1am Mon-Sat; 12.30pm-1am Sun. **Credit** MC, V. **Map** p332 F8 & p336 B4 ③⑥

Sandwiched between the lads-night-out chaos of Lothian Road and the lap-dancing bars at the top of the West Port, the Blue Blazer is a cosy place to hide away and chat with a decent pint of cask ale, especially in the wee room through the back.

★ Canny Man's

237 Morningside Road (447 1484). Bus 11, 15, 15A, 16, 41. **Open** 11.30am-11pm Mon-Wed, Sun; 11.30am-midnight Thur, Sat; 11.30am-1am Fri. *Food served* noon-3pm, 6.30-9.30pm Mon-Thur; 6.30-9.30pm Sat; 12.30-3pm Sun. **No credit cards.**

It's been around since 1871. It looks as if it was decorated by a mad maiden aunt from the Victorian era. It has a good wine list, a tiny beer garden and a truly exceptional selection of single malt whiskies. The catch? No backpackers, no mobiles, no cameras and 'dress smart but casual', which divides opinion more effectively than the Church of Scotland's 1843 Disruption. Loved and loathed in equal measure, the Canny Man's is a fabulous place to drink if you can get through the door.

★ Cloisters

26 Brougham Street (221 9997). Bus 11, 15, 15A, 16, 23, 45. **Open** noon-midnight Mon-Thur; noon-1am Fri, Sat; 12.30pm-midnight Sun. *Food served* noon-8pm Mon-Thur; noon-5pm Fri, Sat. **Credit** MC, V. **Map** p332 F9 ③⑦

The decor at Cloisters, housed in a former manse, is nice enough, but it's the rare cask ales that are the selling point: a selection of Scottish ales is permanently on tap, along with a weekly-changing list of guest beers. For beer, it's one of the city's very best. It puts on a good showing on the whisky front as well, with around 40 varieties; there's pub grub, too.

★ Dragonfly

52 West Port (228 4543, www.dragonfly cocktailbar.com). Bus 2, 35. **Open** 4pm-1am daily. *Food served* 4-10pm daily. **Credit** AmEx, MC, V. **Map** p332 F8 ③⑧

A hangout for the beautiful people since 2004, Dragonfly is still one of Edinburgh's best cocktails bars. With a serious approach to drink and reimagined retro-analogue interior design, it was an instant hit. This is the kind of place where staff will experiment with Finnish vodka, strawberries and something balsamic to create a cocktail that tastes like a Michelin-starred dessert.

Earl of Marchmont

22 Marchmont Crescent (662 1877). Bus 24, 41. **Open** 11am-1am Mon-Sat; 11am-midnight Sun. *Food served* noon-9pm daily. **Credit** AmEx, MC, V. **Map** p332 H11 ③⑨

From Bruntsfield in the west to Newington in the east, there is a swathe of South Edinburgh that is desperately residential. Pubs are rare and the old Earl of Marchmont didn't set many pulses racing. In 2008, however, it was taken over by the people who own the Renroc café (*see p153*). Now the place has a more up-to-date feel, the bar food is decent and that residential desert is somewhat better off.

Pear Tree House

36 West Nicolson Street (667 7533). Nicolson Street–North Bridge buses. **Open** 11am-midnight Mon-Thur; 11am-1am Fri, Sat; 12.30pm-midnight Sun. **Credit** MC, V. **Map** p333 J9 ④⓪

Just over the road from Edinburgh University's George Square campus, the Pear Tree's cobbled beer garden has played host to generations of thirsty students. Inside, the decor is classic trad Scots pub, with the addition of a big screen for the football. Outside term-time, it's fairly placid.

Whisky Galore

A brief history of Scotland's most famous export.

A brief history of whisky-making in Scotland runs something like this: centuries of unfettered production, 17th-century taxes, some strife, 18th-century taxes, lots more strife, legislation in 1823, and a commercial industry thereafter. An array of 19th-century technological developments buoyed the industry, which received a major boost from the 1860s when French brandy production started to collapse because of the insect pest phylloxera. By the late 19th century, whisky was the country's spirit of choice.

This was simple blended whisky, mind. The intense and occasionally erratic single-malt varieties produced by small distilleries were deemed too wild, and so various single-malt whiskies were married to bulk grain whiskies to create blends. These blended whiskies have dominated the market ever since; today's big-sellers include Bell's, the Famous Grouse, Chivas Regal and Johnny Walker Black Label.

But over the last half-century, the whisky industry has rediscovered the wonders of single-malt scotch in its own right. Glenfiddich was the first to dip a toe in the water in the 1960s, since when the floodgates have opened and the business has grown beyond all expectation. There are now roughly 95 distilleries across the country producing single-malt whisky.

It should follows that these 95 distilleries are producing 95 whiskies, but things aren't quite that simple. Take the aforementioned Glenfiddish, for instance. The label sells huge amounts of 12-year-old single malt, but its business has expanded greatly through the marketing of another seven varieties, from a different 12-year-old to a very expensive 50-year-old. In similar fashion, Glenmorangie is rightly celebrated for its ten-year-old whisky, now sold as the 'Original', but it also offers another five in its basic range. And then there are the multitudes of specialist expressions and limited-edition single-cask bottlings found at the likes of **Scotch Malt Whisky Society** (*see p182*).

The result of all this divergence has been a through-the-roof increase in the number of single-malt varieties over the last few decades. A recent edition of the annual *Jim Murray's Whisky Bible*, for instance, had tasting notes for a daunting 2,000-plus varieties. With such an insane level of choice, personal preference comes to the fore. Sometimes it really is best simply to head to a decent whisky pub such as the **Bow Bar** (*see p167*) and try a few, but more hands-on help is also available. The **Scotch Whisky Experience** (*see p59*) schedules supervised tastings and runs a formal one-day course; the Scotch Malt Whisky Society also runs supervised tastings for members; and you can ask staff at **Cadenhead's** whisky shop (*see p171*) about the tasting sessions it holds in a local pub. *Sláinte.*

CONSUME

Get the local experience

Over 50 of the world's top destinations available.

Café-bars

56 North
2-8 West Crosscauseway (662 8860, www.fifty sixnorth.co.uk). Bus 13 or Nicolson Street–North Bridge buses. **Open** noon-1am daily. *Food served* noon-9pm daily. **Credit** AmEx, MC, V. **Map** p333 J9 ④①
Back in the 1990s this place was known as Bar Ce Lona, then it became the Human Be-in and finally, in 2008, it morphed into 56 North. All that time it has been a student neighbourhood café-bar. Now its food includes gourmet burgers, flatbreads with the likes of salmon and avocado, salads, and dishes like gammon steak with duck egg.

Filmhouse Café Bar
88 Lothian Road (229 5932, www.filmhouse cinema.com). Bus 1, 2, 10, 11, 15, 15A, 16, 23, 24, 27, 34, 35, 45. **Open** 10am-11.30pm Mon-Thur, Sun; 10am-12.30am Fri, Sat. *Food served* 10am-10pm daily. **Credit** MC, V. **Map** p332 E6 & p336 A4 ④②
The city's independent arthouse cinema has been around since the 1980s and continues to draw a loyal crowd of cinephiles. With coffee, snacks, light meals and a couple of good beers on tap, the Filmhouse's café-bar is the perfect place to meet friends before or after a movie.
▶ *For the cinema itself, see p226.*

Montpeliers
159-161 Bruntsfield Place (229 3115, www. montpeliersedinburgh.co.uk). Bus 11, 15, 15A, 16, 23, 45. **Open** 9am-1am daily. *Food served* 9am-10pm daily. **Credit** MC, V.
Although it's been trading since 1992, the odd refurb has ensured that Montpeliers hasn't become dated or dowdy. The decor is currently clean cut, with sofas by the window and dark woods galore. The bar is to one side, with the dining space partitioned off to the other; here, you can sample the celebrated breakfast, along with salads, steaks, burgers or comfort food (Irish stew, perhaps).

Traverse Theatre Bar
10 Cambridge Street (228 5383, www.traverse. co.uk). Bus 1, 2, 10, 11, 15, 15A, 16, 23, 24, 27, 34, 35, 45. **Open** 10.30am-midnight Mon-Wed; 10.30am-1am Thur-Sat. *Food served* 10.30am-10pm daily. **Credit** MC, V. **Map** p332 E8 & p336 A3 ④③
The bar at the Trav gets very busy pre-and post-performance, especially during the Fringe. The modern, roomy establishment is generally open-plan, but there's a more closed-off dining space in one corner. It attracts a typical café-bar crowd: you can pick up anything from a veggie sausage roll or haggis roll for breakfast to nachos or a crayfish salad at night. There's free Wi-Fi.
▶ *For the theatre, see p254.*

WEST EDINBURGH
Pubs & bars

Caley Sample Room
58 Angle Park Terrace (337 7204, www.thecaley sampleroom.co.uk). Bus 2, 3, 3A, 4, 25, 33, 44, 44A. **Open** 11am-midnight Mon-Thur; 10am-1am Sat; 10am-midnight Sun. *Food served* noon-9pm Mon-Thur, Sun; noon-10pm Sat. **Credit** AmEx, MC, V. **Map** p331 A11 ④④
The Caley is red brick on the outside and roomy on the inside, with wooden benches and simple, functional decor. With good cask ales on offer, it invariably packed before Hearts games at nearby Tynecastle. In recent years, its menu has picked up no end; you'll find people popping in for good-quality sirloin steak and chips, bar snacks such as pitta with houmous, feta and chorizo, or even a full-on Sunday lunch.

Golden Rule
28-30 Yeaman Place (229 3413). Bus 22, 30. **Open** noon-midnight Mon-Sat; noon-11pm Sun. **Credit** MC, V. **Map** p331 B11 ④⑤
The Golden Rule is a friendly, old-fashioned pub with some cask ales, plus a more contemporary lounge bar downstairs that has won a reputation for its excellent jukebox. The western suburbs of the city tend to be a bit of a desert when it comes to decent pubs, so this one stands out all the more.

LEITH & THE COAST
Pubs & bars

★ Boda
229 Leith Walk, Leith (553 5900, www.boda bar.com). Bus 7, 10, 12, 14, 16, 22, 25, 49. **Open** 2pm-1am Mon-Fri; noon-1am Sat; 1pm-midnight Sun. **Credit** AmEx, MC, V. **Map** p329 L2 ④⑥
Run by a Swedish couple with a friendly and laid-back style, Boda operates like an inclusive neighbourhood pub, albeit one with cheese platters and

---

INSIDE TRACK LOCAL WHISKY

Although no one makes very much fuss about it, West Edinburgh boasts its very own whisky distillery. Unlike some of the more attractive single malt distilleries in the Scottish countryside, the **North British** near Tynecastle football stadium is an industrial-scale grain distillery, producing the anonymous grain whisky that goes into blends such as the Famous Grouse, J&B Rare and Johnny Walker Black Label. In operation since 1887, it's now distilled more than two billion litres.

CONSUME

Bond No.9. *See p182.*

moose sausages on the menu. Its owners have since built a mini-empire for themselves, with Sofi's (63 Henderson Street, Leith, 555 7019), the Victoria (265 Leith Walk, Leith, 555 1638) and Joseph Pearce's (23 Elm Row, Calton Hill & Broughton, 556 4140). *See also p171* **Size Matters**.

Cramond Inn

30 Cramond Glebe Road, Cramond (336 2035). Bus 24, 41. **Open** 11am-11pm Mon-Thur; 11am-midnight Fri, Sat; 12.30-11pm Sun. *Food served* noon-9pm Mon-Sat; 12.30-6pm Sun. **Credit** AmEx, MC, V.

On the coast stretching west from Leith, tucked away in a conservation village on the banks of the River Almond, this cosy, family-friendly venue is full of welcoming nooks and crannies. It's particularly busy on summer Sundays, when Edinburgh folk come up to these parts for a walk. Dating from the 17th century, the inn is now owned by Yorkshire brewery Samuel Smith's, and does basic pub grub.

Dalriada

77 The Promenade, Portobello (454 4500, www.dalriadabar.co.uk). Bus 12, 15, 15A, 32, 42, 49. **Open** 11am-11pm Mon-Thur, Sun; 11am-midnight Fri, Sat. **Credit** MC, V.

At this pub down at Portobello beach about three miles east of Leith, this former hotel is an ideal stop if you've been walking along the Esplanade. You can get a decent pint of cask ale or a coffee and sit in the front garden overlooking the sands, head for the enclosed beer garden at the back, or just hang out in the spacious interior.

Esplanade

62-64 Bath Street, Portobello (669 0082, www. the-espy.com). Bus 12, 15, 15A, 32, 42, 49. **Open** 11am-11pm Mon-Wed; 11am-1am Thur, Fri; 10am-1am Sat; 10am-11pm Sun. *Food served* noon-3pm, 5-10pm Mon-Fri; 10-11.45am, noon-10pm Sat; 10-11.45am, noon-9pm Sun. **Credit** AmEx, MC, V.

Right by the beach at Portobello, the Esplanade (the Espy to its friends) sits in premises that have been home to several bars over the years. Locals appreciate the basic but comfortable decor and the family-friendly ambience, whether stopping in for a drink or some food (burgers, nachos, salads and more). Like the Dalriada, it's a good stop-for-a-pint option if you're down at the beach.

Guilty Lily

284 Bonnington Road, Leith (554 5824, http://guiltylily.com). Bus 1, 10, 16, 22, 35, 36. **Open** noon-midnight Mon-Wed, Sun; noon-1am Thur-Sat. *Food served* noon-3pm, 5-10pm daily. **Credit** AmEx, MC, V.

From the people who brought you the Esplanade (*see above*), Guilty Lily arrived in late 2008 and functions like a modern neighbourhood pub in this still-changing part of Edinburgh. Food is a big feature, with inventive breakfasts (poached eggs and pesto mushrooms on toast) through to the popular home-made burgers.

King's Wark

36 The Shore, Leith (554 9260). Bus 1, 10, 16, 22, 35, 36. **Open** noon-11pm Mon-Thur;

noon-midnight Fri, Sat; 11am-11pm Sun. *Food served* noon-10pm Mon-Sat; 11am-3pm, 6-10pm Sun. **Credit** MC, V. **Map** p326 Y3 ⑰
The King's Wark stands on the site of a long-gone 15th-century building. There have probably been taverns here since the 17th century; the current building may be around 300 years old. The main room is simply a well-worn, welcoming pub, but there's a smaller space to one side for slightly more formal dining. The beer-battered fish and chips is always a winner.

Malt & Hops
45 The Shore, Leith (555 0083). Bus 1, 10, 16, 22, 35, 36. **Open** noon-11pm Mon, Tue; noon-midnight Wed, Thur; noon-1am Fri, Sat; 12.30-11pm Sun. *Food served* noon-2pm Wed-Fri. **Credit** AmEx, MC, V. **Map** p326 Y3 ⑲
No more and no less than the best cask ale bar in Leith sits right on the Water of Leith. It's a basic, old-fashioned, one-room pub with an open fire, seats outside in summer, a fine selection of regular and guest ales and a fair whisky choice. No one's here to see and be seen; you go for a pint and a chat.

Ocean Bar
Ocean Terminal, Ocean Drive, Leith (555 6222). Bus 1, 10, 16, 22, 35, 36. **Open** 10am-11pm Mon-Thur, Sun; 10am-midnight Fri, Sat. *Food served* 10am-9pm daily. **Credit** AmEx, MC, V. **Map** p326 X1 ⑲
On the first floor of the Ocean Terminal shopping mall, the Ocean Kitchen Bar & Grill has great views out over the Western Harbour, home of the

Royal Yacht Britannia. The bar side of the operation is particularly good for cocktails, though it's all at its best when you can go outside to the balcony and look out over the water. One of the more unusual places to drink in the city.
▶ *For the Ocean Terminal mall itself, see p185.*

Old Chain Pier
32 Trinity Crescent, by Newhaven (552 1233). Bus 10, 11, 16, 32. **Open** noon-10.30pm Mon-Thur; noon-midnight Fri, Sat; 12.30-10.30pm Sun. *Food served* noon-8pm Mon-Thur; noon-8.45pm Fri, Sat; 12.30-8pm Sun. **Credit** MC, V.
Sitting on the coast between the small harbours at Newhaven and Granton, the Old Chain Pier was built on the site of – yes, you guessed – an old chain pier that was constructed in 1821 and swept away in a storm in 1898. Today, it functions as a friendly neighbourhood pub, with a conservatory for more formal dining. However, it's best for a simple pint and a bar meal while gazing out over the Forth.

Pond
2 Bath Road, Leith (467 3825). Bus 1, 10, 16, 22, 35, 36. **Open** 4pm-midnight Mon-Thur, Sun; 4pm-1am Fri, Sat. **Credit** AmEx, MC, V.
The encroachment of new apartment blocks has put paid to the Pond's former reputation as 'the pub at the end of the universe', but it's still on a fairly unlovely street between Leith Links and the docks (albeit not far from the Shore and the heart of Leith). It has the look of a hand-knitted university common room, but with a decent pint in hand and a seat on one of the sofas, it can seem like a home from home.

CONSUME

Port o' Leith

58 Constitution Street (554 3568). Bus 1, 10, 16, 22, 35, 36. **Open** *9am-1am Mon-Sat; 12.30pm-1am Sun.* **No credit cards.** **Map** p326 Z3 ⑩
Both this pub and its proprietor, Mary Moriarty, are legends on the Edinburgh pub scene. It's a small, neatly kept venue, patronised by everyone from merchant mariners to locals and students, and can get a little robust at times. Still, you could sit for hours looking at the details: ships' flags, lifebelts, snuff for sale and so on. The true essence of Leith.

★ Roseleaf

23-24 Sandport Place, Leith (476 5268, http://roseleaf.co.uk). Bus 1, 10, 16, 22, 35, 36. **Open** *10am-midnight Mon-Thur, Sun; 10am-1am Fri, Sat. Food served 10am-10pm daily.* **Credit** MC, V. **Map** p326 X3 ⑪
Once a fairly unremarkable pub, this place was transformed in 2007, and is now a friendly, considered and attractive environment where people are as likely to pop in for food – or decent tea in a china cup – as they are for a beer at the bar. The Cullen skink (smoked fish soup) is among the city's best; there are also some excellent breakfast choices.

★ Scotch Malt Whisky Society Members' Room

The Vaults, 87 Giles Street (555 2266, www.smws.com). Bus 1, 10, 16, 22, 35, 36. **Open** *10am-11pm Mon-Wed; 10am-midnight Thur-Sat; 11am-10pm Sun. Food served noon-9pm Mon-Wed; noon-10pm Thur-Sat; noon-2.30pm, 6-8.30pm Sun.* **Credit** AmEx, MC, V. **Map** p326 Y3 ⑫
The SMWS was set up in 1983 to buy individual casks of whisky from distilleries, bottle them and sell them to members. The atmosphere is tranquil, the food is decent and the range of whiskies is terrific. The catch: it's open to members and guests only; membership is £100 for the first year, cheaper thereafter. If you go with a member, they can sign you in. **Other locations** 28 Queen Street, New Town (220 2044).

INSIDE TRACK
THE PAST IN A GLASS

The most resonant place to drink wine in Edinburgh is the **Vintners Rooms** restaurant in Leith (*see p166*). Monks began importing wine into Leith in the 12th century; this particular building has a history as a wine store that dates back to the 15th century, if not earlier. The more ornate of the restaurant's two dining areas dates to the 18th century and used to be a wine auction room. Sipping your 1986 Margaux there today (£880) means following in a very old tradition.

Shore

3-4 The Shore, Leith (553 5080, www.theshore.biz). Bus 1, 10, 16, 22, 35, 36. **Open** *noon-1am daily. Food served noon-10pm daily.* **Credit** MC, V. **Map** p326 Y2 ⑬
The Shore has a small, bustling bar and tables outside on the pavement; you can even take your drink across the street to the quayside and sit watching the Water of Leith flow into the docks. It's essentially a gastropub: the bar menu is fabulous, and an adjoining room operates as a restaurant, serving some excellent fish dishes.
► *It's now owned by the people behind Fishers next door; see p163.*

Starbank Inn

64 Laverockbank Road, by Newhaven (552 4141, www.starbankinn.co.uk). Bus 10, 11, 16, 32. **Open** *11am-11pm Mon-Wed; 11am-midnight Thur-Sat; 12.30-11pm Sun. Food served noon-2.30pm, 6-9pm Mon-Fri; noon-9pm Sat; 12.30-9pm Sun.* **Credit** AmEx, MC, V.
Set back and slightly raised on the other side of the street from the sea wall, the Starbank arguably has better views of the Forth than the nearby Old Chain Pier (*see p181*). Like its neighbour, it offers good cask ales, but is the more patrician of the two establishments. The menu offers solid, traditional fare; roast lamb and mint sauce, poached salmon, ploughman's lunch and the like.

Café-bars

Bond No.9

84 Commercial Street, Leith (555 5578, www.bondno9.co.uk). Bus 1, 10, 16, 22, 35, 36. **Open** *11am-1am daily. Food served 11am-10pm daily.* **Credit** AmEx, MC, V. **Map** p326 Y2 ⑭
Housed in an old warehouse in Leith, this champagne and cocktail bar opened just in time for the 2008 credit crunch. The timing may have been a little off, but there's no arguing with the quality of product: great bar staff and very good cocktails indeed. The menu (the likes of prawn and chorizo salad, followed by pasta with meatballs in tomato sauce) isn't bad either. *Photos pp180-181.*

Malmaison Bar

1 Tower Place (468 5000, www.malmaison.com). Bus 1, 10, 16, 22, 35, 36. **Open** *9am-1am daily. Food served 11am-8pm daily.* **Credit** AmEx, DC, MC, V. **Map** p326 Y2 ⑮
The name is now well known thanks to a string of boutique hotels across the UK, but this was the very first Malmaison in the country. The ground floor has a fine contemporary bar space, with outdoor seating on the terrace that overlooks the water. The food here is good, but the Malmaison Brasserie next door has a more extensive menu.
► *For the hotel, see p132.*

Shops & Services

Any colour as long as it's tartan...

Your impressions of Edinburgh's shopping scene depend on where you shop. If you stick to the Royal Mile in the Old Town, you might assume that all the city has to offer is shortbread, whisky and a baffling variety of tartan tat. If you limit yourself to Princes Street, you'd be forgiven for thinking you were on any high street in the UK. But if you get off the well-trodden tourist trail, you'll find everything from big-name designer stores (George Street) to tiny antiques shops (Stockbridge), all of which combine to lend character to the neighbourhoods in which they sit.

General shop opening hours are from 9am or 10am until 6pm from Monday to Saturday. However, lots of shops stay open late on Thursday, and some are also open on Sunday. During August and in the run-up to Christmas, many shops extend their opening hours; call ahead to check.

General

DEPARTMENT STORES

All the UK's big department stores have branches in Edinburgh. Most are on Princes Street.

Debenhams
109-112 Princes Street, New Town (0844 561 6161, www.debenhams.com). Princes Street buses. **Open** 9.30am-6.30pm Mon-Wed, Fri; 9.30am-8pm Thur; 9am-6.30pm Sat; 11am-6pm Sun. **Credit** AmEx, MC, V. **Map** p332 F7 & p336 B2.
Once you've negotiated the various levels, you'll find a good fashion selection: the Designers at Debenhams range features clothes by the likes of Ben de Lisi, Pearce Fionda, Betty Jackson and John Rocha. There are also decent ranges of homewares, accessories and cosmetics.
Other locations Ocean Terminal, Leith (08445 616161).

Harvey Nichols
30-34 St Andrew Square, New Town (524 8388, www.harveynichols.com). Princes Street buses.

About the author
Kaye McAlpine has lived and worked in Edinburgh for more than 20 years. As well as working on guidebooks, she has several academic publications to her name.

Open 10am-6pm Mon-Wed; 10am-8pm Thur; 10am-7pm Fri, Sat; 11am-6pm Sun. **Credit** AmEx, DC, MC, V. **Map** p328 H5 & p336 E1.
With four floors of glossy-magazine clothing, this is a fashionista's delight. As well as the clothes, priced highly, you'll find exclusive cosmetics and fragrance brands, a Charlie Miller salon, a personal shopping service, and the Forth Floor bar and restaurant, with breathtaking views.

Jenners
48 Princes Street, New Town (0844 800 3725, www.houseoffraser.co.uk). Princes Street buses. **Open** 9.30am-6pm Mon-Wed, Fri, Sat; 9.30am-7pm Thur; 9am-6pm Sat; 11.30am-5.30pm Sun. **Credit** AmEx, DC, MC, V. **Map** p328 & p332 G6, p336 E2.
Based at this Princes Street location since 1838 but now owned by House of Fraser, Jenners retains a loyal following. The six floors offer a wide range of fashion brands, with names such as Superdry, Canali and Paul Smith for men and Diesel Premium and Jaeger for women. The cosmetics department has names such as Kiehls and Biotherm on its roster; the food hall is now run by Valvona & Crolla. A refurbishment has highlighted the shop's striking architectural features. *Photos p184.*
▶ *Parent company House of Fraser has its own store further along Princes Street (no.145, 0844 800 3724).*

Jenners. *See p183.*

★ John Lewis

69 St James Centre, Leith Street, New Town (556 9121, www.johnlewis.com). Princes Street buses. **Open** 9am-6pm Mon-Wed; 9am-8pm Thur; 9am-6pm Fri; 9am-6.30pm Sat; 10am-6pm Sun. **Credit** MC, V. **Map** p328 H5.

Four floors offer the usual sensible, mainstream John Lewis range of technology, beauty, fashion and homewares, all with the 'never knowingly undersold' guarantee. Following a £25m refurbishment a few years back, this branch has a modern feel. John Lewis stocks Apple computers, one of the few city-centre sources. The café has great views over the city and the Forth of Firth.

Marks & Spencer

54 Princes Street, New Town (225 2301, www.marksandspencer.com). Princes Street buses. **Open** 9am-7pm Mon-Wed, Fri; 9am-8pm Thur; 8.30am-7pm Sat; 11am-6pm Sun. **Credit** AmEx, MC, V. **Map** p328 & p332 G6, p336 D2.

Recently refurbished, the Princes Street branch is M&S's flagship Edinburgh store, stocking all the brand's ranges. Women's fashions, menswear, childrenswear and homewares are now all under the one roof, after years of being in two different Princes Street locations. There's also a large food hall, plus two cafés.
Other locations 21 Gyle Avenue, West Edinburgh (317 1333).

MALLS

Most malls in the Edinburgh area contain the same retailers you'll find on the high street. However, a few also house cinemas, all have places to eat and most will keep you dry when it's raining outside.

Cameron Toll

6 Lady Road, South Edinburgh (666 2777, www.camerontoll.co.uk). Bus 24, 29, 31, 37, 38, 42. **Open** 10am-6pm Mon-Wed, Sat; 10am-7pm Thur, Fri; 11am-5pm Sun: some stores, such as Sainsbury's are open later.

A ten-minute bus ride south of the city centre, Cameron Toll houses around 40 stores, most of which are high-street names (Boots, Waterstone's, Game and plenty of others where they came from). There's also a sizeable Sainsbury's.

★ Fort Kinnaird

Newcraighall Road, South Edinburgh (669 9090, www.fortkinnaird.com). Bus 30. **Open** 10am-8pm Mon-Fri; 9am-6pm Sat; 10am-6pm Sun.

Recently renovated, sprawling Fort Kinnaird is home to dozens of familiar stores, including Marks & Spencer, Toys R Us, H&M, Monsoon, Next and Edinburgh's only Borders. The leisure venues were demolished as part of the facelift, but there are plenty of cafés inside the stores.

Gyle Centre
South Gyle Broadway, West Edinburgh (539 8828, www.gyleshopping.co.uk). Bus 12, 21, 24 58 or Edinburgh Park rail. **Open** 9.30am-8pm Mon-Wed, Fri; 9.30am-9pm Thur; 9am-6pm Sat; 10am-6pm Sun.

A 20-minute drive west of the city, the Gyle is home to Morrison's at one end and Marks & Spencer at the other. In the expanse between, you'll find stores such as Gap, Next, New Look, Austin Reed, Monsoon and other well-known high street names.

★ Ocean Terminal
Ocean Drive, Leith (555 8888, www.ocean terminal.com). Bus 1, 11, 22, 34, 35, 36. **Open** 10am-8pm Mon-Fri; 10am-7pm Sat; 11am-6pm Sun. **Map** p326 X1.

A mall with a difference – not everyone has the Queen's old yacht moored outside. As well as the Royal Yacht *Britannia*, Ocean Terminal has a freesport facility on the top floor, a Vue cinema, a Pure spa and a soft play area for young children. Shops include Fat Face, White Stuff, Xile, Korres, French Connection, Faith, Joy, Baxters, a Charlie Miller hair salon and Ness, as well as more typical mall stores such as Bhs and Debenhams.

Princes Mall
Princes Street, New Town (557 3759, www. princesmall-edinburgh.co.uk). Princes Street buses. **Open** 9am-6pm Mon-Wed, Fri, Sat; 9am-7pm Thur; 11am-5pm Sun. **Map** p328 & p332 H6, p336 E2.

Right next door to Waverley train station, Princes Mall houses a Kookai and Oasis, as well as Warehouse, Joy and a branch of New Look. There are also a number of smaller stores, a Regis hair salon, a Costa, and a selection of fast food options.

Where to Shop

Edinburgh's best shopping neighbourhoods in brief.

THE OLD TOWN
Along the **Royal Mile**, it's pretty much wall-to-wall souvenirs. But away from the main drag, there's more of note. **Cockburn Street** contains a mix of record stores (Avalanche, Underground Solush'n), independent fashion stores (Cookie) and other unusual gift stores. At the bottom sits the **Grassmarket**, with vintage clothing stores, antiques shops and the occasional market.

THE NEW TOWN
The heart of Edinburgh's shopping culture is in the New Town, especially along **Princes Street**. You'll find many big names from the British high street: department stores such as Debenhams and House of Fraser, fashion favourites including H&M and Gap, and newer names such as Zara and Urban Outfitters. The street has suffered from a certain malaise in recent years, and the stores at the West End pumping out electro-bagpipe music haven't helped; however, it still draws the crowds.

Stroll north from here up **Castle**, **Frederick** or **Hanover Streets**, and the landscape changes immediately. In Georgian and Victorian buildings that once housed banking institutions and offices, you'll find the likes of Whistles, Jigsaw, Karen Millen, the White Company and Phase Eight. Running parallel to Princes Street, **George Street** is home to numerous designer labels, beauty stores and other worthwhile enterprises; scattered in between them are a decent selection of bars and cafés, as well as the ubiquitous coffee franchises.

At the eastern end of George Street, through St Andrew Square, stands Harvey Nichols. It's the gateway to **Multrees Walk**: one of Edinburgh's newest streets, it's lined with upscale designer stores. West of George Street, meanwhile, sits **William Street**, home to gorgeous boutiques and other independent stores.

CALTON HILL & BROUGHTON
Just north of the hulking St James Centre, **Broughton Street** is the commercial hub of this part of town. You'll find a number of interesting shops along here, chiefly in the fashion and food fields.

STOCKBRIDGE
Along the western part of **St Stephen Street**, **North West Circus Place**, **Deanhaugh Street** and, especially, **Raeburn Place** (Stockbridge's main drag), a huge number of independent shops deal in everything from upscale fashion to antique furniture. This corner of Stockbridge is one of the city's most interesting shopping areas.

LEITH & THE COAST
Shopping in Leith is dominated by the massive **Ocean Terminal** mall, which holds an array of big and familiar names. However, there are a few other shops of note scattered around the neighbourhood.

St James Centre
Leith Street, New Town (557 0050, www.stjames shopping.com). Playhouse or Princes Street buses. **Open** 9am-6pm Mon-Wed, Fri, Sat; 9am-7pm Thu; 10am-6pm Sun. **Map** p328 H5.
The main draw here is John Lewis (*see p184*), which claims to be Scotland's largest department store. Among the other attractions are familiar names such as HMV, Next and Topshop and a post office. The much-criticised concrete exterior is on its way out: there are plans to revamp the entire site.

MARKETS

In recent years, a combination of new buildings and trading standards clampdowns have put paid to some of the city's markets and boot sales. However, temporary specialist markets are often set up in the city centre, especially around the Grassmarket and Castle Street, during August's festivals and in the run-up to Christmas. For the city's farmers' market, *see p199*.

Specialist
BOOKS & MAGAZINES
General

Edinburgh is home to branches of two major chains, both good all-rounders. **Waterstone's** (www.waterstones.co.uk) are at 13 and 128 Princes Street and at Ocean Terminal in Leith, while **Blackwells** (www.blackwells.co.uk) are at 53-62 South Bridge, Old Town.

Travellers in search of news from home should try the **International Newsagents** (351 High Street, Old Town, 225 4827).

Specialist

Analogue
102 West Bow, Old Town (220 0601, www. analoguebooks.co.uk). Bus 2, 23, 27, 41, 42. **Open** 10am-5.30pm Mon-Sat. **Credit** MC, V. **Map** p332 G8 & p336 D4.
Books on design, photography and contemporary culture, glossy tomes on fashion, illustration, graffiti and graphic design, and interesting T-shirts, magazines and prints.
▶ *There's also a gallery here; see p228.*

★ Beyond Words
42-44 Cockburn Street, Old Town (226 6636, www.beyondwords.co.uk). Bus 35 or Nicolson Street–North Bridge buses. **Open** 10am-6pm Mon-Sat; 1-6pm Sun. **Credit** MC, V. **Map** p332 H7 & p336 F3.
Scotland's premier photographic bookshop stocks an impressive range of books, from coffee table-friendly tomes to technical manuals.

★ Children's Bookshop
219 Bruntsfield Place, South Edinburgh (447 1917, www.fidrabooks.com). Bus 11, 15, 15A, 16, 23, 45. **Open** 10am-5pm Mon-Sat. **Credit** MC, V. **Map** p332 E11.
Set up by publisher Fidra, this newish enterprise does just what it says on the tin. As well as Fidra's own titles, the shop sells the best in children's contemporary fiction and non-fiction.

CONSUME

Analogue.

Concrete Wardrobe. *See p191.*

CONSUME

Deadhead Comics

27 Candlemaker Row, Old Town (226 2774, www.deadheadcomics.com). Bus 2, 23, 27, 41, 42. **Open** 10am-6pm Mon-Sat; noon-6pm Sun. **Credit** AmEx, MC, V. **Map** p332 H8.

Everything a comic shop should be: small, stacked, and staffed by guys who really know their stuff. Deadhead offers American superhero titles, lesser-known indie works and some secondhand comics.

Word Power

43 West Nicolson Street, South Edinburgh (662 9112, www.word-power.co.uk). Nicolson Street–North Bridge buses. **Open** 10am-6pm Mon- Sat; noon-5pm Sun. **Credit** AmEx, MC, V. **Map** p333 J9.

An old-school giant-fighter, this radical bookstore sells titles from new writers and small presses alongside magazines and mainstream radical books. It hosts a Radical Book Fair in October and a Fringe alternative to the International Book Festival in August.

Used & antiquarian

Armchair Books

72-74 West Port, South Edinburgh (229 5927, www.mochaholic.org/acb). Bus 2, 35. **Open** 10am-7pm Mon-Sun. **Credit** MC, V. **Map** p332 F8.

Armchair is an archetypal secondhand bookshop, its teeming shelves stacked with old volumes. Armchair specialises in Victorian, illustrated and antiquarian books, and is a real browser's paradise.

Old Town Bookshop

8 Victoria Street, Old Town (225 9237, www.oldtownbookshop.com). Bus 23, 27, 41, 42. **Open** 10.30am-5.30pm Mon-Sat. **Credit** MC, V. **Map** p332 H7 & p336 D4.

Specialists in antiquarian titles in art and architecture, Scottish history and topographical studies. There are also good collections of maps and prints.

Oxfam Bookshops

109 High Street, Old Town (557 3539, www. oxfam.org.uk). Nicolson Street–North Bridge buses. **Open** call for details. **No credit cards**. **Map** p333 J7.

Oxfam has several outlets dedicated to books in the city. The High Street store is the most central and the most mainstream, but the branch in Stockbridge (25 Raeburn Place, 332 9632) feels more like a 'proper' bookshop, with some antiquarian titles.

CHILDREN

Fashion

Bliss

5 Raeburn Place, Stockbridge (332 4605) Bus 24, 29, 42. **Open** Mon-Sat 10am-5.30pm; 1pm-5pm Sun. **Credit** MC, V. **Map** p327 D4.

Babies' and toddlers' clothes from labels such as Trumpette, Starchild, Katvig and Brights & Stripes. Gifts and cards are also sold.

Other locations 111A Broughton Street, New Town (556 3311).

★ Maddie & Mark's
1 Craigcrook Place, North Edinburgh (315 3322, www.maddieandmarks.co.uk). Bus 24, 41. **Open** 9.30am-5.30pm Mon-Sat (also Sun in Aug). **Credit** MC, V.
An independent shoe shopt, with brands including Lelli Kelly, Umi, Stones & Bones, Geox, as well as Startrite and the ubiquitous Crocs.
Other locations 205 Bruntsfield Place, South Edinburgh (447 9779).

Nippers
131 Bruntsfield Place, South Edinburgh (228 5086, www.nippersforkids.com). Bus 11, 15, 15A, 16, 23, 45. **Open** 9.30am-5.30pm Mon-Sat; noon-4pm Sun. **Credit** MC, V. **Map** p332 E11.
Karen Mackay's company has been producing practical clothing for children up to around six years old for more than 20 years. Her shop also stocks brands such as Bob & Blossom and No Added Sugar.

Toys

For the **Children's Bookshop**, *see p187.*

Aha Ha Ha
99 West Bow, Old Town (220 5252). Bus 2, 23, 27, 41, 42. **Open** 10am-6pm Mon-Sat. **Credit** MC, V. **Map** p332 G8 & p336 D4.
The city's best-known joke shop is flagged by an oversized Groucho moustache and glasses above the front door. You'll also find stage make-up, magic tricks and dressing-up costumes.

Hatches, Matches & Dispatches
166 Bruntsfield Place, South Edinburgh (228 4441). Bus 11, 15, 15A, 16, 23, 45. **Open** 9am-5.30pm Mon-Sat. **Credit** AmEx, MC, V. **Map** p332 E11.
With sturdy painted wooden toys that are very much built to last, this shop is sheer heaven for plastic-hating parents.

Seesaw
109 Broughton Street, Broughton (556 9672). Bus 8. **Open** 9.30am-6pm Mon-Sat; noon-5pm Sun. **Credit** AmEx, MC, V. **Map** p328 H4.
Seesaw sells wooden toys that don't bleep or light up. There are also selections of soft toys, mobiles and rattles for the youngest babies, plus washable nappies, wraps and slings.

★ Toys Galore
193 Morningside Road, South Edinburgh (447 1006). Bus 11, 15, 15A, 16, 41. **Open** 9.30am-5.30pm Mon-Sat. **Credit** MC, V.
All of the leading toy brands (Playmobil, Brio et al) are sold here, as are specialist lines from the likes of Steiff Bears and Alberon Dolls.

Wonderland
97 & 101 Lothian Road, West Edinburgh (229 6428, www.wonderlandmodels.com). Bus 1, 2, 10, 11, 15, 15A, 16, 23, 24, 27, 34, 35, 45. **Open** *Jan-Sept* 9.30am-6pm Mon-Fri; 9am-6pm Sat. *Oct-Dec* 9.30am-6pm Mon-Fri; 9am-6pm Sat; noon-5pm Sun. **Credit** AmEx, MC, V. **Map** p332 E8 & p336 A4.
Wonderland stocks a huge range of craft, model, and toy paraphernalia, including Scalextric, Meccano, model figures (Breyer, Papo, Schleich, King & Country), trains, dolls' houses and much more.

ELECTRONICS & PHOTOGRAPHY

General

Basic electronics and computing needs can be met on Princes Street or at one of the out-of-town retail parks, most of which are home to the likes of Currys or PC World.

Specialist

For gamers, there's a branch of **Game** at 127 Princes Street (225 3453, www.game.net). In the unlikely event that you need to rent a mobile phone for your stay, contact **Cellhire** (www.cellhire.com).

Blacks & Lizars
6 Shandwick Place, New Town (225 2195, www.blacksandlizars.com). Bus 3, 3A, 4, 12, 25, 26, 31, 33, 44. **Open** 9am-5.30pm

CONSUME

Mon-Wed, Fri; 9am-7pm Thur; 9am-5pm Sat.
Credit AmEx, MC, V. **Map** p331 D7.
Although they're best known as optometrists,
Blacks & Lizars also specialises in photographic
equipment: digital, compact and SLR cameras, plus
camcorders, lenses and all kinds of accessories.

Ideal Computing

*78 Bruntsfield Place, South Edinburgh (0871
700 0150, www.idealcomputing.co.uk). Bus 11,
15, 15A, 16, 23, 45.* **Open** 9am-6pm daily.
Credit MC, V. **Map** p332 E11.
If you're overwhelmed by the PC superstores, this
small outlet, which custom-builds and sells its own
systems, is a good alternative.

FASHION

Designer

A few major designer stores have branches on
Multrees Walk, off St Andrew Square in the
New Town. Among them are **Emporio
Armani** (no.23, 523 1580, www.emporioarmani.
com), **Louis Vuitton** (nos.1-2, 652 5900, www.
louisvuitton.com) and leather label **Mulberry**
(no.6, 557 5439, www.mulberry.com).

Arkangel

*4 William Street, New Town (226 4466, www.
arkangelfashion.co.uk). Bus 3, 3A, 4, 12, 25, 26,
31, 33, 44.* **Open** 10am-5.30pm Mon-Wed, Fri, Sat;
10am-6.30pm Thur. **Credit** MC, V. **Map** p331 D7.
Easily identifiable from its pink exterior, Arkangel
is one of Edinburgh's best loved independently
owned boutiques, home to a delectable range of chic
clothing. The pieces, from the likes of Lilith, Marion
Foale, Öslem Süer and Antoine & Lili, should delight
anyone who's looking for a more individualistic
look. There's also a great range of costume jewellery.

★ Corniche

*2 Jeffrey Street, Old Town (556 3707, www.
corniche.org.uk). Bus 35 or Nicolson Street–North
Bridge buses.* **Open** 10.30am-5.30pm Mon-Sat.
Credit AmEx, MC, V. **Map** p329 & p333 J6.
For more than 30 years, Corniche has been the
byword for designer shopping in the city. Designers
such as Westwood, Nigel Cabourne and Gaultier are
represented year-round.

INSIDE TRACK SHORTCUTS

Feet getting tired on the fashion trail?
Try cutting through from George Street
to Rose Street via the close between the
Dome (14 George Street) and **Le Monde**
(16 George Street). You'll come out
opposite M&S and very near Jenners.

Cruise

*94 George Street, New Town (226 3524, www.
cruiseclothing.co.uk). Bus 13, 23, 27, 42 or Princes
Street buses.* **Open** 9.30am-6pm Mon-Wed, Fri,
Sat; 10am-8pm Thur; 11am-5.30pm Sun. **Credit**
AmEx, MC, V. **Map** p328 & p332 F6, p336 C1.
Cruise has been catering to fashion-conscious Scots
for 20 years now. Brands include Armani, Dior,
Prada, Gucci, John Smedley, Dolce & Gabbana,
Ghost and Galliano.
Other locations Cruise Jeans, 80 George Street,
New Town (226 0840).

Jane Davidson

*52 Thistle Street, New Town (225 3280, www.
janedavidson.co.uk). Bus 13, 23, 27, 42 or
Princes Street buses.* **Open** 9.30am-6pm Mon-
Wed, Fri, Sat; 9am-7pm Thur. **Credit** AmEx,
MC, V. **Map** p328 G5.
Davidson has been attracting in-the-know locals
since 1969. Labels include Ben de Lisi, Christian
Lacroix, Diane von Furstenberg, Missoni and more.
New international lines are frequently added.

Sam Thomas

*18 Stafford Street, New Town (226 1126,
www.sam-thomas.co.uk). Bus 3, 3A, 4, 12, 25,
26, 31, 33, 44.* **Open** 9.30am-6pm Mon-Wed,
Fri, Sat; 9.30am-6.30pm Thur; 12.30-5pm Sun.
Credit AmEx, MC, V. **Map** p331 D7.
With labels such as great Plains, Nougat and Avoca
laid out on colour-coordinated rails, clothes here feel
smart enough, but the prices won't break the bank.
A branch at 5 William Street stocks accessories.

Discount

Edinburgh isn't great for discount shopping,
but there are branches of cheapy chain
TK Maxx at Meadowbank Retail Park
(London Road, Calton Hill, 661 6611, www.
tkmaxx.co.uk) and **Craigleith Retail Park**
(32 South Groathill Avenue, 315 3600,
www.thequarrycraigleith.co.uk).

General

The question of whether **Princes Street** is
still Edinburgh's premier shopping street is
open to debate, but it remains home to most
of the high-street fashion retailers. Chains such
as **Gap** (no.48, 220 2846), **Top Shop** (no.30,
556 0151), **Zara** (no.104, 240 3230) and **H&M**
(no.85, 226 0790) all have large outlets here.
   A couple of blocks north, **George Street** is
home to more upmarket chains such as **Karen
Millen** (no.53, 220 1589), **Whistles** (no.97, 226
4398) and **Hobbs** (no.47, 220 5386). However,
venture beyond the high street and you'll
find an inspiring range of boutiques, stocking
everything from urban labels to local designers.

Ragamuffin. *See p195.*

See p195.

CONSUME

Bohemia

17 Roseneath Street, South Edinburgh (478 9609, www.bohemiadesign.co.uk). Bus 24, 41. **Open** 10am-6pm Mon-Sat; 1-5pm Sun. **Credit** MC, V. **Map** p332 H11.

The clothes in this lovely South Edinburgh boutique come from Swedish label Odd Molly, plus the likes of American Vintage, Bensimon and Totem Praia. There are cosmetics from Ortigia, MOR and Paul & Joe, plus cute kidswear.

★ Concrete Wardrobe

50A Broughton Street, New Town (558 7130, www.concretewardrobe.co.uk). Bus 8. **Open** 10am-6pm Mon-Sat noon-4pm Sun. **Credit** AmEx, MC, V. **Map** p328 H4.

Concrete Wardrobe is staffed by some of the designers whose work is sold in it, so expect some expert help with making your choice. There's a lot to enjoy here: fashion, great accessories and unique gifts.

Cookie

29A-31 Cockburn Street, Old Town (622 7260). Bus 35 or Nicolson Street–North Bridge buses. **Open** 9.30am-6pm Mon-Wed, Fri, Sat; 9.30am-7pm Thur; 11am-5pm Sun. **Credit** AmEx, MC, V. **Map** p332 H7 & p336 F3.

Its ranges of colourful dresses, pretty tops and skirts make Cookie feel like a vintage shop. The twist is that all the stock is new, and includes plenty of unusual labels.

Cult Clothing

7-9 North Bridge, Old Town (556 5003, www.cult.co.uk). Nicolson Street–North Bridge buses. **Open** 9.30am-6pm Mon-Wed, Fri, Sat; 10am-7pm Thur; noon-5pm Sun. **Credit** AmEx, MC, V. **Map** p328 & p332 H6, p336 F3.

Cult caters to casual twentysomethings with a variety of brands: Superdry, Electro Honey, Breed and the like. If it's on-trend, it'll be here.

Cupboard

10 William Street, New Town (226 6580, www.thecupboard.co.uk). Bus 3, 3A, 4, 12, 25, 26, 31, 33, 44. **Open** 10am-5.30pm Mon-Wed, Fri; 10am-6.30pm Thur; 9.30am-5.30pm Sat. **Credit** AmEx, MC, V. **Map** p331 D7.

The Cupboard is one of those rare fashion shops in which the customer is always valued and isn't

TimeOut

timeout.com/travel
Get the local experience

Dream deli counter at Franchi, in the Prati district, **Rome**

placed a poor second to the clothes. With labels such as Annette Görtz, James Lakeland, Ischiko and Absolut in stock, this is a delightful boutique, stocking stylish labels that don't stop at size 14.

Eden
18 North West Circus Place, New Town (225 5222, www.edenretail.co.uk). Bus 24, 29, 42. **Open** 10am-5.30pm Tue-Sat. **Credit** MC, V. **Map** p328 E5.
Eden stocks clothes you won't find elsewhere in the city, from designers such as Noli and Desigual. Accessory brands include Anna Lou of London.

Godiva
9 West Port, South Edinburgh (221 9212, www. godivaboutique.co.uk). Bus 2, 35. **Open** 10am-6.30pm Mon-Fri; 10.30am-6pm Sat; 10.30am-5pm Sun. **Credit** MC, V. **Map** p332 G8.
As well as stocking quality vintage clothing, Godiva champions new and local designers, and has also branched out into made-to-measure pieces.

Joey D
54 Broughton Street, Broughton (557 6672, www.joey-d.co.uk). Bus 8, 13, 17. **Open** 10.30am-6pm daily. **Credit** MC, V. **Map** p328 H4.
The garments here are best described as deconstructed then reconstructed. Vintage clothes are ripped up and put back together to create something different. Accessories are equally left-field.

Psycho-Moda
22 St Mary's Street, Old Town (557 6777). Bus 35 or Nicolson Street–North Bridge buses. **Open** 11am-6pm Mon-Sat. **Credit** MC, V. **Map** p333 J7.
This small boutique deals in own-label clothing for women, including dresses in luxurious fabrics. It also offers a made-to-measure service.

Slater Menswear
100 George Street, New Town (220 4343, www.slaters.co.uk). Bus 13, 23, 27, 42 or Princes Street buses. **Open** 8.30am-5.30pm Mon-Wed, Fri, Sat; 8.30am-7.30pm Thur; 11.30am-4.30pm Sun. **Credit** AmEx, MC, V. **Map** p328 & p332 F6, p336 B1.
Slater stocks a range of classic brands for men, such as Dents, Farah, Aquascutum and Dockers, as well as the likes of Caterpillar, Calvin Klein and Everlast. It also offers formal hire and kilt hire.

Swish
22-24 Victoria Street, Old Town (220 0615, www.swishonthe.com). Bus 2, 23, 27, 41, 42. **Open** 10.30am-6pm Mon-Sat; noon-5pm Sun. **Credit** AmEx, MC, V. **Map** p332 J7 & p336 D4.
Swish offers urban chic for men, women and kids in a store that spans two floors. Labels include Bench, Religion and Gsus. There's also a range of quirky accessories alongside the clothes.

Xile
Princes Mall, Princes Street, New Town (556 6508, www.xileclothing.com). Princes Street buses. **Open** 9.30am-6pm Mon-Sat; 11am-5pm Sun. **Credit** MC, V. **Map** p328 & p332 H6, p336 E2.
There are three Xile stores in Princes Mall, all with a slightly different stock: the Directional store has more cutting-edge labels; and you'll find the largest stock of Lyle and Scott's luxury knits in any independent outlet in the Casualwear store, as well the likes of Barbour, Luke and Paul & Shark.
Other locations Ocean Terminal, Leith (555 3088, 561 4496).

Traditional

See p194 **If the Kilt Fits....**

★ Belinda Robertson
13A Dundas Street, New Town (557 8118, www.belindarobertson.com). Bus 23, 27. **Open** 9.30am-6pm Mon-Fri; 10am-6pm Sat; noon-5pm Sun. **Credit** AmEx, MC, V. **Map** p328 F5.
Belinda Robertson offers a blend of traditional and more contemporary designs in cashmere. There are two labels: White Label is the more affordable, but Black Label is made entirely in Scotland.

Geoffrey (Tailor) Kiltmakers & Weavers
57-61 High Street, Old Town (557 0256, www. geoffreykilts.co.uk). Bus 35 or Nicolson Street–North Bridge buses. **Open** 9am-5.30pm Mon-Wed, Fri, Sat; 9am-7pm Thur; 10am-5pm Sun. **Credit** AmEx, MC, V. **Map** p333 J7.
One of the city's best Highland outfitters stocks kilts (including children's kilts), ladies' kilted skirts and all the relevant accessories.

★ 21st Century Kilts
48 Thistle Street, New Town (220 9450, www.21stcenturykilts.com). Bus 13, 23, 24, 27, 42. **Open** 10am-6pm Tue, Wed, Fri, Sat; 10am-7pm Thur. **Credit** AmEx, MC, V. **Map** p328 & p332 F6.
Howie Nicholson's take on the kilt has helped alter the garment's image. You'll find camouflage, black, denim, leather and PVC kilt options for men and women, and even a few for kids. If you're going to go for the casual kilt look, boys, wear 'em with big boots and your socks shoved down to your ankles.

Hawick Cashmere
71 Grassmarket, Old Town (225 8634, www. hawickcashmere.com). Bus 2, 23, 27, 28, 42, 45. **Open** 10am-6pm Mon-Sat. **Credit** AmEx, MC, V. **Map** p332 G8 & p336 D4.
Hawick has been trading since 1874, but the shop is testament to the fact that traditional clothing need not be staid. The colourful racks are loaded with everything from socks to sweaters.

CONSUME

CONSUME

If The Kilt Fits…

How to be Scottish, in a manner of speaking.

It's Scotland's national dress. It's available in countless different styles and colours. If campaigners get their way, it may even be lent some kind of European protected status. However, although it may seem a straightforward process to put it on, do it up and stride off into the sunset, there's much more to the kilt than you might imagine.

First of all, it bears stressing that you get what you pay for. If you're in the market for the real thing, go to a proper kilt-maker, such as **Geoffrey (Tailor)** (*see p193*). Hand-stitched from around eight yards of 16- to 17-ounce worsted, kilts don't come cheap: a pretty standard kilt could cost from £375 to £700, with the price rising to four figures if you want all the necessary accessories (belt, sporran, socks, flashes, *sgian dubh* and so on). A kilt should be a once-in-a-lifetime purchase, and maybe more – some are passed down from father to son.

The heavier the material, the better it'll keep its shape, and the better the swing you'll get with it when you walk. Your kilt should fall to the middle of your knees, with the apron (the flat bit) at the front and the pleats at the back. If you're hiring a kilt to wear at a wedding, remember to turn your sporran to your hip when you're dancing – it's the easy way to avoid impact damage during any particularly wild stripping of the willows.

Recently, the concept of the 'casual' kilt has come to the fore. This new kind of kilt is still made of worsted, but there's less yardage, it's machine stitched, and it sits lower down on the hips. Howie Nicholsby of **21st Century Kilts** (*see p193*) has been at the forefront of the casual kilt phenomenon. At his shop you can choose a kilt in camouflage or pinstripes, leather or PVC.

If you don't want to spend too much on a kilt, a machine-stitched item in a lightweight worsted might set you back around £200- £300. **Slanj** (14 St Mary's Street, Old Town, 557 1666) or **McCalls** (21-22A Haddington Place, Leith Walk, 557 3979) are both worth a visit. Alternatively, **Armstrong's** (*see right*) often stock second-hand kilts. But whatever you do, avoid those £20 offerings in the gift shops. The kilt may be flammable, the polyviscose won't wear well and, most crucially, the garment won't have the requisite weight – you may end up showing a lot more than you reckoned on.

21st Century Kilts.

Ness

*336-340 Lawnmarket, Old Town (225 8815,
www.nessbypost.com). Bus 2, 23, 27, 41, 42.*
Open 10am-6pm daily. **Credit** AmEx, MC, V.
Map p332 G7 & p336 D4.
Pretty bags, vibrant jackets, hats and skirts, and
even tartan wellies. Ness also stocks blankets, luggage, cutesy bunnies and tweed corsages.
Other locations 367 High Street, Old Town
(226 5227); Ocean Terminal, Leith (554 5231).

Ragamuffin

*278 Canongate, Old Town (557 6007, www.
ragamuffinonline.com). Bus 35, 36 or Nicolson
Street–North Bridge buses.* **Open** *Aug* 10am-7pm
Mon-Sat; 10am-6pm Sun. *Apr-July, Sept* 10am-
6pm Mon-Sat; noon-6pm Sun. *Oct-Mar* 10am-6pm
Mon-Sat; noon-5pm Sun. **Credit** AmEx, MC, V.
Map p333 J7.
Ragamuffin is packed full of designer knitwear, all
guaranteed to keep the wearer warm and toasty. As
well as their own Angels Don't Trudge label, the
shop stocks around 50 other designers. Expect
quirky knits and relaxed styles, plus accessories in
a range of colours. *Photos p191.*

Used & vintage

★ Armstrongs

*83 Grassmarket, Old Town (220 5557, www.
armstrongsvintage.co.uk). Bus 2, 23, 27, 41, 42.*
Open *Aug* 10am-7.30pm daily. *Sept-July* 10am-
5.30pm Mon-Thur; 10am-6pm Fri, Sat; noon-6pm
Sun. **Credit** MC, V. **Map** p332 G8 & p336 D4.
Diving into this emporium is a glorious journey into
decades, if not centuries, of fashion. Armstrongs has
just about everything from 1920s glamour to 1980s
kitsch; there are also some real gems of Victoriana.
Other locations 14 Teviot Place, Old Town
(226 4634); 64-66 Clerk Street, South Edinburgh
(667 3056).

Herman Brown

*151 West Port, South Edinburgh (228 2589).
Bus 2, 35.* **Open** 12.30-6pm Mon-Sat. **Credit**
AmEx, MC, V. **Map** p332 F8.
With an emphasis on the 1950s to '80s, this family-
run shop specialises in top-end vintage finds. There
are lots of glamorous accessories too, such as super
hat pins and original cool shades.

FASHION ACCESSORIES
Cleaning & repairs

City Alterations

*123 Hanover Street, New Town (220 6004,
www.cityalterations.co.uk). Bus 13, 23, 27, 42
or Princes Street buses.* **Open** 8.30am-7.30pm
Mon-Fri; 8.30am-6.30pm Sat; 11am-5pm Sun.
No credit cards. Map p328 & p332 G6.

A city-centre stop for dry cleaning, repairs – including invisible mending – and alterations.

Kleen Cleaners

*10 St Mary's Street, Old Town (556 4337). Bus
35 or Nicolson Street–North Bridge buses.* **Open**
9am-5pm Mon-Fri; 10am-4pm Sat. **Credit** AmEx,
MC, V. **Map** p333 J7.
Instantly recognisable by the display of wedding
dresses in the window, this store offers dry cleaning
– with a specialised service for delicate fabrics such
as cashmere – as well as alterations and repairs.

Clothing hire

See p193 **Fashion: Traditional**.

Hats

Fabhatrix

*13 Cowgatehead, Old Town (225 9222, www.
fabhatrix.com). Nicolson Street–North Bridge
buses.* **Open** 10.30am-6pm Mon-Fri; 10.30am-
5.30pm Sat; noon-5pm Sun. **Credit** AmEx,
MC, V. **Map** p332 G8 & p336 D4.
All kinds of hats, from cloches and summer straw
to top hats and fascinators. Many are constructed in
hand-dyed felts, with tweed, feather or wool detailing. There are also wraps, scarves and accessories.

Yvette Jelfs

*4 Albany Street, New Town (556 8388, www.
yvettejelfs.com). Bus 8.* **Open** 10am-6pm Tue-Sat.
Credit MC, V. **Map** p328 H4.
Milliner Yvette Jelfs' boutique is home to a beautiful array of headwear, plus a selection of fashion and
ethical jewellery. There's everything from demure
flat-top boaters to ornate fascinators.

Jewellery

Argento

*18a Frederick Street, New Town (226 1704, www.
argentosilver.com). Bus 13, 23, 27, 42 or Princes
Street buses.* **Open** 9.30am-6pm Mon-Wed, Fri,
Sat; 9.30am-7.30pm Thur; noon-5pm Sun. **Credit**
MC, V. **Map** p328 & p332 F6, p336 C1.
Enjoy some new silver and stones without breaking
the budget, with brands such as Pandora, Pilgrim,
Kit Heath and Hot Diamonds. There are also some
celtic and Rennie Mackintosh designs.

Arkangel

*4 William Street, New Town (226 4466, www.
arkangelfashion.co.uk). Bus 3, 3A, 4, 12, 25,
26, 31, 33, 44.* **Open** 10am-5.30pm Mon-Wed,
Fri, Sat; 10am-6.30pm Thur. **Credit** MC, V.
Map p331 D7.
Try Arkangel for a statement piece of costume jew-
ellery – Butler & Wilson, Ziio, Phillipe Audibert, Les
Nereides – or some gorgeous clothing.

★ Galerie Mirage
46a Raeburn Place, Stockbridge (315 2603).
Bus 24, 29, 42. **Open** 10am-5.30pm Mon-Fri;
10am-6pm Sat; 12.30pm-5pm Sun. **Credit** MC,
V. **Map** p327 C4.
Materials at Mirage include amber, silver and semi-precious stones, as well as more exotic materials such as mammoth bone and vegetable ivory. Great for something a little different.

Hamilton & Inches
87 George Street, New Town (225 4898, www.
hamiltonandinches.com). Bus 13, 23, 27, 42 or
Princes Street buses. **Open** 9.30am-5.30pm Mon-Fri; 9am-5pm Sat. **Credit** AmEx, MC, V. **Map**
p328 & p332 F6, p336 C1.
The pieces here are every bit as grand as you might expect from a silversmith by appointment to the Queen. As well as traditional jewellery, H&I makes fine silver tableware.

Joseph Bonnar
72 Thistle Street, New Town (226 2811, www.
josephbonnar.com). Bus 13, 23, 27, 42 or Princes
Street buses. **Open** 10.30am-5pm Tue-Sat.
Credit AmEx, MC, V. **Map** p328 G5.
Joseph Bonnar stocks beautiful pieces of antique and period jewellery, including parures. You'll find exotic stones here such as alexandrite and chiastolite, as well as the more usual diamonds, rubies, sapphires and emeralds.

Lingerie

There's a branch of **Calvin Klein Underwear** at 6 Multrees Walk, by St Andrew Square (557 6971, www.cku.com), while high-street staple **La Senza** can be found at 117 Princes Street (226 1689), Ocean Terminal in Leith (*see p185*; 553 7174) and the Gyle Centre (*see p185*; 339 0551). Most of the city's department stores have good lingerie departments.

★ Boudiche
15 Frederick Street, New Town (226 5255,
www.boudiche.co.uk). Bus 13, 23, 27, 42 or
Princes Street buses. **Open** 10am-6pm Mon-Wed, Fri, Sat; 10am-7pm Thur; noon-5pm Sun. **Credit** MC, V. **Map** p328 & p332 F6, p336 C2.
This dark, decadent lingerie boutique has daywear, occasion wear and all kinds of flirtatious frippery. Brands include Elle Macpherson Intimates, La Perla, Fifi Chachnil and Damaris. Boudiche also stocks DD+ lingerie, boudoir gifts and pampering treats.

Bravissimo
20 Multrees Walk, New Town (550 3620,
www.bravissimo.com). Princes Street buses.
Open 10am-6pm Mon-Wed, Fri; 10am-7pm
Thur; 9.30am-6pm Sat; 11am-5pm Sun. **Credit**
MC, V. **Map** p328 H5 & p336 F1.

Pretty lingerie and swimwear in D to K cup sizes, with brands including Freya, Miss Mandalay and Masquerade as well as the shop's own label.

Luggage & leather goods

Mackenzie Bags
23a Dundas Street, New Town (557 6444,
www.mackenziebags.co.uk). Bus 23, 27. **Open**
Summer 10am-5.30pm Mon-Sat. *Winter* 10am-5pm
Mon-Sat. **Credit** AmEx, MC, V. **Map** p328 F4.
Mackenzie's hand-finished bags – Gladstone bags, briefcases, shoulder bags, totes, rucksacks and micro bags – come with a lifetime guarantee.

Shoes

Clarks (no.79, 220 1261) and **Russell & Bromley** (no.106, 225 7444) are among the shoe shops on Princes Street. On-trend **Schuh** has three branches in the city, one on Frederick Street (no.6-6A, 220 0290), one on North Bridge (no.32, 225 6552) and a third in Ocean Terminal (555 3766). For children's shoes, *see p188*.

Helen Bateman
16 William Street, New Town (220 4495, www.
helenbateman.com). **Open** 9.30am-6pm Mon-Sat. **Credit** MC, V. **Map** p331 D7.
Helen Bateman's designs come in a basic range, retained year-round. There are also funkier seasonal sandals and slingbacks, plus special-occasion shoes.

★ Pam Jenkins
41 Thistle Street, New Town (225 3242, www.
pamjenkins.co.uk). Bus 13, 23, 27, 42 or Princes
Street buses. **Open** 10am-5.30pm Mon-Sat.
Credit AmEx, MC, V. **Map** p328 G5.
With the likes of Jimmy Choo, Nicole Farhi, Christian Louboutin, Alexander McQueen and Kate Spade all under one roof, this is heaven for shoe lovers.

Rogerson Fine Footwear
126-128 Rose Street, New Town (220 1775,
www.rogersonshoes.com). Bus 13, 23, 27, 42 or
Princes Street buses. **Open** 9.30am-6pm Mon-Wed, Fri, Sat; 9.30am-7pm Thur; noon-5pm Sun.
Credit MC, V. **Map** p328 & p332 F6, p336 C1.
High-quality European footwear from a long-established Scottish firm, including shoes from Ecco, Hispanitas, Think and Mephisto.

Sole
16 Multrees Walk, New Town (556 6660, www.
sole.co.uk). Princes Street buses. **Open** 9am-6pm
Mon-Wed, Fri, Sat; 9am-7pm Thur; 11am-5pm Sun.
Credit AmEx, MC, V. **Map** p328 H5 & p336 F1.
Expect an array of higher-end brands, such as D&G, Paul Smith, Patrick Cox and Hugo Boss, along with couture sport lines and casual names such as Rocketdog, Diesel, Ugg and Birkenstock.

FOOD & DRINK

Bakeries

You can't beat **Falko Konditorei**, a bakery with an attached café that specialises in German breads, pretzels and sweet things. *See p155.*

Drinks

For the **Scotch Whisky Experience**, *see p59.*

Cadenhead's Whisky Shop

172 Canongate, Old Town (556 5864, http:// edinburgh.wmcadenhead.com). Bus 35, 36. **Open** 10.30am-5.30pm Mon-Sat. **Credit** MC, V. **Map** p333 K7.
Belonging to Scotland's oldest independent bottler (established 1842), this store has a grand selection of whiskies. It also runs whisky tastings in local pubs.

Demijohn

32 Victoria Street, Old Town (225 3265, www. demijohn.co.uk). Bus 2, 23, 27, 41, 42. **Open** 10am-6pm Mon-Sat; 12.30-5pm Sun. **Credit** MC, V. **Map** p332 J7 & p336 D4.
This 'liquid deli' allows you to try drinks before you buy. There are unusual British-sourced liqueurs, such as elderflower vodka and damson gin.

Royal Mile Whiskies

379 High Street, Old Town (225 3383, www.royal milewhiskies.com). Bus 35 or Nicolson Street–

North Bridge buses. **Open** 10am-6pm Mon-Sat; 12.30-6pm Sun. **Credit** MC, V. **Map** p332 H7 & p336 E4.
Hundreds of whiskies, some extremely rare and expensive, are on offer at this award-winning shop. Other liqueurs are also stocked, including absinthe.

Villeneuve Wines

49a Broughton Street, Broughton (558 8441, www.villeneuvewines.com). Bus 8, 13, 17. **Open** noon-10pm Mon-Wed; 10am-10pm Thur-Sat; 1-8pm Sun. **Credit** AmEx, MC, V. **Map** p328 H4.
A very well-stocked and reasonably priced fine wine and whisky shop. Staff are knowledgeable and happy to make recommendations.

General

For basic foods, try **Marks & Spencer** (54 Princes Street, 225 2301) or **Sainsbury's** (9-10 St Andrew's Square, 225 8400).

Beets

49 Bernard Street, Leith (476 5086). Bus 16, 22, 35, 36. **Open** 8.30am-6.30pm Mon-Fri; 11am-6pm Sat. **Credit** MC, V. **Map** p326 Y3.
Fair Trade, organic, vegan and vegetarian goods, including cheeses, spreads and groceries. There's also a good range of coffees and teas.

Henderson's

92-94 Hanover Street, New Town (225 6694, www.hendersonsofedinburgh.co.uk). Princes Street

Falko Konditorei.

CONSUME

IJ Mellis, Cheesemonger.

buses. **Open** 8am-7pm Mon-Fri; 9.30am-6pm Sat.
Credit MC, V. **Map** p326 & p330 G6, p336 D1.
Henderson's has been promoting natural food in
Scotland for over 40 years. You'll find a good sup-
ply of artisan breads, Fair Trade and organic pro-
duce, cheeses and healthy snacks.

Henri's Fine Food & Wine

*376 Morningside Road, Morningside (447 8877,
www.henrisofedinburgh.co.uk). Bus 11, 15, 15A,
16, 23.* **Open** 8.30am-6pm Mon-Fri; 8.30am-5.30pm
Sat; 9am-3.30pm Sun. **Credit** AmEx, MC, V.
Breads, charcuterie, artisanal cheeses, sausages
and all kinds of jarred and bottled delights, with
some Scottish produce alongside the French.

★ Herbie of Edinburgh

*66 Raeburn Place, Stockbridge (332 9888,
www.herbieofedinburgh.co.uk). Bus 24, 29,
42.* **Open** 9.30am-7pm Mon-Fri; 9am-6pm
Sat. **Credit** AmEx, MC, V. **Map** p327 C4.
This deli has plenty of fresh-baked breads and an
extensive range of cheeses that you can try before
you buy. The second branch also has a café.
Other locations 1 North West Circus Place,
Stockbridge (226 7212).

Real Foods

*37 Broughton Street, Broughton (557 1911,
www.realfoods.co.uk). Bus 8, 13, 17.* **Open** 9am-
7pm Mon-Wed, Fri; 9am-8pm Thur; 9am-6.30pm
Sat; 10am-6pm Sun. **Credit** MC, V. **Map** p328 H4.
Open since 1975, this is the place to go for natural,
organic, fair trade and vegetarian food, or foods
catering for special diets.
Other locations 8 Brougham Place, South
Edinburgh (228 1201).

Store

*13 Comely Bank Road, Stockbridge (315 0030,
www.thestorecompany.co.uk). Bus 24, 29, 42.*
Open 10am-6.30 Mon-Thu; 9am-6pm Fri, Sat;
11am-5pm Sun. **Credit** MC, V. **Map** p327 B4.
The plainly named Store is a blend of farm shop,
mini-greengrocer and quality deli and there are
always treats to catch the eye – breads, artisanal
cheeses and more join matured beef and lamb fresh
from the farm. Hampers are also available.

★ Valvona & Crolla

*19 Elm Row, Leith Walk, Broughton (556 6066,
www.valvonacrolla.com). Bus 7, 10, 12, 14, 16,
22, 25, 49.* **Open** 8.30am-6pm Mon-Thu; 8am-
6pm Fri-Sat; 10.30am-4pm Sun. **Credit** AmEx,
MC, V. **Map** p329 G4.
Edinburgh's best known stop-off for deli goodies
and gourmet treats has been trading at this address
since 1934. The range of comestibles is wide and
the quality is top notch. There's a well-known
Italian-oriented café-bar in the back of the store;
you may need to book to eat here at busy times; for
more, *see p145*.
▶ *V&C also run the food concession at Jenners;
see p183.*

INSIDE TRACK
TAKE HOME A HAGGIS

Made in Edinburgh, **Macsween's haggises**
are generally considered to be some of the
best available. You can find them in most
supermarkets. The company also makes a
good vegetarian version.

CONSUME

Markets

Farmers' Market
*Castle Terrace, South Edinburgh (www.edinburgh
farmersmarket.com). Lothian Road buses.* **Open**
9am-2pm Sat. **Map** p332 F8 & p336 B4.
More than 65 stalls set up on Castle Terrace sell
meat, fish, free-range eggs, cheeses, fruit and veg,
along with all manner of homemade chutneys,
breads and chocolates. Most of the stallholders are
also producers. For more, *see p147* **Market Forces**.

Specialist

Coco
*174 Bruntsfield Place, South Edinburgh (228
4526, www.cocochocolate.co.uk). Bus 11, 15,
15A, 16, 23, 45.* **Open** 10am-6pm Mon-Sat;
noon-4pm Sun. **Credit** MC, V. **Map** p332 E11.
All of the chocolates produced and sold here are
organic and ethically traded. Gorgeous gift boxes
are available.

Crombie's of Edinburgh
*97-101 Broughton Street, Broughton (557 0111,
www.sausages.co.uk). Bus 8, 13, 17.* **Open** 8am-
5.30pm Mon-Fri; 8am-5pm Sat. **Credit** MC, V.
Map p328 H4.
This high-quality butcher is best known for its
extensive array of sausages: the likes of wild boar,
apricot and stilton, or venison, port and calvados
versions sit aside more traditional sausages.

★ IJ Mellis, Cheesemonger
*30A Victoria Street, Old Town (226 6215, www.
mellischeese.co.uk). Bus 2, 23, 27, 41, 42.* **Open**
10am-5.30pm Mon-Wed; 9.30am-6.30pm Thu-Sat.
Credit MC, V. **Map** p332 J7 & p336 D4.
A perfect place to sample Scottish cheeses, as well
as the best of the rest of the UK, France, Holland,
Italy and Spain. It sells artisan bread, too, so it's perfect for picnic supplies.
Other locations 6 Bakers Place, Stockbridge
(225 6566); 330 Morningside Road, South
Edinburgh (447 8889).

GIFTS & SOUVENIRS

There's no shortage of cheap tartan rubbish for
sale on and near the Royal Mile, but there are
many more interesting alternatives to be found.

Flux
*55 Bernard Street, Leith (554 4075, www.
get2flux.co.uk). Bus 12, 16, 35, 36.* **Open** 11am-
6pm Mon-Sat; noon-5pm Sun. **Credit** MC, V.
Map p326 Y3.
British-made crafts are a speciality here, as are fairly
traded and recycled goods; if you're looking for a
souvenir of Scotland that's actually been made in the
country, this may be a good choice.

Just Scottish
*4-6 North Bank Street, Old Town (226 4806).
Bus 2, 23, 27, 41, 42.* **Open** 10am-6pm Mon-Sat;
noon-4pm Sun. **Credit** AmEx, MC, V. **Map** p332
G7 & p336 D3.
This gallery space and attached gift shop is home
to quality Scottish merchandise, including jewellery,
textiles, silver, and metalwork.

★ Mr Wood's Fossils
*5 Cowgatehead, Grassmarket (220 1344,
www.mrwoodsfossils.co.uk) North Bridge buses.*
Open 10am-5.30pm Mon-Sat. Also open Sun
in July, Aug & Dec; call for hrs. **Credit** MC, V.
Map p332 G8 & p336 D4.
Fossils of all sizes and to suit all budgets are sold
here, as well as a good range of minerals, both pol-
ished and unpolished, and jewellery incorporating
stones or, yes, fossils.

One World Shop
*St John's Church, Princes Street, New Town
(229 4541, www.oneworldshop.co.uk). Princes
Street buses.* **Open** 10am-5.30pm Mon-Sat;
11am-4.30pm Sun. **Credit** AmEx, MC,V.
Map p332 E7 & p336 A2.
A wide selection of crafts, textiles, toys, clothing
and foodstuffs. All goods are ethically sourced and
fairly traded.

Organic Pleasures
*71 Broughton Street, Broughton (558 2777,
www.organicpleasures.co.uk). Bus 8.* **Open**
11am-7pm Tue-Sat; 1pm-5pm Sun in Aug
& Dec. **Credit** AmEx, MC, V. **Map** p328 H4.
Proud to be the first erotic boutique of its kind
('provoking new moves in the world of sensual
pleasure', according to its website), Organic
Pleasures takes care with its sourcing: goods are
manufactured in the UK, and its oils and sex toys
are eco-friendly.

Paper Tiger
*6A-8 Stafford Street, New Town (226 2390,
www.papertiger.ltd.uk). Bus 3, 3A, 4, 12, 25, 26,
31, 33, 44.* **Open** 9am-6pm Mon-Wed, Fri, Sat;
9am-7pm Thur; 11am-5pm Sun. **Credit** MC,V.
Map p331 D7.
A good range of upmarket stationery, journals, greet-
ings cards and wrapping paper. Card publishers

CONSUME

INSIDE TRACK LOST MURAL

For a little glimpse of the lost grandeur of
George Street, have a peep in **Paperchase**
(77A George Street, New Town, 226 4323).
At the rear of the store is a fragment of a
large mural that once covered the wall of
the building.

stocked here include Urban Graphics and Roger la Borde; Moleskine notebooks are also available.
Other locations 53 Lothian Road, West Edinburgh (228 2790).

Russian Shop
18 St Mary's Street, Old Town (556 0181, www.therussianshop.co.uk). Bus 35 or Nicolson Street–North Bridge buses. **Open** 10am-5.30pm Mon-Sat. **Credit** AmEx, MC, V. **Map** p333 J7.
Stocks an array of Matryoshka dolls, Russian dolls, ceramics, laquerwork, wooden crafts and icons.

★ Studio One
10-16 Stafford Street, New Town (226 5812). Bus 3, 3A, 4, 12, 25, 26, 31, 33, 44. **Open** 9.30am-6pm Mon-Wed, Fri, Sat; 9.30am-7pm Thur; 11am-5pm Sun. **Credit** MC, V. **Map** p331 D7.
Studio One stocks a great selection of gifts, along with pampering treats, toys, jewellery and all kinds of household items.
Other locations Studio One Furniture, 71 Morningside Road, South Edinburgh (447 0452).

The Gift of Scotland

It's not just the thought that counts.

A wander through the gift shops on the Royal Mile can be a dispiriting experience: the Scottish capital has more than its fair share of tourist tat. Still, it's not all bad news; careful browsing will lead to something that says 'Scotland' with a little more dignity.

The only Scottish gift shop on the Royal Mile where the owner can proudly display her clan plaque (she's a Campbell), **Neanie Scott** (131 Canongate, Old Town, 558 3528, www.neaniescott.com) sells gift boxes of hand-tied fishing flies by George Cowie of Ballater, supplier to Prince Charles when he's fishing at nearby Balmoral. Also available: hand-made Highland dirks, by sword designer John Barnett, and hand-knitted Arran sweaters. You can choose the wool and pattern, and then have the sweater shipped to you anywhere in the world.

Not far from here, the **Just Scottish Gallery & Gift Shop** (*see p199*) stages exhibitions, with works by artists and craftspeople living and working in Scotland, including textiles, paintings, sculptures, jewellery and prints. All are for sale. Also on an artistic level, the middle two weeks in June is usually when the doors open on the annual **Edinburgh College of Art Student Degree Show**, showing and selling works by over 400 students. See www.eca.ac.uk for more information.

So, what do you get the man who has everything? How about an eco-friendly fur-free sporran, the original Scottish manbag? Robincraft, a sporran manufacturer based in Bonnyrigg, has created a sporran from synthetic material that comes in different luxurious 'skins' such as imitation chinchilla or American badger. You can pick one up at **McCalls** (21-22A Haddington Place, Calton Hill, 557 3979, www.mccalls.co.uk).

Women, meanwhile, may go for the jewellery made by sisters Lyndsey Bowditch and Gillian Crawford. **Tartan Twist** (www.tartantwist.com), the pair's company, supplied the official pendant for 'the Gathering', a huge clan convergence during the Homecoming Scotland 2009 celebrations that were organised to encouraged those with Scottish roots to visit. Scottish contemporary design is combined with traditional tartans in a range of sterling silver, freshwater pearl and Murano glass pieces. Look for the range at the **National Museum of Scotland** (*see p76*).

Dunoon Mugs makes the only Scottish mass-produced bone china. You can pick up one with your clan tartan, or the saltire, the blue flag of Scotland with the white St Andrew's cross, at **Cuttea Sark** (26 Victoria St, Old Town, 226 6245, www.cutteasark. co.uk). But if your friends or family might prefer something a little older, you can pick up historical maps and prints of Edinburgh and Scotland on the Canongate at **Carson Clark Gallery** (no.181-183, 556 4710, www.carsonclarkgallery.co.uk) or at the **Royal Mile Gallery** (no.272, 558 1702, www.royalmilegallery.com).

CONSUME

HEALTH & BEAUTY
Complementary medicine

Edinburgh Floatarium
29 North West Circus Place, Stockbridge (225 3350, www.edinburghfloatarium.co.uk). Bus 24, 29, 36, 42. **Open** *9am-7pm Tue-Fri; 9am-6pm Sat.* **Credit** *MC, V.* **Map** *p328 E5.*
As well as the floatation tank, relaxing experiences on offer here include various massage techniques, reflexology, chiropody, reiki and shiatsu.

Glover's Integrated Healthcare
10 William Street, New Town (225 3161, www. glovers-health.co.uk). Bus 3, 3A, 12, 25, 26, 31, 33, 41. **Open** *10am-3pm Mon-Fri.* **Credit** *MC, V.* **Map** *p331 D7.*
Christine Glover, a former president of the Royal Pharmaceutical Society, sells a wide range of alternative health products. The clinic offers homeopathy, reflexology and other therapies, as well as food intolerance testing.

★ Napiers Dispensary
18 Bristo Place, Old Town (225 5542, www. napiers.net). Bus 2, 23, 27, 41, 42. **Open** *10am-6pm Mon; 9am-6pm Tue-Fri; 9am-5.30pm Sat.* **Credit** *MC, V.* **Map** *p332 H8.*
Napiers offers consultations, treatments and therapies from herbalists, acupuncturists and various other practioners. The shop is well stocked with homeopathic and herbal medicines, and also carries natural cosmetics.
Other locations 35 Hamilton Place, Stockbridge, New Town (315 2130).

Hairdressers & barbers

In addition to the salons listed below, the city has plenty of old-school barbers; just look for the red and white poles.

Charlie Miller
13 Stafford Street, New Town (226 5550, www. charliemiller.com). Bus 3, 3A, 4, 12, 25, 26, 31, 33, 44. **Open** *9am-5.30pm Mon-Wed, Fri; 9am-6.30pm Thur; 8.30am-5pm Sat.* **Credit** *AmEx, MC, V.* **Map** *p331 D7.*
This award-winning and popular local hairdressing name has a number of salons throughout the city, including at Ocean Terminal and Harvey Nichols.
Other locations throughout the city.

Medusa
6-7 Teviot Place, Old Town (225 6627, www. medusahair.co.uk). Bus 2, 41, 42. **Open** *9am-6pm Mon-Wed, Fri; 9am-8.30pm Thur; 9am-4.30pm Sat.* **Credit** *MC, V.* **Map** *p332 H8.*
No matter the time of day, this hairdresser always seems to be busy – it's always a safe bet for a good

cut or colour. The Bread Street premises includes a beauty salon called the Inner Sanctuary.
Other locations 26 Bread Street, South Edinburgh (622 7277).

★ Sesh Hairdressing
50-52 Bernard Street, Leith (555 0708). Bus 12, 16, 35, 36. **Open** *10am-7pm Mon-Wed, Fri; 11am-8pm Thu; 9am-4pm Sat; 10am-4pm Sun.* **Credit** *MC, V.* **Map** *p326 Y2.*
Sesh has a loyal following among Leithers and Edinburgh folk alike. Bright, relaxed surroundings make for an all round enjoyable experience.

Opticians

The **Dollond & Aitchison** (558 1149, www. danda.co.uk) and **Vision Express** (556 5656, www.visionexpress.co.uk) chains have stores at the St James Centre (*see p187*).

Eyes Optometrist
63 Thistle Street, New Town (225 4004). Princes Street buses. **Open** *9.30am-5.30pm Mon-Fri; 9.30am-4pm Sat.* **Credit** *AmEx, MC, V.* **Map** *p328 G5.*
An independent operation specialising in handmade spectacle frames. Designer names such as Philippe Starck and Eye DC are also represented.

Pharmacies

Edinburgh doesn't have a 24-hour pharmacy, but some of the pharmacies attached to larger supermarkets remain open into the evening.

Boots
101-103 Princes Street, New Town (225 8331, www.boots.co.uk). Princes Street buses. **Open** *8am-6.30pm Mon-Wed, Fri, Sat; 8am-8pm Thur; 10am-6pm Sun.* **Credit** *AmEx, MC, V.* **Map** *p328 & p332 F6, p336 C2.*
The largest of several branches of Boots stores scattered around Edinburgh has huge ranges of toiletries and cosmetics; there is also a pharmacy and an optician on the premises.
Other locations throughout the city.

Shops

It's also worth checking the beauty counters in big department stores (*see pp183-184*) and the Princes Street branches of **Lush** (no.44, 557 3177) and **Body Shop** (no.90A, 220 6330).

★ Dolly Leo Apothecary
22 Raeburn Place, Stockbridge (315 2035, www.dollyleo.co.uk). Bus 24, 29, 42. **Open** *10am-5pm Mon, Tue; 10am-5.30pm Wed; 10am-6.30pm Thur; 10am-6pm Fri, Sat; noon-5pm Sun.* **Credit** *AmEx, MC, V.* **Map** *p327 D4.*

CONSUME

Zen Lifestyle.

This is a sumptuous, independently owned cosmetics and beauty boutique, with products from Becca, Mama Mio, Anqelique, Alive and Well, Korres and many more. Beauty treaments are also available.

Jo Malone
93 George Street, New Town (0870 192 5161, www.jomalone.co.uk). Princes Street buses. **Open** 10am-6pm Mon-Wed; 10am-7pm Thur; 9.30am-6pm Fri, Sat; noon-5pm Sun. **Credit** AmEx, MC, V. **Map** p328 & p332 F6, p336 B1.

All Jo Malone's sought-after products are here. Staff can also help you find your bespoke scent, and offer hand and arm massages and skincare consultations.

Space NK
97-103 George Street, New Town (225 6371, www.spacenk.co.uk). Bus 13, 23, 27, 42 or Princes Street buses. **Open** 9.30am-5.30pm Mon-Wed, Fri, Sat; 9.30am-6.30pm Thur; noon-5pm Sun. **Credit** AmEx, MC, V. **Map** p328 & p332 F6, p336 B1.

This chic store stocks brands including Kiehl's, Ren, Eve Lom, NARS, Caudalie and Chantecaille.

Spas & salons

One Spa
8 Conference Square, Western Approach Road, West Edinburgh (221 7777, http://onespa.com). Bus 2, 3, 3A, 4, 25, 33, 44, 44A. **Open** 6.30am-10pm Mon-Fri; 7am-9pm Sat, Sun. **Credit** AmEx, MC, V. **Map** p331 D8.

From the rooftop whirlpool to the heat and steam experiences, One Spa offers plenty of luxury. Opt for a simple manicure or check in for an entire day of blissful pampering.

Pure
Ocean Terminal, Leith (561 1320, www.pure spauk.com). Bus 1, 11, 22, 34, 35, 36. **Open** 10am-9pm Mon-Fri; 10am-7pm Sat; 11am-6pm Sun. **Credit** AmEx, MC, V. **Map** p326 X1.

Along with its full-day and half-day packages, Pure has a full range of relaxation and beauty treatments and therapies.

Zen Lifestyle
9 Bruntsfield Place, South Edinburgh (477 3535, www.zen-lifestyle.com). Bus 11, 15, 15A, 16, 23, 45. **Open** 8am-10pm Mon-Fri; 9am-6pm Sat; 10am-6pm Sun. **Credit** AmEx, MC, V. **Map** p332 E10.

This award-winning urban retreat offers a range of relaxation treatments, as well as beauty essentials and treats for men and women, including massage, facials, waxing and many more.

Other locations 2-3 Teviot Place, Old Town (226 6777).

HOUSE & HOME
Antiques

Anteaques
17 Clerk Street, South Edinburgh (667 8466, www.anteaques.co.uk). Nicolson Street–North Bridge buses. **Open** 10am-7pm Fri, Sat; 11am-6pm Sun. **Credit** MC, V. **Map** p333 K9.

The clue's in the name. Anteaques offers a mix of antiques, with vintage silver a speciality, and tea, in its sweet café (scones and cakes are also available).

Edinburgh Architectural Salvage Yard
31 West Bowling Green Street, Leith (554 7077, www.easy-arch-salv.co.uk). Bus 7, 11, 14, 21. **Open** 9am-5pm Mon-Fri; noon-5pm Sat. **Credit** MC, V. **Map** p326 W4.

Recovered pieces from the Georgian, Victorian, and Edwardian eras can be found here, alongside art nouveau and art deco objects.

Georgian Antiques

10 Pattison Street, Leith (553 7286, www.
georgianantiques.net). Bus 21. **Open** 8.30am-
5.30pm Mon-Fri; 10am-2pm Sat. **Credit** MC, V.
Map p326 Z3.
Spread over 50,000sq ft in a converted whisky bond,
this is the largest collection of quality antiques and
collectibles in town.

General

Anta

Crocket's Land, 91-93 West Bow, Old Town
(225 4616, www.anta.co.uk). Bus 2, 23, 27,
41, 42. **Open** 10am-6pm Mon-Sat; noon-5.30pm
Sun. **Credit** AmEx, MC, V. **Map** p332 G8 &
p336 D4.
A family-run design company, Anta sells a selection
of hand-painted stoneware and contemporary textiles, plus quirky accessories. The shop also has a
corsetière, who can help create an original corset.
Other locations 73 Grassmarket, Old Town
(225 9096); 32 North West Circus Place, New
Town (220 1693).

Designshop UK

116-120 Causewayside, South Edinburgh (0870
2424 128, www.designshopuk.com). Bus 2, 3, 3A,
5, 7, 8, 14, 29, 30, 31, 33, 37, 47, 49. **Open**
10am-6pm Tue-Sat. **Credit** MC, V. **Map** p333 K11.
Covetable contemporary furniture and accessories
from world-famous names such as Vitra and Panton.

★ Inhouse

28 Howe Street, New Town (225 2888, www.
inhouse-uk.com). Bus 24, 29, 42. **Open** 9.30am-
5.30pm Tue, Wed, Fri, Sat; 10am-7pm Thur.
Credit AmEx, MC, V. **Map** p328 F5.
In addition to contemporary minimalist furniture,
you'll find a large range of modern accessories,
including plenty of Alessi designs.

MUSIC

CDs, records & DVDs

Avalanche

63 Cockburn Street, Old Town (225 3939, www.
avalancherecords.co.uk). Nicolson Street–North
Bridge buses. **Open** 10am-6.30pm Mon-Sat; noon-
6pm Sun. **Credit** MC, V. **Map** p333 H7 & p336 F3.
Probably the best independent music shop in town.
Alongside new CDs, a range dominated by indie
artists, there's a decent selection of cut-price DVDs
and a mixed bag of second-hand discs.

★ Coda Music

12 Bank Street, Old Town (622 7246, www.coda
music.co.uk). Bus 2, 23, 27, 41, 42. **Open** 9.30am-
5.30pm Mon-Sat; 11am-5pm Sun. **Credit** MC, V.
Map p332 H7 & p336 E3.

The Beauty Principle

Where to find the finishing touches.

You have the outfit and you have the
shoes, but sometimes, you just need
that extra beauty boost. One of these
businesses should be able to help
complete your look.

If you've run out of your favourite Bobbi
Brown lippy or foundation, then a trip to
Jenners (*see p183*) or **John Lewis** (*see
p184*) are your only hopes in Edinburgh.
For a decent range of Annick Goutal
fragrances, head to **Harvey Nichols** (*see
p183*). Bare Minerals foundation is also
stocked in Jenners, but **Lisa V Beauty**
(25 Hamilton Place, Stockbridge, 343
2308) stocks the Bare Escentuals range.

It's been a long time coming, but
eyebrow threading is finally available
in central Edinburgh. Expect to pay
between £15 and £25. Appointments
are not always necessary in **Debenhams**
(*see p183*) or Shavata in **Harvey Nichols**
(*see p183*). At **Neal's Yard** (102 Hanover
Street, Old Town, 226 3223), it's on offer
the first Saturday of every month, thanks
to Sabrina, and tends to be popular.
Or pop down to **Dolly Leo** (*see p201*),
where specialist Tara is on hand, but
phone first to avoid disappointment.

Dolly Leo.

The focus here is on Scottish folk music in all its forms, but you'll also find plenty of other traditional music from around the globe.

Fopp
7-15 Rose Street, New Town (243 0870, www.foppreturns.com). Princes Street buses. **Open** 9am-6pm Mon-Wed, Fri, Sat; 9am-7pm Thu; 11am-6pm Sun. **Credit** AmEx, MC, V. **Map** p328 & p332 G6, p336 D1.

Two floors of new releases and back-catalogue surprises, plus good selections of books and DVDs, make this a great place for bargains.

McAlister Matheson Music
1 Grindlay Street, South Edinburgh (228 3827, www.mmmusic.co.uk). Bus 1, 2, 10, 11, 15, 15A, 16, 23, 24, 27, 34, 35, 45. **Open** 9.30am-6pm Mon-Thu; 9.30am-6.30pm Fri; 9am-5.30pm Sat. **Credit** AmEx, MC, V. **Map** p332 E8.

Classical music and opera are the focus at McAlister Matheson. The shop stays open later when there's a concert at Usher Hall.

Ripping Music & Tickets
91 South Bridge, Old Town (226 7010, www. rippingrecords.com). Bus 35 or Nicolson Street–North Bridge buses. **Open** 9.30am-6.30pm Mon-Sat; 12.30-5.30pm Sun. **Credit** AmEx, MC, V. **Map** p333 J8.

There's a good selection of rock, pop, dance and indie CDs in stock, but Ripping's main attraction is the range of gig tickets. Everything that's available is pinned up in the window display, from local nights to stadium shows.

Underground Solu'shn
9 Cockburn Street, Old Town (226 2242, www. undergroundsolushn.com). Bus 35 or Nicolson Street–North Bridge buses. **Open** 10am-6pm Mon-Wed, Fri, Sat; 10am-7pm Thur; noon-6pm Sun. **Credit** AmEx, MC, V. **Map** p332 H7 & p336 E3.

Pretty much unbeatable for vinyl dance imports, with a huge choice of house, garage, techno and jungle sounds in stock. The vibe is friendly rather than intimidating and the shop also sells tickets for club nights.

Instruments

Imported Instruments
Ocean Terminal, Leith (0800 756 1312, www.importedinstruments.com). Bus 1, 11, 22, 34, 35, 36. **Open** 10am-8pm Mon-Fri, 10am-7pm Sat; 11am-6pm Sun. **Credit** AmEx, MC, V. **Map** p326 X1.

An independent guitar store, Imported Instruments stocks brands including Dean, Fender, Gibson, Tanglewood and Korg. Services include basic restringing, and guitar and bass repairs.

Stringers
13 York Place, New Town (557 5432, www. stringersmusic.com). Bus 8, 10, 11, 12, 15, 15A, 16, 45. **Open** 9.30-5.30 Mon-Sat. **Credit** MC, V. **Map** p327 H5.

A niche shop for violins, violas, cellos and double basses, plus all the necessary accessories. There's a repair service for all stocked instruments.

SPORTS & FITNESS

Boardwise
4 Lady Lawson Street, South Edinburgh (229 5887, www.boardwise.com). Bus 2, 35. **Open** 10am-6pm Mon-Sat. **Credit** AmEx, MC, V. **Map** p332 F8.

Whether your board of choice rides on snow, surf or wheels, you'll find what you need here, alongside skater and surfing clothing labels.

Edinburgh Bicycle Cooperative
8 Alvanley Terrace, South Edinburgh (228 3565, www.edinburghbicycle.com). Bus 11, 15, 15A, 16, 23, 45. **Open** 10am-7pm Mon-Fri; 10am-6pm Sat, Sun. **Credit** AmEx, MC, V. **Map** p332 F11.

Scotland's first co-operatively run bike shop has been open for 30 years. Staff know their stuff, and are happy to offer advice on local routes. There's an extensive selection of bikes and accessories.

★ Tiso
123-125 Rose Street, New Town (225 9486, www.tiso.com). Bus 13, 23, 27, 42 or Princes Street buses. **Open** 9.30am-5.30pm Mon, Tue, Fri, Sat; 10am-5.30pm Wed; 9.30am-7.30pm Thur; 11am-5pm Sun. **Credit** MC, V. **Map** p328 & p332 F6, p336 B2.

With four floors of clothing, equipment, books and maps, Tiso is effectively Scotland's outdoors superstore. The store contains North Face and Berghaus 'super shops' and a Blues the Ski Shop concession. The Leith branch has a mini climbing wall and a Gore-Tex waterproof test shower.

Other locations 41 Commercial Street, Leith (554 0804).

TICKETS

Tickets for gigs, plays and other shows are generally sold through the venues themselves, but some are also sold through **Ticketmaster** (www.ticketmaster.co.uk). For gigs, you can also try **Underground Solu'shn**, which stocks tickets for most shows in the city, and **Ripping Music & Tickets** (for both, *see above*).

TRAVELLERS' NEEDS

For computer repairs and mobile phone rental, *see pp189-190*. For luggage, *see p196*. For shipping, *see p305*.

Arts & Entertainment

Ingleby Gallery. *See p230.*

Festival Edinburgh

Everyone's welcome at the planet's biggest arts celebration.

For 11 months of the year, Edinburgh is a relaxed, sedate city, revelling in the benefits of its capital status while enjoying the calm that comes with a smallish population. But come August, it's all change. The population doubles, the atmosphere becomes almost continental, and the grey stone façades burst into colour. It's the largest arts celebration in the world, drawing performers from Uppsala to Uluru and all points in between.

Not everyone is enamoured of this dramatic shift in the city's character. Many locals jump ship and rent their properties to visitors for massive fees, while others simply stay and grumble. However, they're in the minority: for most, the array of festivals held during August together comprise the highlight of the city's cultural calendar. Unique is an overused word, but it absolutely applies here. August in Edinburgh is like no place else on earth.

A FESTIVALS PRIMER

The first thing to note about August in Edinburgh is that the hundreds of events that take place are not part of a single cultural festival. The traditional primacy of the Edinburgh International Festival has meant that August's events are often referred to as, simply, 'the festival'. However, there are a huge bundle of administratively separate jamborees taking place at the same time, dedicated to different artistic disciplines. Many of them came together to form **Festivals Edinburgh**, an umbrella organisation that works with all the various organisers in a bid to improve their lot in the city, but they're ultimately separate and very distinct enterprises. This chapter attempts to make sense of them all.

During August, legions of notable writers, artists and performers descend on the city. Famous cinematic faces arrive to revive their careers with cameo stage roles, and the usually busy London comedy circuit closes for a month. But Edinburgh also fills with rank amateurs on a wing and a prayer, making one last tilt at fame before the money runs out. You might have to stand in line for hours to get into the latest hot-ticket show or you might be the only person in the audience. You might be moved to tears by dramatic theatre and sent into paroxysms of laughter by a stand-up comic. Or, of course, vice versa.

The August festivities began in 1947 with the launch of the **Edinburgh International Festival (EIF)**, established with the express aim of providing war-torn Europe with a focus for the best in new drama, music and the visual arts. The organisers hoped the festival would unite the continent's culture while the great festivals of Salzburg and Munich found their feet again in the aftermath of World War II. Some blend of the programme, the scale of the city and good fortune meant they achieved their ambitions many times over. After more than six decades, the EIF, and its various offshoots and specialist competitors, has come to define the city in the eyes of the outside world.

EIF Director Jonathan Mills, an Australian composer and former director of the Melbourne Festival, launched his first programme in 2007. Believing in evolution rather than revolution, he combined a professorial interest in the EIF's history with his own personal passions for early music and theatre/music crossovers. He likes to give each programme a coherent theme – cultural and geographical borders in 2008, the Scottish Enlightenment in 2009 – in order to lend the event a sense of purpose. Under Mills, the festival has taken in visual art (every other year), which had previously been absent from the programme for years.

The **Edinburgh Festival Fringe** (which, from now on, we'll just call the Fringe) began in modest circumstances in 1947, when eight companies not invited to the EIF decided to hold their own unofficial shows during it. Today, the anarchic, chaotic event dwarfs its grander rival: it routinely stages in excess of 2,000 shows across 250 venues. The Fringe broke away from the EIF in 1998, and now starts and finishes a week earlier.

The Fringe differs from all Edinburgh's other festivals, and most cultural festivals in Europe, in that there is no quality control. Anyone can put on a show, provided they can hire a venue, find accommodation and live on fresh air and dreams for a month or so. The only thing most acts have in common is their willingness to pay £300-odd to the Festival Fringe Society in order to guarantee a listing in the Fringe Programme, a 250-page brochure that emerges each June.

The Fringe attracts a bewildering array of aspiring young talent, consummate crowd-pleasers, once-in-a-lifetime amateurs and wily old pros. But don't be fooled by the sheen of amateurism: the Fringe is a well-oiled machine. Comedy and theatre are the mainstays, but dance, music and, to a lesser degree, visual art all feature in the programme. Venues vary wildly, from multi-theatre operations to big tops, moving vehicles and people's living rooms. The only rule is that there are no rules.

The **Edinburgh International Film Festival** also arrived in 1947, after the Edinburgh Film Guild grew piqued that the EIF had omitted film from its remit. It's since become an important date in the industry calendar, and has gained an even higher profile since director Hannah McGill shunted the festival back to June a few years ago. (It's the only festival in this chapter that isn't held during August.) It's popular with the local cinemagoing public, who get to see a wide selection of flicks before their UK release dates.

Three years after the Film Festival arrived, a decidedly different event made its entrance: the **Edinburgh Military Tattoo**, a soldiers' parade of music, dance and athleticism. It's grown into the single most popular event in the city each August, shifting more than 200,000 tickets each year and inspiring what many believe are the world's longest queues. The Tattoo is held on the Castle Esplanade.

As the city attracted greater crowds, other festivals sprang up, hoping for a piece of the action. Held a week before the Fringe, the **Edinburgh Jazz & Blues Festival** began in 1979. The **Edinburgh International Book Festival** was launched four years later and is now the largest event of its type in the world. The low-key **Edinburgh Art Festival** was launched in 2004 and has grown steadily in profile. In the same year, the first ever **Festival of Politics** was staged, inspired by the opening of the Scottish Parliament. Two events are

aimed at locals: the **Edinburgh Mela**, a two-day outdoor event that celebrates Asian culture in the city with performances, food stalls and a bazaar; and the politically minded **Edinburgh People's Festival**, which aims to 'bring the arts to the ignored indigenous communities' by staging shows in the city's more deprived areas. And two events are industry jamborees: the **Edinburgh International Television Festival**, founded in 1976, and the **Edinburgh Interactive Entertainment Festival**, which briefly opens its doors to the public for demonstrations of upcoming video games.

The remainder of this chapter is divided into the various artistic disciplines covered by the various festivals. At the end of the section (*see pp214-215*), you'll find all the nuts and bolts information on each one: dates, contact details and the like.

CULTURE DURING THE FESTIVALS

Art

Festivals *Edinburgh International Festival, Edinburgh Art Festival*

The visual arts have traditionally been cast aside during August in Edinburgh, forgotten in favour of the performing arts. However, things are gradually changing.

In 2004, around 30 galleries in the city established the low-key **Edinburgh Art Festival**. The festival has since grown in profile, with special events supplementing the exhibitions already staged in the city's galleries and museums. With the support of the Scottish Government's Expo Fund, the festival is building a £250,000 pot of money that will be used for commissioning and promoting work for 2010 and beyond.

INSIDE TRACK
LAST NIGHT FIREWORKS

The EIF's **closing concert** in Princes Street Gardens, held on the final Sunday of the festival, is accompanied by some spectacular explosions lighting up the night sky above the castle. The concert is ticketed and always sold out, but the fireworks are free and best viewed from North Bridge, Princes Street, Calton Hill, Salisbury Crags or the Royal Botanic Garden. The 40-minute extravaganza is a great popular attraction. And wherever your viewing point, you can tune in to the concert on local radio.

August in Edinburgh.

Under Jonathan Mills, the **EIF** has become involved in the visual arts for the first time in years. In 2009, the festival offered a series of shows covering the broad umbrella theme of 'The Enlightenments', and now looks set to feature a visual-arts strand every two years.

Comedy

Festivals *Edinburgh Festival Fringe*

Each year's Fringe brings a new controversy, and the hot topic in 2008 was the launch of something called the **Edinburgh Comedy Festival**. Critics pointed out that it wasn't a festival so much as a marketing exercise by the four biggest venues (any comic who wasn't performing at the Assembly Rooms, the Gilded Balloon, the Pleasance or the Underbelly was excluded); the venues responded by saying that they were only trying to get more people to enjoy the festival.

The debate will rumble on for as long as the ECF continues to return, which it did in 2009, but the argument wouldn't even be necessary without the extraordinary volume of comedy on offer during August. A massive array of comics head here from all corners of the globe in the hope of landing an agent, securing a touring contract, signing a TV deal and – almost as an afterthought, it sometimes feels – making the paying punters laugh.

The popularity of the Fringe as a comedic career-maker can be traced to 1960, when Oxbridge revue *Beyond the Fringe* (starring Peter Cook, Dudley Moore, Jonathan Miller and Alan Bennett) made its debut before going on to extended runs in the West End and on Broadway. The show was actually part of the EIF (that's why it was, yes, 'beyond the Fringe'). However, its success – playing to 120 per cent houses, thanks to audiences being prepared to stand – set a precedent for comics to head north during August.

It wasn't until the 1980s that the Fringe's reputation as a hotbed of new comedy began to translate into mainstream success. Launched in 1981, the Perrier Award was set up to draw attention to what its judges believed to be the best comedy and/or cabaret show on the Fringe. Many of the acts who won the Perrier in the early and mid 1980s have since faded, but the roll call of then-unknown winners in the late '80s and early '90s established the award's cachet. Jeremy Hardy (1988), Frank Skinner (1991), Steve Coogan (1992) and Lee Evans (1993) all became stars after winning the prize, which now goes under the sponsorless name of the Edinburgh Comedy Awards.

It's this 1990s golden age, and its seemingly concomitant guarantee of national fame, that

arguably still drives the Fringe's comedy component. After all, what else could possibly persuade hordes of hard-up comics to spend August haemorrhaging most of the cash they've earned over the other 11 months of the year on usually futile attempts to crack the big time? Competition is insanely fierce, but the chance that the show you bring to the Fringe could be Your Big Break is, for most aspiring funnymen, simply too tempting to pass up.

The largest comedy gathering in the world is also, for its performers, the most gruelling. Most comedy festivals last for a week, tops, and generally consist of one-off showcases at which acts have to make crowds laugh for 20 minutes. Edinburgh demands more. Although a few big-name comics fly in for short and often lucrative theatrical engagements, those on the lower rungs commonly take to the stage six days a week for a three-week stretch. Aided by their existing reputations (and a knockout agent), a lucky few land evening slots at prestigious venues. Others are quickly forced to resign themselves to the fact that, if the sun comes out, their daily 3.10pm slot in a scruffy pub cellar may not sell out. Indeed, they may be the only person in the room.

If they're not too dispirited, exhausted or drunk, a handful of comics each year get the opportunity to play the Late & Live show at the Gilded Balloon, a bearpit of a comedy club that starts at 1am every night. Unlike most laugh-ins, the set-up welcomes boozed-up hecklers and positively encourages audiences to waylay the four performers, who each have a half-hour to fill. A good showing here can make a comic's career; more often, it breaks them, at least until the next day, when they have to head back to their regular gig and start again.

The primary comedy venues on the Fringe are the Assembly Rooms, the Pleasance, the Gilded Balloon, the Underbelly and the Stand. Still, don't limit yourself: comics play in a multitude of smaller locations around the city, many for free. It's all something of a lottery, but every lottery has a winner… doesn't it?

Film & television

Festivals *Edinburgh International Film Festival, Edinburgh International Television Festival*

The **Edinburgh International Film Festival** started life as a gala celebration of documentaries, but now presents a mix of new features and shorts, animated flicks and factual programming, retrospectives and revivals. Director John Huston described it in 1972 as 'the only film festival worth a damn'. Although it's since been overtaken in prominence by Cannes

ARTS & ENTERTAINMENT

ARTS & ENTERTAINMENT

and Sundance, it remains an important date in the cinema calendar. There's a strong industry presence at the events – official delegates are recognisable by their ever-present half-full wine glasses and all-black outfits – but there are also plenty of tickets available to regular punters.

Since moving from August to June in 2008, the Film Festival has found it easier not only to distinguish itself from the city's other big festivals, but also to strike a clearer identity on the international circuit. There are many UK premières, often on show months before their release (assuming they get one; many don't), as well as retrospectives of cinema's great names. Screenings ranges from the annual Directors' Showcase, billed as 'classics of the future' by established auteurs, to the Rosebud strand, dedicated to first- and second-time directors.

Although the festival made space for *Wall-E* in 2008, and there's always at least some red-carpet action, blockbusters are few and far between. Instead, short films, experimental novelties and animations feature prominently. Documentaries have come back into fashion of late; an award for the best documentary was introduced in 2006. Alongside the screenings are a range of talks and discussions featuring cast, crew and critics.

The EIFF's audience-friendliness stands in contrast to the weekend-long **Edinburgh International Television Festival**, aimed pretty much exclusively at insiders. Media folks are past masters at navel-gazing, and nowhere are their talents more apparent than at the range of lectures, discussions and debates about the past, present and future of the idiot box. It's an industry-only event, the importance of which is later amplified by the excessive coverage it receives from those who forked out the sizeable delegate fee to attend.

Literature & debate

Festivals *Edinburgh International Book Festival, Festival of Politics*

Pitching its well-appointed marquees in the gardens of Robert Adam-designed Charlotte Square (*see p83*), the **Edinburgh International Book Festival** is a cultured haven that carefully sets itself apart from the chaotic throngs in the Old Town. Compared with its competitors, the event moves at a genteel pace, fuelled not by deep-fried pizza and Tennent's Extra but by dry white and canapés.

The programme comprises a range of talks, readings and discussions, grouped into broad themes that change each year. The organisers are keen to encourage participation: debates are a prominent part of the programme, as are events for children, who can romp safely in the enclosed gardens. Aspiring writers are encouraged to join one of several writers' workshops and to visit the writers' retreat hidden among the trees.

Most authors make only a single appearance at the event, but the truly stellar – or the truly tenacious – may show up several times during the two-week programme. Big names in recent years have included Ian Rankin, Zadie Smith, Richard Dawkins, Salman Rushdie, Seamus Heaney and Doris Lessing. The festival isn't above the odd nod to populism – Sean Connery was a sell-out in 2008 – but, more typically, the event is a hotbed of politically engaged debate. Alongside the expected slew of novelists, poets and critics, John Prescott, Tony Benn, Alex Salmond and Gordon Brown have made appearances, as have a host of philosophers, environmentalists and radical thinkers.

Those interested in current events should also investigate the five-day **Festival of Politics**. Launched in 2005 and held at the Scottish Parliament building, the festival includes an array of talks, debates and discussions from prominent figures such as Vanessa Redgrave, Kate Adie and Mark Thomas. Admission to most events is free.

Music

Festivals *Edinburgh International Festival, Edinburgh Festival Fringe, Edinburgh Jazz & Blues Festival*

Edinburgh is an old-fashioned city in many respects, not least of which is its range of music programming during August's festivals. Though a few daring types have attempted to bring rock and pop to the fore, classical music and opera still dominate.

More than theatre and dance, classical music is at the heart of the **EIF**. The Usher Hall stages concerts nightly, supplemented by an all-day line-up at the Queen's Hall and half a dozen major operas at the Festival Theatre. Standards are high and top international names make regular appearances. Programming, split roughly 50-50 between orchestral concerts and chamber recitals, draws on the canon; events in 2009 included a Bach series. However, there have been recent signs that the EIF's music programme may be expanding under director Jonathan Mills; 2009 saw folk brought to the fore in a series called the Caledonian Sessions. The highly popular Fireworks Concert in Princes Street Gardens (*see p78*) draws proceedings to a close with a suitable flash and a bang, bringing audiences out to every possible viewing station throughout the city centre.

There's also a surprising amount of classical music on offer at the **Fringe**, much of it very

Edinburgh International Film Festival

worthwhile. Young musicians dominate, generally performing in one-off concerts or short-run recital series. The Festival of British Youth Orchestras takes place annually as part of the programme and is often worth a look, as are the free daily lunchtime shows at St Mary's Cathedral (see p95).

The rest of the Fringe's musical programme is an anything-goes jumble that takes in everything from Scottish folk to wink-wink cabaret. After years in the wilderness, rock has reestablished itself thanks to the event once known as T on the Fringe but now called the **Edge Festival** (www.theedgefestival.com), which encompasses everything from scuzzy indie kids getting a foot on the ladder to major names at the Corn Exchange; Radiohead, Morrissey, Franz Ferdinand and Arcade Fire have all passed through.

Although you won't find their details in any official programme, the town's clubs and music venues take full advantage of the influx of hedonists and book big-name DJs during August. Sessions often last until 5am, when clubbers emerge blinking into the dawn. Promoters are keen to attract festivalgoers, but few book DJs far enough ahead to get into the Fringe brochure. Check flyers and *The List* for details on what's going on while you're in town.

The **Edinburgh Jazz & Blues Festival** can get a little lost in all these crazy goings-on, partly because it begins a week before the Fringe. However, while its programme is chiefly populated by local musicians, it does draw the occasional big name: Dionne Warwick, Wynton Marsalis and Jools Holland have all performed here. More or less every strand of jazz is covered at the event, with concerts staged throughout the day and night.

Theatre & dance

Festivals *Edinburgh International Festival; Edinburgh Festival Fringe*

Those of a theatrical bent should investigate the programmes of both the **EIF** and the **Fringe**. The latter offers plenty of variety, although the quality control is more predictable at the former.

The roster of theatre and dance at the EIF is small, grand and expensive to stage, although prices can be less than you'd pay on the Fringe if you book ahead. The programmes put together by Jonathan Mills have ranged from established names of the avant garde, such as the Wooster Group and Mabou Mines, to collaborations with companies closer to home, such as Dublin's Gate and the city's own

Edinburgh Mela.

Traverse. It's also the place to see major names in dance, whether crowd-pleasers such as Michael Clark and Matthew Bourne, famous classical ensembles or edgy European troupes.

Although the Fringe has the reputation for pushing boundaries, it's often the EIF that provides the biggest and most provocative revelations. But while you might find acclaimed international acts making their UK debuts as part of the Festival, you won't see brand new acts breaking through into the big time. The EIF generally leaves that to its pals on the Fringe. That said, it has made some recent concessions via the Edinburgh International Festival Fringe Prize, which always gives an up-and-coming company a low-key place in the festival.

Comparatively speaking, the variety of theatre and dance on the Fringe is baffling, dazzling and, at times, off-putting. Everybody from amateurish private school ensembles to well-known American troupes come to the party, performing everything from classic Edwardian costume drama to sexually explicit modern ballet. Shock and controversy are touchstones; the more attention a show receives, the more tickets it sells.

Among the countless venues, the Traverse (see p254) prides itself on staging cutting-edge drama, and is the beating heart of Fringe theatre. Its bar is the essential hangout for many a luvvie. Meanwhile, dance fans should head to the Grassmarket for round-the-clock moves at Dance Base (see p254).

VISITING THE FESTIVAL

With so much to see in such a short space of time, planning your August itinerary can be a daunting prospect. The chaotic, spontaneous vibe is all part of the experience, but a little forward planning is crucial if you're to get the best out of it. (This is particularly vital when it comes to accommodation; see pp135-166.)

Try and approach the festivals with some measure of organisation. Military precision isn't essential, but it helps: unless you're in an improv troupe, it's best not to turn up and make it up as you go along. Have a look at the programme(s) before you arrive, and keep your ear to the ground. You can just rock up without any tickets and let nature take its course, but don't come crying to us when the only show you can get into is the Aberystwyth Amateur Dramatics Society's production of *Carousel*. In Welsh.

In addition to its printed programme, each festival has its own website at which you can find out what's on and book tickets for future events. Perhaps the most useful online resource, though, is **www.edinburghfestivals.co.uk**, which contains a searchable database listing what's on across all the major festivals. The catch-all set-up makes it that much easier to plan your schedule.

So, how do you go about sorting the diamonds from the rough? Well, this is the one time of the year when press coverage really counts. Ignore the publicity stunts and read the reviews instead. The daily festivals supplement published by the *Scotsman* is hard to beat for comprehensiveness. Arguably the most reliable reviews are found in the *Guardian*, which dedicates at least a page a day to the event, as do the *Edinburgh Evening News* and the *Herald*. The *Scotsman* and the *Herald* give out, respectively, Fringe Firsts and Angel Awards to new plays, comedies, concerts and films that have impressed their critics; tickets for them immediately start selling like the proverbial hot cakes. And *The List* offers comprehensive coverage of the festivals; usually published fortnightly, it comes out every Thursday during August. For more on local media, see p308.

Several free festival newspapers, staffed by young writers and aspirant culture vultures, litter bars and cafés during August. Containing news, reviews, interviews, features, listings and scurrilous gossip, they make up in enthusiasm what they lack in professionalism. *Three Weeks* is the longest established of this breed; *The Skinny* is an increasingly important year-round venture. And then, of course, there's good old-fashioned word of mouth. Don't be shy: pitch in and ask those folks sitting a few seats away if they've seen anything good, or if they've spent good money on any absolute stinkers.

Profile Faith Liddell

The director of Festivals Edinburgh on the inspiration of her home town.

Faith Liddell began working in the Traverse bar as a student, and has worked in theatres and festivals here ever since. The former director of the Edinburgh International Book Festival, she's now director of Festivals Edinburgh, an umbrella organisation set up by Edinburgh's 12 major festivals.

'I love the textures of the city, its astonishing combination of dramatic landscapes and the striking historical and contemporary architecture all sitting in fabulous intimacy with each other. It's this proximity that allows the cultural textures of the city to weave so vibrantly into its life, to occupy its spaces so energetically and to draw its residents and visitors into its spell.

'My favourite places in Edinburgh are the Shore in Leith, a fabulous gastronomic haven with a waterside atmosphere and its own sense of community. I love the High Street too, the wonderful stretch of the Old Town from the castle through the heartland of the festivals to the palace and parliament, set against the remarkable backdrop of Arthur's Seat. It's an astonishing mile of history, culture and topography.

'There's a real sense of magic in the transforming power that a great festival brings to a city. It's almost impossible for anyone who hasn't experienced it to imagine the intensity of that magic in Edinburgh, with not one festival but seven in the space of just four weeks. From late July to early September, our city is immersed in art, ideas and entertainment. It's a source of inspiration for over 10,000 artists and producers, and for hundreds of thousands of visitors.

'With 12 major festivals throughout the year, Edinburgh is an astonishing place to live and visit. Our festivals inhabit every corner of the historic heart of the city, from the castle esplanade to the ancient bowels of the Cowgate, from Charlotte Square to the narrow cobbled closes of the High Street, from the grandeur of the Festival Theatre to the dark intimacy of the city's underground passages.

'Edinburgh is a romantic place even for those of us that live here but, during the peak August festival period, it's like the biggest and most cultured speed dating event in the universe. Remember, though, that, like the festivals, part of the appeal is that it's all so ephemeral.'

Booking tickets

In theory, booking tickets for the thousands of performances held over the various August festivals should be a nightmare. But glossing over the major box-office meltdown suffered by the Fringe in 2008 (things were a lot smoother the following year), buying tickets for shows at most of the festivals is generally very straightforward, whether you'd rather purchase online, by phone, via mail or in person.

The easiest way to book tickets before arriving in Edinburgh is by going online. All the major festivals take internet bookings; in most cases, you can choose either to have your tickets sent to you or to collect them from the relevant festival's box office when you arrive. Once you're in town, it's best to book either by phone or at one of the walk-up box offices: the **Fringe** has an office on the High Street; the **Edinburgh International Film Festival** sells tickets through the Filmhouse; and tickets for the **EIF**, the **Festival of Politics** and the **Edinburgh Jazz & Blues Festival** are all available from the Hub.

Advance booking will almost certainly be necessary. Many events staged as part of the **EIF**, the **Edinburgh International Book Festival** and the **Edinburgh International Film Festival** are one-offs, and those featuring big names do tend to sell out ahead of time. Many comedy and theatre shows on the **Fringe** run for far longer, in some cases nightly over a three-week period, which means you may have less trouble picking up tickets when you arrive. Others, though, run for limited periods (in some cases, only a single night); booking ahead is advisable.

If you're heading north purely to take in the Fringe, consider heading up there for the first weekend, when punters can buy two tickets for the price of one for most shows. The caveat? Many of the shows are at 'preview' stage and are more than a little ragged around the edges. Alternatively, head for the Fringe's **Half Price Hut**, on the corner of Waverley Bridge and Princes Street. Open 11am to 9pm daily throughout the Fringe, the hut offers 50 per cent discounts on tickets to many of that day's shows. And it's also worth hanging around the main comedy and theatre venues in the early evening to catch promoters handing out free tickets for shows that are selling poorly in an attempt to conjure up an audience.

DIRECTORY

All dates and prices listed are tbc; contact the festivals directly before making plans.

Edinburgh Art Festival
Venue: various venues. Information: 07825 336782, www.edinburghartfestival.org. **Tickets** generally follow museum admission fees; most exhibitions are free. *Advance booking* not required. **Dates** 6wks, late July-early Sept.

Edinburgh Festival Fringe
Venue: various venues. Information & tickets: Fringe Office, 180 High Street, Old Town, EH1 1QS (226 0026 information, 226 0000 box office, www.edfringe.com). **Tickets** mostly £6-£12, though some are cheaper (or even free) and others are more expensive (£15-£35). *Advance booking* online, by phone, by post & in person from mid June. **Dates** 3wks, Aug.

ARTS & ENTERTAINMENT

Edinburgh Military Tattoo.

Edinburgh Interactive Entertainment Festival

Venue: various venues. Information & tickets: 01462 456780, www.eief.co.uk. **Tickets** games screenings, the sole portion of the event open to the public, are free. *Advance booking* online only. **Dates** 2 days, mid Aug.

Edinburgh International Book Festival

Venue: Charlotte Square Gardens, New Town. Information & tickets: 5a Charlotte Square, New Town, EH2 4DR (718 5666 information, 0845 373 5888 box office, www.edbookfest.co.uk). **Tickets** mostly £6-£9 (£4 for children's events), plus some free events. *Advance booking* online and by post from mid June, by phone and in person from 1mth before festival. **Dates** 17 days, ending on last Mon in Aug (Aug 14-30 2010; Aug 13-29 2011; Aug 11-27 2012).

Edinburgh International Festival

Venue: various venues. Information & tickets: The Hub, Castlehill, Old Town, EH1 2NE (473 2099 administration, 473 2000 box office, www.eif.co.uk). **Tickets** many events cost around £10-£25 or £10-£40, with some cheaper concerts (around £17), one or two more expensive operas (£10-£65) and some free events mixed into the schedule. *Advance booking* online, by phone, by post & in person from early Apr. **Dates** 24 days, ending on 1st Sun in Sept (13 Aug-5 Sept 2010; 12 Aug-4 Sept 2011; 10 Aug-2 Sept 2012).

Edinburgh International Film Festival

Venue: various cinemas & theatres. Information & tickets: Filmhouse, 88 Lothian Road, Old Town, EH3 9BZ (228 4051 administration, 623 8030 box office, www.edfilmfest.org.uk). **Tickets** most films are around £6-£9, with the opening and closing galas costing £15. *Advance booking* online, by phone & in person from early May. **Dates** 12 days in late June.

Edinburgh International Television Festival

Venue: Edinburgh International Conference Centre. Information & tickets: 117 Farringdon Road, London EC1R 3BX (0131 519 4131, www.mgeitf.co.uk). **Tickets** by delegate pass. *Advance booking* Online, phone & postal bookings from early in the yr. **Dates** 3 days, ending on last Sun in Aug (Aug 27-29 2010; Aug 26-28 2011; Aug 24-26 2012).

Edinburgh Jazz & Blues Festival

Venue: various venues. Information & tickets: Hub, Castlehill, Old Town, EH1 2NE (467 5200 information, 473 2000 box office, www.edinburghjazzfestival.co.uk). **Tickets** mostly £8-£15, with some shows costing up to £30 and

others free. *Advance booking* online, by phone & by post from early in the year. **Dates** 10 days, late July-mid Aug.

Edinburgh Mela

Venue: Pilrig Park, Leith. Information: North Edinburgh Art Centre, 15A Pennywell Court, EH4 4TZ (332 2888, www.edinburgh-mela.co.uk). **Tickets** £2 day pass covers most events; headline shows are around £10. *Advance booking* online, by phone and in person (from the Hub) from July. **Dates** 6-8 Aug 2010; 2-4 Sep 2011.

Edinburgh Military Tattoo

Venue: Castle Esplanade, Old Town. Information & tickets: 32-34 Market Street, Old Town, EH1 1QB (0870 755 5118, www.edintattoo.co.uk). **Tickets** around £15-£50. *Advance booking* online, by phone, by post & in person from early Dec. **Dates** 23 days in Aug (6-28 Aug 2010; 5-27 Aug 2011).

Edinburgh People's Festival

Venue: various venues. Information & tickets: Out of the Blue Drill Hall (see p253) (www.edinburghpeoplesfestival.org.uk). **Tickets** most events are free; those with a ticket price usually cost less than £5. *Advance booking* not required. **Dates** several weeks, Aug.

Festival of Politics

Venue, information & tickets: Scottish Parliament, Holyrood, EH99 1SP (348 5000, www.festivalofpolitics.org.uk. **Tickets** free; a handful of paid-for events are around £6. *Advance booking* from the Scottish Parliament or the Hub from early July. **Dates** 5 days, late Aug (17-21 Aug 2010; subsequent years tbc).

ARTS & ENTERTAINMENT

Calendar

What to do between September and July.

The concentration of cultural events that takes place in Edinburgh during August captures the headlines (and gets its own chapter in this guide; *see pp206-215*), but plenty of other festivals brighten up the rest of the year. The revival of **Beltane** has turned into a late-night spectacular with an audience of thousands; summer sees Scotland's best breweries take over the Assembly Rooms for a few days; **Doors Open Day** is a fascinating glimpse behind the scenes of otherwise inaccessible buildings in the autumn; and winter brings the **Capital Christmas** and **Edinburgh's Hogmanay**. All are worth taking into account when planning a trip. Note, though, that dates can vary; always check the website before making plans.

SPRING

Mary King's Ghost Fest
Various venues, Old Town (08702 430160, www.marykingsghostfest.com). **Date** late Mar.
Ten days of talks, bus tours, clairvoyant gatherings, ghost-hunts and vigils. It's either the city's most feeble excuse for a festival or a spooky excursion into the paranormal, depending how sceptical you feel.

Ceilidh Culture Festival
Various venues (228 1155, www.ceilidhculture. co.uk). **Date** late Mar/early Apr.
Backed by the local authority, this is a community-focused celebration of traditional Scottish music, dance, song and storytelling. City-wide over a period of nearly four weeks, prices vary by event.

Edinburgh International Harp Festival
Merchiston Castle School, Colinton Road, West Edinburgh (468 0593, www.harpfestival.co.uk). **Date** 9-14 Apr.
Six days of concerts, classes and workshops with the harp – or *clarsach* – taking centre stage.

★ Edinburgh International Science Festival
Various venues (558 7776, www.sciencefestival. co.uk). **Date** 2wks, early Apr.
This hugely enjoyably festival gives an accessible slant on difficult subjects without dumbing down. Running for more than 20 years, it's the UK's largest science jamboree, attracting more than 60,000 people to its many talks, events and workshops.

Beltane Fire Festival
Calton Hill, Calton Hill & Broughton (www.beltane.org). **Date** Apr 30.
An ancient tradition marking the transition from winter to spring, Beltane was revived in the 1980s and has grown into quite a drama: fire, costume, body-paint, dancing and drumming on the late-night backdrop of Calton Hill. If the weather holds, it can attract up to 12,000 people. Tickets cost around £5 in advance from the Hub (*see p59*); a limited number are available for £7 on the night.

SUMMER

★ Royal Highland Show
Royal Highland Centre, Ingliston, West Edinburgh (335 6200, www.royalhighland show.org.uk). **Date** June.
See *p104* **Down on the Farm**.

Scottish Real Ale Festival
Assembly Rooms, George Street, New Town (www.scottishbeerfestival.org.uk). **Date** late June.
Beer enthusiasts take over the Assembly Rooms for three days each June, getting to grips with around 130 different ales from 30 Scottish breweries based as far afield as Orkney and the Borders. The entry price of £5 includes a free beer glass.

AUTUMN

Doors Open Day
Various venues (557 8686, www.cockburn association.org.uk). **Date** wknd, late Sept.

Each year, heritage body the Cockburn Association collaborates with organisations and individuals to allow public access to buildings that few people usually get to see – everything from private homes to lighthouses. It's all free.

Edinburgh Independent Radical Book Fair

Out of the Blue, the Drill Hall, 36 Dalmeny Street, off Leith Walk, Leith (662 9112, www.word-power.co.uk). **Date** late Oct/Nov.
Five days of readings and discussions, focusing on independent and radical publishing houses. For more, contact Word Power (*see p188*).

Samhuinn (Hallowe'en)

High Street, Old Town (www.beltane.org). **Date** 31 Oct.
Samhuinn marks the end of the Celtic summer, six months after Beltane. The Beltane Fire Society takes to the streets once again, from Castle Esplanade, down the Royal Mile to Parliament Square, where the summer court, led by the Green Man, is banished to the magical realm for winter.

WINTER

Bonfire Night

Various venues. **Date** 5 Nov.
Guy Fawkes was a Yorkshire-born terrorist, part of a Catholic group who were opposed to the Protestant establishment and decided to try and blow up Parliament while James I & VI was inside. The plot was foiled on 5 Nov 1605; ever since, bonfires have been lit on that date to celebrate. The big fireworks display is at Meadowbank Stadium (*see p249*); it focuses on pyrotechnics, not Jacobean politics.

St Andrew's Day

Various venues. **Date** 30 Nov.
St Andrew's Day is nowhere near as debauched for the Scots as St Patrick's Day is for the Irish, but it's still a decent reason to raise a glass. In 2007, the Scottish Parliament designated it as a public holiday, and efforts are now being made to make it a little more festive than it's been in the past.

Capital Christmas

Various venues (www.edinburghschristmas.com). **Date** late Nov-early Jan.
What started out as a few casual events has grown into a large, popular, city-wide festival. The centrepiece is the Winter Wonderland in Princes Street Gardens, complete with fairground rides, crafts market, skating rink and the Edinburgh Wheel (a Ferris wheel next to the Scott Monument).

★ Edinburgh's Hogmanay

Throughout the city (www.edinburghshogmanay. org). **Date** 29 Dec-1 Jan.
Edinburgh's modern Hogmanay celebration is a four-day festival, featuring a torchlight procession, bands in Princes Street Gardens, street performers, fireworks and even, for the hardy, a mini-triathlon on New Year's Day. The street party on the evening of 31 Dec sees the city centre cordoned off for safety reasons, with a maximum of 100,000 ticket-holders admitted; see the website for details on how to book tickets. Some locals love it; others, though, view it as an open-air binge drinking session for young singles and couples, and prefer the more family-friendly events. The last few years have seen a few problems hit the party – last-minute cancellations because of severe weather, cutbacks following loss-making years in 2007 and 2008 – but the event is still worth tens of millions of pounds to Edinburgh's economy.

Burns Night

Throughout the city (www.visitscotland.com). **Date** 25 Jan.
In his short life, Robert Burns (1759-96) built a reputation as a fine poet, but it was only after his death that he came to be regarded as Scotland's national bard. Burns Suppers, dinners in his memory, have been run for more than 200 years by Burns societies, churches, masonic lodges and other community groups. Held around the anniversary of his birth (25 January, Burns Night), they follow a traditional format, including recitation of the poem 'Address to a Haggis', and a meal including haggis, 'chappit neeps' (mashed swede), mashed potatoes and whisky. There's no single, set-piece Edinburgh event, but watch out for themed exhibitions and Burns Suppers in hotels and restaurants.

Edinburgh's Hogmanay.

ARTS & ENTERTAINMENT

Children

Whatever the weather, there's something for the kids here.

Come rain, shine or the dark, dreich days of winter, you'll want to keep your kids entertained. Happily, Edinburgh loves children, and children love it right back. The acres of parkland and the huge volcano (it is dormant, isn't it?) allows for plenty of outdoor romping when the weather holds. And when it doesn't, the higgledy old houses and gloriously gory history should keep even the most jaded of teenagers switched on to the city and its delights.

If you're here in August, your kids will enjoy whiling away many cash-free hours on the High Street watching Fringe performers drumming up trade for their shows. And if you're here at the end of December, don't miss the **Torchlight Procession** (*see p217*), as well as whatever free street theatre the **Hogmanay** programme brings (*see p217*).

GETTING AROUND

The good news: most of the major sights in Edinburgh are confined within a few square miles. The bad news: many are separated by hills, some of which are pretty steep.

If it's too far or too high to walk, Edinburgh's bus network should come to the rescue. Under fives travel free (up to two children per adult), while under-15s will pay 70p for a single fare (adults are charged £1.20). Foldable pushchairs are fine on the buses, but traditional prams are a complete no-go. On popular routes, parents with pushchairs may find that if the bus is busy, or if there's another pushchair, travel system or a wheelchair already on board, you may have to wait for the next bus. If you've got a very young baby and plan to make a number of journeys, it may be worth considering a sling. For more on buses, *see p302*.

INSIDE TRACK
IN CASE OF EMERGENCY

If your child gets ill or injured while in Edinburgh, your best bet is the **Royal Hospital for Sick Children** (23 Sciennes Road, South Edinburgh, 536 0000), orientated to the needs of babies and children up to the age of 13. There's direct A&E access from Sylvan Place.

Edinburgh's city centre is well served by black cabs. They can be costly but they do seat five, and you shouldn't need to fold your pushchair. Some cabs also have fold-down concealed toddler seats (ask the driver before getting in). For more on cabs, *see p303*.

SIGHTS
Around the Royal Mile

Perhaps surprisingly, **Edinburgh Castle** (*see p56*) doesn't have too much to hold little ones' interest. However, they may be taken by the castle's creepier corners (look out for David's Tower, especially the eerie light show that tells of the murderous Black Dinner) and the real-life soldiers and the One O'Clock Gun (*see p56* **Bang!**). The gun goes off with quite a crack: and, yes, it will make big and little kids jump if they're not expecting it.

Down on Castlehill is the **Camera Obscura** (*see p56*), Edinburgh's oldest purpose-built tourist attraction. Again, kids may not go for the main attraction, but you should have better luck with the other four floors of illusions, holographs and visual delights. The outside of the building has distorting mirrors that can entertain younger children for a few minutes.

East along Market Street sits the **Edinburgh Dungeon** (*see p65*), run by the same company that operates the London and York Dungeons and focusing on the horrors of Scotland and

Edinburgh's gory past. The dungeons claim to be family-friendly, but they're not recommended for under-10s; or, for that matter, anybody on the nervous side.

Due south of here (take the George IV Bridge) sit the **Royal Museum** and the **National Museum of Scotland** (*see p75*), which both have plenty to engage the kids' attention. At the former, the robots, generators, rockets and other gadgets in the Connect Gallery will have boys swooning. And at the latter, seek out the Discovery Zones, which hold games, dressing-up opportunities (the Roman helmet does fit adult heads, even if the chainmail is too small) and other ways to absorb Scotland's history. The buildings have well-appointed toilets, nappy-changing facilities and feeding rooms.

Back on the Royal Mile, continue east and you'll find the **Museum of Childhood** (*see p66*). It may be fascinating for adults or for any school-aged kids doing projects on the past, but it might not hold children's interest for long. In its favour, though, admission is free and the gift shop has some cute stock.

To learn about Scotland's geography, head east to the Earthscape Scotland exhibition outside **Our Dynamic Earth** (*see p69*). Inside, this purpose-built venue charts the geologic evolution of our entire planet: you can witness the Big Bang, touch an iceberg and experience the sounds and smells of an erupting volcano, all without leaving the city. 2009 saw the launch of a highly engaging new exhibit, a 360° presentation under a dome called We Are Astronomers, narrated by David Tennant. Also of note is the Ocean Commotion play area.

Outside the centre

Respectively to the west and east of Edinburgh, both the **Almond Valley Heritage Centre** in Livingston (01506 414957, www.almondvalley. co.uk) and Dunbar's **East Links Family Park** (01368 863607, www.eastlinks.co.uk) delight kids with train rides, farm animals, play zones and soft play areas. East Links is the larger of the two, but both are worth a visit. However, it may be a good idea to pack a change of clothes, as there are wet and/or muddy areas at both.

Edinburgh's proximity to the Firth of Forth means there are a few beach escapes within easy reach of the city. You could go rock-pooling on **Granton Beach** or take a trip to **Portobello** (*see p112*). However, the best of all is **Belhaven Beach** within **John Muir Country Park**. Other lovely beaches within striking distance include those at **North Berwick**, **Gullane**, which has a paying car park with a playpark and toilets nearby, and **Yellowcraig**, where amenities include a recently renovated playpark with a toddler area, toilets and a dog-walking area close to the beach. For more, *see pp292-300*.

ACTIVITIES

Animal attractions

★ **Craigies**
West Craigie Farm, South Queensferry (319 1048, www.craigies.co.uk). No bus. **Open** 9am-5pm daily. **Credit** MC, V.
At this fruit farm, you can pick your own soft fruit (also available by the punnet), enjoy some ravishing

Kiss the Fish. See p221.

ARTS & ENTERTAINMENT

It's Easy Being Green

Take the kids to one of Edinburgh's numerous parks.

Yes, this is a capital city, and yes, there are opportunities to spend money everywhere you turn. But yes, there are also plenty of ways to take young children out in Edinburgh without breaking the bank, many of them allied to the city's wonderful parks. Edinburgh is dotted with open spaces, most of which are great for families (depending, as ever, on the weather).

None of them are more central than **Princes Street Gardens** (*see p78*), divided into East and West by the Mound. In summer, a floral clock is laid out in West Princes Street Gardens, just at the entrance on the Mound; in winter, the same site usually holds a nativity scene. Slightly further west, the footbridge across the railway behind the Ross Bandstand offers perfect views of trains emerging from Waverley Station. On a good day, a friendly wave will get a toot from the drivers. At the westernmost reaches of the park, you'll find toilets, a snack bar and a small play park. East Princes Street Gardens, meanwhile, usually hosts a Winter Wonderland in the weeks before Christmas (*see p217*).

Inquisitive minds may wonder what that great big hill is in the centre of the city. But if **Arthur's Seat** (*see pp96-98*) looks too demanding a hike for the little ones, consider the surprisingly easy walk along Salisbury Crags or aim, instead, for St Margaret's Loch at the east end of **Holyrood Park**. Having been entertained by the ducks, geese and swans, you can scramble up the hillside to the ruined St Anthony's Chapel, dating from the 15th century.

For information on children's activities, contact the Holyrood Park rangers (140 Holyrood Road, 652 8150, www.historic-scotland.gov.uk, open 10am-4pm Mon-Fri); there's always something on at Easter.

South-west of Holyrood Park are the **Meadows**, popular with local adults and kids. There's a great play area at the eastern end, complete with a climbing wall, a water zone and a 'death' slide. Some of the groovier apparatus is perhaps best for older children, but there are also swings for little ones. At the northern end of Middle Meadow Walk, **Peter's Yard** (*see p157*) is a good spot in which to grab something nice to eat.

All the way north, beyond Stockbridge, is **Inverleith Park**, which offers acres of play space, a pirate-boat themed play park, a large pond with a raised wooden walkway over the reed beds and even a pétanque club (Tue & Thur evenings, Wed & Sun afternoons).

Opposite the park's western exit, you'll find the **Royal Botanic Gardens** (*see p89*), which is coming to the end of an extensive renovation to its entrance and visitors' centre. As well as all kinds of plants, there are waterfowl to feed and squirrels to encourage (or avoid), plus glasshouses with tropical palms. At the centre, there's a self-service café/restaurant, with high chairs, nappy-changing facilities and an outdoor eating area. The Botanics, as they're known, are very popular with families, but do remember that it's not a park and so ball games, picnics and cycling are all forbidden.

views over to Fife and down the Firth of Forth, and get some real fresh air. As well as the fruit, Craigies is a working farm, so it doesn't feel too commercialised. There are free-range hens pecking around their enclosure, so kids can see the birds that have laid the eggs that are on sale in the farm shop. There's a café, too, with a tasty if fairly small menu.

★ Edinburgh Zoo
Corstorphine Road, Murrayfield (334 9171, www.edinburghzoo.org.uk). Bus 12, 26, 31. **Open** *Apr-Sept* 9am-6pm daily. *Oct-Mar* 9am-4.30pm daily. **Admission** £14; £9.50-£12 discounts; free under-3s; £29-£50 family. **Credit** MC, V.
Edinburgh Zoo's greatest claim to kids' attention is the Penguin Parade. It's scheduled for 2.15pm daily (Apr-Aug) subject to the penguins' attitudes; given that one of them, Sir Nils Olav, has an honorary knighthood, attitudes have to be respected. The zoo has maintained a self-sustaining penguin colony for nearly a century; it's now the largest in Europe.

But if Nils and the gang won't play, there should be something else to take the eye. Wow-factor mammals include chimpanzees, rhinos and pygmy hippos; in 2008, the zoo pulled off a conservation coup by breeding a Grevy's zebra (called Flo), a species that's endangered in the wild. There are several play areas for children, plus two cafés and several kiosks.

Gorgie City Farm
Gorgie Road, West Edinburgh (337 4202, www.gorgiecityfarm.org.uk). Bus 1, 2, 3, 21, 25, 33, 34, 38. **Open** *Mar-Oct* 9.30am-4.30pm daily. *Nov-Feb* 9.30am-4pm daily. **Admission** free; donations welcome.
This lovely, informal spot is a working farm. As well as the usual farmyard favourites (a Jersey cow, old-breed pigs, sheep, goats and ponies), a pet lodge houses guinea pigs, rabbits, fish, tortoises and the like, and there's even an owl and a pussycat. There's also a playground and a good café with high chairs.

Scottish Seabird Centre
Harbour, North Berwick (01620 890202, www.seabird.org). North Berwick rail then 10min walk. **Open** *Apr-Oct* 10am-6pm daily. *Feb-Mar, Oct* 10am-5pm Mon-Fri, 10am-5.30pm Sat, Sun. *Nov-Jan* 10am-4pm Mon-Fri; 10am-5.30pm Sat, Sun. **Admission** £7.15; £4.05-£5.35 discounts; under-4s free. **Credit** MC, V.
With its seashore location, state-of-the-art cameras and live-feed webcams, this is a great place to view seabirds. You can also book Sea.fari trips out into the Firth of Forth from here if you book ahead. Amenities include a café, which serves meals and snacks, plus good nappy-changing facilities.

Sea.fari Adventures
Newhaven Harbour (331 4857, www.seafari.co.uk). Bus 7, 10, 11, 16, 17, 22, 25. **Admission** £20; £18 discounts. **Credit** MC, V.

Head down to the harbour and hop aboard for a one-hour trip out into the Firth of Forth and around the islands – there should be seals and seabirds galore. All trips should be booked in advance. In sunny weather, remember to bring sunglasses and suncream; whenever you go, bring warm clothes, as the wind can be fierce.

Arts & culture

If your children are more into making art than looking at it, there are a number of studios in Edinburgh in which they can learn some new skills. **Kiss the Fish** in Stockbridge (9 Dean Park Street, 332 8912, www.kissthefishstudios.com) offers kids the chance to decorate all kinds of objects using paint, paper and glitter. If you want your objects glazed, you can pick them up the next day.

In Marchmont sits **Doodles Ceramic Workshop** (29 Marchmont Crescent, 229 1399, www.doodlesscotland.co.uk), Edinburgh's first paint-your-own-pottery enterprise. Kids (and adults) can decorate a variety of white unglazed pottery items with stencils, stamps and paints; staff then glaze the item for you. A similar kind of experience is available at **Ceramic Experience** (www.theceramicexperience.com) has two locations in the city, one near Ocean Terminal in Leith (118 Ocean Drive, 554 4455) and one in Marchmont (28-30 Marchmont Crescent, 662 6666). If you use acrylics, you can take your work away right then; glazing takes a few days.

Finally, **Lauriston Castle** (*see p106*) often runs arts and craft family workshops. For details, call ahead.

Indoor play centres

The popularity of Edinburgh's various play centres seem to go in cycles. Sometimes it's simply a case of the newer ones boasting greater novelty value than their rivals. Below are two of the options.

> ### INSIDE TRACK FEEDING TIME
>
> If you're visiting the city with very young children, it's worth remembering that it's a criminal offence in Scotland to harass or otherwise prevent a mother from breastfeeding a child under two years old; the law also covers other carers feeding milk to children. This applies to all public places, buses, and non-licensed and licensed premises where children are welcome, such as cafés and family-friendly pubs.

ARTS & ENTERTAINMENT

Molly's

Ocean Terminal, Leith (0845 123 5593). Bus 1, 11, 22, 34, 35, 36. **Open** 10am-6pm Mon-Fri; 11am-6pm Sun. **Admission** *1hr session* £3.50 3-12yrs; £3 1-3yrs; £1.50 under-1yrs. **Credit** MC, V.

Molly's offers a multi-tier soft play area, with a toddler zone. It's in a shopping mall and can get busy, especially at weekends, but it can also be a welcome break from shopping. Payment is by the hour.

▶ *For more on Ocean Terminal, see p185.*

★ Time Twisters

Unit 5, Catalyst Trade Park, 2B Bankhead Drive, Sighthill, West Edinburgh (308 2464, www.time twisters.co.uk). Bus 18, 25, 32, 34, 35. **Open** 9.30am-6pm daily. **Admission** *1hr session* £3.95 3-12yrs; £2.95 1-3yrs; free under-1yrs. **Credit** MC, V.

Edinburgh's newest play centre has an Egyptian theme, and is a dream location for any children into mummies, crocodiles, pyramids and the like. The centre is zoned for different age groups, with the line drawn at kids over the age of 12 or taller than 145cm. Admission is on an hourly basis; however, if you think you're going to be in for longer than one hour, pay for two hours when you arrive in order to save money. The food at the café is pretty healthy.

EATING & DRINKING

If self-styled 'family restaurants' aren't your scene, there are numerous places in the city that welcome children without making a song and dance about it. Many cafés and restaurants around town offer drawing materials to make everyone's visit a little easier.

All six branches of **Pizza Express** (www. pizzaexpress.com) are family-friendly, but those at the Shore (Waterview House, 554 4332) and in Deanhaugh (1 Deanhaugh Street, 332 7229) are very popular with kids. Alternatively, kids can make their own pizzas at **Ti Amo** (16 Nicolson Street, South Edinburgh, 556 5678, http://tiamorestaurant.co.uk) or **Giuliano's on the Shore** (1 Commercial Street, Leith, 554 5272, www.giulianos.co.uk).

INSIDE TRACK
WORLD OF SPORT

Active kids aren't limited to the play centres listed above. If you have streetsport-mad older child, head to **Trangresssion Park** (*see p250*), which offers skateboarding and BMXing facilities. If wall-climbing's more their thing, try **Alien Rock** or the **Edinburgh International Climbing Arena** (for both, *see p249*).

For fish, try **Loch Fyne** (25 Pier Place, Newhaven Harbour, Leith, 559 3900, www. lochfyne.com), which has a set-price two-course kids' menu. In the evening, you'll get lovely views of the sun setting over the Forth.

Tapas can be a great option. Try **Dionika** (3-6 Canonmills Bridge, Canonmills, New Town, 652 3993, www.dionika.com) or **Café Andaluz** (77b George Street, New Town, 220 9980, www. cafeandaluz.com). Fans of elephants and Harry Potter should love the **Elephant House** (*see p137*). And by the Meadows, **Peter's Yard** (*see p157*) offers delicious snacks and meals to eat in or take away.

Pubs that serve full meals are, at the staff's discretion, allowed to admit kids until 8pm. Try the **Baillie** (*see p173*); there isn't a children's menu as such, but the starters and some mains (club sandwiches, for instance) are good options. The **Standing Order** (62-66 George Street, New Town, 225 4460), part of the JD Wetherspoon's chain, has a family dining room.

ARTS & ENTERTAINMENT

While many of the festivals held throughout the year in Edinburgh have family-friendly aspects, several events cater purely for younger audiences. Every Easter, the Scotland-wide **Puppet Animation Festival** (www.puppet animationfestival.org) brings a number of performances to Edinburgh. In the last week in May, **Imaginate** (www.imaginate.org.uk) is devoted entirely to performing arts for children, staged in various child-friendly venues and usually with a free crèche for under-fives. And in October, the **Scottish International Storytelling Festival** at the Scottish Storytelling Centre (*see p66*) delivers plenty to entertain younger and older audiences.

Sticking with the theatre, several annual Christmas shows are usually worth a look. The **Royal Lyceum** (*see p253*) offers its own reinterpretation of a classic story, which generally holds the attention and imagination of five- to ten-year-olds. Alternatively, for a traditional panto, head to the **King's Theatre** (2 Leven Street, 529 6000, www.eft.co.uk).

Several local cinemas now offer film screenings for parents and carers with babies (not to be confused with children's screenings, such as the Saturday Kids AM series at **Vue Ocean Terminal**). Once a week, **Cineworld**, the **Cameo** and the **Filmhouse** hold morning film screenings for parents and carers with babies, respectively entitled Cinebabies, The Big Scream and For Crying Out Loud!. The Cameo offers screenings that may be suitable for children and other moviegoers with autism. For all cinemas, *see pp225-227*.

Comedy

It's a laugh a minute in August, but a joke at others…

All praise the **Stand**. If it wasn't for the tireless efforts of this grungy basement comedy club on the edge of the New Town, Edinburgh's comedy scene would look decidedly patchy. That is, of course, excluding August, when the Fringe presents more comedy turns than anywhere else on the planet.

The two extremes, August on the one hand and the rest of the year on the other, make Edinburgh the feast-or-famine capital of comedy. This is particularly the case when it comes to top-of-the-range comedians, who flood here for the Fringe but otherwise limit their appearances to occasional forays into major venues such as the **Queen's Hall** (*see p236*), the **Edinburgh Playhouse** (*see p253*) and the **Edinburgh Festival Theatre** (*see p254*). In other words, if comedy's your thing, choose your dates with care.

ARTS & ENTERTAINMENT

COMEDY VENUES

So how do you like your laughter: poured from a can, or served fresh using hand-picked local ingredients? This, in essence, is the choice that's available in Edinburgh for 11 months a year. In one corner is the **Stand**, which has officially banned stag and hen parties; 'The Stand is aimed at couples and groups of friends who appreciate comedy,' says head man Tommy Sheppard. And in the other corner is **Jongleurs**, which depends on those selfsame big groups. At Jongleurs, you always know exactly what you're going to get, which is the chain's greatest strength and biggest weakness. At the Stand, which operates seven days a week, the superior environment makes up for the occasional blips in line-ups that mix home-grown talent with luminaries from the international circuit.

Elsewhere on the scene, comedy nights launched by local promoters and frustrated stand-ups come and go with alarming regularity, making it virtually impossible to predict which ones will still be running in a few months' time. Jongleurs was put on the market by Regent Inns in 2008, although it continues to trade as normal; but at the same time, London's Comedy Store has expressed ambitions to open a venue in the city. The best source for online and printed listings remains *The List* (www.list.co.uk).

Fit o' the Giggles: Absolute Beginners

Beehive Inn, Grassmarket, Old Town (225 7171, www.fitothegiggles.com). Bus 2, 23, 27, 41, 42. **Shows** Mon. **Admission** £2; £1 students. **Credit** AmEx, MC, V. **Map** p332 G8 & p336 D4.

This showcase for new acts and new material enlivens Mondays. There are around ten comedians each week – four new, four not so new – plus a compère and weekly headliner. The club also presented bigger names at the Mercat bar, but pulled out in 2009. It intends to reappear elsewhere.

Heresy Comedy Club

Jekyll & Hyde, 112 Hanover Street, New Town (225 2002, www.heresycomedy.com). Bus 13, 23, 27, 42 or Princes Street buses. **Shows** 9pm Thur. **Admission** free. **No credit cards**. **Map** p328 & p332 G6.

Free evenings of stand-up by a lively mix of newcomers attracted by a philosophy described by the club as 'anti-religion, anti-racism, anti-weapons proliferation and pro-comedy'.

Jongleurs

Unit 6/7, Omni Centre, Greenside Place, Calton Hill (08707 870707, www.jongleurs.com). Playhouse buses. **Shows** 8.30pm Fri, Sat. **Tickets** £12.50-£15.50. **Credit** AmEx, MC, V. **Map** p329 J5.

You're likely to find some of the biggest names in the business taking the mic at Jongleurs. But this is also, unashamedly, comedy for the masses, so even comics known for edgy material may jettison their

THE BEST LOCAL COMEDIANS

Kevin Bridges
Still in his early twenties, the Clydebank comic has a bright future.

AL Kennedy
The novelist-turned-comic is a regular at the Stand.

Fred MacAulay
When he's not presenting his radio show on BBC Radio Scotland (10-11.30am Mon-Fri), the likeable Scot occasionally takes to the stage.

Bruce Morton
After 20 years on the scene, the pioneering Glasgwegian stand-up is still going strong.

Jojo Sutherland
The self-described 'Comedy Mother' plays often at the Stand and Jongleurs.

riskier gags in favour of the crowd-pleasers; not for nothing has the club's empire spread from humble beginnings to an astonishing 15 UK branches. The ticket price includes entrance to the post-gig club; no wonder it's popular with large parties.

★ Stand
5 York Place, New Town (558 7272, www.the stand.co.uk). Playhouse or Princes Street buses. **Shows** 8.30pm (doors 7.30pm) Mon-Wed; 9pm (doors 7pm) Thur-Sat; 1pm (doors 12.30pm), 8.30pm (doors 7.30pm) Sun. **Tickets** free-£13. **No credit cards**. **Map** p328 H5.

The Stand's 160-capacity basement space is at its uproarious best at the big weekend shows; arrive early for a good seat. But this is a seven-day operation, and the feelgood weekday shows are full of surprises. Established performers such as Miles Jupp and Craig Hill cut their teeth at Monday's popular Red Raw newcomers' night (£2); other shows focus on sketch comedy, satire, female comics and even gay comedy. Sunday afternoons have a more laid-back vibe, with battered sofas, a simple menu and improvised comedy. During the Fringe, the Stand takes over a number of additional spaces in the area.

Stand-up at the Still
Illicit Still, 2 Brougham Street, South Edinburgh (228 2633, www.theillicitstill.com/comedy.html). Bus 11, 15, 15A, 16, 23, 45. **Shows** 1st and 3rd Tue of mth. **Admission** free. **Credit** MC, V. **Map** p332 F9.
If you like your laughs up close and personal, try the comedy at this intimate pub backroom, where twice-monthly Tuesday-night shows generally offer around six up-and-coming comics plus a headliner. Turning up early doesn't just guarantee you the best seat in the house – it may be the only way of getting any kind of a pew.

Voodoo Rooms
19a West Register Street, New Town (556 7060, www.thevoodoorooms.com). Princes Street buses. **Shows** call for details. **Credit** AmEx, MC, V. **Map** p328 & p332 H6, p336 F1.
As well as nightclubs and rock gigs, this atmospheric venue above the Café Royal has a taste for gothic cabaret and burlesque. Fitted out in black (black walls, black ceilings, black bar fittings) with gold trim on the Georgian cornicing, it's a perfect match for the rococo glamour of the alternative variety nights.
▶ For rock shows and club nights, see p241.

Stand.

Film

Edinburgh's love affair with movies shows no signs of abating

After one trip to **Brass Monkey** (14 Drummond Street), you'll realise Edinburgh adores its film. One room of this Old Town bar has been decorated with a collage of movie posters, with cushions scattered across the floor like a giant bed. Every afternoon around 3pm, staff roll down a screen and show films from the bar's DVD collection.

For all their endeavours, though, the staff at Brass Monkey are only continuing a trend that goes back as far as the foundation in 1929 of the still-thriving **Edinburgh Film Guild** (http://edinburghfilmguild.org.uk), which organises thrice-weekly screenings at the **Filmhouse** (*see p226*). There are big multi-screen cinemas, of course, offering popcorn, hot dogs and Hollywood blockbusters. But the heart of Edinburgh's movie scene lies away from the cineplexes.

CINEMAS

Filmgoers in Edinburgh depend on a number of multiplexes and a handful of independent, cinephile-friendly operations. In the former category are operations run by Odeon and Vue, both nationwide chains. In the latter sit the more characterful likes of the **Dominion** (*see p226*), which harks back to the days before popcorn and Coke, and the **Cameo** (*see below*), which supplements screenings with talks and Q&As. On the fringes sit specialist enterprises such as the noteworthy **Scottish Documentary Institute** (www.scottishdocinstitute.com), which organises regular screenings.

Cinema programmes change on Fridays; see *Metro*, the *Edinburgh Evening News*, *The Scotsman*, *The Herald*, *The List* and online for listings. Films are classified as follows: (U) – universal viewing; (PG) – parental guidance advised for young children; (12a) – under-12s must be accompanied by an adult; (15), (18) – no entry for under-15s and under-18s respectively. Most (but not all) of the city's cinemas are fully disabled-accessible; call ahead to check.

★ Cameo Picturehouse
38 Home Street, South Edinburgh (0870 755 1231, www.picturehouses.co.uk). Bus 11, 15, 15A, 16, 23, 45. **Tickets** *Mon £4.50. Tue-Sun £5.80-£6.80; £4.50-5.20 discounts.* **Credit** MC, V. **Map** p332 E9.

Nestled in Tollcross, this indie cinema is a real treat, picking around eight films a week from the edges of the mainstream. Chat up the friendly staff at the bar, then take your pint through when the film begins. Look out for European matinées and cheap-rate Sunday afternoon double-bills, a 20-year tradition. There are screenings for parents with babies under

INSIDE TRACK FILM FESTIVALS

The **Edinburgh International Film Festival** (*see p209 and p215*) is far from the only game in town – the city's cinemas host a string of specialist film festivals. At the **Filmhouse** (*see p226*), there are festivals devoted to everything from horror (April's **Dead by Dawn**; www.deadbydawn.co.uk) to dance (May's **Dance:Film**; www.dancefilm scotland.com) and even African short films (October's **Africa in Motion**; www.africa-in-motion.org.uk). The venue also serves as the Edinburgh anchor for the **Italian Film Festival** (April; www.italianfilmfestival.org.uk) and the **French Film Festival UK** (November; www.frenchfilmfestival.org.uk), both nationwide events. Elsewhere, it's worth looking out for the **Edinburgh Mountain Film Festival** (www.edinburgh mountainff.com), a festival of movies devoted to climbing and exploration that's held at Edinburgh University in October.

ARTS & ENTERTAINMENT

12 months, and autism-friendly screenings (managed in partnership with the National Autistic Society) with low lights left on and the sound turned down.
▶ *Short films from around the world are shown regularly at the Cameo as part of Future Shorts (www.futureshorts.com).*

Cineworld Fountain Park

Fountain Park, 130-133 Dundee Street, West Edinburgh (0871 200 2000, www.cineworld.co.uk). Bus 2, 3, 3A, 4, 25, 33, 44, 44A. **Tickets** £3-£7.30; £4.70 discounts. **Credit** AmEx, MC, V. **Map** p331 C10.
Located in Sean Connery's old stomping ground of Fountainbridge, Cineworld is a sprawling, comprehensive 13-screener. Unusually for a multiplex, standard Hollywood fare is often supplemented with riskier film choices, particularly on Monday evenings and other off-peak times.

Dominion

18 Newbattle Terrace, Morningside, South Edinburgh (447 2660 information, 447 4771 tickets, www.dominioncinemas.net). Bus 11, 15, 15A, 16, 41. **Tickets** £4.90-£12.50; £6-£7.90 discounts. *Before 6pm Mon-Fri* £4.90. **Credit** MC, V.
A beautiful reminder of what cinemas used to be like in the days before the multiplex, the Dominion's art deco interior dates from 1938. The more expensive tickets are for impossibly comfortable reclining armchairs and Pullman seats. A full hot menu is available before 6pm in the basement café/bar, with sandwiches on offer until 9pm. Selected screenings welcome carers with babies.

Filmhouse.

★ Filmhouse

88 Lothian Road, South Edinburgh (228 2689 information, 228 2688 tickets, www.filmhouse cinema.com). Bus 1, 2, 10, 11, 15, 15A, 16, 23, 24, 27, 34, 35, 45. **Tickets** £3.40-£6.50; £2.10-£4.90 discounts. **Credit** MC, V. **Map** p332 E8 & p336 A4.
The Filmhouse offers a mix of arty new films and classics. Look out for screenings on Wednesdays, Fridays and Sundays organised by the Edinburgh Film Guild (http://edinburghfilmguild.org.uk), especially the traditional Halloween and Christmas movies. The café/bar serves drinks and home-cooked food to moviegoers who don't mind the slow service. Selected screenings are for carers and babies only.

Odeon Lothian Road

118 Lothian Road, South Edinburgh (221 1477 information, 0871 224 4007 tickets, www.odeon. co.uk). Bus 1, 2, 10, 11, 15, 15A, 16, 23, 24, 27, 34, 35, 45. **Tickets** £7.75; £5.50 discounts. **Credit** MC, V. **Map** p332 E8.
Filling both a geographical and cultural gap between its independent neighbours, the Cameo and the Filmhouse, the Odeon supplies the city centre with mainstream and family films.
Other locations *Odeon Wester Hailes* Westside Plaza, 120 Wester Hailes Road, West Edinburgh (453 1569 information, 0871 224 4007 tickets).

Scotsman Screening Room

Scotsman Hotel, 20 North Bridge, Old Town (www.scotsmanscreenings.com). Nicolson Street-North Bridge buses. **Tickets** *Movie* £8.50. *Movie & meal* £39. **Credit** MC, V. **Map** p332 H7 & p336 F3.
The leather armchairs lend this intimate and luxurious cinema the feel of a private viewing room; unsurprising, since that's what it is during the week. The Sunday-night public programme concentrates on classic films that rarely get an outing on the big screen. Tickets are pricey but probably worth it, especially when combined with dinner in the hotel's North Bridge Brasserie. A nice place for a date.
▶ *For the North Bridge Brasserie, see p139; for the hotel itself, see p117.*

★ Vue Omni Centre

Omni Centre, Greenside Place, New Town (0870 240 6020 information, 0871 224 0240 tickets, www.myvue.com). Playhouse or Princes Street buses. **Tickets** £6.50; £4.90-£5.55 discounts. **Credit** MC, V. **Map** p329 J5.
The giant glass cheesecake at the top of Leith Walk houses the closest cinema to Princes Street, a comfortable multiplex set-up. Expect big releases rather than arthouse flicks. Nonetheless, with 12 screens at each Vue, you should be able to find something you want to see.
▶ *The sister cineplex at Leith's Ocean Terminal (0871 224 0240) offers more of the same.*

On Location

Moviemakers take to the streets of Edinburgh, with mixed results.

Trainspotting.

Some corners of Edinburgh are so picturesque that you may feel as if you're walking through a film set. In all likelihood, you are. If **William Street** in the West End feels familiar, for example, it's because it's doubled for all manner of historical streets on TV and film. At the opposite end of the New Town, **Abercromby Place** has cropped up in *Quite Ugly One Morning*, *Death Defying Acts* and pretty much anything else that aims to carry a little Georgian class.

Directors in search of a darker ambience often turn to the closes off the Royal Mile (*see pp60-61*). You can see **Advocates Close** in *The Debt Collector* and *Driving Lessons*. **Bakehouse Close** appears in *Greyfriars Bobby*, while **Fishmarket Close** can be spotted in Robert Carlyle vehicle *Looking After Jo Jo*. **Greyfriars Kirkyard** (*see p75*) is another favourite; you can see it in *Jude* and *The Prime of Miss Jean Brodie*. The latter was mainly shot at what was then Donaldson's College (a school for deaf children), now **Edinburgh Academy**.

The city is also proud of *Chariots of Fire*, with its sequences in **Holyrood Park** (*see pp86-89*), the **Assembly Hall** on the Mound and the **Café Royal** (*see p171*). The 1948 version of *Journey to the Centre of the Earth* took off from the university's **Old College Quad**. And the two versions of *The Thirty-Nine Steps* exploited the grandeur of the **Forth Rail Bridge** (*see p295*).

Further from the mainstream, Richard Jobson used the city as a backdrop for *Sixteen Years of Alcohol* and *Woman in Winter*, while fans of David Mackenzie's *Hallam Foe* and *Young Adam* will spot locations such as the **City Art Centre** (*see p228*), **Cockburn Street** (*see p65*) and the **Union Canal**. And there's no better introduction to the overkill of Edinburgh in August than Annie Griffin's *Festival*, which features everywhere from the sedate **Caledonian Hilton** (*see p121*) to the grungey **Stand** comedy club (*see p224*).

It's little surprise that adaptations of Edinburgh-set novels have made rich use of iconic locations around the city. TV treatments of Ian Rankin's Rebus novels have featured the likes of the **National Museum of Scotland** (*see p76*) and the **Scottish Parliament** (*see p70*); learn about these and others on a Rebus Tour (*see p304*). Just outside the city, **Rosslyn Chapel** (*see p294*) figures in both the book and the movie of *The Da Vinci Code*.

In terms of putting Edinburgh on the filmic map, however, you can't do better than the opening scene of *Trainspotting*, which features Ewan McGregor and Ewan Bremner being chased down **Princes Street** and on to **Calton Road**. McGregor gets held up by a car but Bremner continues running – presumably all the way to Glasgow, which is where the rest of the movie was shot.

Galleries

The art of Midlothian.

Edinburgh's compact geography means that locals have tended to ignore anything located more than a 15-minute walk away. The city's contemporary art galleries are clearly wise to this state of affairs: many are clustered around Waverley Station, while **Doggerfisher** and **Edinburgh Printmakers** are near the top of Leith Walk and the **Talbot Rice Gallery** is just a couple of blocks up the South Bridge. As such a contemporary arts tour is less of a pilgrimage and more of an easy stroll.

In the shape of the **Royal Scottish Academy** and the **National Galleries**, Edinburgh's artistic old guard still stands firm. However, both enterprises have done much to boost interest in contemporary art, helping to challenge the city's unadventurous buying climate. The more parochial galleries on Dundas Street remain wedded to tradition, but there's modernity on show here if you know where to look.

GALLERIES

For information on exhibitions, pick up *The List* (*see p308*) or see www.list.co.uk. Note that the hours given in this chapter only apply when there is an exhibition ongoing; always check online before making a special trip, just in case the gallery in question is between shows.

During August, the **Edinburgh Art Festival** (*see p207 and p214*) gives a collective voice to the profusion of summer exhibitions across the city, and is even starting to commission work. Visual art has often been drowned out by the clamour of the performing arts in August, which is one reason why the festival has been a welcome addition.

Analogue

102 West Bow, Old Town (220 0601, www. analoguebooks.co.uk). Bus 2, 23, 27, 41, 42. **Open** 10am-5.30pm Mon-Sat. **Credit** MC, V. **Map** p332 G8, p336 D4.

Stowed away behind Edinburgh's finest graphic arts shop, this intimate space packs in works from Britain's hippest illustrators and designers. The gallery functions as an extension to the shop floor, with shows rotating on a monthly basis; works can also be viewed and purchased online.
► *For the shop, see p187.*

City Art Centre

2 Market Street, Old Town (529 3993, www. cac.org.uk). Princes Street buses. **Open** call for details. **Credit** MC, V. **Map** p332 H7 & p336 F3.

Hosting civic shows alongside large touring exhibitions (for which there's sometimes an admission charge), treading the thin line between public edutainment and contemporary art, this six-floor gallery has previously had problems grappling with its size. However, it's possible that a recent refurbishment may help matters a little; you can find out from May 2010, when the gallery, shop and café reopen for business after a period of closure.

Collective

22-28 Cockburn Street, Old Town (220 1260, www.collectivegallery.net). Bus 35 or Nicolson Street–North Bridge buses. **Open** noon-5pm Tue-Sat. **No credit cards. Map** p332 H7 & p336 E3.

This artist-led gallery has provided a small but influential platform for diverse up-and-coming local talents, as well as internationally established artists, since opening in 1984. The addition of the Black Cube space has allowed for regular exhibitions of video art and film from around the world.

▶ *The gallery is right by Stills; see p231.*

Corn Exchange Gallery

Constitution Street, Leith (561 7300, www.corn exchangegallery.com). Bus 12, 16, 35. **Open** 11am-4.30pm Tue-Fri; also by appointment. **No credit cards. Map** p326 Z3.

Making use of the lobby space of Navyblue, a forward-thinking design company, this airy Leith gallery runs a busy programme of up-and-coming artists from around the world. Director Caroline Alexander takes a strong artistic lead, producing shows that, for a private gallery, have an uncommonly contemporary edge.

The Art of Shopping

How to fill your home with art without emptying your wallet.

Although a little money would come in handy, you don't need to be independently wealthy to shop in Edinburgh's galleries. Those of us on more modest incomes can take pleasure in the knowledge that the city's art galleries are home to some of its most interesting gift shops.

In particular, the National Galleries are between them home to some of the more interesting gift stores in town, offering both novelty value and a degree of cultural credibility. The shop at the **Scottish National Gallery of Modern Art** (*see p90*) is squashed into a rather cramped ground-floor room, but its stock is impressive: the books run from coffee-table tomes to studies of contemporary artists, many selected to tie in with the current exhibitions. Over the road at the **Dean Gallery** (*see p90*), the more spacious shop adds calendars, posters, mugs

and jewellery to its range of literature. At the bottom of the Mound, the spacious **National Galleries Shop** (*see p79*) exploits the most iconic images in the galleries' collection in an assortment of gifts, books, jewellery, tableware and toys. And there'll surely be more of the same at the **Scottish National Portrait Gallery** (*see p83*) when it reopens at the end of 2011.

In addition to a stock of hard-to-find art magazines, the shop at the **Fruitmarket Gallery** (*see p230*) is great for quirky cards, unusual children's books, off-beat publications and gorgeous studies of contemporary art and design. Over the road at the **City Art Centre** (*see left*), there's a more mainstream selection of books, toys, stationery and exhibition-related gifts. For photography anthologies, try the **Stills** (*see p231*); and for prints, check out **Edinburgh Printmakers** (*see p230*).

ARTS & ENTERTAINMENT

National Galleries Shop.

Ingleby Gallery.

ARTS & ENTERTAINMENT

★ Doggerfisher
11 Gayfield Square, Broughton (558 7110, www. doggerfisher.com). Playhouse buses. **Open** 10am-6pm Tue-Fri; noon-5pm Sat; also by appointment. **Credit** AmEx, MC, V. **Map** p329 J4.
Housed in a converted tyre garage, Doggerfisher has promoted an impressive roster of mainly Scottish artists since its 2001 inception – among them Moyna Flannigan, Nathan Coley, Rosalind Nashashibi and Lucy Skaer – and is an increasingly conspicuous player at art fairs around the world. Prices can be high, but the gallery's penchant for delicate materials and fine crafts means it's always worth a visit.

Edinburgh Printmakers
23 Union Street, Broughton (557 2479, www. edinburgh-printmakers.co.uk). Playhouse buses. **Open** 10am-6pm Tue-Sat. **Credit** MC, V. **Map** p329 J4.
This pioneering open-access printmaking workshop often shows prints by its in-house artists alongside works by more well known names, including Tracey Emin and Gillian Wearing. Much of the work is archived, but staff can help you sift through prints. Hands-on types can enrol on print-making courses or one-day taster workshops.

Embassy
Roxy Art House, 2 Roxburgh Place, Old Town (www.embassygallery.org). Nicolson Street–North Bridge buses. **Open** noon-6pm Thur-Sun; also by appointment. **No credit cards. Map** p333 J8.
Although it's sometimes criticised as a cliquey second home for art-school grads, this committee-run space nonetheless sticks a forever-young V-sign

to the Edinburgh bourgeoisie while playing host to emerging European artists. The endearingly shambolic approach means the gallery's own website is the best way to keep up with forthcoming events.

★ Fruitmarket Gallery
45 Market Street, Old Town (225 2383, www. fruitmarket.co.uk). Princes Street buses. **Open** 11am-6pm Mon-Sat; noon-5pm Sun. **Credit** MC, V. **Map** p332 H7 & p336 F3.
Expect thoroughbred shows by the likes of Clare Barclay, Lucy Skaer and Callum Innes at the Fruitmarket, Edinburgh's leading venue for contemporary art. The pint-sized bookshop sells a wide range of art book ephemera.
▶ *There's also a nice café here; see p137.*

Henderson Gallery
4 Thistle Street Lane NW, New Town (225 7464, www.thehendersongallery.com). Bus 13, 23, 27, 42 or Princes Street buses. **Open** 11am-6pm Tue-Sat. **Credit** AmEx, MC, V. **Map** p328 & p332 F6, p336 D1.
From the people who brought you Henderson's, Edinburgh's longest standing vegetarian restaurant, comes this bright and intimate gallery dedicated to new young artists.
▶ *For the restaurant, see p145.*

★ Ingleby Gallery
15 Calton Road (556 4441, www.inglebygallery. com). Nicolson Street–North Bridge & Princes Street buses. **Open** 10am-6pm Mon-Wed, Fri, Sat; 10am-7pm Thur. **Credit** AmEx, MC, V. **Map** p329 & p333 J6.

Established in 1998 and largely devoted to abstract art, the Ingleby moved in 2008 from a sedate Georgian townhouse to this bright and spacious three-floor gallery at the back of Waverley Station. The move has allowed the pace-setting space to do more justice to its impressive clutch of prints and paintings, which are predominantly by Scottish artists such as Ian Hamilton Finlay, Andy Goldsworthy and Alison Watt.

▶ *Art isn't confined to the interior: look out for the billboard on the side of the building, which is given over to a different artist every few weeks.*

★ Jupiter Artland

Bonnington House, near Wilkieston, west of Edinburgh (257 4170, www.jupiterartland.org). Bus 27. **Open** 10am-4pm Thur-Sun. **Admission** £5; £3 discounts; free under-5s. **No credit cards.**

Open since May 2009, this sculpture park in the grounds of a 17th-century mansion house has been a stunning addition to the Edinburgh art scene. For the past few years, owners Robert and Nicky Wilson have been commissioning major artists to build pieces responsive to the landscape. They include the grassy slopes of Charles Jencks' *Life Mounds* as well as woodland work by Andy Goldsworthy, the late Ian Hamilton Finlay, Anish Kapoor and Antony Gormley. Wear sensible shoes and allow two hours to take it all in; and if you're driving, you'll need to book your car a space in advance.

▶ *There's more Jencks in the shape of* Landform, *a not-too-dissimilar piece to* Life Mounds, *in front of the Scottish National Gallery of Modern Art; see p90.*

Patriothall Gallery

Patriothall Studios, off 48 Hamilton Place, Stockbridge (226 7126, www.patriothallgallery. co.uk). Bus 24, 29, 42. **Open** 10am-4pm Thur-Sun. **No credit cards.** **Map** p328 E4.

In 1988, Workshop & Artists Studio Provision Scotland (WASPS) turned a former Stockbridge bakery, hidden in a back lane off the main road, into a series of roomy gallery spaces. The result is an artist-led venture that clocks up 20 exhibitions a year and feels like a hotbed of creativity.

Red Door

42 Victoria Street, Old Town (477 3255, www.edinburghart.com). Bus 2, 23, 27, 41, 42. **Open** 11am-5.30pm Mon-Sat; noon-5pm Sun. **Credit** MC, V. **Map** p332 G7 & p336 D4.

Sandwiched into a narrow space on Victoria Street, this mini-gallery touts a selection of works by local designers, graphic artists, Lomographers and contemporary jewellers. Prices are generally reasonable.

Scottish Gallery

16 Dundas Street, New Town (558 1200, www.scottish-gallery.co.uk). Bus 13, 23, 27. **Open** 10am-6pm Mon-Fri; 10am-4pm Sat. **Credit** MC, V. **Map** p328 F5.

The Scottish Gallery's rather drab name belies the merit of the work it houses. The lower floor is one of the best spots in town for contemporary ceramics; upstairs, modern paintings rub shoulders with works by recent graduates and emerging Scottish artists. 'Traditional' is not a dirty word here: open since 1842, the gallery is headed up by Guy Peploe, the grandson of Scottish colourist SJ Peploe.

Sleeper

6 Darnaway Street, New Town (225 8444, www.sleeper1.com). Bus 19, 24, 29, 36, 37, 42, 47. **Open** 2-5pm Mon-Fri. **No credit cards.** **Map** p328 E5.

Running chiefly on word-of-mouth publicity, Sleeper is a wilfully under-promoted white cube found under the offices of Reiach & Hall Architects. After explaining why you're here to the firm's receptionist, walk along the plushly-carpeted corridor and down the stairs to find the gallery. Past exhibitors have included Bruce Nauman and Douglas Gordon.

Stills

23 Cockburn Street, Old Town (622 6200, www.stills.org). Bus 35 or Nicolson Street–North Bridge. **Open** 11am-6pm daily. **Credit** MC, V. **Map** p332 H7 & p336 E3.

The city's leading photography venue, Stills is important not only for its year-round programme of shows, but also for its on-site resources for photographers, including darkrooms, editing suites and digital labs. It runs a number of photography and design-based courses for the public.

INSIDE TRACK
GOING UNDERGROUND

Although Edinburgh's art scene hasn't mushroomed as greatly as that of Glasgow, things have moved away from a conservative modus operandi towards a youthful miscellany of artist-led initiatives. Thanks to ambitious graduates of the **Edinburgh College of Art (ECA)**, the city has benefited from an enthusiastic, irreverent DIY attitude towards exhibitions. By keeping an eye out for fliers stacked in established galleries, or by checking the noticeboards at the ECA (74 Lauriston Place, Old Town, 221 6000, www.eca. ac.uk) or the **Forest Café** and its **TotalKunst** gallery (3 Bristo Place, Old Town, 220 4538, www.theforest.org.uk), the eager art tourist can track down one-off shows squatting in temporary shop-lets, private flats, bars, cafés and other off-site areas around town.

ARTS & ENTERTAINMENT

Gay & Lesbian

The scene gets heard.

The preponderance of students and young professionals in Edinburgh means that the pace of its gay scene is fast. Yet there's refreshingly little attitude on show here: if you try talking to someone you don't know, you can expect a demure and even shy friendliness that's typical of the capital as a whole. Many young gay men and lesbians here favour bleached hair and tight clothes, but not fitting into this stereotype is unlikely to raise an immaculately plucked eyebrow or cause bouncers to question your sexuality. Taking in restaurants, bars, cafés and a never-ending roster of club nights, the scene is as welcoming as you'll find.

THE GAY SCENE

Centred on an area known as the **Pink Triangle**, bounded on two sides by Broughton Street and Leith Walk, Edinburgh's gay scene thrives on drinking and late-night hedonism. Outside the dedicated gay bars and clubs, a diverse variety of gay nights at otherwise straight venues around the city provide plenty of entertainment. The quality and quantity of LGBT bars has also increased substantially, leaving the scene in healthy shape.

The big event in the gay calendar is June's **Pride Scotia**, a huge annual festival held alternately in Edinburgh (2011, 2013 and so on) and Glasgow (2010, 2012, et cetera). Each spring and autumn, the **Lothian Gay & Lesbian Switchboard** (*see p306*) organises a ceilidh, where you'll reel past midnight in homo-friendly surroundings. And look out for the **London Lesbian & Gay Film Festival on Tour**, which brings the best in gay cinema to the **Filmhouse** (*see p226*) each July.

The most comprehensive coverage on the local scene is in **Scotsgay**, which can be found in bars or online at www.scotsgay.co.uk. The gay section of *The List* has previews and listings, as does free listings newspaper *The Skinny* (www.theskinny.co.uk).

One of the scene's focal points is the **Edinburgh LGBT Centre** (58-60 Broughton Street), where you'll find meeting facilities – many gay community groups get together here – and the Café Nom de Plume. For other local organisations, *see p306*.

RESTAURANTS & CAFES

★ **Blue Moon Café**

1 Barony Street, Broughton (556 2788, www. bluemooncafe.co.uk). Bus 8, 13 and Playhouse buses. **Open** 10am-10pm daily. **Main courses** £7. **Credit** MC, V. **Map** p328 H4.

Right at the heart of Edinburgh's gay scene, the welcoming, laid-back Blue Moon Café offers good food and drink. The staff are cute and sassy: ask here if you have any questions or need any information about what's on in the local clubs.

► *The owners are also behind Deep Blue, the neighbouring bar; see right.*

Café Nom de Plume

60 Broughton Street, Broughton (478 1372). Bus 8, 13 and Playhouse buses. **Open** 11am-11pm Mon-Thur; 11am-1am Fri, Sat; noon-11pm Sun. **Main courses** £8. **Credit** AmEx, MC, V. **Map** p328 H4.

Housed in the LGBT Centre on Broughton Street (*see left*), this café welcomes all-comers. You can come here for a sit-down meal, but it's also good for a quick beer or a coffee. Other attractions here, aside from the heart-of-the-Pink-Triangle location, include free wireless.

BARS

The division between gay bars and gay-friendly bars is not always clear in Edinburgh in general and the Pink Triangle in particular, an area which gays and straights mix and mingle in generally perfect harmony. Outside the scene, a variety of other bars draw a good proportion of gay drinkers, among them **Black Bo's** (*see p167*), the **Basement** (*see p175*) and the **Elbow** (*see p175*). Many venues extend their hours during August's festival.

Café Habana

22 Greenside Place, Leith Walk, Calton Hill (558 1270, www.cafehabanaeh1.com). Playhouse buses. **Open** 1pm-1am daily. **No credit cards**. **Map** p329 J5.

The distinguishing feature of this favourite is the balcony that overlooks the hubbub of the colourful, energetic and sociable bar. Look down on proceedings, and it's likely you'll find the gay community, perhaps joined by the odd hen party, having a fabulous time. Be warned: there's regular karaoke.

CC Blooms

23-24 Greenside Place, Calton Hill (556 9331). Playhouse buses. **Open** 6pm-3am daily. **Admission** free. **Credit** MC, V. **Map** p327 J5.

Ah, CC's, where great romances start and end, often in the same evening. There are nights when this full-time gay nightclub has more cheese than IJ Mellis (*see p199*), but its cheeky charm attracts girls and boys alike. There are DJs here nightly and, at weekends, occasional queues to get in.

Deep Blue

1 Barony Street, Broughton (556 2788, www.bluemooncafe.co.uk). Bus 8, 13 and Playhouse buses. **Open** 4pm-1am daily. **Credit** MC, V. **Map** p328 H4.

Brought to you by the folks behind the neighbouring Blue Moon Café, Deep Blue is one of the mellower venues on the Edinburgh gay scene. It's a good spot in which to start the evening before things get a little crazier elsewhere.

Frenchies

89 Rose Street North Lane, New Town (07711 862813). Princes Street buses. **Open** noon-11pm Mon-Thur; noon-1am Fri, Sat; 2pm-1am Sun. **No credit cards**. **Map** p328 & p332 F6, p336 B1.

Although it was renovated in 2009 and is now under new management, Frenchies is the oldest gay hangout in Edinburgh. Despite its central location, the bar is quite difficult to spot. Happy hour runs from 6pm until 8pm daily.

★ GHQ

4 Picardy Place, Calton Hill (0845 166 6024, www.socialanimal.co.uk). Playhouse buses. **Open** 11pm-3am Mon-Thur, Sun; 9pm-3am Fri, Sat. **Admission** varies. **No credit cards**. **Map** p329 J5.

Café Habana.

ARTS & ENTERTAINMENT

One of the sleeker venues on the Edinburgh gay scene, GHQ hosts a number of the circuit's favourite gay club nights. There are DJs most nights.

Newtown Bar

26b Dublin Street, New Town (538 7775, www.newtownbar.co.uk). Bus 4, 8, 10, 11, 12, 15, 15A, 16, 26, 44, 45. **Open** noon-1am Mon-Thur; noon-2am Fri, Sat; 12.30pm-1am Sun. **Credit** MC, V. **Map** p328 G4.

This venue has been a stop on the gay scene for years under a variety of different names. Now the Newtown Bar, it's an approachable café-bar during the day with a club downstairs that gets regular use; some nights in the club are men only (the local Bears group meets here on the second Sat of the month).

Priscilla's Cabaret Bar

17 Albert Place, Leith (554 8962). Bus 7, 10, 12, 14, 16, 22, 25, 49. **Open** noon-1am Mon-Fri; 5am-noon, 4pm-1am Sat; 12.30pm-1am Sun. **No credit cards. Map** p329 K3.

Only a short walk from the Pink Triangle), Priscilla's is all about fun. The programme of events includes quizzes and karaoke nights, but the highlights are the outlandish drag cabaret shows at weekends.

★ Regent

2 Montrose Terrace, Calton Hill (661 8198). Bus 1, 4, 5, 15, 15A, 19, 26, 34, 35, 44, 44A, 45. **Open** 11am-1am Mon-Sat; 12.30pm-1am Sun. **Credit** MC, V. **Map** p329 M5.

Proud of its credentials as a real ale pub, this boozer eschews the jukebox in favour of encouraging conversation. The atmosphere is in keeping with the pub's traditional decor, and staff are friendly. A fine alternative to the city's more frenetic bars and clubs, if a little bit out of the way. There's free Wi-Fi access.

Street

2 Picardy Place, Calton Hill (556 4272). Playhouse buses. **Open** noon-1am Mon-Sat; 12.30am-1am Sun. **Credit** MC, V. **Map** p329 J5.

Located on the corner of Broughton Street, this long-time favourite is co-run by Trendy Wendy, the scene's most famous face. The regular DJs at weekends are supplemented by other special events, such as board-game nights, quizzes and cocktail specials.

Club nights

Below are a list of Edinburgh's regular gay and lesbian nights. In the local bars, look out for flyers granting money off the entrance fee, and don't worry about any dress code they might claim to enforce: none of the clubs are too strict.

Booty

GHQ (see p233). www.club-booty.com. **Open** 10pm-3am last Sun of mth. **Admission** free. **No credit cards.**

Around in the city since 2003, when it started life as Bootylushous, Booty grooves on with funk, disco, soul and R&B for an open-minded audience. Cheap drink deals are an added bonus.

Fever

Faith, 207 Cowgate, Old Town (225 9764, taste-clubs.com). Nicolson Street–North Bridge buses. **Open** 11pm-3am 3rd Sat of mth. **Admission** £7-£10. **No credit cards. Map** p333 J7.

The guys behind Taste (*see below*) decamp to Faith once a month to spin quality dance music to a similarly mixed/gay audience. The pre-club party is held at the Street (*see left*).

★ Fur Burger

GHQ (see p233). www.club-booty.com. **Open** 11pm-3am 2nd Fri of mth. **Admission** £5. **No credit cards. Map** p329 J5.

This delightfully named ladies' night aims to offer 'rhythmic pulses from the grrls your mother warned you about'. There's a pre-club party at gay-friendly bar Planet (6 Baxter's Place), where free passes for the club are usually available.

▸ *The other main women's night on the scene is Velvet. Appearances have been sporadic, but it's worth checking www.myspace.com/clubvelvet to see if it's happening while you're in town.*

★ Taste

GRV (see p244). www.taste-clubs.com. **Open** 11pm-3am 1st Sun of mth. **Admission** £5-£6. **No credit cards.**

Taste is gay-friendly rather than exclusively gay, which makes for a better night out. Whether you like your house music deep, American or just plain ready-salted, resident DJs Brian Fisher and Mark Price (plus assorted guest players) will sort you out.

SHOPS & SERVICES

Q Store

5 Barony Street, New Town (477 4756). Bus 8, 13, 17. **Open** 11am-7pm Mon-Fri; 11am-6pm Sat; 1-5pm Sun. **Credit** MC, V. **Map** p328 H4.

Just off Broughton Street, this queer shop is pleasingly clean and airy. Head here to buy mucky DVDs and magazines, as well as skimpy underwear and a full range of sex contraptions and accoutrements. It's the only licensed gay store north of the border.

Saunas

The city's two gay saunas are **Steamworks** (5 Broughton Market, Broughton, 477 3567, www.steamworks-sauna.co.uk, 11am-11pm daily) and **Number 18** (18 Albert Place, Leith Walk, Leith, 553 3222, www.number18sauna.com, noon-10pm Mon-Thur, noon-11am Fri-Sun). Expect to pay around £5-£10 for entrance depending on the time of day.

Music & Nightlife

The Scottish capital continues its longtime rivalry with Glasgow

When it comes to music, Edinburgh's cosmopolitanism works in its favour, with a steady influx of international traffic that helps sustain and nurture an eclectic array of entertainment. From folk sessions in backstreet pubs to classical concerts at historic halls, via underground electronic gigs and late-night jazz sessions, most things are on offer if you look.

But the looking is key. Unlike the neighbouring city of Glasgow, Edinburgh doesn't talk up its wares. Combine this reticence with a city centre in which residential flats coexist alongside cultural venues, and you'll need to try that little bit harder to find what's out there. And don't be fooled by the myth that things only happen in Edinburgh in August: thanks in part to the recent arrival of several new venues, the rest of the year round is busier than ever.

ARTS & ENTERTAINMENT

Music

CLASSICAL & OPERA

Classical music in Edinburgh really began to take off in the 18th century, after the Edinburgh Musical Society moved into **St Cecilia's Hall** on the Cowgate. Named in honour of the patron saint of music and musicians and completed in 1763, it was the first purpose-built concert hall in Scotland. Despite outbreaks of fire, plague and urban regeneration, St Cecilia's, tucked inconspicuously away on the Cowgate, still stands and hosts concerts to this day (Niddry Street, Cowgate, Old Town, 650 2805), as well as one of the finest collections of original instruments in the world. The best part of this high-ceilinged, oval-shaped room is that the acoustics were so well planned that if anything is amplified, it invariably sounds rubbish. For unamplified music, though, it's perfection.

The two most notable ensembles playing regularly in the city are the **Royal Scottish National Orchestra** (www.rsno.org.uk) and the **Scottish Chamber Orchestra** (www.sco.org.uk). The RSNO performs a lively programme of concerts, highlighted by a

Proms season in June at both the Usher Hall and Glasgow's Royal Concert Hall. The SCO, meanwhile, mainly divides its time between the Usher Hall and the Queens Hall, both in Edinburgh, and the Glasgow City Halls.

A few other native groups play frequently in the city, chief among them the **BBC Scottish Symphony Orchestra** (www.bbc.co.uk/scotland/bbcsso). The **Scottish Ensemble** (www.scottishensemble.co.uk) and the **Paragon Ensemble** (www.paragon-ensemble.com) specialise in less celebrated works that may not otherwise see the light of day. And keep a eye out for performances from **Mr McFall's Chamber** (www.mcfalls.co.uk), an ingenious experimental project that unites SCO players and other talented, broadminded musicians who are equally at home tackling Frank Zappa as they are Franz Liszt.

With this in mind, it's also worth looking out for **Noisy Nights**, a monthly Monday-night programme of new compositions presented by **Seven Things** (www.seventhings.com). Composers submit scores of short works, seven or eight of which are performed by a resident ensemble in the Traverse Theatre bar. There's more modern music in the occasional programmes offered by the **Edinburgh Contemporary Arts Trust** (www.ecat. org.uk), which promotes everyone from the Estonian Chamber Choir to crazed Dutch jazzers the Instant Composers Pool Orchestra.

About the author

Neil Cooper *is a writer for the* Herald *in Edinburgh, and has also written for* The Times, *the* Independent, *the* Wire *and* Plan B.

Royal Scottish National Orchestra.

Edinburgh has no dedicated opera house, a shortcoming that was the subject of much inept political wrangling a couple of decades ago. However, **Scottish Opera** (www.scottish opera.org.uk) have shrugged off assorted financial woes to provide a rolling programme at the glass-fronted Edinburgh Festival Theatre and the Theatre Royal in Glasgow.

Major venues

Queens Hall
85-89 Clerk Street, South Edinburgh (668 2019 box office, 668 3456 administration, www.the queenshall.net). Nicolson Street–North Bridge buses. **Box office** *In person* 10am-5.30pm Mon-Sat (or until 15mins after showtime). *By phone* 10am-5pm Mon-Sat. **Tickets** £9-£25. **Credit** AmEx, MC, V. **Map** p333 K10.
Classical music makes up approximately half the programming at this 900-seat venue, a former church that retains its old pews. The Scottish Ensemble, the Paragon Ensemble and the Edinburgh Contemporary Arts Trust all perform regularly at the hall, which is also one of the major concert venues for the Edinburgh International Festival in August. Pop, rock and jazz round out the roster.

Reid Concert Hall
Bristo Square, Old Town (650 2427, www. music.ed.ac.uk). Bus 2, 41, 42. **Concerts** *Lunchtime Oct-May* 1.10pm Tue, Fri. **Tickets** free-£7. **No credit cards. Map** p332 H8.
On selected days during termtime, you can wander in and enjoy a free lunchtime concert from students at the University of Edinburgh's music faculty, or from more established performers such as the Edinburgh Quartet. The hall also hosts a roots music series in August, and offers occasional experimental events.

Usher Hall
Lothian Road, South Edinburgh (228 1155 box office, 228 8616 administration, www.usherhall. co.uk). Bus 1, 2, 10, 11, 15, 15A, 16, 23, 24, 27, 34, 35, 45. **Box office** 10am-5.30pm Mon-Sat (or until 15mins after showtime). **Tickets** free-£50. **Credit** AmEx, MC, V. **Map** p332 E8, p336 A4.
A great deal of time and money has been spent in recent years returning the Usher Hall to its former glory, from cosmetic refurbishments of the hall to the restoration of the pipe organ. First opened in 1914, it's in demand by everyone from the RSNO to rock acts such as the Flaming Lips. Most major classical music events during August's Edinburgh International Festival are held here.

Churches

Some of Edinburgh's old churches are used as concert venues, particularly during the Fringe. **Canongate Kirk** (153 Canongate, Old Town, 668 2019, www.canongatekirk.com), the Queen's place of worship when she's at Holyroodhouse, stages shows by small choral groups and chamber orchestras. As well as holding free concerts at 6pm most Sundays, the **High Kirk of St Giles** (*see p64*) plays host to travelling choirs; regular concerts are also held at the central **Greyfriars Kirk** (*see p75*).

St Mary's Episcopal Cathedral
Palmerston Place, New Town (225 6293, www. cathedral.net). Bus 12, 13, 26, 31, 38. **Open** *Evensong* 5.30pm Mon-Wed, Fri, Sat; 3.30pm Sun. *Sung Eucharist* 5.30pm Thur; 10.30am Sun. **Tickets** *Concerts* prices vary. **No credit cards. Map** p331 C8.
St Mary's is unique in Scotland in maintaining daily sung services. Organ recitals at 4.30pm on Sundays during the festival are another musical highlight.

ROCK, POP & DANCE

Once considered the prissy bridesmaid to Glasgow, Edinburgh has at last developed a network of venues large and small to house its burgeoning set of scenes. Only a few years ago, you could have counted the number of interesting local acts on one hand. But today, there's a promiscuous amount of acts plying their trade in a variety of styles, from indie quartet **Ballboy** to electronic duo **Boards of Canada**, and from the anti-folk sounds heard in shows staged by the **Tracer Trails** and the **Gentle Invasion** to the experimental noise of **Giant Tank** and **Grind Sight Open Eye**. The same is true of the city's variety of venues: the once-loved likes of the Tap o'Laurieston, La Belle Angele and the Liquid Rooms have all gone, but newer spots such as **Cabaret Voltaire** have stepped into the breach.

Most shows tend to run between 7pm and 10pm or 11pm, after which venues stage clubs that are more often than not worth sticking around for. Note, though, that the early gig finishes often catch out visiting punters, who arrive fashionably late to avoid the support band and find they've missed nearly all of the headline act. Check stage times before setting out to avoid making the same mistake.

During August, contemporary pop and rock doesn't have much of a profile, although the **Edge** festival (*see p211*) does offer some interesting shows. Elsewhere in the calendar, **Tigerfest** (www.tigerfest.co.uk) offers a month of indie shows in the spring (it was in May in 2009); the low-key **Dialogues Festival** (www.dialogues-festival.org) uses a variety of venues at various times of year to showcase everything from electronica to contemporary classical music; and the **Leith Festival** sometimes features bands in the Queen Charlotte Rooms and the Leith Dockers Club.

Information & tickets

To find out what's on when you're in town, check the individual venue websites listed in this chapter, or keep your eyes peeled for posters around the more interesting areas of town and follow your nose. For a more comprehensive guide, *The List* (online and in print) and freesheet *The Skinny* are your best bets. Online, *Jockrock* (www.jockrock.org) is chock-a-block with record and gig reviews.

The main ticket outlets in Edinburgh are **Ripping Music** (*see p204*) and **Ticketmaster** (*see p204*); **Tickets Scotland** (www.tickets-scotland.com) may also be of assistance.

Venues

In addition to the venues, a couple of the city's concert halls also stage regular rock and pop shows. The **Queens Hall** (*see left*) has hosted gigs by the likes of Edwyn Collins and PJ Harvey & John Parrish; and the **Usher Hall** (*see left*) has featured, among others, Belle & Sebastian and Lemon Jelly. The **Edinburgh Playhouse** (*see p253*) supplements its theatrical blockbusters with shows from big names such as Lou Reed, Neil Young and, for his only UK date in 2008, Tom Waits.

ARTS & ENTERTAINMENT

Queens Hall.

Capital Records

A brief history of pop and rock in Edinburgh.

Prior to the late 1970s, Edinburgh hadn't given the pop world much more than '60s Brit-girl duo the **McKinleys** and teeny-bopper boy-band the **Bay City Rollers**. Punk blew all that indifference out of the Forth. In Scotland, it was not Glasgow but Edinburgh that became the new music's creative epicentre.

Much of the action was centred on Edinburgh College of Art, which sired **The Rezillos**; Jo Callis, the group's guitarist, went on to pen million-selling pop singles for the Sheffield-based Human League.

Bob Last's short-lived Fast Product Records caught Edinburgh's artsy spirit, but also looked beyond the city: Gang of Four, the Mekons and the Human League all started out on Fast before signing to majors. Fast eventually morphed into the glossier Pop Aural, leaving Last to champion glossy 1980s New Pop. Around the same time, **Josef K**, **The Scars** and **The Fire Engines** all made waves beyond their hometown, as did Dundee émigrés **The Associates**.

During the '80s, a local band by the name **Goodbye Mr Mackenzie** were forever on the cusp of a breakthrough. They never achieved it, but the group's backing singer Shirley Manson eventually found fame of her own as the singer with Garbage.

While Goodbye Mr Mackenzie were trying to reach the mainstream, a healthy and incestuous indie-pop scene emerged, with the likes of **The Thanes**, **Jesse Garon & the Desperadoes**, **The Fizzbombs** and **The Shop Assistants** playing every cellar bar in town.

The 1990s brought Human Condition Records, who put out **Idlewild**'s first ever single, and SL Records, who championed John Peel favourites **Ballboy** and **Khaya**; the latter eventually morphed into **Desc**

and, recently, the **Leg**. **The Beta Band**'s roots were in Fife, but their indie hybrid was honed at Edinburgh College of Art. **Boards of Canada** took their inspiration from local club Pure, as did many of the laptop-toting acts on Benbecula Records.

Current Edinburgh bands worth watching include 4AD signings **Broken Records**, **Meursault**, **Frightened Rabbit**, **Found** and **Eagleowl**, among others. **Unicorn Kid**, aka Oli Sabin, has drawn a buzz and landed a gig remixing the Pet Shop Boys; not bad for a 17-year-old just out of Leith Academy. The preppy mix of Afrodelic guitars, Talking Heads stylings and twin-drummer rhythms toted by **Jesus H Foxx** predates Vampire Weekend to make for a decidedly groovy proposition.

Then there's Fence Records, the cottage-industry empire from nearby Fife led by the likes of **King Creosote** and **James Yorkston**, or former Rough Trade-signed Edinburgh band **Aberfeldy**, elder statesmen these days. Riley Briggs' band have recently been sharingstages with **The Gillyflowers**, a honey-coated country act fronted by Maria McKee-alike Kirsten Adamson.

Some of the old Sound of Young Scotland scenesters remain on the Edinburgh scene. Ex-Josef K and Orange Juice guitarist Malcolm Ross has joined former Fire Engines drummer Russell Burn and his actor brother Tam Dean Burn as Robert-Burns-meets-Iggy-Pop showband **The Bum-Clocks**. And Davey Henderson, the original Fire Engines frontman (and, in the 1980s, leader of local nearly-men Win) has resurfaced with **The Sexual Objects**. Check local listings and you may find one of more of these cats playing while you're in the city.

There are two major open-air venues in the city. **Murrayfield Stadium** (*see p246*) has welcomed the likes of REM and Oasis, while **Edinburgh Castle** (*see p56*) hosts summer shows from acts including Leonard Cohen and Girls Aloud (though not, sadly, on the same bill). At the other end of the scale, small Old Town pub **Whistlebinkies** (*see p168*) hosts singer-songwriters and bands most nights; the **Bongo Club** (*see p244*) sometimes features live acts; and the **Wee Red Bar** (*see p244*) runs a showcase every Friday at 6pm during termtime.

Ark

5-7 Waterloo Place, Calton Hill (623 7147, www.thearkvenue.com). Princes Street buses. **Admission** free-£5. **No credit cards. Map** p328 & p332 H6, p336 F2.

This long, thin venue has one of the best views of Edinburgh city centre. Musically, it caters for a hotch-potch of local-band triple-bills, rock nights and tribute acts, with the occasional group of note thrown in. An essential service to local bands finding their feet in a low-key manner.

▶ *The venue has affiliations to Henry's Cellar Bar; see below.*

Bannermans

212 Cowgate, Old Town (556 3254, www. myspace.com/bannermanslive). Nicolson Street–North Bridge buses. **Admission** £4-£5. **Credit** AmEx, MC, V. **Map** p333 J7 & p336 F4.

If you walk under the bridge on the Cowgate that runs adjacent to this cavernous venue, you'll reach a spot where you can hear, at full blast ,what's going on inside. These days, the line-ups at Bannermans are heavy on indie-schmindie, having hosted early shows by the likes of Idlewild and Biffy Clyro before they both discovered tunes. The main room hosts triple-band bills on most evenings; the maze-like layout hosts several bars if you want a breather.

Bowery

Roxy Art House, 2 Roxburgh Place, Old Town (www.thebowery.org.uk). Nicolson Street–North Bridge buses. **Admission** free-£10. **No credit cards. Map** p333 J8.

Open since the end of 2008, the Bowery has since become the unofficial home for the city's burgeoning anti-folk scene, while also staging a few experimental shows. It's housed in the basement of a former church that, during the Fringe, trades as the Roxy Art House.

▶ *The Embassy gallery is housed in the same building; see p230.*

Cabaret Voltaire

36 Blair Street, Old Town (220 4638, www.the cabaretvoltaire.com). Nicolson Street–North Bridge buses. **Admission** free-£15. **Credit** MC, V. **Map** p333 J7 & p336 F4.

Its name nodding both to a Swiss nightclub favoured by the original Surrealists and to the hugely influential electronic act, Cabaret Voltaire helped reinvigorate Edinburgh's music scene during the early 21st century. The programme is a fine mix of local bands and touring acts, from bigger names such as Glenn Tilbrook to the 3-4-3 nights that offer three upcoming Edinburgh acts for £3. The Speakeasy space in the club's basement, once home to rehearsal rooms in which assorted Edinburgh luminaries learned their trade, offers a TV relay of events upstairs. After the bands, there are regular club nights.

Corn Exchange

11 New Market Road, South Edinburgh (477 3500, www.ece.uk.com). Bus 4, 20, 34, 35, 44, 44A. **Admission** £14-£28. **Credit** MC, V.

The main problem with this 2,500-capacity former slaughterhouse is its location out of the city centre. That said, the ambience at this oversized barn isn't that great, either, although that doesn't seem to deter fans wishing to see the likes of Mercury Prize-winners Elbow and others en route to stadium status.

Forest

3 Bristo Place, Old Town (220 4538, www. theforest.org.uk). Bus 2, 42, 42. **Admission** free. **No credit cards. Map** p332 H8.

A hippy vibe pervades this collective-run venue in a former church, with bands playing either in the café-bar area or in the upstairs hall. For sensitive Nick Drake types living out their private 1960s fantasy, it's perfect, and isn't without an unlicensed charm. Much of the fare on offer is underground to the point of near-invisibility, as the out-of-date website generally proves.

Henry's Cellar Bar

8-16 Morrison Street, West Edinburgh (221 1288, www.myspace.com/henrysvenue). Bus 1, 2, 10, 11, 15, 15A, 16, 23, 24, 27, 34, 35, 45. **Admission** £4-£5. **No credit cards. Map** p332 E8.

INSIDE TRACK SHHHH!

A few years ago, Finlay Quaye announced from the stage at the Ross Bandstand in Princes Street Gardens that he'd be playing a secret show in **Henry's Cellar Bar** (*see above*) later that evening. This was news to the audience, but also to Henry's. Out of the several thousand people watching at the Ross Bandstand, those that managed to get in eventually saw Quaye, though they also saw the bemused band who had been scheduled to appear at Henry's wondering where on earth their audience had come from.

ARTS & ENTERTAINMENT

WHEREVER CRIMES AGAINST HUMANITY ARE PERPETRATED.

Across borders and above politics.
Against the most heinous abuses
and the most dangerous oppressors.
From conduct in wartime
to economic, social, and cultural rights.
Everywhere we go,
we build an unimpeachable case
for change and advocate action
at the highest levels.

HUMAN RIGHTS WATCH TYRANNY HAS A WITNESS

WWW.HRW.ORG

HUMAN
RIGHTS
WATCH

HMV Picture House.

Situated beneath and connected by a stairwell to a Chinese restaurant, this basement bar was once a jazz joint, but has broadened its remit to encompass everything from punk noiseniks and swingin' '60s revivalists to alternative singer-songwriters such as Jeffrey Lewis, who performed a secret show here. Acts play earlyish shows most nights, with club nights filling the later slots at weekends.

HMV Picture House
31 Lothian Road, South Edinburgh (221 2280 office, 0844 847 1740 box office, www.edinburgh-picturehouse.co.uk). Bus 1, 2, 10, 11, 15, 15A, 16, 23, 24, 27, 34, 35, 45. **Admission** £10-£30. **Credit** MC, V. **Map** p332 E8 & p336 A3.
For years, Edinburgh was crying out for a central, mid-sized venue that could accommodate major touring bands. The city finally got its wish with the 2008 reopening of this old cinema, which hosted '80s gigs by the likes of New Order and the Smiths under its former identity of the Caley Palais. It spent the intervening years as a succession of tacky night-clubs, but the new owners stripped the walls back to their original art deco interior before booking the likes of Jarvis Cocker and Doves on to an impressive gig roster. There are also a few club nights.

Sneaky Pete's
73 Cowgate, Old Town (225 1757, www.sneaky petes.co.uk). Nicolson Street–North Bridge buses. **Admission** £5-£10. **No credit cards**. **Map** p332 H8 & p336 D4.
Once upon a time, this bijou bar was the last port of call for Saturday-night desperadoes who weren't too fussy about the company they kept. However, a major makeover has transformed both clientele and venue, which now plays hosts to local groups and bubbling-under cult acts from elsewhere such as

Crystal Stilts and Heartbreak. It's the perfect space to check out an act who in a year's time might well be playing venues five times the size. Gigs finish around 10-11pm, after which club nights feature dubstep and other electronic curiosities.

Studio 24
24-26 Calton Road, Calton Hill (558 3758, www.myspace.com/studio24edinburgh). Nicolson Street–North Bridge buses. **Admission** free-£10. **No credit cards**. **Map** p329 & p333 J6.
Two decades ago, as Calton Studios, this venue hosted early shows from the likes of Mudhoney and Teenage Fanclub. During the early 21st century, the emphasis fell more on goth and emo, but there are still plenty of indie acts on the bill. Noise complaints from neighbours, the majority of whom moved into the area long after the venue set up shop, caused the council to pull the plug for several months in 2009, but the venue eventually had its licence restored.

Voodoo Rooms
19a West Register Street, New Town (556 7060, www.thevoodoorooms.com). Princes Street buses. **Admission** free-£15. **Credit** AmEx, MC, V. **Map** p328 & p332 H6, p336 F2.
This glorified pub function room and its assorted bar and restaurant areas comprise the plushest venue in town. The booking policy stretches to relatively leftfield names: Pharoah Sanders, the Blackbyrds and Ulrich Schnauss have all played, and Adrian Sherwood's mix of a Mark Stewart & the Maffia show took advantage of the to-die-for sound system in a way that no one has matched. Thursday's indie night Limbo mixes carefully curated triple bills of local, out-of-town and international acts. The main bar is pop-ulated at weekends by a cocktail-drinking crowd who seem to think they're in *Sex and the City. Photo p242.*

Voodoo Rooms. *See p241.*

ARTS & ENTERTAINMENT

FOLK & ROOTS

In the years since Hamish Henderson, poet, founder of the School of Scottish Studies and composer of national-though-not-nationalist-anthem-in-waiting 'Freedom Come All Ye', spearheaded the 1960s Scottish folk revival by founding the Edinburgh Folk Club, a welter of bar-room activity has provided an informal focus on keeping the old traditions alive. The best way to discover the genuine article is to head to one of the various pub sessions. The best are held at **Sandy Bell's** and the **Royal Oak** (for both, *see p168*), the latter also home to Sunday's Wee Folk Club, but they're the tip of the iceberg.

Venues

Edinburgh Folk Club
Pleasance, 60 Pleasance, South Edinburgh (605 2458, www.edinburghfolkclub.org.uk). Nicolson Street–North Bridge buses. **Gigs** *Sept-July* 8pm Wed. **Admission** £8; £7 reductions. **No credit cards. Map** p333 K8.
The Pleasance's Cabaret Bar hosts the Edinburgh Folk Club's weekly sessions for 11 months in every 12; the exception is August, when the venue becomes subsumed by the Fringe.

INSIDE TRACK ARE YOU SITTING COMFORTABLY?

The **Waverley Bar** (St Mary's Street, Old Town, 556 8855) was one of the original homes of the Scottish folk revival, and hosted the likes of Billy Connolly. The bar, which looks as if it hasn't had a makeover since those heady days, now hosts a monthly storytelling night called the **Guid Crack Club**, which captures a similar vibe.

Village
16 South Fort Street, Leith (478 7810). Bus 7, 11, 14. **Gigs** *Leith Folk Club* 7.30pm Tue. **Admission** £6. **Credit** AmEx, MC, V. **Map** p326 W3.
Currently the home of Leith Folk Club, this bijou second room of a compact bar plays host to an increasing amount of shows these days, with artists from home and abroad who stretch the idea of what folk music is. Arrive early, as it fills up very quickly.

JAZZ

Edinburgh's jazz scene is effectively down to the one-man machine that is drummer and promoter Bill Kyle, whose **Jazz Bar** rose from the ashes of the Bridge Jazz Bar. There's also jazz at the **Lot**; at the **Queens Hall** (*see p236*), which offers less regular but worth-the-wait bigger shows; and at August's **Edinburgh Jazz & Blues Festival** (*see p211 and p215*).

Wester Hailes-born saxophonist Tommy Smith remains the figurehead of the local scene, his involvement with the **Scottish National Youth Jazz Orchestra** (www.nyos.co.uk) nurturing a welter of new players. The **Scottish National Jazz Orchestra** (www.snjo.co.uk), which plays several times a year at the Queens Hall, is worth a peek. But there's plenty of note on a grassroots level, from bands such as **Trio AAB** and **Trianglehead** and from roving musicians including saxophonist **Konrad Wiszniewski**, trumpeter **Colin Steele** and guitarist **Haftor Medbøe**.

Venues

Jazz Bar
1a Chambers Street, Old Town (220 4298, www.thejazzbar.co.uk). Nicolson Street–North Bridge buses. **Gigs** from 9pm, midnight Mon; from 5pm, 9pm, midnight Tue-Fri, Sun; from 3pm, 5pm, 9pm, midnight Sat. **Admission** free-£10. **No credit cards. Map** p333 J8.

One of the vicitims of the Old Town fire of 2002 was the Bridge Jazz Bar. Proprietor Bill Kyle asked local jazz stalwarts for their help backing a new venture to replace the much-loved old place; aficionados dug deep, and the Jazz Bar duly arrived on Chambers Street. There are three gigs a night (four on Saturdays) from local and visiting groups; late nights slide into a funkier club vibe. Oddly, the Jazz Bar doesn't play a part in the Edinburgh International Jazz & Blues Festival, which is missing a trick by not providing a focal point for night-owl players.

Jazz Centre at the Lot
4-6 Grassmarket, Old Town (225 9922, www. jazzcentre.co.uk). Bus 2, 23, 27, 28, 42, 45.
Gigs phone for details. **Admission** £8.
Credit MC, V. **Map** p332 G8, p336 C4.
Used sporadically by promoters Assembly Direct (www.jazzmusic.co.uk), this bijou upstairs venue occasionally hosts international acts such as the Necks, but it more usually welcomes Scottish stalwarts, including quality work from the likes of drummer Tom Bancroft and trumpeter Colin Steele.

Nightlife

Edinburgh clubland can be a murky place. If all you want to do is pull in a cheesy, irony-free environment, innumerable city-centre dives will suffice. More discerning punters, however, should find something a little more interesting on the scene by keeping their eyes open and their ear to the ground.

The List and *The Skinny* both carry details on the latest nights around town. Information on the venue's own websites isn't always up to date, so word of mouth may be the best bet when identifying the week's buzz nights.

Ask in record shops such as **Underground Solu'shn** (*see p208*) or any of the bars detailed below; most will also have an array of flyers.

The prices listed here should be taken as guidelines rather than gospel. When new nights launch, prices often change, and rates often rise substantially on weekends. Note, too, that hours for many of these venues will be extended during August's festival spell. And while many nights are long-established, others can vanish after a few weeks. But, hey, that's fashion…

PRE-CLUB BARS

The **City Café** (19 Blair Street, 220 0125) is a good starting point for any night on the town. This was Edinburgh's first style bar; while its once voguish deco interior has faded somewhat, it's worth a visit, if only to pick up whatever flyers are lying around the place.

On the next street, **Black Bo's** (*see p167*) is an ideal meeting place if you're going to the Bongo Club, Cabaret Voltaire, Sneaky Pete's or anywhere in the Cowgate axis. Up near Broughton Street, the **Outhouse** (12 Broughton Street Lane, 557 6668) is similarly party-friendly, with a large courtyard that's ideal for barbecues. Past the Grassmarket, **Dragonfly** hosts DJs playing for the beautiful people, as do the **Voodoo Rooms** (*see p241*) and the **Villager** (49-50 George IV Bridge, 226 2781).

A number of bars are allowed to open beyond the usual curfew of 1am until the club curfew of 3am, which is in turn extended to 5am during August and the week leading up to Hogmanay. **Pivo** (*see p175*) is the most renowned of these late-openers, its loose Czech theme adding little to what is an already bustling bar that can get pretty messy once all the nearby pubs have

Bongo Club. *See p244.*

shut. House and techno DJs play seven nights a week. **Opium** (71 Cowgate, 225 8382) offers a similar vibe within a two-level space; **Medina** (*see p168*) is enlivened by a dynamic mix of house and funk. If you want to rub shoulders with footballers and orange-tanned ladies, try the **Opal Lounge** (51a George Street, New Town, 226 2275, www.opallounge.co.uk).

NIGHTCLUBS

Several of Edinburgh's live music venues morph into nightclubs after the bands have finished. The most notable of them is **Cabaret Voltaire** (*see p239*), which welcomes an array of different nights; among them is a monthly Saturday-night slot for legendary Glasgow club Optimo, with resident DJs Twitch and Wilkes messing up and rebuilding seminal sounds like no other team in town. There are also decent club nights at **Sneaky Pete's** (*see p241*).

Bongo Club

37 Holyrood Road, Old Town (558 7604, www.thebongoclub.co.uk). Nicolson Street–North Bridge buses. **Open** times vary. **Admission** £3-£9. **No credit cards**. **Map** p333 K7.

Housed in the former Moray House students' union building, the Bongo Club offers a worthwhile array of club nights that stretch from reggae and hip hop to, at Confusion is Sex, burlesque and experimental music. Occasional gigs and other special events complete the programme. *Photo p243*.

Caves

12 Niddry Street South, Old Town (557 8989, www.thecavesedinburgh.com). Bus 35 or Nicolson Street–North Bridge buses. **Open** times vary. **Admission** free-£10. **No credit cards**. **Map** p333 J7.

Another venue with a name that gives the game away, the Caves is an irregular but top-quality venue for well-heeled student types who hire out the place for one-offs, usually of a funky variety. The most regular draw is funk, Latin and afrobeat fiesta Departure Lounge (www.departurelounge.me.uk); on a very different level, Fence Records hosts an occasional Fence Club here. When it gets busy, it pays not to get stuck under the arches.

Citrus Club

40-42 Grindlay Street, South Edinburgh (622 7086, www.citrus-club.co.uk). Bus 1, 2, 10, 11, 15, 15A, 16, 23, 24, 27, 34, 35, 45. **Open** times vary. **Admission** free-£6. **No credit cards**. **Map** p332 E8 & p336 A4.

This former student union is a cheap and cheerful affair that mines a lager-spattered vein of indie and '80s retro for those who don't take things too seriously. Oddly, the occasional band nights have made the Citrus a mecca of sorts for veteran ska acts.

Electric Circus

36-39 Market Street, Old Town (226 4224, www.theelectriccircus.biz). Nicolson Street–North Bridge buses. **Open** 5pm-1am Tue-Thur; 5pm-3am Fri; 6pm-1am Sat; 7pm-1am Sun. **Admission** free. **Credit** AmEx, MC, V. **Map** p332 H7 & p336 E1.

Now, this is a novelty. Formerly known as Massa, Buster's and a host of other names, the Electric Circus has been subject to an extensive refurbishment that divided its sole large space into smaller rooms that can be hired by groups for karaoke parties. There's also a stage area, where local bands play on a weekly basis. The idea is that on any given night, there's something different happening in each corner of the club.

GRV

7 Guthrie Street, Old Town (220 2987, www.grv.com). Nicolson Street–North Bridge buses. **Open** times vary. **Admission** free-£15. **No credit cards**. **Map** p333 J8.

Duck down a smelly alley off the Cowgate, look left to see where the Cowgate fire of 2002 claimed one of its biggest scalps in the shape of defunct club La Belle Angele, then turn right. Through a door is GRV (formerly the Green Room Venue), a multi-floor fun palace that houses a club and various art spaces. The plethora of nights is headlined by gay-friendly long-runner Taste.

Hive

15-17 Niddry Street, Old Town (0131 556 0444, www.clubhive.co.uk). Bus 35 or Nicolson Street–North Bridge buses. **Open** 11pm-3am daily. **Admission** free-£4. **No credit cards**. **Map** p333 J7 & p336 F4.

As the name suggests, this club is made up of a series of interlocking rooms, which host a series of student-friendly nights across two dancefloors and several bar areas. Occasionally used for gigs, the Hive can be a lively spot. However, if you don't know the place well, it's easy to lose your friends in the labyrinthine layout.

Wee Red Bar

Edinburgh College of Art, Lauriston Place, South Edinburgh (229 1442 office, 229 1003 bar, www.weeredbar.co.uk). Bus 2, 23, 27. **Open** *Club nights* 10.30pm-3am Fri; 11pm-3am Sat. **Admission** £2.50-£5. **No credit cards**. **Map** p332 F9.

The spiritual home of Edinburgh's original art-punk scene (the Rezillos, the Fire Engines et al), the ECA's scarlet-painted students' union continues to provide a platform for intimate happenings of every persuasion. The Egg, held every Saturday, is the city's longest standing indie disco; every Friday at 6pm during termtime, there's a free showcase of local talent, which gave rise to a compilation DVD entitled *The Art School Dance*.

Sport & Fitness

The Scots' passion for sports extends to playing as well as watching.

Its assorted teams may not win much, but Edinburgh is still quite a centre for professional sport. There are football, ice hockey and rugby clubs, and the city hosts international matches in both cricket and rugby. Nearby Musselburgh has a racecourse, and the Muirfield golf course in East Lothia will host the Open Championship in 2013.

For those who want to be active, there's arguably even more on offer: easily accessible golf courses, world-class indoor rock climbing, lovely Victorian swimming pools and mass participation road races where enthusiasts can run for fun, or to raise money for charity. When it comes to sport, you can watch or take part, and in Edinburgh, there's ample opportunity to do both.

Spectator Sports

CRICKET

Cricket has taken giant strides since Scotland (www.cricketscotland.com) joined the International Cricket Council (ICC) in 1994, even appearing at the 2007 World Cup. Most matches are at the **Grange** in Stockbridge (Portgower Place, 332 2148, www.grangecricket.org); the season runs from April to August. In recent years, the Grange has hosted Friends Provident Trophy ties against English county sides and some one-day internationals (Australia in 2009).

FOOTBALL

Edinburgh's two football teams, **Heart of Midlothian** (Hearts) and **Hibernian** (Hibs), hail from opposite ends of the city: respectively, Gorgie in the west and Leith in the north-east. Both teams have brought trophies back to Edinburgh in the last decade – Hearts won the Scottish Cup in 2006, Hibs the League Cup in 2007 – but the two Glasgow sides, Celtic and Rangers, still dominate Scottish football. While the Edinburgh derbies are always passionate affairs, there's little of the bigotry that has plagued football in the West of Scotland.

★ **Heart of Midlothian FC**
Tynecastle Stadium, Gorgie Road, West Edinburgh (0871 663 1874, www.heartsfc.co.uk). Bus 1, 2, 3, 3A, 4, 22, 25, 30, 33, 44, 44A.

Open *Shop* 9.30am-5.30pm Mon-Fri; 9.30am-1.30pm match days. *Ticket office* 9am-5pm Mon-Fri; 10am-2pm Sat; 10am-kickoff match days. **Tickets** £16-£28. **Credit** MC, V.

After some success when Vladimir Romanov took over the club in 2005, the tidy and atmospheric Tynecastle operated close to its 17,420 capacity for a couple of seasons. But with a managerial revolving door and high player turnover, disillusionment saw average attendances drop again by the end of the decade. Tickets aren't that hard to come by, unless you want to see a European tie or the local derby.

★ **Hibernian FC**
Easter Road Stadium, 12 Albion Place, Leith (0844 844 1875, www.hibernianfc.co.uk). Bus 1, 34, 35, 39. **Open** *Shop* 9am-5pm Mon-Sat. *Ticket office* 9am-5pm Mon, Tue, Thur, Fri; 10am-5pm Wed; 9am-3pm Sat; 9am-kickoff match days. **Tickets** £22-£28. **Credit** MC, V.

INSIDE TRACK WAR MEMORIAL

When World War I broke out, a large number of **Hearts** footballers joined the British Army, and in the course of the conflict, seven first-team members were killed. Every year on Remembrance Sunday (the second Sunday in November), club officials, players and fans gather at the war memorial at Haymarket, West Edinburgh to pay their respects.

Cricket in Edinburgh. See p245.

ICE HOCKEY

Ice hockey in the city started in 1952, although the current club, **Edinburgh Capitals**, was founded as recently as 1998; it plays in the UK's Elite Ice Hockey League (Sept-Mar). The club plays at the Murrayfield Ice Rink (*see p249*).

RUGBY UNION

Since the Five Nations international was expanded into the Six Nations in 2000, Scotland have cultivated an appalling record, better only than newcomers Italy. Despite this, support is still as strong as ever. International matches at the 67,130-capacity **Murrayfield Stadium** (West Edinburgh, 0844 335 3933, www.scottish rugby.org) still draw sell-out crowds; try and buy tickets well in advance. As long as a big match isn't coming up, 75-minute stadium tours are available weekdays only (£6 adults, £3.50 under-16s). Call 346 5160 for more details.

Scottish club rugby has been looking for a way forward since the game went professional in the mid 1990s. Traditionally, clubs were based either in small communities or tied to fee-paying schools. The problem of the last 15 years has been turning that into a professional structure; the answer, at least so far, has been superclubs. Along with the Glasgow Warriors, **Edinburgh Rugby** (346 5252, www.edinburgh rugby.org) takes on teams from Ireland and Wales in the Magners League from September to May. The team plays at Murrayfield ('the Castle' in this context) but draws small crowds. Tickets can be bought on the day (Murrayfield Ticket Centre by Gate A, off Roseburn Street).

In the last decade, Hearts has been a conveyor belt for Scottish talent, but it was all sold to balance the books: crucially, they lost Kevin Thomson and Steven Whittaker to Rangers, and Scott Brown to Celtic, all in 2007. Despite the regular loss of key players, they still manage usually to finish in the top half of the Scottish Premier League. As with Hearts, tickets are widely available except for local derbies.

GOLF

Golf was born in Scotland, and the historic courses here regularly host major tournaments. The 2013 Open Championship will be just outside Edinburgh at Muirfield in East Lothian (www.muirfield.org.uk), home to the **Honourable Company of Edinburgh Golfers**. For more on playing golf in the region, *see right*.

HORSE RACING

Horse racing has a long local tradition. Races initially took place on Leith Links from at least the 17th century, then moved to **Musselburgh**, East Lothian, in 1816. Racing attracted massive crowds for decades, but it declined from the 1960s, when betting shops were legalised in the UK. In the 1980s, it looked as if Musselburgh Racecourse would close, but it was reprieved thanks to new technology: the ability to sell televised race coverage direct to betting shops.

Musselburgh Racecourse

Musselburgh, East Lothian (665 2859, www.musselburgh-racecourse.co.uk).
Musselburgh hosts around 25 race days a year. Jump meetings dominate the winter (Nov-Feb), but the majority of the meets are on the flat (Apr-Oct).

Active Sports

CYCLING

Local transport chiefs have joined European cities such as Madrid and Milan by signing up to ambitious new cycling targets with the aim that by 2020 one in every six journeys will be by bike. Year-round, **Spokes**, the Lothian Cycle Campaign (313 2114, www.spokes.org.uk), and the **Edinburgh Bicycle Cooperative** (0845 257 0808, www.edinburghbicycle.com) both offer information on cycling in Edinburgh, and on the city's cycle paths (for which *see right* **Riding the Rails**). **Sustrans Scotland** (www.sustrans.org.uk) publishes a free booklet, *National Cycle Network – Go Traffic-Free in Scotland*, on cycle paths, including ex-railway lines, in Edinburgh, Fife, Central Scotland and the Borders. Both **Biketrax** (11-13 Lochrin Place, South Edinburgh, 228 6633, www.biketrax.co.uk) and **Cycle Scotland**

(29 Blackfriars Street, Old Town, 556 5560, www.cyclescotland.co.uk) offer rentals. Expect to pay £10-£20/day or £50-£80/week.

Members of affiliated clubs get to use the velodrome at **Meadowbank Sports Centre** (*see p249*) for training, while **Scottish Cycling** (317 9704, www.scuonline.org), based in West Edinburgh, has details of clubs and races all over the country.

GOLF

Scotland is the home of golf, something readily apparent from a map of Edinburgh: there are more than 30 courses within easy reach of the city, and dozens more within driving distance. The majority welcome visitors with open arms, but don't expect just to turn up and get a tee time: always book in advance. Prices listed in this section are for peak season, but discounted green fees may be available in winter. If you're hoping to hire clubs, be sure to bring a credit

card to act as a deposit. Casual golfers may enjoy **Bruntsfield Links**, a fun pitch-and-putt course adjacent to the Meadows. All courses below are open dawn-dusk daily unless stated.

★ Braid Hills No.1

22 Braid Hills Approach, South Edinburgh (447 6666, www.edinburghleisure.co.uk). Bus 11, 15, 15A. **Green fee** £19 Mon-Fri; £23 Sat, Sun. **Club hire** £17. **Credit** AmEx, MC, V.
This tricky municipal course represents one of the city's best bargains. Situated against the backdrop of the Pentland Hills to the south and the Firth of Forth to the north, it provides perhaps the most stunning views in Edinburgh. There's also a nine-hole course (Braid Hill Princes). Book well ahead. *Photo p248.*

Duddingston

Duddingston Road West, Arthur's Seat (661 7688, www.duddingstongolfclub.co.uk). Bus 4, 42, 44, 44A, 45. **Green fee** £35. **Club hire** £15. **Credit** MC, V.

Riding the Rails

Edinburgh's old train tracks are reborn for two-wheeled vehicles.

During the 1960s, one-third of Britain's rail network – capillaries, veins and even arteries – was removed in a sweeping cost-cutting move. Two decades later, happily, many of these disused lines began to be revived as bicycle and walking paths.

In Edinburgh, almost all the former railway lines have been adapted, making for a virtually continuous network. You can ride along them, weather permitting; for information on bike hire shops, *see above*. The three main inner-city disused-railway routes are listed below.

NORTH EDINBURGH PATHS

7.5 miles; tarmac with one short earth stretch (can get muddy); no major gradients.
Part of National Cycle Route 75, this runs between the Shore at Leith and Roseburn, near Murrayfield Stadium. Offshoots along the way lead to Canonmills, the Newhaven harbour and the picturesque waterside village of Cramond.

INNOCENT RAILWAY PATH

5 miles; tarmac; drop down the Innocent Tunnel but otherwise pretty flat.
Connecting the St Leonard's Gate entrance to Holyrood Park to Musselburgh, this route takes in the 50-yard long Victorian tunnel through which ran Edinburgh's very first railway line. Just before St Leonard's Gate

opposite the university's Pollock Halls, take a left along East Parkside into a newish housing development. After about 50 yards, take a sharp right at the Resident Parking Only sign and you'll enter the now-paved tunnel, built in 1831.

WATER OF LEITH PATH

9 miles; tarmac with some earth surfaces and some steps; some hills.
This green corridor through Edinburgh is rich in woodland, wildlife and heritage (including the remains of water-driven mills). If time doesn't permit you to do the full route, the first part, Dean Village to Slateford (four miles), makes for a very pleasant outing.

A demanding, tree-lined course set in undulating parkland south-east of Arthur's Seat. The Braid Burn (stream) winds throughout the course, and is in play on a disturbing number of holes.

Lothianburn

106a Biggar Road, Hillend, South Edinburgh (445 5067, 445 2288 shop, www.lothianburngc. co.uk). Bus 4, 15, 15A. **Green fee** £25-£30. **Club hire** £14. **Credit** MC, V.

A swooping, testing hillside course perched around 270 metres above sea level, again affording great views of the city. One of the cheaper private courses in or near the city.

Muirfield

Duncur Road, Muirfield, Gullane (01620 842123, www.muirfield.org.uk). **Open** dawn-dusk Tue, Thur. **Green fee** *Summer* £185. *Winter* £105. **Club hire** call for details. **Credit** MC, V.

It's possible to follow in the footsteps of Tiger by playing one of the world's finest links courses, but visitors are only allowed two days a week and a single round is the opposite of cheap.

Murrayfield

43 Murrayfield Road, West Edinburgh (337 3478, www.murrayfieldgolfclub.co.uk). Bus 12, 13, 26, 31. **Open** *Non-members* 8am-4.30pm Mon-Fri. **Green fee** £40. **Club hire** £15. **Credit** AmEx, MC, V.

Murrayfield's handsome 18-hole course is set around Corstorphine Hill to the west of the city. Visitors must book in advance.

Musselburgh Links Old Golf Club

Balcarres Road, Musselburgh (665 5438, www.musselburgholdlinks.co.uk). Bus 30. **Green fee** £12.30/9 holes. **Club hire** £15.50-£28.50. **Credit** MC, V.

It's worth a visit here simply to pay homage to the world's oldest active golf course, although it's only a nine-hole links. Golf was played here in the 17th century, and quite possibly before.

Prestonfield

6 Priestfield Road North, Prestonfield (667 9665, www.prestonfieldgolf.com). Bus 2, 14, 30, 33. **Green fee** £20-£15. **Credit** V.

A not-too-taxing parkland course with great views of Arthur's Seat, within easy reach of the city centre.

★ St Andrews

West Sands Road, St Andrews, Fife (01334 466666, www.standrews.org.uk). **Green fee** varies. **Club hire** £25. **Credit** AmEx, MC, V.

The world's most famous golf complex is only an 50-mile drive from Edinburgh and offers seven courses. For the world-famous Old Course, the minimum handicap is 24 (men) and 36 (women). Open Monday to Saturday, the course is booked months in advance, though half the slots are available daily via a ballot system. The other five 18-hole courses can all be booked online (reserve at least one month ahead except for Saturday play, which can only be booked 24 hours ahead); reservations aren't accepted on the nine-hole Balgove course. In winter, the Balgove costs just £8 for nine holes, the economical way to play at St Andrews.

GYMS & FITNESS CENTRES

In addition to the stand-alone gyms below, a number of city centre hotels have fitness clubs. The **Caledonian Hilton** (*see p121*) is home to a fairly basic LivingWell (www.livingwell.com); the facilities at both the **Scotsman** (*see p117*) and the **Sheraton Grand** (*see p130*), with its One Spa, are rather more plush.

Braid Hills No.1. *See p247.*

Edinburgh International Climbing Arena Ratho. *See p250.*

Bannatyne's

43 Queen Street, New Town (225 8384, www. bannatyne.co.uk). Bus 4, 8, 10, 11, 12, 15, 15A, 16, 26, 44, 45. **Open** 6.30am-10pm Mon-Fri; 8am-8pm Sat-Sun. **Rates** phone for details. **Credit** MC, V.

A gym, a pool, a steam room, a sauna and an aerobics studio, all in the city centre. Its sister club on the eastern fringe of the city is enormous. **Other locations** 89 Newcraighall Road, East Edinburgh (657 6800).

Meadowbank Sports Centre

139 London Road, Abbeyhill, Leith (661 5351, www.edinburghleisure.co.uk). Bus 4, 5, 15, 15A, 19, 26, 34, 44, 44A, 45. **Open** 7.30am-10pm daily. **Rates** vary. **Credit** MC, V.

Meadowbank has facilities for athletics, badminton, squash, basketball and football, as well as a velodrome; there are classes for children, adults and the over-50s in everything from archery to martial arts. The stand-out part is Meadowbank Stadium, which opened for the 1970 Commonwealth Games.

In 2006, a proposal arose to demolish it, sell off the land for housing and build a new centre elsewhere. Two years later, the scheme was in disarray, but the local authority still believes the stadium is in poor shape and in danger of permanent closure.

Pleasance Sports Centre

46 Pleasance, South Edinburgh (650 2585, www.ed.ac.uk/schools-departments/sport-exercise). Nicolson Street–North Bridge buses. **Open** 7am-10.25pm Mon-Fri; 8.50am-5.30pm Sat; 10am-5.30pm Sun. **Rates** phone for details. **Credit** MC, V. **Map** p333 K8.

The University of Edinburgh's sports centre has an impressive gym and sports injury clinic, plus badminton, squash, basketball facilities, a climbing wall and more. A £4.8 million improvement programme should be completed by summer 2010. Memberships lasting one, three, six or 12 months are available.

Virgin Active – Edinburgh Omni

Omni Centre, Greenside Place, Calton Hill & Broughton (550 1650, www.virginactive.co.uk). Playhouse buses. **Open** 6.30am-10.30pm Mon-Fri; 8am-8pm Sat, Sun. **Rates** phone for details. **Credit** MC, V. **Map** p329 J5.

This stylish members-only complex offers separate male and female sauna and steam rooms, spa baths, a health and beauty clinic, and a restaurant. The centrepiece is the 25m stainless steel pool.

ICE-SKATING

Murrayfield Ice Rink

Riversdale Crescent, West Edinburgh (337 6933, www.murrayfieldicerinkltd.co.uk). Bus 12, 26, 31. **Open** times vary. **Admission** £3.80-£5.80. **Skate hire** £1.20-£1.70. **Credit** MC, V.

Home to the Edinburgh Capitals (*see p246*), this large rink is also used for public skating sessions and curling. Disco skating sessions on Friday and Saturday nights attract a young crowd; family sessions take place on Thursday nights and Saturday mornings; and Sunday lunchtimes are set aside for learn-to-skate sessions.

ROCK CLIMBING

In addition to these dedicated centres, the **Meadowbank Sports Centre** (*see left*) has an old-fashioned, mainly brick wall; the University of Edinburgh's **Pleasance Sport Centre** (*see left*) also has a wall.

Alien Rock

8 Pier Place, Newhaven (552 7211, www.alien rock.co.uk). Bus 10, 11, 16, 32. **Open** *Summer* 11am-10pm Mon-Fri, 10am-7pm Sat, Sun. *Winter* 11am-11pm Mon-Thur; 11am-10pm Fri; 10am-8pm Sat, Sun. **Admission** £6.80-£7.50; £4.50-£7 reductions. **Credit** MC, V. **Map** p326 U1.

Located in a former church, Alien Rock offers around 200 ever-changing routes, 40 top-roped lines, a 4.8m bouldering wall and 12 overhanging lead lines. All equipment can be hired, though novices will need to take an introductory course.
Other locations Alien 2, 23-53 West Bowling Green Street, Leith (552 7211).

★ Edinburgh International Climbing Arena Ratho

South Platt Hill, Newbridge, West Edinburgh (333 6333, www.eica-ratho.com). Bus X48, then 10min along canal. **Open** *Arena* 10am-10pm Mon-Fri; 10am-7pm Sat, Sun. *Aerial Assault* 4.30pm-8pm Thur, Fri; 10.30am-5pm Sat, Sun. **Admission** *Arena* £8-£8.75; *Aerial Assault* £7.50-£9.50. **Credit** MC, V.

This multi-million-pound climbing arena was the biggest in the world when it opened in 2003, but soon ran into financial problems. After the local authority lent a hand, the venue was relaunched in spring 2007. Based in an old quarry, it's a hugely ambitious facility, with walls from 12m to 35m high, freestanding boulders and a suspended aerial assault course. *Photo p249.*

SKATEBOARDING

Transgression Park

Second Floor, Ocean Terminal (555 3755, www.transgressionpark.co.uk). **Open** 10am-10pm daily. **Admission** £5.50, plus £2 day membership. **Credit** MC, V.

This custom-built urban streetsports facility offers a skatepark for BMX, inline skating and skateboarding. You have to be a member to join, but daily membership is available, as is any equipment you might need to hire. There's a girls-only night once a month.

SKIING

Midlothian Snowsports Centre

Biggar Road, Hillend (445 4433, www.midlothian.gov.uk). Bus 4, 15, 15A. **Open** *May-Aug* 9am-7.15pm daily. *Sept-Apr* 9am-9pm Mon-Sat; 9am-7.15pm Sun. **Rates** *Main slope/nursery slopes* £9.30 first hr, £3.90 extra hr; £6.30 discounts, £2.70 extra hr. **Credit** MC, V.

INSIDE TRACK
RUN TO THE HILLS

June's annual 14-mile **Seven Hills of Edinburgh** race (www.seven-hills.org.uk) takes in the summits of all of the city's hills, including Arthur's Seat, with a total climb of 670 metres. In 2009, the winning runner, David Simpson, finished in one hour, 43 minutes.

The Midlothian Centre is in proud possession of the longest artificial ski slope in Europe, measuring 400m, as well as a jump slope and learning slopes. Ski prices include the hire of boots, skis and poles.

SWIMMING

Aside from those in gyms and fitness centres (*see p249*), public pools are run by Edinburgh Leisure (www.edinburghleisure.co.uk). Its website details prices and opening times for 12 pools; the **Portobello Swim Centre** is probably the pick of the bunch. The website also has details of **Leith Waterworld**, with flumes, wave machine, water cannon and more.

Portobello Swim Centre

57 Promenade, Portobello (669 6888, www.edinburghleisure.co.uk). Bus 12, 15, 15A, 26, 32, 42, 49. **Open** *Pool* 6am-10pm Mon-Fri; 9am-5pm Sat; 9am-8pm Sun. **Admission** *Pool* £2.90-£3.90; £2 discounts; free under-5s. **Credit** MC, V.

Housed in an elaborate building that dates back to 1901, the old Portobello Baths have had a couple of facelifts in their century-plus lifespan. A Lottery grant in 1998 turned the splendid old pile into the Portobello Swim Centre, adding new fitness facilities and a family-friendly café with views out to the beach. There are also Turkish baths, where some days are designated as men- or women-only.

TENNIS

There are also 16 courts in the Meadows, officially open from April to September; *see p101.*

★ Craiglockhart Tennis & Leisure Centre

177 Colinton Road, Craiglockhart (443 0101, www.edinburghleisure.co.uk). Bus 4, 10, 27, 45. **Open** 9am-10.30pm Mon-Fri; 9am-6pm Sat; 9am-10pm Sun. **Rates** phone for details. **Credit** AmEx, MC, V.

Scotland's most comprehensive tennis centre has indoor and outdoor courts, and provides coaching to all standards. The leisure centre has a gym, badminton and squash courts, and also runs classes.

TRACK & FIELD

Most athletic activities are organised around the **Meadowbank Sports Centre** (*see p249*). Edinburgh Leisure (www.edinburghleisure.co.uk) has details of others. The city has plenty of green spaces for joggers, including the **Meadows** (*see p101*) and **Holyrood Park** (*see p96*). There are several mass-participation events, such as May's Great Edinburgh Run (10km, www.greatrun.org), and June's women-only Race for Life (5km, www.raceforlife.org).

Theatre & Dance

Edinburgh's performing arts scene isn't just a one-month wonder.

You may get the chance to see big stars treading the Edinburgh boards during your stay; David Tennant, Brian Cox and Alan Cumming have all taken their turn in recent years. However, the theatre scene in the city is not driven by celebrity or glamour. Audiences are just as likely to be attracted to the standard of the ensemble in question or the promise of a new work by one of Scotland's many celebrated playwrights (among them David Greig, Liz Lochhead, David Harrower, Jo Clifford, Zinnie Harris and Gregory Burke). In this regard, theatre is keenly attuned to the broader cultural life of Scotland; at its best, it can provide an illuminating snapshot of a nation.

Theatre

The majority of venues used for theatre during August's festival season revert to other functions for the rest of the year, but a handful of full-time theatres and arts centres keep things ticking over. If you're looking for large-scale mainstream entertainment, it's most likely you'll end up at the **King's Theatre**, the **Playhouse** or the **Edinburgh Festival Theatre**; meanwhile, the city's two main producing houses, the **Traverse** (for the new and untried) and the **Royal Lyceum** (for the more established), sit back-to-back near the **Usher Hall** (*see p236*). However, despite several attempts across a number of years to set one up, the city lacks a dedicated space for up-and-coming performers.

Many imaginative touring companies are based in the city, and often stage shows in less conventional spaces. The best include **Grid Iron** (www.gridiron.org.uk), renowned for site-specific performances held everywhere from the supposedly haunted Mary King's Close to Edinburgh Airport; **Wee Stories** (www.wee storiestheatre.org), which specialises in family-friendly plays both large-scale and small; and **Stellar Quines** (www.stellarquines.com), which offers a high-quality pro-female drama programme. And last but hardly least, standing apart from the crowd is the **National Theatre of Scotland** (*see p252* **Profile**), a roving company that's still in its infancy but has already made its mark with a number of powerful and engaging new works.

INFORMATION & TICKETS

The List (www.list.co.uk) remains the best source for theatre listings in Edinburgh, but it's also worth taking a look at the extensive array of links to events, companies and artists at **www.theatrescotland.com**. Tickets for many major venues can be booked through **Ticketline** or **Ticketmaster**; *see p204*.

VENUES

For the **Edinburgh Festival Theatre**, which stages theatrical events, *see p254*.

Bedlam Theatre

11B Bristo Place, Old Town (225 9873 information, 225 9893 box office, www.bedlam theatre.co.uk). Bus 2, 41, 42. **Box office** from 45mins before performance. **Tickets** £2-£10. **Credit** *Festival only* MC, V. **Map** p332 H8. The Bedlam Theatre is home to the Edinburgh University Theatre Company, which produces a rolling programme of student drama every week of

---

INSIDE TRACK
CHILDREN'S THEATRE

Kids are well served by the high-quality junior entertainment provided at the **Imaginate** children's theatre festival in May and the **Puppet Animation Festival** in April. For both, *see p222*.

Profile National Theatre of Scotland

Inspiring and itinerant, the country's theatre continues to impress.

If you've arrived in Edinburgh in search of the National Galleries of Scotland or the National Library of Scotland, you'll have little difficulty finding them. However, if you're in search of the National Theatre of Scotland (NTS), you'll need to look a little harder. That's because this is a national theatre with no theatre.

Instead of investing in red carpets, this fleet-footed, streamlined organisation has put its money on other people's stages since launching in 2006. In Edinburgh, it's worked with the Royal Lyceum (*see p253*) on a production of *Six Characters in Search of an Author*; with the Traverse (*see p254*) on a series of new plays by first-time writers; and with local companies such as Wee Stories on *The Emperor's New Kilt*, a big children's show, and *Grid Iron on Roam*, performed beyond the check-in desks of Edinburgh Airport.

This arrangement means that a tremendous variety of theatre, from community shows to classic dramas, can be awarded national status, which in turn allows the NTS the freedom to

Duncan McLean in *Long Gone Lonesome*.

move in whichever direction the artistic energy lies. While other national theatres embody a very particular type of traditional, proscenium-arch drama, this open-plan operation can shift shape at will. NTS shows have taken place on a ferry boat, in a prehistoric glen and before the great and the good of the Edinburgh International Festival.

Artistic director Vicky Featherstone's company also stages pieces entirely of its own devising. Among such works was 2006's *Black Watch*, a highly theatrical retelling of the story of Scotland's oldest military regiment and its engagement in Iraq. Written by Gregory Burke and directed by John Tiffany, the show was first performed in a drill hall on the Edinburgh Fringe before journeying to London, New York, Sydney and beyond; on its travels, it picked up more than 20 awards, including four Oliviers. *Black Watch* was a perfect demonstration of the National Theatre of Scotland's ability to respond to current events with imagination, immediacy and passion. It'll be interesting to see how they grow as a company in future years.

Siobhan Redmond in *The House of Bernarda Alba*.

SHOW TIME
For details of the NTS's productions, see www. national theatre scotland.com.

the academic year. Alumni include Ian Charleson, comedian Miles Jupp, actor Kevin McKidd and Greg Wise, otherwise known as Mr Emma Thompson and the honorary president of the Friends of Bedlam.

Brunton Theatre

Bridge Street, Musselburgh (665 2240, www. bruntontheatre.co.uk). Bus 15, 15A, 26, 30, 44, 44A. **Box office** 10am-7.30pm Mon-Fri; 10am-2.30pm, 3.30-7.30pm Sat. **Tickets** £8-£15.50. **Credit** MC, V.

A 20-minute bus ride out of town, this comfortable, 300-seat civic theatre produces its own pantomime at Christmas. For the rest of the year, it hosts adult and children's companies on the touring circuit and the occasional community show, while also forging relationships with touring groups such as the excellent Catherine Wheels children's theatre company.

Edinburgh Playhouse

18-22 Greenside Place, Calton Hill (0844 847 1660, www.edinburghplayhouse.org.uk). Playhouse buses. **Box office** *In person* 10am-8pm Mon-Sat (10am-6pm on non-performance days). *By phone* 24hrs daily. **Tickets** £15-£38.50. **Credit** AmEx, MC, V. **Map** p329 J5.

Run by global entertainment conglomerate Live Nation, the 3,000-seat Playhouse is the regular home for touring West End musicals such as *Mamma Mia!* and *We Will Rock You*. The Edinburgh International Festival regularly uses the auditorium, the largest of its kind in the UK, for bigger dance and opera productions, while grown-up rock stars and big-name comedians treat the Playhouse as a stopping-off point: Anthony and the Johnsons and Ricky Gervais have both visited recently.

GRV (Green Room Venue)

37 Guthrie Street, Old Town (220 2987/www. thegrv.com). Nicolson Street–North Bridge buses. **Tickets** call for prices. **No credit cards**. **Map** p333 J8.

A recent addition to the local arts scene, the GRV is primarily a music and club venue. However, one of its party rooms – known as the Cube – doubles as a small-scale theatre for young companies.

King's Theatre

2 Leven Street, Tollcross, South Edinburgh (529 6000, www.eft.co.uk). Bus 11, 15, 15A, 16, 23, 45. **Box office** *In person* 10am-8pm Mon-Sat (10am-6pm on non-performance days). *By phone* 11am-8pm Mon-Sat (11am-6pm on non-performance days). **Tickets** £14.50-£60. **Credit** MC, V. **Map** p332 F10.

Built in 1905, this elegant old-time institution is managed, along with the Edinburgh Festival Theatre, by the Festival City Theatres Trust. The programme mixes musicals with star-studded serious drama, usually on pre- or post-West End tours; highlights of recent seasons have included Sir Ian McKellen and Patrick Stewart in *Waiting for Godot* and Neil Morrissey in *Rain Man*. Every December, there's a highly popular pantomime.

North Edinburgh Arts Centre

15a Pennywell Court, Muirhouse (315 2151, www.northedinburgharts.co.uk). Bus 27, 37, 42. **Box office** 10am-5pm Mon-Fri; 9.30am-11.30am Sat. **Tickets** £3-£8. **Credit** MC, V.

Tucked away behind one of the least inviting shopping arcades in the city, this community centre is getting back on its feet again after a short period of closure. The busy programme includes small-scale touring productions aimed at children and adults.

Out of the Blue Drill Hall

36 Dalmeny Street, Leith (555 7101, www.out oftheblue.org.uk). Bus 7, 10, 12, 14, 16, 22, 25, 49. **Box office** call for details. **Tickets** call for details. **No credit cards. Map** p329 L2.

Primarily a studio space, Out of the Blue has undergone a £500,000 redevelopment in order to make it suitable for performances, rehearsals and screenings. It's a likely home for oddball Fringe events.
▶ *The venue usually also features in the Leith Festival; see p216.*

★ Royal Lyceum

Grindlay Street, South Edinburgh (248 4800 information, 248 4848 box office, www.lyceum. org.uk). Bus 1, 2, 10, 11, 15, 15A, 16, 23, 24, 27, 34, 35, 45. **Box office** 10am-7.45pm Mon-Sat (10am-6pm on non-performance days). **Tickets** £1-£27. **Credit** AmEx, MC, V. **Map** p332 E8 & p336 A4.

Bedlam. *See p251.*

At its peak in the 1970s, the Lyceum was at the vanguard of a renaissance of local theatrical culture, and a breeding ground for leading directors such as Bill Bryden and Richard Eyre. The intervening decades were less radical but audiences remained loyal; since 2003, artistic director David Mark Thomson has built the company into one of the most popular in Scotland. A typical season might include some Shakespeare, Arthur Miller, the occasional new play and fresh translations of European classics.

Roxy Art House
2 Roxburgh Place, Old Town (629 0039, www.roxyarthouse.org). Nicolson Street–North Bridge buses. **Tickets** call for prices. **No credit cards.** **Map** p333 J8.
After coming into its own as a busy Fringe venue in recent times, the Roxy was taken on by Edinburgh University Settlement (a social action centre) at the start of 2009 with the intention of developing its capacity as a year-round workshop, rehearsal space, theatre and exhibition space.

Scottish Storytelling Centre
43-45 High Street, Old Town (556 9579, www.scottishstorytellingcentre.co.uk). Bus 35 or Nicolson Street–North Bridge buses. **Box office** 10am-6pm Mon-Sat; later on performance days. **Tickets** £4-£10. **Credit** MC, V. **Map** p333 J7.
The refurbished former Netherbow Arts Centre now serves as a home for storytelling, arguably Scotland's one indigenous art form. The venue presents regular storytelling events pitched at all ages, with opportunities both to hear stories and to tell them.
► *For more on the centre, see p66.*

Theatre Workshop
34 Hamilton Place, Stockbridge (226 5425, www.theatre-workshop.com). Bus 23, 27, 36. **Box office** 9.30am-5.30pm Mon-Fri (during show runs only). **Tickets** £10; £6 discounts. **Credit** MC, V. **Map** p328 E4.
Anyone who recalls this small, boho establishment as the centre of Stockbridge life will be saddened to see how underused it is these days. Things are especially uncertain since the resident company, dedicated to addressing social issues (especially to do with disability), lost its Scottish Arts Council funding.

★ Traverse Theatre
10 Cambridge Street, South Edinburgh (228 1404, www.traverse.co.uk). Bus 1, 2, 10, 11, 15, 15A, 16, 23, 24, 27, 34, 35, 45. **Box office** 10am-8pm Mon-Sat (10am-6pm on non-performance days); from 2hrs before performance Sun. **Tickets** £5-£18. **Credit** MC, V. **Map** p332 E8, p336 A3.
Founded in the 1960s, the Traverse was first housed in a former brothel on the High Street; a legend was born on its second night when actor Colette O'Neill was accidentally stabbed during a production of Sartre's *Huis Clos*. By the time the theatre moved to its second home in the Grassmarket in the late '60s, the emphasis on European experimentalism had begun to shift towards homegrown fare from writers such as John Byrne and Tom McGrath. Then, in 1992, the theatre moved to this purpose-built expanse beneath an office complex. Two spaces showcase a lively array of new plays from writers developed by the company – among them David Greig, David Harrower and Zinnie Harris – as well as a rolling programme of touring shows. In August, it's always one of the hottest spots on the Fringe.
► *For the bar, see p179.*

Dance

The fan base for ballet and dance in Edinburgh is a devoted one, adventurous enough to enjoy regular visits from the likes of Mark Morris, Nederlands Dans Theater and Michael Clark, as well as Ashley Page's rejuvenated **Scottish Ballet** (www.scottishballet.co.uk). Smaller companies regularly tour to the **Traverse** (*see above*) and the **Brunton** (*see p253*).

VENUES

★ Dance Base
14-16 Grassmarket, Old Town (225 5525, www.dancebase.co.uk). Bus 2, 23, 27, 41, 42. **Box office** 10am-6pm Mon-Fri; 10am-2pm Sat. **Tickets** prices vary. **Credit** MC, V. **Map** p332 G8, p336 C4.
This beautifully airy, purpose-built state-of-the-art venue has become the focal point for the capital's dance community. With four studios housing an extensive programme of classes and workshops, it accommodates all levels and areas of interest. Ever wanted to learn Highland or gumboot dancing? Feldenkrais and Alexander technique? Head here.

Edinburgh Festival Theatre
13-29 Nicolson Street, South Edinburgh (529 6000, www.eft.co.uk). Nicolson Street–North Bridge buses. **Box office** *In person* 10am-8pm Mon-Sat (10am-6pm on non-performance days); 4pm-start of performance Sun. *By phone* 11am-8pm Mon-Sat (10am-6pm on non-performance days); 4pm-start of performance Sun. **Tickets** £10-£62. **Credit** MC, V. **Map** p333 J8.
The EFT began life as the Empire Palace Theatre, hosting the biggest old-time variety stars. By the mid 1980s, it was another story: then the run-down Empire bingo hall, it suffered the indignity of staging shows by the likes of trash-sleaze merchants the Cramps. However, a 1994 restoration turned it into the most opulent of receiving houses, with one of the biggest dance stages in the UK. Its programme is a mix of dance, opera and large-scale theatrical productions; it's a major venue for opera and dance during the Edinburgh International Festival.

Escapes & Excursions

Dirleton Castle. *See p293.*

Getting Started

How to leave Edinburgh behind…

Edinburgh's relatively compact size gives the tourist two great advantages. The first is that the city is easy to explore; the second is that it's easy to escape. In less than an hour, you can find yourself in the countryside of **East Lothian**, the fishing villages of **Fife** or the cosmopolitan bustle of **Glasgow**; with a little more time, you can reach corners of Scotland that are the closest Britain comes to genuine wilderness.

In the following pages, we concentrate on Glasgow, in the midst of a cultural renaissance that's been building for nigh on 15 years. On a less frenetic note, we highlight the attractions of the Lothians, Stirling and Fife, and offer hints about how to get further afield.

PLANNING A TRIP

The **Edinburgh & Lothians Tourist Board** (*see p310*) can provide information on travel, sightseeing and accommodation throughout Scotland. If you're planning on heading into the wilds, it's worth investing in good maps from Ordnance Survey (OS), which has the whole of Great Britain mapped in intimate detail. The two series likely to prove of greatest use are the Landranger (scale 1:50,000) and the Explorer (scale 1:25,000); buy them at TSO Scotland (71 Lothian Road, South Edinburgh, 659 7036, www.tso.co.uk) and most major bookshops.

Getting around

Many of Scotland's more rural regions are ill-served by public transport. Driving is often the best option and sometimes the only option. For details of car hire firms, *see p303*.

The rail system provides a network of trains to most of the larger towns. First Scotrail (*see p302*) sells a variety of flexible travel passes that allow you to roam by train, bus and ferry, chief among them the **Freedom of Scotland Travelpass** (£111 for four days' travel over an eight-day period, or £148 for eight days' travel over 15 consecutive days). The **Central Scotland Rover** (£32 for three days' travel over a seven-day period) covers a more limited area. If you're heading to the Highlands, invest in an eight-day **Highland Rover** pass (£72 for four days' travel, including ferries to, and bus

travel on, Mull and Skye) and discover parts of Scotland that aren't accessible by car.

Bus travel is another possibility, although bear in mind that services in more remote areas may be as infrequent as twice a week. Buses from Edinburgh usually depart from St Andrew Square Bus Station (*see p302*).

Precautions

Scotland's mountain scenery is one of the country's greatest assets, but is also potentially dangerous for hillwalkers and climbers who do not observe these basic safety precautions.

► Don't overestimate your ability and fitness.
► Always tell someone where you're going and what time you plan to get back.
► Take a map, a compass and a torch.
► Wear suitable footwear and always carry waterproof clothing.
► Carry a water bottle and emergency rations.
► Pay close attention to the weather, which can change very quickly; if it looks like turning bad, get off the mountain.

If you're travelling to the Highlands, prepare for midges, tiny flying insects with a voracious appetite for human blood. Midges breed on boggy ground and prefer still days, and are at their worst between late May and early August. No one has yet found a repellent for them that works; however, they are deterred by citronella and herb oils such as thyme or bog myrtle.

Glasgow

…And never the twain shall meet.

The marketing wizards have tried to sell Glasgow in various ways. Campaigns to pep up its image started in 1983 with 'Glasgow's Miles Better', before 'Glasgow's Alive' and, since 2004, 'Glasgow: Scotland with Style'. The gradual shift in emphasis is telling. 'Glasgow's Miles Better' was an attempt to reboot the self-respect of a city devastated by industrial decay. Then, though, came millions of pounds of investment, bringing new attractions, bars, restaurants and plush apartment blocks. The more recent slogan is more confident and outward-looking, much like the city itself.

It's not, though, much like Edinburgh. While the Scottish capital is calmer, prettier and more genteel, Glasgow is brasher, tougher and livelier. Visitors and locals both have their preferences, but one city makes more sense when seen next to the other. Taken together, they're a scintillating pair.

INTRODUCTION

The shipbuilding and heavy industry that underpinned it may have gone, but no matter. Glasgow has changed with the times, growing into an enclave for the cultured and creative, and offering its own range of urban diversions and possibilities. Between 1990, when it was nominated European City of Culture, and 1999, when it was appointed UK City of Architecture and Design, Glasgow spent serious time and money on remodelling, redirection and rebranding, a process that continues. A dark period of post-war and post-industrial decline, with the associated unemployment and poverty, was painstakingly shifted into a brighter future of high-tech business, service-based commerce and hyperactivity in the arts and media.

These days, the city is image-conscious to the point of vanity. At the upper end of the market, there's an infatuation with designer clothing, while at the lower end lies an obsession with curing the natural pallor: Glasgow has dozens of tanning salons, and fake tan is far from unknown. In similar fashion, many of the changes in the city in recent years have been cosmetic. The old problems haven't been wholly solved: they've just been pushed to outer estates and overspill towns as the centre becomes busily middle-class. The conditions in certain peripheral areas are still defined by chronic deprivation and startlingly low life expectancy.

Glasgow's history of sectarianism, a lingering product of antagonism between Irish Catholic and Scottish Protestant workers and unions, still finds ugly expression in the 'Old Firm' football clashes between Celtic and Rangers. But any fears that the city might be forgetting its long traditions of industriousness, socialism, free-thinking and fun-loving have so far proved unfounded. Glasgow always adapts to the times, but its physical character remains essentially unchanged, a compact grid of grand, bold architecture graced in places by the magnificent work of Charles Rennie Mackintosh and Alexander 'Greek' Thomson.

Glasgow's personality remains progressive, curious, innovative and sociable. Entertainment

---

INSIDE TRACK EASY ACCESS

During the week, trains run in both directions between Edinburgh Waverley and Glasgow Queen Street stations every 15 minutes from 6.30am until 7.30pm, then every half-hour until 11.30pm. The journey usually takes around 50 minutes. There are fewer trains at weekends, but you still won't have to wait too long at either end. For more on travelling to and from the city, *see p290*.

Glasgow

Scotland St School
Museum of Education

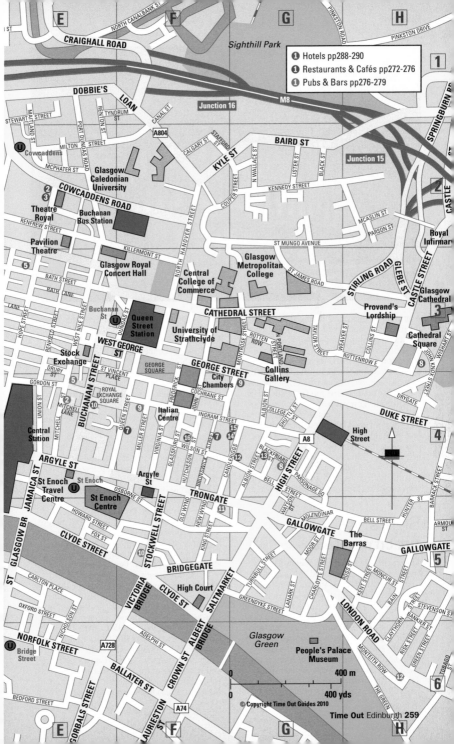

Sighthill Park

1 Hotels pp288-290
1 Restaurants & Cafés pp272-276
1 Pubs & Bars pp276-279

CRAIGHALL ROAD

NORTH CANAL BANK ST

Junction 16

M8

DOBBIE'S LOAN

CANAL ST

A804

KYLE ST

BAIRD ST

Junction 15

Cowcaddens

COWCADDENS ROAD

Glasgow Caledonian University

Theatre Royal

Buchanan Bus Station

KENNEDY STREET

St Mungo Avenue

Pavilion Theatre

KILLERMONT ST

Glasgow Royal Concert Hall

Central College of Commerce

Glasgow Metropolitan College

Royal Infirmary

Buchanan St

Queen Street Station

CATHEDRAL STREET

Glasgow Cathedral

Provand's Lordship

Stock Exchange

WEST GEORGE ST

University of Strathclyde

ROTTENROW E

Cathedral Square

GEORGE STREET

GEORGE SQUARE

City Chambers

Collins Gallery

DUKE STREET

ROYAL EXCHANGE SQUARE

Italian Centre

INGRAM STREET

High Street

Central Station

ARGYLE ST

WILSON ST

A8

BLACKFRIARS ST

PARSONAGE SQ

St Enoch Travel Centre

St Enoch

Argyle St

St Enoch Centre

TRONGATE

GALLOWGATE

The Barras

GALLOWGATE

CLYDE STREET

STOCKWELL STREET

BRIDGEGATE

High Court

CLYDE ST

SALTMARKET

LONDON ROAD

Victoria Bridge

Albert Bridge

Glasgow Green

People's Palace Museum

NORFOLK STREET

Bridge Street

BALLATER ST

A74

0   400 m

0   400 yds

© Copyright Time Out Guides 2010

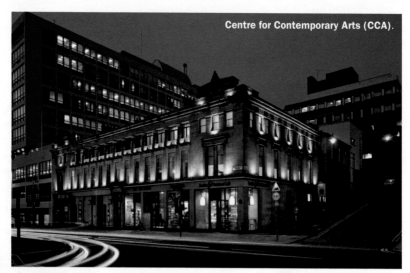

Centre for Contemporary Arts (CCA).

is prized and thrillingly indulged every night of the week, without any of the self-consciousness that can make hip city-dwellers reluctant to be seen having a good time. A night in the Ben Nevis bar (*see p278*), listening to awesomely talented folk musicians, is just as worthwhile an experience as clubbing at the Soundhaus (*see p285*), tuned to awesomely talented DJs.

While Glasgow's reputation for toughness and drunkenness isn't unjustified, neither are reports of its good humour and friendliness, and the frank, realist brand of joie de vivre that permeates the character of the city's residents is infectious. Outsiders often imagine a huge rivalry between Edinburgh and Glasgow, but, in truth, both cities are happy to get on with their own lives in their very different ways.

Sights

THE CITY CENTRE

The wealth generated by Glasgow's once-dominant place in the world of trade and commerce transformed the semi-rural city into one of the most elegant urban centres in Scotland. It's a small but tidy arrangement of decorative stone canyons, laid out in an easily negotiable grid that dates to Victorian times.

The heart of Glasgow is **George Square**, a former swamp first laid out in the late 18th century; it's benefited handsomely from renovation and today looks in good shape. The square's centrepiece is a soaring statue of Sir Walter Scott; it's not as grand as the tribute

paid to him in Edinburgh's Princes Street Gardens, but it's impressive all the same. Robert Burns, William Gladstone and Queen Victoria are commemorated in other statues around the square. The most notable building is the magnificent **City Chambers** to the east: opened by Queen Victoria in 1888, it's a potent reminder of Glasgow's former importance in the British Empire. The square hosts a year-round programme of public events, including the city's rowdy Hogmanay celebrations.

Queen Street station sits at the north-west side of George Square, with Buchanan Street underground adjacent. **Buchanan Street** itself is a major shopping drag, a pedestrianised road that pulses with activity on weekends.

Following Buchanan Street north past the vast **Buchanan Galleries** mall (*see p279*) and the **Royal Concert Hall** (*see p283*), you'll connect with busy **Sauchiehall Street**, a boring commercial thoroughfare at its eastern extremity but increasingly interesting the further west you walk along it. As you do so, stop in at the **Willow Tea Rooms** (no.217, 0141 332 0521, www.willowtearooms.co.uk): commissioned by the formidable Kate Cranston, a pioneer of the art tearoom society prevalent in 19th-century Glasgow, it was designed by Charles Rennie Mackintosh and remains a beautiful spot. Close by, the **Centre for Contemporary Arts** (CCA; *see right*) is housed in a building by Alexander 'Greek' Thomson, Glasgow's other visionary architect, and is now one of the UK's most stylish venues for visual and performance art. This section of the street is also home to a number of decent bars and music venues, among them the **ABC** (*see p284*) and **Nice 'n' Sleazy** (*see p276*).

A sharp incline to the north leads up **Garnethill**, a mainly residential area that's the centre of Glasgow's small Chinese community. The **Glasgow School of Art** (*see p262*), Mackintosh's masterpiece, balances on this perilously steep hill; the view south from here takes in the exotic spire of the **St Vincent Street Free Church**, another Thomson construction. Even today, these two great architects still battle for mastery of Glasgow's skyline. Further west are two other notable sights: **Garnethill Synagogue** (129 Hill Street), the oldest Jewish place of worship in the city, and **Tenement House** (*see p262*).

Back at Buchanan Street, you're within easy reach of two of the city's more engaging cultural institutions. To the east, dominating handsome **Royal Exchange Square**, is the **Gallery of Modern Art** (GOMA; *see right*). And just off to the west on Mitchell Lane is the first public building designed by Charles Rennie Mackintosh, constructed in 1895 to house the offices of the *Glasgow Herald*. An ultramodern makeover has transformed it into the **Lighthouse**, an architecture and design centre (*see p262*).

Centre for Contemporary Arts (CCA)

350 Sauchiehall Street (0141 352 4900, www. cca-glasgow.com). Cowcaddens underground. **Open** *Centre* 10am-11pm Tue-Thur; 10am-midnight Fri, Sat. *Gallery* 11am-6pm Tue-Sat. **Admission** free. **Credit** MC, V. **Map** p258 D2.

Since 1992, the CCA has hosted challenging work in the fields of visual arts, music and performance. Six major exhibitions a year, with art from home and abroad, are supplemented by adventurous live music, DJ nights in its Scott Street Bar, studio theatre shows and arthouse movies. The café has a courtyard feel.
▶ *Glasgow School of Art is just around the corner; see p262.*

★ FREE Gallery of Modern Art (GOMA)

Queen Street (0141 287 3050, www.glasgow museums.com). Buchanan Street underground or Queen Street rail. **Open** 10am-5pm Mon-Wed, Sat; 10am-8pm Thur; 11am-5pm Fri, Sun. **Admission** free. **Map** p259 E4.

The traffic cone now almost permanently attached to the equestrian statue of the Duke of Wellington

Gallery of Modern Art (GOMA).

ESCAPES & EXCURSIONS

gives a neat Glaswegian touch to the classical grandeur of the Gallery of Modern Art, widely known as GOMA to locals. Built in 1778, the Cunningham Mansion was previously used as a town house for a tobacco baron and as offices for the Royal Bank of Scotland. Today, it's the second most visited contemporary art gallery in the UK outside London. The permanent collection contains works by Scots such as John Bellany, Christine Borland, Ken Currie and Douglas Gordon, but also major international artists; it's supplemented by first-class touring shows.

Glasgow School of Art

167 Renfrew Street (0141 353 4500, www.gsa. ac.uk). Cowcaddens underground or Charing Cross rail. **Tours** *Apr-Sept* 10am, 11am, noon, 2pm, 3pm, 4pm, 5pm daily. *Oct-Mar* 11am, 3pm Mon-Sat. **Admission** £7.75; £3.75-£5.75 discounts; free under-10s; £19.75 family. **Credit** AmEx, MC, V. **Map** p258 D2.

An icon of 20th-century design and arguably the world's first modernist building, Mackintosh's masterpiece is full of surprising details. The best angles are around the façades of the north and west wings. The interior is open only for tours, for which reservations are required, but it's well worth booking for a stroll that takes in the extraordinary library.

Lighthouse

11 Mitchell Lane (0141 221 6362, www.thelighthouse.co.uk). Buchanan Street or St Enoch underground, or Central Station rail. **Open** 10.30am-5pm Mon, Wed-Sat; 11am-5pm Tue; noon-5pm Sun. **Admission** £4; £1.50-£2 discounts. **Credit** MC, V. **Map** p259 E4.

Tucked away down an alleyway off Buchanan Street, Mackintosh's *Glasgow Herald* building is now the Centre for Architecture, Design & the City, and its programme of exhibitions and events continues to make it an exciting part of the cultural scene. The well-contextualised Mackintosh Interpretation Centre ('the Mack') leads to a daunting helical staircase that offers views over the whole city; the Doocot café-bar is a cut above your average arts venue café.

Tenement House

145 Buccleuch Street (0141 333 0183, www.nts.org.uk). Cowcaddens underground or Charing Cross rail. **Open** *Mar-Oct* 1-5pm daily. **Admission** £5.50; £4.50 discounts; free under-5s; £15 family. **No credit cards.** **Map** p258 C2.

The former home of Miss Agnes Toward, an ordinary Glaswegian shorthand typist, offers a remarkable glimpse into late Victorian home life, with its bed recesses in the kitchen and lounge and perfectly preserved knick-knacks. An exhibition on the ground floor about tenement life, the clearance of the slums and the city's continuing gentrification gives a real insight into Glasgow's journey.

THE MERCHANT CITY

Spreading away from the south-east of George Square, the Merchant City was developed in the 18th century by the city's sugar and tobacco traders, who conducted their business on the nearby River Clyde and built mansions here in order to make their daily commute easier. In the 19th century, a number of markets sprung up in the area, before it steadily declined. However, the boom years of the '90s spurred a revival, spawning new bars, cafés, boutiques, arts venues and expensive apartment conversions.

Running east from Royal Exchange Square, **Ingram Street** connects the Merchant City to the centre proper. The street and those surrounding it are dotted with high-fashion boutiques such as **Ralph Lauren** and **Cruise** (*see p281*); while neighbouring Buchanan Street is dominated by fairly familiar chains, the Merchant City offers more exclusive – and, it follows, expensive – shopping opportunities. A few streets east is **Candleriggs**, home to a number of restaurants and bars. And just past it is the old **Glasgow City Halls** complex, now enjoying a new lease of life as a concert venue (*see p283*). One of its halls was built as a market in the 19th century; its name, the Old Fruitmarket, pays homage to its history.

To the south, more or less parallel to Ingram Street, lies the slightly ragged but still imposing **Trongate**. The obvious 16th-century clock tower belongs to vital local playhouse the **Tron Theatre** (*see p287*), built as a church. In autumn 2009, the arrival of **Trongate 103** (www.trongate103.com) gave the city's arts scene its biggest shot in the arm for years. An £8.5-million revival of a six-storey Edwardian warehouse, it occupies virtually an entire city block. Organisations calling it home include the **Transmission Gallery** (0141 552 7141, www.transmissiongallery.org), the **Glasgow Print Studio** (0141 552 0704, www.gpsart.co. uk), **Street Level Photoworks** (0141 552 2151, www.streetlevelphotoworks.org) and the incredible **Sharmanka Kinetic Theatre** (0141 552 7080, www.sharmanka.com). Behind Trongate 103, Parnie Street and nearby Chisholm Street are composed of an eye-catching fusion of red and yellow sandstone tenements and dotted with an unlikely mix of shops: if you want to get a tattoo, browse some rare comics or buy a tropical fish, you're in luck.

Head west on the Trongate and it becomes **Argyle Street**, the shabbiest of Glasgow's big shopping thoroughfares. The **Argyle Arcade**, an airy Victorian glass-roofed passageway lined with jewellers' shops, hooks off Argyle Street to the north and connects with Buchanan Street. However, there's more of interest to the south: gentrification has been slower to arrive in the

Lighthouse.

roads and alleys below Argyle Street and the Trongate, and Old Glasgow remains appealingly tangible. Nowhere is this more the case than in the three pubs that make up the Stockwell Triangle on Stockwell Street, chief among them the 18th-century **Scotia** (*see p277*). Together, this trio almost gives off a more palpable, atmospheric sense of Glasgow's history than any of the city's museums.

At the eastern end of the Trongate, at its intersection with High Street, Gallowgate, London Road and Saltmarket, is **Glasgow Cross**. The junction is marked by the seven-storey **Tolbooth Steeple**, formerly part of the city's long-vanished Tolbooth. It's the point at which the City Centre becomes the East End.

THE EAST END

Although Glasgow has redefined itself many times over the centuries, it's tended to do so while moving west, leaving a rich vein of history in its wake. From the earliest records of Glasgow Cathedral in 1136 through to the wealth-driven expansions of the 19th century, the East End essentially was Glasgow. And it is in the East End, with all its adversity and good humour, that the Glaswegian spirit persists.

Glasgow's origin myth says it was founded at the point where the Molendinar Burn flowed into the Clyde, now the site of the High Court. Opposite the court stands the **McLennan Arch**, which originally formed part of Robert Adam's Assembly Rooms. When the rooms were demolished, local MP James McLennan funded their reconstruction in the Barras. The arch was moved to its present location in 1922, and now marks the entrance to Glasgow Green.

Dating back to the 15th century, when King James II designated the land as grazing ground, **Glasgow Green** is Europe's oldest public park. It once doubled as a fairground and a hanging place; these days, the public events it hosts – Proms in the Park, say – are more sedate. The **People's Palace** and the **Winter Gardens** (*see p265*) are the main permanent attractions. Just north of the Green, meanwhile, is **St Andrew's in the Square** (0141 559 5902, www.standrewsinthesquare.com), a former church that now hosts concerts and a decent café-bar, Café Source.

Edging further north, the twin thoroughfares of Gallowgate and London Road form part of the boundary of the **Barras**, Glasgow's monumental weekend market (*see p279*). Next door is the legendary **Barrowland** ballroom (*see p284*). The gigantic neon sign outside the venue was temporarily removed during World War II, when it was realised that German bombers were using it as a guiding light. And up the High Street, north of Gallowgate, sit **Glasgow Cathedral**, **Provand's Lordship**, the **Necropolis** and the **St Mungo Museum of Religious Life & Art** (for all, *see below and right*). This little corner is all that gives an impression of medieval Glasgow, and seems increasingly strange and wonderful amid the 21st-century metropolis that surrounds it.

★ FREE Glasgow Cathedral

Castle Street (0141 552 6891, www.glasgow cathedral.org.uk). High Street rail. **Open** *Apr-Sept* 9.30am-5pm Mon-Sat; 1-5pm Sun. *Oct-Mar* 9.30am-4pm Mon-Sat; 1-4pm Sun. **Admission** free. **Map** p259 H3.

People's Palace & Winter Gardens.

Before it developed a reputation for commerce, Glasgow was known as an ecclesiastical town. Pilgrims came here to visit the tomb of St Mungo, who's said to have founded a church at the site of the modern cathedral in the late sixth century (supposedly the same site as a fifth-century Christian burial ground). The earliest parts of the current building date back 800 years or more, though it was regularly amended and extended through to the 19th century. The exterior is grimy, but it's still an impressive example of Gothic architecture.

▶ *If you want to stay in this part of town, try the Cathedral House Hotel; see p289.*

★ FREE Necropolis

Glasgow Necropolis Cemetery, 50 Cathedral Square (0141 552 3145). High Street rail. **Open** 24hrs daily. **Admission** free.

The first interdenominational 'hygienic' graveyard in Scotland was inspired by the famed Père Lachaise cemetery in Paris. The first burial took place in 1832; years later, it's now a deeply atmospheric place, dotted with the ornate but now-crumbling tombs of Glasgow's great and good.

FREE People's Palace
& Winter Gardens

Glasgow Green (0141 276 0788, www.glasgow museums.com). Bridgeton rail. **Open** 10am-5pm Mon-Thur, Sat; 11am-5pm Fri, Sun. **Admission** free. **Map** p259 G6.

Built in 1898, the red sandstone People's Palace originally served as a municipal and cultural centre for the city's working classes. It now houses a cherished exhibition that covers all aspects of Glaswegian life, but pays particular attention to the city's social and industrial history since the mid 18th century. The adjoining Winter Gardens is one of the most elegant Victorian glasshouses in Scotland. Just outside the palace is the Doulton Fountain: built to celebrate Queen Victoria's rule over the Empire, it's the largest terracotta fountain in the world.

FREE Provand's Lordship

3 Castle Street (0141 552 8819, www.glasgow museums.com). High Street rail. **Open** 10am-5pm Mon-Thur, Sat; 11am-5pm Fri, Sun. **Admission** free. **Map** p259 H3.

Glasgow's oldest house, built in 1471, is a delightful refuge on wet afternoons. A well-worn staircase leads to a homely recreation of the former Bishop's bedroom; a physic garden provides some meditative calm away from the din of cars outside.

FREE St Mungo Museum of Religious Life & Art

2 Castle Street (0141 276 1625, www.glasgow museums.com). High Street rail. **Open** 10am-5pm Mon-Thur, Sat; 11am-5pm Fri, Sun. **Admission** free. **Map** p259 H3.

Glasgow's ugly sectarianism is quickly forgotten in this wide ranging museum that investigates how different cultures have dealt with life's most fundamental concerns. Temporary exhibitions provide further food for thought, engaging with modern problems from other cultures. There's also a Zen garden here.

THE WATERFRONT

Essentially where Glasgow began when St Mungo settled here in the sixth century, the **River Clyde** is where the city is most visibly regenerating itself. A stroll along its banks offers insights into how today's city fathers would like to see Glasgow continue to grow.

Along the north bank, the **Clyde Walkway** runs underneath the numerous city-centre bridges. You can pick it up at the west end of Glasgow Green, then head westwards along Clyde Street, then the Broomielaw, and Anderston and Lancefield Quays, until you arrive at the city's sci-fi riverside landmarks.

Among the new apartment blocks, the **Clyde Arc**, also known as the 'Squinty Bridge', opened in 2006, the first new river crossing for 37 years. Not controversy-free, it closed for some months in 2008 because of cable damage, but it's a handsome piece of contemporary design all the same. On the north side of the river nearby sits evidence of Glasgow's industrial heritage in the shape of the huge **Finnieston Crane**, completed in 1932, while the **Clyde Auditorium** (*see p284*), almost in the crane's shadow, takes the area back to the future. Inevitably nicknamed 'the Armadillo', it's an impressive building, but its hard, funky glisten was later eclipsed by the spectacular shine of the **Glasgow Science Centre** (*see p266*), across the Clyde at Pacific Quay.

Directly adjacent to the Science Centre stands the sleek, 127-metre **Glasgow Tower**, the tallest free-standing structure in the city and also the only building on the planet that can rotate 360 degrees. It affords unsurpassed views but, like its Squinty Bridge neighbour, has not enjoyed a trouble-free life. Since 2007, Pacific Quay has also hosted the state-of-the-art headquarters of BBC Scotland, adding to the forward-looking feel of the area.

ESCAPES & EXCURSIONS

Glasgow Waterfront.

Back on the north side of the river, and a little further west, you come to another historical remnant: the **Tall Ship at Glasgow Harbour** (*see right*), the SV *Glenlee*, one of the few Clyde-built sailing ships still in existence. If all goes according to plan, it will have a slick new neighbour from 2011: the **Riverside Museum**, a replacement for the **Museum of Transport** at Kelvin Hall (*see p271*). Around this stretch of the Clyde, look out for the **Waverley** (0845 130 4647, www.waverley excursions.co.uk). The world's only sea-going paddle steamer, it takes passengers for pleasure cruises 'doon the watter'.

Clydebuilt

King's Inch Road, Braehead (0141 886 1013, www.scottishmaritimemuseum.org). Bus 23, 101. **Open** 10am-5.30pm Mon-Sat; 11am-5.30pm Sun. **Admission** £4.25; £2.50-£3 discounts; family £10. **No credit cards.**
One of the Scottish Maritime Museum's three sites (the others are at Dumbarton and Irvine), Clydebuilt tells the worthwhile, intertwined story of Glasgow and the Clyde, from trading to shipbuilding.

INSIDE TRACK TAKE-OFF!

The last word in Glasgow transport is provided by **Loch Lomond Seaplanes** (08702 421457, www.lochlomondsea planes.com), which has a floating dock by the Science Centre. From March to November, it offers flights in its small seaplane to Oban Bay (25 minutes), Tobermory Bay on Mull (35 minutes) and tours over the Clyde and Argyll (45 minutes). Taking off from the water in the heart of Glasgow is a thrill.

★ Glasgow Science Centre

Pacific Quay (0141 420 5000, www.glasgow sciencecentre.org). Exhibition Centre rail. **Open** *Science Mall* 10am-5pm daily. *IMAX* times vary. **Admission** *Science Mall* £8.25; £6.25 discounts. *Planetarium, Tower, IMAX* £2.50 each. *IMAX feature* £8.95; £6.95 discounts. **Credit** MC, V.
This futuristic titanium and glass structure boasts three stimulating floors of hands-on science and technology exhibits as part of the Science Mall. Since opening in 2001, it's become deservedly popular with kids and armchair scientists for its well-run displays and its excellent planetarium. The centre also houses an IMAX cinema, and the adjacent Glasgow Tower offers the very best views in the city.

Tall Ship at Glasgow Harbour

Stobcross Road (0141 222 2513, www.thetall ship.com). Exhibition Centre rail. **Open** *Mar-Oct* 10am-5pm daily. *Nov-Feb* 11am-4pm daily. **Admission** £5.95; £4.65 discounts. **Credit** MC, V. **Map** p258 A4.
The SV *Glenlee* is one of only five Clydebuilt sailing ships that remain afloat. Launched in 1896, she stands as an impressive reminder of the Clyde's shipbuilding legacy. The accompanying exhibitions explore what life was like on the open seas, touching on everything from pirates to mermaids.

THE SOUTH SIDE

The West End may be the city's bohemian quarter, but Glasgow's sprawling South Side is much more cosmopolitan: diverse, fascinating and under-visited. Most of it is residential, from distant and affluent districts such as **Newton Mearns** to less monied housing estates like **Castlemilk**. The area also boasts several notable cultural institutions, chief among them the **Citizens' Theatre** and the challenging **Tramway** in Pollokshields. For both, *see p287*.

Some of the best examples of Alexander 'Greek' Thomson's architecture stand on the South Side, among them the Acropolis-inspired **Caledonia Road Church** (1856) off Cathcart Road. A fire in 1965 destroyed the painted interior, leaving only the portico and tower intact. In 2009, a proposal was put forward that would see part of the building become a centre to celebrate Thomson's work, but it's a long way from confirmation, much less completion. The Thomson-designed terraces of Regent Park, in the Strathbungo district, have fared rather better, and have been a designated conservation area since the 1970s. Both Thomson and Mackintosh lived here.

The South Side opens out into several parks; indeed, the city as a whole boasts more parks per head than any other in Europe. Among them is **Bellahouston**, which holds the **House for an Art Lover** (*see p269*), a modern construction based on plans submitted by Mackintosh in 1901. In **Pollok Park**, Glasgow's largest, you'll find the main South Side attractions: **Pollok House** (*see p269*) and the phantasmagorical **Burrell Collection** (*see below*). But most visitors to the South Side are heading to **Hampden**, the national football stadium and venue for Scotland's home games. The stadium contains a museum (*see p269*) with permanent displays and temporary exhibitions on Scottish football's finest moments.

★ FREE Burrell Collection

Pollok Park, 2060 Pollokshaws Road (0141 287 2550, www.glasgowmuseums.com). Pollokshaws West rail. **Open** 10am-5pm Mon-Thur, Sat; 11am-5pm Fri, Sun. **Admission** free.

When Sir William Burrell gave his collection of art and artefacts to the city of Glasgow in 1944, he stipulated it must be kept at least 16 miles from the city centre to prevent it from being covered in soot. The air has improved since he died, and his estate agreed to it being moved to Pollok Park. The collection encompasses treasures from ancient Egypt, Greece and Rome, ceramics from various Chinese dynasties, and an assortment of European decorative arts, including rare tapestries and stained glass. It also boasts one of the finest collections of Impressionist and post-Impressionist paintings and drawings in the world. Come on a sunny day, when the reflected light in the interior glass-roofed courtyard is breathtaking.

FREE Glasgow Museums Resource Centre

200 Woodhead Road, South Nitshill Industrial Estate (0141 276 9300, www.glasgowmuseums. com). Nitshill rail. **Open** *Pre-booked tours only* 2.45pm. **Admission** free.

Space constraints mean that only five per cent of Glasgow Museums' works are displayed at any one time. Much of the remainder are stored in this modern day Aladdin's cave, open for tours to members of the public who book ahead.

Holmwood House

61-63 Netherlee Road, Cathcart (08444 932204, www.nts.org.uk). Cathcart rail. **Open** *Apr-Oct* 1-5pm Mon, Thur-Sun. **Admission** £5.50; £4.50 discounts; £15 family. **No credit cards**.

'Greek' Thomson was given carte blanche by paper mill owner James Couper when designing Holmwood in the middle of the 19th century; the freedom he was granted inspired his most elaborate villa. The richly ornamental classical interior is a testament to his lovable eccentricities.

Glasgow Science Centre.

Sport for All

Glasgow gears up for the Commonwealth Games in 2014.

For a dozen days in the summer of 2014, the Commonwealth Games will sprinkle some fairy dust on Glasgow. Understandably, the games' local organisers are keen to show the world the best of their city. Glasgow already has a great deal of the necessary infrastructure in place, but there are plans to complement the existing venues with new facilities that will, it's hoped, help regenerate downtrodden neighbourhoods, encourage Glaswegians to take up sport and, perhaps, make some impact on the city's woeful health statistics.

Perhaps the most useful development is at Dalmarnock, south-east of the city centre, where an athletes village is being built. After the games, it will be developed as a residential area. Dalmarnock will also be the site for the National Indoor Sports Arena and the Sir Chris Hoy Velodrome, and a new Scottish National Arena by the SECC on the Clyde will be constructed before the games. Last but by no means least, public transport will also be improved.

The origins of the games themselves are interesting, and offer a revealing glimpse at how Britain used to live. The first British Empire Games, as the event was then called, was held in Canada in 1930, and there were two further gatherings before the games' suspension because of World War II. The games resumed in 1954 and went through a couple of name changes until all mention of 'British' was dropped;

the simple and more politically neutral title of the Commonwealth Games has been preferred since 1978.

Even as the remains of the British Empire flew apart, from Indian independence in 1947 to Hong Kong being handed back to China in 1997, a quadrennial sports gathering inspired by that very empire built up an unstoppable head of steam. When Edinburgh hosted the games in 1986, for example, a number of African, Asian and Caribbean nations boycotted the games because of the British government's refusal to impose economic sanctions on South Africa over apartheid. But four years later, it was business as usual.

England, Northern Ireland, Scotland and Wales take part in the games as separate nations, along with an A-Z of existing and former colonies, dominions, mandates, protectorates and other territories from the Commonwealth, a loose association of countries linked by their relationship to the old imperial power. Given the absence of big hitters such as China, Germany, Russia and the US, a Commonwealth Games medal doesn't carry the weight of its Olympic or World Championship equivalent. But bringing together top performers from the UK, Africa, Australia, Canada, the Caribbean, India, New Zealand and beyond, results in a competitive spectacle that merits its place on the international calendar.

▶ *For more on the games, see www.glasgow2014.com.*

Plans for the new velodrome.

House for an Art Lover
Bellahouston Park, 10 Dumbreck Road (0141 353 4770, www.houseforanartlover.co.uk). Dumbreck rail. **Open** times vary. **Admission** £4.50; £3 discounts. **Credit** MC, V.

Built according to plans Mackintosh submitted to a German architecture competition in 1901, the House for an Art Lover was completed in 1996 to mixed reactions. Externally, it has stark Modernist curves; inside, though, the grids and flowers seem more Mockintosh than Mackintosh.

Pollok House
Pollok Park, 2060 Pollokshaws Road (0844 493 2204, www.glasgowmuseums.com). Pollokshaws West rail. **Open** 10am-5pm daily. **Admission** £5.50; £4.50 discounts; £21 family. **Credit** MC, V.

This magnificent 18th-century mansion displays the Stirling Maxwell collection of Spanish and European paintings, including beautiful works by Goya, El Greco and Murillo. The highlight, though, is William Blake's exquisite tempera painting of Chaucer's Canterbury pilgrims.

FREE Scotland Street School Museum
225 Scotland Street (0141 287 0500, www.glasgowmuseums.com). Shields Road underground. **Open** 10am-5pm Mon-Thur, Sat; 11am-5pm Fri, Sun. **Admission** free. **Map** p258 B6.

A Mackintosh treat, this majestic school building is now a museum offering an insight into Glaswegian schooling in the first half of the 20th century. It presents a detailed look at the architectural plans of Mackintosh's final commission in Glasgow, showing how he added numerous ornamental details once the drafts had been approved (much to the understandable annoyance of the School Board).

Scottish Football Museum
National Stadium, Hampden (0141 616 6139, www.scottishfootballmuseum.org.uk). King's Park or Mount Florida rail. **Open** 10am-5pm Mon-Sat; 11am-5pm Sun. **Admission** *Museum* £6; £3 discounts; free under-5s. *Stadium tour* £6; £3 discounts; free under-5s. **Credit** MC, V.

This display of Scottish football history is comprehensive to the point of obsession, documenting all the players, kits and trophies since 1867 – you even get to see the dressing rooms. While the Scottish national side hasn't reached any international finals for more than a dozen years, hope springs eternal.

THE WEST END

Beginning at the huge dome and imposing façade of the Mitchell Library just beyond the M8 motorway, the West End has a character all of its own: it's Glasgow all right, but it doesn't seem to fit with the rest of the city. Leafy, hilly, prettier and lazier than the city's other quarters,

the West End remains a middle-class enclave, populated mainly by students, rich folks and creative types. A high-quality range of bars, coffee shops, delis and record stores cater for most of their tastes.

The main artery through the West End is the long, straight **Great Western Road**, built in 1836 so Glasgow's bourgeoisie could get out of the crowded, soot-blackened city centre in a hurry. Nowadays, it's often a choked snarl of traffic, heading out past the **Botanic Gardens** (*see below*) and towards Loch Lomond. South of the road sit an array of domestic terraced buildings; from the 19th century, they remain among the city's most beautiful. Flanking Great Western Road, **Great Western Terrace** is perhaps the finest example of such architecture in the city: another Alexander 'Greek' Thomson design from 1867. Just up from here is Devonshire Gardens, where you'll find one of the city's most impressive hotels (*see p289*).

Around a mile to the south-east there are more fine residential streets, **Park Circus** (1857-63) and **Park Terrace** (1855) for example, mere steps away from the eastern reaches of **Kelvingrove Park**. First laid out as pleasure grounds in the 1850s, the park becomes packed on sunny days with dogs, bongo players and cheerful displays of public drunkenness. The **Kelvingrove Art Gallery & Museum** (*see p271*), a striking red Victorian palace, dominates the western end of the park. On those rare evenings when the sunset hits it, Glasgow takes on an exotic, storybook magic.

Just beyond the park is the **University of Glasgow**, whose dark fairytale neo-Gothic tower dominates the West End. The bizarre concrete façade of the Mackintosh House at the **Hunterian Art Gallery** next door (*see p271*) helps shape a strange and beautiful skyline. And just beyond all this is **Byres Road**, the heart of the West End. An assortment of little streets edge off this main thoroughfare, host to a variety of stores selling vintage clothes and unusual gifts. The busiest and most beautiful is **Ashton Lane**, home to the **Grosvenor** cinema and bar complex (*see p282*) and the **Ubiquitous Chip** bar-restaurant (*see p275*).

FREE Botanic Gardens & Kibble Palace
730 Great Western Road (0141 334 2422, www.glasgow.gov.uk). Hillhead underground. **Open** *Palace* Apr-Oct 10am-6pm daily. Nov-Mar 10am-4.15pm daily. *Gardens* 7am-dusk daily. **Admission** free.

Glasgow's Botanic Gardens are dominated by the huge dome of Kibble Palace, a marvel of Victorian engineering restored to its original glory in 2006. Look out, too, for the abandoned railway station, the extensive herb garden and, in summer, concerts.

FREE Fossil Grove

Victoria Park (0141 950 1448, www.glasgow museums.com). Jordanhill rail or 44 bus. **Open** *Apr-Sept* 10am-3.30pm daily. **Admission** free.
The petrified remains of a 300-million-year-old carboniferous forest at Fossil Grove give visitors pause to reflect on the transience of life. Discovered when Victoria Park was created on the site of a disused quarry, the fossils are housed in a Victorian ironwork warehouse, an antique in its own right.

FREE Hunterian Museum & Art Gallery

University of Glasgow, Hillhead Street (0141 330 4221, www.hunterian.gla.ac.uk). Hillhead underground. **Open** *Museum & Art Gallery* 9.30am-5pm Mon-Sat. *Mackintosh House* 9.30am-5pm Mon-Sat. **Admission** free. *Mackintosh House* £3; £2 discounts. **No credit cards**.
The Hunterian is divided into two distinct parts. The museum, amid the Gothic grandeur of the Gilbert Scott building, features dinosaurs, archaeological finds and an engaging hands-on display of Glasgow scientist Lord Kelvin's inventions and experiments. The gallery across the road houses Scotland's largest print collection and some fine Scottish paintings; there's also a room devoted to Whistler. The gallery leads on to the Mackintosh House, which recreates the architect's home in Southpark Avenue.

★ FREE Kelvingrove Art Gallery & Museum

Argyle Street (0141 287 2699, www.glasgow museums.com). Kelvinhall underground or Partick rail. **Open** 10am-5pm Mon-Thur, Sat; 11am-5pm Fri, Sun. **Admission** free.
The Kelvingrove has always been Glasgow's must-see museum; these days, after a 2006 refurbishment, it's in great shape. Cleaned of a century of grime, the impressive atrium sparkles in the light that floods in through the windows. The ground-floor exhibitions cover every subject under the sun, from Darwin and evolution to Doctor Who; on the first floor, masterpieces by Dali, Rembrandt, Van Gogh and Botticelli add up to an embarrassment of riches.

FREE Mitchell Library

North Street (0141 287 2999, www.mitchell library.org). Charing Cross rail. **Open** 9am-8pm Mon-Thur; 9am-5pm Fri, Sat. **Map** p258 C2.
Despite its imposing appearance, the Mitchell is a welcoming place for quiet study and local research. Containing more than one million books and documents, the library also has a huge collection of photographic prints and lithographs that vividly illustrate Glasgow's past.

FREE Museum of Transport

1 Bunhouse Road, Kelvinhall (0141 287 2720, www.glasgowmuseums.com). Partick rail or Kelvinhall underground. **Open** 10am-5pm Mon-Thur, Sat; 11am-5pm Fri, Sun. **Admission** free.

Kelvingrove Art Gallery & Museum.

The Museum of Transport's plans to move to the new Riverside Museum at Glasgow Harbour on the Clyde by 2011 means that the exhibits are suffering disruption as the removal date gets closer. But there are still trains and trams, cars and bikes to ponder, plus the cherished recreation of an old 1930s street. Check the website for updates on the new museum.

Consume

RESTAURANTS & CAFES
The City Centre

★ Brian Maule at the Chardon d'Or
176 West Regent Street (0141 248 3801, www. brianmaule.com). Cowcaddens underground or Charing Cross rail. **Open** noon-2.30pm, 6-10pm Mon-Thur; noon-2.30pm, 6-10.30pm Fri; 6-10.30pm Sat. **Main courses** £23. **Credit** AmEx, MC, V. **Map** p258 D3 **❶ Modern European**
Ayrshire lad trains in France, becomes head chef at Le Gavroche in London, then returns to Scotland to open his own place in 2001. Since its launch, Maule's restaurant has been consistently rated as among the best in the city. The interior is modern, if polite, and the classic cuisine remains confident and unfussy. Try a light bar lunch if the evening menu is beyond the reach of your credit card.

Café Hula
321 Hope Street (0141 353 1660, www.cafe hula.co.uk). Buchanan Street or Cowcaddens underground, or Queen Street rail. **Open** 8am-8pm Mon-Thur; 8am-midnight Fri, Sat. **Main courses** £8. **Credit** AmEx, MC, V. **Map** p259 E2 **❷ Modern European**
Eschewing cutting-edge style in favour of scatter-cushion hippy chic, Café Hula is a decidedly un-Glaswegian eaterie. Food may include the likes of chickpea and chorizo stew, simple pastas and something happily, comfortably vegetarian (goat cheese and Mediterranean vegetables); sandwiches are available for takeaway.

Dragon-i
311-313 Hope Street (0141 332 7728, www. dragon-i.co.uk). Buchanan Street or Cowcaddens underground, or Charing Cross rail. **Open** noon-2pm, 5-11pm Mon-Fri; 5-11pm Sat; 5-10pm Sun. **Main courses** £16. **Credit** MC, V. **Map** p259 E2 **❸ Chinese**
The food at Dragon-i is more Asian-eclectic than straightforward Chinese, but there are no Madame Butterfly design clichés here: the dining room is characterised by rich reds and blues, and dark wood fittings. The wine list shows some thought, and the desserts aren't half bad.
▶ *Like Café Hula on the same street, it's handy for the Theatre Royal; see p287.*

Fifi & Ally
80 Wellington Street (0141 226 2286, www. fifiandally.com). Buchanan Street underground or Queen Street rail. **Open** 9am-6pm Mon, Tue; 9am-11pm Wed; 9am-midnight Thur-Sat. **Main courses** £14. **Credit** AmEx, MC, V. **Map** p258 D4 **❹ Modern European**
Originally a fine café and shop in Princes Square mall, Fifi & Ally proved such a hit that cousins Fiona Hamilton and Alison Fielding opened this second venue in 2007: a plush restaurant with a small café area and another shop. The striking restaurant has long been one of Glasgow's destination diners, serving a mix of dishes (fondue, Moroccan spiced chicken). **Other locations** 51-52 Princes Square, Buchanan Street (0141 229 0386).

Fratelli Sarti
133 Wellington Street (0141 248 2228, www. sarti.co.uk). Buchanan Street underground or Queen Street rail. **Open** 8am-10pm Mon-Thur; 8am-10.30pm Fri, Sat; noon-10pm Sun. **Main courses** £9. **Credit** AmEx, MC, V. **Map** p258 D3 **❺ Italian**
A Glasgow institution, Fratelli Sarti now has several branches in the city, but the deli-and-trat in Wellington Street still retains its appeal as a welcoming and unpretentious place to stop for a plate of pasta and a glass of wine – basic Italian fare made with fresh, flavoursome ingredients.
Other locations 121 Bath Street (0141 204 0440); 42 Renfield Street (0141 572 7000).

Gamba
225a West George Street (0141 572 0899, www. gamba.co.uk). Buchanan Street underground or Queen Street rail. **Open** noon-2.30pm, 5-10.30pm Mon-Sat. **Main courses** £17. **Credit** AmEx, MC, V. **Map** p258 D3 **❻ Seafood**
For years, this unassuming basement joint has been the city's favourite upmarket seafood restaurant. The approach is simple enough: source good raw materials and let their quality shine through. The menu has the odd international twist, but also includes more traditional fare. It's far from cheap, but the pre-theatre menu is decent value.

Ichiban
50 Queen Street (0141 204 4200, www.ichiban. co.uk). St Enoch underground or Argyle Street rail. **Open** noon-10pm Mon-Thur; noon-11pm Fri, Sat; 1-10pm Sun. **Main courses** £8. **Credit** AmEx, MC, V. **Map** p259 F4 **❼ Japanese**
We have Wagamama to thank for the formula: noodles, served in a sparse, modern first-floor room, eaten by diners perched on benches and sharing their table with others. However, Ichiban deserves credit for being the first restaurant to bring the dining style to Scotland back in 1998.
Other locations 184 Dumbarton Road, West End (0141 334 9222).

★ MC @ ABode

ABode Hotel, 129 Bath Street (0141 221 6789, www.abodehotels.co.uk). Buchanan Street or Cowcaddens underground, or Queen Street rail. **Open** noon-2.30pm, 6-10pm Tue-Sat. **Main courses** £20. **Credit** AmEx, MC, V. **Map** p258 D3 ❽ **Modern European**

A contender for the accolade of Glasgow's best restaurant, MC is the brainchild of Michelin-starred chef Michael Caines. There are now six ABodes in the UK and Mr Caines can't be everywhere; fortunately, local boy Craig Dunn is a more than capable head chef. If the carte is beyond your means, the set lunches (£12.95 or £15.95) are more affordable.

Red Onion

247 West Campbell Street (0141 221 6000, www.red-onion.co.uk). Buchanan Street or Cowcaddens underground, or Queen Street rail. **Open** 11am-10pm daily. **Main courses** £14. **Credit** AmEx, MC, V. **Map** p258 D3 ❾ **Modern European**

After travelling the world working as the private chef to a slew of rock stars, John Quigley returned home to open an upmarket restaurant under his own name, before turning his hand to Red Onion in 2005. A flexible place, it offers salads, sandwiches and an eclectic main menu (chicken breast with black pudding, say, or beer-braised shin of beef).

Rogano

11 Exchange Place (0141 248 4055, www.rogano glasgow.com). Buchanan Street or St Enoch underground, or Argyle Street or Queen Street rail. **Open** noon-11pm Mon-Thur; noon-midnight Fri, Sat. **Main courses** £25. **Credit** AmEx, MC, V. **Map** p259 E4 ❿ **Modern European**

This Glasgow classic has a beautiful 1935 art deco interior, created at the same time that the RMS *Queen Mary* was built at Clydebank. Snacks are served at the bar, with a fuller menu offered in the café and the restaurant. Once upon a time, this was the city's premier destination diner; locals still hold it in high esteem, but the decor is the draw for visitors.

Two Fat Ladies

118a Blythswood Street (0141 847 0088, www.twofatladiesrestaurant.com). Buchanan Street or St Enoch underground, or Central Station rail. **Open** noon-3pm, 5-10.30pm Mon-Sat. **Main courses** £18. **Credit** AmEx, MC, V. **Map** p258 D3 ⓫ **Seafood**

The second space from Two Fat Ladies is a modish, contemporary room, buzzing more often than not. As at the original Dumbarton Road operation, the kitchen specialises in seafood. They also run another two West End venues, neither exclusively fishy: the beautiful Two Fat Ladies at the Buttery, and the bistro-like Shandon Belles in its basement.
Other locations 88 Dumbarton Road (0141 339 1944); Two Fat Ladies & Shandon Belles, 652 Argyle Street (0141 221 8188).

The Merchant City & the East End

Arisaig

1 Merchant Square, Candleriggs (0141 553 1010, www.arisaigrestaurant.co.uk). St Enoch underground or Argyle Street rail. **Open** noon-midnight Mon-Sat; 12.30pm-midnight Sun. **Main courses** £11.95. **Credit** AmEx, MC, V. **Map** p259 G4 ⓬ **Scottish**

Named after the coastal chunk of the country south of Mallaig, this is Glasgow's most accessible Scots dining experience. There's a downstairs brasserie, with a bar and restaurant upstairs with an emphasis on fish: try langoustines in garlic butter, then poached hake with sea fennel mash. *Photos p274.*

Café Gandolfi & Bar Gandolfi

64 Albion Street (0141 552 6813, www.cafe gandolfi.co.uk). St Enoch underground, or Argyle Street or High Street rail. **Open** 9am-11.30pm Mon-Sat; noon-11.30pm Sun. **Main courses** £12. **Credit** AmEx, MC, V. **Map** p259 G4 ⓭ **Modern European**

Established back in 1979, this stalwart is as popular as ever. The distinctive L-shaped room is decorated with attractive, tactile wooden furniture by the late, great Tim Stead; the kitchen offers keenly-priced, Scottish-slanted food such as Arbroath smokies. Pop in for a sandwich and a glass of wine, or tuck into three full-on courses of good, solid cooking. Upstairs is the buzzing Bar Gandolfi; a few doors along is Gandolfi Fish. *Photo p277.*
Other locations Gandolfi Fish, 84 Albion Street, Merchant City (0141 552 9475).

City Merchant

97-99 Candleriggs (0141 553 1577, www.city merchant.co.uk). Buchanan Street or St Enoch underground, or Argyle Street or High Street rail. **Open** noon-10.30pm Mon-Sat. **Main courses** £16. **Credit** AmEx, MC, V. **Map** p259 F4 ⓮ **Modern European**

The City Merchant was one of the first restaurants to venture into the Merchant City more than 20 years ago, and has endured while the area has gentrified around it. You can order a decent rib-eye steak, but they also do well with seafood here. The two-course pre-theatre menu (£12) is the economical option; pushing the boat out on the seafood platter for two with extra lobster can get very expensive indeed.

Arisaig. *See p273.*

Dakhin

89 Candleriggs (0141 553 2585, www.dakhin. com). Buchanan Street or St Enoch underground, or Argyle Street or High Street rail. **Open** noon-2pm, 5-11pm Mon-Fri; 1-11pm Sat, Sun. **Main courses** £13. **Credit** AmEx, MC, V. **Map** p259 G4 ⑮ **Indian**

Glasgow has loved its robust Indian food, invariably and inevitably washed down with gallons of lager. More mature Indian restaurants have come to the fore in the last decade, and none have impressed as much as Dakhin. Housed in an open, first-floor room, it specialises in south Indian cuisine. Nearby Dhabba (44 Candleriggs (0141 553 1249, www.thedhabba. com) is the restaurant's north Indian sister business.

Rab Ha's

83 Hutcheson Street (0141 572 0400, www. rabhas.com). Buchanan Street or St Enoch underground, or Argyle Street or High Street rail. **Open** 5.30-10pm daily. **Main courses** £10. **Credit** AmEx, MC, V. **Map** p259 F4 ⑯ **Modern European**

Rab Ha's doubles as a small hotel and bar, but it's best known for its basement restaurant (honey-roast pork, seared duck, rib eye steak) and the derivation of its name: the original Rab Ha', Robert Hall, was a 19th-century Glasgow trencherman whose appetite even inspired children's songs. You can also grab a salad or a burger in the ground-floor bar.

The West End

Ashoka

108 Elderslie Street (0141 221 1761, www. ashokaglasgow.com). Charing Cross or Exhibition Centre rail. **Open** noon-midnight daily. **Main courses** £13. **Credit** AmEx, MC, V. **Map** p258 B2 ⑰ **Indian**

Nothing to do with the chain of the same name, the Ashoka is located just west of the M8. You can come here for karaoke, belly dancing, palm readings and balloons tethered to the table, or you can try the quieter dining area where the food is fresh and includes decent vegetarian choices. A Glasgow Indian experience par excellence since 1982.

Cail Bruich West

725 Great Western Road (0141 334 6265, www.cailbruich.co.uk). Hillhead underground. **Open** noon-3pm, 5-9.30pm Tue-Sat; 12.30-3.30pm, 5-9pm Sun. **Main courses** £17. **Credit** AmEx, MC, V. **Modern European**
A 2008 arrival in the West End, this is a smart, little restaurant with red leather seating, approachable waiting staff and good-value menus (two courses for lunch, pre-theatre: £9.50, £13.50). In the evening, you could try the scallops with fennel and rosti to start, then sirloin with whisky sauce as a main.

Firebird

1321 Argyle Street (0141 334 0594, www.fire birdglasgow.com). Kelvinhall underground. **Open** 11.30am-midnight Mon-Thur; 11.30am-1am Fri, Sat; 12.30pm-midnight Sun. **Main courses** £11. **Credit** MC, V. **Modern European**
Not far from Kelvingrove Park, this bright, open-plan café-bar has funky paintings on its walls and simple but well-executed dishes on its menu, among them fennel-scented leg of lamb. The pizzas are among the best in the city; there are also pasta dishes, salads and specials, all made to order.

★ Mother India

28 Westminster Terrace (0141 221 1663, www. motherindiaglasgow.co.uk). Exhibition Centre rail. **Open** 5-10.30pm Mon, Tue; noon-2.30pm, 5.30-10.30pm Wed, Thur; noon-11pm Fri, Sat; noon-10pm Sun. **Main courses** £12. **Credit** AmEx, MC, V. **Map** p258 A2 ⓭ **Indian**
Often acclaimed as Glasgow's best Indian restaurant, Mother India opened up its basement to create an additional dining space in 2006, dub. Its other Glasgow branch sits opposite the Kelvingrove Art Gallery & Museum; unusually for an Indian restaurant, the café's menu comes tapas-style for sharing. **Other locations** Mother India's Café, 1355 Argyle Street, West End (0141 339 9145).

★ No.16

16 Byres Road (0141 339 2544, www.number16. co.uk). Kelvinhall underground. **Open** noon-2.30pm, 5.30-10pm Mon-Sat; 1-10pm Sun. **Main courses** £15. **Credit** MC, V. **Modern European**
No.16 regularly pops up on 'best of' surveys, satisfying even the most recalcitrant of critics. The menu, French-influenced with international leanings, is a testament to the creativity of chef Grant Neil, who stuck around when ownership changed in 2009. Space is limited, so book ahead for dishes such as hake with tzatziki and basil mash.

La Parmigiana

447 Great Western Road (0141 334 0686, www. laparmigiana.co.uk). Kelvinbridge underground. **Open** noon-2.30pm, 6-11pm Mon-Sat. **Main courses** £16. **Credit** AmEx, MC, V. **Italian**

The Giovanazzi family has been serving yer classic Italian posh nosh since 1978; the only thing to have changed substantially in those three decades is the decor. Come here for grilled langoustines followed by chunky seafood risotto, or perhaps some duck breast. Further tribute to the restaurant's authenticity is paid by the city's Italian residents, some of whom seem to use it as a community centre.

Shish Mahal

66-68 Park Road (0141 334 7899, www.shish mahal.co.uk). Kelvinbridge underground. **Open** noon-2pm, 5-11pm Mon-Thur; noon-11.30pm Fri, Sat; 5-11pm Sun. **Main courses** £10. **Credit** AmEx, MC, V. **Indian**
Since 1964, this curry house has shaped the tastebuds of Glaswegians. The extensive menu contains all the familiar dishes, sometimes because people who've been eating here for decades demand them. The place has a familiarity that Johnny-come-lately competitors can't hope to match, but makeovers have kept the Shish looking contemporary.

The Sisters, Kelvingrove

36 Kelvingrove Street (0141 564 1157, www.thesisters.co.uk). Kelvinhall underground. **Open** noon-2.30pm, 5.30-9pm Tue-Sat; noon-7pm Sun. **Main courses** £17. **Credit** MC, V. **Map** p258 A2 ⓯ **Scottish**
This second establishment run by the two O'Donnell sisters (the other is in suburban Jordanhill) has won over the West End girls and boys. The room is contemporary and smart but by no means stuffy, while the food is modern, Scottish and generally excellent: scallops and black pudding for example, or venison with raspberry and balsamic. **Other locations** 1a Ashwood Gardens, Jordanhill (0141 434 1179).

Stravaigin

28-30 Gibson Street (0141 334 2665, www. stravaigin.com). Kelvinbridge underground. **Open** 5-11pm Tue-Thur; noon-4pm, 5-11pm Fri, Sat; 12.30-4pm, 5-11pm Sun. **Main courses** £16. **Credit** AmEx, MC, V. **Fusion**
The 'think global, eat local' approach to cooking at this basement restaurant and ground-floor café-bar has made it one of Glasgow's leading eateries. The menu is as appealing as it is eclectic: Oaxacacan dressed Shetland crab, say, then Tuscan lamb with cavalo nero, polenta and fig compote. They also have a pub, the Liquid Ship (*see p278*). **Other locations** Stravaigin 2, 8 Ruthven Lane, West End (0141 334 7165).

★ Ubiquitous Chip

12 Ashton Lane (0141 334 5007, www. ubiquitouschip.co.uk). Hillhead underground. **Open** noon-2.30pm, 5.30-11pm Mon-Sat; 12.30-3pm, 6.30-11pm Sun. **Set meal** £34.95 2 courses; £39.95 3 courses. **Credit** AmEx, MC, V. **Scottish**

ESCAPES & EXCURSIONS

The Chip has evolved into a complex of venues since it opened in 1971. At last count, up in Ashton Lane, it had a covered, cobbled courtyard restaurant, a more conventional dining room adjacent, a brasserie, a mezzanine dining space and three pubs. The signature dish is venison haggis as a starter; mains offer solid fare (Aberdeen Angus steak, roast Perthshire pigeon, Scottish-landed lobster).

Vallée Blanche

360 Byres Road (0141 334 3333, www.lavallee blanche.com). Hillhead underground. **Open** noon-2.15pm, 5.30-10.30pm Tue-Fri; 11am-10.30pm Sat; noon-10.30pm Sun. **Main courses** £16. **Credit** AmEx, MC, V. **Modern European**

Once you get up a flight of stairs into this venue, you might think you've found some sort of Alpine lodge. The menu offers starters such as braised pig cheek, and mains like Peterhead-landed halibut or roast lamb. Chef Neil Clark used to be at the acclaimed but now-closed Étain in the City Centre; the food here lives up to the standards he set over there.

PUBS & BARS
The City Centre

Arches Café-Bar

253 Argyle Street (0141 565 1035, www.the arches.co.uk). St Enoch underground or Argyle Street rail. **Open** 11am-midnight Mon-Sat; noon-midnight Sun. *Food served* noon-9pm daily. **Credit** AmEx, MC, V. **Map** p258 D4 ❶

Housed under Central Station, the cavernous Arches is all things to all people: a cultural centre known for its theatre productions (*see p287*), a music venue, a gallery space, an integral part of the city's club scene (*see p285*) and an above-average café-bar. Both the lunchtime and evening menus are extensive, but it's also a good spot for a simple drink or two.

Bar 10

10 Mitchell Lane (0141 572 1448). St Enoch underground or Argyle Street rail. **Open** 10am-midnight daily. *Food served* 10am-7.30pm Mon-Thur; 10am-4.30pm Fri; 10am-6.30pm Sat; noon-6pm Sun. **Credit** MC, V. **Map** p259 E4 ❷

One of Glasgow's original style bars, Bar 10 bears the unmistakable mishmash appearance of having once been something else entirely. Relaxed and perhaps a little down-at-heel, it's loveable nonetheless. A fullish menu is served during the day, but the kitchen winds down in the evenings.

Bunker

193-199 Bath Street (0141 229 1427, www. the bunkerbar.com). Buchanan Street or Cowcaddens underground, or Charing Cross rail. **Open** noon-midnight Mon-Wed; noon-2am Thur-Sat; 12.30pm-midnight Sun. *Food served* noon-9pm daily. **Credit** MC, V. **Map** p258 D3 ❸

Glasgow loves its style bars: it seems as though barely a month passes before someone attempts another variation. It makes the 2003-vintage Bunker an established presence. As the evening progresses, it morphs from café-bar into pre-club hangout.

Griffin

266 Bath Street (0141 331 5171). Cowcaddens underground. **Open** 11am-midnight daily. *Food served* noon-9pm daily. **Credit** AmEx, MC, V. **Map** p258 C2 ❹

This Edwardian-era survivor is made up of an attractive old bar and a couple of adjoining spaces for pub grub. People spill out of the performances at the theatre and come here for a drink; it's also popular with staff from nearby offices after work.

★ Horseshoe

17-19 Drury Street (0141 204 4056, www.horse shoebar.co.uk). St Enoch underground or Argyle Street rail. **Open** 11am-midnight Mon-Sat; 12.30pm-midnight Sun. *Food served* noon-9pm Mon-Sat; 12.30-5pm Sun. **Credit** AmEx, MC, V. **Map** p259 E4 ❺

Very near to Central Station, the Horseshoe is a classic old-school Glasgow bar. There are few nods to the 20th century here, let alone the 21st: customers come for beer and ludicrously cheap pub grub. There's a basic restaurant space upstairs.

Nice 'n' Sleazy

421 Sauchiehall Street (0141 333 0900, www. nicensleazy.com). Cowcaddens underground. **Open** 12.30pm-3.30am daily. *Food served* 12.30-9pm daily. **No credit cards. Map** p258 C2 ❻

Anyone who's anyone on the Glasgow music scene will show their bearded face and skinny frame in here at regular intervals, probably after enjoying the same combination of wicked cocktails, good food and cheap bands downstairs as the rest of us. Not nice, exactly, but not especially sleazy, either – and with brilliant tunes on the sound system.

Variety Bar

401 Sauchiehall Street (0141 332 4449). Cowcaddens underground. **Open** 11am-midnight Mon-Sat; 12.30pm-midnight Sun. **No credit cards. Map** p258 C2 ❼

Looking as though it once imagined itself as a retro American diner but at some point during the redecorations thought better of it, this charismatic and welcoming Sauchiehall Street spot attracts a good pre- and post-gig crowd from the nearby ABC (*see p284*). The daytime atmosphere is less hectic.

The Merchant City & the East End

Babbity Bowster

16-18 Blackfriars Street (0141 552 5055). Buchanan Street underground or Argyle Street or High Street rail. **Open** 11am-midnight Mon-Sat;

12.30pm-midnight Sun. *Food served* noon-10pm Mon-Sat; 12.30pm-10pm Sun. **Credit** AmEx, MC, V. **Map** p259 G4 ❽

You may not get many chances here to bask in the sunshine with a pint, but the tables outside Babbity Bowster's offer such a privilege. Drinks include cask ales and the menu takes in Scottish dishes and the occasional French favourite. The venue also has hotel rooms and a first-floor restaurant (Scottische).

Corinthian

191 Ingram Street (0141 552 1101, www.social animal.co.uk). Buchanan Street or St Enoch underground or High Street rail. **Open** *Lite Bar & Piano Bar* 11am-midnight Mon-Thur, Sun; 11am-3am Fri, Sat. *Food served: Lite Bar* noon-5pm.* **Credit** AmEx, MC, V. **Map** p259 F4 ❾

This entertainment complex is a beautifully extravagant spot. Housed in an ornate Victorian bank (later the High Court), it now contains several bars, a club and a restaurant. If you don't have the time to eat here, at least have a drink in the enormous Lite Bar, resplendent with gold leaf, cornicing and, directly overhead, an enormous glass dome.

★ Scotia

112 Stockwell Street (0141 552 8681, www. scotiabar.net). St Enoch underground or Argyle Street rail. **Open** 11am-midnight Mon-Sat; 12.30pm-midnight Sun. *Food served* noon-3pm Mon-Fri; 12.30-4pm Sat, Sun. **Credit** MC, V. **Map** p259 F5 ❿

Behind Argyle Street, new Glasgow falls apart, and you get a sense of what the city was like a long time ago. Enter the Scotia, and you're transported back to the late 18th century. The wood-panelled walls and old pictures convince you that this is the city's oldest bar, a prime place for music, beer and whisky. ▶ *Along with the Victoria Bar (159 Bridgegate, 0141 552 6040) and the folky Clutha Vaults (167 Stockwell Street, 0141 552 7520), it's part of the Stockwell Triangle, a trio of old-school boozers.*

Tron Theatre Bar

63 Trongate (0141 552 8587, www.tron.co.uk). St Enoch underground or Argyle Street rail. **Open** 10am-6pm Mon; 10am-midnight Tue-Sat; 11am-6pm Sun. *Food served* noon-4pm Mon, Sun; 10am-8pm Tue-Sat. **Credit** MC, V. **Map** p259 F5 ⓫

Although parts of this building date back to the 16th century, it's only been in use as a theatre since 1980. Take your pick between the attractive Victorian restaurant, with its wooden-vaulted ceiling, or the light and bright modern conservatory bar to the side of the building. Either is worth a visit, whether or not you're planning on seeing a play here.

★ West Brewing Company

Binnie Place, off Glasgow Green (0141 550 0135, www.westbeer.com). St Enoch underground or High Street rail. **Open** 10am-11pm Mon-Thur; 10am-midnight Fri, Sat; 11am-11pm Sun. *Food served* 10am-9pm Mon-Sat; 11am-9pm Sun. **Credit** AmEx, MC, V. **Map** p259 H6 ⓬

One of Glasgow's most notable newcomers, the West Brewing Company launched in 2006 in the former Templeton Carpet Factory. The beer, brewed on site, aims for German authenticity, and the pub has a Bavarian theme. The menu has the usual burgers but also throws in the odd German sausage.

ESCAPES & EXCURSIONS

Café Gandolfi. *See p273.*

The West End

★ Ben Nevis

1147 Argyle Street (0141 576 5204). Exhibition Centre rail. **Open** *noon-midnight. Food served noon-6pm daily.* **No credit cards. Map** p258 A2 ⓭

There's no way Ben Nevis could be described as a designer bar, although it was clearly assembled with a kind of Neolithic chic in mind: dark wood and stone abound. With a wide whisky selection, decent beer, music sessions and pub grub, it's a nice surprise at the Kelvingrove end of Argyle Street.

★ Bon Accord

153 North Street (0141 248 4427, www.thebon accord.com). Charing Cross rail. **Open** *11am-midnight Mon-Sat; 12.30-11pm Sun. Food served noon-7.45pm Mon-Sat; 12.30-7.45pm Sun.* **Credit** AmEx, MC, V. **Map** p258 C3 ⓮

Often acclaimed as the best real ale pub in the city, Bon Accord has a healthy selection of beers on tap, all in excellent condition. Other attractions include fine music sessions, decent bar meals and a good range of single malt whiskies served in proper tumblers. The only downside is the location above the M8 motorway, but you won't notice once inside.

★ Chinaski's

239 North Street (0141 221 0061, www. chinaskis.com). Charing Cross rail. **Open** *noon-midnight daily. Food served noon-9pm daily.* **Credit** MC, V. **Map** p258 C2 ⓯

Chinaski's is something of a departure for Glasgow: a style bar that's actually quite stylish, rather than just a glitzy excuse to raise the price of lager. The menu is good, and there's even a pleasant 'bourbon and cigar garden' out the back (bourbon and cigars not mandatory). Heaven knows what Charles Bukowski, from whose writings the bar takes its name, would have made of it. In 2008, the owners opened another venue next door, Black Sparrow (0141 221 5530), which has upped the food ante.

Drawing Room

1055 Sauchiehall Street (0141 339 2999, www. drawingroombar.co.uk). Kelvinhall underground or Partick rail. **Open** *4pm-midnight Mon-Thur; 4pm-1am Fri; noon-1am Sat; noon-midnight Sun. Food served 4-9pm Mon-Thur; 4-10pm Fri; noon-10pm Sat; noon-9pm Sun.* **Credit** MC, V.

Handy for Kelvingrove Art Gallery & Museum, this hard-working bar has a stone-walled, common room feel. It runs an exhibition programme for local artists and also has plays, pub quizzes, live music and food (steaks, burgers, vegetarian curries). Of course, you could also just go for a beer.

Goat

1287 Argyle Street (0141 357 7373, www.the goat.co.uk). Bus 9, 62 or Kelvinhall underground. **Open** *noon-midnight daily. Food served noon-9pm daily.* **Credit** MC, V.

The Goat is essentially a gastropub: drinkers tend to congregate downstairs, leaving the mezzanine area for diners munching on the decent food (including a good bar bites menu). Other selling points include occasional bands and DJs, free Wi-Fi access, and leather sofas on which to lounge and watch the football. An excellent all-rounder.

Lansdowne Bar

7A Lansdowne Crescent (0141 334 4653, www. lansdownebar.co.uk). Bus 59 or Kelvinbridge underground. **Open** *noon-midnight Mon-Sat; 12.30pm-midnight Sun. Food served noon-2pm, 5-9pm Mon-Thur; noon-10pm Fri, Sat; 12.30-8pm Sun.* **Credit** MC, V.

Just off the Great Western Road, the Lansdowne is a basement bar with a modern feel, its decor characterised by clean lines and wooden fittings. The superior pub grub is best enjoyed with a decent pint of Deuchars IPA. Other attractions include occasional DJs and, out back, a conservatory.

Liquid Ship

171 Great Western Road (0141 331 1901, www. stravaigin.com). St George's Cross underground. **Open** *10am-midnight Mon-Sat; 11am-midnight Sun. Food served 10am-10pm Mon-Sat; 11am-10pm Sun.* **Credit** MC, V.

Liquid Ship comes from the same stable of businesses as Stravaigin (*see p275*), which makes the emphasis it places on food no surprise. The menu is more about salads, snacks and platters than sit-down dinners, but is done well all the same. The Ship has also built up a reputation as a music venue.

Lismore

206 Dumbarton Road (0141 576 0102). Bus 8, 16, 20, 62, 64, 89 or Kelvinhall underground. **Open** *11am-midnight daily.* **No credit cards.**

Taking its name from a small Inner Hebridean island, the Lismore is a straightforward, unpretentious and traditional folk music pub with one of the best selections of single malt whisky in Glasgow. The pub's decorative features include stained-glass and references to the Highland Clearances.

Lock 27

1100 Crow Road, Anniesland (0141 958 0853, www.lock27.com). Anniesland rail. **Open** *noon-11pm Mon-Wed; noon-midnight Thur-Sat; 12.30pm-midnight Sun. Food served noon-9pm Mon-Sat; 12.30-9pm Sun.* **Credit** MC, V.

Glasgow has few places to drink alfresco and even fewer by the waterside. Lock 27, then, occupies a fairly privileged niche, sitting on the Forth & Clyde Canal just beyond the West End. It has a fairly extensive menu and bargain wines, but really comes into its own on sunny days.

Òran Mór

Top of Byres Road (0141 357 6200, www.oran-mor.co.uk). Hillhead underground. **Open** 9am-2am Mon-Sat; 11.30am-2am Sun. *Food served* 9am-9pm Mon-Thur, Sun; 9am-10pm Fri, Sat. **Credit** MC, V. The cavernous bar at this converted church at the corner of Byres Road and the Great Western Road is supplemented by some lively arts programming and a worthwhile restaurant. The ceiling mural in the main auditorium was painted by Alasdair Gray, and is one of Glasgow's most extensive pieces of public art. The Play, Pie and a Pint seasons, lunchtime theatre performances where the ticket price includes a pie and a drink, are popular.

SHOPS & SERVICES

Second only to London among UK cities, Glasgow loves to shop. Virtually every one of the country's favourite high-street chains and big department stores are represented, but there are also plenty of independent retailers around town, hawking all manner of specialist goods to the hordes of local shopaholics.

In the **City Centre**, three streets dominate the shopping landscape: **Argyle Street**, which crosses the bottom of **Buchanan Street**, which in turn connects with **Sauchiehall Street**. All three are pedestrianised for much of their extents; a good job, given the massive volume of foot traffic that descends upon them at weekends. The busiest of the trio is Buchanan Street, home to malls, mainstream stores, and a handful of comparatively rare chains such as Diesel and Jones the Bootmaker.

Just east of here, the **Merchant City** is home to the majority of Glasgow's smarter clothing boutiques. Some are operated by individual designers: Emporio Armani and Ralph Lauren both have shops in the area. But others, such as Cruise, stock a wide and almost indiscriminate range of catwalk names.

Standing apart from the heady consumerist familiarity of the City Centre, Glasgow's **West End** has its own commercial buzz, dotted with lively fashion boutiques and unusual gift shops. The main shopping streets are **Byres Road** and the **Great Western Road**, home to a jumble of music shops, clothing stores, grocers' shops and cafés.

One-stop shopping

Glasgow's department stores generally think big, and none think bigger than **House of Fraser** (45 Buchanan Street, 08448 003728, www.houseoffraser.co.uk). The huge Victorian building is home to everything from Juicy Couture shower gel to Vero Moda batwing jumpers and Smeg coffee machines at over £1,000. Frasers represents historical Glasgow

as the business was founded here in 1849, making **John Lewis** (Buchanan Galleries, 0141 353 6677, www.johnlewis.com), here since 1999, a fresh-faced incomer. As well as clothes, the store also has toys, homewares, haberdashery and more. **Debenhams** (97 Argyle Street, 08445 616161, www.debenhams.com) has most basics, while **Marks & Spencer** (2-12 Argyle Street, 0141 552 4546, www.marksandspencer.com) is as popular for its above-average food hall as for its inexpensive undies.

Several large malls dot the city centre, each holding a large number of names familiar to British shoppers from high streets across the UK. The most popular of the malls – and, not coincidentally, the most mainstream – is the shiny **Buchanan Galleries** (220 Buchanan Street, 0141 333 9898, www.buchanangalleries.co.uk), home to the likes of Fred Perry, Phase Eight and the Disney Store. The **St Enoch Centre** (55 St Enoch Square, 0141 204 3900, www.st-enoch.co.uk), Europe's largest glass structure, is similarly stocked with stores such as HMV, H Samuel, Dorothy Perkins and Gap.

Some variation on the mall theme is provided by **Princes Square** (48 Buchanan Street, 0141 221 0324, www.princessquare.co.uk). You'll find Jo Malone, Lacoste and Ted Baker here, but also the less ubiquitous likes of jeweller Dower & Hall, and a Vivienne Westwood outlet. By far the town's most interesting mall isn't really a mall at all: the chain-free **De Courcy's Arcade** (5-21 Cresswell Lane, West End), home to a smile-inducing mix of cafes, vintage record shops and antique stores. (Cresswell Lane runs parallel to the east side of Byres Road, just behind Hillhead underground station.)

Two regular markets merit mention. The **Barras** (244 Gallowgate, 0141 552 4601, www.glasgow-barrowland.com, 10am-5pm Sat & Sun) comes alive with hundreds of traders and shopkeepers offering you – yes, *you!* – the bargain of a lifetime. Sports socks, tea towels, clothes, CDs, DVDs and just about everything else you can think of is on offer, although you might wonder where some of it came from. Even if you have no use for old videos or a polyester bra, it's worth the journey simply to hear the local dialect in full flow. For a less full-on experience, head to the weekend Merchant

---

INSIDE TRACK
SELFRIDGES IN GLASGOW?

For years there has been gossip about the major London department store **Selfridges** opening in Glasgow. The company does own a site in the Merchant City; keep an eye out for progress.

ESCAPES & EXCURSIONS

Explore Britain

Essential ideas for your weekend breaks.

City Market (Merchant Square, Candleriggs, www.merchantsquareglasgow.com, 10am-6pm Sat, noon-6pm Sun) for arts, gifts and gewgaws.

Books

Perhaps surprisingly for a city of its size and stature, Glasgow isn't especially well served by bookshops. The City Centre contains branches of **Borders** (98 Buchanan Street, 0141 222 7700, www.borders.co.uk) and **Waterstone's** (153-157 Sauchiehall Street, 0141 332 9105, www.waterstones.co.uk), both of which should cover most mainstream book needs. The two leading second-hand bookstores in the city are the relatively organised **Caledonia Books** (483 Great Western Road, 0141 334 9663, www.caledoniabooks.co.uk) and the decidedly cluttered **Voltaire & Rousseau** (12-14 Otago Lane, 0141 339 1811).

Fashion

Edinburgh might have Harvey Nichols and Multrees Walk these days, but shoppers in search of designer labels will find a wider range in Glasgow. For starters, head to the Merchant City and **Cruise** (180 Ingram Street, 0141 572 3232; also Cruise Jeans, 223 Ingram Street, 0141 229 0000, www.cruisefashion.co.uk): one of the city's favourite independent retailers, it offers everything from sharp suits to ragged jeans from labels including Dolce & Gabbana, Prada and Burberry. Other options include branches of **Emporio Armani** (19 John Street, 0141 552 2277, www.emporioarmani.com), **Versace** (162 Ingram Street, 0141 552 6510) and **Ralph Lauren** (208 Ingram Street, 0141 242 6000, www.ralphlauren.co.uk).

If all you really want is a good quality suit, head for **Slaters** (165 Howard Street, 0141 552 7171, www.slaters.co.uk). And while Glasgow is better known for fashion-forward clothing than traditional clobber, you can get kitted out in full Highland regalia. Try **Geoffrey (Tailor) Kiltmakers & Weavers** (309 Sauchiehall Street, 0141 331 2388, www.geoffreykilts.co.uk; *see p193*) or **Hector Russell, RG Lawrie Kiltmakers** (110 Buchanan Street, 0141 221 0217, www.hector-russell.com), which hawks everything from cashmere to shortbread.

The city is dotted with independent boutiques. On the top floor of Princes Square and run by two cousins, **Fifi & Ally** (Princes Square, 0141 229 0386, www.fifiandally.com) is the hippest, specialising in casually bohemian clothes, jewellery and more. (For the restaurant, *see p272*.) Other city centre treats include **All Saints** (GPO Building, Ingram Street, 0141 248 6437; 83-85 Buchanan Street, 0141 285 7970; also in House of Fraser, www.allsaints.com),

a fashion label where old meets new (think skinny jeans combined with Victoriana). The West End is also home to a pleasing array of one-off shops. Perhaps chief among them is **Felix & Oscar** (459 Great Western Road, 0141 339 8585, www.felixandoscar.co.uk), great for funky clothing and accessories.

For retro gear in the City Centre, visit **Mr Ben** (Kings Court, 99 King Street, 0141 553 1936, www.mrbenretroclothing.com), where the focus is on 1970s and '80s clothing. Going back in time, the **Victorian Village** (93 West Regent Street, 0141 332 0808) has antique and jewellery shops as well as **Saratoga Trunk**, a vintage clothing emporium. It's just the tip of the iceberg though; to visit the company's warehouse, the source for outfits worn in films such as *Star Wars: The Phantom Menace*, you'll need to make an appointment.

If you're after something more contemporary, try **Aspecto** (18-20 West Nile Street, 0141 248 5349, www.aspecto.co.uk), which stocks sportswear by brands such as Duffer, G-Star and Adidas. **Cult Clothing** (63 Queen Street, 0141 226 6822, www.cult.co.uk) also takes care of Glaswegian's urban style needs, with labels such as AngelEye and Superdry.

If you're looking for jewellery, the best port of call is the **Argyll Arcade** (30 Buchanan Street, 0141 248 5257, www.argyll-arcade.com). Built in 1827, this ornate arcade features 30 jewellery shops, selling antique and cutting-edge pieces. Other options include **Brazen Studios** (58 Albion Street, 0141 552 4551, www.brazen studios.co.uk), which showcases jewellery by some of Britain's best new designers, and **Orro Contemporary Jewellery** (12 Wilson Street, 0141 552 7888, www.orro.co.uk), where the innovative designs are made of anything from platinum to plastic.

Health & beauty

The city's department stores (*see p279*) have a wide selection of cosmetics and fragrances by all the big brands. Large branches of **Boots**, in the St Enoch Centre and Buchanan Galleries, have good ranges, as well as health essentials. For a designer fix from Eve Lom, Stila or REN, go to **Space NK** (Princes Square, 0141 248 7931, www.spacenk.co.uk).

Other chains include **Molton Brown Cosmetics** (59 Buchanan Street, 0141 248 9288, www.moltonbrown.co.uk), ever-colourful **Lush** (116 Buchanan Street, 0141 243 2522; 136 Sauchiehall Street, 0141 333 9912; www.lush.co.uk) and **Neal's Yard Remedies** (11 Royal Exchange Square, 0141 248 4230, www.neals yardremedies.com), which has lots of sweet-smelling jars of potions made with essential oils and herbal extracts. If you prefer the natural

ESCAPES & EXCURSIONS

Monorail.

approach, **Napiers** (61-63 Cresswell Street, 0141 339 5859; www.napiers.net) is well stocked with herbal and homeopathic remedies.

Those in need of pampering are directed to the **Beauty Store** (1 Royal Exchange Court, 0141 204 2244, www.thebeautystore.biz). As well as a full range of beauty treatments, it also offers an extensive selection of luxury cosmetics. Complete your grooming with a haircut at **Taylor Ferguson** (106 Bath Street, 0141 332 0397, www.taylorferguson.com) or **Rainbow Room International** (125 Buchanan Street, 0141 248 5300, www.rainbow roominternational.com). Gents can get the works at the **City Barbers** (99 West Nile Street, 0141 332 7114, www.citybarbers-glasgow.co.uk).

Music

It's not too hard to find what's left of the major record chains in Glasgow, but **Fopp** is more fun and has two branches in the city (19 Union Street, 0141 285 7190; 358 Byres Road, 0141 337 7490; www.fopp.co.uk). A few smaller independent shops battle to be heard. **Avalanche** (34 Dundas Street, 0141 332 2099, www.avalancheglasgow.co.uk) stocks music from across the board, but is best approached for its indie discs. Bijou **Monorail** (12 Kings Court, King Street, 0141 552 9458, www.mono railmusic.com) has a hand-picked selection of alternative music in all manner of genres; **23rd Precinct** (23 Bath Street, 0141 332 4806, www.23rdprecinct.co.uk) specialises in dance, electronica and hip hop, while **Classics in the**

City (54 Dundas Street, 0141 353 6915, www.classicsinthecity.co.uk) should cover all your classical and opera needs.

ARTS & ENTERTAINMENT
Comedy

Year-round, the local scene is well served by the Glasgow outpost of the **Stand** (333 Woodlands Road, West End, 0870 600 6055, www.thestand. co.uk; *see p224* for the Edinburgh branch), which stages events nightly. It's also one of the main venues for March's two-week **Glasgow International Comedy Festival** (0141 552 2070, www.glasgowcomedyfestival.com), a mix of big names and circuit regulars. The city is also home to a branch of unavoidable national chain **Jongleurs**, in the same block as the Cineworld movie house (11 Renfrew Street, City Centre, 0844 499 4067, www.jongleurs.com).

Film

Glasgow is dotted with first-run cinemas, among them the centrally located **Cineworld** on the corner of Renfrew Street and West Nile Street (08712 002000, www.cineworld.co.uk) and the West End's **Grosvenor Cinema** (Ashton Lane, 08451 666002, www.social animal.co.uk). Lovers of independent cinema are directed to the **Glasgow Film Theatre** (12 Rose Street, 0141 332 6535, www.gft.org.uk), which supplements arthouse flicks with older movies and occasional special events.

5761, www.bennetsnightclub.co.uk), a cheery nightclub, and **Delmonica's** (68 Virginia Street, 0141 552 4803, www.socialanimal.co.uk) quiet during the day but busier at night.

The annual **Pride Scotia** festival is held alternately in Edinburgh and Glasgow; it'll be at the latter in 2010 and 2012. The city holds its own citywide celebration of queer culture each year: **Glasgay!** (0141 552 7575, www.glasgay. co.uk), whose month-long programme takes in film screenings, theatrical performances and art exhibitions. It's held over a month or so each October/November.

MUSIC & NIGHTLIFE

Classical & opera

Scottish Opera's Glasgow home is the **Theatre Royal** (*see p287*).

Glasgow Royal Concert Hall

2 Sauchiehall Street, City Centre (0141 353 8000, www.glasgowconcerthalls.com). Buchanan Street underground or Queen Street rail. **Box office** *In person & by phone* 10am-6pm Mon-Sat; until 9pm on concert days. **Tickets** £25-£75. **Credit** MC, V. **Map** p259 E3.
Opened in 1990 when Glasgow was European City of Culture, the 'new' Royal Concert Hall has come to be regarded as one of the leading venues of its type in the UK. The classical programming features the Royal Scottish National Orchestra; other events range from popular Christmas concerts to the Celtic Connections festival in January.

★ Glasgow City Halls & Old Fruitmarket

Candleriggs, Merchant City (0141 353 8000, www.glasgowconcerthalls.com). Buchanan Street underground or Queen Street rail. **Box office** *In person & by phone* noon-6pm Mon-Sat; until 9pm on concert days. **Tickets** £25-£75. **Credit** MC, V. **Map** p259 G4.
Built in the 19th century, this complex of venues reopened in 2006 after extensive refurbishments, and is in terrific shape. The roster of concerts in the impressive, 1,000-capacity Grand Hall is highlighted by regular shows from the BBC Scottish Symphony Orchestra. The Old Fruitmarket specialises in jazz and folk events and can hold up to 1,600; there's also a rather more modest Recital Hall, usually given over to chamber music.

Royal Scottish Academy of Music & Drama

100 Renfrew Street, City Centre (0141 332 4101 information, 0141 332 5057 box office, www. rsamd.ac.uk). Cowcaddens underground. **Box office** *By phone* 9am-5pm Mon-Sat. **Tickets** £5-£25. **Credit** MC, V. **Map** p258 D2.

Galleries

In addition to major spaces such as the **Burrell Collection** (*see p267*), **GOMA** (*see p261*), the **Lighthouse** (*see p262*), the **CCA** (*see p261*), the **Glasgow School of Art** (*see p262*) and the **Kelvingrove Art Gallery & Museum** (*see p271*), Glasgow boasts a number of small, independent galleries. Aside from those at **Trongate 103** (*see p262*), it's worth checking **Sorcha Dallas** (5-9 St Margaret's Place, 0141 553 2662, www.sorchadallas.com); the gallery spaces at the **Arches** and the **Tramway** (for both, *see p287*) stage engaging shows.

The **Glasgow School of Art Degree Show**, a free exhibition of student work held for a week or so each June at the Renfrew Street college (*see p262*), is one of the local arts community's social events of the year, with fine art from tomorrow's Turner Prize-winners and a suitably wild street party. The work is often superb, but the event is also a great opportunity to explore the Mackintosh Building. And look out for the **Glasgow International Festival of Visual Art** (www.glasgowinternational. org), an arts biennial that's growing in confidence and size. It's next due to be staged in April-May 2010, then again in 2012.

Gay & lesbian

Aside from the **Polo Lounge** (*see p285*), which can draw a slightly mixed crowd on weekends, two of the city's best gay venues are **Bennets** (80 Glassford Street, Merchant City, 0141 552

INSIDE TRACK GLASGOW JAZZ

Big jazz names do trot through town as part of British or European tours, particularly during the two-week **Glasgow International Jazz Festival** held around June/July (0141 552 3552, www.jazzfest.co.uk), but the scene is otherwise small. The **Old Fruitmarket** (see p283) hosts many of the touring acts; for details of smaller venues, see the GlasJazz website (www.mcmultimedia. co.uk/glasjazzindex.html).

The concert hall of the Royal Scottish Academy of Music & Drama stages a regular array of recitals and masterclasses.

Rock, pop & dance

In addition to the venues featured below, **Nice 'n' Sleazy** (see p276) stages regular live music in its basement space, and there are frequent gigs at **Òran Mór** (see p279), the **Arches** (see right) and many other venues around the city. For up-to-date listings, check the local fortnightly events magazine The List. **Glasgow Royal Concert Hall** (see p283) is also used for rock and pop as well as being a key venue for **Celtic Connections**, the annual folk festival (0141 353 8000, www.celticconnections.com) which runs for a fortnight each January. Previous years have seen Scottish groups such as Capercaillie or Runrig appear alongside American artists like Alison Krauss and Beth Nielsen Chapman. Meanwhile the **Glasgow Americana** festival has been going since 2007, organised by the Fallen Angels Club (www.fallenangels club.com). Held every May, it showcases rootsy North American performers.

Barrowland

244 Gallowgate, East End (0141 552 4601, www.glasgow-barrowland.com). Argyle Street or High Street rail. **Admission** £12-£35. **No credit cards. Map** p259 H5.
For years one of the greatest live music venues in the UK, the Barrowland is still going strong. Apart from the garish, gigantic neon sign, it's not much to look at, but the crowd of up to 1,900 regard it as their historical duty to go wild.

Ferry

25 Anderston Quay, West End (0141 248 5376, www.the-ferry.co.uk). **Admission** £10-£20. **Credit** AmEx, MC, V.
This is a West End venue in the sense that it's beyond the M8, but close to the City Centre and on the Clyde. It's hosted events since the 1980s; since a 2005 refurbishment, and now stages regular gigs from musicians of all stripes.

★ O2 ABC

300 Sauchiehall Street, City Centre (0141 332 2232, www.abcglasgow.com). Cowcaddens underground or Charing Cross rail. **Admission** £5-£22.50. **No credit cards. Map** p259 D2.
The two halls at this old cinema between them stage a variety of events: everyone from David Gray to the Gang of Four, with a concentration on rock and pop. Once the bands have finished, DJs take over, spinning music of a primarily indie bent. A sponsorship naming-rights deal with a phone company has stripped it of a little dignity, but it's still worth a look.

O2 Academy Glasgow

121 Eglinton Street, South Side (0141 418 3000, www.o2academyglasgow.co.uk). West Street underground. **Admission** £5-£30. **Credit** AmEx, MC, V. **Map** p258 D6.
First an art deco cinema, then a bingo hall and now Glasgow's newest mid-sized live music venue, the Carling Academy is a pleasantly grubby space. Massive Attack, the Flaming Lips and Florence & the Machine have all played of late.

Grand Ole Opry

2-4 Govan Road, South Side (0141 429 5396, www.glasgowsgrandoleopry.co.uk). Shields Road underground. **Open** 7pm-1am Fri, Sat. **Admission** £4-£5. **No credit cards.**
The Opry is a South Side institution for Glasgow's legions of country-music fans, who gather every weekend in this tacky hall, decorated in Confederate memorabilia, to imbibe cheap liquor, line-dance, witness the fake shoot-out and – yee-haw! – play bingo. Founded in 1974, it's like nowhere else in Britain.

★ King Tut's Wah Wah Hut

272A St Vincent Street, City Centre (0141 221 5279, www.kingtuts.co.uk). Central Station rail. **Admission** £6-£17. **No credit cards. Map** p258 D3.
Founded in 1990, this storied space in the middle of town is still the venue of choice for touring acts on their way up – or down – the NME ladder.

Scottish Exhibition & Conference Centre (SECC), Clyde Auditorium

Exhibition Way, City Centre (0141 248 3000 information, 0870 395 4000 tickets, www.ticket soup.com). Exhibition Centre rail. **Admission** £10-£75. **Credit** MC, V. **Map** p258 A3.
The SECC is a vast aircraft hangar of an arena, the main venue for big touring acts as they pass through Scotland. The smaller Clyde Auditorium (aka the 'Armadillo') provides the sit-down atmosphere sought by more mature performers (and audiences).

Nightclubs

In clubbing terms, Edinburgh has a head start on its West Coast rival simply by dint of the fact that its city fathers have made it far easier for bar and club owners to obtain a late alcohol licence. However, while the scene in Edinburgh has more than its fair share of cheesy indie nights and cornball retro-disco piss-ups, Glasgow's nightlife circuit retains an edge. In addition to the clubs below, a handful of music venues also stage club nights once the bands have finished. Among them are the **O2 ABC** (*see left*) and **Nice 'n' Sleazy** (*see p276*).

Arches

30 Midland Street, City Centre (0141 565 1000, www.thearches.co.uk). St Enoch underground or Central Station rail. **Open** hrs vary. **Admission** varies. **Credit** MC, V. **Map** p259 E4.

Reclaimed from the huge network of tunnels beneath Glasgow's sizeable Central Station, this multi-purpose venue hosts theatre performances (*see p287*), exhibits works by local artists and serves an above-average menu in its café-bar (*see p276*). It's also, though, a consistently terrific club venue with a varied programme.

Buff Club

142 Bath Lane, City Centre (0141 248 1777, www.thebuffclub.com). Cowcaddens underground or Charing Cross rail. **Open** 11pm-3am Mon-Fri; 10.30pm-late Sat, Sun. **Admission** £3-£6. **No credit cards. Map** p258 D3.

The Buff Club's primary focus is disco, funk and soul, but it also offers other tunes through its seven-night opening schedule: Monday's Killer Kitsch turns over electro and house.

★ Glasgow School of Art

168 Renfrew Street, City Centre (0141 353 4690, www.theartschool.co.uk). Cowcaddens underground or Charing Cross rail. **Open** 10pm-3am Thur-Sat. **Admission** free-£7. **No credit cards. Map** p258 D2.

The bar and club nights at Glasgow's Art School are venerated among the city's indie cognoscenti. Regular nights include Mixed Bizness on Thursdays (underground and dancefloor classics).

Polo Lounge

84 Wilson Street, Merchant City (0845 659 5905, www.socialanimal.co.uk). Buchanan Street underground or Queen Street rail. **Open** 9pm-3am Wed, Thur, Sun; 5pm-3am Fri, Sat. **Admission** free-£5. **Credit** MC, V. **Map** p259 F4.

One of Glasgow's leading gay clubs (for others, *see p283*), the Polo Lounge opens its doors every night of the week. The DJs generally don't challenge the punters too much, but the queues here on weekends are testament to the fact that the punters don't mind.

Soundhaus

47 Hydepark Street, Anderston (0141 221 4659, www.soundhaus.co.uk). Anderston rail. **Open** hrs vary. **Admission** by membership only. **No credit cards. Map** p258 B4.

It's located on an industrial estate a short distance out from the city centre, and it's members only so you have to join or get signed in, but it's still worth the walk for hard-edged styles in an agreeably underground atmosphere.

Barrowland.

Discover the city from your back pocket

Essential for your weekend break, 25 top cities available.

★ Sub Club
22 Jamaica Street, City Centre (0141 248 4600, www.subclub.co.uk). St Enoch underground or Central Station rail. **Open** 10pm-3am Wed-Sun. **Admission** free-£12. **No credit cards.** **Map** p259 E4.

Favouring experimentalism over commercialism, up-and-comers over veterans, this small but perfectly formed enterprise encapsulates all that can be great about Glasgow clubbing. Sunday's anything-goes Optimo is commonly regarded as one of Scotland's finest regular club nights.

Theatre & dance

Two very different events enliven the city's theatrical calendar. Over several weeks each February-March, arts production company New Moves International stages the **New Territories** (www.newmoves.co.uk), bringing an array of challenging contemporary dance and performance art to the Tramway. And then, in June-July, it's time for Scotland's only outdoor Shakespeare festival: **Bard in the Botanics** (www.bardinthebotanics.org), staged in the fragrant surroundings of the Botanic Gardens. Picnicking is encouraged.

★ Arches Theatre
253 Argyle Street, City Centre (0870 240 7528, www.thearches.co.uk). St Enoch underground or Central Station rail. **Box office** 9am-8pm Mon-Sat; noon-6pm Sun. **Tickets** £4-£10. **Credit** MC, V. **Map** p259 E4.

The most atmospheric theatre in Scotland, this subterranean warren has built itself into a vital creative hub for nearly 20 years. The hugely popular nightclub (*see p285*) and café-bar (*see p276*) keep the money flowing in, allowing young theatre-makers to take their first experimental steps and the resident company to stage adventurous productions of 20th-century classics. The best shows use the myriad rooms for spooky promenade performances, as disorientating as they are dramatic. The venue is a keen supporter of up-and-coming talent, through forums such as the Arches Theatre Festival in the spring and autumn's Arches Live. *Photo p288.*

Citizens' Theatre
119 Gorbals Street, South Side (0141 429 5561 information, 0141 429 0022 box office, www.citz.co.uk). Bridge Street underground. **Box office** 10am-6pm Mon-Sat. **Tickets** £7-£17. **Credit** MC, V. **Map** p259 E6.

For more than 30 years, under the directorial triumvirate of Giles Havergal, Robert David MacDonald and Philip Prowse, the Citz was one of Europe's great theatrical powerhouses, famed for its blend of high camp, high risk and high intelligence. Since Jeremy Raison took over in 2003, the company has redefined itself for a new era without losing its old identity. As

well as the attractive horseshoe auditorium, two studios are often used for touring productions.

King's Theatre
297 Bath Street, City Centre (0141 240 1111, www.ambassadortickets.com/king's-theatre). Charing Cross rail. **Box office** *In person & by phone* 10am-8pm Mon-Sat. **Tickets** £11-£40. **Credit** AmEx, MC, V. **Map** p258 C2.

Under joint management with the Theatre Royal, the King's has a true place in the city's heart, not least for its earthy annual pantomime. Outside the Christmas season, the traditional theatre, built in 1904, hosts large-scale touring productions on post-West End runs, as well as some amateur musicals.

Pavilion Theatre
121 Renfield Street (0141 332 1846, www.paviliontheatre.co.uk). Cowcaddens underground or Queen Street rail. **Box office** 10am-8pm daily. **Tickets** £11-£22. **Credit** MC, V. **Map** p259 E2.

The Pavilion is that rare thing: a large, traditional theatre run without subsidy by an independent management. Unashamedly populist, it offers broad comedies, often with a Glasgow setting, as well as bands, comedians and risqué hypnotists. The raucous Christmas pantomime is a hoot.

Theatre Royal
282 Hope Street, City Centre (0141 332 9000, www.ambassadortickets.com). Cowcaddens underground. **Box office** 10am-6pm Mon-Sat. **Tickets** £6-£30 (more for Scottish Opera productions). **Credit** AmEx, MC, V. **Map** p259 E2.

To ease its perennial financial woes, Scottish Opera handed over the operation of the Theatre Royal to the Ambassador Theatre Group in 2005, which means this grandest of Glasgow theatres shares its management with the King's Theatre. The association with Scottish Opera and Scottish Ballet endures, sustaining the Victorian theatre's reputation for the high arts; you're likely to come across serious drama and large-scale Shakespeare productions.

Tramway
25 Albert Drive, Pollokshields (0856 330 3501, www.tramway.org). Pollokshields East rail. **Box office** *In person & by phone* 10am-8pm Tue-Sat; noon-6pm Sun. **Tickets** £2-£18. **Credit** MC, V.

Cutting edge art, theatre and performance, plus a year-round garden of tranquillity. The big warehouse-style space enjoyed its salad days in the early 1990s after Glasgow's stint as European City of Culture when visitors included Peter Brook and the Wooster Group. But it's still a hive of activity and innovation, with performers from home and abroad.

Tron Theatre
63 Trongate, City Centre (0141 552 4267, www.tron.co.uk). St Enoch underground. **Box office**

ESCAPES & EXCURSIONS

10am-6pm Mon-Sat. **Tickets** £6.50-£14.50.
Credit MC, V. **Map** p259 F5.
From middle class family meltdown dramas to cult pantomine, hard-hitting plays about women in war-zones to gay musicals, the Tron is the hardest-working theatre in showbiz. Away from the varied programme, the restaurant and bar hum with discussions between local dramatists.

HOTELS
The City Centre

ABode
129 Bath Street, G2 2SZ (0141 572 6000, www.abodehotels.co.uk/glasgow). Cowcaddens underground or Charing Cross rail. **Rates** £79-£175 double. **Credit** AmEx, DC, MC, V. **Map** p258 D3 ❶
This City Centre hotel found a measure of success under its former name, Arthouse. However, since a rebranding as part of the ABode mini-chain in late 2005, it's picked up even more plaudits. Part of this is down to the involvement of chef Michael Caines (*see p273*), who lends his name to the kitchen at MC @ Abode (*see p273*). The rooms are pleasant and modern in an undemonstrative way.

★ Blythswood Square
Blythswood Square, G2 4AD (0141 208 2458, www.townhousecompany.com/blythswoodsquare). Buchanan Street or St Enoch underground, or Central Station rail. **Rates** £195-£1,500 double. **Credit** AmEx, MC, V. **Map** p258 D3 ❷

The Town House Collection, which runs a number of high-end hotels in Edinburgh, decided to branch out into Glasgow and launched this luxury spa hotel at Blythwood Square in late 2009. With 93 rooms, six suites, a penthouse and the best spa in Glasgow, all within premises that date to the 1820s, it made a big splash when it opened.

City Inn Glasgow
Finnieston Quay, G3 8HN (0141 240 1002, www.cityinn.com/glasgow). Exhibition Centre rail. **Rates** £69-£175 double. **Credit** AmEx, MC, V. **Map** p258 A4 ❸
This modern hotel isn't bang in the City Centre, and counts among its neighbours such attractions as the Finnieston Crane and the Science Centre. Its restaurant is decent enough, and the hotel offers free broadband access. However, the selling point is the views afforded by the river-facing rooms. Specify when you book. *Photos pp290-291.*
▶ *It's useful if you're seeing a gig at the SECC or the Clyde Auditorium; see p284.*

Malmaison
278 West George Street, G2 4LL (0141 572 1000, www.malmaison-glasgow.com). Buchanan Street or Cowcaddens underground, or Charing Cross rail. **Rates** £170-£355 double. **Credit** AmEx, DC, MC, V. **Map** p258 D3 ❹
The second hotel in the chain to open (Edinburgh was first, a month earlier), this Malmaison is housed for the most part in a 19th-century Greek Orthodox church. It's an impressive setting: check out the handsome, below-stairs restaurant, complete with

Arches Theatre. *See p287.*

ESCAPES & EXCURSIONS

The Rivals

The two big Glasgow teams continue to dominate Scottish football.

The Scottish Football League started in 1890 with 11 clubs. Astonishingly, ten of them came from in or around Glasgow. Among them were **Celtic** (who play at Parkhead; 0871 226 1888, www.celticfc. net) and **Rangers** (who play at Ibrox; 0871 702 1972, www.rangersfc.co.uk). Known jointly as the Old Firm, the teams have bossed the Scottish game ever since, attracting the biggest crowds, the best players and the largest incomes. No team outside the Old Firm has won the Scottish championship since 1985.

For all that, though, Celtic and Rangers have struggled in European competitions.

The problem is one of scale: because the country has a population of just five million, TV advertising revenues are comparatively small. In terms of attendances, Celtic and Rangers may be among the top 20 clubs in Europe, but a lack of cash – and, perhaps, a lack of competition at local level – has excluded them from the continent's elite.

Some years ago, the teams hit a glass ceiling, and the grouchiness is growing as the pair contemplate the riches above. For now, they spend just enough in Scotland to render the Scottish Premier League almost meaningless as a competition, a disaster for the game's viability north of the border.

---

stunning vaulted ceilings. The handsome, comfortable rooms are individually decorated; none are more individual than the Big Yin Suite with tartan rolltop bath, named in tribute to Billy Connolly.

Marks Hotel

110 Bath Street, G2 2EN (0141 353 0800, www.markshotels.com). Cowcaddens underground or Charing Cross rail. **Rates** £79-£155 double. **Credit** MC, V. **Map** p259 D4 ⑤
Opened in 2000 as Bewleys, this was taken over by a new owner, upgraded and relaunched as Marks in 2007; its stepped, overhanging façade, protuberant roof and glass frontage still make it hard to miss. Bold wallpapers, complementary fabrics, free wireless and a central location are all in its favour, a definite improvement on its earlier incarnation.

Radisson SAS

301 Argyle Street, G2 8DL (0141 204 3333, www.radissonblu.co.uk). St Enoch underground or Central Station rail. **Credit** AmEx, DC, MC, V. **Map** p258 D4 ⑥
Just as the Malmaison makes a virtue of its historic building, so the Radisson isn't afraid to advertise its brash modernity. It opened in 2004 in a striking, purpose-built structure close to Central Station. The interior isn't quite as memorable as the exterior, but the rooms are nonetheless crisp, comfortable and welcoming. Its restaurant is the Mediterranean-flavoured Collage.

The Merchant City & the East End

Brunswick

106-108 Brunswick Street, G1 1TF (0141 552 0001, www.brunswickhotel.co.uk). Buchanan Street underground or Queen Street rail. **Rates** £50-£95 double. **Credit** AmEx, MC, V. **Map** p259 F4 ⑦

No two of the Brunswick's 18 rooms are quite alike, but all are plain, stylish and devoid of clutter. Whoever named the hotel's carefully chic café-bar Brutti Ma Buoni ('ugly but good') clearly had a sense of humour. The location is handy, and prices are keen. Small, independent and nicely formed.

Cathedral House

28-32 Cathedral Square, G4 0XA (0141 552 3519, www.cathedralhousehotel.org). High Street rail. **Rates** £79 double. **Credit** MC, V. **Map** p259 H3 ⑧
The Cathedral House started life in 1877 as a halfway house for a local prison, before being transformed into the diocesan headquarters of the Catholic Church. Today's operation attempts to balance this history with modern facilities, and does so quite nicely. There aren't too many frills in the eight rooms, but the prices make them quite hard to resist.

Premier Inn Glasgow City Centre

187 George Street, G1 1YU (08702 383320, www.premierinn.com). Buchanan Street or St Enoch underground, or Argyle Street or High Street rail. **Rates** £68-£150 double. **Credit** AmEx, MC, V. **Map** p259 G4 ⑨
Cheap, basic and central (a couple of minutes' walk from George Square), it's exactly like any other Premier Inn anywhere. But of all the budget bed boxes in the city, this might be the most amenable. Nice people on the front desk.

The West End

★ Hotel du Vin at One Devonshire Gardens

1 Devonshire Gardens, G12 0UX (0141 339 2001, www.hotelduvin.com). **Rates** £150-£510 double. **Credit** AmEx, MC, V.

ESCAPES & EXCURSIONS

City Inn. *See p288.*

The Hotel du Vin had a reputation as the city's smartest hotel before Blythswood Square arrived. It sits in a leafy row of Victorian terraces, handsome, elegant and luxurious but never flashy. The rooms are supplemented by an array of appetising services and amenities: an award-winning bistro, luxury linens, free wireless and so on.

South Side

Sherbrooke Castle Hotel

11 Sherbrooke Avenue, Pollokshields (0141 427 4227, www.sherbrooke.co.uk). Dumbreck rail. **Rates** £95-£155. **Credit** AmEx, MC, V.
Tucked away in the south-west, this late Victorian baronial mansion that has been a hotel since the postwar period. With its dark wood fixtures, it very much looks the part of the traditional Scottish hotel, with very friendly staff. Not actually a castle, it's handy for the Burrell Collection (*see p267*).

Directory
ARRIVING & LEAVING
By air

Glasgow Airport (0844 481 5555, www. glasgowairport.com) is around eight miles west of the city, at Junction 28 of the M8. Bus services from the airport into the city include the 500, which is fastest and most direct (every ten minutes at peak times, £4.20 single, £6.20 return); the 747 and 757 (every half hour, £4, £5) go by slightly different routes and are not as fast. Alternatively, a taxi will take about 20 minutes and cost about £18-£20. There's no

direct rail link; Paisley Gilmour Street is the nearest station (a mile and a half to the south).

Some flights arrive at **Glasgow Prestwick Airport** (0871 223 0700, www.gpia.co.uk), around 35 miles south-west of the city. There's a regular train service to Glasgow's Central Station; journey time is 45 minutes.

By bus or coach

Long-distance buses arrive at and depart from **Buchanan Street Bus Station** (0141 333 3708, www.spt.co.uk/bus) at Killermont Street. Citylink runs a service to and from Edinburgh every 15 minutes at peak times; journey time is around 80 minutes and the standard return is £8.90 (it may be cheaper if you book ahead).

By car

Despite its all-ensnaring motorway system, Glasgow is actually easy to access by car. The M8 from Edinburgh delivers you into the heart of the city. Take junction 15 for the East End and Old Town, junction 16 for Garnethill, junction 18 for the West End, junction 19 for the City Centre and junction 20 for the South Side.

By train

Glasgow has two main-line train stations. **Queen Street Station** (West George Street) serves Edinburgh (trains every 15 minutes) and the north of Scotland, while **Central Station** (Gordon Street) serves the West Coast and south to England. The stations are centrally located and are within walking distance of each other. For more on rail travel, *see p256*.

The service during the day is aimed at people with emergency dental needs who aren't registered with a dentist; you can access it by calling the number above. For anyone else, call NHS 24 on 0845 424 2424; you'll be connected to a dental expert who will make an evening appointment at the EDTC if necessary. Either way, the EDTC is not a walk-in centre and you'll only be seen with an appointment.

Glasgow Royal Infirmary, Accident & Emergency

84 Castle Street, East End (0141 211 4484). High Street rail. **Open** *Accident & emergency* 24hrs daily. **Map** p259 H2.

Western Infirmary, Accident & Emergency

Dumbarton Road, Partick, West End (0141 211 2409). Kelvinhall underground or Partick rail. **Open** Accident & emergency 24hrs daily.

POSTAL SERVICES

There are post offices throughout the city, the majority open during usual post office hours (*see p309*). For details of your nearest, call 0845 722 3344 or see www.royalmail.com.

TELEPHONES

The area code for Glasgow is 0141.

TOURIST INFORMATION

Glasgow Visitor Information Centre

11 George Square, City Centre (0141 204 4400, www.seeglasgow.com). Buchanan Street underground. **Open** *Oct-Easter* 9am-6pm Mon-Sat. *Easter-May* 9am-6pm Mon-Sat; 10am-6pm Sun. *June* 9am-7pm Mon-Sat; 10am-6pm Sun. *July, Aug* 9am-8pm Mon-Sat; 10am-6pm Sun. *Sept* 9am-7pm Mon-Sat; 10am-6pm Sun. **Credit** MC, V. **Map** p259 F3.
The Information Centre will take credit card bookings for accommodation, and can also answer general enquiries about sightseeing and local events.

GETTING AROUND

Central Glasgow is easy to negotiate on foot, but you'll need to use public transport or hire a car to go further afield. Nearly all the listings in this chapter refer only to the underground or the overground rail service. However, the frequent bus services are well signed at the regular bus stops. Glasgow is also served by a fleet of black taxis. They're fairly cheap compared to Edinburgh, but elusive in the early hours. For more on public transport, contact Traveline Scotland (0871 200 2233, www.travelinescotland.com)

As for trains, besides the inter-city services, there's a good network of low-level trains serving Glasgow's suburbs, which is run by Scotrail. The slightly ramshackle underground system, affectionately known as the Clockwork Orange, is a single, circular line that loops between the centre, just south of the Clyde and the West End.

RESOURCES

Health

The general website for **NHS Greater Glasgow & Clyde** is www.nhsgg.org.uk. The 24-hour NHS helpline for all urgent medical queries is 0845 424 2424.

Emergency Dental Treatment Centre

Glasgow Dental Hospital & School, 378 Sauchiehall Street, City Centre, G2 3JZ (0141 232 6323). Cowcaddens underground. **Open** *Emergency clinic* 8.30am-5.15pm then 7pm-10pm Mon-Fri. Appointments only. **Map** p258 D2.

> ### INSIDE TRACK
> ### GET OUT OF TOWN
>
> Glasgow scores over Edinburgh in its proximity to the islands off the West Coast. You can get a train from Central Station to **Ardrossan Harbour** (54 minutes), from where you can catch the ferry to Brodick on Arran, or to **Wemyss Bay** (52 minutes), the departure point for Rothesay on Bute. For ferries, see www.calmac.co.uk.

Around Edinburgh

Escape the city for a very different side of Scotland.

The area immediately surrounding Edinburgh doesn't offer any of the capital's built-up urban charms, which is precisely its appeal. Things are different out here: just as marked by history, certainly, but altogether wilder, quieter and, in places, even hillier.

Due east of the city, along the coast, lie a string of handsome towns and villages listed here under the catch-all term of **East Lothian**. To the south lies the rest of **Midlothian**, home to the Pentland Hills and a succession of charming historic sights; nearby **West Lothian** is where you'll find the breathtaking Forth Bridges. And slightly further afield, **Stirling** and the **Borders** each hold plenty of appeal.

EAST LOTHIAN

The coastal town of **Musselburgh** is only about five miles from the bustle of the Royal Mile, but it feels much further away. It was settled by the Romans, who established a port at the mouth of the River Esk as far back as AD80, and it remains proud of its history. Since the early 14th century, it's been known as the 'honest toun', a sobriquet gained when the locals refused to claim a reward offered to them after they cared for Randolph, Earl of Moray, through illness.

Post-war development hasn't been kind to Musselburgh's outer reaches, but its centre remains handsome; the chief attractions are run by the National Trust. Towards Edinburgh sits **Newhailes** (Newhailes Road, Musselburgh, 0844 493 2125, www.nts.org.uk, closed Tue, Wed & Oct-Apr, £10.50, £7.50 discounts), at its core an 17th-century house with rococo interiors and an 18th-century garden. And don't miss **Inveresk Lodge** (24 Inveresk Village, 0844 493 2126, www.nts.org.uk, £3, £2 discounts): the building is private but the sublime gardens, sloping down to the Esk's peaceful banks, are open to all. Even so, most visitors tend to head here for sporting reasons, to play the famous **Musselburgh Links** (*see p248*) or for a day at **Musselburgh Racecourse** (*see p246*).

After the racecourse, take the B1348 along the coast road, through the small towns of **Prestonpans**, **Cockenzie** (with a huge power station) and **Port Seton**. Once you get past the village of **Longniddry**, the scenic impact of the East Lothian coast really hits. Wildlife thrives here: the **Aberlady Bay Local Nature Reserve**, reached by crossing the footbridge from the car park just east of Aberlady village, is open all year, its sandy mudflats a big pull for bird-watchers. Golfers flock here, too.

Virtually the entire coastline in this area is beach. It starts at Seton Sands, then goes round by Gosford Bay into Aberlady Bay. The most popular beach is **Gullane**, a shallow mile-long crescent behind the town. Then comes another two miles of quiet, contemplative coastline to the north-east before the spacious **Yellowcraig Beach** near Dirleton. The weather may not allow sunbathing or swimming most of the year, but these East Lothian beaches have a beauty all their own.

Set a little way back from the coast, a mile or so past Gullane, the chocolate-box pretty village of **Dirleton** has the impressive remains of the 13th-century **Dirleton Castle** (01620 850330, www.historic-scotland.gov.uk, £4.70, £2.35-£3.70 discounts). The castle sits atop a hill surrounded by handsome gardens: the north garden is associated with the Arts and Crafts movement of the 1920s, while the west garden was late Victorian and was reconstructed to its original plan in 1993.

Two miles east sits the larger and busier town of **North Berwick**, a seaside settlement; Edinburghers head here during the summer to take advantage of the clean sands flanking the old harbour. Behind the town, **North Berwick**

Law rises to a modest 187 metres, but it's a popular climb on a fine day and offers great views; geologically, it's the same as Arthur's Seat in Edinburgh, a basalt volcanic plug. But the main attraction is the **Scottish Seabird Centre** (01620 890202, www. seabird.org, £7.15, £4.05-£5.35 discounts); dolphins and otters have been spotted around here, but seabirds obviously predominate. **Seafari** (01620 890202) runs daily boat trips from the harbour, weather permitting, from Easter to October.

The coast past North Berwick is dominated by **Tantallon Castle** (01620 892727, www. historic-scotland.gov.uk, £4.70, £2.35-£3.70 discounts), a formidable cliff-edge fortification largely built in the 14th century. Past here, continue along the A198 until you reach the A1. Immediately east, by Dunbar, is the **John Muir Country Park**, which provides various habitats for wildlife. Muir lived in Dunbar until he was 11, when his family emigrated; he was later a hugely influential naturalist in the US.

Back along the A1, towards Edinburgh again, is the village of **East Linton**. Make a diversion into the minor roads south-west of the village and you find the atmospheric remains of the 13th-century **Hailes Castle** overlooking the River Tyne (www.historic-scotland.gov.uk, free). And just a short drive north of the A1, at a former World War II airfield, sits the popular **National Museum of Flight** (East Fortune Airfield, East Fortune, 247 4238, www.nms.ac. uk/flight, closed weekdays Nov-Mar, £8.50, £6.50 discounts, free under-12s).

Keep heading west on the A1 and you soon come to the Royal Burgh of **Haddington**, a well-heeled market town. The main attraction is the 14th-century **St Mary's Parish Church**, also known as the Lamp of Lothian (www.st maryskirk.com) and keenly preserved by locals. However, an even more delightful settlement sits just four miles south along the B6369. Built by the Marquis of Tweeddale in the 18th century for his estate workers, **Gifford** is too charming for words. Continuing further south still and Longyester affords access to the **Lammermuir Hills**, popular with walkers.

Where to eat & drink

For some of the most elevated cooking in East Lothian, try **La Potinière** in Gullane (01620 843214, www.la-potiniere.co.uk, set meals £18-£40) which takes a classic and polite French approach to its cuisine. At the Kilspindie House Hotel in Aberlady, **Ducks** also has a kitchen operating to high standards (01875 870682, www.ducks-aberlady.co.uk, main courses £15); it's run by Malcolm Duck, who had a fine restaurant in Edinburgh for many years.

In Dunbar, the **Creel** (01368 863279, www. creelrestaurant.co.uk, main courses £13) is a bistro with carefully sourced food, while the **Rocks** (01368 862287, www.experiencethe rocks.co.uk, main courses £15) is more of an inn that specialises in seafood; it also has rooms. In a different vein, the original **S Luca** (32-38 High Street, Musselburgh, 665 2237, www. s-luca.co.uk) sells the best ice-cream on the East Lothian coast; it's a sister venue to the branch in Edinburgh (*see p157*). Also in Musselburgh, the striking **Glasshouse at Eskmills** (Stuart,

Dirleton Castle.

ESCAPES & EXCURSIONS

ESCAPES & EXCURSIONS

Little Sparta.

House, Station Road, 273 5240, www.the glasshouseeateskmills.com, main courses £13) brings contemporary decor and modern European cooking to a former mill building.

Where to stay

There are nice hotels here: Aberlady's 17th-century **Kilspindie House Hotel** (01875 870682, www.kilspindie.co.uk, double £115), part of the same operation that contains Ducks (*see above*); North Berwick's stately, Victorian **Marine Hotel & Spa** (Cromwell Road, 0844 879 9130, www.macdonaldhotels.co.uk, double £115-£230); Gifford's **Tweeddale Arms Hotel** (01620 810240, double £95); Haddington's upscale **B&B One West Road** (01620 829863, www.onewestroad.com, double £90-£100). But the area is close enough to Edinburgh that you may prefer to stay in town.

Getting there

By bus Lothian Buses runs services that go to Musselburgh then on towards Port Seton. Further afield, First Bus has more useful routes from the city to North Berwick and Dunbar, and also to Haddington. For more on buses, *see p256.*
By car For Haddington or Dunbar, take the A1 east out of the city. For all the towns and attractions along the coast, however, take the A198. From the A1, follow signs for Longniddry and pick up the A198 from there. Alternatively, just follow the coast road from Musselburgh.
By train A service runs from Waverley to Musselburgh, Wallyford, Prestonpans, Longniddry, Drem and North Berwick.

Tourist information

Dunbar *143a High Street (01368 863353).*
Open *Mid Mar-Oct* 9am-6pm daily.
North Berwick *Quality Street (01620 892197).*
Open *Jan, Feb, Nov, Dec* 9.30am-6pm Fri-Sun.
Mar 9.30am-5pm Mon, Wed-Sat; 11am-4pm Sun.
Apr, May 9.30am-6pm Mon-Sat. *Jun* 9.30am-6pm
Mon-Sat; 11am-4pm Sun. *Jul, Aug* 9.30am-7pm
Mon-Sat; 11am-6pm Sun. *Sept* 9.30am-6pm Mon-Sat; 11am-4pm Sun. *Oct* 9.30am-5pm Mon-Sat.

MIDLOTHIAN

The Pentland Hills rise south of Edinburgh and form the backbone of the **Pentland Hills Regional Park**, which sprawls from the city bypass down to the village of Carlops in the south-east and the area around Harperrig Reservoir in the south-west. The park takes in a succession of summits, various lochs, 60 miles of signposted paths, two visitor centres and evidence of settlement going back around 2,500 years. Serious hillwalkers will be in heaven.

There's an entrance to the park just by the Flotterstone Inn (*see right*), less than four miles south of the city bypass on the A702; this is also where you'll find one of the park's visitor centres. Less than a mile from the car park, the **Glencorse Reservoir** sits among heather-covered hills, a visual combination that forms one of those classic images of Scotland. If you're feeling energetic, you can keep walking around Glencorse Reservoir and on to nearby Loganlea Reservoir, all on a good surface. Of course, the further you walk, the longer it will take to get back to the Flotterstone Inn for a drink.

Way down at the south end of the Pentlands, not far from the village of Dolphinton on the A702 (take the turning to Dunsyre), is **Little Sparta** (www.littlesparta. co.uk, £10), a fascinating sculpture garden created by the late artist Ian Hamilton Finlay. Mysterious, calming and full of subtle surprises, the garden is open only three afternoons a week from June to September, but it's well worth making the effort to see this quietly extraordinary place.

To the east side of the Pentlands is the village of Roslin, its fame boosted enormously by the appearance of the **Rosslyn Chapel** (0131 440 2159, www.rosslynchapel.org.uk, £7.50, £6 discounts, free under-16s) in Dan Brown's 2003 thriller *The Da Vinci Code* and the subsequent 2006 movie. (To get there, take the A701 from Edinburgh towards Penicuik but turn off left on the B7006 to Roslin.) Sir William Sinclair (or St Clair), the Earl of Caithness and Orkney, decided to build the chapel in 1446, but the project may well have been unfinished by the time Sir William died in 1484. At any rate, the chapel has stood in its current form for more than 500 years. The latest round of repairs, a £13 million project, should be completed during 2010.

With hints of Celtic and Norse beliefs sitting alongside the Christian elements, the carvings are remarkable throughout. One flourish has been interpreted as an ear of corn, which was unknown in Scotland in the 15th century; it's seen as evidence that one of the Sinclair family had visited North America before that chap Columbus. However large a pinch of salt you take with such information, the chapel remains a strongly evocative place.

If you have the appetite for another ancient pile, try **Crichton Castle** (Crichton, 01875 320017, www.historic-scotland.gov.uk, £3.70, £1.85-£3 discounts). The residence of the Crichtons and then the Earls of Bothwell, the ruins contain a 14th-century tower house, a 15th-century great hall and an impressive diamond-dotted façade from the late 16th century. To reach it, take the A68 south from the town of Dalkeith, then head south on the B6367 when you reach Pathhead. There's car parking, but the final approach to the ruins is 600 metres on foot along a rough track.

The Pentlands, Roslin and the likes of Crichton Castle are engaging but Midlothian is better known for its associations with coal mining. A string of towns and villages form the county's centre of gravity, each running into the next, though there are few reasons to visit any of them. The exception is Newtongrange, where the **Scottish Mining Museum** (Lady Victoria Colliery, 663 7519, www.scottishmining museum.com, £6.50, £4.50 discounts) shows

visitors what drove the local economy before the mines closed down. The colliery in which it's housed employed 2,000 people at its peak, produced 40 million tons of coal in its lifetime and has a 500-metre shaft underground.

Where to eat & drink

If you're anywhere near West Linton (around 12 miles south of the city bypass on the A702), then the **Old Bakehouse** on Main Street is worth a look (01968 660830, www.west-linton. org.uk/the_old_bakehouse.html, closed Mon & Tue, main courses £12). Closer to Edinburgh but still on the A702, the **Flotterstone Inn** (01968 673717, www.flotterstoneinn.com, main courses £11) offers bar and restaurant menus. At Lothianbridge, the **Sun Inn** (663 2456, www.thesuninnedinburgh.co.uk, main courses £12) does decent beer and good pub grub. Finally, the **Howgate** (at Howgate village near Penicuik, 01968 670000, www.howgate. com, main courses £12) is also out of the way: if you're driving to Penicuik on the A701, branch off on the B7026 before reaching the town and carry on for three miles. It looks like everyone's idealised notion of a farmhouse restaurant, but it also does good steaks.

Where to stay

Aside from the 13th-century **Dalhousie Castle** (01875 820153, www.dalhousiecastle. co.uk, double £125-£295), just off the B704 south-east of Bonnyrigg, and the 15th-century Borthwick Castle (01875 820514, www.borth wickcastle.com, double £130-£240), which looks as if it should be besieged rather than patronised, the accommodation isn't anything special, and you're better off staying in the city.

Getting there

By bus Both Lothian Buses and First Bus have services from central Edinburgh that will take you to Roslin or Newtongrange. MacEwan's Coach Services operates a route down the A702 that will drop you off by the Flotterstone Inn. For general bus details, *see p256*, or call Traveline Scotland on 0871 200 2233. If you want to get to Crichton Castle, you'll need a car. **By car** The Ordnance Survey Landranger map no.66 (Edinburgh) covers most of Midlothian. **By train** There are no train services.

Tourist information

Newtongrange *Scottish Mining Museum, Lady Victoria Colliery, Newtongrange (663 4262).* **Open** *Apr-Sept* 10am-5pm Mon-Sat. Closed Oct-Mar.

ESCAPES & EXCURSIONS

WEST LOTHIAN

Like its Midlothian neighbour, West Lothian has its share of old mining towns, but also a post-war new town in the shape of **Livingston**, built to take overspill from Glasgow. Driving through the county on either of its main routes, there's little of obvious interest to detain the visitor, but it's worth seeking out the main attractions.

Between Edinburgh and Queensferry, for example, is the village of **Dalmeny**. The main attraction here is 12th-century **St Cuthbert's**, one of the finest Romanesque churches in Scotland. Nearby sits **Dalmeny House** (331 1888, www.dalmeny.co.uk, £6, £4-£5 discounts), a Gothic-revival mansion designed by William Wilkins in 1814 and home of the Earls of Rosebery. The property boasts a grand interior and, incongruously, an extensive collection of Napoleonic memorabilia. It's only open for very limited hours, though, generally for just three days a week during June and July; call before setting out.

Just beyond the house is **Queensferry**, also known as South Queensferry to distinguish it from North Queensferry in Fife. This is the best place from which to see the enormous Forth rail and road bridges. The latter, a vast suspension bridge completed in 1964, is a continuing source of controversy: despite its relative youth, the bridge is deteriorating and traffic restrictions may be in place within a few years, but a new bridge would come with a price tag that makes the bill for the Scottish Parliament or the Edinburgh tram system look like small change. By contrast, the wonderful rail bridge, a mile and a half long, is more impressive and less troublesome despite the fact that it was completed in 1890.

The other main reason to visit Queensferry is to catch the Maid of the Forth ferry (call for times on 331 5000, or see www.maidoftheforth. co.uk), which sails from South Queensferry to **Inchcolm Abbey** (01383 823332, www. historic-scotland.gov.uk, £4.70, £2.35-£3.70 discounts) on Inchcolm Island in the Firth of Forth. Founded in 1123, the abbey comprises a clutch of wonderfully preserved monastic buildings. Seal sightings are common during the boat trip.

West of Queensferry stands the astonishing **Hopetoun House** (331 2451, www.hopetoun house.com, closed Oct-Mar, £8, £4.25-£7 discounts), designed by William Bruce in 1699 and enlarged by William Adam in 1721. The elegant simplicity of the building belies the opulence within: it really is quite extraordinary inside. Further west is **Blackness Castle** (01506 834807, www.historic-scotland.gov.uk, closed Thur & Fri Nov-Mar, £4.20, £2.10-£3.20

discounts), used by Zeffirelli in his 1990 film version of *Hamlet*. Its walls have crumbled since they were built in the 1440s, but the view across the Forth from the castle promontory remains spectacular.

Just four miles south-west of Blackness is the attractive Royal Burgh of **Linlithgow**, most celebrated for the beautiful ruins of **Linlithgow Palace** (01506 842896. www. historic-scotland.gov.uk, £5.20, £2.60-£4.20 discounts) where Mary, Queen of Scots was born in 1542. The palace overlooks **Linlithgow Loch**, a scenic spot for a circular walk. Behind Linlithgow railway station lies the Union Canal Basin; you'll find the **Linlithgow Canal Centre** (01506 671215, www.lucs.org.uk, closed Sept-Easter, hours vary Easter-Sept, free), which includes a museum and a tearoom. For deeper local history, head to **Cairnpapple Hill** (01506 634622, www.historic-scotland. gov.uk, closed Oct-Mar, £3.70, £1.85-£3 discounts), off the minor roads between Linlithgow and Bathgate. This 5,000-year-old, Neolithic burial site sits on top of a hill with views that range up and down the Forth.

Where to eat & drink

Driving out of Edinburgh to the Forth Road Bridge on the A90, the black, space age building on the right, just before the bridge, is the **Dakota Forth Bridge** (*see right*; main courses £15), where the contemporary Grill restaurant has good seafood and steaks. In Queensferry itself, **Orocco Pier** (*see right*; main courses £17) offers decent bistro cooking and views of the bridges. A couple of doors along, the **Boat House** (22 High Street, 331 5429, www.theboathouse-sq.co.uk, main courses £18) has excellent views and acclaimed seafood. For a pint or pub grub with literary associations, try the **Hawes Inn** (7 Newhalls Road, 331 1990, main courses £9); Robert Louis Stevenson wrote part of *Kidnapped* here back in the 1880s.

The other main centre for food and drink in West Lothian is Linlithgow. **Livingston's** (52 High Street, 01506 846565, www. livingstons-restaurant.co.uk, set menus £30-£37) is a traditional Franco-Scottish affair; **Epulum** (121 High Street, 01506 844411, www.epulum.net, main courses £15) is more cosmopolitan. The best pint in the area can be had at the **Four Marys** (111 High Street, 01506 842171, www.thefourmarys.co.uk, main courses £8), which also does bar food. But the best restaurant in West Lothian is just outside Linlithgow via the northbound A803: the **Champany Inn** (01506 834532, www.champany.com), which was awarded a Michelin star in 2008.

Fishing for Culture

The Pittenweem Arts Festival brings culture to a corner of Fife.

The pretty fishing village of Pittenweem has attracted many artists over the years. There are roughly 30 resident in the small hamlet at present, with more in the chain of communities strung out along the lovely coastline known as the East Neuk (corner) of Fife. Appropriate, then, that it's home to one of Britain's most pleasurable art festivals, a mix of exhibitions, workshops, talks, demonstrations and performances.

According to Jean Duncan, the chair of the **Pittenweem Arts Festival**, the village's location is key. 'By bringing artists to a beautiful rural location [and using] makeshift galleries, art suddenly seems accessible and friendly to many who do not visit city galleries. We want people to experience art in a very relaxing and welcoming place. There is an emotional link in Pittenweem between enjoying the atmosphere of a day out, the fantastic views of the sea and the old harbour or being able to talk to the artists whose picture you are looking at and possibly the scene he or she has painted. And there's no face painting, burgers or candy floss!'

Ian Hamilton Finlay, the first artist invited to the festival, used his show 'Diamond Studded Fishnets' to establish a tradition of linking new work with Pittenweem's heritage. In later years, Tom McGrath wrote a one-man play about the arrival of the monk St Fillan, which was performed in the cave which bears his name.

Each year the Festival invites a number of internationally known artists as well as emerging artists from the local area. In recognition of the difficulties young artists face in getting their work exhibited and brought to the attention of buyers, in 2008 the Festival established two bursary awards.

Fast approaching its 30th birthday, the festival now includes around 100 exhibitions, which draw an estimated 20,000 visitors to this sleepy spot. The event always starts on the first Saturday in August and ends on the second Sunday. For more on the festival, including details of its annual programme, see www.pittenweemartsfestival.co.uk.

Where to stay

At Queensferry, try the imposing and modern **Dakota Forth Bridge** (319 3690, www.dakota forthbridge.co.uk, double £99-£119), on the edge of town, or the smaller-scale **Orocco Pier** (17 High Street, 0870 118 1664, www.orocco pier.co.uk, double £85-£160). In parts of West Lothian where few tourists venture, the **Macdonald Houstoun House** (Uphall, 01506 853831, www.macdonaldhotels.co.uk, double £85-£165) dates to the 17th century but has modern leisure facilities. Otherwise you can always head back to Edinburgh; the train from Linlithgow to Waverley takes all of 22 minutes.

Getting there

By bus Lothian Buses has a service to Ratho; for anything else, it's First Bus and other providers. For general bus information, *see p256*, or call Traveline Scotland on 0871 200 2233.

By car From the western edge of Edinburgh, the M9 will take you to Linlithgow, then on to Stirling; the M8 goes to Livingston, Bathgate and eventually Glasgow. For detailed navigation, the Ordnance Survey Landranger map no.65 (Falkirk & Linlithgow) covers West Lothian.

By train Linlithgow and Dalmeny (beside Queensferry) are on main lines and well served by trains from both Waverley and Haymarket. Suburban lines going west, also from Waverley and Haymarket, will take you to Livingston's two stations (North and South) and Bathgate.

Tourist information

Linlithgow *County Buildings, High Street (01506 775320).* **Open** 8.30am-5pm Mon-Thur; 8.30am-4pm Fri; 10am-6pm Sat; 10am-4pm Sun.

ESCAPES & EXCURSIONS

STIRLING & AROUND

Given its associations with battles, military strategy, the Highlands and the Lowlands, plus control of the vital Forth Valley, **Stirling** can almost claim to be the historical heart of Scotland. A prominent castle on a rock, not unlike Edinburgh's, is the cherry on the cake.

Two of the country's most significant medieval victories against England took place near here: William Wallace's at Stirling Bridge in 1297 and Robert the Bruce's at Bannockburn in 1314, and both are commemorated in the town. Wallace is celebrated by the **National Wallace Monument** on the northern edge of Stirling (Abbey Craig, 01786 472140, www. nationalwallacemonument.com, £6.50, £4-£4.90 discounts), a Victorian tower that dominates the skyline. There's plenty of Wallace memorabilia on display, including his broadsword, and the views from the top are extraordinary. The story of Bannockburn, meanwhile, is told at the **Bannockburn Heritage Centre** (Glasgow Road, 01786 812664, www.nts.org.uk, closed Nov-Feb, £5.50, £4.50 discounts).

Stirling Castle Rock was probably first occupied in the 7th century, yet today's **Stirling Castle** (01786 450000, www.historic-scotland.gov.uk, £9, £4.50-£7 discounts) dates mainly from the 15th and 16th centuries. A magnificent sight, it's one of the finest in Scotland. Displays detail the history of the building: Alexander I died here in 1124; James II was born within its walls; Mary, Queen of Scots was crowned here; and Mary's son James I & VI was christened in the chapel. The Great Hall is impressive but the castle's exterior is its greatest asset: a dramatic structure that's particularly haunting at night. (Note that James V's Palace within the castle is undergoing refurbishment and will reopen in 2011.)

Below, on Castle Wynd, is **Argyll's Lodging** (Castle Wynd, 668 8831, www.historic-scotland. gov.uk, pre-booked tours only), a 17th-century townhouse with 16th-century elements that's named in honour of the ninth Earl of Argyll. Over the way is **Mar's Wark**, the impressive stone remains of what was once a grand, Renaissance-style house built by the Earl of Mar in the 16th century. Next door is the **Church of the Holy Rude** (www.holyrude. org), which has one of the few surviving medieval timber roofs in Scotland; the intended rebuild was halted by the Reformation.

Sightseeing in Stirling is dominated by its history. However, the town is also at the centre of old Stirlingshire, where you don't have to look too hard for evidence of 19th and 20th century industries; take, for instance, the gargantuan Grangemouth petrochemical refinery on the Forth. On the other side of

National Wallace Monument.

the M9 from Grangemouth, the otherwise undistinguished town of Falkirk has one of Scotland's most extraordinary attractions. The **Falkirk Wheel** (Lime Road, Tamfourhill, Falkirk, 0870 050 0208, www.falkirk-wheel.com, boat trip £8.50, £4.25-£6.50 discounts) acts as a link between the Union Canal and the Forth & Clyde Canal making it possible to travel from Edinburgh to Glasgow by boat. Although that may not sound too thrilling, there's a twist: the Union Canal is around 30 metres above the Forth & Clyde where they meet, and the wheel lifts canal boats from one to the other. It's a smooth marvel of modern engineering. You can watch it all happen from the sidelines, or take a boat ride and have a whirl on the wheel.

East of Falkirk, there's a different kind of transport by Bo'ness: the steam-powered trains of the **Bo'ness & Kinneil Railway** (01506 822298, www.srps.org.uk/railway, call or check online for ride times, £6, £3-£5 discounts) regularly chug along the Firth of Forth to the Birkhill Claymines, where visitors can take a tour. Close to **Linlithgow** (*see p296*), Bo'ness is one of those administratively in-between places: VisitScotland thinks it's in Stirlingshire, others believe it's in West Lothian.

Where to eat & drink

Between Falkirk and Kilsyth, **Glenskirlie House** (*see below*; main courses £20) is a hotel with elevated dining options. Back in Stirling town, the best bet is **Hermann's** on Broad

Street (01786 450632, www.hermanns.co.uk, main courses £18), a modern Austro-Caledonian crossover; the chef-proprietor is from the Tirol and does a cool schnitzel. For a pint, pop into the **Portcullis Hotel** near the castle (01786 472290, www.theportcullishotel.com).

Where to stay

If you can stand the drive and the damage to your credit card, then **Gleneagles** is the pick of the bunch (01764 662231, www.gleneagles. com, double £199-£380); **Glenskirlie House** (01324 840201, www.glenskirliehouse.com, double £155-£235) is not bad either. In town, the **Barcelo Stirling Highland** (Spittal Street, 01786 272727, www.barcelo-hotels.co.uk, double £87-£167), housed in the old former high school, has modern decor, a health club and all the trimmings. Alternatively, the **Golden Lion** (King Street, 01786 475351, www.thegoldenlionstirling.com, double £89-£169) is a winning boutique, although you would never guess as much from the outside.

Getting there

By bus Scottish Citylink runs the main service from Edinburgh to Stirling and buses leave from St Andrew Square bus station once an hour. The journey, centre to centre, takes 63 minutes. For the Citylink service, call 08705 505050.
By car Stirling is about 45 miles north-west of Edinburgh via the M9 motorway.
By train There are regular trains from Waverley and Haymarket to Stirling. The journey takes about 50 minutes.

Tourist information

Bo'ness *Bo'ness & Kinneil Railway, Union Street (08452 255121).* **Open** *July, Aug* phone ahead for information.
Falkirk *Falkirk Wheel, Lime Road, Tamfourhill (08452 255121).* **Open** *Mar-Oct* 9.30am-6pm daily. *Nov-Feb* 9am-4.30pm daily.
Stirling *41 Dumbarton Road (08452 255121).* **Open** 10am-5pm daily.

THE BORDERS

The Borders covers the bottom right-hand corner of Scotland: everything between the Lothians and England, including the stretch of coast with the nature reserve at **St Abb's Head** and the fishing village of **Eyemouth**, towns such as **Galashiels**, **Hawick** and **Selkirk**, assorted abbey ruins, the **River Tweed**, some very handsome hill country and recurring associations with Sir Walter Scott. The Borders uplands may lack the drama of the

Scottish Highlands further north, but at beauty spots such as **Scott's View**, looking over the triple-peaked Eildon Hill (on the B6356 east of Melrose), the proportions of the landscape create a work of art.

It's here that the extent of the Borders' abbeys hits home. A series of institutions founded in the 12th century, with the most celebrated at **Kelso**, **Jedburgh** and **Dryburgh** (by the village of St Boswells), they lie in ruins today, but remain highly evocative; **Melrose Abbey** (Abbey Street, 01896 822562, www.historic-scotland. gov.uk, £5.20, £2.60-£4.20 discounts) may even have been where Robert the Bruce's heart was buried. (Historic Scotland also runs the other main abbeys; check its website for details.)

Away from the ruins, a couple of gardens merit mention. **Dawyck Botanic Garden** (Stobo, on the B712, 01721 760254, www.rbge. org.uk, closed Jan & Dec, £4, £1-£3.50 discounts) is an outpost of Edinburgh's Royal Botanic Garden. And just east of Peebles lies lovely **Kailzie Gardens** (Kailzie, 01721 720007, www.kailziegardens.com).

Around five miles south-east of Peebles is the tidy village of **Innerleithen**, where you'll find **Traquair House** (Innerleithen, 01896 830323, www.traquair.co.uk, closed Dec-Mar, £7, £4-£6.50 discounts). Reputedly the oldest inhabited dwelling in Scotland, it has served as a court for William the Lion, a hunting lodge for Scottish royalty, a refuge for Catholic priests and a centre for Jacobite sympathies. In late July, it hosts the two-day Traquair Fair, with craft

Falkirk Wheel.

stalls, food and drink, music and theatre. For literary buffs, Sir Walter Scott's former home at Abbotsford **Abbotsford** (Melrose, 01896 752043, www.scottsabbotsford.co.uk, closed Nov-mid Mar, £7, £3.50 discounts) on the banks of the Tweed, is unmissable: baronial, gothic and romantic, just like the man himself.

Where to eat & drink

In Melrose, **Burts Hotel** (*see right*; set menus £29-£35) has been a favourite for years, with polite decor and good Scottish ingredients. Also in Melrose, **Marmions** (Buccleuch Street, 01896 822245, www.marmionsbrasserie.co.uk, main courses £15) has a brasserie menu.

In the village of Ednam, north of Kelso, **Edenwater House** (01573 224070, www.edenwaterhouse.co.uk, set menu £35) does rather good things with local produce. Further west in Peebles, there's an international influence on the cooking at the **Halcyon** (39 Eastgates, 01721 725100, www.halcyon-restaurant.co.uk, main courses £14), while Ally McGrath's **Osso** (1 Innerleithen Road, 01721 724477, www.ossorestaurant.com, main courses £15) is very accomplished.

Where to stay

At Peebles, the **Peebles Hydro** (01721 720602, www.peebleshotelhydro.co.uk, double £170-£260) is a monster of a hotel, with everything from woodland trails to swimming pools.

North of town, **Cringletie House** (01721 725750, www.cringletie.com) is a 19th-century baronial pile. Another stand-out country house is the **Roxburghe** (01573 450331, www.roxburghe.net, double £159-£375), just south of Kelso; it has its own golf course.

In Melrose, **Burts Hotel** (01896 822285, www.burtshotel.co.uk, double £90-£130) dates to the 18th century and has the feel of a well-appointed inn. The nearby **Townhouse** (01896 822645, www.thetownhousemelrose.co.uk, double £120-£142) provides the hotel with a little competition: both are in Market Square. And in Selkirk, attractions at the **Philipburn Country House** (01750 720747, www.philipburnhousehotel.co.uk, double £125-£225) include a bistro, serving hearty food, and a quaint pool.

Getting there

By bus Buses depart from St Andrew Square Bus Station. Call Traveline Scotland on 0871 200 2233 for details.

By car The main route is the A68, but there are several other routes south from Edinburgh. Take the A701 through Penicuik, then branch off on the A703 and you'll reach Peebles. Go down the A7, past Gorebridge and North Middleton, then take the B7007 off to the right and you'll be up into the Moorfoot Hills. Alternatively, continue on the A7 and you'll reach Galashiels, with Selkirk and Melrose nearby.

By train There are no trains to the Borders.

Tourist information

Eyemouth *Auld Kirk, Market Square (01890 750 678).* **Open** *Summer* 10am-5pm Sat; 11am-2pm Sun. *Winter* closed.
Hawick *1 Tower Mill, Heart of Hawick Campus (01450 373 993).* **Open** 10am-5.30pm Mon, Wed; 10am-6.15pm Tue, Thur; 10am-7.45pm Fri, Sat; noon-3.30pm Sun.
Jedburgh *Murray's Green, Abbey Place (01835 863 170).* **Open** *Summer* 9am-6.30pm Mon-Sat; 10am-5pm Sun. *Winter* 10am-4pm Mon-Sat.
Kelso *Town House, the Square (01573 228 055).* **Open** *Summer* 10am-5pm Mon-Sat; 10am-2pm Sun. *Winter* 10am-2pm Fri, Sat. *Dec-Mar* closed.
Melrose *Abbey House, Abbey Street (01896 822 283).* **Open** *Summer* 9.30am-5.30pm Mon-Sat; noon-5pm Sun. *Winter* 10am-2pm Fri, Sat.
Peebles *23 High Street (01721 723 159).* **Open** *Summer* 9am-6pm Mon-Sat; 10am-4pm Sun. *Nov, Dec* 9.30am-4pm Mon-Sat; 11am-3pm Sun. *Jan-Mar* 9.30am-4pm Mon-Sat.
Selkirk *Halliwell's House, Market Place (01750 20054).* **Open** *Summer* 10am-5pm Mon-Sat; 11am-3pm Sun. *Winter* closed.

Abbotsford.

Directory

Getting Around

ARRIVING & LEAVING

By air

Edinburgh Airport *0844 481 8989, www.edinburghairport.com.* Edinburgh Airport is about ten miles west of the city centre. The airport is served by all major UK airlines, but the only direct US flights are run by **Delta** (to New York JFK; www.delta.com) and **Continental** (to New York Newark; www.continental.com).

The best way to and from the airport is on the **Airlink 100 bus service** (www.flybybus.com), which stops at Maybury, Drum Brae, Edinburgh Zoo, Murrayfield, the Haymarket, the West End and Waverley Bridge. Buses leave stand 19 at the airport every 15mins from 4.50am to 6.50am, then every 10mins until 00.22am; outside these hours, you can take the N22 from the airport to Waverley Steps by the station (every 30mins). To the airport, buses leave Waverley Bridge every 15mins from 4.20am until 6.05am, then every 10mins until 11.45pm; the N22, which leaves Waverley Steps at 15 and 45 mins past the hour, fills the night-time gap. The Airlink 100 journey takes 25mins and costs £3.50 for a single or £6 return; for the N22, the single fare is £3.

The **taxi** journey to central Edinburgh usually takes around 25 minutes and costs around £20.

By road

National Express (0870 580 8080, www.nationalexpress.com) operates coach services between Edinburgh and destinations in England and Wales. Buses run by **Scottish Citylink** (0870 550 5050, www.citylink.co.uk) serve a variety of towns around Scotland, while **Megabus** (www.megabus.com) runs budget bus services from Edinburgh to half a dozen Scottish destinations (including Glasgow) and a few in England. All buses and coaches arrive and depart from St Andrew Square Bus Station.

St Andrew Square Bus Station *Elder Street, New Town. Princes Street buses.* **Open** 6am-midnight daily. **Map** p328 H5 & p336 F1.

By train

Waverley Station *Waverley Bridge, New Town (0845 748 4950, www.nationalrail.co.uk).* *Princes Street buses.* **Map** p328 & p332 H6, p336 F2.
From here, you can catch trains to London (on the East Coast main line), Glasgow (every 15mins daily, less often on Sun) and to a panoply of Scottish destinations. Check www.nationalrail.co.uk for details.

PUBLIC TRANSPORT

Notwithstanding disruption caused by the construction of the tram network, public transport in the centre of Edinburgh is reasonably fast and reliable, and is certainly a better option than driving. For getting around **Glasgow**, *see p291*; for other areas, *see p256*. For lost property, *see pp307-308*.

Buses

The city and its suburbs are very well served by a comprehensive bus network. **Lothian Buses** (555 6363, www.lothianbuses.com) runs the majority of services throughout Edinburgh and into Mid and East Lothian; it's these services that are listed throughout the guide.

Several parts of town are served by a large number of buses. In these cases, rather than list each bus on every occasion, we've broken them into groupings. Below are the groupings used in the guide, together with a list of routes that serve the respective streets or areas.

Nicolson Street–North Bridge buses 3, 3A, 5, 7, 8, 14, 29, 30, 31, 33, 37, 47, 49.
Playhouse buses 1, 4, 5, 7, 8, 10, 11, 12, 14, 15, 15A, 16, 19, 22, 25, 26, 34, 44, 45, 49.
Princes Street buses 1, 3, 3A, 4, 10, 11, 12, 15, 15A, 16, 19, 22, 24, 25, 26, 29, 31, 33, 34, 36, 37, 44, 47.

Night Buses, operated by Lothian Buses, run nightly on ten routes around the city. Most routes run hourly from around midnight, but a few are more frequent (including the N22 between Ocean Terminal and the airport; *see left*). For more, see www.nightbuses.com.

Single journeys in Edinburgh cost £1.20 for adults or 70p for children aged 5-15; under-5s travel free, up to a maximum of two kids per adult passenger. There are no single fares on the city's Night Bus network; unlimited travel on it costs £3 a night. Exact change is required for all single fares.

Daytickets allow for unlimited travel on Lothian Buses (excluding the Airlink 100 bus, tour services and Night Buses). Daytickets cost £3 (£2.40 for children aged 5-15), and are available when you board your first bus of the day.

For longer periods, the **Ridacard** affords the holder unlimited travel on the network. The card costs £15 for one week (£13 for students aged 16-25, £10 for 5-15s) or £45 for four weeks (£38 for students, £30 for 5-15s). Ridacards aren't valid on tour buses and Night Buses, though they do entitle riders to half-price travel on the latter. You can buy a Ridacard from Lothian Buses Travelshops (*see below*).

LOTHIAN BUSES TRAVELSHOPS
27 Hanover Street *New Town. Princes Street buses.* **Open** 8.15am-6pm Mon-Sat. **Map** p328 & p332 G6, p336 E2.
7 Shandwick Place *New Town. Princes Street buses.* **Open** 8.15am-6pm Mon-Sat. **Map** p331 D7.
Waverley Bridge *New Town. Princes Street buses.* **Open** 8.15am-6pm Mon-Sat; 9.30am-5.15pm Sun. **Map** p328 & p332 H6, p336E2.

In addition to Lothian Buses, **First Group** (0871 200 2233, www.firstgroup.co.uk) runs a handful of services between Edinburgh and outlying areas. Tickets are not transferable.

Trains

The majority of Scottish rail services are run by **First Scotrail**. Details are available from National Rail Enquiries on 0845 748 4950 or www.nationalrail.co.uk. The information desk at Waverley station (*see left*) can also help.

As well as Waverley and Haymarket stations, the city has several suburban stations; check with National Rail Enquiries for full details.

Trams

The construction of Edinburgh's new tram network has been beset by delays and financial difficulties (*see p33*). It's hoped that the first phase of the network, linking Edinburgh Airport with Leith via Murrayfield, Haymarket, Princes Street and Waverley Station, will be ready to open in summer 2011, but no one's holding their breath. When the system does open, it will be integrated with the Lothian Buses network; Ridacards (*see left*) will be valid on both trams and buses.

TAXIS

Black cabs

Most of Edinburgh's taxis are black cabs, which take up to five passengers. When a taxi's yellow 'For Hire' light is on, you can hail it in the street. The basic fare, for the pick-up and the first 450m or 90 seconds of waiting time, costs £1.60 (£2.70 between 6pm and 6am); each additional 210m (242m after 9.30pm) or 45 seconds costs 25p. There's a 20p charge for every additional passenger over two.

Phoning for a taxi is advisable at night or if you're outside the city centre. To book, contact **Central Taxis** (229 2468, www.taxis-edinburgh.co.uk), **City Cabs** (228 1211, www.citycabs.co.uk) or **Computer Cabs** (272 8000, www.comcab-edinburgh.co.uk). Most taxis accept only cash. For lost property, *see pp307-308*.

Private hire cars

Minicabs (saloon cars) are generally cheaper than black cabs and may be able to carry more passengers (specify when booking). Cars must be booked in advance. Reputable firms include **Bluebird** (621 6666) and **Persevere** (555 2323). Call around first to get the best price.

Complaints

Complaints about a taxicab or private hire company journey should be made in writing to the Edinburgh Council Licensing Section, 249 High Street, Edinburgh EH1 1YJ. Be sure to make a note of the date and time of the journey and the licence number of the vehicle.

DRIVING

If you're planning on staying within Edinburgh during your visit,

driving isn't recommended. For one thing, the town is reasonably small and thus very accessible either on foot or via the public transport system (*see left*). For another, the preponderance of pedestrianised and one-way streets means the traffic can be terrible. And parking (*see below*) is difficult and pricey.

If you're a member of a motoring organisation in your home country, check to see if it has a reciprocal agreement with a British equivalent.

AA (Automobile Association)
0870 600 0371 enquiries, 0800 887766 emergencies, 08457 887766 emergencies from mobiles, www.theaa.com.
RAC (Royal Automobile Club)
08705 722722 enquiries, 0800 828282 emergencies, www.rac.co.uk.

Car hire

All firms below have branches at the airport; several also have offices in the city centre. Shop around for the best rate; always check the level of insurance included in the price.

Alamo *UK: 0870 400 4562, www.alamo.co.uk. US: 1-877 222 9075, www.alamo.com.*
Arnold Clark *UK & US: 0844 576 5425, www.arnoldclarkrental.co.uk.*
Avis *UK: 0844 544 3407, www.avis.co.uk. US: 1-800 331 1212, www.avis.com.*
Budget *UK: 0844 544 3439, www.budget.co.uk. US: 1-800 472 3325, www.budget.com.*
Enterprise *UK: 0870 350 3000, www.enterprise.co.uk. US: 1-800 261 7331, www.enterprise.com.*
Europcar *UK: 0870 607 5000, www.europcar.co.uk. US: 1-877 940 6900, www.europcar.com.*
Hertz *UK: 0870 844 8844, www.hertz.co.uk. US: 1-800 654 3001, www.hertz.com.*
National *UK: 0870 400 4552, www.nationalcar.co.uk. US: 1-800 222 9058, www.nationalcar.com.*
Thrifty *UK: 01494 751500, www.thrifty.co.uk. US: 1-800 847 4389, www.thrifty.com.*

Parking

The city is divided up into central and peripheral parking zones. In the central zone, you must pay to park between 8.30am and 6.30pm, Mon-Sat; in the peripheral zone, the controlled hours are 8.30am-5.30pm Mon-Fri. Parking costs £1.20-£2 an hour; maximum stays vary from three to six hours. You can pay at a

pay-and-display machine or by mobile with mPark (instructions will be on the pay-and-display machine). Information on parking in Edinburgh, including a map of parking locations, is at www.edinburgh.gov.uk/parking.

If you park illegally, you may get a ticket (the fine is £60, reduced to £30 if it is paid within 14 days) or even towed (a release fee of £105 plus £12 a day). If you fear your car has been towed, call the police on 0131 311 3131, who have a record of all towed cars. They will tell you how to get back your vehicle.

If you don't fancy taking your chances with street parking, consider one of the car parks around the city. It's more expensive than street parking but less hassle, and there's no limit on the amount of time you can park your car. All the car parks detailed below are open 24 hours a day. Rates vary; call for details. There's a full list of city centre car parks, complete with a map, online at www.edinburgh.gov.uk/parking.

Castle Terrace *Old Town (0845 050 7080, www.ncp.co.uk).* **Rates** from £4.80/2hrs up to £23/24hrs. **Map** p328 E8, p336 A3.
Greenside Place *Calton Hill & Broughton (0845 050 7080, www.ncp.co.uk).* **Rates** from £3.50/2hrs up to £20/24hrs. **Map** p333 J5.
St James Centre *Leith Walk, Broughton (0845 050 7080, www.ncp.co.uk).* **Rates** from £3/2hrs up to £19/24hrs. **Map** p333 J5.
St John's Hill *2 Viewcraig Gardens, Old Town (0845 050 7080, www.ncp.co.uk).* **Rates** from £3/2hrs up to £16/24hrs. **Map** p333 K7.

CYCLING

Thanks to some successful lobbying by the local cycle campaign **Spokes**, Edinburgh is a pretty decent place for cyclists. The city council has invested in some off-road cycle paths and road-edge cycle lanes; although it's not compulsory for motorists to observe the latter, the lanes ease the flow of cyclists during rush hours and make some roads safer. Cyclists can travel freely along bus lanes.

Be sensible when tethering a bike in the street: bikes left on the Grassmarket and Rose Street are prone to vandalism and theft. Otherwise, the only real worries for cyclists are the steep and cobbled streets around the Old Town.

DIRECTORY

Spokes produces four cycle maps that show the cycle routes in Edinburgh and the Lothians. All cost £4.95 and are available from the Spokes website. For more on cycling, *see p247*.

WALKING

To fully appreciate the beauty, elegance, charm and contrasts of the city centre and its environs, Edinburgh is best explored on foot. Although the usual caution should be exercised at night, especially around those areas of the city with abundant and rowdy nightlife (Lothian Road and the Cowgate, to name but two), walking around the city is safe and rewarding.

GUIDED TOURS

Bus tours

Edinburgh Bus Tours *220 0770, www.edinburghtour.com.* **Rates** *One bus tour* £12; £5-£11 discounts. *Four bus tours* £15; £6-£13 discounts. *Bus & boat tour* £18; £7-£16 discounts.
Lothian Buses (*see p302*) runs a number of different double-decker bus tours: City Sightseeing, a sights primer in nine languages; the Edinburgh Tour, more of the same but with live English commentary; MacTours, conducted on vintage buses; and the Majestic Tour, which runs to Holyroodhouse and Ocean Terminal. In summer, there's also a Bus & Boat tour, which takes in a boat trip on the Firth of Forth. The bus services start around 9-10am and finish at 5-6pm (later in summer, earlier in winter). All tours depart regularly from Waverley Bridge, and booking isn't required; tickets allow riders to alight and rejoin the tour at any point over a 24-hour period.

Walking tours

Auld Reekie Tours *557 4700, www.auldreekietours.com.* **Tours** *Ghost & Torture* hourly, 6-9pm daily. *Terror Tour* 10pm & 10.30pm daily. *Underground Tour* hourly, 12.30-5.30pm daily. **Meeting point** Tron Kirk, High Street, Old Town. **Tickets** *Ghost & Torture* £8.50; £7.50 discounts. *Terror Tour* £10; £9 discounts. *Underground Tour* £7; £6 discounts. **Credit** AmEx, MC, V. **Map** p333 J7 & p336 F4.
Sacrificing some factual accuracy for engaging pantomime, tour guides lead you through the streets

of Edinburgh to a section of the Underground Vaults, where you'll allegedly find a pagan temple.

City of the Dead Tours *225 9044, www.blackhart.uk.com.* **Tours** *Underground City of the Dead* Easter-Oct 1.30pm, 2.30pm, 7.30pm, 8pm, 9pm daily. Nov-Easter 1.30pm, 3.30pm 7.30pm, 9pm daily. *City of the Dead Haunted Graveyard Tour* Easter-Oct 8.30pm, 10pm daily. Nov-Easter 8.30pm. 9.30pm daily. **Meeting point** Mercat Cross, High Kirk of St Giles, High Street, Old Town. **Tickets** £8.50; £6.50 discounts. **No credit cards**. **Map** p332 H7 & p336 E4.
The haunted graveyard in question is at Greyfriars, and is said by people who believe in this sort of thing to be home to a poltergeist. The underground tour, meanwhile, takes you to what's billed as 'the closest place to hell on earth'.

Edinburgh Literary Pub Tour *0800 169 7410, www.edinburgh literarypubtour.co.uk.* **Tours** *May-Sept* 7.30pm daily. *Mar, Apr, Oct* 7.30pm Thur-Sun. *Nov-Feb* 7.30pm Fri. **Meeting point** Beehive Inn, Grassmarket. **Tickets** £8; £7 discounts. **Credit** MC, V (advance bookings). **Map** p332 G8.
A lively guide to the city's literary history, from Burns to Welsh via most points in between. Prebooking (recommended) saves £1-£2 on the ticket price.

Mercat Walking Tours *557 6464, www.mercattours.com.* **Tours** *Ghosts & Ghouls* Apr-Sept 7pm, 8pm, 9pm daily. Oct-Mar 7pm, 8pm daily. *Ghosthunter* Aug 9.45pm, 10.30pm daily. Apr-July, Sept 9.45pm Mon-Wed, Sun; 9.45pm, 10.30pm Thur-Sat. Oct-Mar 9.45pm daily. *Gallows to Graveyard* Apr-Sept 9.30pm Fri, Sat. Oct-Mar 9.30pm Sat. *Ghostly Underground* 3pm daily. *Paranormal Underground* 5.45pm Mon-Thur, Sun; 4.45pm, 5.45pm Fri, Sat. *Historic Vaults* Apr-Sept noon, 2pm, 4pm daily. Oct-Mar 2pm, 4pm daily. *Secrets of the Royal Mile* 2.15pm daily. **Meeting point** Mercat Cross, High Kirk of St Giles, High Street, Old Town. **Tickets** *Ghosts & Ghouls* £11; £6.50-£10 discounts. *Ghosthunter* £8.50; £7.50 discounts. *Gallows to Graveyard, Paranormal Underground, Secrets of the Royal Mile* £8.50; £5-£7.50 discounts. *Ghostly Underground, Historic Vaults* £7.50; £4-£6.50 discounts. **Credit** AmEx, MC, V. **Map** p332 H7 & p336 E4.

The longest established and most professional of all the companies prides itself on historical accuracy. Don't expect a lecture, though: the black-cloaked guides feed the customers a grisly portrait of Old Edinburgh. Mercat's walks pass through the extensive Underground Vaults. The earlier tours are less sinister than those staged in the evenings.

Real Mary King's Close *0870 243 0160, www.realmarykingsclose. com.* **Tours** *Apr-Oct* every 20mins, 10am-9pm daily. *Nov-Mar* every 20mins, 10am-5pm Mon-Fri, Sun; every 20mins, 10am-9pm Sat. **Meeting point** Mary King's Close, via Warriston Close. **Admission** £10.50; £6-£9.50 discounts. **Credit** MC, V. **Map** p332 H7 & p336 E3.
The remains of a street beneath the City Chambers have been turned into an historical attraction, overseen by a costumed guide. It's a fascinating look at life in the city over the years. More supernaturally focused tours are usually scheduled to run around Hallowe'en; call or check online for details.

Rebustours *553 7473, www.rebus tours.com.* **Tours** usually noon & 3pm Sat. **Meeting point** Royal Oak, Infirmary Street, Old Town. **Tickets** £10; £9 discounts. **No credit cards**. **Map** p333 J8.
Ian Rankin's Edinburgh is uncovered on a pair of walking tours run by knowledgeable enthusiast Colin Brown. Booking is required, but payment is on the day and in cash only.

Witchery Tours *225 6745, www.witcherytours.com.* **Tours** *Murder & Mystery* Apr 7.30pm, 8.30pm, 9pm, 9.30pm daily. May-Aug 8.30pm, 9pm, 9.30pm daily. Sept 8.30pm, 9pm daily. Oct-Mar 7pm, 7.30pm, 8.30pm, 9pm daily. *Ghosts & Gore* Apr 7pm daily. May-Sept 7pm, 7.30pm daily. **Meeting point** outside Witchery restaurant, 352 Castlehill, Old Town. **Tickets** £7.50; £5 discounts. **Credit** AmEx, MC, V. **Map** p332 G7.
Moving from the castle through the Cowgate, a character guide entertains in agreeably light-hearted fashion, with other characters – including Burke and Hare, the bodysnatchers – frequently popping up to startle the unwary tourist. It's an amusing evening out. The summer-only Ghosts & Gore tour is a daylight reworking of the same event.

DIRECTORY

Resources A-Z

AGE RESTRICTIONS

You have to be 18 to drink in Scotland, although some bars and clubs admit only over-21s. The legal age for driving is 17; however, most car rental firms won't hire cars to under-21s. The age of consent is 16.

ATTITUDE & ETIQUETTE

Edinburgh is, on the whole, an informal city. A handful of high-end restaurants may insist on jacket or jacket and tie (call ahead to check if you're unsure), but this is generally a pretty relaxed place, whether you're here doing business or on holiday.

BUSINESS

Conventions & conferences

Edinburgh Convention Bureau *29 Drumsheugh Gardens, EH3 7RN (473 3666, www.convention edinburgh.com).* Assistance on arranging a conference.
Edinburgh International Conference Centre *The Exchange, 150 Morrison Street, West Edinburgh, EH3 8EE (300 3000, www.eicc.co.uk). Bus 2, 3, 3A, 4, 25, 33, 44, 44A.* **Map** p331 D8. In the modern surroundings of the city's new financial centre, the EICC's main space can accommodate up to 1,200 delegates.

Couriers & shippers

DHL *0844 248 0999, www.dhl.co.uk.*
FedEx *08456 070809, http://fedex.com/gb.*
UPS *08457 877877, www.ups.com/gb.*

Office services

Integrated Language Services *451 3159, www.hw.ac.uk/ils.* Translation and interpretation service, based at Heriot-Watt University's School of Languages.
Regus *Conference House, The Exchange, 152 Morrison Street, West Edinburgh, EH3 8EB (200 6000, www.regus.co.uk). Bus 2, 3, 3A, 4, 25, 33, 44, 44A.* **Map** p331 D8. Conference and office spaces, located conveniently close to the EICC.
Office Angels *95 George Street, New Town, EH2 3ES (226 6112, www.office-angels.com).* Recruitment consultants.

Useful organisations

Edinburgh Chamber of Commerce *Capital House, 2 Festival Square, West Edinburgh, EH3 9SU (0844 736 2992, www.edinburghchamber.co.uk).* Advice and support for businesses.
Scottish Enterprise *Apex House, 99 Haymarket Terrace, West Edinburgh, EH12 5HD (313 4000, www.scottish-enterprise.com).* A government-funded economic development agency.
Scottish Executive *St Andrew's House, Regent Road, Calton Hill, EH1 3DG (556 8400, www.scotland.gov.uk).* Access to government departments.

CONSUMER

If you pay with a credit card, you can cancel payment or get reimbursed if there's a problem. The **Citizens Advice Bureau** and the local trading standards office at the **Advice Shop** (for both, *see p307*) can also help.

CUSTOMS

Citizens entering the UK from outside the EU must adhere to duty-free import limits:

● 200 cigarettes or 100 cigarillos or 50 cigars or 250g of tobacco
● 2 litres still table wine plus either 1 litre spirits or strong liqueurs (above 22% abv) or 2 litres fortified wine (under 22% abv), sparkling wine or other liqueurs
● 60cc/ml perfume
● 250cc/ml toilet water
● other goods to the value of no more than £145

The import of meat, poultry, fruit, plants, flowers and protected animals is restricted or forbidden; there are no restrictions on the import or export of currency.

People over the age of 17 arriving from an EU country are able to import unlimited goods for their own personal use, if bought tax-paid (ie not duty-free). For more details, see www.hmrc.gov.uk.

DISABLED

It's forbidden to widen the entrances of or add ramps to listed buildings, and parts of the Old Town have wheelchair-unfriendly narrow pavements. However, equal-opportunity legislation requires that new buildings are fully disabled-accessible.

Lothian Buses' new fleet of vehicles are accessible to passengers in wheelchairs. Some routes still rely on older buses, but more than half the buses are now accessible. Call 555 6363 for details. Newer **black taxis** (*see p303*) are wheelchair-accessible; always specify when booking.

DIRECTORY

Most theatres and cinemas are fitted with induction loops for the hard of hearing. Ask when booking.

For more on disabled living in Edinburgh, contact **Grapevine**, part of the Lothian Centre for Integrated Living.

Grapevine *Norton Park, 57 Albion Road, Calton Hill, EH7 5QY (475 2370, www.lothiancil.org.uk).* **Open** *By phone* 9.30am-4pm Mon-Fri.

DRUGS

Although cannabis was briefly and confusingly reclassified as a class-C soft drug a few years ago (the decision has since been reversed), both hard and soft drugs are illegal in Scotland, as they are in the rest of the UK.

ELECTRICITY

The UK electricity supply is 220-240 volt, 50-cycle AC rather than the 110-120 volt, 60-cycle AC used in the US. Foreign visitors will need to run appliances via an adaptor. TV and video use different systems to the US.

EMBASSIES & CONSULATES

For a list of local consular offices, check the *Yellow Pages*, or see www.edinburgh.gov.uk/internet/city_living/cec_consulates. The majority of embassies and consulates (the US is an exception) do not accept personal callers without an appointment.

Australian Consulate *Edinburgh Chamber of Commerce, Capital House, 2 Festival Square, EH3 9SU (228 4771, www.australia.org.uk).* **Consulate of Canada** *5 St Margaret's Road, EH9 1AZ (07702 359916 mobile, www.cic.gc.ca).* **Irish Consulate General** *16 Randolph Crescent, EH3 7TT (0131 226 7711, www.irish consulatescotland.co.uk).* **US Consulate General** *3 Regent Terrace, Calton Hill, EH7 5BW (556 8315 enquiries, 01224 857097 after-hours emergencies, www.usembassy.org.uk/scotland).*

EMERGENCIES

In the event of a serious accident, fire or incident, call 999 and specify whether you require an ambulance, the fire service or the police. *See also right* **Helplines**.

GAY & LESBIAN

Several campaigning groups maintain offices in Edinburgh, such as **Stonewall Scotland** (557 3679, www.stonewallscotland.org.uk) and the **Equality Network** (07020 933952, www.equality-network. org). Young people should check the **LGBT Youth Scotland** website at www.lgbtyouth.org.uk. Among the city's special-interest groups are the **Edinburgh Gay Women's Group**, which runs a social at the Regent (*see p233*) from 7.30pm on the third Wednesday of the month, from 8.30pm every Wednesday; there's a comprehensive list of the others at the **Lothian Gay & Lesbian Switchboard** website (*see below*).

For more on the local gay scene, including a full list of local bars and cafés, *see pp232-234*.

Edinburgh LGBT Health & Wellbeing Centre *9 Howe Street, New Town (523 1100, www.lgbt health.org.uk). Bus 24, 29, 36, 42.* **Open** hours vary. **Map** p328 F5. Health advice and support, along with other social events. **Lothian Gay & Lesbian Switchboard** *556 4049 main line, 557 0751 lesbian line, www.lgls. co.uk.* **Open** *Main line* 7.30-10pm daily. *Lesbian line* 7.30-10pm Mon. Advice and support, with occasional social events.

HEALTH

National Health Service (NHS) treatment is free to EU nationals, UK residents and those studying here. All can register with a doctor (commonly known as a general practitioner, or GP). There are no NHS charges for accident and emergency treatment, treatment of some communicable diseases (including STDs) and family planning. If you aren't eligible to see an NHS doctor, you will be charged the cost price for medicines prescribed by a private doctor.

If you don't fit into any of the above categories but want to find out if you still qualify for free treatment, see www.nhslothian. scot.nhs.uk.

Accident & emergency

Royal Infirmary of Edinburgh *51 Little France Crescent, Old Dalkeith Road, EH16 (536 1000).* Bus 8, 18, 24, 33, 38, 49. Edinburgh's 24-hour casualty department.

Complementary medicine

See p201.

Contraception & abortion

Caledonia Youth *5 Castle Terrace, South Edinburgh (229 3596, www.caledoniayouth.org). Bus 1, 10, 11, 15, 15A, 16, 22, 24, 30, 34.* **Open** noon-6pm Mon-Thur; noon-3.30pm Fri; noon-2.30pm Sat. **Map** p332 E8 & p336 A3. Advice on contraception, abortion and sexual health for under-25s. Staff can offer referrals to local hospitals or clinics. **Family Planning & Well Woman Services** *18 Dean Terrace, Stockbridge (332 7941). Bus 24, 29, 42.* **Open** *By appointment* 9.30am-7.30pm Mon-Thur; 9am-3.30pm Fri. *Drop-in clinic (under-25s)* 9.30am-noon Sat. **Map** p327 D4. Confidential advice, contraceptive provision, pregnancy tests and abortion referral.

Dentists

Chalmers Dental Centre *3 Chalmers Street, South Edinburgh (www.nhslothian.scot.nhs.uk). Bus 35.* **Open** 9am-4.45pm Mon-Thur; 9am-4.15pm Fri. **Map** p332 G9. A walk-in clinic offering emergency care. Out of hours, phone the Lothian Dental Advice Line on 0131 536 4800; staff can arrange for you to receive emergency care if necessary.

Hospitals

See above **Accident & emergency**.

Opticians

The **Alexandra Pavilion** offers a free walk-in service for emergency eye complaints. For dispensing opticians, *see p201*.

Princess Alexandra Eye Pavilion *Chalmers Street, South Edinburgh (536 1000). Bus 35.* **Open** 8.30am-5pm Mon-Fri. **Map** p332 G9.

Pharmacies

See p201.

STDs, HIV & AIDS

The **Genito-Urinary Medicine Clinic** (GUM), affiliated with the Royal Infirmary of Edinburgh, provides free, confidential advice and treatment of STDs, and offers

HIV tests by appointment. The **Solas Centre** is the city's HIV and AIDS support resource.

Genito-Urinary Medicine Clinic

Lauriston Building, Lauriston Place, South Edinburgh (536 2103). Bus 35. **Open** *Phone for appointments* 9am-4.30pm Mon-Fri. **Map** p332 G9.

Waverley Care Solas *3 Mansfield Place, New Town (558 1425, www.waverleycare.org.uk). Bus 8.* **Open** 10am-4pm Mon-Thur (closed 1st Wed of mth); 10am-1pm Fri. **Map** p328 H4.

HELPLINES

Alcoholics Anonymous *0845 769 7555, www.alcoholics-anonymous. org.uk.* **Open** 24hrs daily.
Childline *0800 1111, www. childline.org.uk.* **Open** 24hrs daily.
Edinburgh Women's Rape & Sexual Abuse Centre *556 9437, www.ewrasac.org.uk.* **Open** hrs vary.
Know the Score Drugs Helpline *0800 587 5879, www.knowthe score.info.* **Open** 24hrs daily.
National AIDS Helpline *0800 567123.* **Open** 24hrs daily.
National Health Service Direct *0800 4546, www.nhsdirect.nhs.uk.* **Open** 24hrs daily.
Samaritans *08457 909090, www. samaritans.org.* **Open** 24hrs daily.
Victim Support *0845 303 0900, www.victimsupport.org.uk.* **Open** 9am-9pm Mon-Fri; 9am-7pm Sat, Sun.

Drop-in centres

Advice Shop *South Bridge, Old Town (225 1255, www.edinburgh. gov.uk). Nicolson Street–North Bridge buses.* **Open** 9.30am-4pm Mon, Wed, Thur; 10am-4pm Tue; 9.30am-3.30pm Fri. **Map** p333 J7 & p336 F4. Advice on consumer problems and welfare benefits.
Citizens Advice Bureau *58 Dundas Street, New Town (557 1500 enquiries, 557 3681 appointments, www.cas.org.uk). Bus 13, 23, 27.* **Open** 9.10am-4pm Mon, Tue, Thur; 9.10am-12.30pm, 1.30-3pm (drop-in), 6-8pm (legal enquiries) Wed. **Map** p332 F4. Free advice on legal, financial and personal matters. Aside from this city-centre branch, there are four other offices around Edinburgh.

ID

ID is not widely required in the UK, but you will need a passport or drivers' licence (with a photograph)

for changing money, cashing travellers' cheques and so on.

INSURANCE

Non-nationals should arrange baggage, trip-cancellation and medical insurance before departures. Medical centres will ask for your insurance company and policy number; keep the details with you at all times.

INTERNET

Public internet access is abundant in Edinburgh. Many cafés and bars offer free Wi-Fi access, as do many hotels; all the reviews in our **Hotels** chapters (*see pp114-134*) include information on the variety and price of internet access offered at each property. In addition, some chain cafés such as Starbucks offer wireless access via a paid-for subscription. However, if you're not toting a laptop or similar, a handful of internet cafés have computers available for rent, usually by the hour.

Coffee Home *28 Crighton Place, Leith Walk (477 8336, www.coffeehome.co.uk). Bus 7, 10, 12, 14, 16, 22, 25, 49.* **Open** 10am-10pm Mon-Sat; noon-10pm Sun. **Map** p329 L2.
easyInternetcafé *58 Rose Street, New Town (226 5971, www.easy internetcafe.com). Princes Street buses.* **Open** 7.30am-10pm daily. **Map** p328 & p332 F6, p336 C1.
West Bow Internet Café *98 West Bow, Old Town (226 5400, www.edininternetcafe.com). Bus 2, 23, 27, 41, 42.* **Open** call for details. **Map** p332 G8 & p336 D4.

LEFT LUGGAGE

Edinburgh Airport *344 3486, www.edinburghairport.com.* **Open** 5.15am-10.45pm daily. Left luggage facilities are located between the check-in area and the internationals arrivals hall.
St Andrew Square Bus Station There are lockers in the station.
Waverley Station *558 3829, www.excess-baggage.com.* **Open** 7am-11pm daily. The left luggage facilities are run by Excess Baggage.

LEGAL HELP

If a legal problem arises, contact your embassy, consulate or high commission (*see left*). You can get advice from any **Citizens Advice Bureau** (*see above*) or one of the

organisations listed below. If you need financial assistance, be sure to ask about Legal Aid eligibility. For leaflets explaining how the system works, write to the **Scottish Legal Aid Board**. Advice on problems concerning visas and immigration can be obtained from the **Immigration Advisory Service**.

Edinburgh & Lothians Race Equality Council *14 Forth Street, EH1 3LH (556 0441, www.elrec.org.uk).*
Immigration Advisory Service *115 Bath Street, Glasgow, G2 2SZ (0141 248 2956 enquiries & appointments, 0141 222 4888 helpline, www.iasuk.org).*
Law Society of Scotland *26 Drumsheugh Gardens, EH3 7YR (226 7411, www.lawscot. org.uk).*
Scottish Legal Aid Board *44 Drumsheugh Gardens, EH3 7SW (226 7061 office, 0845 122 8686 helpline, www.slab.org.uk).*

LIBRARIES

The **Central Library** (*see p61*) stocks an enormous range of publications, and has a large reference section. You don't need to live locally to use the library for reference, but only local residents are permitted to join the lending library.

The **National Library of Scotland** (*see p63*) is a deposit library. The Reading Rooms are open for reference and research; admission is by ticket only to approved applicants.

University of Edinburgh Main Library *George Square, South Edinburgh (650 3409, www.lib.ed. ac.uk). Bus 2, 41, 42.* **Open** *Term-time* 8.30am-midnight Mon-Sat; noon-midnight Sun. *Holidays* 8.30am-8pm Mon-Thur; 8.30am-5pm Fri; 10am-8pm Sat; noon-8pm Sun. **Map** p332 H9. Students who aren't studying at the university may use it for reference purposes. Other users get research access, but at a cost (which depends on your personal and professional status).

LOST PROPERTY

Always inform the police if you lose anything, if only to validate insurance claims. A lost passport should also be reported at once to your embassy or consulate, if relevant (*see left*). Below are the details of the lost property offices for items left on public transport.

DIRECTORY

Edinburgh Airport *344 3486,*
www.edinburghairport.com.
Open 5.15am-10.45pm daily.
The lost property office is located
in the international arrivals hall.
Lothian Buses *Annandale Street,*
Broughton (558 8858, www.lothian
buses.com). Bus 7, 10, 12, 14, 16,
22, 25, 49. **Open** 10am-1.30pm
Mon-Fri. **Map** p329 J3.
Taxis *Edinburgh Police, Fettes*
Avenue, Stockbridge (311 3141).
Bus 19, 24, 29, 37, 38, 42, 47.
Open 9am-5pm Mon-Fri.
Map p327 A4.
All property that has been left in a
black cab, as well as in the street or
in shops, gets sent here.
Waverley Station *558 3829,*
www.excess-baggage.com. **Open**
8am-5.30pm daily. Waverley's lost
property facilities are operated by
Excess Baggage. For items lost in
other stations or on trains, contact
the individual station.

MEDIA

Most of Scotland's newspapers,
and much of its TV output, operate
on a quasi-national basis pitched
somewhere between the regional
media and London's self-styled
'national' press. The attitudes on
display in the newspapers both
reflect and illuminate the current
state of that nebulous beast known
as Scottish identity. The cultural
divergences that impelled the
devolution campaign continue
to pervade the media here, with
mixed results.

Newspapers

Much of the London-based press
now prints Scottish editions.
Nationals such as the *Guardian*
and Sunday sibling the *Observer*
(left-leaning, arts-friendly), the
Times and the *Sunday Times*
(right-slanted, business-heavy),
and the *Sun* and Sunday's *News
of the World* (trashy, gossipy) are
all widely sold; London's flimsy
Metro freesheet also publishes a
Scottish edition. Alongside the
imports sit a number of exclusively
Scottish papers, listed below.

**The Scotsman &
Scotland on Sunday**
www.scotsman.com & http://
scotlandonsunday.scotsman.com.
Based in Edinburgh, *The Scotsman*
has gone a little downmarket in
recent years. The editorial line
tends to the right; arts and features
have an east coast bias. *Scotland
on Sunday* is its sister paper.

The Herald & Sunday Herald
www.theherald.co.uk &
www.sundayherald.com.
This Glasgow-based broadsheet
has the edge over the *Scotsman* in
terms of news. Any Glaswegian
bias in its features coverage
complements the *Scotsman*'s east
coast orientation. The *Sunday
Herald* is the sister paper.
Daily Record & Sunday Mail
www.dailyrecord.co.uk &
www.sundaymail.co.uk.
Published by the Mirror Group in
Glasgow, Scotland's best-selling
daily and its Sunday sibling are
frothy, although sports coverage
is strong. Both papers have a
campaigning instinct.
Evening News
http://edinburghnews.scotsman.com.
Edinburgh's daily evening tabloid.
The latest headlines from around
the world are combined with a
strong local Edinburgh flavour.

Magazines

The city's most high-profile
magazine is **The List** (£2.20,
www.list.co.uk). Issued fortnightly
on Thursdays (weekly during
August), it contains full cultural
listings for Edinburgh and Glasgow,
and also publishes an annual
Eating & Drinking Guide to
both cities (£5.95). *The List* has
competition from **The Skinny**
(free, www.theskinny.co.uk).
 Tradition still has a place on
Scots magazine shelves. In print
since 1739, the monthly **Scots
Magazine** (£1.80, www.scots
magazine.com) is a kind of
McReader's Digest, while the
fresher **Scottish Field** (£3.50,
www.scottishfield.co.uk) offers
lifestyle features. The literary
scene is covered by the biannual
Edinburgh Review (£5.95,
www.englit.ed.ac.uk/edinburgh
review) and the sporadically
published **Chapman** (£5.50,
www.chapman-pub.co.uk).

Radio

Most UK national stations are
accessible in Edinburgh, chief
among them the five main BBC
stations (www.bbc.co.uk/radio):
Radio 1 (97.6-99.8 FM, youth-
slanted pop), **Radio 2** (88-90.2 FM,
adult pop and rock), **Radio 3** (90.2-
92.4 FM, classical), **Radio 4** (92.4-
94.6 FM, current affairs and culture)
and **Radio 5 Live** (693 & 909 MW,
news and sport). There are also a
number of other national stations
available solely on digital radio.

Several stations are unique to
Scotland. **BBC Radio Scotland**
(92.4-94.7 FM) commands respect
for its mix of talk and music-
based programming. **Forth 1**
(97.3 FM, www.forthone.com) is
a sort of Scottish Radio 1 with
added commercials, while **Forth
2** (1548 AM, www.forth2.com)
plays older music. **Real Radio**
(100.3-101.1 FM, www.realradio-
scotland.co.uk) is a downmarket
mix of music and chat, and
Galaxy (105.7-106.1 FM, www.
galaxyscotland.co.uk) offers
familiar favourites.

Television

Both the BBC and ITV in Scotland
opt in and out of the UK-wide
output, with BBC Scotland and
the independent Scottish Television
(STV) contributing regularly to
their respective networks.

MONEY

Britain's currency is the pound
sterling (£). One pound equals
100 pence (p). 1p and 2p coins are
copper; 5p, 10p, 20p and 50p coins
are silver; the £1 coin is gold; the
£2 coin is silver with a gold edge.
The euro may be accepted in some
shops in tourist areas.
 Three Scottish banks – **Bank
of Scotland**, the **Royal Bank
of Scotland** and the **Clydesdale
Bank** – issue their own paper
notes. The colours of the notes
varies between the three, but
they're not far from the following
schema: green £1; blue £5; brown
£10; purple/pink £20; red or green
£50; bold red £100.

Banks & ATMs

In general, banks are open 9am to
4pm Mon-Fri, but some remain
open later. ATMs, usually situated
outside banks, give 24-hour access
to cash; most will also allow you to
draw money on a card tied to an
international network such as Visa.
 There are branches of the three
Scottish clearing banks throughout
the city. Customers of English
banks should be able to draw
money from their ATMs at no
charge; check with your bank.
Some English banks do maintain
a limited presence in the city; the
main branches are listed below.

Barclays *1 St Andrew Square,
New Town (08457 555555,
www.barclays.co.uk). Princes
Street buses.* **Open** 9.30am-4.30pm

Mon-Fri; 9.30am-12.30pm Sat.
Map p328 G5 & p336 E1.
HSBC *76 Hanover Street, New Town (08457 404404, www.hsbc. co.uk). Bus 13, 23, 27 or Princes Street buses.* **Open** 9am-5pm Mon, Wed-Fri; 9.30am-5pm Tue.
Map p328 & p332 G6.
Lloyds TSB *28 Hanover Street, New Town (0845 300 0000, www. lloydstsb.com). Bus 13, 23, 27 or Princes Street buses.* **Open** 9am-5pm Mon, Tue; 10am-5pm Wed; 9am-7pm Thur; 9am-6pm Fri; 10am-4pm Sat.* **Map** p328 & p332 G6.
National Westminster *8 George Street, New Town (0845 366 1965, www.natwest.com). Princes Street buses.* **Open** 9am-5pm Mon, Tue, Thur, Fri; 9am-5pm Wed; 10am-3pm Sat.* **Map** p328 & p332 G6, p336 E1.

Bureaux de change

Bureaux de change charge fees for cashing travellers' cheques or exchanging currency. Commission rates vary greatly; it pays to shop around. There are bureaux de change at the airport and Waverley Station; others are scattered around in areas popular with tourists.

Most banks offer currency exchange; rates are usually better than at bureaux de change. Commission is often charged for cashing travellers' cheques in foreign currencies, but not for sterling travellers' cheques, provided you cash them at a bank affiliated to the issuing bank. Get a list when you buy your cheques.

When changing currency or travellers' cheques, you'll need photo ID, such as a passport or drivers' licence.

Lost/stolen credit cards

Report lost or stolen credit cards both to the police and the 24-hour phone lines listed below. Inform your bank by phone and in writing.

American Express *01273 696933, www.americanexpress.com.*
Diners Club *0870 190 0011, www.dinersclub.co.uk.*
MasterCard *0800 964767, www.mastercard.com.*
Visa *0800 891725, www.visa.com.*

Tax

By law, sales tax is included in all prices advertised in UK shops. However, a handful of hotels may quote you rates that exclude tax. Always check when booking.

OPENING HOURS

In general, business hours are 9.30am-5.30pm Mon-Fri. Most shops are open 9am-5.30pm Mon-Sat and 11am-5pm on Sun. Many restaurants are open all day; some stay open well beyond 11pm. Officially, closing time for pubs is 11pm, but most pubs have licences to sell alcohol until 1am. Many shops, restaurants, pubs and clubs operate longer hours during the August festivals.

POLICE

If you've been the victim of a crime, look under 'Police' in the phone directory for the nearest police station, or call directory enquiries (*see p310*). The **Police Information Centre** in the Old Town (*see p65*) is both a museum and a working police centre. For emergencies, *see p306*.

POSTAL SERVICES

The UK has a fairly reliable postal service. If you have a query, contact Customer Services on 08457 740740. For business enquiries, call 08457 950950.

Post offices are usually open 9am-5.30pm during the week and 9am-noon on Saturdays, although some post offices shut for lunch and smaller offices may close for one or more afternoons each week. Three central post offices, two in the New Town and one in the Old Town are listed below; for others, call the **Royal Mail** on 08457 223344 or check online at www.royalmail.com.

You can buy individual stamps at post offices, and books of four or 12 first- or second-class stamps at newsagents and supermarkets that display the appropriate red sign. A first-class stamp for a regular letter costs 39p; second-class stamps are 30p. It costs 62p to send a postcard abroad. For details of other rates, see www.royalmail.com.

Frederick Street Post Office
40 Frederick Street, New Town (08457 223344). Bus 28, 37, 41, 42 or Princes Street buses. **Open** 9am-5.30pm Mon, Wed-Fri; 9.30am-5.30pm Tue; 9am-12.30pm Sat.* **Map** p328 & p332 F6, p336 C1.
St James Centre Post Office
8-10 Kings Mall, St James Centre, New Town (08457 223344). Princes Street buses. **Open** 9am-5.30pm Mon, Wed-Sat; 9.30am-5.30pm Tue.* **Map** p328 H5.

St Mary's Street Post Office
46 St Mary's Street, Old Town (08457 223344). Nicolson Street– North Bridge buses. **Open** 9am-5.30pm Mon-Fri; 9am-12.30pm Sat.* **Map** p333 J7.

Poste restante

If you intend to travel around the UK, friends from home can write to you care of a post office, where mail will be kept at the enquiries desk for up to one month. The envelope should be marked 'Poste Restante' in the top left-hand corner, with your name displayed above the address of the post office where you want to collect the mail. Take photo ID (a driving licence or passport) when you collect your post. The post office at the St James Centre (*see above*) offers this service.

RELIGION

BAPTIST: Charlotte Baptist Chapel *204 Rose Street, New Town (225 4812, www.charlotte chapel.org). Princes Street buses.* **Services** 11am, 6.30pm Sun.
Map p332 E7 & p336 A1.
BUDDHIST: The Portobello Buddhist Priory (27 Brighton Place, Portobello, 669 9622, www. portobellobuddhist.org.uk) offers daily Zen Buddhist meditation; the **Edinburgh Buddhist Centre** (30 Melville Terrace, Marchmont, 662 6699, www.edinburghbuddhist centre.org.uk) offers classes and meditation sessions.
CATHOLIC: St Mary's Cathedral *61 York Place, New Town (556 1798, www.stmaryscathedral.co.uk). Playhouse buses.* **Services** 10am, 12.45pm Mon-Fri; 10am, 6pm (vigil) Sat; 9.30am, 11.30am, 6pm (vigil), 7.30pm Sun. **Map** p328 H5.
CHURCH OF SCOTLAND: St Giles' Cathedral *High Street, Old Town (225 4363, www.stgiles cathedral.org.uk). Bus 2, 23, 27, 41, 42, 45.* **Services** noon Mon-Thur, Sat; 8am, noon Fri; 8am, 10am, 11.30am, 6pm, 8pm Sun.
Map p332 H7 & p336 E4.
EPISCOPALIAN: St Mary's Cathedral *Palmerston Place, New Town (225 6293, www.cathedral. net). Bus 2, 3, 3A, 4, 12, 25, 26, 31, 33, 38, 44, 44A.* **Services** 7.30am, 1.05pm, 5.30pm Mon-Wed, Fri; 7.30am, 11.30am, 1.05pm, 5.30pm Thur; 7.30am Sat; 8am, 10.30am, 3.30pm Sun. **Map** p331 C8.
HINDU: Hindu Mandir & Cultural Centre *St Andrew Place, Leith (440 0084, www.edinburghhindu mandir.myfreeola.com). Bus 12, 16,*

DIRECTORY

35. **Meetings** 2pm 2nd & 4th Sun of mth. **Map** p326 Y4.

ISLAM: Edinburgh Central Mosque *50 Potterrow, South Edinburgh (667 1777). Bus 2, 41, 42.* **Prayer times** phone for details. **Map** p333 J8.

JEWISH: Edinburgh Hebrew Congregation *4 Salisbury Road, South Edinburgh (667 3144, www.ehcong.com). Bus 2, 14, 30, 33.* **Services** times vary; phone for details. **Map** p333 L11.

METHODIST: City of Edinburgh Methodist Church *25 Nicolson Square, South Edinburgh (667 1465, www.edinburghandforth methodistcircuit.org.uk). Nicolson Street–North Bridge buses.* **Services** 6.30pm Sun. **Map** p333 J8.

QUAKER: Quaker Meeting House *7 Victoria Terrace, Victoria Street, Old Town (225 4825, www.quakerscotland.org). Bus 2, 23, 27, 41, 42, 45.* **Meetings** 12.30pm Wed; 11am Sun. **Map** p332 G7 & p336 D4.

SIKH: Guru Nanak Sikh Gurdwara *1 Mill Lane, Leith (553 7207). Bus 1, 7, 10, 11, 14, 21, 34.* **Services** phone for details. **Map** p336 X3.

SAFETY & SECURITY

Violent crime is relatively rare in central Edinburgh, but it still pays to use common sense. Keep your wallet and other valuables out of sight; and never leave bags, coats and purses unattended.

Edinburgh's city centre is a pretty safe and civilised place, but the lairy pub culture on the Cowgate and Lothian Road can be a little unpleasant at closing time. Ill-lit parks such as the Meadows have been the scene of (infrequent) assaults down the years. Women should avoid the Leith backstreets, one of the region's main red-light districts. Away from the centre at Edinburgh's various peripheral housing schemes, things get a lot dicier; these areas are best avoided.

SMOKING

Smoking is now banned in enclosed public spaces across Scotland, including all restaurants and pubs. The law is strictly enforced, as fines for establishments that break it are punitively high.

STUDY

A good deal of Edinburgh's character is defined by its big student population. Most study at one of four universities, of which the most prestigious is the **University of Edinburgh** (Old College, South Bridge, South Edinburgh, 650 1000, www.ed.ac.uk). Founded in 1583, it's since been joined by **Heriot-Watt University** (Riccarton Campus, Currie, 449 5111, www.hw.ac.uk), **Napier University** (Craiglockhart Campus, 219 Colinton Road, South Edinburgh, 0845 260 6040, www.napier.ac.uk) and **Queen Margaret University** (Clerwood Terrace, West Edinburgh, 474 0000, www.qmuc.ac.uk). There's also the **Edinburgh College of Art** (Lauriston Place, South Edinburgh, 221 6000, www.eca.ac.uk).

TELEPHONES

Dialling & codes

The area code for Edinburgh is 0131; Glasgow's area code is 0141. To reach a UK number from abroad, dial the international access code (011 if you're in the US) or the '+' symbol on a mobile phone; then 44 for the UK; then the area code, omitting the first 0; then the seven-digit number. So to call **Edinburgh Castle** (*see p56*) from the US, for example, dial 011 44 131 225 9846.

Numbers beginning 075, 077, 078 and 079 are mobile phones. Phone numbers beginning 080 are toll-free; those prefixed 084 and 087 are charged at up to 10p a minute; and numbers beginning 09 are billed at premium rates.

To call abroad from Edinburgh, dial the international access code (00) or the '+' symbol, then the country code (61 for Australia, 33 for France, 1 for the US), then the local number.

Mobile phones

Mobile phones in the UK operate on the 900 MHz and 1800 MHz GSM frequencies common throughout most of Europe. If you're travelling to the UK from Europe, your phone should be compatible; if you're travelling from the US, you'll need a tri-band handset. Either way, you should check that your phone is enabled for international roaming, and that your service provider at home has a reciprocal arrangement with a UK provider.

Operator services

Operator 100.
Automated alarm calls *55*.
Directory enquiries 118 500.

Public phones

Public payphones take coins, credit cards or prepaid phonecards. The minimum cost is 20p. Phonecards are available from post offices and many newsagents in denominations of £2, £5, £10 and £20. Most public phones in the city centre now also have an integrated internet facility.

TIME

Edinburgh operates on Greenwich Mean Time (GMT). Clocks move an hour forward to run on British Summer Time (BST) at 1am on the last Sunday in March, and return to GMT on the last Sunday in October.

TIPPING

Tipping 10-15% in taxis, restaurants, hairdressers and some bars (but not pubs) is normal. Some restaurants and bars add service automatically to all bills; always check to avoid paying twice.

TOILETS

It's generally not acceptable to use the toilets of cafés or bars unless you're a customer or have a small child in tow. However, major department stores on and around Princes Street have public toilets, while the city maintains a decent number of public toilets around town: the most central are on Castlehill, Nicolson Square and Tollcross in Old Town, and on the Mound and Princes Street Gardens. All except Castlehill have disabled facilities; the Tollcross toilet also has baby-changing facilities.

TOURIST INFORMATION

The **Edinburgh & Lothians Tourist Board** operates the main tourist office in the city, at the east end of Princes Street. As well as distributing a wealth of information on tours and attractions, staff can book hotels and event tickets, car hire and coach trips. There's also internet access and a bureau de change. The information point at the airport has a smaller range of services, but can help with tours and hotels. There are other centres around the Lothians; see www.edinburgh.org for details.

For tourist information in Glasgow, *see p291*. For tourist information in other destinations, see the relevant section of the Escapes & Excursions chapter (*pp292-300*).

**Edinburgh & Scotland
Information Centre** *Above
Princes Mall, 3 Princes Street, New
Town, EH2 2QP (0845 225 5121,
www.edinburgh.org). Princes Street
buses.* **Open** *Apr, Oct* 9am-6pm
Mon-Sat; 10am-6pm Sun. *May,
June, Sept* 9am-7pm Mon-Sat; 10am-
7pm Sun. *July, Aug* 9am-8pm Mon-
Sat; 10am-8pm Sun. *Nov-Mar*
9am-5pm Mon-Sat; 10am-5pm Sun.
Map p328 & p332 H6, p336 F2.
**Edinburgh Airport Tourist
Information Desk** *Edinburgh
Airport (0870 040 0007,
www.edinburgh.org).* **Open**
Apr-Oct 6.30am-10.30pm daily.
Nov-Mar 7am-9pm daily.

VISAS & IMMIGRATION

EU citizens do not require a visa to
visit the UK; citizens of the USA,
Canada, Australia, South Africa
and New Zealand can also enter
with only a passport for tourist
visits of up to six months as long
as they can show they can support
themselves during their visit
and plan to return. Go online to
www.ukvisas.gov.uk to check your
visa status well before you travel,
or contact the British embassy,
consulate or high commission in
your own country. You can arrange
visas online at www.fco.gov.uk.
For work permits, *see below*.

**Home Office Immigration &
Nationality Bureau** *Lunar House,
40 Wellesley Road, Croydon, CR9
1AT (0870 606 7766 enquiries,
0870 241 0645 applications,
www.homeoffice.gov.uk).*

WEIGHTS & MEASURES

As part of Europe, Scotland uses
kilos and metres, but only
nominally: natives still tend to
think in Imperial measures.

WHEN TO GO

There isn't really a best or a worst
time to visit Edinburgh: it all
depends on what you want from
your visit. The cultural festivals
means August is the liveliest and
most interesting month of the year.
However, it's also the busiest: the
pavements are awash with tourists
and street performers, and there
are queues virtually everywhere.
Similarly, the Hogmanay
celebrations draw hordes each
year, but aren't to everyone's taste.
For more on August's festivals,
see pp206-215; for other special
events, *see pp216-217*.

THE LOCAL CLIMATE

Average temperatures and monthly rainfall in Edinburgh.

	High (°C/°F)	Low (°C/°F)	Rainfall (mm/in)
Jan	6 / 43	1 / 34	64 / 2.5
Feb	7 / 45	1 / 34	45 / 1.8
Mar	9 / 48	2 / 36	52 / 2.0
Apr	11 / 52	3 / 37	43 / 1.7
May	14 / 57	6 / 43	49 / 1.9
June	17 / 63	9 / 48	53 / 2.1
July	19 / 66	11 / 52	58 / 2.3
Aug	19 / 66	10 / 50	53 / 2.1
Sept	16 / 61	9 / 48	62 / 2.4
Oct	13 / 55	6 / 43	70 / 2.8
Nov	9 / 48	3 / 37	61 / 2.4
Dec	7 / 45	1 / 34	67 / 2.6

The changeable Scottish weather
further complicates matters.
Winters can be quite chilly and
summers are generally pleasant,
but the rain is a constant threat all
year round. There's no guarantee
of good weather at any time, but
between the months of May and
October, when the days get longer
and you can finally get your
thermals off, the city is probably
at its best. For a chart detailing the
local climate, *see above*.

Public holidays

Edinburgh shares some public
holidays with the whole of the UK
and others with only the rest of
Scotland, and even has one holiday
of its own. Many shops remain
open on public holidays, but public
transport services are less frequent.
Almost everything is closed
on Christmas Day, and most
businesses are shut on New Year's
Day. Below is a list of the city's
public holidays.

New Year's Day
Jan 1 (or following Mon if it falls on
a weekend)
January 2 Holiday
Jan 2 (or first non-holiday weekday
if it falls on a weekend)
Good Friday varies
Early May Bank Holiday
first Mon in May
Spring Bank Holiday
last Mon in May
Victoria Day (Edinburgh only)
Mon before May 24
Summer Bank Holiday
first Mon in Aug
St Andrew's Day
Nov 30 (or following Mon if it falls
on a weekend)
Christmas Day
Dec 25 (or following Mon if it falls
on a weekend)

Boxing Day
Dec 26 (or first non-holiday
weekday if it falls on a weekend)

WOMEN

Women travelling on their own
face the usual hassles, but this
is generally a safe city. Take the
same precautions you'd take in
any big city. Many of the city's
black cab firms now give priority
to lone women, whether booked
by phone (recommended after
midnight) or flagged in the street.
See left for general safety and
security tips.

WORKING IN
EDINBURGH

Finding temporary work in
Edinburgh can tough. However,
if you speak English and are an
EU citizen or the owner of a work
permit, you should be able to find
a job in catering or labouring, or in
a bar, pub, café or shop. Graduates
with an English or foreign-language
degree could try teaching.
    To find work, check the *Scotsman*
and other national newspapers, and
windows of newsagents. There's
often temporary and unskilled work
available: look in the *Yellow Pages*
under 'Employment Agencies'.
Restaurants and bars often
advertise jobs in their windows.

Work permits

EEA citizens, residents of Gibraltar
and certain categories of other
overseas nationals (such as citizens
of other Commonwealth countries
aged 17-27) do not require a work
permit. However, Citizens of non-
European Economic Area (EEA)
countries need a permit to work
legally in the UK.

DIRECTORY

Further Reference

BOOKS

Fiction

Kate Atkinson *One Good Turn*
The fifth novel by York-born,
Edinburgh-based Atkinson is set
at the International Festival.
Iain Banks *Complicity*
A visceral, body-littered thriller,
with spot-on characterisation of
both the city and the protagonists.
Ron Butlin *Night Visits*
'Edinburgh at its grandest, coldest
and hardest,' as the *TLS* put it.
Laura Hird *Born Free*
Family life on a modern Edinburgh
housing estate.
James Hogg
Confessions of a Justified Sinner
An ironic jibe against religious
bigotry in the 17th and 18th
centuries, set in Edinburgh.
Paul Johnston *The Bone Yard*;
Body Politic; *Water of Death*
Futuristic detective fiction set in
a nightmare vision of Edinburgh
as a city state with a year-round
Festival, where the impoverished
populace lives to serve the needs
of the tourists. Some locals will tell
you this book is non-fiction.
Alexander McCall Smith
The Sunday Philosophy Club;
44 Scotland Street
The prolific professor's output
includes a detective series and a
collection of whimsical stories.
Ian Rankin *Inspector Rebus* novels
Hardbitten Rebus inhabits a city
that many locals see as their own.
JK Rowling *Harry Potter and
the Philosopher's Stone*, et al
Rowling wrote the first Potter
books in cafés around Edinburgh.
Sir Walter Scott
The Heart of Midlothian
Scott's 1818 novel contains, among
many other tales, an account of the
Porteous lynching of 1736.
Robert Louis Stevenson
Edinburgh: Picturesque Notes; *The
Strange Case of Dr Jekyll & Mr Hyde*
A perceptive study; fiction inspired
by local criminal Deacon Brodie.
Muriel Spark
The Prime of Miss Jean Brodie
A schoolteacher Jean Brodie makes
a stand against the city's moral
intransigence and conventionality.
Irvine Welsh *Trainspotting*;
Porno; *Filth*; *The Acid House*
The city's underbelly uncovered.

Non-fiction

Neil Ascherson *Stone Voices*
An unusual, insightful and tender
meditation on Scotland.
Donald Campbell *Edinburgh:
A Cultural and Literary History*
A digressionary wander through
Edinburgh's cultural past.
David Daitches *Edinburgh*
A highly readable and academically
sound history of the city.
Jan-Andrew Henderson
The Town Below the Ground
The Old Town's underground slums.
James U Thomson
Edinburgh Curiosities
A look at the city's history that
reveals its dark underbelly and
quirky nature.
AJ Youngson *The Making
of Classical Edinburgh*
An exhaustive account.

Poetry

Robert Burns
Complete Poems & Songs
Scotland's national poet.
William Dunbar *Selected Poems*
Vibrant, bawdy poems by the local
poet, priest and member of James
IV's court.
Robert Fergusson
Selected Poems
Born in Edinburgh in 1750,
Fergusson died in poverty in the
city's Bedlam just 24 years later.
William McGonagall
Poetic Gems
Was he serious? Was it all one big
prank? Decide for yourself in this
collection by Edinburgh-born
McGonagall, widely acknowledged
to be one of the worst published
poets in literary history.

FILMS

Chariots of Fire
dir David Puttnam (1981)
Based on the 1924 Olympics, David
Puttnam's film has spectacular
shots of Salisbury Crags.
The Da Vinci Code
dir Ron Howard (2006)
Rosslyn Chapel plays a key role in
Ron Howard's blockbuster
adaptation of Dan Brown's novel.
The Debt Collector
dir Anthony Neilson (1999)
Although it was shot for the most
part in Glasgow, this thriller –
starring Billy Connolly – was
nonetheless set in Edinburgh.
**The Prime of Miss Jean
Brodie** *dir Ronald Neame (1969)*
Maggie Smith as Edinburgh's
best-known schoolmarm.
Shallow Grave
dir Danny Boyle (1994)
Three Edinburgh yuppies get stuck
with a suitcase full of drug money
and a dead body.
The 39 Steps
dir Alfred Hitchcock (1935)
Hitchcock's loose adaptation
of John Buchan's novel; Ralph
Thomas's 1959 remake featured
the city more prominently.
Trainspotting
dir Danny Boyle (1996)
Shot mostly in Glasgow, but its
opening was filmed in Edinburgh.

WEBSITES

Edinburgh City Council
www.edinburgh.gov.uk
The local government.
**Edinburgh & Lothians
Tourist Board**
www.edinburgh.org
The 'official' guide to the city.
Edinburgh Festivals
www.edinburgh-festivals.com
Scotsman-powered diary.
Edinburgh's Hogmanay
www.edinburghshogmanay.com
Happy new year…
General Register Office
www.gro-scotland.gov.uk
Trace your family history.
Historic Scotland
www.historic-scotland.gov.uk
The government body in charge of
Scotland's historic monuments.
The List *www.list.co.uk*
The best online resource for event
listings in the city.
National Trust for Scotland
www.nts.org.uk
Information on all NTS properties
around the country.
Scotch Malt Whisky Society
www.smws.co.uk
With a useful malt whisky primer.
Scottish Executive
www.scotland.gov.uk
Useful information.
Scottish Parliament
www.scottish.parliament.uk
A user-friendly guide.
Scottish Tourist Board
www.visitscotland.com
The countrywide tourist agency.

Index

Note: Page numbers in **bold** indicate section(s) giving key information on a topic; *italics* indicate photos.

A

INDEX

INDEX

Advertisers' Index

Please refer to the relevant pages for contact details.

Maps

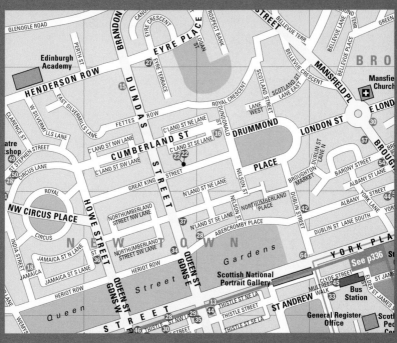

Legend	
Major sight or landmark	
Railway station	
Park	
College/Hospital	
Neighbourhood	LEITH
Pedestrian street	

Scotland

0 ——————— 75 miles
0 ——————— 120 km
© Copyright Time Out Guides 2010

Edinburgh by Area

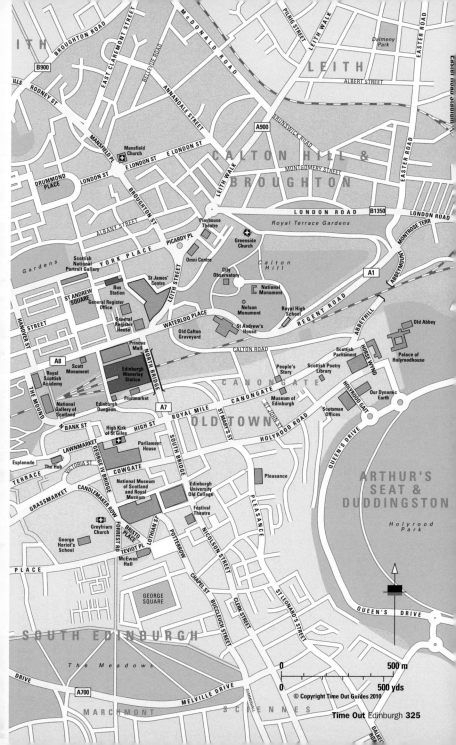

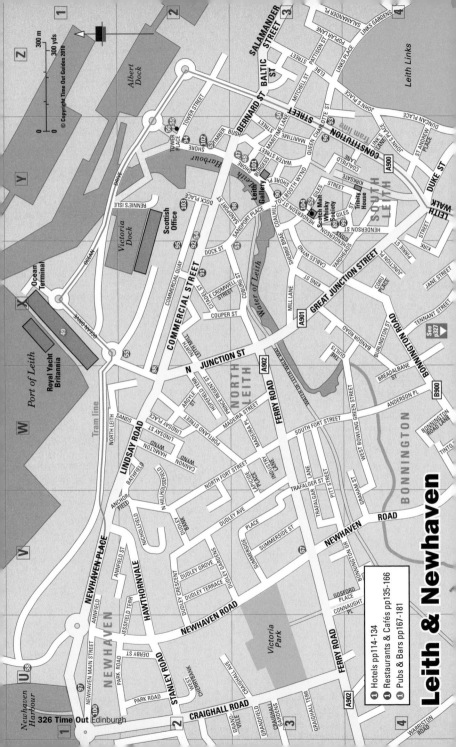

Leith & Newhaven

❶ Hotels pp114-134
❷ Restaurants & Cafés pp135-166
❸ Pubs & Bars pp167-181

© Copyright Time Out Guides 2010

300 m
300 yds

Newhaven Harbour

Port of Leith
Royal Yacht Britannia

Ocean Terminal

Albert Dock

Victoria Dock

Scottish Office

Rennie's Isle

Leith Harbour

Water of Leith

Leith Gallery

Scotch Malt Whisky Society

Trinity House

SOUTH LEITH

NORTH LEITH

BONNINGTON

NEWHAVEN

Victoria Park

SALAMANDER STREET
BALTIC ST
BERNARD ST
CONSTITUTION STREET
LEITH WALK
DUKE ST

Leith Links

COMMERCIAL STREET
OCEAN DRIVE
LINDSAY ROAD
HAWTHORNVALE
NEWHAVEN PLACE
STANLEY ROAD
CRAIGHALL ROAD
NEWHAVEN ROAD
FERRY ROAD

JUNCTION ST
GREAT JUNCTION STREET
BONNINGTON ROAD

Tram line

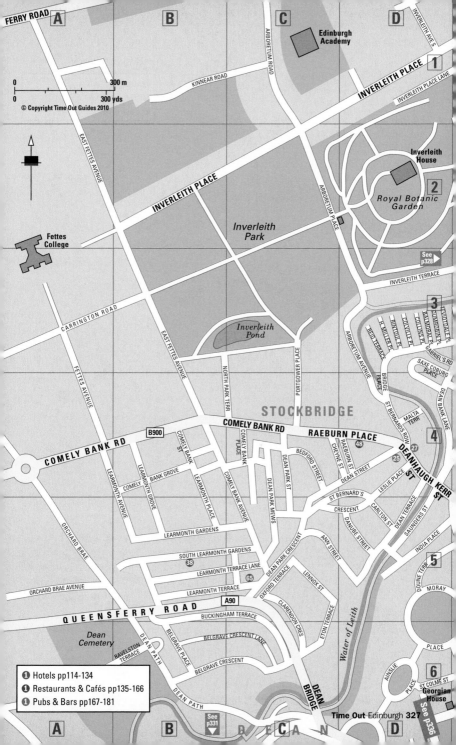

FERRY ROAD

A **B** **C** **D**

1

Edinburgh Academy

INVERLEITH PLACE

INVERLEITH PLACE LANE

ARBORETUM ROAD

KINNEAR ROAD

300 m
300 yds

© Copyright Time Out Guides 2010

EAST FETTES AVENUE

INVERLEITH PLACE

Inverleith House

2

Royal Botanic Garden

ARBORETUM PLACE

Inverleith Park

Fettes College

See p328 ▶

INVERLEITH TERRACE

CARRINGTON ROAD

3

TL MILLER PL
RINTOUL PL
DANUBE ST
COLLINS PL
BALMORAL PL
DUMBIEDYKES
EILDON ST
GABRIEL'S RD

FETTES AVENUE

EAST FETTES AVENUE

Inverleith Pond

REID TERRACE

BRIDGE PLACE

ARBORETUM AVENUE

SAXE COBURG PLACE

DEAN BANK LANE

NORTH PARK TERR

PORTGOWER PLACE

STOCKBRIDGE

ST BERNARDS ROW

MALTA TERR

4

COMELY BANK RD

COMELY BANK RD

Comely Bank PLACE

COMELY BANK

RAEBURN PLACE

DEANHAUGH ST

KERR ST

B900

48

27

COMELY BANK GROVE

LEARMONTH AVENUE

LEARMONTH GROVE

COMELY BANK AVENUE

LEARMONTH PLACE

DEAN PARK ST
BEDFORD STREET
CHEYNE ST
RAEBURN ST
DEAN STREET

25

LESLIE PLACE

DEAN STREET

DEAN TERRACE

SAUNDERS ST

INDIA PLACE

ORCHARD BRAE

LEARMONTH GARDENS

DEAN PARK MEWS

ST BERNARD'S CRESCENT

CARLTON ST

DANUBE STREET

SOUTH LEARMONTH GARDENS

38

LEARMONTH TERRACE LANE

65

DEAN PARK CRESCENT

ANN STREET

DOUNE TERR

5

ORCHARD BRAE AVENUE

LEARMONTH TERRACE

OXFORD TERRACE
LENNOX ST

MORAY

QUEENSFERRY ROAD

A90

BUCKINGHAM TERRACE

CLARENDON CRES

ETON TERRACE

Water of Leith

PLACE

Dean Cemetery

RAVELSTON TERRACE

DEAN PATH

BELGRAVE PLACE

BELGRAVE CRESCENT LANE

BELGRAVE CRESCENT

AINSLIE PLACE

6

DEAN PATH

DEAN BRIDGE

ST COLME ST

Georgian House

See p331 ▼

See p336 ▶

R E C A N

Time Out Edinburgh **327**

❶ Hotels pp114-134
❶ Restaurants & Cafés pp135-166
❶ Pubs & Bars pp167-181

A **B** **C** **D**

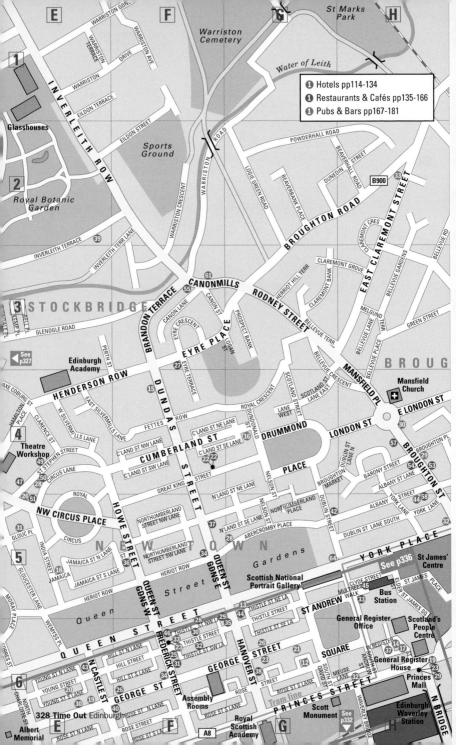

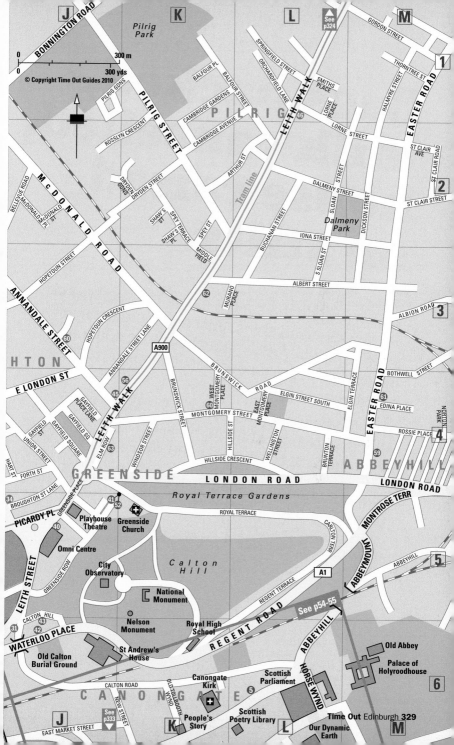

Bags packed, milk cancelled, house raised on stilts.

You've packed the suntan lotion, the snorkel set, the stay-pressed shirts. Just one more thing left to do – your bit for climate change. In some of the world's poorest countries, changing weather patterns are destroying lives.

You can help people to deal with the extreme effects of climate change. Raising houses in flood-prone regions is just one life-saving solution.

**Climate change costs lives.
Give £5 and let's sort it *Here & Now***

www.oxfam.org.uk/climate-change

Be Humankind Oxfam

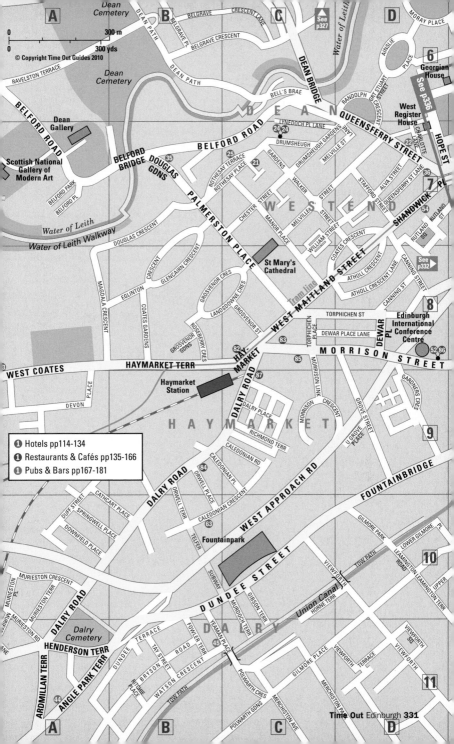

© Copyright Time Out Guides 2010

❶ Hotels pp114-134
❶ Restaurants & Cafés pp135-166
❶ Pubs & Bars pp167-181

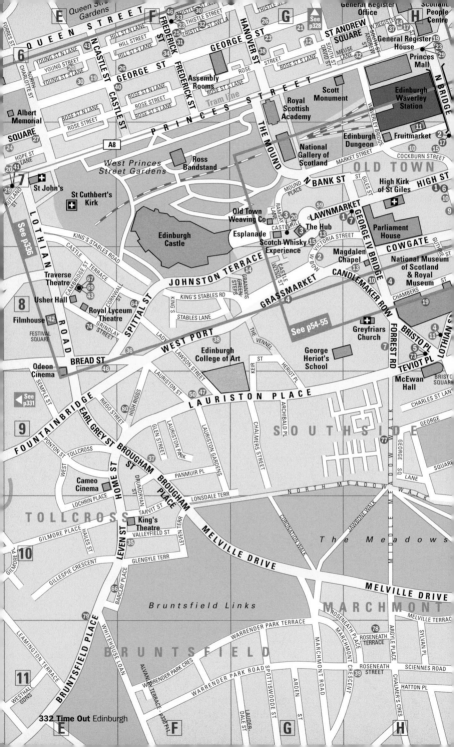

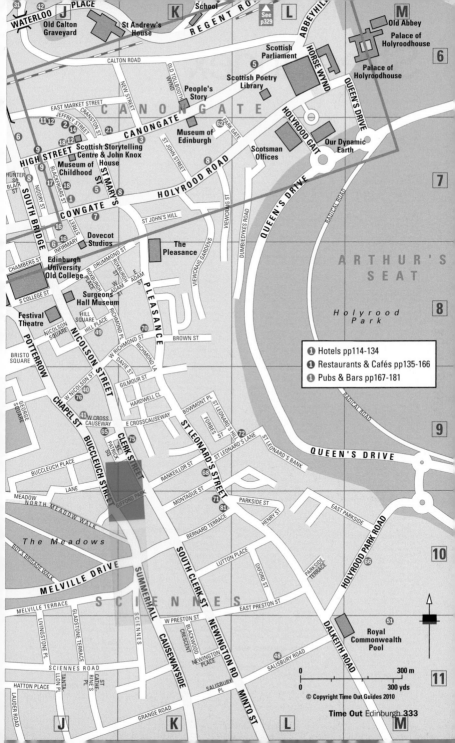

Street Index

STREET INDEX

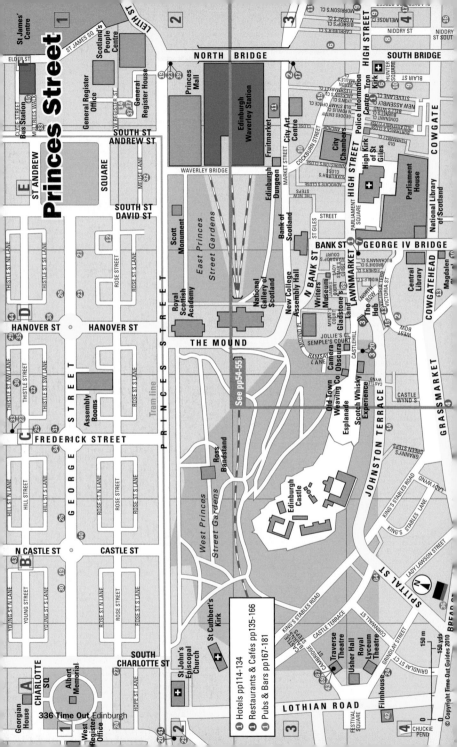

Princes Street

St James' Centre
LEITH ST
ST JAMES ST
St James Sq
Scotland's People Centre
ELDER ST
CLYDE STREET
Bus Station
MULTREES WALK
General Register Office
W REGISTER ST
General Register House
SOUTH ST ANDREW ST
ST ANDREW SQUARE
MEUSE LANE
SOUTH ST DAVID ST
THISTLE ST NE LANE
ROSE STREET
ROSE ST LANE
HANOVER ST
HANOVER ST
THISTLE ST NW LANE
THISTLE STREET
ROSE STREET
ROSE ST LANE
Assembly Rooms
FREDERICK STREET
HILL ST N LANE
HILL STREET
HILL ST S LANE
ROSE ST N LANE
ROSE STREET
ROSE ST S LANE
GEORGE STREET
Tram line
N CASTLE ST
CASTLE ST
YOUNG ST N LANE
YOUNG STREET
YOUNG ST S LANE
ROSE ST N LANE
ROSE STREET
ROSE ST S LANE
CHARLOTTE SQ
A
Georgian House
Albert Memorial
HOPE STREET
West Register Office
SOUTH CHARLOTTE ST
St John's Episcopal Church
St Cuthbert's Kirk

PRINCES STREET
Scott Monument
East Princes Street Gardens
Royal Scottish Academy
National Gallery of Scotland
THE MOUND
See pp54-55
Ross Bandstand
West Princes Street Gardens
Edinburgh Castle

NORTH BRIDGE
Princes Mall
Edinburgh Waverley Station
Fruitmarket
City Art Centre
MARKET STREET
Edinburgh Dungeon
WAVERLEY BRIDGE
COCKBURN STREET
Bank of Scotland
ST GILES STREET
New College Assembly Hall
MOUND PL
Writers' Museum
Gladstone's Land
JOLLIE'S CL
SEMPLE'S COURT
Camera Obscura
RAMSAY LANE
CASTLEHILL
Old Town Weaving Co
Scotch Whisky Experience
Esplanade

SOUTH BRIDGE
NIDDRY ST
NIDDRY ST SOUT
MELROSE CT
HIGH STREET
Police Information Centre
NEW ASSEMBLY CLOSE
Tron Kirk
BLAIR ST
HUNTER SQUARE
City Chambers
High Kirk of St Giles
Parliament House
National Library of Scotland
COWGATE
BANK ST
ADVOCATE'S CLOSE
PARLIAMENT SQUARE
LAWNMARKET
GEORGE IV BRIDGE
LADY STAIR'S CLOSE
Central Library
Magdalen
VICTORIA ST
The Bow
LAWNMKT
WEST BOW
CASTLE WYND
COWGATEHEAD
GRASSMARKET
JOHNSTON TERRACE
GRANNY'S GREEN STEPS
KING'S STABLES ROAD
KING'S STABLES LANE
LADY WYND
SPITTAL ST
LADY LAWSON STREET
King's Stables Road
CASTLE TERRACE
CAMBRIDGE ST
CORNWALL STREET
GRINDLAY STREET
Traverse Theatre
Usher Hall
Royal Lyceum Theatre
Filmhouse
FESTIVAL SQUARE
LOTHIAN ROAD
CHUCKIE PEND
BREAD ST

150 m
150 yds

Hotels pp114-134
Restaurants & Cafés pp135-166
Pubs & Bars pp167-181

336 Time Out Edinburgh

© Copyright Time Out Guides 2010